JOHN J. CRITTENDEN

taking full account of his relationship with Clay seemed utterly impracticable. The first part of the study, therefore, is devoted to an analysis of Crittenden's apprenticeship to Harry of the West.

The second phase of Crittenden's career was his emergence as a mature statesman after Clay receded from the center of the national political stage in the mid-1840s. As a leader of the Whig party, he was well equipped. His excellent family connections allied him with the Jeffersons, the Lees, the Taylors, the Inneses, and the Todds. Well-educated, urbane, a facile debater, he could hold his own in any company of public men. His great affability made for him friends in all sections who were devoted to him both as a person and as a political leader. More important still, the mantle of Clay as champion of compromise—that favorite device for American political effectiveness—seemed to many to fit him more snugly than it had even Clay himself. His reputation for integrity, for fair dealing, for moderation in partisan affairs, and for adherence to principle fitted him in a peculiar way for leadership. So much so, indeed, that it is a cause for wonder that he did not become a candidate for the Presidency.

Crittenden's qualities were not unnoticed by his contemporaries. Again and again came appeals from influential men in all sections urging him to become a candidate. Never, however, did Crittenden reveal either in public statement or in his private correspondence that he was tempted by these proffers of support. It can hardly be said that he regarded himself as unworthy. Although a man of sufficient modesty, he could not have considered himself inferior to many of the mediocrities who sought the Presidency in his day.

In seeking an explanation for Crittenden's refusal to enter the lists for the Presidency, one might first look back to his long association with Clay. In those years Crittenden had learned to subordinate his own ambitions to those of his party and its leader. So many times had he demonstrated this attitude that it might have become part of his nature. But the changing times provide yet another explanation. Crittenden emerged as an independent leader during the period when the importance of loyalty to party was gaining emphasis in the nation. Then, too, Crittenden assumed leadership of his party just as the slavery issue was producing a fateful national crisis, and no other principle was as clear and as dear to him as the necessity for preservation of the Union. In his own border state he

had watched for decades the conflicts over issues which later were
to divide the nation—tariff, banking, internal improvements, and
slavery. There, nourished by Clay's passionate devotion to the developing nation, Crittenden had formed a deep conviction of the
importance of preventing dissolution of the Union. As the struggle
grew more intense and the crisis deepened, Crittenden felt more
and more that personal ambition must be sacrificed. He had seen
in Clay's experience the handicaps borne by a peacemaker who is
preoccupied with his own political ambitions. Crittenden thus was
able willingly, almost joyously, to renounce all thought of the Presidency and devote all his energies to saving the Union.

ACKNOWLEDGMENTS

MY THANKS for aid in the preparation of this book must go to many persons and institutions. First of all I am indebted to my colleague, Thomas D. Clark, who suggested to me the need for a biography of Crittenden, who lightened my departmental duties so that I could undertake the study, who encouraged me throughout the enterprise, and who gave me valued criticism while the manuscript was in preparation. The administration at the University of Kentucky relieved me of teaching and administrative responsibilities over a period encompassing three semesters and several summers. I was also given substantial assistance by the University of Kentucky Research Fund, which generously subsidized my travels of many months in gathering materials and also provided me with a research assistant over a period of several years. This assistant, Frank Mathias, a doctoral candidate in history at the University of Kentucky, examined almost inumerable newspaper files and periodicals and checked bibliographical data. The meticulous and conscientious manner in which he performed these tasks for me expedited the completion of the biography by many months. I am most grateful, too, to the John Simon Guggenheim Foundation for its generous grant which enabled me to devote full time to the study during 1960-1961 and thus advanced considerably the date of publication.

My thanks are due, too, to the staffs of many libraries: the Library of Congress, especially the Division of Manuscripts; the Duke University Library and its archivist, Miss Mattie Russell, an old friend and former schoolmate; the University of Kentucky Library, where Dr. Jacqueline Bull and her associates aided me beyond the call of duty; Yale University Library, Rochester University Library, the Alderman Library of the University of Virginia, the library of the Missouri

Historical Society, the library of the Chicago Historical Society, the Detroit Public Library, the library of the Historical Society of Pennsylvania, the Illinois State Historical Society, the library of the Peabody Institute, the Kentucky Historical Society, and the Filson Club.

My colleagues at the University of Kentucky, Mary Wilma Hargreaves, James F. Hopkins, Clement Eaton, and Holman Hamilton, all of whom are familiar with the period covered by this work, read the manuscript and made suggestions which saved me from errors. To all of these colleagues I am grateful, and all of them are hereby exonerated of all responsibility for whatever errors still remain. To Professor Hopkins I am additionally indebted for bibliographical aid mentioned in the essay at the end. My sister, Susan McDevitt, has helped with the numerous typings, has checked footnotes, and has read the manuscript with such care that her untrained eye caught several errors which had escaped detection by professionals.

Finally, my appreciation must go in full measure to my wife Betty. From its inception this study has been a joint venture and a most happy one. She accompanied me on all my researches. She took notes and kept my files. She typed draft after draft and verified or corrected doubtful statements. In all but the actual writing she has been a full partner, and even in the composition her advice was constantly sought and generally followed. Indeed, she is so much a part of this book that it is affectionately dedicated to her.

CONTENTS

Book Three
THE PATRIOT

ILLUSTRATIONS

Book One

CLAY'S LIEUTENANT

CHAPTER I

The Making
of a Frontier Lawyer

It was in the autumn of 1783 that Major John Crittenden brought his bride, Judith Harris, to Kentucky. For many of the company with whom they traveled from the Valley of Virginia, this was their first sight of the fabled Bluegrass region, but to the young major it was homecoming. Eight years before, he had made his first visit, spending long months with George Rogers Clark and others surveying and staking land claims. Part of the land he then acquired was in the Woodford section of Fayette County, and it was here that he brought Judith, probably to a log cabin already prepared for her. Here they would live their lives.

Within eighteen months their first child was born, a girl whom they named Harriet. Then on September 10, 1786, Judith gave birth to a son, John Jordan.[1] In the ensuing years seven more children were born: Thomas in 1788, Margaret in 1790, Henry in 1792, Obedience in 1795, Robert in 1797, Caroline in 1799, and Lucy in 1802. All lived to maturity except Obedience, who died in August, 1796, at the tender age of eighteen months.[2]

Of Major Crittenden's early life little is known. His great-grandfather, Richard Crittenden, migrated to Virginia from Essex County, England, sometime between 1663 and 1674, as a redemptioner to George Billips. A grandson of Richard, Henry Crittenden, settled in Essex County, Virginia, and married Margaret Butler. Henry and Margaret had six children, one of them John, who was born about 1752 or shortly before.[3] About this same time Henry moved his young family to Northampton County, North Carolina. There John grew to young manhood, hunting, exploring the wilderness, and fighting Indians, like most frontiersmen. By the time he was twenty-one he was an accomplished woodsman, able to sustain himself indefinitely in wilderness country. Somehow he also managed to obtain an exceptionally good education, for the few writings he left are highly literate.

Like other restless, enterprising frontiersmen John Crittenden early sought his fortune in the West. In July, 1775, he was at Fort Wheeling, Virginia, with a party on its way to Kentucky "to improve and take up lands for themselves and some gentlemen in Virginia."[4] From Wheeling the party went down the Ohio to the mouth of the Kentucky, where they separated, some proceeding down the Ohio to the falls, while Crittenden and others went up the Kentucky to Leestown, near the present site of Frankfort. Here Crittenden met George Rogers Clark, who was deputy to Hancock Lee, the chief surveyor of the Ohio Land Company. Clark joined Crittenden's party, which moved on to Boonesboro and later to Harrodsburg.

Throughout the autumn and winter of 1775 and the spring of 1776 Crittenden, Luke Kennon (Cannon), Clark, Thornton Farron, and others were busy locating and staking land claims throughout central Kentucky: at Buck Lick, at Grassy Lick, on Stoner Creek.

---

[1] Many authorities, including Crittenden's daughter, give the date as September 10, 1787. See Mrs. Chapman Coleman, *The Life of John J. Crittenden, with Selections from His Correspondence and Speeches*, 2 vols. (Philadelphia, 1871), I, 13; H. H. Crittenden, *The Crittenden Memoirs* (New York, 1936), 25, 515; Nelson Osgood Rhoades, *Colonial Families of the United States of America . . .*, 10 vols. (Baltimore and Los Angeles, 1920), VII, 489. But in the Crittenden Papers at Duke University Library there is a letter to Crittenden from his brother Thomas, dated September 1, 1814, which clearly establishes 1786 as the correct date of Crittenden's birth. This is confirmed by a letter from Crittenden's wife to Orlando Brown, n. d., in Orlando Brown Papers, Kentucky Historical Society (Frankfort), Folder 213.

[2] Memorandum in Crittenden Papers (Duke).

[3] Francis H. Oxx, "The Kentucky Crittendens . . ." (microfilm copy of manuscript in Kentucky Historical Society), 24-27.

[4] Deposition of Elias Tobin, in *Register of the Kentucky State Historical Society*, XXXI (1933), 237 (hereinafter, *Kentucky Register*).

Their operations extended along the Kentucky River from Boonesboro to its mouth, along the Licking River in what is now Harrison, Pendleton, and Campbell counties, and along the Ohio from Carroll to Kenton.[5]

The claims of Crittenden and his associates were soon threatened by the operations of Richard Henderson and his Transylvania Company. In June, 1776, Crittenden, Clark, John Bowman, James Harrod, Isaac Hite, and nine others met at Harrodsburg and drew up a petition to the Virginia legislature urging it to break up the Transylvania Company and incorporate Kentucky as part of Virginia. Crittenden was selected to represent the settlers of West Fincastle (Kentucky) in presenting this petition to the legislature.[6]

Meantime, war had come. When Crittenden reached Virginia, he enlisted in the Eleventh Regiment of the Continental Line and was given the rank of lieutenant. This regiment became part of Daniel Morgan's famed Riflemen, made up altogether of sharpshooting frontiersmen. Crittenden must have gone north with Morgan and served in the campaign against Burgoyne, for there is a record of his presence in the neighborhood of Saratoga some months after Burgoyne's capture. In February, 1781, he was discharged from Morgan's Riflemen with the rank of brigade major, and a few months later he was on his way back to Kentucky to serve under his old friend Clark. En route, however, he stopped off in Powhatan County to visit two of his war comrades, John and Jordan Harris, sons of Colonel John Harris, whose wife, Obedience Turpin, was a first cousin of Thomas Jefferson. Here Crittenden met and fell in love with Judith, the sister of his friends. But even romance did not cause the young major to linger long, and he soon departed for the West.[7]

Clark had already made his successful campaign culminating in the capture of Colonel Henry Hamilton at Vincennes, and the power

[5] George Rogers Clark to Jonathan Clark, April 1, 1775, quoted in Samuel M. Wilson, "The Ohio Company of Virginia," in *Kentucky Law Journal*, XIV (1926), 304-305; Oxx, "The Kentucky Crittendens," 43-44; depositions of John Fuqua, Hugh Forbes, and Patrick Jordan, in *Kentucky Register*, XXX (1932), 284, 286, 287, XXXI (1933), 234.

[6] Rhoades, *Colonial Families*, VII, 489; deposition of John Fuqua, 284; Oxx, "The Kentucky Crittendens," 44.

[7] Oxx, "The Kentucky Crittendens," 5, 46-48, 50-52; "Virginia Officers and Men in the Continental Line," in *Virginia Magazine of History and Biography*, II (1894), 251; Charles R. Staples, "Cornelius Darnell and His Application for Revolutionary War Pension," in *Kentucky Register*, V (1907), 186; Rhoades, *Colonial Families*, VII, 489; Thomas M. Green, *Historic Families of Kentucky* (Cincinnati, 1889), 247-48.

of the British in the western country was broken. But the Indians were still a menace, their war parties making sporadic raids across the Ohio into Kentucky. Clark conceived a plan of patrolling the Ohio with a fleet of armed boats, and Crittenden superintended their construction.[8] But this plan proved ineffective, and in October, 1781, Clark dispatched Major Crittenden to the Virginia legislature to ask for support of an expedition to exterminate Indian villages around Detroit. But the plea was futile, for by the time Crittenden reached Richmond, Cornwallis had surrendered and the legislature was war-weary; Virginia had already agreed to cede the Northwest Territory to the Continental Congress and would spend no more of her own treasure in its preservation. By November, 1782, Major Crittenden was back in Kentucky in time to participate in a foray across the Ohio in which seven Indian villages were destroyed and thousands of bushels of corn were burned.[9]

With the Revolution ended, Major Crittenden was chosen to represent Fayette County, then including all of central and north-eastern Kentucky, in the Virginia legislature. After the session was ended in 1783, he stopped off once more in Powhatan to further his suit with Judith. He was successful not only in winning her favor but in gaining her father's approval as well. The young couple were married on August 21, 1783, at the bride's home and set out at once for Kentucky.[10]

Life in Kentucky at this time was little different from frontier life in other areas. There were hardships to be overcome, but there were also rewards for the enterprising settler. The area around Lexington was extraordinarily fertile and was even then attractive to settlers beginning to pour into the region from beyond the Alleghenies. Land values in such a situation could not fail to rise, and Major Crittenden's time was profitably spent in acquiring vast holdings. Titles acquired under the Ohio Company had been voided by the Virginia legislature in 1779, but provision was made for limited grants to those who could prove actual settlement and the planting of a crop prior to that date. Nor was Virginia niggardly in rewarding her

[8] Charles G. Talbert, "A Roof for Kentucky," in *Filson Club History Quarterly*, XXIX (1955), 145-65 (hereinafter, *Filson Quarterly*).

[9] Oxx, "The Kentucky Crittendens," 53-55; Charles G. Talbert, "Kentucky Invades Ohio—1782," in *Kentucky Register*, LIII (1955), 293.

[10] Rhoades, *Colonial Families*, VII, 489; Green, *Historic Families*, 247-48; Allen E. Ragan, "John J. Crittenden, 1787-1863," in *Filson Quarterly*, XVIII (1944), 4; Oxx, "The Kentucky Crittendens," 48.

war veterans. By 1783 Major Crittenden had already perfected title to his 1,400 acres in Fayette County and had been issued warrants for more than 2,500 acres of undesignated land, together with additional acreage in Jefferson County to the west of Fayette. By one means or another he soon secured title to 1,400 acres on South Elkhorn, purchased from Abraham Buford 15,000 acres on Licking River near its junction with the Ohio, secured 9,000 acres on Red River in Fayette County jointly with Luke Kennon, and with his old friend Clark acquired joint title to 8,000 acres on Locust Creek in Bracken County. At one time his holdings included almost 75,000 acres of unimproved land, located principally in what was later Campbell, Clark, Franklin, and Montgomery counties.[11] Although he never amassed great wealth, Major Crittenden prospered, and his family grew up in more than ordinary comfort. The father had stature in the community. He was a charter member of the Order of the Cincinnati. He was a man of affairs who knew his way around governmental offices, and when the assembly met, he was able to perform useful chores for his Kentucky neighbors, such as perfecting titles to land claims.

Woodford County was formed in 1788 from part of Fayette, and four years later the town of Versailles was established and its affairs placed in the hands of seven trustees. John Crittenden was one of these, and he, Colonel Richard Young, and Robert Alexander were appointed by the county court to supervise the construction of a permanent courthouse. Crittenden was probably not a man of imperturbable temper, for in 1790 he was indicted for "profane swearing." The indictment was dismissed and apparently did no damage to his reputation, for by 1792 he had been named a trustee of Transylvania Seminary. A few years later he was appointed by the governor to be justice of the peace for Woodford County in place of

11 William E. Railey, *History of Woodford County* (Frankfort, 1828), 49-50; Katherine G. Healy, "Calendar of Early Jefferson County, Kentucky, Wills," in *Kentucky Register*, VI (1908), 317; "Certificate Book of the Virginia Land Commission," in *Kentucky Register*, XXI (1923), 107, 283, 284, 288, 307; copy of deed attested by John Bradford, in Crittenden Papers, University of Kentucky Library; Oxx, "The Kentucky Crittendens," 47; deed to John Crittenden for 10,000 acres on Licking River, signed and sealed by Gov. Patrick Henry, July 15, 1786, John Crittenden to Colonel George Nicholas, April, 1791, in Crittenden Papers (Kentucky); Woodford County Deed Book C-1, p. 50; Woodford County Tax Books, 1794-1806 (microfilm copy, Reel 394, Kentucky Historical Society); Willard Rouse Jillson, *The Kentucky Land Grants*, Filson Club Publications No. XXXIII (Louisville, 1925), 37; William Leavy, "Memoir of Lexington and its Vicinity . . . ," in *Kentucky Register*, XLII (1944) 47; Rhoades, *Colonial Families*, VII, 489; Ragan, "John J. Crittenden," 4.

Thomas Marshall, and he served in this office until his resignation in 1798.[12]

Until June, 1792, Kentucky was part of Virginia and, had it not been for the mountain barrier between them, would probably have remained so. But difficulty of communication between the two regions created a difference in perspective which made separation inevitable. Problems that were matters of life and death to the struggling settlers of the new country—of defense against the Indians and of trade through the Spanish port of New Orleans—were not of great moment to the people east of the mountains, who were not eager to make great sacrifices for the security and comfort of their emigrants to the west. As a result, a separation movement early developed in Kentucky, punctuated by the quasi-treasonable movements of James Wilkinson and Benjamin Sebastian. Both these men were in the pay of the Spanish governor at New Orleans, and their plans called for the separation of Kentucky not only from Virginia but from the United States as well. At the same time, British agents in Kentucky were attempting to induce the people to separate from the Union and place Kentucky under the protection of Great Britain.

Such intrigues of empire would excite the imagination of any impressionable boy, and the youthful John Jordan Crittenden must have been stirred by talk of them around his father's hearth. There was talk, too, of high adventure. Clark's expedition against the British a decade before had been decisive in breaking British power in the Northwest, but it did not permanently pacify the Indians of the region. Raids from north of the Ohio continued. These were never made by formidable war parties but by small bands that moved stealthily through the forests, pouncing upon small hunting parties or attacking outlying farmhouses. It is estimated that in the decade following the Revolution more than fifteen hundred Kentuckians were victims of these savage raids.

The more thickly settled portions of the country, such as Woodford County, generally escaped depredation. Yet on occasion the Indians were bold enough to penetrate into the neighborhood of even

[12] "Kentucky State Papers, Excerpts from Executive Journal No. 1 of Governor Isaac Shelby," in *Kentucky Register*, XXVII (1929), 591; "Excerpts from Executive Journal of Governor James Garrard," *Kentucky Register*, XXIX (1931), 348; Leavy, "Memoir of Lexington," 127; Lewis Collins and Richard Collins, *History of Kentucky*, 2 vols. (Covington, 1874), II, 763; Versailles *Woodford Sun*, June 13, 1929; Woodford County Court, Order Book A (1790), 93, 114.

the strongest settlements. In 1792, when young Crittenden was not yet six years of age, Jacob Coffman, a farmer in Anderson County just across the Kentucky River from Woodford, was killed and scalped, and Crittenden's father was probably one of the party who fruitlessly pursued the Indians. In the same year a Captain Todd, of neighboring Franklin County, was waylaid and scalped as he was riding down the hill across the river from the village of Frankfort.

A few months later a party of several dozen Indians surprised and captured John Dinint in Woodford County. The party then encamped in a rocky cliff on Glenn's Creek, less than ten miles from Versailles, while several hundred men gathered to seek them out. The Indians were discovered, routed, and pursued, but they managed to cross the Ohio with safety. Dinint, who for some reason had not been killed by the Indians, escaped during the crossing.[13] Dramatic events like these, which only the older Crittenden children were able to remember, were related over and over to the younger ones. Doubtless the tales grew in the retelling, and must have enlivened many a winter's evening.

Meanwhile, the education of the Crittenden children was being looked to. More than likely the children were taught to read, write, and "cipher" by their parents. The boys, at least, were given the best formal training available. They were sent to nearby Pisgah Academy for at least a year, and then to boarding school in Jessamine County, where they had as fellow students John and Thomas A. Marshall, cousins of the Chief Justice, J. Cabell Breckinridge, Hubbard Taylor, and Francis Preston Blair. Here John Jordan showed great delight in the study of the classics. Here, too, he made lasting friendships with his schoolfellows, particularly with Blair, a friendship that even bitter political feuds in later days could not destroy.[14]

Crittenden was in his seventeenth year when his schooling in Jessamine ended. He had already decided on the law, the most lucrative of professions in Kentucky, where unending litigation arose from confused land titles. Law schools in that day, rare in the East, were practically unknown in the West. To prepare themselves for the practice, young men would study under some experienced attorney until prepared to strike out for themselves. To this end young Crittenden moved to Lexington to the home of George M. Bibb, a

---

[13] Collins, *History of Kentucky*, II, 763-67.
[14] Ragan, "John J. Crittenden," 4; Coleman, *Crittenden*, I, 14.

young barrister friend of Major Crittenden's who had already attained eminence at the Kentucky bar.

After completing his studies with Bibb, Crittenden wished to prepare himself more broadly than such limited and casual instruction permitted. Accordingly, he enrolled in Washington Academy in Lexington, Virginia, an institution that has grown into the present Washington and Lee University. About forty students were in attendance at the time; one of them, Hugh Lawson White, was to be a close associate and fast friend of Crittenden's in later years. Here Crittenden spent two years studying "belles-lettres and mathematics."[15]

The curriculum of Washington Academy was the traditional one for American colleges at the beginning of the nineteenth century, an adaptation of the British version of the medieval liberal arts. The Latin and Greek classics, Hebrew, rhetoric, mathematics, and the "reformed" philosophy of Aristotle made up his college studies. The concept was, as Hofstadter says, that there was "a more or less fixed body of knowledge" that all "liberally educated gentlemen should know," and curriculums were "designed to create among them a common core of knowledge that would make them a community of the educated."[16] The level of instruction was low in America in the days immediately following the Revolution, and it is unlikely that Crittenden received much more than routine linguistic and mathematical drill in his classes; certainly he did not go far into the spirit of classical culture. Nevertheless, with his father's Virginia background and with his own association with young Kentuckians and Virginians of some culture, Crittenden could not fail to absorb the genteel tradition.

But even the reformed philosophy of Aristotle was not congenial with the spirit of equality, of liberty, and of religious skepticism that had come to America from Europe and pervaded the Kentucky frontier. The classics may have seemed stiff and dull to the young Kentuckian, for in the autumn of 1804 he moved to the College of William and Mary in Williamsburg, Virginia, where other spirited young Kentuckians were gathered.

---

[15] Crittenden to Messrs. White and Craighill, May 22 [1803?], in Coleman, *Crittenden*, I, 14, 74-75; William N. Craighill to Crittenden, Feb. 19, 1844, John B. Bibb to Mrs. Coleman, Nov. 26, 1867, in Crittenden Papers (Duke).

[16] Richard Hofstadter and C. DeWitt Hardy, *The Development and Scope of Higher Education in the United States* (New York, 1952), 10-12.

Here was an institution that more than a quarter of a century before, under the influence of Jefferson, had broken with tradition and adopted a curriculum permeated with Enlightenment philosophy. The break was so drastic that it became known as the French Revolution. Spurred on by Jefferson, the governing board had revamped the William and Mary curriculum, discontinued the preparatory school, and instituted the elective system. Under this system no preliminary credits were required, and any student could come and take such courses as he desired, save Greek and Latin, which were no longer offered. The Divinity School had been eliminated, and modern languages were taught for the first time in any American college. The courses included law, medicine, mathematics, fine arts, and natural and moral philosophy.

When Crittenden enrolled, William and Mary was an exciting place with young ideas of joyful revolt against the past, of spirited dreams for the future. Jefferson's influence was at its height; he was almost deified by the students. A spirit of anti-Federalism and of intense Republicanism pervaded the college and the town, so much so that even the reverend president of the college, Bishop James Madison, is said to have referred in religious services not to the Kingdom but to the "Republic" of Heaven. The deism which had made skeptics of orthodox Calvinists was so rife at William and Mary that Bishop William Meade expected to " 'find a skeptic, if not an avowed unbeliever,' in every educated young man he met for years."[17]

Instead of Aristophanes and Plato, young Crittenden at William and Mary was exposed to Molière and Descartes, but also to Rousseau and Voltaire and the other Encyclopedists. Books from the British Enlightenment included John Locke's *On Toleration*, William Lawrence Brown's *On Equality*, William Godwin's *Political Justice*, Dugald Stewart's *Philosophy of Mind*, and Duncan's *Elements of Logic*. Other books discussed by the students were David Hume's skeptical essays, Shakespeare's plays, Gibbon's *Decline and Fall of the Roman Empire*, Hugh Blair's *Lecture on Rhetoric*, Adam Smith's *Wealth of Nations*, Vattel's *Law of Nations*, Coke's *Commentary*

[17] E. G. Swen, "Kentuckians at William and Mary College before 1861 with a Sketch of the College before that Date," in *Filson Quarterly*, XXIII (1949), 173-98; Ragan, "John J. Crittenden," 4; Donald G. Tewksbury, *The Founding of American Colleges and Universities before the Civil War* (New York, 1932), 55; Coleman, *Crittenden*, I, 14.

upon Littleton, Blackstone's *Commentaries,* and *The Federalist.* With this intellectual fare and with such liberal instructors as Madison in philosophy and St. George Tucker in law, it is not surprising that there was an "independent political and literary spirit" among the students. The numerous Kentuckians among them seemed particularly imbued "with the visions of a free and flexible political life."

These were happy, carefree days for young Crittenden. He already had a great capacity for making and keeping friends. Here he became acquainted with John Tyler, whose path would again cross his in a crucial period for both of them. He loved to play at cards and seems to have contributed his share to the frolicking and merrymaking at the Raleigh Tavern, the center for college gaiety. Students could board either in Wren or in Town, as they chose. There was no planned recreation, but there was at William and Mary a freedom from rigid discipline remarkable for that day, but in keeping with the liberal spirit of the college. Students were frequently guests at balls at the Raleigh, or in homes, or at private dinner parties or outdoor barbecues.

There were no female students at the college, but cordial relations prevailed between the students and the young ladies of the town. A fellow student of Crittenden's remarked at the time that "such another place, perhaps, does not exist where the pure pleasure of society can be enjoyed without those banes which ordinarily attend it." In spite of these distractions an academic atmosphere seems to have prevailed, for another student wrote at the same time, "Study is our principal amusement. . . . If a person comes here for improvement he must study hard, but if pleasure be his object, it is as fine a place for spending money as ever I saw."[18]

If pleasure appealed to Crittenden, so apparently did study, for he possessed an inquiring and studious mind. Records of the college for these years were lost in a fire during the Civil War, so that it is not known what specific courses he took nor what grades he earned, but his later career suggests that he read avidly, not only in law, but in history and philosophy. Literary societies were active at William and Mary, as at most colleges of the eighteenth and nineteenth centuries, and it would be strange indeed if Crittenden with his gift

[18] Swen, "Kentuckians at William and Mary College," 185-86, 188, 197.

for oratory was not a frequent participant in the formal debates which were one of the great intellectual pastimes of the day.

Lectures were the general method of instruction. Recitation was not approved, but there was discussion in class after lectures. It was common for students to rise at sunup, read until about eleven, then attend lectures until two o'clock. Dinner was at three, and most students relaxed in recreation until sundown. The favorite sport seems to have been a game of handball played against a brick wall. Reading was resumed until about eleven or midnight, when the students retired.

Probably Crittenden had completed one year's study at William and Mary and was in his second year when his father died. According to his granddaughter, Major Crittenden was killed by a falling tree, but the date of his death is unknown. He was alive in 1804, but had died before October, 1806, when Judith renounced in Woodford county court her right to administer his estate and George M. Bibb was appointed in her place. The home place in Woodford had been reduced by sales to 318 acres, and Major Crittenden's unimproved lands had dwindled to 6,000 acres in Franklin, and 22,000 in Pulaski. The farm was productive; it had nine horses and twenty-one head of cattle. In addition, Major Crittenden owned seventeen slaves, valued at almost $5,000. It was not, however, a bountiful estate for a widow with a young family.[19]

John Jordan was twenty years of age. His sister, Harriet, was a year and a half older, but there were six younger brothers and sisters, the youngest of whom was just five. Nevertheless, John was able to finish the year at Williamsburg and received his diploma in June. The night before he left for home, his friends gave a "frolic" in his honor at the Raleigh Tavern.[20]

His college years (considerable for that day) equipped Crittenden with an education peculiarly suited for the practice of law and politics on the Kentucky frontier. He had been introduced both to the

[19] Woodford County Tax Lists, 1804, 1806; Oxx, "The Kentucky Crittendens," 60-62; various dates are given for the accident, but it seems to have occurred in the autumn of 1806. Ragan, "John J. Crittenden," 4; Rhoades, *Colonial Families*, VII, 489; Railey, *Woodford County*, 49; Woodford County Will Book D, 153; Woodford County Deed Book G, 137, 138, Deed Book H, 12.

[20] Railey, *Woodford County*, 49-50; Ragan, "John J. Crittenden," 4; Coleman, *Crittenden*, I, 13-14; *Kentucky Register*, XLII (1944), 12-13; J. Speed Smith to Crittenden, April 17, 1849, in Crittenden Papers (Duke).

classics and to the Enlightenment, but he had not yet become aware of the deep contradictions between the views of the Aristotelian gentleman and the egalitarian rationalist. He was therefore able for a while to move happily in both worlds.

Back in Kentucky, Crittenden hung out his shingle in Versailles shortly before his twenty-first birthday. For the next few months he remained there, living in his mother's home and helping with the management of the farm and with the care of his young brothers and sisters. By late autumn of 1807 the family was recovering from the shock of the father's sudden death. Judith Crittenden's affairs were in order, and the young lawyer so recently fired by new ideas grew restless.

Land titles had been pretty firmly established by this time in Woodford and in central Kentucky generally. The courts were busy enough, with routine litigation, but opportunities seemed more promising in a newer, freer region. In the western part of the state south of Green River there had sprung up a thriving community of people who had migrated principally from the area around Nashville, Tennessee. John Jordan Crittenden resolved to try his fortune in the Green River country.[21] The business center of southwestern Kentucky in 1807 and for some years after was Russellville, county seat of Logan. In the whole state there were but a half-dozen larger communities, and probably only Lexington and Louisville had greater business importance, for this was the commercial center not only for southern Kentucky but for a considerable portion of north Tennessee as well.[22]

Crittenden was accepted into the community at once. There were no blemishes in his character or background, and not many young men in the country could boast of as broad and thorough an education. Trained in the law by the renowned St. George Tucker at William and Mary, he had also been shown preferment by the prominent Kentucky jurist, George M. Bibb. He had distinguished family connections, a father who had sat in the Virginia legislature and a mother who called Thomas Jefferson cousin. Within a few weeks after his arrival in Russellville, Crittenden had made many new and warm friends. He was unanimously elected to membership in

[21] John B. Bibb to Mrs. Chapman Coleman, Nov. 26, 1867, in Crittenden Papers (Duke); Coleman, *Crittenden*, I, 14.
[22] Collins, *History of Kentucky*, II, 487.

the Masonic Order recently installed there. He took an active part in the affairs of the lodge, and within two months he had been raised to the second degree.

Crittenden was personable but not handsome. Of little more than average height, his slender and angular body made him appear tall. His deep-set black eyes, framed under heavy dark brows and separated by an unusually high-bridged nose, were calm and reassuring to clients who sought his advice. He was described by a contemporary as "homely, which is increased by the defective arrangement of his teeth." His skin was clear but somewhat weatherbeaten by much exposure to sun and wind. A lock from his straight, black hair sometimes strayed forward over his high, broad forehead.[23]

Two factions, the Mauldings and the Ewings, had struggled for political power in Logan in the decade prior to Crittenden's settlement there. By the time of his arrival the Ewings had won out, and they and their allies held all political offices, both local and state. Preferment was to be had only with their approval, unless one should be so bold or foolhardy as to attempt to unseat them. To an ambitious young barrister, freshly launched upon his career, the latter alternative held little promise. Accordingly, Crittenden allied himself with the Ewings. There was nothing unusual in this; it was customary for young men to begin their political apprenticeship by joining forces with older and established patrons.[24]

Among the leaders of the Ewing clan was Ninian Edwards. He had come to Logan from Nelson County in 1798 and soon became a leader of the bar, then judge of the circuit court. In 1806 he had been appointed to the court of appeals, and two years later, chief justice.[25] In 1809 President James Madison named him governor of the Illinois Territory. Just how or when Edwards first became acquainted with Crittenden is not known. Crittenden had been living in Russellville little more than a year, and for most of that time, certainly, Edwards' duties as chief justice had kept him in Frankfort.

23 Alexander C. Finley, *History of Russellville and Logan County* (Russellville, Ky., 1878-1879), 72-75; Collins, *History of Kentucky*, I, 28; Arndt M. Stickles (ed.), "Joseph R. Underwood's Fragmentary Journal on the New and Old Court Contest in Kentucky," in *Filson Quarterly*, XIII (1939), 207; Richmond (Va.) *Enquirer*, quoted in Lexington *Kentucky Reporter*, May 9, 1825.

24 Finley, *History of Russellville and Logan County*, 23.

25 Clarence E. Carter (ed.), *The Territorial Papers of the United States*, XVI, *The Territory of Illinois 1809-1814* (Washington, 1948), 45.

In any event, by early autumn of 1809, Crittenden and Edwards were on intimate terms, and at the beginning of the following year Edwards appointed Crittenden his aide and attorney general for Illinois Territory. He participated in only one case of which there is record during this period, a murder trial against Michael Jones, register of the land office. Charges against Jones were evidently framed by conspirators, and when the case was tried on April 10, 1810, Crittenden soon became convinced that his witnesses were lying. Jones was acquitted, and indictments for perjury were returned against two of the prosecution witnesses.[26] It is not likely that the unfortunate episode was the cause of Crittenden's resignation from this office, which soon followed, for he was able to secure the place for his brother Thomas, who had followed him to Russellville, studied law in his office, and now was prepared to start his own career.

Back in Russellville, Crittenden found his practice growing. Litigation over land titles was abundant; grants of land had been made with little discrimination by both Virginia and Kentucky, and frequently the same land had many claimants. Crittenden was able to attract clients, and fledgling lawyers soon were seeking him out to direct their legal training.[27]

Before Crittenden left Woodford County, he had formed an attachment for comely Sarah Lee, eldest daughter of a neighbor and Revolutionary comrade-in-arms of his father. Both Sarah's mother and her father were grandchildren of Richard Lee, founder of the famous family of the Old Dominion, and her mother was also a first cousin of Zachary Taylor, the future President. By the spring of 1811 Crittenden had been away from Woodford more than three years. He and Sarah surely exchanged many letters during that time, for it was a hard four days' journey by horseback from Russellville to Woodford, and Crittenden was too busy to make that journey often. But no letters between them have been preserved.

Crittenden and Sarah were married on May 27, 1811, at the bride's home in Woodford, and Crittenden took Sarah back to Russellville,

[26] Commission signed by Edwards, Jan. 1, 1810, copy in possession of Thomas Joyes, Louisville, Kentucky. Crittenden to Ninian Edwards, Oct. 9, 1809, Feb. 24, March 4, 1810, in Autograph Letterbooks, XLVIII, Chicago Historical Society; E. B. Washburne (ed.), *The Edwards Papers*, Chicago Historical Society Collection Vol. III (Chicago, 1884), 56; Carter, *Territorial Papers*, XVI, 58, 95; Coleman, *Crittenden*, I, 14-15.

[27] Two future governors of the state, Charles S. Morehead and his cousin James T. Morehead, studied in Crittenden's office during this period. Collins, *History of Kentucky*, II, 437; Finley, *History of Russellville and Logan County*, 83.

where they lived in a house built by Dr. R. K. Call at the southwest corner of Ninth and Main streets. Call later married Sarah's younger sister Lucinda. In Russellville, Crittenden and Sarah spent eight happy years, and here four of their seven children were born.[28]

In the summer of 1811 Crittenden prepared to dive into political waters. Most political careers in that day began in the legislature. There was popular voting in Kentucky, and the legislature and the executive each drew authority directly from the people. The governor occupied a position of distinction, but the legislature had more influence, not only in state affairs but in national. It chose United States senators and instructed them how to vote on issues before the Congress. Frequently it adopted resolutions on federal questions, and it even advised members of the lower house of Congress concerning their votes on national legislation. Counties or groups of counties were given representation in the legislature in approximate ratio to qualified voters, which included all white men. Logan County had two seats in the lower house, and it was to one of these that Crittenden was elected.[29]

Records of debates are not preserved in the official journals, and detailed accounts of legislative proceedings must be sought in the contemporary press. The only mention Crittenden received in his first session concerned the right of the legislature to instruct the state's senators on issues in Congress. Ben Hardin of Nelson County argued for senatorial independence. State legislatures, he said, should confine their activities to local affairs. Where in the Constitution, he asked, was there any mention of the right of the legislature to give such instruction? He was answered by J. H. Hawkins of Fayette. The legislature, said Hawkins, was the guardian of the people's rights. Since a senator represented his state in the national government, it followed naturally that the legislature had the right to command him.

Crittenden joined in the debate on the side of Hawkins and argued for instruction.[30] This was his maiden speech and it was well received. One who witnessed the debate called Crittenden "a young

28 Rhoades, *Colonial Families*, VII, 489-90; William Meade, *Old Churches, Ministers, and Families of Virginia*, 2 vols. (Philadelphia, 1861), II, 85, 135; G. Glenn Clift, "Kentucky Marriages and Obituaries, 1787-1860," in *Kentucky Register*, XXXVI (1938), 166; genealogical memorandum in Crittenden Papers (Duke); Coleman, *Crittenden*, I, 19; Margaret Barnes Stratton, *Place-Names of Logan County and Oft-Told Tales* (Russellville, 1950), 44.

29 Coleman, *Crittenden*, I, 15; *The Biographical Encyclopaedia of Kentucky . . . of the Nineteenth Century* (Cincinnati, 1878), 62.

30 Lexington (Ky.), *Reporter*, Jan. 4, 1812.

gentleman of fine oratorical abilities, and a very enlightened liberal mind." News of the good impression Crittenden made in this effort soon was carried back to Russellville, and his friends there were rejoiced to learn of his growing reputation.[31] Little is recorded of Crittenden's further actions in this session of the legislature. That he satisfied his constituents is certain, for the legislatures were elected annually at that time, and Crittenden was returned by the voters of Logan for the succeeding term.

Meanwhile, Indian restlessness and hostility across the Ohio had intensified. Tecumseh was attempting to unite the tribes for a concerted resistance to the extension of the white man's settlement. It was universally believed in the western country that the Indians were spurred on and supplied by the British from Canada, and clamor for war against the British and their red allies grew intense. Crittenden had reached Frankfort for the legislative session in November, 1811, almost simultaneously with news of the Battle of Tippecanoe, and the war cry that went up from the Kentucky capital that winter made all other issues seem meaningless. With the declaration of war came high enthusiasm in the state. The news was hailed as "a second decree of independence," and Kentuckians immediately prepared to march "to the lakes, to the plains of Abraham, or the consecrated field of Tippecanoe."[32]

Crittenden was as eager for the war as were his neighbors; he had been kept informed of the situation in Washington by Henry Clay, leader of the War Hawks there.[33] Almost as soon as war was declared, an expedition into the Illinois country was planned, and Crittenden secured a post as aide to General Samuel Hopkins, who had raised a division of two thousand mounted volunteers in western Kentucky. Hopkins crossed the Ohio River in early October and marched to Fort Harrison on the Wabash. There he received orders from General William Henry Harrison to proceed to the upper Illinois country to cooperate with Governor Ninian Edwards in an expedition against the Kickapoos.

In the prairie lands Hopkins was misled by his guides and never reached the rendezvous. After wandering for a week, the men sensed

[31] A[nthony] Butler to Crittenden, Dec. 31, 1811, in Crittenden Papers, Library of Congress. (Unless otherwise indicated, citations of the Crittenden Papers refer to the Library of Congress collection.)

[32] *Niles' Register*, II (1812), 239, 335.

[33] Henry Clay to Crittenden, May 28, 1812, in Crittenden Papers.

that something was amiss. Although the officers attempted to dissuade them, they insisted on returning to the base at Vincennes. Frontier democracy was not compatible with strict military discipline, and so Hopkins had to capitulate. Chagrined at his failure, he led his force up the Wabash, destroying several deserted Indian villages on the way. By this time winter was near, the term of enlistment was coming to an end, and further operations were curtailed. The expedition was therefore less than a brilliant success. Not only had Hopkins' force marched and countermarched to no avail, but his failure to join with Edwards had prevented the governor from accomplishing his objective.[34]

By the time the expedition was over, the legislature was once more in session, and Crittenden hurried back to Frankfort for his second term. It was to a sobered and disturbed capital that he returned. The war and its shocking reversals demanded attention. Instead of achieving the conquest of Canada, which Clay and others had boasted would be but a matter of weeks, the United States had lost two-thirds of the Northwest Territory to the British. Through a combination of inefficiency, unpreparedness, and lack of valor, Detroit had been surrendered, the American stronghold at Michilimackinac had been captured, the American garrison at Fort Dearborn had been surprised and massacred, and the British and their Indian allies were carrying the war deep into the settlements in Ohio, Indiana, and Illinois. Through the deep winter months of December and January, fighting had slowed, and the legislature in this breathing spell spent the weeks debating levies and supply for the summer campaign.

Then, on February 2, came electrifying news. Governor Isaac Shelby, hero of King's Mountain and veteran of numerous battles, together with most of the legislature, was at the theater when messengers arrived to tell of General James Winchester's disastrous defeat at the River Raisin by British General Proctor and the massacre by Indians of American prisoners—among whom were many Kentuckians. As the news spread, people poured from the theater and from their homes to stand in the cold night transfixed with horror and grief.

Quickly answering a plea from Harrison for aid, the legislature

34 William Russell to Secretary of War, Oct. 31, 1812, in Carter, *Territorial Papers*, XVI, 268-69; Collins, *History of Kentucky*, II, 345; Coleman, *Crittenden*, I, 15; *Biographical Encyclopaedia of Kentucky*, 62.

authorized the veteran Shelby to raise an additional 3,000 militia for six months and to take command of them in person. At Shelby's proclamation, 7,000 men came forward. "All seem to be aroused," wrote a native that spring, "men above 45, and boys under 17 years of age, are volunteering, anxious for an opportunity to avenge the blood of their slaughtered friends." Of the 3,000 men selected, half were dispatched at once under General Green Clay to reinforce Harrison. But when Harrison decided to postpone the invasion of Canada until control of Lake Erie was secured, the remaining 1,500 were disbanded except for a mounted regiment which was sent out under Colonel Richard M. Johnson.[35]

It was late summer before Commodore Oliver Hazard Perry was prepared to move against the British flotilla on Lake Erie, and the long months of inactivity had dulled the morale of the Kentuckians already in the field and diminished the enthusiasm of those at home. When Harrison requested the balance of the militia, he thought it wise to urge Shelby to take the field himself, offering even to subordinate himself to the old general so that Shelby would be the "guiding Head" while Harrison would be "The Hand."[36]

Shelby, instead of waiting to levy a draft of militia, decided that the way to bring out the best men (some of whom were no longer on the muster rolls) would be to send out a call for officers "and others possessing influence" to rendezvous at Newport on August 31 with mounted volunteers. When Shelby arrived there, he was greeted by 3,500 mounted volunteers. They represented all classes in the commonwealth. Some were rich, but some were so poor that they had to go into debt to acquire necessary equipment. Some had come from the Green River country, traveling three hundred miles to reach Newport.[37]

Among the volunteers was Crittenden, who, undaunted by the

[35] Logan Esarey, *Messages and Letters of William Henry Harrison*, 2 vols. (Indianapolis, 1922), II, 353, 411, 420; Milo M. Quaife (ed.), "Governor Shelby's Army in the River Thames Campaign," in *Filson Quarterly*, X (1936), 135-38; Isaac Shelby to Secretary of War, March 20, 1813, in Official Correspondence of Governor Isaac Shelby during his Second Administration as Governor of the Commonwealth of Kentucky, Letter Book A, transcript copy, in University of Kentucky Library (hereinafter, Shelby Papers); *Niles' Register* (1812-1813), III, 408.

[36] Shelby to Secretary of War, Aug. 1, 1813, Harrison to Shelby, July 20, 1813, in Shelby Papers.

[37] Shelby to Harrison, Aug. 1, 1813, in Shelby Papers; Shelby to Harrison, Aug. 8, 11, 1813, in Esarey, *Harrison Letters*, II, 504, 518, 522; Shelby to Harrison, Sept. 1, 1813, Daniel Parker to Shelby, Sept. 27, 1813, in Shelby Papers; Anthony Butler to Crittenden, Aug. 30, 1813, in Crittenden Papers (Duke).

ill-fated Hopkins campaign of the year before, eagerly accepted appointment as aide to Shelby. This was an important post, for much depended on the efficiency of the staff of the energetic and resourceful old warrior, even though he declined to allow Harrison to relinquish to him command of the campaign. Realizing that even a day's delay might prove disastrous, Shelby ordered his force to march at once to join Harrison. They crossed the Ohio on September 1, not waiting to organize. When the force halted for ammunition and hospital stores at Urbana, Ohio, on September 6, Shelby formed his army into eleven regiments, five brigades, and two divisions, with Joseph Desha and William Henry as divisional commanders. The ratio of officers to men seems high by contemporary standards, but it was not illogical in view of the notorious lack of discipline of frontier troops.[38]

Named with Crittenden as aide to Shelby was John Adair, and William T. Barry was appointed Shelby's secretary. That the general's aides were busy might be surmised from the rapid progress made by the untrained troops. On September 9 the march was resumed at a forced pace, and by September 15 the troops reached Seneca at the mouth of the Portage River. Here horses were left with caretakers while the men embarked stores and artillery in boats that had been prepared for the crossing of Lake Erie.

By September 22, Perry's victory had freed Lake Erie, and Harrison quickly set sail with his men to throw his force to the rear of the British army under Proctor. But Proctor had been warned of their coming, and by the time they landed at Malden, he had abandoned the town and moved to Amherstburg. Harrison reembarked and followed, landing three miles below the town on September 27; but again he was too late. After destroying the fort and all the public buildings, Proctor had retreated up the Thames River, forty miles from Malden.

Meanwhile, Colonel Richard M. Johnson's mounted regiment had come up from Detroit to join Harrison, who resumed pursuit of Proctor. After a preliminary skirmish to take a bridge at Dolson's, the army camped on the night of October 5. Next morning, with Johnson's cavalry in front, Shelby's dismounted men moved to Arnold's Mills, where the road crossed the river again. The ford was too deep for infantry, but with the aid of Indian canoes and with

<hr />

[38] Quaife, "Gov. Shelby's Army," 138-42; Shelby to Secretary of War, Aug. 4, 1814, in Shelby Papers; *Kentucky House Journal, 1815*, pp. 19-20; Esarey, *Harrison Letters*, II, 532-33.

each horseman taking an infantryman behind him, they were able to cross by noon. Eight miles farther on, signs of the quarry multiplied. Here the road passed for a few miles through a forest on the bank of the river. For two or three hundred yards a swamp paralleled the river, with several hundred yards of dry ground in between. The British and Indians were formed, their left on the river and their right on the swamp.

Putting Johnson's men in front and Shelby's infantry in support, Harrison ordered the attack. Johnson broke through the British regulars on the right at the first charge, and in a few minutes the battle in front was over. The British, already demoralized, were in hopeless disorder, and the mounted Kentuckians wheeled and poured a galling fire into scattered groups, which surrendered as rapidly as they could find captors. On the left, however, the Indians were more stubborn and poured a volley into Johnson's flank. At the same time, the Indians advanced on the front line of infantry and seriously threatened it. At this point Shelby brought up a regiment in reserve, which fired pointblank into the Indians' front while Johnson's cavalry gained their rear. The Indians broke precipitately, and the battle was over.[39]

The enemy force was completely destroyed. The British regulars were either killed or captured, but the heaviest enemy losses were among the Indians, for the word on every Kentuckian's tongue was "Remember the Raisin." There was little disposition to show mercy to the red men, and those who did not escape were put to the sword. Destruction of enemy property and military stores was estimated at between two and three million pounds sterling. More important than all else, territorial gains resulting from the campaign cut the British intercourse with the Indian tribes in the Northwest. This would give security and tranquillity to the frontier and put an end to the incessant warfare that had been so distressing to the people of the West. On the other hand, American losses were only seven killed and twenty-two wounded. "When all things are considered," wrote Shelby, "it is probably the cheapest campaign that has happened in this or any other country."[40]

[39] Shelby to Harrison, April 21, 1816, in Esarey, *Harrison Letters*, II, 544-65, 568-70; Quaife, "Gen. Shelby's Army," 146-53; Shelby to Secretary of War, Aug. 4, 1814, in Shelby Papers; Collins, *History of Kentucky*, II, 401-404, 867-68.

[40] Shelby to Secretary of War, Nov. 17, 1813, in Shelby Papers; letter of Crittenden in Lexington *Reporter*, Oct. 23, 1813.

It had been an unequal battle from the first. With Shelby's and Johnson's combined forces, Harrison had almost five thousand men, whereas according to Harrison's own estimate Proctor had only a few hundred British regulars and about a thousand Indians, perhaps fifteen hundred in all. Harrison contended, however, that the position held by the British equalized the advantage he had in numbers. Victory, he said, was due to the superior bravery of the Kentuckians. He was generous in his eulogy of Shelby and Johnson, and he paid special notice to Crittenden, Barry, and Adair. Their performance, he reported, "could not be surpassed."[41]

With the battle won and the campaign aims achieved, Harrison turned command of the army back to Shelby, and the homeward journey was now begun. Stormy weather made recrossing of the lake impracticable, so the army moved overland to Detroit. From there it moved along the lakefront over a new and difficult road, through Fort Meigs to the camp where the horses had been left at the mouth of the Portage. Here it arrived on October 19. After resting his men for two days, Shelby renewed the long trek.

Now began the severest hardships of the entire campaign. The army was entirely without tents. Many of the prisoners were wounded and had to be carried on horses. In addition, great numbers of camp followers and children were taken prisoner. Many of these were too young, others too ill, to walk. Horses, therefore, had to be taken from the men to provide for the weak and the feeble, so that many of the conquering heroes trudged home afoot while their captives rode.

Despite this, the army pushed forward at a steady pace of twenty to twenty-five miles a day, fording streams, sleeping in rain and frost. Many became ill of chills and fever, and to make matters worse, there was an acute shortage of food. Half rations were ordered, but sometimes even these were not available, and the men had to go as long as twenty-four hours at a time without food. Many of the sick would die during the night, and soldiers starting out next day would note fresh graves. "The whole movements of the army since the action," wrote one of Crittenden's companions, "does exceed anything in the annals of history. . . . It appeared to me more like a beaten army retreating before the enemy than a victorious army returning at ease with the trophies of success." After two grueling weeks the

41 Harrison to Secretary of War, Oct. 9, 1813, in Esarey, *Harrison Letters*, II, 563-64.

army crossed the Ohio at Limestone (Maysville) November 4, and was disbanded.[42]

As Crittenden and his fellow veterans made their way home through the state, they were everywhere given a hero's welcome. All hardships and difficulties were now forgotten in the warm sunshine of favor and preferment. The campaign had, indeed, not been an ordinary one. To have raised 3,500 armed men on only a few weeks' notice, to have marched them five hundred miles, inadequately organized and undisciplined, into a primitive country through dismal swamps occupied by a savage foe, to have defeated that enemy and returned home in little more than sixty days was not a discreditable achievement either for the commanding general or for his aides.

[42] Esarey, *Harrison Letters*, II, 565; Quaife, "Gen. Shelby's Army," 153-65; A. C. Quisenberry (ed.), "Captain James Sympson's Diary and Memoranda of the Thames Campaign," in *Kentucky Register*, XI (1913), 27.

CHAPTER II

Frontier Politics

THE THAMES River campaign was an important milestone in Crittenden's career, both in its effect on his prospects and in its influence on his thinking. His life on the frontier, his acquaintance with the spirit of Jeffersonian Republicanism gained at William and Mary, and his engaging, gregarious nature augured much for a young man of political ambition. It is not surprising, therefore, that he should have impressed the Virginia gentlemen who dominated Kentucky politics in the early 1800s. Yet even these qualities were not all that was needed for success in Kentucky politics; since pioneer days, men of culture who were identified with the landed gentry had been looked upon with suspicion by the frontiersman and were to be increasingly under attack as time passed. But the frontiersman who distrusted culture recognized and valued courage, and Crittenden discovered early in his career that a war record gave a gentleman a basis for *rapprochement* with the equalitarian backwoodsman. For the next half century, according to a contemporary, "to have fought at the Thames was the 'open sesame' to public and political honor" in Kentucky.[1] Indeed, as Crittenden himself was to discover, military service became the favorite means by which the conservative in American politics tried to halt the rising tide of egalitarianism. Crittenden would later use this means with temporary success but with ironic consequences in two crucial moments in the nation's history.

Crittenden knew that a military record had to be accompanied by success in order to be effective in frontier politics. Even though he could not be blamed in any way for the failure of the Hopkins expedition, the fact of failure itself was a political reality which mattered most to the pragmatic Kentucky voter, and there was no profit to be gained by anyone who had a part in it. Aware of this, Crittenden had been eagerly seeking military service when Shelby's commission reached him. An impartial observer might not have seen a great deal of honor in the defeat of so small a force of British and Indians at the Thames by such a large army of Americans. But it was revenge for the Raisin disaster, and in a war in which American victories in the West were so few, there was more than enough glory in the campaign for all who took part in it. For from the army that fought at the Thames there were to come three governors, four United States senators, more than a score of congressmen, and an untold number of legislators, judges, and local leaders.

In Crittenden's case, moreover, it should be remembered that not only had he served worthily as a comrade-in-arms with older men prominent in the state's political affairs, but he had also earned citations both from Shelby and from Harrison. From this time on he would be an intimate friend and adviser to Shelby, the most respected and best loved of all Kentuckians of his generation, and he was to become an associate of the younger men who were destined to political distinction, partly as a result of this campaign.

Crittenden's potential for success in Kentucky politics was thus peculiarly well balanced by his military record and by his connections with great families both in Kentucky and in Virginia. These same factors would be assets even in national politics. For Kentucky by 1813 epitomized in miniature the political struggles that were soon to rock the nation. Class antagonisms of Virginia had been perpetuated in Kentucky, although the power of the aristocracy had been greatly attenuated on the frontier. For the pioneer, with his hardy inde-

---

[1] A. C. Quisenberry, "One Hundred Years Ago—The Battle of the Thames," in *Kentucky Register*, XI (1913), 21.

pendence, was a much more formidable force than the small farmer of the East. Swarming into Transappalachia to grapple with the hardships of wild terrain and Indian warfare before the gentry arrived to claim the land, the pioneers created an ethos of their own. By nature children of the Enlightenment, they were "Reckless, exuberant, lawless, violent, brave."[2]

Although they were not overtly rebelling against society, they probably wished to achieve in the West a way of life unimpeded by the tradition of the past—not only the tradition of Europe, but of Virginia, too. "Such an expectation of unalloyed freedom," according to Arthur Moore, "precipitated irresponsible acts ranging from gross to foolish." Having endured the privations of the raw frontier, they had reason to be suspicious of Virginia aristocracy. As time went on, the real pioneers like the Harrods, McAfees, Calloways, Bryans, Logans, and Floyds figured progressively less in the affairs of the state, gradually giving way before the men of wealth and education. Actually, aristocratic Virginians had taken a relatively minor part in the early struggle for the land; they had waited to procure desirable tracts by grant from the Old Dominion. Many of the pioneers, like Daniel Boone, who had settled some of this very land, had later to surrender it when lawyers found their titles inferior to the Virginia grants.

By 1813 many pioneers by endless litigation had been divested of the choicest lands in Kentucky. The backwoodsman was thus learning that he now had to contend with a superior class in the West, just as he had had to do in Virginia and North Carolina. There were rich planters and "sons of planters denied estates by entail and primogeniture, and yeomen risen through wealth to a genteel condition."[3] These gentry, who not unreasonably felt that they were adding substantially to the wealth and culture of the West, tended to protect their interests through the familiar medium of law and government once the settlement was stabilized. And they were generally successful in holding their positions despite such equalitarian political instruments as Kentucky's constitution of 1792, which had granted equal suffrage and freedom of expression. If in their political strategy Virginians often assumed democratic airs, this is

[2] Arthur K. Moore, *The Frontier Mind, a Cultural Analysis of the Kentucky Frontiersman* (Lexington, 1957), 67.

[3] Moore, 71.

only a tribute to the understanding and grace with which they went about establishing order in the new frontier as well as to their genuine appreciation of the hardihood and courage of the frontiersmen.

Also by 1813, stimulated largely by the insatiable demands of Europe for foodstuffs and war materials for the death struggle with Napoleon, Kentucky had achieved an economic importance. The mountains were an effective barrier to commercial as well as to political intercourse with the East, but a flourishing trade had developed with the South, as tobacco, whisky, hemp, and other products could be transported down the Ohio and Mississippi rivers to New Orleans. Industrial development was also significant. The rising class of tradesmen and craftsmen who had moved down the Ohio into Kentucky from Pennsylvania and New York brought a new element into the agrarian alignment established earlier. By 1810 they had already fitted out fifteen cotton factories, thirteen hemp mills, thirty-eight ropeworks, thirty-three fulling mills, and numerous distilleries. The thriving agriculture and the trade to the South tended to make Kentucky almost independent of the East.[4] But these newly arrived craftsmen and mechanics were becoming a rising political power in the state, vociferously advancing their commercial interests, at first allied for strategic purposes with the Jeffersonian frontiersmen, later with the agrarian aristocrats in power. Finally, they emerged, with Clay as their leader, into a powerful political force in the West.

The isolation from eastern influences, the heightened social mobility common to a new land, the variety and complexity of its culture, and above all the presence in great force of the western equalitarian principles that would capture the nation made Kentucky an ideal training ground for the politician who later would have a voice in shaping national policy. For someone with Crittenden's background to succeed in Kentucky politics in the early years of the nineteenth century was not remarkable, for political leadership had been captured by the aristocracy. But for him to maintain his leadership through the period of Jacksonian democracy up to the Civil War argues political acumen of a high order.

Kentucky politics were complex not only because of the early presence of contending social and cultural interests there but because

---

[4] Thomas D. Clark, *A History of Kentucky* (New York, 1937), 164-72; Frances L. S. Dugan and Jacqueline P. Bull (eds.), *Bluegrass Craftsman* (Lexington, 1960), 23.

of its position as a border state. The distinctions already emerging between the agrarian South and the burgeoning industrial North were cultural streams that flowed together in Kentucky; Kentucky political leaders would soon learn that they must deal with both sides of the conflict developing between powerful forces on the slavery issue in their state. And Kentucky's very complexity helped to establish such figures as Clay and Crittenden as men able to deal with these issues on a national scale.

Although Kentucky was an arena in those years where were fought out in microcosm the fundamental issues which later were to find expression in national parties, there were no political parties in the modern sense in the state at this early date. The Federalist party, already on its last legs in the East, had never had substantial following in Kentucky, where only a few public men dared openly to oppose the policies of Jefferson. The political struggles found expression in a loose alliance of factions throughout the state centered in some individual family, such as the Ewings of Logan County or the Prestons or Breckinridges elsewhere; this was a pattern familiar to Virginia. Yet factional struggles were not entirely devoid of issues that divided social and economic classes, so that alliances of individuals and families sometimes took on the semblance of party unity.

As already noted, the war boom had brought on an inflation welcomed by frontier farmers but feared by commercial and banking interests. Clay, as spokesman for the latter groups, urged measures to protect their interests, such as a stable currency to be regulated by a national bank chartered by Congress. Soon Clay would expand his program to include protective tariff for industry and federal subsidy for internal improvements. All these called for the kind of national government strikingly reminiscent of that formerly advocated by the discredited Federalists. As panic and depression followed in the wake of the boom, agrarians of the Jeffersonian school aligned themselves against these neo-Federalist measures. Leader of the agrarians, until he departed for Tennessee, was Felix Grundy.

In 1813 the war had shifted away from Kentucky to distant regions east and south. Two of Crittenden's brothers moved off to other battlefields, Henry in an expedition to recapture Michilimackinac and Robert with Andrew Jackson in Alabama. But Crittenden returned to Logan County, for he now had a family to support. A son, George Bibb, had been born to Sarah in March, 1812, and just thirteen months later a daughter whom they named Ann Mary.[5]

Crittenden built a profitable law practice in Russellville. As a rule his fees did not exceed fifty or sixty dollars, but there were many of them. He was making more money than he could easily spend in that simple rural community. By 1815 he had acquired four hundred acres of land in neighboring Hopkins County, had invested in a local vineyard, and had been appointed trustee and attorney for the Pendleton Academy. Money seemed to mean little to Crittenden, and he was constantly lending his friends sums ranging from ten to five hundred dollars. He kept a record of these transactions in a little memorandum book, noting payments made and balances due. At the end of 1815 more than two thousand dollars was owed him from seven different borrowers, all friends and business associates. In only two cases is there any evidence of indebtedness other than the notation in the book. In no case was there any mention of security or of interest charge.[6]

A young man marked for a brilliant career as was Crittenden would not long remain aloof from the political wars. By 1814 he was back in the legislature. His old friend and mentor George M. Bibb was at the time United States senator from Kentucky. After the legislature adjourned, Bibb resigned, and Governor Shelby had the responsibility of appointing his successor. In view of Crittenden's youth and comparative inexperience, it seems surprising that he should have been considered for Bibb's place, but he was. Probably family connections, influential friends (including Shelby himself), and personal popularity all contributed to his promotion. Shelby had already dispatched an offer of the appointment to Crittenden when he learned that Crittenden was only twenty-seven years of age and thus was ineligible.[7]

[5] C. C. Trabue to Crittenden, April 7, 1851, in Crittenden Papers; Thomas T. Crittenden to Crittenden, Sept. 1, 1814, genealogical memorandum, in Crittenden Papers (Duke).

[6] Transfer deed of William French to Rezin Davidge and John Crittenden, Assignment by Joseph Ficklin of five shares in Logan Vineyard Company, Crittenden to Dr. W. R. Wilmoth, 1811, Crittenden's Memorandum Book, 1815, in Crittenden Papers.

[7] Thomas T. Crittenden to Crittenden, Sept. 1, 1814, in Crittenden Papers (Duke); J. J. Hawkins to Crittenden, Sept. 27, 1814, R. C. Anderson to Crittenden, n. d., in Crittenden Papers.

Instead of going to the United States Senate, therefore, Crittenden returned to the legislature the following winter. This time he was urged from many quarters to become a candidate for the speakership—evidence of the regard in which he was now held. His chief opponent was John Rowan of Nelson County, an able and distinguished lawyer a dozen years older than Crittenden. Rowan had long been in public life, a member of the state constitutional convention of 1799, secretary of state in 1804, and representative in the Eleventh Congress in 1807. But Crittenden had won favor with friends of both Shelby and Clay, and with such support the young Logan County lawyer was not to be denied. Crittenden won out over the older man, being elected speaker on the second ballot, 40 to 27.[8] He presided over the house with an impartial but friendly dignity that was later to prove one of his great political assets. His rulings appear to have been fair and judicious; at least, there were no appeals from them, and the following year he was again elected speaker, this time without opposition.[9]

But now arose a conflict growing out of the kind of odd turn of political fortune that was later to confront Crittenden twice on the national scene. George Madison had been unanimously elected governor in August, 1816, and Gabriel Slaughter, in a close contest, was elected lieutenant governor. In October, Madison suddenly died, and Slaughter succeeded to his office. Almost at once Slaughter's conservative leanings got him into difficulty. He dismissed the popular Charles S. Todd from the office of secretary of state and appointed John Pope as his successor. This move was unwise on many counts, for Pope had voted in Congress against the declaration of war in 1812 and was suspected of sympathy with the Federalist party. He was also undisputed leader of a faction hostile to Henry Clay, the most influential man in the state since the retirement of Shelby.

Slaughter followed this with another appointment equally unpopular. When Governor Shelby had discovered that Crittenden was too young to serve in the Senate, he had appointed William T. Barry to Bibb's unexpired term. Now Barry resigned, and Slaughter appointed General M. D. Hardin to succeed him. Hardin, too, was

---

8 Collins, *History of Kentucky*, II, 693; *Kentucky House Journal, 1815*, pp. 4-5.

9 *Kentucky House Journal, 1815, passim; 1816*, pp. 4-5.

thought to be a Federalist, and this was too much for Jeffersonian Kentucky. When the legislature met, it was openly hostile to Slaughter. Never before had a Kentucky governor died in office, and it was now claimed by his opponents that Slaughter was not actually governor. The constitution, they said, provided that in such a contingency the lieutenant governor should serve only until a new election could be called and a qualified successor chosen. A bill calling for such an election the next August actually was presented in the house.

State political leaders both in and out of the legislature accepted this tortuous constitutional interpretation. Joseph Cabell Breckinridge was the spokesman of the movement in the legislature, and former United States Senators Jesse Bledsoe, Bibb, and Barry were also outspoken in its support. Henry Clay, triumphantly returned from Ghent, where he had helped negotiate the peace treaty, was also believed to favor the election bill. But conservative forces, led by Pope and George Robertson, were too strong. The election bill was voted down in the house, 63 to 28, and a similar one in the senate by an equally large majority.[10]

The struggle was not yet over, however. Republican extremists, as Slaughter's opponents might well be called, continued their clamor, hoping to make his assumption of office an issue in the legislative elections the following summer. At that time they won an overwhelming victory. One-fourth of the senate was to be elected that year, and practically all of these seats went to Slaughter's opponents; they also gained a majority of twenty-six in the house. When the new legislature met, a bill to call a special gubernatorial election passed the house by a vote of 56 to 30; it was defeated in the senate by a margin of only two votes.[11]

As speaker, Crittenden had taken no part in the house debates on the subject, but he gave open support to the election bill. That this was sound strategy, even if narrow partisanship, was apparent when the legislature met in December, 1816, to choose a successor to Hardin, whose Senate term was to end the following March. Crittenden was eager for the place. He had recently passed his

---

[10] Charles Kerr (ed.), *History of Kentucky*, 5 vols. (Chicago and New York, 1922), II (by E. Merton Coulter and William E. Connelley), 582-87; Ragan, "John J. Crittenden," in *Filson Quarterly*, XVIII (1944), 5-6.

[11] Kerr, *History of Kentucky*, II, 588-91.

thirtieth birthday, and his youth was no longer a constitutional barrier. He was by now one of the most popular men in the state. He had won the friendship and confidence of Henry Clay and had just been reelected to his third term as speaker of the Kentucky legislature, again without opposition. The senatorial election was held on December 10, and Crittenden was chosen on the second ballot by a vote of 72 to 47 over General John Adair, his fellow aide to Shelby at the battle of the Thames.[12]

When the first session of the Fifteenth Congress assembled on December 1, 1817, Crittenden was on hand to take the oath. He was appointed to a special committee to consider that part of the President's message pertaining to Indian affairs, and to a committee for "conducting business in the Senate." He was also given a place on the Committee on Judiciary and the Committee on Naval Affairs, exceptional consideration for a fledgling senator. His first opportunity to speak came in late January in debate on a Revolutionary soldiers pension bill, but there is no record of what he said.[13] Full accounts of debates in that period were not recorded, and apparently this one was not considered sufficiently important for the *Annals*.

A friendly observer who was present, however, became so captivated by Crittenden's oratory that he forgot to report what the speaker said. He did note that Crittenden seemed a little nervous when he began, but that as he proceeded, his voice became "clear and sonorous," and his language "rich, chaste and nervous." He held his audience from beginning to end by his "impassioned" manner, his "terrible" invective, and his "irresistible" arguments. His eloquence, wrote his friend, "puts a spell upon our senses, and makes our very blood run cold." Admitting that this picture might sound exaggerated, he nevertheless concluded that "of all the speakers I have ever heard, he is unquestionably the most powerful and efficient in debate."[14] Another reporter, a stranger to Crittenden, who had not been impressed by his nondescript appearance before he heard him, now wrote that "were you to hear him speak . . . your enraptured faculties would award to him the highest elevation of genius; the fire of his eye, the expression of his features, the volubility of his speech, and the

---

12 *Kentucky House Journal, 1816-1817*, pp. 46-47; *Kentucky Senate Journal, 1816-1817*, pp. 40-41.

13 *Annals of Congress*, 15 Cong., 1 Sess., 11.

14 John H. Todd to Thomas Speed, Feb. 4, 1818 (copy), in Crittenden Papers.

superior force of his mind, would fill you with astonishment. Archimedes-like, he wants only a fulcrum on which to rest his lever, to overturn his adversary's system."[15]

If Crittenden had further occasion to exercise these seductive powers at that session, there is no record of it. Opportunity did present itself, however, at the next session. Matthew Lyon, a Vermont editor, had been fined and imprisoned in 1798 under the Sedition Act for his bitter denunciation of John Adams' administration. He had moved to Eddyville, Kentucky, in 1801, and since 1811 he had been vainly petitioning Congress for refund of the fine of more than a thousand dollars. When the Senate Judiciary Committee reported his 1818 petition unfavorably in early December, Crittenden offered an amendment, the effect of which would have been to establish a rule that all persons fined under that act should be reimbursed. In the debate that followed, Crittenden gave full support to the Jeffersonian doctrine that the Constitution offers a protective shield for civil liberties. Despite Crittenden's persuasive and lengthy arguments, however, and despite the ascendancy of the Jeffersonian party, Crittenden's substitute was voted down.[16] Not until long after Lyon was in his grave was the fine recovered by his heirs.

At this session Crittenden spoke for another proposition that deserved better consideration than it received. Kentucky and Tennessee had long been involved in a boundary dispute. The charters of both Virginia and North Carolina fixed 36° 30' north latitude as the dividing line between them, and the extension of this line, of course, established the boundary between their western offspring. Thomas Walker, who surveyed the western boundary, erred, however, and only later was it discovered that about 2,500 square miles that should be in Kentucky lay south of Walker's line and had, in ignorance, been appropriated by Tennessee. Efforts at an adjustment whereby Kentucky might be compensated with lands in an unsettled portion of western Tennessee failed.

At this session of Congress, Crittenden supported a bill authorizing the Supreme Court to pass on such disputes between states. The states needed "a distinguished friend," he said, to help settle their disputes, and a judgment from the Supreme Court would carry

[15] Richmond (Va.) *Enquirer*, quoted in Lexington *Kentucky Reporter*, May 9, 1825.
[16] *Annals of Congress*, 15 Cong., 2 Sess., 48, 60, 64; *Niles' Register*, XV (1818-1819), 285.

such moral force that it would "execute itself silently and effectually." Kentucky, he said, in her present dispute with Tennessee was faced with the alternative either of surrendering to Tennessee's arbitrary refusal to compromise or else of resorting to the sword. Crittenden's bill had merit, and his arguments in support of it were sound, but sentiment for state rights proved too strong. The Senate rejected his bill 17 to 20.[17]

These were years of calm in the national capital before the storms that were soon to break. The Tallmadge amendment to the Missouri bill was introduced in the House of Representatives in February, 1819, but Congress adjourned before the controversy reached the Senate. Nothing substantial enough to be called a party opposed the Monroe administration. Ambitious men, of whom Henry Clay was one, had already begun their political infighting for the succession to Monroe, but this struggle had six full years to germinate before it would divide the country in the winter of 1825.[18] "There is nothing new or interesting here," Crittenden wrote from Washington early in his second term. "Congress is proceeding very dully with the mere drudgery of legislation."[19]

Crittenden was proud of his position as a United States senator and soon developed a genuine affection for many of his associates there. But he had pecuniary problems. Members of Congress were paid only five dollars a day at that time, soon to be increased to eight. The body was in session generally for only the three winter months, and when it adjourned, pay stopped. Long service in the Senate, therefore, took either a man of independent wealth or one like Daniel Webster, whose friends would privately subsidize him. But Crittenden was a young man with neither of these resources. He did have, however, increased responsibilities. A third child, Cornelia, had joined the family circle in 1816, and a fourth, Thomas Leonidas, would make his appearance in May, 1819. Hard times, which had struck the East a year before, were being felt in Kentucky now. Crittenden's law business, flourishing at the time of his election, was

[17] Annals of Congress, 15 Cong., 2 Sess., 193-94, 200.

[18] See entries for Dec. 6, 24, 1817, Dec. 17, 25, 1818, Jan. 25, 1819, March 31, 1820, in Charles Francis Adams (ed.), Memoirs of John Quincy Adams, Comprising Portions of His Diary from 1795 to 1848, 12 vols. (Philadelphia, 1874-1877), IV, 28, 30, 193, 197-98, 212, 215-16, 228-30, V, 52-53.

[19] Crittenden to Isaac Shelby, Dec. 18, 1818, in Crittenden Collection, Chicago Historical Society.

languishing, and Sarah was urging him to remain at home for the welfare of his family. Reluctantly he agreed that he must give up his cherished post and devote himself to his law practice. He sent in his resignation to the legislature, but at the same time he privately resolved "to quit . . . business as soon as ever I can make a decent fortune, if ever that should happen." Then he hoped he might return to the Senate. "I have so set it down on my tablet," he wrote.[20]

Crittenden was too much a man of affairs ever to become profoundly learned in the law, but he was a very effective trial lawyer, winning a disproportionately large number of his cases. A keen judge of men and a skilled tactician, he seemed to sense precisely the fragments of testimony that would appeal to a jury and to hammer these home in his arguments.

On one occasion Crittenden was employed to defend a street brawler indicted for biting off the ear of an antagonist. Judge H. P. Brodnax, who presided over the Logan circuit court, was a "stately, high toned Virginia gentleman," who dressed in knee pants and silk stockings. He detested rough or uncouth behavior and insisted on a high degree of dignity in his court. It was with some difficulty that a jury was selected to try the ear biter, for Crittenden insisted upon rejecting all reputable citizens. After much delay, eleven had been obtained, but one more was needed. Finally the sheriff brought in a man who would have been unwelcome in almost any company. His old straw hat had half the brim off, his face bore the marks of many a battle, and he had only a part of a nose, the rest having been lost in some groghouse brawl. Crittenden, pretending impatience at longer delay of the trial, agreed to accept him. But Judge Brodnax's patience now was exhausted. Surveying the jury with some disdain, he remarked disparagingly about its nondescript appearance. Crittenden, feigning surprise, observed that he thought it quite a respectable jury. The defendant was acquitted in short order.[21]

Soon after Crittenden resigned from the Senate, he removed his family from Russellville to Frankfort, the capital of the state. Frankfort was also the county seat of Franklin County, which lay athwart the Kentucky River on the western border of his native county of

[20] Crittenden to John Williams, Jan. 5, 1820, Crittenden to David Daggett, Feb. 10, 1820, in Crittenden Papers, Yale University Library; Henry Clay to Crittenden, Dec. 14, 1819, in Coleman, *Crittenden*, I, 39.

[21] John B. Bibb to Mrs. Chapman Coleman, Nov. 26, 1867, in Crittenden Papers (Duke).

Woodford. Ages before, the Kentucky River had cut a deep gorge through the limestone soil of this region, whose rolling, undulating fields and rich bottom lands produced an abundant surplus of such crops as hemp, tobacco, cereals, and livestock for export.

In 1819 Frankfort was a village of little more than fifteen hundred persons. Nestled in a bend of the river, it was almost entirely surrounded by what were then heavily wooded hills, and the view from the hills above or from the town below was equally picturesque. In the older part of the town, in a quadrant formed by the intersection of Broadway and Washington streets with each other and with the bending river, stood stately, graceful homes. Here families of rich landowners and prosperous lawyers lived a close-knit, neighborly existence.

In the winter months when the legislature met or when the court of appeals was in session, Frankfort was busy and exciting. The inns and private homes were crowded to overflowing; balls were held weekly; and Dan Weisiger, the tavernkeeper and caterer for the community, and Hopping Dick Taylor, at the Mansion House, were taxed to the utmost to meet the demands for their services. But nine months of the year Frankfort was a peaceful, drowsy, little village, roused only by the coming and going of the steamboats on the river or the mailcoach from Lexington or Louisville.

It was not caprice that prompted Crittenden to exchange his bright prospects in bustling Russellville for a home in this sleepy, idyllic village. Winning cases in the Green River country had not proved too difficult for him, but most legal business in any rural community is relatively trifling and the fees small. Only occasionally would a big case come along, and when it did, the decision of the circuit court was invariably appealed. The Kentucky court of appeals in Frankfort was too distant in those days for lawyers from outlying towns to be able to prosecute their own cases in the higher court. An attorney at or near Frankfort had to be employed and the fee divided with him. Consequently, once a lawyer's reputation had been made in a remote section of the state, he frequently found it advantageous to move to Frankfort, where he might devote his time largely to the more important cases coming before the court of appeals, referred to him by his lawyer friends throughout the state.

A few months after he moved to Frankfort, Crittenden could write that he was seated "obscurely & contentedly . . . in my little law shop, watching for fees and for clients."[22] He did not have long to wait. Within little more than two years he was to appear in 428 cases before the court of appeals, and the fees for about five-sixths of these totaled more than eight thousand dollars. (No fee is indicated in his books for the remainder.) Not only were his cases referred to him from the Green River country; they came to him from the Bluegrass counties as well. Joseph Underwood, James T. Morehead, Presley Edwards, and John Breathitt were his most frequent associates from the western and southern part of the state. From the Bluegrass, Robert J. Breckinridge, Robert P. Letcher, Squire Turner, George Robertson, and Henry Clay all used his services at one time or another.[23]

A few years after Crittenden moved to Frankfort, Clay began employing him, and as time went on, he referred cases to him more and more.[24] On at least one occasion they appeared as cocounsel in Lexington, defending Charles Wickliffe, son of Robert Wickliffe, who had killed the editor of the *Kentucky Gazette.* In their summary of the case Crittenden expounded the law of self-defense and its precedents, making what Clay's biographer called "an able and eloquent defense." Clay then made a highly impassioned plea, and the jury rendered a verdict of acquittal within a few minutes after the case was submitted to them.[25] When Clay became Secretary of State in March, 1825, he was prepared to recommend Crittenden as his successor as chief counsel in Kentucky for the Bank of the United States. But the bank's business was declining to such an extent at that time that the directors decided not to employ a replacement.[26]

[22] Crittenden to John Williams, Jan. 5, 1820, Crittenden to David Daggett, Feb. 10, 1820, in Crittenden Papers (Yale).

[23] Journal of Cases Practiced before the Court of Appeals, Nov., 1819, to April, 1822, Account of Crittenden with John Breathitt for Law Business, Dec., 1821, in Crittenden Papers. See also volumes for succeeding years.

[24] Clay to Crittenden, Nov. 10, 1824, July 25, Oct. 20 (unsigned fragment), 1825, March 10, 1826, Jan. 25, 1827, Nov. 20, 1831, April 15, 1832, in Crittenden Papers; Crittenden to Clay, Jan. 12, 1827, Nov. 26, 1832, in Crittenden Papers (Duke).

[25] Calvin Colton, *The Life, Correspondence, and Speeches of Henry Clay,* 6 vols. (New York, 1864), I, 90-92; J. Winston Coleman, Jr., *The Trotter-Wickliffe Duel* (Frankfort, 1950), 5.

[26] Clay to Langdon Cheves, Sept. 13, 1822, in Dreer Collection, Historical Society of Pennsylvania; Francis Preston Blair to Clay, March 7, 1825, in Clay Papers, Library of Congress (hereinafter without depository indicated); Clay to Thomas Todd, March 27, 1825, in Clay Papers, Kentucky State Historical Society. Unless otherwise designated, the Clay manuscripts cited are from typescript copies in possession of the Henry Clay Project at the University of Kentucky.

In addition to Clay, Crittenden's most distinguished clients during this period were former Presidents James Madison and James Monroe, and Colonel Richard M. Johnson, colorful United States senator and a hero of the Battle of the Thames.[27] But Crittenden represented people in all walks of life, and in an infinite variety of causes. His reputation as a successful practitioner grew, and after he had been in Frankfort only a year, judges of the state's highest court were speaking of him "in the warmest terms of admiration." Within a few years his old schoolmate Francis Preston Blair, now Crittenden's neighbor in Frankfort, thought him the "ablest and worthiest" member of the Kentucky bar. This was at a time when George M. Bibb, after hearing William Wirt, Daniel Webster, John Sergeant, and Hugh Lawson White plead before the United States Supreme Court, was writing that in his opinion "the bar of Kentucky . . . contain[s] as much talent and force as any other bar in the Union." Bibb may have been biased, but at least he was an experienced judge of legal talent.[28]

Crittenden's fees for his practice before the court of appeals were generally arranged between him and the referring lawyer. Crittenden seems to have been strangely unconcerned in this highly important phase of business. His charges were probably adequate but not exorbitant. A Maysville lawyer, after telling his client that Crittenden's compensation for representing him in the court of appeals would "not be less than $100," reported that the client would be pleased to pay that sum. John Helm, writing from Elizabethtown to engage Crittenden's services, told him to name his fee and it would be paid. In another case Helm promised "a generous fee" when the case was disposed of.[29]

Sometimes clients in distress wrote direct, making brave promises of payment. One, involved in a suit "of mighty consequence," wrote that if he triumphed, Crittenden would "be well paid, *yea* overpaid." "I hope," he added, "you will not desert me." Hugh Mercer of Fredericksburg, Virginia, transferred his legal business in Kentucky

27 Power of attorney executed by James Monroe to Crittenden, [?] 1828, James Madison to Crittenden, July 8, 1830, in Crittenden Papers (Duke); Richard M. Johnson to Crittenden, March 7, 1824, Feb. 6, 1827, in Crittenden Papers.

28 Robert P. Letcher to Crittenden, Nov. 30, 1821, in Crittenden Papers; Blair to Clay, March 7, 1825, in Clay Papers; George M. Bibb to Crittenden, March 8, 1824, in Coleman, *Crittenden*, I, 61.

29 John Chambers to Crittenden, Sept. 11, 1827, John L. Helm to Crittenden, March 20, 1833, in Crittenden Papers.

to Crittenden as a result of Crittenden's reputation for "efficient and faithful" devotion to business. He promised to "make any compensation" which Crittenden would see fit to charge. But Richard M. Johnson, in heavy debt to the Bank of the United States, exhorted Crittenden to defend him in a suit which Green Clay had brought against him, promising only that "Heaven will reward you. I shall never be able to do it." Future relations between this client and Crittenden would warrant the opinion that Johnson was conscientiously defended.[30]

Some of Crittenden's cases during this early period were of more than passing interest. In one, Crittenden defended a Transylvania University student from the Deep South who had killed a fellow student in a brawl. So great was the feeling in Lexington that change of venue was obtained to Woodford, and the case was tried in Versailles. The prosecutor urged the jury to make an example of the student in order to combat the "lawlessness of the times" that was undermining "the majesty of the law." Agreeing in principle with his "stern and learned friend" that an example "even among the young and thoughtless" might check violence and passion, Crittenden said there were ample opportunities for such example "from among our own people." Do not, he pleaded, "seize upon the youthful stranger, who came confidingly among us," for such a sacrifice. There were, he said, unhappily too many opportunities to make examples of "our own sons, in our own borders. Let us do this, then, when the occasion offers," and send this young man back home to his family, who had entrusted him to their care. Admitting that his client had committed a great crime, he urged that acquittal, under the circumstances, would be "honorable to our great State, and do no damage to the laws." The lad was acquitted.[31]

For a half-dozen years after he moved to Frankfort, Crittenden remained out of public office. But his good judgment and power of persuasion were too well known for him to remain a private citizen. The Kentucky-Tennessee boundary dispute, thrown back to the states by Congress, was still unsettled. In January, 1820, Crittenden and John Rowan, now judge of the court of appeals, were chosen by

---

[30] Letters to Crittenden from John Hanna, Feb. 16, 1832, from Mercer, May 7, 1831, and from Johnson, March 7, 1824, Crittenden Papers; Frankfort *Commonwealth*, April 16, 1833; Coleman, *Crittenden*, I, 83.

[31] Coleman, *Crittenden*, I, 23-25.

the legislature to "confer and agree" with commissioners from Tennessee on an adjustment.

The Kentucky commissioners made two proposals: let the erroneous Walker line remain the boundary from the Cumberland Mountains to the Tennessee River, and let Tennessee compensate Kentucky by equivalent territory west of the Tennessee River; or establish 36° 30' throughout. The Tennessee commissioners rejected both proposals and countered with an offer that Walker's line be accepted east of the Tennessee River and a more southerly line west, with reciprocal engagements by both states confirming land grants made by Virginia and North Carolina lying between the two lines. Crittenden was willing to accept this proposal, but Rowan was not. The Kentucky commissioners then proposed submitting the dispute to arbitration, but the Tennessee commissioners would not agree.

The Kentucky commissioners reported to the legislature their failure, but Crittenden recommended in a further report that the legislature accept the Tennessee proposal. He did not think this arrangement right in the abstract, for Kentucky's claim for the land between Walker's line and 36° 30' was technically correct. But under the circumstances the Tennessee proposal was the most politic and most equitable arrangement that could be secured. He pointed out that the Walker line east of the Tennessee River had been accepted by all parties for forty years, that counties and towns had been laid out in conformity with it, and that moving the boundary a few miles to the south not only would disturb municipal regulations but would confound already confused land titles and force Tennessee citizens into a reluctant subjection to Kentucky. With minor adjustments the legislature accepted Crittenden's recommendation, and the articles of agreement were signed in Frankfort on February 2, 1820. In little more than a month this bitter controversy, which threatened to impair good relations between the two states, had been settled to the satisfaction of almost everyone.[32]

Crittenden was called frequently for other civic duties. In June, 1823, probably through Henry Clay's influence, he was unanimously elected to the Transylvania University board of trustees. He participated actively in the affairs of the board, and a year later he was

[32] *Kentucky House Journal*, 1819, pp. 84-86, 249-54, 282, Appendix, 1-40; Nashville *Clarion*, quoted in Russellville (Ky.) *Weekly Messenger*, Feb. 22, 1820, see also March 7, 1820.

awarded an honorary degree of doctor of laws by the faculty. He served as trustee and attorney for the Kentucky Seminary, an academy in Frankfort, and in 1824 he was one of seven commissioners named by the legislature to rebuild the state capitol, which had been destroyed by fire. These commissioners employed Gideon Shryock as architect, raised funds by popular subscription to supplement the $15,000 appropriated by the legislature, and built the beautiful Ionic-columned structure that still stands in the old part of the city. The following May, when Lafayette visited the city, Crittenden, George M. Bibb, Thomas Bodley, and Solomon P. Sharp arranged a sumptuous dinner in honor of the great Frenchman. On this occasion Crittenden's twelve-year-old daughter, Ann Mary, read a poem that she had composed in Lafayette's honor.[33]

Public business, however, did not preclude acts of personal kindness for old friends. When Isaac Shelby, grown feeble in the service of his state and his country, was bitterly attacked by William C. Preston, Crittenden came to the aid of his former benefactor. Shelby, reminiscing over the Battle of King's Mountain in private correspondence with his old comrade John Sevier, had mentioned that William Campbell, one of his aides, had not been present at the British surrender there but had arrived on the scene some fifteen or twenty minutes later. After Sevier's death, his son ill-advisedly published some of his correspondence, including the letter from Shelby. This enraged Preston, who thought it reflected upon the courage of William Campbell, his grandfather. He issued a pamphlet denouncing Shelby as a mountebank and discrediting Shelby's own contribution to the victory. Shelby, now paralyzed, was determined to answer Preston and vindicate his own name. Unable to write, he enlisted the aid of Crittenden and M. D. Hardin. Together these two gathered certificates from survivors of the battle and prepared and published an answer in Shelby's name. The statement gave documentary proof both of Shelby's good conduct in the battle and of

[33] Raymond F. McLain, "The Record of the Board of Trustees Transylvania University, 1821-1823," in *Filson Quarterly*, XXI (1947), 208; Robert and Johanna Peter, *Transylvania University, Its Origin, Rise, Decline, and Fall*, Filson Club Publications No. 11 (Louisville, 1896), 126; Charles Humphreys to Crittenden, July 18, 1825, in Crittenden Papers; "Minutes of the Board of Trustees of the Kentucky Seminary from January, 1812, to January, 1830," in *Kentucky Register*, XLVIII (1950), 19-23; L. F. Johnson, *History of Franklin County, Kentucky* (Frankfort, 1912), 76; receipted expense voucher by Richard Taylor for Lafayette Dinner, May 10, 1825, in Brown Papers, Kentucky Historical Society; Alice Elizabeth Trabue, *A Corner in Celebrities* (Louisville, 1923), 39.

Campbell's absence at the climax of the struggle. It was a complete vindication of the old governor.[34]

On another occasion Crittenden helped prevent a duel between two of his friends, Robert J. Breckinridge and Robert Wickliffe. Learning that the two men had arranged a meeting, Crittenden wrote Clay, asking aid in forestalling it. Clay thereupon addressed a letter to both men and forwarded it to Crittenden, who also signed it and delivered it to the antagonists and their seconds. Crittenden was prepared to obtain a warrant placing both men under a peace bond, but this proved unnecessary.[35]

When Crittenden first moved to Frankfort, he lived for more than a year in a small cottage purchased from Dr. L. Wilkinson. But these quarters were too small for his growing family. In addition to Thomas, born shortly before he moved to Frankfort, Sarah was to present him with three more children in the next five years, a third son, Robert, and two daughters, Eugenia and Sarah Lee, whose familiar name was Maria. Therefore, by the spring of 1821 Crittenden was seeking a larger home. He found it at the southwest corner of Washington and Main streets, a site once owned by Aaron Burr.

It was a spacious, rambling, L-shaped brick house, probably built about the turn of the century and modeled somewhat after the houses of colonial Philadelphia. The front door opened directly on Main Street and was elevated only a step above the street. Inside, a spacious central hall separated the two front parlors, and from this hallway a graceful staircase ascended the left wall to a landing, and from there to halls opening upon sleeping rooms on the upper floors. Crittenden bought the house from Joseph Scott, who had recently purchased it from Charles Sproul. In exchange he gave Scott the house the Crittendens had been living in, fifteen shares of stock in the Bank of Kentucky, $1,250 in notes of the Bank of the Commonwealth, worth perhaps half their face value, and assumed a $3,000 mortgage held by the Bank of Kentucky.[36]

34 Shelby to ————, Nov. 14, 1822, M. D. Hardin and Crittenden to Shelby, n. d., microfilm copy, in Shelby Papers (Kentucky); Lexington *Kentucky Reporter*, April 14, 1823; Charles S. Todd to Mrs. Chapman Coleman, April 4, 1870, in Crittenden Papers (Duke).

35 Clay to Crittenden, Sept. 13, 1823, in Crittenden Papers.

36 Genealogical memorandum, in Crittenden Papers (Duke); Deed of Exchange with Joseph Scott, June 7, 1821, Receipt of Scott, dated June 28, 1821, in Crittenden Papers; *Kentucky Register*, LVII (1959), 76; George C. Downing, "The Home of Governor Crittenden, Frankfort, Kentucky," *Kentucky Register*, III (1905), 23-24; Coleman, *Crittenden*, I, 42.

Behind the house was a small garden, enclosed by a high brick wall. At the front of the house, on the edge of the sidewalk, was a semicircular carriage block of Kentucky marble. From this block in the years to come Crittenden would address many a gathering of his neighbors, when they came to welcome him home from his labors in Washington. But that time was not yet, and in the next decade the carriage block served mainly as a resting place for the children in the long summer evenings, seated opposite their parents on the front doorstep. Here neighbors often gathered—Robert Letcher and his wife "the Queen," who lived directly behind the Crittendens on Wapping Street; the Orlando Browns and the Mason Browns, who lived around the corner on Wilkinson Street; the Swigerts, who lived directly across Main Street; the Moreheads, who lived in a house diagonally across the corner of Main and Washington; the Burnleys and Carneals from Wapping Street. Or perhaps some visitors from out of town—Henry Clay or Robert J. Breckinridge or Madison C. Johnson from Lexington, or George D. Prentice or Humphrey Marshall or Samuel S. Nicholas from Louisville.

As the neighbors gathered, the boys inside the house passed chairs through the front windows to accommodate them. If all were of the same political faith, then the talk would touch upon the questions of the day: of stay laws and relief, of the Old Court–New Court controversy, of John Quincy Adams and Andrew Jackson and the controversial contest between them, of tariff and banks and internal improvements. These were subjects children never could entirely understand; even so, they remained unnaturally quiet so as to catch every word of the adult conversation. If any of the visitors were, perchance, members of the New Court party, or later, Jackson men, then politics must be eschewed. Sometimes the talk turned to still more dramatic doings—to an exciting legal trial, or perhaps to tales of local violence. On such occasions the children were reluctant to go to their beds in the upper chambers when their hour had struck, for they feared to leave the protective circle of their elders.

In this home Crittenden lived for the next four decades, gathering his children and his grandchildren about him as often as he could persuade them to visit him. Here he welcomed his friends. He gave three simple dinners a week during the legislative session, so that by the end he had entertained them all. Fish, venison, and oysters were his favorite dishes and were frequently served. He always served bourbon whisky, and took a cup or two himself—on infrequent occasions, too many. And finally, in this house, when his labors were ended, he died, full of years and honors but still animated by the zest for life.

Massive trees, still standing, surrounded the house, on the pavement next to the street and in the garden to the rear—lindens and maples and spreading oaks. Crittenden loved these trees and watched over them closely, seeing that they were topped and pruned periodically. The gnarled, twisted oak at the very tip of the corner sidewalks was a special favorite. Almost every morning when he was at home, he strolled outdoors before breakfast. On such occasions he would stop by the side of this old friend, tap it with his walking stick, and look up into its dense foliage, as if almost to converse with it.

Crittenden had a habit of talking aloud to himself on occasion, gesticulating earnestly, to the great amusement of his children. If guests were about and asked who his companion might be, the children, a finger to their lips, beckoned the visitors to the window, there to watch in silent amusement as the tall, slender figure of their host strode up and down, up and down, in ardent conversation with an imaginary companion.[37]

These were happy days for the young Crittenden family, but they were not to go on uninterrupted. After little more than a dozen years of married life, Sarah, the wife and mother, died in mid-September, 1824. We know nothing of the cause of Sarah's death; as a matter of fact, we know little of Sarah as a person. As already noted, letters from her are nonexistent, and most of the children were too young to recall much about her in later years. She was laid to rest in the old Bellevue Cemetery on the Leestown Road, barely a mile from her home. She left Crittenden with seven children, the eldest, George, twelve years of age, and the youngest not yet two.[38]

Crittenden was torn with grief, but he had little time for self-pity. He now had added responsibility for the care of his children, in addition to other extraordinary demands on him. He was embroiled in a political struggle that was raging in Kentucky, one which would greatly influence his future. The outcome was in doubt, but the contest was rapidly reaching a climax.

[37] Downing, "Home of Governor Crittenden," III, 23-24; H. H. Crittenden, *Memoirs*, 32; Coleman, *Crittenden*, I, 42-43.
[38] C. Glenn Clift, "Kentucky Marriages and Obituaries," in *Kentucky Register*, XXXIX (1941), 127; Oxx, "The Kentucky Crittendens," 182.

CHAPTER III

Old Court–New Court

HENRY CLAY, to whose leadership Crittenden was to give unquestioning loyalty for more than thirty years and to whose fortunes Crittenden's were so inextricably bound, had learned Republicanism from his mentor, Chancellor George Wythe of Virginia. Indeed, one of the reasons Clay decided to cross the mountains to Kentucky in 1797 was to escape the "Mock Republicanism" of Washington and to find a place "endowing naturally its owners with ease & affluence as well as preserving them from the infection of prodigality & the poison of Aristocracy," a place that "gave promise of freedom from a corrupt and enslaving past."[1] In Kentucky, Prince Hal, with his Jeffersonian principles, quickly became the political hero of the "liberty-bellowing, Indian-killing" frontiersmen.[2]

But Clay's alliance by marriage with the ruling families of Kentucky had also given him opportunities for investments and handsome fees, and for association with Virginia gentlemen who were anything but "mobocrats." These relationships were to attenuate Clay's Jeffersonian leanings more and more as time went on, until his American System was to be virtually a western-oriented version of Federalism. It was the irony of Clay's career and one that was to cost him his lifelong dream, the Presidency, that he was never able to recognize the essential conflict between wealth and Republicanism. The money that permitted him to live so graciously was to become a fateful issue to Clay, and his growing conservatism in this regard was to have a significant effect also upon Crittenden's career.

Clay's first real conflict over money and banking came in his two-year battle to renew the charter of the Kentucky Insurance Company. His adversary was Felix Grundy, the democratic "upstart" who was beginning to challenge Clay's leadership. The insurance company had adroitly inserted a clause in its charter permitting unlimited issuance of notes "payable to bearer" and had thereby become the banking institution of the state. The need for a stable currency in a growing young economy was of course obvious to businessmen, but a central bank and the Federalism with which it was associated were anathema to any disciple of Jefferson, and in opposing the renewal, Felix Grundy was more consistent than Clay. Clay was victorious in the brilliant parliamentary duel with Grundy and the charter was renewed in 1806, but it was an ominous victory; for Grundy went south to Tennessee, where he helped raise up the champion that was to prove Clay's nemesis.[3]

Although this battle on behalf of the business interests increased Clay's reputation as a political tactician and was on the whole a tribute to his intelligence and foresight, it marked the beginning of the inconsistencies in his financial views that were to haunt him at vital moments. After the charter triumph, Clay went straight back to Republicanism, even enlisting Felix Grundy among his War Hawks, who were to incite the nation to throw down the gauntlet against Great Britain. In this campaign there was an alliance between the commercial interests in the West and the interests of the small farmer and frontiersman, for the Napoleonic wars had made the new American West the source of supply for foodstuffs and for materials of war. The enormous stimulus thus given to the new land by war-created foreign markets meant flush times, in which everyone shared an interest in prosperity. Until the real nature of Napoleon revealed

[1] Samuel Hopkins to John Breckinridge, March 29, 1794, quoted in Bernard Mayo, *Henry Clay, Spokesman of the New West* (Boston, 1937), 47.

[2] Mayo, 58.

[3] Clement Eaton, *Henry Clay and the Art of American Politics* (Boston, 1957), 14-17.

itself, the attempts of the French to spread Enlightenment doctrines also had the sympathy of the Republican West, especially since its produce was shipped abroad to Napoleon's Europe down the Ohio and Mississippi rivers without much reliance on New England shipping. A war that promised western expansion and punishment for England for interfering with profitable commerce was bound to win favor in the West, and Clay made the most of this situation.

On a wave of fiery enthusiasm Clay felt that his power was growing among western equalitarian Republicans. Borne along by this feeling, he reversed in 1811 the position he had taken in Kentucky in 1806 and led the fight in Congress for the repeal of the national bank. Clay was later to regret this rash, although politically expedient, move; for although the Bank of the United States was a creature of the hated Federalists and although a great deal of its stock was owned in England, it did represent a stabilizing influence in an economy feeling the inflationary pulls of the European war. Indeed, despite his Republican repugnance for central banking, Jefferson had recognized the necessity for the bank, and had even strengthened it. England was attempting to withdraw specie from America at this time, and there was growing pressure from numerous state banks issuing notes unbacked by specie, so that the destruction of the one stable force in the economy was to have disastrous effects. And in the destruction of this first Bank of the United States, Henry Clay "as much as any other man could be held responsible."[4]

Five years later, with the war ended, Clay again reversed his stand on the monetary question. There was now a growing need to resume trade relations with the East and its manufactures, as well as to develop western industry. The currency of the nation was in a sad condition, for specie was moving steadily to New England to pay for finished goods, and the totally unreliable currency of the recently spawned state banks was retarding commercial development. Although to Calhoun must go the credit for developing the bill that reestablished the national bank in 1816, Clay, as Speaker of the House, was most responsible for its passage.[5]

Significantly, just at this time Clay's popularity slumped in his home state. Historians have attributed this slump to the fact that Clay had voted to increase the pay of congressmen from about nine

[4] Mayo, *Henry Clay*, 377.
[5] Glyndon G. Van Deusen, *Life of Henry Clay* (Boston, 1937), 112.

hundred dollars a year to fifteen hundred dollars. Frontiersmen no doubt resented Clay's stand, which reflected the growing power of government, but the ease with which this issue was fanned into flame by Clay's opponents suggests deeper grievances. Henry Clay seemed oblivious of the changing political forces around him. His associates were in the upper strata of business and society; and the logic of his American System of internal improvements, tariff, and sound money in building the industry and prosperity of the West after the loss of much European trade seemed so reasonable to him and his associates that he apparently never understood the persistent hostility of the rank and file toward banks and the financial power they represented. He seemed not to realize that the sound logic of his own position, which his experience with banking and currency had made clear to him, was not grasped by everyone concerned with the welfare of the West. Clay overestimated the ability of the small farmer to consider the logic and the long-range good of the economy when his own immediate welfare was concerned. He was to find that plain people were inclined to hold the "evil man" view of society: when times were booming, it was the bankers who withheld the credit that would have permitted the struggling farmer or small merchant to expand to take advantage of the rising markets; and when the boom collapsed, it was the bankers who with fiendish malice had plotted this development and who were delighted to foreclose the mortgages that had been contracted for in good times.

During the extreme vacillations of the economy of the nation after 1819, Henry Clay should have kept more closely in touch with the money and banking issue in Kentucky. Foreshadowing its appearance as a national issue, it tore Kentucky apart during the 1820s and precipitated a constitutional crisis centered on the court of appeals. Had Clay's duties and the advice of his friends permitted him to take more interest in this struggle, he might have been better prepared for the rise, under Jackson, of the equalitarian forces, whose power he so consistently underestimated. In his early spectacular western Republicanism, which had made him the Cock of Kentucky to his eastern associates, Clay had militantly followed the course of Jeffersonian democracy; but as the mantle of leadership fell more snugly about his shoulders, he seemed to expect that the westerners would be guided by his judgment as to what was for their welfare. With his own personal associations and his own experiences assuring him of the long-range wisdom of his course, Clay could not see that his American System, with its tariffs, internal improvements, strong military establishments, and central banking, was very like the original Federalism against which he had tilted so vehemently.[6] That his followers should realize this better than he, and that westerners should decide to follow leadership more consistent with the original principles of Republicanism, should have surprised Clay only if he were beguiled into believing the democratic farmer was following him on the road to economic conservatism. Clay would have profited by sharing the experiences of his friend Crittenden in Kentucky's struggle over "relief."

The end of the Napoleonic wars in 1815 brought prosperity to America. Then, as European industry and agriculture recovered sufficiently to reduce their needs for the products of the American West, and as American businessmen saw foreign markets disappearing, cautious lenders resumed the demand for payment in specie that struck at the heart of the war-induced inflation. Lost markets combined with tightened currency to produce the usual effect—sudden and devastating depression. As early as 1818, financial troubles began to appear in the East. The fall was in proportion to the dizzy heights the inflationary spiral had attained. Bankruptcies came on an enormous scale to business houses both in Europe and in America. Sales of western lands dwindled, and land prices plummeted, as did prices for crops, manufactured goods, and slaves. A house and lot on Limestone Street in Lexington, which had been bought for $15,000 a few years before, sold under the hammer for $1,300. Slaves whose hire brought in a hundred dollars the year before sold for only three or four hundred dollars. Corn was selling at ten cents a bushel, and wheat for twenty cents. The depression had come.[7]

Bankers, who had tried vainly to stem the expansion, were already under attack for their conservative policies. Until 1818 there had been only two banks operating in Kentucky: the Bank of the United States, with branches at Louisville and Lexington, and the Bank of Kentucky, about a fifth of whose stock was owned by the state and a majority of whose directors were chosen by the legislature. Although the great mass of people had been suspicious of banknotes since

[6] Eaton, *Henry Clay*, chap. iii, *passim*.

[7] Collins, *History of Kentucky*, II, 878; Adams, *Memoirs*, IV, 349, 370; *Niles' Register*, XVII (1819-1820), 84, 85, XIX (1820-1821), 16, XX (1821), 85.

their experience with Continental currency a few decades before, they were now resentful because not enough currency was available. The huge expansion of business immediately after the war led to such pressure by small businessmen for an expanded currency that the legislature in 1818 chartered forty-six banks, soon to be known as the Forty Thieves.[8] Total capitalization of these banks was nearly $9,000,000, almost none of it in specie. Their practice was to issue a flood of notes, lend these out to purchasers of land or for other speculative schemes, and, on the strength of mortgages to secure these loans, issue more banknotes to lend to an ever-growing army of speculators.

But the branches of the Bank of the United States would not accept the notes of these flimsy creatures, and consequently their notes circulated at a huge discount. There was widespread resentment of the Bank of the United States during the boom years for this restrictive policy. A goodly portion of the population of Kentucky was interested in speculation, and a resolution was offered in the legislature in 1819 calling for a tax of $60,000 annually on each branch of the national bank. Another resolution called on the bank to close its Kentucky branches.

When the bubble burst at the end of the boom, public opinion reversed itself. Now the obliging Forty Thieves, who had resisted the attempts of the Bank of the United States to curtail their unsound notes, were themselves the object of the ire of the people and the legislature. The legislature annulled the charters of the Forty Thieves, but the damage had already been done. Debts caused by the collapse of speculative enterprises were staggering. Gross debts due all banks amounted to an estimated $10,000,000, much of it owed by small farmers and mechanics. Now the debtors and many others, feeling the pinch of depression, called public meetings to urge a special legislative session to pass relief measures. Jeffersonian hostility toward strong government, prominent in prosperity, was not so strong in times of depression and want.[9]

Public clamor was difficult for a democratically chosen body to resist. When the legislature met, it created a second state bank, the

[8] A. M. Stickles, *The Critical Court Struggle in Kentucky, 1819-1829* (Bloomington, Ind., 1929), 5-25.

[9] Collins, *History of Kentucky*, II, 878; Nathaniel S. Shaler, *Kentucky, a Pioneer Commonwealth* (Boston and New York, 1884), 177-78; *Niles' Register*, XV (1818-1819), 385, XVI (1819), 260, 261.

Bank of the Commonwealth, with a capital stock of $2,000,000, and with authority to issue $3,000,000 in notes not redeemable in specie, for the bank had no specie. Instead, $2,000,000 of its notes were secured only by state stock in the Bank of Kentucky, and by the promise to redeem from receipts of future taxation and from sale of state-owned lands west of the Tennessee River. Loans were limited to $1,000, except that directors might borrow twice that amount, and could be obtained simply by personal endorsement if the borrower had no real estate to mortgage. All borrowers must swear to use the loan either to pay debts or to purchase domestic products. The bank's president and board of directors were chosen annually by the legislature, and they were given great discretion both in making loans and in determining when to call payments.[10]

Crittenden was elected president of the bank, and Francis Preston Blair treasurer. As soon as notes could be prepared, they were distributed to branches to be put in circulation. The legislature took stock, money, and business away from its stable financial institution, the Bank of Kentucky, and hoping to buoy the new institution by the superior credit of the old, sought to have the Bank of Kentucky accept the Commonwealth banknotes at par. Crittenden attempted to work out such an arrangement with his friend John Harvie, president of the Bank of Kentucky. But Harvie, fearing the credit of his own institution would be endangered, agreed only to token acceptance.

From the very beginning, Commonwealth banknotes depreciated, first to seventy cents on the dollar, then to sixty, soon to forty, and even lower outside the state. Moreover, the transfer of state business to the new bank threatened the old; and its notes declined also, although not so rapidly as those of the new bank. Even so, Crittenden and his directors tried various schemes to remedy this decline. First they reduced the number and size of loans and increased interest rates to as high as 2 percent per month. When this did not succeed, they began in 1823, with the legislature's permission, to refuse new loans and to retire the notes as they came back into the bank. At the beginning of 1824 three-quarters of a million dollars were destroyed in public bonfires in the streets of Frankfort, and at the end of that year another half million. By that time the bank had stopped

[10] *Kentucky House Journal,* 1820, pp. 270-73; Shaler, *Kentucky,* 178; Collins, *History of Kentucky,* II, 878-79.

making any new loans, confining its activities to collections of loans already made. These practices soon brought the value of the notes remaining in circulation on a par with those of the Bank of Kentucky.

Although the experiment of the Bank of the Commonwealth was a departure from sound economic policies of the time, it was not a complete failure. That the bank had issued notes without a cent of specie, had made possible the payments of debts and taxes when the notes were heavily discounted, and yet had wound up with its notes at par seemed to many to defy the laws of economics. "A miracle," sneered one of its critics, "whereby something was made out of nothing." Those who felt that this new banking experiment would halt speculation or improve economic conditions were soon disappointed, however.[11]

Another relief measure of 1820 involving the Bank of the Commonwealth was a stay law, which provided that if a creditor should agree to accept notes either of the Bank of the Commonwealth or of the Bank of Kentucky, he might execute judgment on his claim after three months. If he refused, however, the debtor might replevy execution for two years.[12] As the new bank's paper sank to a fraction of its value, pulling that of the old along with it, the creditor faced a dilemma: whether to accept part payment in these discounted notes in satisfaction for all the debt or to wait two years, hoping to collect all at the end of that time but facing the risk of new delays or even total loss then. Creditors became highly incensed at this seeming injustice, and raised cries of indignation. They complained that it was folly for the legislature to attempt to "legislate the people out of debt." Debtors, meanwhile, taking advantage of the law and of public sentiment, pressed harsh terms of settlement, and the unhappiness of creditors grew. Some of them refused to make loans, thus contributing further to business stagnation.[13]

Soon the people of the state organized into rival factions, a

11 Collins, History of Kentucky, II, 879; Kentucky House Journal, 1820, pp. 291-92, 1821, pp. 69, 94-115, 1822, p. 113, 1824-1825, p. 63; Shaler, Kentucky, 178; Niles' Register, XX (1821), 52; Orlando Brown, "The Governors of Kentucky, [1792-1824] with Biographical Sketch and Notes by G. Glenn Clift," in Kentucky Register, XLIX (1951), 221; Lexington Kentucky Reporter, Nov. 4, Dec. 9, 1822, Nov. 29, 1824; Johnson, Franklin County, 76-77.

12 Kentucky House Journal, 1820, p. 358.

13 Stickles, The Critical Court Struggle, 23; Johnson, Franklin County, 76-77; Shaler, Kentucky, 178; J. H. Hawkins to Crittenden, June 18, John Holoway to Crittenden, July 21, 1821, Arnold Thomas to Charles P. Bacon, June 7, 1823, in Crittenden Papers; Niles' Register, XX (1821), 52.

division paralleling national party alignments. One faction wanted to repeal the obnoxious stay law, the other to sustain it. The antirelief party, opposed to the law, was composed generally of well-to-do farmers, lawyers, and merchants, although its following included some humbler folk. Conversely, the relief party was based on the debtors, most of whom were small farmers and mechanics. Kentucky's ablest political leaders were divided. Some leaders of the relief party were eminent members of the bar: John Rowan and George M. Bibb, former justices of the court of appeals; William T. Barry and Governor John Adair, Crittenden's old comrades on Shelby's staff; and Solomon P. Sharp. Antirelief leaders were of equal eminence: Robert Wickliffe, Ben Hardin, George Robertson, and Thomas Flournoy.[14]

Although the worst of bad times was over by the spring of 1822, the issue produced a crisis in May of that year, when Judge James Clark decided in a case in the Bourbon circuit court that the stay law was unconstitutional and void because it conflicted with state and national constitutional provisions against laws nullifying contractural obligations.[15] Excitement was so great that Governor John Adair called the legislature into special session, and that body cited Clark to appear before it, a step preliminary to impeachment. Clark did not appear but firmly defended his action in a written response. Meanwhile, an appeal from Clark's decision was pending before the court of appeals. In October, 1823, this court, composed of John Boyle, William Owsley, and Benjamin Mills, sustained the Clark opinion, and the rage of the relief party knew no bounds. Public passion was now diverted from Clark to the court, which had dared to overrule and nullify what the people saw as their august will.

A few weeks after the court of appeals handed down its decision, the legislature met and adopted resolutions denouncing the tyranny of the judges. A bill to impeach them secured a majority, although not the two-thirds vote required by the constitution. But the relief party was not through. Its leaders determined to make removing the judges the issue in the election of the succeeding legislature, and during the next six months, all other questions were forgotten while the two parties agitated the state. Mass meetings were held in all

[14] Collins, *History of Kentucky*, II, 879; Lexington *Kentucky Reporter*, May 2, 1825; Kerr, *History of Kentucky*, II, 607-22.
[15] Stickles, *The Critical Court Struggle*, 27.

sections, and rival candidates harangued the people. In August the relief party triumphed. Not only did it win a majority in each house, but it also chose by an overwhelming majority a governor, Joseph Desha, who favored removal of the judges.

When the newly elected legislature met in December, the three judges were summoned to appear before it and show cause why they should not be removed. Their calm, well-reasoned answers were countered by Rowan, Bibb, and Barry, the high command of the relief party. But when the removal bill was presented, it still could not muster the two-thirds majority required by the constitution. It received only sixty-nine affirmative to thirty-nine negative votes in the house, and its majority was one less than two-thirds in the senate.

Cheated once more of what they regarded as the just rewards of their victory, the relief advocates resorted to the specious device of reorganizing the court. Late at night on Christmas Eve, with Governor Desha on the floor marshaling the relief forces, the house passed a senate bill reorganizing the court of appeals. (The margin was less than two-thirds in both houses, but since this was a simple legislative act, it did not require the same constitutional majority as the more honest impeachment bill.) By this act the old court of appeals was abolished, the three judges with it, and a new court of four judges was created. The new appointees were all relief men: William T. Barry, chief justice, and John Trimble, B. W. Patton, and R. H. Davidge, associates.[16]

The battle was won but the war was not ended. The old court disregarded the reorganization act, claiming it was irregular and unconstitutional. It merely adjourned, planning to meet again in late January. But the new court lost little time in getting down to business. It chose Francis Preston Blair as its clerk; and when Achilles Sneed, clerk of the old court, refused to surrender his records on demand, Blair took them by force. When the old court returned, it resumed jurisdiction of such cases as were brought before it, so that the state was now plagued with the judicial anarchy of two competing courts of last resort. Some lawyers practiced before one, some before the other, and some before both; but the sympathies of at least nine-tenths of them were with the old judges. Meanwhile,

16 Kerr, *History of Kentucky*, II, 623-31; Collins, *History of Kentucky*, II, 879-82; Shaler, *Kentucky*, 178; Johnson, *Franklin County*, 76-77; Amos Kendall to Henry Clay, Dec. 22, 1824, typescript copy in Clay Papers, University of Kentucky Library.

the antirelief party in the legislature presented a masterful protest prepared by George Robertson. It was unceremoniously rejected, however, and the lawmakers adjourned in mid-January in great bitterness.[17]

Up to this time Crittenden had been more a bystander than a participant in the struggle. He practiced before the new court in the spring and summer of 1825, and he had even served on a committee appointed by the new judges to draw up rules for the conduct of the court's business. When he failed to appear before the short session held by the old court that spring, his absence was noted, and it was thought that he had joined the relief party. Crittenden, however, hesitated to enter the fray. He had warm and powerful friends in both camps. He had political ambitions, too, and he doubtless would have welcomed an opportunity to emulate his friend Clay, who though privately in sympathy with the antirelief party refused to commit himself publicly and continued to correspond with members of both factions. Clay was in Washington much of the time, but Crittenden was in Frankfort, the vortex of the controversy, and thus could not long remain on the sidelines. In April, when it was publicly stated that Crittenden's sympathies were with the new court, he published a letter placing himself unequivocally on the side of the old court. "I retain," he said, "a firm and decided conviction that the late act of the Legislature to abolish the Court of Appeals and to reorganize it, merely to effect a change of Judges, is unconstitutional."[18]

Although he had feared that taking a stand would affect his political future, Crittenden was in the long run to benefit from his experience with this struggle. Of necessity he became intimately acquainted here with the deep-seated ramifications of economic class conflict, a harbinger of coming national issues. Here, too, he could devise the sort of strategy to deal with these ramifications that would help later in the national political scene. It is not surprising that Crittenden would finally take a stand for a conservative monetary policy. As president of the dubious Bank of the Commonwealth, he had become acquainted with the dangers of unstable and ill-considered currency policies. His close friends, like Clay's, were the Virginia

[17] James Cowan to Henry Clay, Jan. 1, 1825, William T. Barry to Clay, Jan. 10, 1825, Clay Papers; Kerr, *History of Kentucky*, II, 632-33; Collins, *History of Kentucky*, II, 882.

[18] Lexington *Kentucky Reporter*, April 4, May 2, 1825.

gentlemen ruling Kentucky, naturally a conservative group, even though a number of them were to take the popular relief side. Further, as the issue came to involve a respect for the law and for the integrity of the courts, Crittenden's natural affection for order and stability would lead him to decide in their favor. Great, indeed, might have been Clay's reward had he been forced to think through the close relationship between economics and politics and to estimate consequences before he made his later decisions on national policy.

Crittenden's avowal was stout support for the antirelief party, who now took on the name Old Court; their adversaries became popularly known as the New Court party. Franklin County was dominated by members of the New Court party, and in order to overcome their preponderance, Crittenden was urged to become a candidate for the legislature. At thirty-eight he was a distinguished public man. He was very popular in Frankfort as lawyer, statesman, and orator, and he was thought to be the only man who had a chance of carrying the Old Court party to victory there. Never a bitter partisan, he had done little thus far to antagonize the opposition. "Crittenden is a man of fine genius," wrote Joseph R. Underwood,[19] and even New Court Clerk Blair, the strongest of partisans, admitted that Crittenden was "a man whose public & private worth has endeared him to all men of all sides in Kentucky." He thought Crittenden possessed "the greatest abilities united to every excellence of the heart," although "his modesty . . . has prevented him from putting forward his pretensions." His great popularity, Blair thought, would make him the choice of the people. "You know his worth," he wrote Clay. "How highly and justly he is valued by the public. You know the unbounded confidence & love which still continues to follow him amidst the bitterest party strife." An impartial observer of the Kentucky scene was equally impressed with Crittenden. "Such is the respect and confidence of both parties in his integrity," he wrote, "that they are willing to confer on him the highest office in their gift."[20]

When Crittenden hesitated to become a candidate, appeals were made to his patriotism. "Kentucky expects and she requires of you to

---

[19] George Robertson to Crittenden, May 25, 1825, in Crittenden Papers; Johnson, *Franklin County*, 78; Lexington *Kentucky Reporter*, May 9, 1825; *Filson Quarterly*, XIII (1939), 207.

[20] Blair to Clay, Jan. 30, 1826, in Clay Papers; Lexington *Kentucky Reporter*, May 9, 1825.

put on your armor and take the field," wrote George Robertson. He owed it, said another, to the state and to himself to strike a blow for constitutional integrity. Pressed from many sides, Crittenden resigned his post as president of the Bank of the Commonwealth and announced his candidacy.[21]

Franklin County was entitled to two representatives in the house. When Crittenden announced for one of the seats, the New Court party looked about to find candidates who could counter his "great abilities." They found them in Solomon P. Sharp, veteran legislator, congressman for two terms during Madison's administration, and one of the ablest lawyers of the state, and in Lewis Sanders. Thus, three candidates were contending for the two seats.[22]

The New Court men held that although the constitution provided for a court of appeals, its makeup was left to the legislature. Thus, it was a creature of the legislature and, as such, could be abolished by it. To this, Crittenden and his party replied that the judges should hold office during good behavior and could only be removed by impeachment of a two-thirds majority in each house of the legislature. The New Court men countered that the constitution also provided that judges' tenure was limited, not only by good behavior, but by "the continuance of their respective courts." Frequently in the past, they said, circuit courts had been abolished and judges had lost their places, and no one had ever charged that this was a violation of the fundamental law. Conceding this, Crittenden and his associates still contended that legislative power to abolish circuit courts did not extend to the court of appeals.

As the campaign progressed, the New Court party pointed to the repeal of the Federal Judiciary Act of 1801, whereby Jefferson had left many of John Adams' "midnight judges" without a court to preside over. They appealed to Jefferson himself, in retirement at Monticello, to speak out in their support. Although he refused, he was thought to be in sympathy with the New Court principles.[23]

The contest grew bitter as election day neared, for the court issue was symbolic of a deeper conflict. Crittenden was noted for his

[21] Robertson to Crittenden, May 25, 1825, in Crittenden Papers; Lexington *Kentucky Reporter*, July 11, 1825; letter of Thomas F. Marshall in Frankfort *Commonwealth*, Dec. 2, 1851.

[22] Letter of Francis Preston Blair in Frankfort (Ky.) *Argus of Western America*, Feb. 22, 1826.

[23] Letters of Amos Kendall in Frankfort *Argus*, May 10, 17, 24, 31, 1826; Collins, *History of Kentucky*, II, 256; Kerr, *History of Kentucky*, II, 632-40.

good temper and equanimity, and at the outset he had presented himself more as a "mediator between contending parties" than as a partisan himself. He had early proposed that a compromise be agreed on whereby all members of both courts would resign and a third court be made up of judges not identified with either party. This was strange doctrine for one who considered the reorganization bill a violation of the constitution, and leaders of the Old Court party would have none of it. In a speech on July 4, however, he repudiated this suggestion; thereafter, according to an adversary, his speeches "assumed by degree a different character." They no longer contained the harmonious sentiments that had so endeared him to all, but breathed "a spirit of denunciation more and more implacable."[24] Crittenden's views were hardening under the heat of battle.

The election in Kentucky was made even more bitter because hard times had increased the litigation over land titles, and many pioneer Kentuckians and naive settlers lost their farms to speculators. Victims of land suits had long resented the courts, and now people saw them as protectors of speculators and of banks, intent on oppressing the poor. The violent feeling aroused here was later to have its counterpart in the whole of the United States, much to the chagrin of Henry Clay.

The 1826 election throughout the state was an astonishing victory for the Old Court party. Sharp and Crittenden were returned to Franklin's two seats, Sharp polling sixty-nine more votes than Crittenden. Fraud was charged on both sides, and with good reason, for in Franklin County alone there were two hundred more votes cast than there were qualified voters.[25]

Although he occasionally resorted to invective in the heat of the contest, Crittenden thought of himself as a mediator. The relief party still regarded him as a restraining influence on the antirelief majority in the legislature, whereas the latter expected him to take the lead in undoing the radical relief legislation of recent years. His problem was not a simple one. The Old Court faction would have a large majority in the lower house, but the senate, where only a fourth of the members were elected annually, was about evenly divided.

24 Lexington *Kentucky Reporter*, May 9, 1825; *Constitutional Advocate*, quoted in Lexington *Kentucky Reporter*, Oct. 31, 1825; George Robertson to Crittenden, May 25, 1825, in Crittenden Papers.
25 F. P. Blair to Henry Clay, Aug. 30, 1825, in Clay Papers; Clay to Crittenden, Aug. 22, 1825, in Crittenden Papers; Stickles, *The Critical Court Struggle*, 80-81; Lexington *Kentucky Reporter*, Sept. 26, Oct. 31, Nov. 28, 1825; Coleman, *Crittenden*, I, 63.

What if the senate should reject, or the governor veto, a bill to repeal the reorganizing act? Crittenden sought advice from Clay. Would it be wise, he asked, to declare by house resolution that Boyle, Owsley, and Mills were the rightful judges, have them resume their offices, and forcefully repossess themselves of the records taken from them by Blair? Or would it be better to refrain from extreme measures, wait another year, then appeal to the voters at the following election?[26] Clay, as might be expected of the Great Pacificator, urged conciliation.[27] But before any measures could be taken to harmoniously restore a constitutional judiciary, a new sensation was to rekindle tempers that might have subsided.

In the early hours of the very morning the legislature was to convene, Crittenden's colleague from Franklin County, Solomon P. Sharp, who lived only a stone's throw from Crittenden, was awakened from sleep and, in the presence of his wife, savagely stabbed to death by an assassin. The cry went up that the Old Court party had instigated the murder. Violence, which had threatened more than once during the campaign, now seemed ready to blaze all over the state. Into this crisis Crittenden stepped.

When the house assembled a few hours later, Crittenden presented resolutions deploring the assassination and offering a reward of $3,000 for the capture of the murderer. Both were unanimously adopted. But in the shock of the tragedy, coming so close on the heels of the bitter political struggle, wild rumors began to circulate. Sharp was perhaps the ablest member of the New Court party who had been returned to the legislature, and it was soon whispered that his killing was inspired by his political enemies. The finger of suspicion pointed to Jeroboam Beauchamp as the assassin. He had been seen in Frankfort the night before the murder and had asked directions to Sharp's house.

Beauchamp was apprehended and brought back to Frankfort, whence he had fled. He sought Crittenden's aid as counsel. It was not often that Crittenden refused to aid a man in difficulty with the law, but this time he declined. For him to have done otherwise would, under the circumstances, have given strong support to the suspicion that the crime had a political motive.

---

[26] Crittenden to Clay, Sept. 22, [Aug. 7] 1825, in Clay Papers (Kentucky); Coleman, *Crittenden*, I, 63; F. P. Blair to Clay, Aug. 30, 1825, in Clay Papers; Lexington *Kentucky Reporter*, Sept. 26, 1825.

[27] Clay to Crittenden, Aug. 22, 1825, in Crittenden Papers.

The sensational trial and resulting revelations showed that the killing had nothing to do with politics. Beauchamp's wife admitted that prior to her marriage to Beauchamp she had borne Sharp's child. Sharp had refused to marry her, she said, and when she made bastardy charges against him, he contended that the child could not be his, for it was black. This had so humiliated and embittered her that she had married Beauchamp only upon his promise to kill Sharp. After making these admissions, she took her life in her husband's cell on the day set for his execution. Because of the bitter political struggle, however, the picture was not so clear-cut. It was charged by Old Court partisans that Governor Desha visited Beauchamp daily in his cell and promised him a pardon if he would implicate leaders of the Old Court party in a conspiracy to take Sharp's life. One of the principal witnesses against Beauchamp was Patrick Darby, editor and Old Court partisan. Beauchamp charged that Darby had testified falsely and had also bribed others to do so. As he was being led to the gallows, he repudiated this and exonerated Darby, but many either did not know of or did not credit this confession.[28]

Meanwhile, the court struggle went on. Leaders of the New Court party, dejected after the August election, had at first seemed inclined to surrender. But when they learned of the balance of parties in the senate, they reconsidered, hoping to obtain better terms. The governor recommended in his message that judges of both courts resign, promising that if they would, he would appoint a new court made up equally of both parties. But the Old Court leaders, unwilling to accept half a loaf, would not agree. They pushed through a bill in the house repealing the reorganization act, but the bill was killed in the senate by the vote of the lieutenant governor.[29]

In the meantime, the Old Court, thinking the issue had been decided by the August election, reassembled in November and prepared to resume business. They sent an order to Blair to deliver up the records in his custody, but Blair refused. With a belligerency

[28] J. Winston Coleman, Jr., *The Beauchamp-Sharp Tragedy* (Frankfort, 1950); Lexington *Kentucky Reporter*, issues from November, 1825, to July, 1826, especially May 22, July 10, 1826; Frankfort *Argus*, same period, especially June 7, 14, 1826; Stickles, "Underwood's Journal," 207; Jeroboam Beauchamp to Crittenden, Nov. 18, 25, 1825, Henry Clay to Crittenden, July 10, 1826, in Crittenden Papers; Lucius P. Little, *Ben Hardin: His Times and Contemporaries* (Louisville, 1887), 140.

[29] F. P. Blair to Henry Clay, Aug. 30, Nov. 28, 1825, in Clay Papers; *Kentucky House Journal, 1825*, pp. 4-5, 14, 437; Lexington *Kentucky Reporter*, Dec. 26, 1825; Kerr, *History of Kentucky*, II, 640-43.

that belied his emaciated appearance, he enlisted assistance, procured muskets, kept around-the-clock vigil in his office, and defied the order of the court. He would surrender the records, he said, only to a court reorganized according to the governor's plan. For a time this plan seemed to hold promise. A bill establishing a court made up equally of both parties was proposed. But a fight on the floor of the house between Ben Hardin and Joseph Haskins, a New Court partisan from Mercer County, so inflamed tempers that no such bill could carry.[30]

In this impasse a committee of six from both houses, with Crittenden as chairman, was chosen to work out an adjustment. But even this group could not reach agreement, and on December 21 Crittenden so reported to the house. His own position was now considerably more definite, perhaps as a result of Blair's belligerence. He peremptorily rejected Governor Desha's proposal, or any other that did not admit the unconstitutionality of the act abolishing the Old Court. "If we are right in supposing that the Legislature has no power to abolish the Court," he said, ". . . we cannot be wrong in rejecting such a compromise, if, indeed, a *compromise* it can be called."[31]

When the legislature adjourned, the courts were in a condition approaching anarchy. Crittenden blamed the failure to resolve the difficulty on the "obstinacy & perverseness" of the governor and a few senators, and he looked forward to the next election, when the people would have an opportunity to remove some of the recalcitrant senators.[32]

But Crittenden was not to have a voice in the final settlement. He campaigned vigorously for reelection, but the New Court majority in Franklin was large, and Crittenden, by his ultimate refusal to support the compromise that he had earlier advocated, lost what support he formerly had secured from New Court advocates. In the August election he ran third behind Lewis Sanders and David White, who defeated him by 112 and 89 votes respectively.[33]

[30] Blair to Clay, Nov. 28, 1825, Jan. 4, 1826, in Clay Papers; *Kentucky House Journal, 1825*, pp. 185-87, 284-85, 293.

[31] Blair to Clay, Nov. 28, 1825, Jan. 4, 1826, in Clay Papers; letters of John Pope in Frankfort *Argus*, April 5, 19, May 17, 1826; *Kentucky House Journal, 1825*, pp. 414-36.

[32] Crittenden to Clay, Dec. 26, 1825, in Crittenden Papers (Duke).

[33] Clay to Crittenden, Aug. 6, 1826, in Crittenden Papers (Duke); Frankfort *Argus*, Feb. 8, Aug. 16, 1826; Little, *Ben Hardin*, 142.

In the state generally, however, the story was different. The Old Court party won a clear majority, and when the legislature convened, it repealed the act abolishing the old court and restored the old judges to full authority. The governor vetoed the act, but the legislature passed it over his veto. The court struggle thus ended, with the relief advocates defeated and discredited. But the bitterness and factionalism which it aroused were to survive and to be reflected for decades to come in political division on other issues.

Defeat, the first he had ever suffered at the hands of his constituents, was a blow to Crittenden, as it always is to the man of ambition, no matter how experienced and broad-minded. From his loss at the polls, however, came hard-won lessons about American politics. Crittenden was beginning now to understand the power and intransigence of the backwoods farmer, who would not abandon allegiance to Jeffersonian democracy, however clear and overwhelming another cause appeared to his political leaders. Crittenden was also learning the penalty for allowing oneself to become definitely identified over a long period with a conservative faction, a lesson the Federalists had learned long ago in Kentucky. Crittenden knew also, as does every politician, that to be effective in politics, he must get himself or his candidate elected. He now was beginning to see that the conservatives were a minority in America and could achieve power only by coalition with some other group. Moreover, Crittenden was beginning to appreciate the necessity of careful strategy and vigorous and skillful conduct of political campaigns, a lesson to be pointed up in 1840. He had also discovered something of the chicanery that was coming increasingly to be practiced at the polls in American elections; the vote in his own county was evidence of this. All of these insights, gained by Crittenden from bitter experience, would have profited Clay greatly.

At this time, however, Crittenden was greatly chagrined at his defeat, as were also his friends. "The result of the Election is . . . most mortifying," wrote Mason Brown; "I do not think that Mr. Crittenden's friends were as active this year as they were last." He doubted, though, that even greater exertion on their part would have prevented defeat.[34] To demonstrate their loyalty to Crittenden, as well as to assuage their own feelings, Crittenden's friends gave a

[34] Mason Brown to Orlando Brown, Aug. 12, 1826, in Brown Papers, Filson Club; Frankfort *Argus*, Aug. 30, 1826.

public barbecue in his honor. More than two hundred of them gathered at Cove Spring a few miles outside the city, to nourish their bodies on rich viands from great iron cooking pots and their spirits on the oratory that flowed so freely on these occasions. Crittenden was toasted as the "able and patriotic defender" of the constitution. Perhaps the occasion soothed to some degree the hurt his pride had suffered. If it did not dispel all his griefs, another event soon would. For at the very time of the August election, romance came once more into Crittenden's life.

His domestic happiness had been shattered two years before by the untimely death of Sarah. Home life had been completely disrupted, of course. George, his eldest son, then twelve, had been sent to boarding school in Lexington; and Ann Mary, thirteen months younger than her brother, had become at her tender age the mistress of her father's home. With five children younger than Ann Mary, the household must have had many problems.

Warm and affectionate by nature, Crittenden mourned the lost Sarah for two years; then it was noted and gossiped that he was "keeping company"[35] with Maria Innes Todd. Her father was Federal Judge Harry Innes, former schoolmate and friend of James Madison, whom Maria as a child had visited in the White House. At the time her beauty, her "good heart," her "amiable disposition," her "good sense," and her "propriety of conduct" had all been remarked upon. Grown to womanhood, she married her first cousin John Harris Todd, son of Justice Thomas Todd of the United States Supreme Court. The Todds were warm friends of the Crittendens even before they became neighbors in Frankfort. Then John Harris Todd died, just two weeks before Sarah Crittenden, leaving Maria with two young daughters and a son.[36]

On his fortieth birthday Crittenden addressed a formal note to Maria: "Mr. Crittenden presents his compliments [to] Mrs. Todd . . . [and requests] that she will honor him so far as to afford him the opportunity of a private interview upon his next visit."[37] The interview was granted and proved fruitful, for ten days later he addressed

[35] Margaret Brown to Orlando Brown, Sept. 20, 1826, in Brown Papers, Filson Club.
[36] John T. Mason to Harry Innes, Dec. 22, 1815 (copy), Innes to Maria Innes, June 18, 1816 (copy), in Crittenden Papers; genealogical memorandum in Crittenden Papers (Duke); Clift, "Kentucky Marriages and Obituaries . . . 1787-1860," in *Kentucky Register*, XXXIX (1941), 127; Trabue, *A Corner in Celebrities*, 31.
[37] Crittenden to Mrs. Maria Todd, Sept. 10, 1826 (copy), in Crittenden Papers.

her as "My dearest Maria," and professed to fear that he would "die *of old age*," before mid-November came around. Maria was living at the time with her widowed mother on a farm a few miles from Frankfort. Crittenden rode out there twice a week, and at other times Maria visited in Frankfort, where they met at the home of friends.

They were married on November 15, and Crittenden brought her to the large house at the corner of Washington and Main. There she presided for the next quarter century over their now-combined families.[38] Her daughter Elizabeth was the same age as Crittenden's youngest child, Sarah Lee. The girls became devoted and inseparable companions, and years later they married brothers. The other daughter, Catherine, fell in love with and married her stepbrother Thomas. It was one of their sons who would bear Crittenden's name, and who would die with Custer at the Little Big Horn precisely a half century after his grandfather and grandmother were married.[39]

[38] Crittenden to Mrs. Maria Todd, Sept. 26, 1826 (copy), in Crittenden Papers; Margaret Brown to Orlando Brown, Oct. 25, 1826, in Brown Papers, Filson Club; Clift, "Kentucky Marriages and Obituaries," in *Kentucky Register*, XXXVI (1938), 262; Coleman, *Crittenden*, I, 21.

[39] Trabue, *A Corner in Celebrities*, 41; genealogical memorandum in Crittenden Papers (Duke).

CHAPTER IV

Bargain
and Corruption

IN THE national capital, meanwhile, a larger struggle was brewing over the same basic issue that had convulsed Kentucky, a struggle in which Clay was to make costly errors in judgment which perhaps marked the turning point of his career. Although Crittenden played only a secondary part in the struggle, it was to cause him great embarrassment and add to Clay's. The outcome had great influence on the futures of both men.

When Andrew Jackson first had appeared in Washington, he had been singled out almost instinctively as a major rival by the Cock of Kentucky. After Old Hickory had exceeded his authority in his highhanded and somewhat brutal Florida campaign, Clay had in 1818 made a veiled attack upon Jackson as a menace to liberty. This had won him the undying hatred of a man as relentless in his political feuds as in his campaigns against Indians. It is hard to determine how much of Clay's conduct in the election of 1824 was reaction to Jackson's militant support of the frontiersman and his equally militant expansionism. At any rate, with his volatile nature aroused by the rising tide of Jacksonian democracy, and possibly deluded by his own followers, Clay was about to play the wrong notes in a political composition in which he had previously displayed his mastery.

Clay had not yet cast his lot publicly and irrevocably with the conservative elements in American politics. Yet his stands on issues raised in the postwar decade were leading him ever more in that direction. His part in championing the nation's first truly protective tariff in 1824, his advocacy of internal improvements, and above all his position on the national bank question and his sympathy for the Old Court party in Kentucky threw him increasingly with those whose political principles had been expressed in Hamilton's concept of a strong central government. Meanwhile, as we have seen, hard times had caused the frontiersman and the laborer to regain their suspicion of banks and business and to shift their allegiance back to traditional Republicanism. Clay had underestimated both the power and the extent of this shift as well as the strength and skill of his western rival. Old Hickory was an opportunist thoroughly versed in the game of playing safe and knew how to steer clear of controversial issues. Although his participation in land speculations had given him an unsavory political record in Tennessee, he managed to present himself as an unassuming hero who was above all a champion of the people.

The presidential election of 1824 was not to be decided in the electoral college, for none of the four candidates received a majority. According to the Constitution, the House of Representatives had to decide among the three candidates who had received the most electoral votes, Jackson, Adams, and William H. Crawford. Clay, to his mortification, was fourth. Since Crawford had suffered a relapse of a serious illness, the contest, for all practical purposes, was between Jackson and Adams. Each state, regardless of size, was entitled to a single vote, to be determined by the majority of its delegation.

With Clay eliminated, Kentuckians who had cast their votes for him now overwhelmingly preferred the Hero of New Orleans over the Puritan from Quincy. Clay, however, had let it be known that he would not support Jackson, and his friends sought to forestall a resolution offered in the Kentucky legislature by Crittenden's brother Henry, requesting the Kentucky delegation to support Jackson. In a move ominous for Clay, the legislature ignored Clay's wishes and passed the resolution by a large majority.[1]

---

[1] Amos Kendall to Clay, Dec. 22, 1824, William T. Barry to Clay, Jan. 10, 1825, in Clay Papers; *Kentucky House Journal, 1824*, pp. 4-5.

Now Clay began a dangerous political game. Partly out of personal ambition, partly out of genuine conviction, he and his friends decided to throw their support to Adams, in an attempt to effect a *rapprochement* between the economic interests of East and West. This move was not inconsistent with the aims of Clay's American System, whereby he sincerely hoped to advance the welfare both of the West and of the nation. It did, however, demonstrate unmistakably that Clay was no longer the Harry of the West who had fought so stoutly against many of the policies he now advocated. Furthermore, for Clay to support Adams was tempting the political fates, when the Kentucky legislature had clearly demonstrated public support for Jackson in the West. It demanded at the very least a thorough calculation of the nature and power of the warring political factions, a quick and disciplined adroitness in handling them, and a cool and realistic appraisal of the risk he was taking with the political fortunes of himself and his friends. Instead, Clay later admitted that he had acted rashly at this crucial moment.[2]

Clay had great influence with the delegations from the western states, which besides Kentucky included Ohio, Illinois, and Missouri, but he found it difficult to persuade them that in the Yankee candidate lay the hope of the West. They demanded a pledge from Adams that their section would not be neglected during his administration. In tangible terms, a prominent place for Clay in the Adams cabinet would constitute such a pledge.[3]

When Congress met, Clay found himself the focus of the maneuvering of the candidates. That Clay did not barter his vote and influence solely for his own personal advantage is now generally agreed, but any astute politician must have known that in view of his equivocal position he would appear to be doing so.[4] For there was enough intercourse between Clay's friends and those of Adams, and even with Adams himself, to arouse suspicion in minds of men less partisan than those in Jackson's camp. On December 3 Adams met with Richard M. Johnson; a week later, with Thomas Metcalfe; the following day, with Robert Letcher, Clay's most intimate friend in the Kentucky delegation. The next day he met with Charles A. Wickliffe and Francis Johnson. On December 12 Adams went to

[2] Van Deusen, *Henry Clay*, 192, 195.

[3] Adams, *Memoirs*, VI, 444-45; Henry A. Wise, *Seven Decades of the Union* . . . (Philadelphia, 1881), 82-84.

[4] Clay to F. P. Blair, Jan. 8, 1824 [1825], in Clay Papers; Adams, *Memoirs*, VI, 464.

Fletcher's boardinghouse, where several of Clay's friends lived; from there he called again on Richard M. Johnson and his brother, finally ending up at Letcher's rooms. On the sixteenth he dined with David White, and on the seventeenth with Letcher. December 29 he met again with Letcher, on January 5 with David Trimble, and twice more with Letcher before the month was out.

Most of what went on at these meetings can only be conjectured. Letcher, whom Adams regarded as Clay's spokesman, mentioned the "convulsed" conditions in Kentucky resulting from the court struggle and told Adams of the pressures that were being brought on the delegation to vote for Jackson. Although Letcher did not profess to be speaking for Clay, Adams gained the impression that "Clay would willingly support me if he could thereby serve himself." By this time, reports that the Kentucky legislature might instruct the delegation to vote for Jackson had reached Washington, but Letcher, Adams recalled, insisted that "if Clay's friends could *know* that he would have a prominent share in the Administration, that might induce them to vote for me, even in the face of legislative instructions."

Adams had Clay to dinner with a large company on December 19, and on Christmas Eve he sat next to Clay at dinner at the Russian Embassy. But Letcher was insisting that Adams have private conversations with his friend, and a meeting was arranged for January 9. They spent the evening, Adams confided to his diary, in a long conversation "explanatory of the past and prospective of the future." Clay disclaimed, according to Adams, any desire for personal advancement as a result of his strategic strength, and would take "that course which might be most conducive to the public interest." His preference, he said, was for Adams, but he wished to satisfy himself as to "some principles of great importance." There is no reason to question Clay's sincerity. Yet if he were to win his friends to vote for Adams, some assurance must be given them that their section would not be neglected by the administration.

Adams must have given such assurances, for almost at once western congressmen, who up until that time had been openly hostile to Adams, began to come around. One of them, the lone representative from Missouri, in pledging his support, told Adams he was "entirely devoted to Mr. Clay" and hoped Clay "would be a member of the next Administration"; and Adams went so far as to pledge that if "elected by the suffrages of the West I should naturally look to the

West for much of the support that I should need." The Missourian departed "apparently satisfied" but returned the following day to tell Adams that his remarks were not to be interpreted as "bargaining." Adams assured him that he had not so regarded them. Three days later, Clay and a majority of the Kentucky delegation announced their determination to vote for Adams.

Adams was elected on the first ballot February 9, with Kentucky and most of the other western states voting for him. Three days later, he offered Clay the first place in his cabinet. Clay hesitated, as well he might. Anonymous charges had already appeared in the press that a bargain had been made whereby Adams would offer Clay the post in exchange for his support. An investigation demanded by Clay had redounded to his advantage when it became known that his accuser was a semiliterate Pennsylvania congressman, George Kremer, who was obviously the tool of Jackson's friends. But if Clay should now accept first place in Adams' cabinet, the charge might be renewed.[5]

Now Clay sensed that he stood at a crossroad; he sought advice from his friends. At first some recommended that he refuse the offer. Others pointed out that whether he accepted or refused, the offer itself would inspire criticism, and that if he should decline, it would be said that "the patriotic Mr. Kremer, by an exposure of the corrupt arrangement, had prevented its consummation." Crittenden had urged Clay to accept even before he knew that Adams had offered him the post. If Adams should be elected, he wrote, "& you will accept a station in his cabinet, all will be quieted in a moment." Charges of the Jackson people, he added, were only intended "to intimidate you . . . from the acceptance of the department of State . . . where they tremble to see you." He urged Clay to "hold on your course unshaken & unaltered by all the calumny, falsehood, & scandal of your enemies." Clay owed it to himself, to his friends, "& to the expectations & wishes of the state, that you should accept the office of Secretary of State, if it should be offered you."[6]

There were others who advised differently, but the opinion expressed by Crittenden prevailed, and Clay accepted.[7] It was a

[5] Adams, *Memoirs*, VI, 435-80, 508; John S. Bassett, *Life of Jackson*, 2 vols. (New York, 1911), I, 362.

[6] Crittenden to Clay, Feb. 15, 1825 (copy), in Crittenden Papers.

[7] Clay to Francis T. Brooke, Feb. 18, 1825, F. P. Blair to Clay, March 7, 1825, Amos Kendall to Clay, Feb. 19, 1825, in Clay Papers; W. H. Harrison to David K. Este, March 3, 1825, in David K. Este Papers, Library of Congress.

fateful decision. It was to be a factor in the division of the country into two political parties whose principles were obscured by the bitter partisanship aroused over the charge of bargain. Buchanan, who acted an innocent but unsophisticated role in the drama, later concluded that it had changed the mainstream of the country's political history and resulted in an illogical party alignment. Exonerating Clay of any intentional wrongdoing, he still thought, twenty years later, that Clay's bad judgment was so egregious as to be unpardonable.[8]

As soon as it was known that Clay was to be Adams' Secretary of State, the storm broke everywhere, even in Kentucky. In Harrodsburg and Lexington there was talk of burning Clay in effigy. Blair wrote that Jackson supporters were "quite vociferous, & consider that your acceptance of the Office of Secretary, a greater outrage" than the defeat of Jackson. Amos Kendall wrote that "the general impression is certainly unfavorable to you." Jackson himself, after Clay had resigned his lucrative position as counsel for the Bank of the United States to accept the cabinet post, remarked that "the Judas of the West has closed the contract and will receive the thirty pieces of silver."[9] Clay's position worsened when David Trimble, one of the Kentucky congressional delegation, frankly admitted in a speech to his constituents, after his return from Washington, that he and his friends "ascertained that if Jackson was President Mr. Clay would not be secretary; if Adams was elected Clay would be secretary"; and that they preferred "Adams with Clay in the cabinet to Jackson without Clay."[10]

Clay visited Kentucky that summer and professed to note no diminution in the enthusiasm of the crowds who greeted him. By the time the legislature met, however, the opposition had become so virulent that Crittenden introduced in the house a resolution indignantly denouncing "the aspersions against . . . Mr. Clay . . . on the occasion of the late . . . election." The resolution provided further that although Adams was not the legislators' choice for the Presi-

8 Buchanan to Letcher, July 27, 1844, in John Bassett Moore (ed.), *The Works of James Buchanan, Comprising his Speeches, State Papers, and Private Correspondence,* 12 vols. (Philadelphia and London, 1908-1911), VI, 59-60 (hereinafter, Buchanan, *Works*).

9 Blair to Clay, March 7, 1825, Kendall to Clay, Feb. 19, 1825, in Clay Papers; Van Deusen, *Henry Clay,* 193.

10 George S. Blakey to Captain Isaac Davis, Feb. 26, 1828, in Isaac Davis Papers, University of Virginia; Frankfort *Argus,* Sept. 19, 1827.

dency, they would "acquiesce cheerfully in the result."[11] This was another mistake, for members of the New Court party were after revenge for the defeat they had suffered in the late legislative election.[12] Even many friends of Clay could not be persuaded to acquiesce in the election of Adams. When Crittenden realized that he had miscalculated, he withdrew the resolution.[13]

But the storm had not yet broken in all its fury. The accusations of corruption that were circulated from time to time throughout the following year had nothing substantial to support them. In the spring of 1827, however, Carter Beverly of Virginia published a letter in the Fayetteville, North Carolina, *Observer* quoting a damaging statement by Jackson. Jackson had told a large company at the Hermitage that Clay's friends had offered to make him President "in one hour," if he would give some indication that he would appoint Clay Secretary of State.[14] When challenged for proof, Jackson called upon Buchanan for support.

The future President, then a young and inexperienced congressman from Pennsylvania, now had his feet to the fire. Before the election in Congress, Buchanan had become a self-appointed intermediary to promote what he thought would be an ideal arrangement. Calling upon Clay and Letcher, he had promised that if they would support Jackson, the State Department would go to Clay. Then, meeting with Jackson, he had promised Clay's support for Old Hickory in return for the State Department. Now, while Jackson was calling on him for vindication, Letcher and Clay were asking Buchanan to disclose what they assumed to be the truth—that he had come to them two years before with a proposition from Jackson himself. To be called upon by each antagonist to support charges against the other, when in fact he had been representing neither, was a fate he did not think he deserved. He faced the issue manfully,

[11] *Kentucky House Journal, 1825*, p. 225; Crittenden to Clay, Dec. 26, 1825 (copy), in Crittenden Papers; Blair to Clay, Jan. 4, 1826, in Clay Papers; Frankfort *Argus*, March 12, 1828.

[12] Clay to Charles Hammond, Dec. 10, 1825, in Clay Papers, Indiana University Library; Kendall to Clay, Oct. 4, 1825, Blair to Clay, Jan. 4, 1826, Clay to James Brown, Oct. 8, 1826, in Clay Papers; Crittenden to Clay, Nov. 25, 1826, in Crittenden Papers (Duke); Frankfort *Argus*, July 9, 1828.

[13] *Kentucky House Journal, 1825*, p. 225; Crittenden to Clay, Dec. 26, 1825 (copy), in Crittenden Papers; Blair to Clay, Jan. 4, 1826, in Clay Papers; Lexington *Kentucky Reporter*, Feb. 6, 1826.

[14] Richard A. Buckner to Clay, May 26, 1826 [1827] in Clay Papers; Frankfort *Argus*, Sept. 19, 1827; Van Deusen, *Henry Clay*, 224; Address of Henry Clay to Public, Dec., 1827, in Thomas J. Clay Papers, Library of Congress.

however, and published a letter exonerating both Clay and Jackson from having given him any commission to act for them.[15]

This letter pleased Clay's friends as greatly as it disappointed Jackson's. But Clay himself was not satisfied. He called upon Crittenden to prepare a careful and elaborate "Address to the Public." Crittenden secured and turned over to Clay statements from all Clay's congressional friends, together with a letter from himself supporting Clay's statement that he had determined to support Adams before he went to Washington in 1824.[16]

But Clay's troubles were just beginning. One of his trusted Frankfort friends, Amos Kendall, editor of the *Argus of Western America* and a leader in the relief or New Court party, now turned against him. In the columns of his paper, Kendall soon was bringing charges against Clay: Clay had used his influence to defeat the hopes of the relief party, and even more important, Clay had written letters to "one of his [Clay's] confidential friends" in January, 1825, urging him to write, and to solicit others to write, letters to the Kentucky congressional delegation urging them to vote for Adams so that Clay might reap the benefit of a bargain he had made. He called upon Clay now to publish these letters.[17]

Clay had indeed written two indiscreet letters to Francis P. Blair. Their publication would be embarrassing now, not because they would prove Kendall's charges, but for an entirely different reason. In these letters Clay had indicated that in deciding between Adams and Jackson, he was faced with Hobson's choice. He would never have chosen Adams "if at liberty to draw from the whole mass of our citizens," he wrote. Adams was really not qualified for the office, but elevation of Jackson to the Presidency was unthinkable. If Blair

15 Buchanan's letter was published in the summer of 1827. See Frankfort *Argus*, Aug. 29, 1827; Buchanan to Letcher, June 27, July 27, 1844, in Buchanan, *Works*, VI, 59-60, 63; Letcher to Clay, Aug. 27, 1827, John Sergeant to Clay, Aug. 17, 1827, in Clay Papers; Crittenden to Clay, Sept. 6, 1827 (copy), in Crittenden Papers; Van Deusen, *Henry Clay*, 225; Philip S. Klein, *President James Buchanan: A Biography* (University Park, Pa., 1962), 49-53, 56-59.

16 Address of Henry Clay to Public, Dec., 1827, in T. J. Clay Papers; John Sergeant to Clay, Aug. 17, 23, 1827, Letcher to Clay, Aug. 27, 1827, in Clay Papers; Crittenden to Clay, Sept. 6, 1827 (copy), in Crittenden Papers; Crittenden to Clay, Oct. 30, 1827, in Crittenden Papers (Duke); Duff Green to Andrew Jackson, Aug. 29, 1827, Green to Thomas Marshall, Dec. 11, 1828, in Duff Green Papers, Library of Congress.

17 Joseph Desha to Kendall, [?] 1831, in Joseph Desha Papers, Library of Congress; Crittenden to Clay, Nov. 25, 1826 [1827], in Crittenden Papers (Duke); Clay to Crittenden, Dec. 12, 1826, in Clay Papers; Frankfort *Argus*, Oct. 10, 1827, Feb. 6, Aug. 6, 1828.

agreed with him, would he, Clay asked, write to members of the delegation and get others to write? Blair would and did. But now that Clay was in Adams' cabinet, to publish his letters demeaning the President was unthinkable, as Kendall well knew.[18]

Kendall turned his venom also upon Crittenden. In early January, 1825, before the decision had been made to swing the Kentucky delegation to Adams, Crittenden had written to Richard K. Call, a member of the Kentucky delegation in Washington. In this letter he had expressed the hope that "we shall succeed in getting a western President and that General Jackson will beat the Yankee."[19] Shortly after writing this, Crittenden had learned from Letcher that Clay's "interests were to be subserved by obtaining the vote of the Kentucky delegation for Mr. A."[20] Crittenden had relayed this information to Blair, who had passed it on to Kendall, at the time a supporter of Clay. Crittenden and Blair had thereafter written to other members of the delegation, urging them to vote for Adams.[21]

In one of these letters Crittenden urged Congressman David White to support Adams despite the legislature's instructions to the contrary. In general he believed that legislative instruction was right, Crittenden wrote White, but not in all cases. In requesting the delegation to vote for Jackson, the legislature had assumed he would win and was "ambitious of having a hand in the matter," he said. He himself would have voted for the instruction resolution, under the circumstances, but he would not now condemn White if he should disregard it. His own personal preference was for Jackson, he went on, provided he would appoint Clay his Secretary of State. But since this was out of the question, he believed that "the common good is more concerned in Clay's being Secretary, than it is in the question whether Jackson or Adams should be President." He cautioned White to treat the letter as confidential, as it contained "a great deal of hasty and trashy politics, which I would not willingly have any other but a friend look upon."[22] Kendall learned of Crittenden's letters to Call

[18] Clay to Blair, Jan. 8, 29, 1825, Blair to Clay, Jan. 24, Feb. 11, 1825, in Clay Papers; Frankfort *Argus*, July 9, 1828.

[19] Crittenden to Call, Jan. 8, 1825, Call to Crittenden, Oct. 13, 1826, in Crittenden Papers (Duke); Lexington *Kentucky Gazette*, quoted in Frankfort *Argus*, Aug. 22, 1827. See also Andrew Jackson to Call, March 9, 1826, in John S. Bassett (ed.), *Correspondence of Andrew Jackson*, 6 vols. and index (Washington, 1926-1935), VI, 482.

[20] Letcher to Crittenden, undated fragment, in Crittenden Papers (Kentucky).

[21] Blair to Clay, Dec. 31, 1827, in Clay Papers.

[22] Crittenden to White, Jan. 19, 1825, published in Frankfort *Argus*, Feb. 6, July 9, Aug. 6, 1828.

and White and charged they would prove that Crittenden was one of the conspirators who had defrauded both Jackson and the people.[23]

The folly of impetuous letterwriting was thus brought home to Crittenden. That he learned his lesson better than Clay, time would reveal. Meanwhile, he delayed answering Kendall's charges and sought advice from Clay and Blair. Kendall had challenged Crittenden to publish his letters to Call and White. This he would not do; instead he made an explanation: he had preferred Jackson to Adams, but like most Kentuckians he preferred Clay to either of them, and he thought either Jackson or Adams "with Mr. Clay associated in the executive department, would form a safer and better administration for the country, than the other without him." His letters to Call and White were not inconsistent with these sentiments, he added weakly.[24]

This was almost admitting Kendall's charges, but not quite. Kendall had charged that Crittenden's letter to White was in response to a letter Clay had written Crittenden. But Kendall was wrong on a technicality. Crittenden had received no letter from Clay on the subject in January, 1825. Instead, as has been seen, Clay wrote Blair, who showed the letter to Crittenden; and Crittenden had shown Blair a letter on the same subject that he had received from Letcher. Like a drowning man, Crittenden clutched at this straw. He stoutly affirmed that he had never heard from Clay or anyone else that Adams would appoint Clay Secretary of State if Clay would support Adams in the election. "If there was any such promise or bargain," he said, "I was ignorant of it." White, in conversation with Crittenden, verified his statement that there was no bargain in the decision to vote for Adams, but, Crittenden observed, he seemed to have "some obscure fear of committing it to writing."[25]

The affair was not to stop with a newspaper war, however. When the legislature met, the Clay-Adams party in the senate unwisely offered a resolution declaring Adams' election innocent of any bargaining and castigating the authors of the accusation as liars and

[23] Crittenden to Clay, Oct. 30, 1827, in Crittenden Papers (Duke); Blair to Clay, Nov. 14, 1827, in Clay Papers.

[24] Crittenden to Clay, Oct. 30, Nov. 15, 1827, in Crittenden Papers (Duke); Lexington Kentucky Reporter, Nov. 14, 1827; Niles' Register, XXXIII (1827-1828), 224.

[25] Niles' Register, XXXIII (1827-1828), 224; Lexington Kentucky Reporter, Nov. 14, 1827; Crittenden to Clay, Oct. 30, Nov. 15, 1827, Clay to Crittenden, Dec. 16, 1827, in Crittenden Papers (Duke); Letcher to Crittenden, March 15, 1828, in Coleman, Crittenden, I, 68-69; Blair to Clay, Feb. [n. d.,] 1828, in Clay Papers.

defamers. Thereupon the Jackson party offered a resolution denouncing the election and calling for an investigation. This placed the Clay faction in a quandary. They had a solid majority and could defeat the opposition resolution, but if they did so, it might appear that the charges could be proved and that they had used their majority to stifle the truth. On the other hand, if they supported the resolution, it would suggest that they had doubted Clay's integrity. They accepted the lesser of the evils and permitted the resolution to pass.[26]

Star witness for the prosecution in the investigation was Amos Kendall, an unlovable creature both in form and in spirit. With his restless, eager eyes, his lean, lank jaws, his awkward manner, and his large, hooked nose, he reminded one of Clay's friends of "a famished wolf."[27] He had been befriended by Clay's wife when he first came to Kentucky, a penniless New England schoolmaster. But that was all forgotten now as he struck out savagely in an effort to destroy his former benefactor. He testified that three or four weeks before Adams' election he was told by Blair that if Adams was elected, Clay would be Secretary of State. Sometime before, Clay had offered him a job in Washington. He told of this, adding that Clay's motive was to draw him away from the relief struggle in Kentucky. Not content with these revelations, Kendall went on to disclose that Clay had paid him for the publication of anti-Adams pamphlets in 1823, when Clay considered Adams his chief rival for the Presidency.[28]

Blair was next called and asked to reveal the contents of the letters he had received from Clay in January, 1825. Although Blair was now a Jackson adherent, he was still on good terms with Clay and Crittenden, and he refused to testify on the ground that to do so would violate an intimate personal relationship. Blair admitted that he had received Clay's letters, and since he would not deny that there was evidence of a bargain in them, it was interpreted by many as proof that a bargain did exist. After all, wrote a New York editor, even though Clay might have been wronged by the charges and

[26] *Kentucky Senate Journal,* 1827, pp. 207-208, 254-57; Lexington *Kentucky Observer,* Feb. 6, 1828; Blair to Clay, Jan. 22, 1828, in Clay Papers; William E. Smith, *The Francis Preston Blair Family in Politics,* 2 vols. (New York, 1933), I, 42-43.

[27] Thomas Stevenson to Clay, Aug. 29, 1848, in T. J. Clay Papers.

[28] *Kentucky Senate Journal,* 1827, pp. 298-99, 303-304, 307-309; Lexington *Kentucky Reporter,* Feb. 6, 1828; Van Deusen, *Henry Clay,* 216-18, 225; Lexington *Kentucky Gazette,* quoted in Frankfort Argus, Aug. 15, 1828.

might have acted "an honorable, distinterested part," yet *"Adams is President and Clay is Premier.* How are we to get over this?"[29]

The investigation ended in a senate resolution exonerating Clay and Adams by a party vote, twenty to fourteen.[30] The house adjourned before the resolution reached that body. Clay's friends hailed the senate resolution as a great victory, but they were whistling past the graveyard. The fact is, they had been sorely wounded. Blair's refusal to disclose the contents of Clay's indiscreet letters, and Kendall's charge that Clay had tried to bribe him with a clerkship, gave credence to the charge of bargain. And Kendall's version of the contents of Crittenden's ridiculously inconsistent letters to Call and White did nothing to dispel the belief.

Kendall followed up his advantage with renewed charges in the *Argus.* He published a letter from Congressman T. P. Moore, who had been shown a letter from Crittenden to Francis Johnson, another member of the Kentucky delegation. According to Moore, Crittenden wrote that Jackson was his choice after Clay, but if Adams would appoint Clay to a place in his cabinet, Crittenden was confident that Johnson's constituents would approve. Close upon this came an address from the Jackson Executive Committee calling on Clay to publish his letters of January 8 to Blair, since Blair would not.[31]

At first Clay declined. The letter would not prove the charges, as the Jackson committee knew; but they also knew how embarrassing it would be for Clay now to disclose the disparaging remarks the letter contained about Adams. These would, as Blair observed, make the President appear "contemptible, & . . . make the world believe that you yourself despised him."[32]

Crittenden at first also opposed publication. But as the clamor of the Jackson men grew, he changed his mind. Silence was doing Clay's cause more harm than a full revelation would. A committee was formed to ask permission to publish the unfortunate letter.[33] Still Clay demurred. He would not, he said, vindicate his own

[29] *Kentucky Senate Journal,* 1827, pp. 307-309; Blair to Clay, Feb. [?], March 4, 1828, in Clay Papers; Frankfort *Argus,* Feb. 6, July 9, Aug. 6, 1828; Lexington *Kentucky Observer,* Feb. 6, 1828; Smith, *Blair Family,* I, 42-43; Coleman, *Crittenden,* I, 67; New York *Enquirer,* quoted in Frankfort *Argus,* Jan. 30, 1828.

[30] *Kentucky Senate Journal,* 1827, pp. 331-32.

[31] Colton, *Clay,* IV, 196; Frankfort *Argus,* June 4, 1828.

[32] Clay to Crittenden, Feb. 14, 1828, Blair to Clay, March 4, 1828, in Clay Papers.

[33] Crittenden to Clay, March 4, 1828, in Crittenden Papers (Duke); John Harvie to Clay, April 14, 1828, in Clay Papers.

reputation "at the sacrifice of a principle." But repeated entreaties from his friends weakened the resolve. Reluctantly he showed a copy of the letter to Adams, then gave his friends permission to show such portions "as relate to the late Presidential election" to "any gentleman, of any party." Under no circumstances must it be published, however.[34]

It is doubtful if Clay's friends thought Kendall met the restrictive qualification. Nevertheless, they permitted him to see it, and despite Clay's stipulation, he proceeded to publish the contents of the letter, although not verbatim. This publication brought further discredit upon Clay, for in addition to the strictures upon Adams in the letter, it revealed that Clay's friends, in voting for Adams, hoped to advance Clay's interests. Clay assured Blair that he urged them to think only of the country. Pointing out that David White, Blair's congressman, had great respect for Blair's opinion, Clay asked Blair to write White so as to "strengthen him in his inclinations."[35] The letter and the conditions that inspired it would haunt Clay for the rest of his days.

All of these embarrassments, of course, were consequences of Clay's mistake in accepting the position of Secretary of State. Since the Treaty of Ghent, Adams had been suspect, and Clay had openly accused him of willingness to sacrifice the interests of the West for the benefit of New England fisheries. Many of Clay's constituents now saw his open alliance with Adams as evidence that he had turned coat for the sake of personal ambition. That his basic views had changed was undeniable, and men like Kendall and Blair could not be blamed for refusing to follow him into National Republicanism. A revelation of embarrassingly intimate correspondence is an incident of most political campaigns, but that Kendall should stoop to it was an unexpected turn of fate for Clay, and for Crittenden as well.

Clay found himself caught in a web of his own making, and his struggles only succeeded in enmeshing him tighter. The irony of his situation was that he had acted from genuinely high motives, consistent with his new principles, in joining Adams. As the great western leader, Clay was in effect forming a coalition between Adams and the westerners—one that the westerners rejected. Even more ironically, part of the effectiveness of this coalition lay in his accepting

[34] Adams, *Memoirs*, VII, 461, VIII, 28; Clay to John Harvie, June 5, 1828, in Lexington *Kentucky Reporter*, July 2, 1828; Frankfort *Argus*, July 2, 1828.
[35] Frankfort *Argus*, July 9, 1828; Lexington *Kentucky Gazette*, Aug. 15, 1828.

the cabinet position. Clay discovered now that the art of compromise itself can be dangerous when the issues are bitter and the alignments hardened.

Nor would Crittenden soon forget lessons learned in the ordeal of this controversy. What he experienced in these years at such pain to Clay and to himself was to provide him with a cautious outlook and a sense of the necessity for realistic appraisal of political situations. These attributes were to lead him on a path which would ultimately estrange him from Clay.

Crittenden's mildly liberal leanings were now to affect him. In the autumn of 1827, just before the conventions to nominate candidates for the gubernatorial election of 1828, Crittenden had seemed to be the clear choice of the Adams-Clay party. But by the time the convention met in mid-December, there were doubts about him. He had favored the occupying-claimant law, whereby an absentee who could prove superior title to occupied land would have to pay for improvements and could not charge rent for the period before the occupant was notified of the superior title. He had also been willing to compromise the court question in a way that his party leaders would not approve. More important, his equivocal position in the revelations just coming to light concerning the election of Adams made him particularly vulnerable. Even now he refused to admit Jackson's unfitness for the Presidency, insisting that he "is a fine old fellow." For three days Crittenden's friends worked in the convention to overcome these objections. Just as they thought they had succeeded, Crittenden suddenly withdrew his name, without consulting them. The convention thereupon nominated Congressman Thomas Metcalfe, a relief advocate who supported Adams and Clay.[36]

Why did Crittenden decline the nomination when he apparently had it in his grasp? As one of Clay's closest advisers and one who had played a leading part in swinging the Kentucky delegation away from the legislature's instructions, he probably knew, as one of his friends wrote, that he would be an opponent upon whom the Jackson party, "possessed with the spirit of the antient Jews, on the subject of the Messiah," could level a powerful attack.[37] Meanwhile, William

---

[36] Adams, *Memoirs*, VII, 388; Lexington *Kentucky Reporter*, Dec. 19, 1827; George Robertson to Clay, Jan. 19, 1828, in Clay Papers; Leonard Curry, "Election Year—Kentucky, 1828," in *Kentucky Register*, LV (1957), 199-200; Frankfort *Argus*, Dec. 26, 1827, Jan. 16, 1828.
[37] Charles Hammond to Clay, March 28, 1827, in Clay Papers.

T. Barry had been nominated by the Jackson party for governor. He was already in the field when Metcalfe, called Old Stone Hammer because in his youth he had been a stonemason, returned to the state upon adjournment of Congress to campaign against Barry.[38]

Crittenden was a candidate for the legislature, but he acted also as campaign manager for Metcalfe and for the administration party. The election of 1827 had returned Jackson majorities to both houses of the legislature, and Crittenden was determined that the next election would not be lost for lack of energy and coordination. He organized county committees all over the state and urged them to "more resolute and systematic exertions." County meetings were held in all sections, and months ahead of the election he reported to Clay that their friends were "determined . . . and prepared for the approaching contest."[39]

Few Kentucky elections have been more bitterly fought or closely contested than the one between Metcalfe and Barry in 1828. Until the upheavals caused by the relief struggle and the election of Adams, Clay had been assumed to be invincible in the state. But that situation no longer prevailed. There was trouble even in the Green River country, where Crittenden's popularity had been great. But now John Breathitt, a popular Old Court lawyer of Logan County, was Jackson's nominee for lieutenant governor.

Both national factions were eager to carry the August election in Kentucky, so as to influence the presidential election a few months later. Election of Metcalfe would be vindication of Clay and approval of Adams; choice of Barry would have the opposite effect. Pamphlets attacking Adams for alleged irregularities in his accounts when he was an envoy in Europe were printed by the thousands and sent into Kentucky by the Jackson managers, only to be countered with newspapers, pamphlets, and handbills making equally scurrilous personal attacks upon Jackson. Adams himself was asked to contribute five or ten thousand dollars "without enquiring how it would be disposed of, but which would be employed to secure the election of Governor Metcalfe." He refused on grounds of both principle and economy.[40]

[38] Letcher to Clay, Aug. 27 [17], 1827, in Clay Papers; Adams, *Memoirs*, VII, 375, 386, VIII, 4, 76.

[39] Thomas Smith to Clay, Oct. 7, 1827, in Clay Papers; Crittenden to Clay, Oct. 30, Nov. 15, 19, 1827 (copies), in Crittenden Papers.

[40] Francis Johnson to Crittenden, April 12, June 6, 1828, in Crittenden Papers; Adams, *Memoirs*, VII, 466-70; Frankfort *Argus*, June 11, 1828.

When the returns were in, neither party could claim a clear-cut victory. Metcalfe was elected by a majority of 709 in a total vote of 77,000. But Breathitt, the Jackson candidate for lieutenant governor, won by 1,087, and the Jackson party claimed a majority of sixteen in the lower house and two in the upper house of the legislature. The Jackson tide was still too strong for Crittenden in Franklin, and he again went down to defeat in the legislative election.[41]

[41] Curry, "Kentucky, 1828," 203-204; Frankfort *Argus*, June 11, Aug. 6, 13, 20, 1828; Lexington *Kentucky Reporter*, July 22, Aug. 20, 1828; Mason Brown to Orlando Brown, Aug. 22, 1828, in Brown Papers, Filson Club.

CHAPTER V

The Rise of Jacksonism

WITH THE coming of the Jacksonian era, differences of age and of background between Clay and Crittenden would create a disparity also in their political development. The idea of party as a systematic and necessary instrument for men in a complex society to express in action their political principles had been developed by Edmund Burke in England barely a half century before.[1] For the young American republic, however, effective use of political parties was a lesson yet to be mastered. Henry Clay had begun his career in the days of personal political partisanship; indeed, he had come into the Bluegrass region of Kentucky as a young adventurer, armed only with his native abilities. The idea of consistent adherence to principles in politics had not found its way into a nation whose institutions were still in the process of formation, and Henry Clay was never to learn fully that his political power was to be derived as much from the various issues that he espoused as from the personal qualities of his leadership.

This dependence upon personal leadership repeatedly caused Clay to fail to perceive either the power of an issue in political action or the damage wrought by his own cavalier disregard of consistency on political questions. Paradoxically, his willingness and ability to compromise, which were to be his chief contributions to American history, sprang partly from this attitude on political issues. His failure to capture the Presidency, the prize he sought all his life, was at least partly due to his intuitive feeling that he must defeat men rather than deal successfully with controversial matters.

Crittenden, as a Kentuckian by birth and as one coming into politics more than a decade after Clay, had from his background a natural love of order and tradition. He entered politics at the time when the embryonic forms of political party action were already being developed. With the coming of Jackson to power, therefore, it was Crittenden who was to learn the meaning of party in politics, and this led him to subordinate his own ambition. This insight, combined with his already well-developed sense of the need for compromise, now was brought home to him.

However sincere Clay had been in his new National Republicanism—and almost all students agree that he was sincere—the emergence of Jacksonism made it painfully clear that he now was taking attitudes toward banking and toward central government directly opposed to those of his Jeffersonian days. To have these principles lead him into an alliance with Adams, whom Clay had previously accused of hostility toward the West, gave pause even to those who admired Prince Hal above all others. Adams' administration did not help Clay greatly with patronage, nor was Clay, partly because of Adams' intransigence, to make much of a record in foreign affairs. Clay professed to be cheerful about the prospects for the reelection of Adams, but even his sanguine mind must have been chilled.

The Kentucky state elections of August, 1828, were an augury for the presidential election. Crittenden, suppressing his own chagrin at his second failure to obtain a seat in the legislature, wrote cheering letters to Clay in Washington. But the odds were too great. Clay as Secretary of State was still under a cloud because of his acceptance of that very position and the revelations brought forth; Calhoun, the Vice President, had broken with Adams over the tariff and was

---

[1] Carl B. Cone, *Burke and the Nature of Politics: The Age of the American Revolution* (Lexington, 1957), chap. vii.

in open alliance with Jackson; the Postmaster General, John McLean, had used his agency to promote Jackson's interests.[2]

The result was a thumping victory for Jackson, not only in the nation but in Kentucky as well. The electoral vote was 178 to 83, and Jackson's popular margin was around 150,000 out of a total vote of about 1,150,000. In Kentucky he carried 57 of 81 counties with a majority of almost 8,000. He was generally strongest in the counties along the fringe of the Bluegrass, the southeastern and southwestern areas, and the Knobs country, the same sections of the state that Barry had carried over Metcalfe three months before.[3]

Crittenden's cup was not yet full, however. In August, 1828, a vacancy had occurred on the United States Supreme Court with the death of Justice Robert Trimble, and Crittenden's friends sought the appointment for him. Adams sent Crittenden's name to the Senate, but the Jackson majority in that body was not disposed to give a Clay man a post on the court when important decisions affecting their party were pending. Crittenden was understandably eager for this position, and he wrote almost frantically to Clay and his other friends to gain it. But he was astute enough to realize that he had no chance several weeks before his nomination failed.[4]

An even more unpleasant surprise was in store for Crittenden, because the introduction of the spoils system with the inauguration of Jackson was to deprive him of his position as United States district attorney for Kentucky, a four-year appointment made by Adams in February, 1827.[5] Until that time, there had been few removals from

[2] William T. Willis to Crittenden, Oct. 1, 1828, Crittenden to Clay, Sept. 23, 1828 (copy), George M. Bibb to Albert T. Burnley, April 5, 1833, in Crittenden Papers; Thomas Smith to Clay, Oct. 7, 1827, in T. J. Clay Papers; Joseph M. Street to Clay, Oct. 16, 1827, B. W. Dudley to Clay, Aug. 17, 1827, William B. Rochester to Clay, Sept. 17, 1827, in Clay Papers; Duff Green to William S. Murphy, Nov. 10, 1828, in Duff Green Letterbook, Library of Congress; Francis Granger to Thurlow Weed, Nov. 30, 1836, in Granger Papers, Library of Congress; Clay to Webster, in Fletcher Webster (ed.), *Private Correspondence of Daniel Webster*, 2 vols. (Boston, 1857), I, 505.

[3] Curry, "Kentucky, 1828," 203-204, 207.

[4] Robert Wickliffe to Clay, Oct. 7, 1828, John Marshall to Clay, Nov. 28, 1828, in Clay Papers; Adams, *Memoirs*, VIII, 78, 82, 112; letters to Crittenden from Charles A. Wickliffe, Dec. 7, 1829 [1828], Richard M. Johnson, Dec. 25, 1828, John Chambers, Dec. 29, 1828, Henry Clay, Jan. 6, 1829, in Crittenden Papers; Crittenden to Clay, Dec. 27, 1828, Jan. 16, Feb. 15, 1829, in Crittenden Papers (Duke); Duff Green to Thomas Marshall, Dec. 11, 1828, in Duff Green Letterbook; Crittenden to Clay, Dec. 3, 1828, in Coleman, *Crittenden*, I, 71.

[5] Clay to Crittenden, Jan. 25, 1827, R. M. Johnson to Crittenden, Feb. 6, 1827, in Crittenden Papers; commission dated Feb. 8, 1827, in Crittenden Papers (Duke).

federal office for political reasons, Adams having removed only twelve officials during his entire administration. But William L. Marcy's dictum, "To the victors belong the spoils," although seemingly inappropriate at the time, soon would be permanently engrafted on American politics. Before two months of Jackson's administration had passed, Crittenden was notified that he must turn over his office to John Speed Smith.[6]

This was the dark hour just before the dawn; already Crittenden thought he had seen a break in the heavy cloud that hovered over his political prospects. With the unpopular Adams' candidacy no longer hanging over the Clay faction in Kentucky, and with relief and court questions settled, many who had supported Jackson for one or another of those reasons now lost much of their bitterness toward Clay and his friends. Crittenden foresaw a split in the Jackson majority in the Kentucky legislature, and hardly had that body met in December, 1828, when his anticipation materialized. As the choicest patronage plums were bestowed invariably on New Court supporters, Old Court partisans who had supported Jackson felt slighted. John Rowan and John Pope especially were growing "tired of their company," and seemed eager to withdraw from the party. Division in the ranks resulted in the failure of Richard M. Johnson to win reelection to the United States Senate.[7]

By the spring of 1829 the changed sentiment extended to the voters in Franklin County, and Crittenden determined once more to run for the legislature. His magnanimous nature made it almost impossible for anyone to remain long embittered toward him. Blair was to furnish ample proof of this. The lifelong friends had parted politically over the election of Adams. Blair was a poor man and had borrowed large sums from Crittenden: two thousand dollars in the summer of 1821, fifteen hundred more in 1825, and a smaller sum in the following year for some articles of clothing for his wife, "without which her situation will be delicate and unpleasant," he wrote.[8]

These debts were still outstanding in the summer of 1829. Blair had offered to give Crittenden a mortgage to secure them, but

[6] Martin Van Buren to Crittenden, May 25, 1829, in Crittenden Papers (Duke).

[7] Duff Green to Thomas Marshall, Dec. 11, 1828, to John Pope, Dec. 11, 1828, Jan. 2, 1829, in Duff Green Letterbook; J. C. Pickett to Joseph Desha, May 5, 1829, in Joseph Desha Papers; Crittenden to Clay, Jan. 16, 1829, in Crittenden Papers (Duke).

[8] Blair to Crittenden, Jan. 19, 1826, in Crittenden Papers.

Crittenden would not hear of it, just as he refused to accept interest on the principal. Despite this personal obligation, Blair militantly opposed Crittenden's legislative candidacy. On the eve of the election they were both scheduled to speak at a meeting in Frankfort. Blair arrived first and made an impassioned address. He vilified the character of his old friend, whom he saw on the outskirts of the crowd. Finished, Blair started to leave, but paused as Crittenden began to speak. One by one Crittenden took up Blair's charges and refuted them without once mentioning Blair's name or attacking him in any way.

Blair was completely mortified by Crittenden's generosity and his own vindictiveness. When they met on the street a few days later, Crittenden saluted him and extended his hand. Blair, at a loss for words to cover his embarrassment and remembering that a son had recently been born to Crittenden and Maria, asked what name Crittenden intended to give him. After a pause, Crittenden calmly replied: "I have been thinking, Preston, of calling him by that name which you have been trying of late to dishonor." According to Blair, this answer, together with Crittenden's "kind and sorrowful glance," went "straight to my heart." It was the only reproach, he said, which Crittenden ever made him. Many years later, after Crittenden's death, Blair would pay tribute to his friend's generous nature. "Tho we sometimes differed in politics," he wrote in 1865, yet Crittenden "was ever my friend & never failed to serve me or mine when necessity called for his purse or the assistance of those glorious talents and that high character which were the riches with which he blessed thousands and which in the countenance they lent me, invigorated my early manhood & fill my heart at this moment with pride & gratitude."[9]

This election Crittenden won by a comfortable margin. He then set himself a further goal. "I must be speaker," he wrote. "It is the only sort of revenge I feel and seek against my proscribers."[10] His

[9] Blair to Harry I. Todd, Oct. 12, 1865, in F. P. Blair Papers, Kentucky Historical Society. See also Blair to Crittenden [1825?], June 10, 1831, in Crittenden Papers; Crittenden to Simon Gratz, July 6, 1821, July 16, 1822, in Crittenden Papers, State Historical Society of Pennsylvania; Blair to Crittenden, 1831, in Coleman, *Crittenden,* I, 33.

[10] Crittenden to Albert T. Burnley, in Coleman, *Crittenden,* I, 78. See also L. Dudley to Clay, July 28, 1829, in Clay Papers; Worden Pope to Martin Van Buren, Aug. 25, 1829, Van Buren Papers, Library of Congress.

fondest expectations were realized when the legislature met in December and he was unanimously chosen speaker. At the same time the house chose as its clerk the future father-in-law of Abraham Lincoln, Robert S. Todd of Fayette County.[11]

Meanwhile, the burgeoning of Jacksonian democracy had made Jackson's opponents almost desperate to find a champion with enough color and popularity to stand up against Old Hickory. Drawn by Clay's magnetism, their eyes began to turn westward toward Lexington, Kentucky. Although the Great Hal was in political retirement there, public honors and dinners were being showered upon him. When he bombarded Jackson, his voice created a stir in the Jackson camp—apparently the only one that could. He first roused Jackson's supporters when he denounced the spoils system and Jackson's habit of appointing congressmen to political offices. He had also denounced Jackson's veto of the Maysville road bill, an act that struck both at Clay's home state and at his principles. Soon he began to develop the issue that was to be most telling, "Executive Usurpation" by a President free in the use of the veto and highhanded in his methods. Clay's attacks on Jackson drew praise from all sections, so that by 1830 he was looked upon as the hope of the anti-Jacksonites to defeat Old Hickory in 1832.

First, however, it was necessary that Clay return to public life so as to have a stage from which he could launch his campaign for the Presidency. A national figure's first duty is to have his own state securely behind him, and there was much pressure from business interests throughout the nation to have Clay returned to the Senate. Crittenden and Clay's other friends were eager to promote his candidacy, but with newly acquired wisdom they were concerned about how best to do it. Jackson's popularity with the backwoodsmen showed no signs of declining, and the very fact that Clay had supporters outside the state made them suspicious. His friends were therefore well aware that a campaign would be risky; on the other hand, if Clay remained too long out of office, he courted political oblivion.

Crittenden felt that Clay should first renew acquaintances without becoming committed and urged him to visit in Frankfort and appear

[11] *Kentucky House Journal*, 1829, pp. 3-4; *Niles' Register* XXXVII (1829-1830), 276.

at prearranged political rallies while the legislature was in session. Accepting this advice Clay made several journeys to Frankfort that winter, and the following autumn he and Crittenden toured the western part of the state.[12] Crittenden had hoped that in this way Clay's once-great popularity with political leaders in the state would be revived, and he might be sent back to Congress when the time "seemed propitious."[13] Such a time could occur when a successor to Senator John Rowan would be chosen in the legislative session in the winter of 1830-1831. Rowan had lost popularity by his vote against the Maysville road bill.

By the summer of 1830, however, Jackson's Democratic Republican party was growing so strong in the state that it seemed too dangerous to risk Clay's defeat in an uncertain contest in the legislature. Clay's friends hoped to have a slight majority there, but Robert Wickliffe, the Old Duke, who had political ambitions himself, was threatening to bolt with a small group of dissidents. Wickliffe, whose father and mother had been among the first settlers in Fayette County, had amassed great wealth at the bar and in planting, and was soon to become the largest slaveowner in the state. A member of the Old Court party who had formerly been opposed to Jackson, his loyalty to Clay was not above question. His political ambitions were not limited to himself but encompassed both his brother, Charles A. Wickliffe of Nelson County, and his own son, Charles. A member of the gentry, his social and economic views were similar to Clay's, but the men were never close. Clay's true friends, among whom Crittenden was by now foremost, knew that Wickliffe's ambitions made him an undependable ally who would not hesitate to desert Clay if by so doing he could advance a Wickliffe.

The strategy finally agreed upon was that Crittenden or Robert Letcher, either of whom was expendable, would be the senatorial candidate of the anti-Jackson party. If, however, Clay's prospects should look good when the legislature met, he might be placed in nomination at the last moment. Accordingly, candidates for the legislature in 1830 were called upon to commit themselves on their choice for senator, and many announced for Crittenden. One

[12] Crittenden to Clay, Feb. 15, 1829, in Crittenden Papers (Duke); Citizens of Christian County to Crittenden, Sept. 7, 1829, Oscar Stuart to Crittenden, Jan. 7, 1861, in Crittenden Papers.
[13] Crittenden to Clay, Feb. 15, 1829, in Crittenden Papers (Duke).

enthusiastic candidate wrote that he hoped Crittenden would "disperse the *whelps* you are now contending with on the outskirts of the forest & then march up tryumphantly & beard the old lyon in his den."[14] Crittenden was himself a candidate for the legislature, and he announced merely that he would not vote for a Jackson man for senator and that he was for Clay for President.[15] Crittenden won his legislative seat in the August election, and when the legislature met, he was again chosen speaker without opposition. There was a majority of more than a dozen anti-Jackson men in the two houses, but it was early ascertained that if Clay were nominated for the Senate, he could not secure a majority. It was agreed, therefore, that Crittenden should be the anti-Jackson candidate, and accordingly he was nominated by friends of Clay.[16]

When balloting began on January 4, four Jacksonites—Richard M. Johnson, John Rowan, Charles A. Wickliffe, and John Breathitt—were brought out in turn to run against Crittenden. Sixty-nine votes were necessary for election, and Crittenden received sixty-eight on fourteen ballots taken over a period of several days. Johnson's high tide was sixty-four votes; Rowan's, forty-nine; Wickliffe's, fifty; and Breathitt's, sixty-six. Throughout the balloting, Crittenden refused to vote, although his ballot would have secured his election. During the deadlock, Clay's candidacy was again explored. Crittenden would cast his ballot for Clay, of course, but several of Crittenden's votes could not be transferred to Clay. Ben Hardin wished to run, and it was said he had no scruple about voting for himself. But he, too, it was learned, would lose several of Crittenden's votes.[17]

As balloting continued, the motives of candidates and their supporters were impeached, and bitterness grew. Threats of proscription were made. The representative from Nicholas County received petitions from a majority of the voters of his district instructing him to vote for one of the Jackson candidates, under threat of "political

14 A. T. Burnley to Crittenden, June 13, 1830, in Crittenden Papers.
15 Clay to Daniel Webster, June 7, 1830, in Webster, *Correspondence*, I, 505; Crittenden to Clay, June 1, 1830, in Crittenden Papers (Duke).
16 *Kentucky House Journal*, 1830, pp. 3, 5; *Niles' Register*, XXXIX (1830-1831), 276; letter of Thomas F. Marshall in Frankfort *Commonwealth*, Dec. 2, 1851.
17 *Kentucky House Journal*, 1830, pp. 177-99; *Niles' Register*, XXXIX (1830-1831), 386; Adams, *Memoirs*, VIII, 254, 262-63; James Taylor to James Madison, Dec. 15, 1830, Jan. 2, 1831, in James A. Padgett (ed.), "The Letters of James Taylor to the Presidents of the United States," in *Kentucky Register*, XXXIV (1936), 34, 388; Little, *Ben Hardin*, 156.

death."[18] When it became certain that the deadlock could not be broken, Crittenden's supporters succeeded in a move to postpone the election to the following year.[19]

The failure of the anti-Jackson party to choose a senator, even when they had a majority, is the more remarkable because they were able to place members of their faction in all other offices chosen by the legislature: state treasurer, two state bank presidents, and public printer. This failure established with certainty the jealousy of Clay that existed within his own party, where faithless friends hoped to lure him into a declaration of his candidacy and then to humiliate him. He was certainly the most popular man in the state, and next to him, Crittenden. Yet Crittenden could not win without his own vote, and Clay could not win even with Crittenden's vote.

The following summer, candidates for the legislature were again asked to indicate whom they would support. Clay's name was not even proposed to them, for fear that if men pledged to him were defeated, his presidential chances the following year would suffer. Crittenden was this time the unqualified choice of the Clay party. He was also a candidate for the legislature again. He won his legislative race, and a clear majority pledged to him for senator were also returned. The legislature met on November 7, and Crittenden was again chosen speaker unanimously. But now came pressure from Lexington. The party and the country needed Clay in Washington, one of Clay's friends wrote, and even though Crittenden had been all along looked on as the candidate, he should press Clay to take the place instead. There would be no difficulty, wrote another, "in making you Gov[ernor]," if Crittenden would stand aside for Clay in the Senate race. Even Daniel Webster was urging Clay's return to the Senate, although he expressed high regard for Crittenden's character and ability. "W[oul]d to God, we could have you both, at this crisis," he wrote.[20] Clay himself never asked that he be given the track in place of his friend.

Some of Crittenden's friends, tired of what they regarded as Clay's unchallenged leadership, urged Crittenden's candidacy, but Crit-

---

[18] William H. Russell to Clay, Dec. 9, 1830, April 15, 1831, in Clay Papers.
[19] *Kentucky House Journal, 1830,* p. 249; *Niles' Register,* XXXIX (1830-1831), 386.
[20] *Kentucky House Journal, 1831,* pp. 3, 5; Thomas Flournoy to Crittenden, Sept. 24, 1831, A. R. Macy to Crittenden, Oct. 14, 1831, in Crittenden Papers; Daniel Webster to Clay, Oct. 5, 1831, in Clay Papers.

tenden gracefully stepped aside.[21] Clay was elected over Richard M. Johnson by a nine-vote majority. "I *could* have gone to the Senate," Crittenden wrote his daughter. "It was but for me to express the wish and Mr. Clay would not have been the candidate. There was no *collusion*, no rivalry, between us. All that was done was with my perfect accordance." He had acted, he added, in a manner "most consistent, with what I trust is my character for disinterestedness, honor and patriotism."[22] But all members of the Crittenden family were not so gracious. His brother Thomas, who had been a neighbor and business associate of Clay's in Lexington, was angry at the treatment Crittenden had received. He charged that Clay himself was responsible, pointing out that it was Clay's friends in Lexington who had started the movement to substitute him for Crittenden.[23]

Clay went to Washington in November, hoping to develop issues that would carry the party to victory in 1832. He was now the acknowledged and indisputable candidate of the conservative wing of the Republican party. First came his bid for support from the South and the West. As the national debt was about to be paid off and present revenue would create a treasury surplus, Clay urged use of the proceeds from the sale of public lands to pay for internal improvements, and reduction of the tariff on noncompetitive items, "applying accidental excesses only to internal improvements." These proposals were to become the credo of the Whig party within a few years.[24] The West would be pleased with the support for internal improvements, and the slight tariff reduction would be a sop to the South. Crittenden, whose inclinations were toward free trade, urged Clay to "go a little further . . . and consent to a reduction of duties on such of our manufactures as are most firmly established." He thought coarse cottons could now flourish without protection, or at least with less than Clay was prepared to offer. A reduction would reassure opponents of the tariff, both in Kentucky and elsewhere, as it would indicate that protection was only a temporary expedient to aid infant industry. It would be a "great triumph," he thought, if it

---

[21] James Taylor to James Madison, Dec. 15, 1830, in Padgett, "Letters of James Taylor," 338; letter of Thomas Marshall in Frankfort *Commonwealth*, Dec. 2, 1851; W. W. Worsley to Clay, Oct. 22, 1831, in Clay Papers.

[22] Crittenden to Mrs. Chapman Coleman, Nov. 18, 1831, in Coleman, *Crittenden*, I, 81-82; Crittenden to Mrs. Coleman, Dec. 4, 1831, in Crittenden Papers (Duke); *Kentucky House Journal*, 1831, p. 47.

[23] W. W. Worsley to Clay, Oct. 22, 1831, in Clay Papers.

[24] Van Deusen, *Henry Clay*, 254.

could be shown that its purpose was already achieved and no longer necessary in any branch of industry.[25] Clay would not be won to his view, however, until the following year.

Under Clay's skillful nurturing, the idea of "Executive Usurpation" was emphasized, and Jackson's temperament gave considerable substance to this theme. But again Clay's hopes were to be confounded by the monetary issue. Clay now decided that he should press rechartering the Bank of the United States. Two years earlier he had told Nicholas Biddle, president of the bank, that he preferred not to propose renewal of the charter until shortly before it expired in 1836. Biddle agreed, but by 1832 both men had changed their minds.[26]

One can only speculate as to what made Clay decide to bring this question before the country prior to the election, but his decision seems to demonstrate his regard for men rather than issues. He had reason to believe that Jackson would veto the bill, and he also knew that the old general, although he opposed centralized banking of any kind, would be embarrassed in his financial plans for paying off the national debt if the charter was not renewed. With Clay, the instinct to strike out at his enemy overcame all else; his mettle had been aroused by his recent Senate battles, and he could see only victory over his enemy, not the implications of the issue itself.

The Bank of the United States was not without faults. Its enormous power had been employed at times unwisely and injudiciously by the handful of capitalists who controlled it; and these mistakes had caused great hardships in various sections of the country. As a symbol of the money monopoly and of strong government, it had been considered by many a threat to freedom. Further, Nicholas Biddle had spent thousands of dollars in propaganda favoring renewal of the charter, a fact which aroused Jacksonian suspicions. When Clay pressed the recharter in the Senate, to the accompaniment of loud huzzas from the opposition press, he was once again identifying himself with an institution unpopular in the West. In the bitter battle in which he saw the bill passed, Clay could be

---

[25] Clay to Crittenden, Nov. 20, 1831, Thomas Metcalfe to Clay, Feb. 14, 1832, in Clay Papers; Duff Green to Richard K. Crallé, Dec. 5, 1831, in Duff Green Papers; Allan Nevins (ed.), *Diary of John Quincy Adams* (New York, 1951), 428; Crittenden to Clay, Feb. 23, 1832, in Crittenden Papers (Duke).

[26] Van Deusen, *Henry Clay*, 256.

flushed with his Senate victory; but Jackson, in vetoing the bill, had the better issue in the eyes of the people.

Eighteen thirty-two was a year of political flux. Out of sectional interests of the period, as well as from the personal followings of political leaders, came the two great parties, Whig and Democratic, that contended for dominance for the next two decades. During Jackson's administration, partisanship reached a degree of bitterness not seen since the Presidency of the elder Adams. His son, John Quincy Adams, viewed the scene in the early 1830s as the beginning of the dissolution of the Union. The country had fallen "into the sere and yellow leaf," he thought, and it could survive but a few years.[27] Another opponent of Jackson's thought that politics had reached a point from which they could descend no lower. The Peggy Eaton affair occupied the center of the national stage, and the only matter of concern seemed to be, he said, "whether a coarse, vulgar, woman is or is not a . . . fit member of society."[28]

But Kentucky had proved a better barometer of the political weather than Clay's friends had supposed. Clay had made his move for recharter too early; ignoring the indications of sentiment against him in his own state, he had again misread the political situation. Jackson, on the other hand, despite his many disadvantages—his high-handedness, his less-than-spotless past, his ignorance on many issues— had one great weapon in his favor: he understood the common man better than his adversaries did. Although he seemed to be unqualified for high political office, he acted with such boldness and courage that he inspired his friends and intimidated and overawed his opposition. Long months before the election, the perceptive among Clay's friends were to despair of unseating the old hero in 1832.[29]

Crittenden was very active in the election that year. He again managed Clay's campaign in Kentucky and also that of the gubernatorial candidate of the party, Richard A. Buckner. Buckner was a weaker candidate than his Democratic opponent, John Breathitt, and Crittenden had tried unsuccessfully to prevent him from running.

[27] Adams, *Memoirs*, VIII, 433, 479-88.
[28] Francis Granger to Thurlow Weed, Aug. 12, 1831, in Granger Papers.
[29] Edward Everett to Francis Granger, Nov. 10, 1831, Thurlow Weed to Granger, Dec. 9, 1831, E. Ledgwick, Jr., to Granger, Aug. 31, 1832, Granger to Ledgwick, Aug. 31, 1832, in Granger Papers; George Poindexter to ————, Jan. 18, 1832, in Poindexter Family Papers, University of Virginia Library; Nathan Sergeant to Crittenden, July 15, 1849, in Crittenden Papers.

Once during the campaign Crittenden remarked that they must elect Buckner, "cost what it will." Someone who overheard him thought that he implied bribing voters, but Crittenden replied convincingly that his words were merely "a common & familiar phrase" and that "only the grossest misconception, or the most sinister spirit could have found in it anything for censure."[30]

The two elections, for governor and for President, showed that party strength in Kentucky was badly divided. Breathitt defeated Buckner in August by little more than a thousand votes, having received a majority of fifteen hundred in the new section of the state known as the Jackson Purchase, between the Tennessee and Mississippi rivers. This victory in August gave the Jackson party great hopes of carrying the state for their champion in November. But they were doomed to disappointment. Clay's friends redoubled their efforts after their faction lost the gubernatorial election; they were determined not to lose Kentucky when Clay himself was the candidate. Their hard work, together with Clay's reviving personal popularity, was decisive. Clay carried his own state by 7,000 votes, but Jackson won in the electoral college by a topheavy vote, 219 to 49.[31]

Discouraged by his crushing defeat, Clay proposed to resign from the Senate so that Crittenden might succeed him. But Crittenden advised him not to do so. He was "not looking forward to the future with any spirit of impatient ambition," he wrote. Besides, Clay had manifested "friendship, liberality, and magnanimity" toward him, and he desired that Clay remain in Washington as long as "the public service may require it." Clay agreed to remain.[32]

But Crittenden's private affairs had now reached a stage where he was prepared and even eager to return to the Senate, and an opportunity soon presented itself. The term of his old friend and political opponent Bibb would expire the next year. Bibb did not wish to succeed himself, and Crittenden determined to take his place. He began to organize local committees to screen prospective candidates for the

[30] Thomas Metcalfe to Clay, June 3, 1832, in Clay Papers; A. R. Macy to Crittenden, Oct. 14, 1832, Richard A. Buckner to Crittenden, Dec. 29, 1831, Crittenden to Clay, Feb. 23, 1832 (copy), Crittenden to Richard A. Buckner, Feb. 27, 1832, Clay to Crittenden, April 15, 1832, Chilton Allen to Crittenden, Nov. 26, 1832, Committee of Seven from Green River to Crittenden, Sept. 9, 1832, in Crittenden Papers.

[31] Kerr, *History of Kentucky*, II, 701-704.

[32] Crittenden to Clay, Nov. 17, 1832, Clay to Crittenden, Nov. 28, 1832, in Crittenden Papers (Duke).

legislature and to prevent "unproper collisions and competitions between our friends."[33]

Political behavior was no better in Kentucky, probably worse, than in many other sections of the country during this period. When Thomas Metcalfe took leave of John Quincy Adams in the spring of 1828 to begin his campaign for governor, the President remarked on the peculiar "usage of that part of the country," where candidates had to travel the state and solicit votes of the people.[34] They did indeed have to travel, and they had to solicit votes. When a campaign reached its peak, Kentuckians seemed to lose the good sense with which they were ordinarily endowed, and visitors from more sedate regions marveled at their outlandish behavior. A newcomer in 1832 wrote: "I have just witnessed that strange thing, a Kentucky Election. . . . Whisky and apple toddy flowed in the cities and villages like the Euphrates through ancient Babylon. . . . Drunkenness stalked triumphant. . . . Runners, each with a whisky bottle poking its long, jolly neck from his pocket, were employed in bribing voters, and each party kept half-a-dozen bullies . . . to flog every poor fellow that should attempt to vote illegally; a half-hundredweight of mortar would scarce fill up the chinks in the skulls that were broken. . . . One of the runners asked me if I were a voter, and replied, when I said I was not: 'Never mind; just take a swig of this'—shaking up a bottle— 'and toss in a vote—I'll fight for you.' " Later he witnessed a brawl between a voter and a challenger in which "slugging, butting, choking" were punctuated by calls from onlookers to "Gouge him!" The newcomer turned away "a confirmed believer in total depravity."[35]

Dear to the hearts of all Kentuckians at this time was the political burgoo. These outdoor meetings, which started long before noon and lasted until nearly dark, were planned for weeks, even months, in advance. Letters went out from the managing committee to famous men in other sections—to Daniel Webster, James Madison, Martin Van Buren, or Andrew Jackson—requesting their presence to discuss the "leading questions of interest to the nation." Rarely, if ever, did these dignitaries honor the occasion with their presence; indeed, they

[33] Crittenden to Henry Clay, Jr., April 13, 1834, in Clay Papers, Ashland, Lexington, Ky.

[34] Adams, *Memoirs*, VIII, 4.

[35] W. C. Barrickman, "Political Nominating Conventions," in *Filson Quarterly*, XVIII (1944), 43.

were not expected to come. But they were expected to answer with a long letter of regret, presenting views of their party and denouncing the wickedness of the opposition. These letters would be read to the gathered multitude during the course of the ceremonies and a number of local politicians would make prodigiously long speeches. Letters and speeches would be published in newspapers that espoused the cause and would even be copied and reprinted by their allies in the more sophisticated metropolitan centers.

Thousands of people gathered for these functions. They came by horseback, carriage, and farm wagon, bringing women and children along. A break in the festivities came about midday, and all gathered around rough tables that had been improvised in some shady spot. In addition to stronger stimulants, refreshments almost invariably centered around a dish called burgoo. The origin of the name is uncertain, but surely no one who tasted the succulent stew ever forgot it. Large quantities of game—venison, squirrel, wild turkey, pheasant—were thrown into a huge iron pot of boiling water. Domestic fowl, beef, pork, and veal were added, together with onions, carrots, turnips, and condiments. The stew cooked for several hours over an open fire under the watchful eye of some accomplished domestic, until the flavors of each component part permeated all. Modern imitations cannot approximate the delights that contemporary accounts tell us this preparation brought to all who tasted it.

Such a meeting as this was called to order by Crittenden at Cove Spring, outside Frankfort, on July 4, 1834. It was the organization meeting of the Whig party in Kentucky, the culmination of a series of local meetings of preceding months. Crittenden prefaced the reading of the Declaration of Independence with an address. A New England visitor who was present remarked upon Crittenden's "dignified" but smiling countenance and his "rich and mellow" voice. He noted also that Crittenden possessed the peculiar oratorical power to "charm the learned and ignorant at the same time." He well deserved, the visitor concluded, "to be a favorite son of Kentucky."[36]

After Crittenden's reading of the Declaration, the company repaired to the feast that had been prepared. After the dinner, Charles S. Morehead read a number of toasts praising Washington, Madison, the Constitution, Henry Clay, womanhood, and the newly formed

[36] Henry Clay, Jr., to Crittenden, April 1, 1834, in Crittenden Papers (Duke); James Love to Crittenden, May 27, 1834, in Crittenden Papers; Frankfort *Commonwealth*, July 8, 1834; Johnson, *Franklin County*, 99.

Whig party, and denouncing Jackson and presidential usurpation. In the afternoon there were more speeches on these same themes, intermingled with music provided by "three splendid bands." After a day of "pure and unalloyed pleasure," the company returned in procession to Frankfort, climaxing the festivities that night with a grand ball at the Mansion House. It was universally admitted to be "the most imposing and most agreeable fourth of July which has ever been commemorated in this section of Kentucky," wrote a Whig editor who was there.

Next day the convention assembled to hear a report prepared by a committee on resolutions, of which Crittenden was chairman. The address, of course, excoriated Jackson. It charged him with gaining election through false charges and misrepresentation and with usurping the authority of Congress. By the tariffs of 1828 and 1832 he had brought the country to the brink of ruin, and it had been saved only by the artistry of Clay. It scored Jackson for corrupting the legislative branch of the government by appointing thirty-eight members of Congress to "high and lucrative posts." It denounced him for the free use of the veto, which was "intended to be used only in extreme cases." It denounced him for removing government deposits from the Bank of the United States, thereby deranging the commerce of the country and producing unparalleled distress. It likened him to the tyrant George III, and his opponents to the Whig patriots of the Revolution. The address and its accompanying resolutions were adopted, and arrangements were made for their printing and wide distribution.[37]

The immediate object of all this was for the Whigs to gain control of the legislature so as to elect Crittenden to the Senate seat he coveted. He had been working quietly but diligently since early May. "For God's sake," he wrote a friend confidentially, "exert yourself to the utmost, and animate our friends all around you."[38] His election was eagerly desired, too, by members of the Kentucky delegation in Congress. "It is the proper theatre for you," wrote one member. "There is not one could come into successful competition with you."[39] The August elections resulted in a great Whig victory, and when the legislature met, Crittenden was chosen to the Senate

[37] Frankfort *Commonwealth*, July 8, 1834.
[38] Crittenden to A. T. Burnley, May 2 [1834], in Coleman, *Crittenden*, I, 87-88.
[39] James T. Morehead to Crittenden, May 17, 1834, James Love to Crittenden, May 27, 1834, in Crittenden Papers.

seat over James Guthrie by a vote of ninety-four to forty. The term was a full one, from March, 1835, to March, 1841.[40]

Meanwhile, changes had taken place in Crittenden's family circle. Besides the three children Maria brought with her into the home, she had presented Crittenden with two sons, John Jordan and Eugene. But there were departures from the home also. George Bibb, the eldest son, who had received an appointment to West Point in the closing days of the Adams administration, had been graduated and was beginning his army service as a lieutenant on the western frontier. Ann Mary, "the tenderest and most dutiful of daughters," had also left the paternal home. In November, 1830, when she was seventeen, she had married Chapman Coleman, an established man of business in Louisville. Coleman was her senior by twenty years, but it was a happy and fruitful marriage. Before Coleman died in 1850, Ann Mary had borne him seven children.[41]

Grief and sorrow came to Crittenden at this time, also. His brother Thomas was striken without warning with a fatal malady at Christmastime, 1832, and Crittenden rushed to his bedside. Thomas was at the time a circuit judge in Jefferson County, but he had several times represented Fayette in the legislature and had served briefly as secretary of state under Metcalfe. "I never knew," Crittenden wrote Maria as he watched his brother's strength ebb, "how dearly I loved this dearest and noblest and best of brothers." Two years later, Robert, the youngest of Crittenden's brothers, who had become a distinguished member of the Arkansas bar, collapsed during a trial in Vicksburg, Mississippi, and died within a few days.[42] Then, only a few weeks later, the last of his brothers, Henry, passed away. Henry had married the daughter of Colonel John Allen and had settled in Shelby County, which he had twice represented in the legislature. In 1833 he had been stabbed by a desperado named John U. Waring for testifying against him in court. The wound never healed, and a year later a fatal infection developed. Crittenden was called to Shelbyville in early December just as the legislature was

[40] *Kentucky House Journal, 1834,* pp. 106-107; *Kentucky Senate Journal, 1834,* p. 115; *Niles' Register,* XLVII (1834-1835), 356.

[41] Genealogical memorandum, Crittenden to Mrs. Coleman, Dec. 4, 1832, June 15, 1833, in Crittenden Papers (Duke); Crittenden to Mrs. Coleman, Nov. 18, 1831, in Coleman, *Crittenden,* I, 81; Frankfort *Argus,* June 13, 1832.

[42] Crittenden to Maria Crittenden, Dec. 25, 1832, in Crittenden Papers (Duke); George M. Moreland, "Some Arkansas Immortals," in Memphis *Commercial Appeal,* Feb. 28, 1926.

assembling. Henry lingered for several weeks but died on December 21. He left three sons, two of whom would gain prominence, one of them distinction. William Logan lost his life in Cuba in 1851 as one of the ill-fated Lopez expedition; Thomas T. was governor of Missouri in the postwar period.[43]

Crittenden was a man of strong family affection. He was devoted to his brothers as well as to his sisters, and he watched over the welfare of their children with as much solicitude as if they were his own. But his disposition did not permit him to be prostrated long by grief. To him life was an experience that was all too short, anyway. The world, especially the world of Washington, was an exciting place where great measures were to be decided. He was now a United States senator with a career of service to his country before him. It was with some sadness, not unmixed with buoyant optimism, therefore, that he looked forward to the next session of Congress.

[43] J. J. Crittenden to Mrs. Coleman, Dec. 14, 1834, in Crittenden Papers (Duke); Green, *Historic Families*, 248; H. H. Crittenden, *Memoirs*, 17, 88-98.

CHAPTER VI

Member of the
Opposition

IN THE day when railroads were either nonexistent or in their infancy, the easiest route from Frankfort to Washington was by steamboat direct to Wheeling, Virginia, and from there by stagecoach over the National Road. But Crittenden had business in Lexington, and so he was obliged to go there by stage and from there to Maysville. At Maysville he was entertained at Langhorne's Hotel with a "wine party." Catching the boat next morning, he proceeded to Wheeling and to Washington, arriving there in time to be presented to the Senate by Clay on December 8. Doubtless through Clay's influence, he was placed at once on two of the most important standing committees, Public Lands and Judiciary.[1]

Washington then was anything but the beautiful city it is today. Although scarce a third of a century had passed since its founding, it already looked rundown. A few large buildings were scattered about. Cows were pastured here and there on public grounds or wandered about seeking forage, and pigs rooted in the public thoroughfares. On windy days in summer or fall, dust clouds on Pennsylvania Avenue blinded pedestrians; in winter the street was a formidable bog. The handful of permanent officials of the government had offices in modest brick buildings on the four corners adjacent to the White House: State, Treasury, War, and Navy. The Capitol, at the other end of the avenue, was a rather unpretentious building; the two graceful wings had not yet been thought of, and the dome would not be finished for three decades longer. John Marshall presided over a Supreme Court that held its sessions in the Capitol basement, in a room that has since been made into a restaurant.[2]

There were not enough houses to accommodate the twenty thousand regular inhabitants nor hotels enough to house members of Congress who might be there only a few months out of the year, if Congress accomplished its business expeditiously. Rents were therefore high, except in Georgetown. Amos Kendall, now serving in Jackson's "kitchen cabinet," found he could rent an adequate house in Georgetown for $125 a year, whereas suitable accommodations in Washington would cost him $1,200.[3] Few members of Congress brought their wives. Instead, the men lived together in small groups, renting a furnished house and contracting also for their meals. These messes were exclusive, and only congenial members of the same party were invited to share accommodations. Many political decisions were made in the privacy of these quarters.

There was much drinking and cardplaying, and the city was notorious for its gambling places. Gadsby's, at the corner of Sixth and Pennsylvania, was a favorite haunt of senators and congressmen. Adjoining clubrooms provided retreats for them as well as other patrons, where brag, *vingt-et-un*, and whist were played, sometimes for large sums. There were, besides, a dozen faro banks within a stone's throw. Congressmen and senators were paid eight dollars a day then, and many squandered this and more in these establishments. Seargent S. Prentiss, brilliant but eccentric young congressman from Mississippi, was said to have lost $30,000 his first winter in Washington. "On the whole," wrote a newcomer to the city about this time, "if there is more extravagance, folly, and corruption anywhere in the world than in this city I do not wish to see the place."

1 Frankfort *Commonwealth*, Dec. 5, 1835; Clay to Lucretia Clay, Dec. 9, 1835, in T. J. Clay Papers; *Congressional Globe*, 24 Cong., 1 Sess., 11; *Senate Journal*, 24 Cong., 1 Sess., 6, 42.
2 William A. Butler, A *Retrospect of Forty Years, 1825-1865* (New York, 1911), 57-58.
3 Amos Kendall, *Autobiography* (New York, 1872), 284, 293.

Crittenden was no Puritan. Besides a congenial game of cards, he indulged in other forms of gambling. A New Englander visiting Kentucky in the spring of 1837 met Crittenden and Clay at a racecourse. He wrote that they were "apparently as much excited, talking as loudly, betting as freely, drinking as deeply, and swearing as excessively as the jockeys themselves." But if Crittenden lost any great sums at Kentucky racetracks or in Washington gambling houses, there is no record of it. Nor would heavy gambling be consistent with his generally conservative disposition. Certainly he liked wine and even stronger drink, as did most men of that day, although he was able to keep all appetites under control except on rare occasions.

One such occasion when Crittenden was intemperate occurred that winter when he dined with a group of his colleagues at John Pendleton Kennedy's. The bowl had flowed rather freely, and late in the evening a cotillion was formed in which Crittenden performed as the partner of Buchanan. The merrymaking went on past midnight. In the early morning hours a dispute arose as to which state had the ugliest native. Crittenden settled the contest by proposing his old Frankfort neighbor Blair, who had now grown prosperous as editor of the *Globe*, but whose haggard, emaciated, cadaverous face had not improved with his fortunes. All conceded that the figurative trophy should go to Kentucky on the strength of this nomination.

Despite the city's limitations, there was a certain extravagant brilliance about its social life. Cabinet members and permanent officials brought their wives to Washington, of course, as did members of the diplomatic corps. The President gave frequent large levees at the White House, sometimes with dancing. In addition, there were grand balls, given either at the embassies or at the home of some local dignitary. There was a constant round of dinners, some of them very elaborate.[4]

During this session and for five years to come, Crittenden, like most other Whigs in Congress, followed Clay's lead. As unofficial leader of the opposition, Clay did all he could to embarrass the Jackson and Van Buren administrations, and Crittenden supported his efforts. Clay favored a protective tariff, and to this Crittenden gave

    [4] Butler, *Retrospect*, 57-58; "Recollections of an Old Stager," in *Harpers' Monthly*, XLVI (1872), 95, XLVII (1873), 255; Kendall, *Autobiography*, 280, 282; Little, *Ben Hardin*, 234; Francis Fessenden, *Life and Public Services of William Pitt Fessenden* (Boston, 1907), I, 13.

only halfhearted support; but Crittenden was in full accord when Clay advocated that proceeds of public land sales be distributed to the states. Crittenden also joined Clay in opposing the Seminole war, Indian removals, the Jackson-Van Buren antibank program, and administration belligerency toward France over spoliation claims. A survey of Senate votes for the next few years shows that Clay and Crittenden rarely were on different sides—never, on an important issue.[5]

Crittenden's first major speech that session came in early February. There was a surplus in the Treasury, and land sales were bringing in enough revenue to take care of ordinary governmental expenditures, so that a high tariff was not needed as a moneyraising device. Partly to forestall tariff reduction, which to many seemed logical, as well as to provide the states with funds to be used for education and for internal improvements, Clay proposed a bill to distribute proceeds of land sales to the states; and Crittenden's Committee on Public Lands reported it favorably. A similar bill had passed in the preceding Congress but had failed to gain Jackson's approval.[6] Thomas Hart Benton, Jackson Democrat from Missouri, saw through Clay's scheme and sought to dispose of the embarrassing surplus in a different way. Using the threat of war with France over a $5,000,000 claim for damages to American citizens during the Napoleonic wars, he proposed to spend $30,000,000 for defense. On the afternoon of February 2, Democratic Senator James Buchanan of Pennsylvania had spoken in support of Benton's program. Crittenden had already prepared to answer Benton, and when Buchanan sat down, he took the floor.

His reputation as an orator had preceded him to Washington. As word spread that he would speak on that day, spectators thronged to the galleries, and a large audience crowded in from the House of Representatives. Crittenden started in a voice so low that it was inaudible to many; and a reporter, unable to hear distinctly, thought he seemed "a trifle dashed." Some, not having heard Crittenden before, exchanged knowing looks at this appearance of discomfiture.

[5] *Niles' Register*, L, (1836), 139, 252, LI, (1836-1837), 330-31, 346; Thomas Hart Benton, *Thirty Years' View; or a History of the American Government for Thirty Years, from 1820 to 1850*, 2 vols. (New York, 1854), I, 625-26, 651, 657-58, 665, 708-709, 711. See also *Congressional Globe*, 24 Cong.—26 Cong., *passim*.
[6] *Senate Documents*, 24 Cong., 1 Sess., Vol. II, No. 89.

But Clay, who sat watching Crittenden's every motion "like a fond father," whispered to Governor James Kent, who sat beside him, that he would "soon hear a display of eloquence worth listening to."

For more than an hour Crittenden spoke, without script and without even a note. His manner was described by an onlooker as "easy, polished, and elegant," his bearing as "dignified." But as he warmed to his subject, his voice became vigorous and clear. At times he spoke rapidly and precisely, much after the fashion of Calhoun. Then he would suddenly swing to the rich, melodious tones of Clay. "If I had not known he was speaking and heard him," wrote a Whig reporter that day, "I would have risked any wager that Calhoun was upon the floor, so exactly were his voice, enunciation and intonation like that great and remarkable man. At another time . . . by the sound of the orator's voice, I should have said at once it was Clay, for his voice had all the expansion and music in it which character-izes that of his great colleague's above that of any other man's who speaks the English language."[7]

Crittenden derided the idea of going to war with France over "a petty, paltry sum of money." Of all motives for war, he thought the recovery of money the most unworthy. He knew of no instance among civilized nations where war had been waged for such an object. If it were a "legitimate" cause for war, "it is surely the most inglorious of them all." He was ready to spend as much as necessary for defense, "and ten times as much," but thought this appropriation unnecessary. Besides, France was our ancient ally, "whose blood had flowed for us, and with our own, in the great struggle that . . . made us a nation!"[8]

The speech was well accepted. A friendly reporter thought that with the exception of a speech made by Webster, Crittenden's was "the happiest and most eloquent display that has been made in Congress during the present session. . . . He more than fulfilled all expectations today." Ben Hardin, who was in Congress at the time and heard the speech, said Crittenden was "inferior to no man in America as a profound lawyer and eloquent orator."[9]

More pleasing to Crittenden, doubtless, than all these plaudits was the effect the speech had on the occupants of the graceful dwell-

[7] Baltimore *Patriot*, Feb. 2, 1836, quoted in Frankfort *Commonwealth*, Feb. 17, 1836.

[8] *Congressional Globe*, 24 Cong., 1 Sess., Appendix, 207-209.

[9] Frankfort *Commonwealth*, Feb. 17, 1836; Little, *Ben Hardin*, 356.

ing on the corner of Main and Washington in Frankfort. A friend who happened by just after newspaper reports of the speech had been read there, described the scene to Crittenden. "There was Mrs. Crittenden," he wrote, *"you know how she generally looks!* but on this occasion there was a glow of exultation in her countenance that gave it a more fascinating expression than I have ever observed it to wear before." The children, catching the excitement of the mother, danced with delight. As he viewed the happy domestic setting the friend thought that "a better looking set could not easily be found."[10]

Benton waged a last-ditch parliamentary battle against the distribution bill, with amendments and with motions to table and to adjourn. Threat of war with France had vanished with the coming of spring, but still Benton stubbornly clung to the idea of spending the surplus for defense, specifically for fortifications on the east coast. Defense would be a nonrecurring expenditure, he argued, whereas if proceeds of public lands were distributed, the government would forever lose a vast resource and a permanent protective policy on imports would be necessary.

In a speech on May 26 Crittenden countered Benton's argument that using the surplus on fortifications would be a one-time expenditure. After the fortifications were built, he said, it would require six thousand men to garrison them. The result would be a standing army requiring two million dollars annually, and calling for more taxes. The fortifications would, therefore, be like "dragon's teeth, over the land, from which hosts of myrmidons would spring up, to eat out the substance of the citizens." Besides, placing men inside fortifications would make cowards of them. Warming to this theme, he let his emotion carry him to a ridiculous extreme. When soldiers "became too good to stand out in the danger," he said, "let them stay home . . . and sustain a mercenary army to fight for them under cover of these fortifications."[11]

But there were other objections to the distribution bill besides those of policy. Strict interpreters of the Constitution, even some who approved of the wisdom of distribution, believed that Congress had no authority to give away the national assets to the states. Jackson was known to hold these views, and it was thought that even if the bill should pass, he would veto it. To quiet these scruples, an amendment was added to a bill that regulated government money in

[10] Orlando Brown to Crittenden, Feb. 11, 1836, in Crittenden Papers.
[11] *Congressional Globe*, 24 Cong., 1 Sess., 404, 503, 505.

state banks. This amendment provided that the Treasury surplus from all sources, taxes as well as land sales, be lent to the states, to be returned to the Treasury whenever Congress should call for it. It was well understood that Congress would never make such a call, but this devious scheme satisfied even Calhoun's constitutional scruples. The bill passed both houses, and the President signed it.[12]

Some auxiliary features of the land debates are of more than passing interest as a reflection of Crittenden's political views. For some years representatives of newer western states, like Illinois and Missouri, where public lands were located, had been advocating a homestead provision in the land laws. Such a provision would enable a settler to acquire a plot of land free on proof of actual settlement there for a term of years. It would be some years before the country would be prepared to accept such a welfare state measure, and an outright homestead bill had been repeatedly defeated.

A step in the direction of free land was preemption, and Benton offered a preemption amendment to the distribution bill. Under its terms a squatter, one who had settled on government land before it was opened to sale, would be permitted to purchase 160 acres, together with any improvements he had made upon the tract, at the minimum price of $1.25 an acre. The tendency of such an amendment, as indeed of all liberal land laws, was to draw settlers to states where the government lands were located, and representatives from states where there were no public lands naturally opposed such measures. Kentucky belonged to the latter class. Besides, there was great interest in internal improvements in Kentucky, and if distribution was to accomplish anything worthwhile, lands must not be sold except to the highest bidder at public auction. Crittenden, therefore, opposed Benton's preemption amendment and voted with the majority that defeated it, twenty-five to twenty.[13]

Debates on distribution and on land occupied most of this first session of the Twenty-fourth Congress. Lesser matters included a bill to recharter local banks in the District of Columbia, which Crittenden supported and which passed by an overwhelming majority. Jackson's appointments also had to be acted on. Crittenden exhibited some narrow partisanship here. He voted against Roger B. Taney, successor to Marshall as Chief Justice, although he supported

[12] *Congressional Globe*, 24 Cong., 1 Sess., 404, 406; Benton, *Thirty Years' View*, I, 651, 657-58.

[13] *Congressional Globe*, 24 Cong., 1 Sess., 416; Benton, *Thirty Years' View*, I, 708.

the nomination of Philip P. Barbour as associate justice. He opposed Andrew Stevenson as minister to Great Britain, but supported his own brother-in-law, Richard K. Call, for governor of Florida Territory. He abstained from voting on Amos Kendall's nomination for Postmaster General. He voted to confirm Jackson's nomination of John Eaton as minister to Spain, although Clay opposed it.[14]

Altogether, Crittenden had not cut a bad figure at the session. He established himself as a ready and able debater—one of the ablest, according to Nathan Sargent. His style of speaking was pleasing, and he never had to resort to a note to refresh his memory. "No Senator ever knocked at his door [in debate]," said Sargent, "and found him unprepared." He was logical, his illustrations were apt, and he could be pungently sarcastic. Yet his sarcasm, according to Sargent, "never left a sting behind or excited an unkind feeling."[15]

All of Crittenden's time was not taken up with national affairs. There were chores to be performed for constituents, and he must also see that his party kept its ascendancy in Kentucky. Ambitious and disappointed politicians like Robert Wickliffe were constantly spreading discord, and those with true grievances required pacifying in order to prevent serious defections. Such a situation was developing in the winter of 1836. Judge James Clark, who was able enough but who had no strong political following, was eager to be governor. James T. Morehead, serving out the unexpired term of Breathitt, who had died in 1834, was eligible but not eager to succeed himself.

Fearful of Clark's political weakness, Crittenden and other leaders finally induced Morehead to consent to run for another term. "Morehead *must* be the candidate for governor," Crittenden wrote. "He is *indispensible* to the present crisis and no excuse ought to be taken from him." He wanted Letcher, now out of Congress, as candidate for lieutenant governor.[16] Clark, claiming that Morehead had told him he would not be a candidate, resented these developments and refused to withdraw. By the spring of 1836 he had drawn to his support a considerable faction of the party. Orlando Brown, editor of the Frankfort *Commonwealth* and one of Crittenden's closest personal and political friends, was hard pressed to prevent a rupture.

14 *Congressional Globe*, 24 Cong., 1 Sess., 531, 535; Benton, *Thirty Years' View*, I, 665; Frankfort *Commonwealth*, March 30, 1836.
15 Nathan Sargent, *Public Men and Events from the Commencement of Mr. Monroe's Administration, in 1817, to the Close of Mr. Fillmore's Administration, in 1853*, 2 vols. (Philadelphia, 1875), II, 47.
16 Crittenden to Orlando Brown, Dec. 27, 1835, in Coleman, *Crittenden*, I, 88-89.

He was discouraged and longed for Crittenden to return home, "if only it were for a week, in order to stimulate the party to action."[17]

From Washington, Crittenden and Clay urged that a nominating convention be held in late April in Frankfort, but before that time, Morehead reconsidered and withdrew. Crittenden was still unwilling to accept Clark, and he now urged Letcher to enter the lists against Clark. But Letcher was unwilling to run unless Clark would "voluntarily" withdraw. When Clark refused, Letcher declined, somewhat reluctantly, to let his name go before the convention, and Clark was nominated with only token opposition. But his prospects were still not good. "Our *fix* is *bad*, very *bad*," wrote Letcher. "Unless a vigorous effort is made very soon we shall lose the election for want of exertion." Responding to this, Crittenden called together the Kentucky Whig delegation and asked each man to write daily letters to his district.[18]

This plan probably contributed to the Whig victory that summer, for the colorless Clark carried the state by eight thousand votes. Crittenden must have been disappointed in his own county, however, for the Democrats carried Franklin by sixty-eight votes. Although he was increasingly prominent in the national capital, he could not overcome the old Democratic predominance in his home county except when he himself was a candidate.[19]

Crittenden loved the excitement of life in Washington and the office of senator. For the next quarter century he left there only when interests of the party demanded it. Yet the long absence from Frankfort that first winter brought pangs of loneliness for home and the loved ones there. He missed especially Orlando Brown and his brother Mason, and Phil Swigert. More than all, he missed the family circle. He wrote often to wife and children, always with expressions of tender affection. "I write merely for the pleasure of writing to you," read one letter to Maria in early April. "It is a sort of mental association that is the best consolation for actual absence." "I have nothing to write unless I should write in the strains of a *mere lover*," he added, but he must avoid this "melting mood."[20]

[17] John Hutchcraft to Henry Clay, Feb. 18, 1836, in Clay Papers; Orlando Brown to Crittenden, Feb. 11, 1836, in Crittenden Papers; Crittenden to Brown, March 13, 1836, in Coleman, *Crittenden*, I, 93.

[18] Letcher to Crittenden, May 3, 1836, in Crittenden Papers.

[19] Frankfort *Commonwealth*, Aug. 17, 1836.

[20] Crittenden to Maria, April 8, 1836, in Coleman, *Crittenden*, I, 93.

He was glad, therefore, when Congress adjourned in early summer, so that he could hasten home. Letcher had written him more than two months earlier that his constituents were saying "many pretty things" about him, and he was flattered to learn that a Kentucky farmer had developed a new type of seed corn and named it for him. But he must have been surprised at the cordiality of his welcome. A crowd of more than a thousand met him at the river landing and escorted him to his home, where they cheered him again and again and would not depart until he had mounted the marble block outside his door and made them a speech. Not content with that, a committee got up a public dinner in order that his old friends might acknowledge "with profound gratitude your eminent services—eminent among the greatest minds in the Senate of the United States." Every man in the community, they added, is "your personal friend." Five hundred turned out for the dinner, held at Bellefonte Springs on the outskirts of the city. John Morris presided, and many toasts paid tribute to Crittenden's "distinguished merits as a public servant."[21]

Then followed a round of barbecues and burgoos, the sponsors of each trying to outdo one another in lavish outlay of food and even more lavish testimonials. The citizens of Woodford insisted on having an opportunity to express their "entire approbation" of Crittenden's "private and public character," and of the "Eloquent and fearless manner" in which he had discharged his duties. The Woodford dinner was held in late July in a forest near his birthplace on the Lexington Road. Clay, Governor Morehead, and Chilton Allen, congressman from the district, were guests, and "several thousand" of both sexes attended. Two months later, Fayette County Whigs celebrated the anniversary of the Battle of the Thames. Crittenden and Clay were again honor guests and were feasted and toasted as at Woodford. Clearly, Crittenden's conduct of his office in Washington had met with the approval of his constituents.[22]

When Crittenden returned to Washington in December, 1836, for the second session of the Twenty-fourth Congress, he temporarily closed his home in Frankfort. George, now an army lieutenant, was

21 Letcher to Crittenden, May 3, 1836, Citizens of Franklin County to Crittenden, July 18, 1836, in Crittenden Papers; *Niles' Register*, L (1836), 403; Frankfort *Commonwealth*, July 13, 27, Aug. 3, Oct. 12, Dec. 6, 1836.
22 Citizens of Woodford to Crittenden, July 13, 1836, in Crittenden Papers; Frankfort *Commonwealth*, Aug. 3, Oct. 12, 1836.

with his regiment in Arkansas Territory, and Ann Mary was busy with her family in Louisville. Thomas had recently gone to New Orleans to try his hand in merchandising. John J. and Eugene, the two sons of Maria and Crittenden, together with Maria's daughter Catherine, were left with their grandmother Innes. Eugenia, whose health was delicate, was sent to spend the winter with Crittenden's youngest sister, Lucy, who had married Harry Innes Thornton and was living in Mobile. The remainder of the family—Maria, Robert, Cornelia, Sarah, and Elizabeth—all started from Frankfort with Crittenden. Robert was dropped off at Oxford, Ohio, where he was enrolled in Miami University. Sarah and Elizabeth, the inseparable stepsisters, were placed in an academy at Steubenville, Ohio. Only Maria and Cornelia went on to Washington with Crittenden, where by early December they were settled for the winter in what Crittenden described only as "pleasant quarters."

In the galaxy of stars that assembled in the Senate that year, Crittenden's light was of the second magnitude. He was now a veteran fifty years of age, respected both as ally and as foe; but he did not have the stature of Clay, Webster, Calhoun, or Benton, giants who grappled continuously with one another for party or personal advantage. On the average they were a decade older than Crittenden, and their experience in national affairs was much broader than his. Yet he was not intimidated by their greater prestige. Aligned with Clay and generally with Webster on policy matters, he never hesitated to contend with Benton or Calhoun on the floor of the Senate. His debate the year before on Benton's resolutions for disposal of the surplus really had been in direct answer to Buchanan and Silas Wright rather than to Benton. His first engagement with Benton in person came early in this session.

Jackson's war on the Bank of the United States left the country without a national depository, and so Treasury funds were placed in select state banks, largely in the West. This created a temporary shortage of specie in the East, where most of the business of the country was centered. Philip Hone, a rich merchant, reported in 1834 "an awful scarcity of money" in New York and a bleak outlook for businessmen who needed credit. Money could not be had on bond or mortgage at 7 percent, and good notes were discounted at 9. Despite this stringency, conservative eastern bankers refused to circulate more notes than their resources warranted, and money in

the East grew increasingly tight. Some critics thought they were encouraging a depression for political advantage, and Nicholas Biddle
was openly accused of it. By summer, 1836, stocks generally were
deflated. Money could not be borrowed on good mortgages for less
than 20 percent, and good paper was selling in Wall Street at a
discount of 3 percent a month.[23]

Such was not the situation in the West. There the elimination of
the Bank of the United States resulted almost immediately in the
creation of a great number of state-chartered banks; their number
more than doubled between 1830 and 1836. The national bank had
discounted local banknotes at their true value, but now that this
restraining influence was gone, these wildcat banks printed notes in
great quantities. A land boom had been building since 1834 in the
West, and these notes were used largely by borrowers to purchase
land. Government land sales, amounting to less than $5,000,000 in
1834, increased fivefold two years later. Until 1836 the government
had freely accepted these banknotes in payment for land. But by
summer of that year Jackson became alarmed at this vast circulation
as well as the inflation that accompanied it and issued his "Specie
Circular" shortly after Congress adjourned. This provided that after
December 15, all government land must be paid for in gold or silver.

Financial derangement quickly followed Jackson's order. The
public had been blindly accepting the notes at face value, unaware
that there was inadequate specie to back them. Now, with shocking
suddenness, the government had made it abundantly clear that it considered banknotes unsafe. "Confidence is shaken to its very center,"
wrote Philip Hone, "and the springs of national and commercial
prosperity are dried up." The circular was especially unpopular in
the West, where it was regarded as a scheme to aid speculators by
bringing sales of government land to an end.[24] As creditors followed
the government in demanding hard money, business and bank failures came, presaging the great panic that was to follow.

When Congress met, therefore, the administration was under
sharper attack, and Benton undertook to defend it. Benton's speeches
are said to read better than they sounded. His voice was unpleasantly
nasal, but he had a mind of extraordinary strength and a storehouse

[23] Allan Nevins (ed.), *The Diary of Philip Hone, 1828-1851* (New York, 1936),
104, 228-29 (hereinafter, Hone, *Diary*); Van Deusen, *Henry Clay*, 283.
[24] Hone, *Diary*, 294; Nathaniel Pope to Crittenden, Aug. 3, 1836, in Crittenden
Papers.

of information that gave him a remarkable facility at illustration. Heavy-set and florid, he was fastidiously neat in dress; and his pince nez, generally in place while he sat at his desk writing or examining heaps of papers, hung on his bosom when he spoke, suspended there on a chain of gold. Few men were liked or hated as much as he. His enemies described him as "contemptible," whereas his friends respected not only his mind but his character. He was an ultra-Democrat, spelled with either a large or a small D, and he was looked upon as Jackson's champion in the Senate. Speaking on December 19, Benton blamed economic distress not on the specie circular but on Whig-sponsored distribution. Moreover, he charged Whig partisan schemes with compounding the error. In order to build up an artificial surplus by January 1, 1837, when distribution was scheduled, he said, Whigs had held up appropriation bills so long during the preceding session that it had proved impossible to spend the money by the end of the year.[25]

Crittenden answered him the next day. He spoke to a full house, for by now his reputation as one of the most accomplished of Senate debaters was established. "When he rises you will not think of departing until you have heard him out," wrote an observer, and "as he approaches his conclusion you[r] regret at his brevity increases." The touch of gray at his temples added to Crittenden's natural dignity and belied a little the impression of extreme youth that his slender figure gave. He spoke now without fire, but developed his argument logically and with convincing fervor and animation. Wit and sarcasm he employed, but not cruel or stern enough to be termed invective. "Decorum and propriety are ever observed in what he utters," added our informer, who described Crittenden as "generous, kind, and popular." Yet, he added, "Few men in debate are more to be feared."[26]

Crittenden conceded that distribution might be a remote cause of the panic in the country, but only because of government awkwardness. It was the circular, he charged, that was the immediate cause of the financial derangement. The sudden call for gold by the government made both banks and noteholders uneasy. Noteholders "pressed the banks for payment, the banks pressed their debtors,

---

[25] ["A Looker On Here in Verona,"] *Sketches of United States Senators of the Session of 1837-1838* (Washington, 1839) (hereinafter, *Sketches by a Looker On*).
[26] *Sketches by a Looker On.*

and withheld their customary accommodations." Under the circular, all the specie had gone into "pet banks," a result that handicapped all other banks and the country in general.

The circular had deranged the state of the currency and given it "a direction inverse to the course of business." For money in a free economy, he said, would move always in the normal course of business transactions. The industrial centers of the East were the natural repositories, and money was worth more there. A westerner, he said, would rather have debts paid him at New York than "at his own door." The government, by forcing specie from east to west, had benefited no one and had injured all. Men might be deluded for a time by such an unnatural movement, but eventually they would see its falseness. He likened the government's action to forcing a compass needle off its natural direction. "You might turn it round and round," he said, "as often as you pleased, but, left to itself, it would still settle at the north."

Turning to Benton's charge that Whigs had held up appropriations in order to create an artificial surplus, Crittenden pointed out that an unprecedented $38,000,000 had been appropriated at the last session. This was "a lavish expenditure," and he freely acknowledged his part in trying to prevent it. He conceded that the "deluge" of state bank paper was disconcerting to trade and should have been curtailed, but he insisted that the government's remedy had been too sudden and too extreme. He twitted Old Bullion on his devotion to gold and silver as a commercial medium. Rather than try to carry on the business of the country without banknotes, he thought the country might as well go back to Spartan bars of iron for specie. He justly censured the administration for the damage it had caused by destroying the Bank of the United States. The bank had maintained a stable currency, Crittenden said, and it was destruction of the national bank that had caused state banks to spring up "like mushrooms" all over the country. The specie circular was a hasty, ill-timed attempt to remedy a bad situation.

Not content with demonstrating that the circular was inexpedient, Crittenden charged that it was unlawful. He recalled that at the preceding session Benton had offered a resolution embodying the very principles later incorporated in the circular. After a full debate, the resolution had been tabled, an action that was "unequivocal condemnation." The vote to table had been overwhelming, only a few besides Benton voting against it. Yet, shortly after adjournment, the circular whose principle Congress had condemned was issued by the President. "The very proposition which was rejected by Congress in April, was enforced as a Treasury order in July." Such action by the executive was usurping the power of Congress and was an insult to the dignity of the Senate. Crittenden would favor rescinding the circular if for no other reason than this. He drew a parallel between it and the executive order a few years before that had withdrawn the deposits from the Bank of the United States just after Congress had declared the money safe there.

But, he declared, the circular was unwarranted on still another ground. It made "an unlawful discrimination between different classes of American Citizens, . . . between debtors for the public lands and all other debtors to the Government." There was also a residence discrimination in the circular, because actual settlers and bona fide residents of the state or territory where lands were offered for sale were exempt from its provisions. In the past, he conceded, Congress had discriminated in favor of settlers and might continue to do so. But this, Crittenden argued, was the exclusive prerogative of Congress. The executive had no such power. The President had no more authority to assign different modes of payment to different classes of citizens than he had to give more lands to one purchaser than to another for the same money.[27]

It was an able speech, moderate and well-reasoned. Duff Green's *Telegraph*, enemy of Jackson and of anyone else who did not espouse Calhoun, thought Crittenden "completely winnowed the subject of the chaff of partisan sophistry." Another friendly editor credited him with completely demolishing Benton's "declamatory tirade" and his "flimsy web of words." Still another critic, after reading the debates, said Crittenden had "killed off a doomed man." This was partisan praise. Benton was not a man to be idly challenged in debate, especially on the subject that he prided himself he knew best—money. Yet Crittenden had dared to touch his shield. Without a note and with complete aplomb, he had stood his ground against Old Bullion and had even, many agreed, drawn blood.[28] The long

[27] *Congressional Globe*, 24 Cong., 2 Sess., 35-36, Appendix, 266-68; *ibid.*, 24 Cong., 1 Sess., 383; Benton, *Thirty Years' View*, I, 698.
[28] Washington *United States Telegraph*, Dec. 24, 1836, and Newark *Advertiser*, quoted in Frankfort *Commonwealth*, Jan. 4, 1837; Nathaniel Pope to Crittenden Jan. 16, 1837, in Crittenden Papers.

BIRTHPLACE OF JOHN J. CRITTENDEN, WOODFORD COUNTY

debates resulted in passage of a bill requiring the government to accept notes of specie-paying banks. But Jackson gave this a pocket veto.[29]

The following winter Crittenden was to find occasion to grapple with Calhoun. At a special session in the fall of 1837 Van Buren, who had succeeded Jackson in the White House six months before, urged that government funds be removed from the pet banks and kept by federal officers in mints, customhouses, and other federal establishments. This plan was crystallized in the independent or subtreasury bill. Whigs generally opposed it, regarding it as an expedient to prevent recharter of the Bank of the United States. One Whig called it "General Jackson's rod . . . wherewith to scourge the refractory merchants." Another said it was the "illegitimate offspring of the little Kinderhooker." The bill passed the administration-controlled Senate but was defeated in the House.[30]

It was reintroduced at the regular session in January, 1838. Few bills ever have been more thoroughly debated. Practically every member of the Senate had his say, long and sometimes often. Amendment after amendment was offered, most of them defeated. In early February, William C. Rives of Virginia moved to substitute a provision retaining not more than twenty-five of the "most solid and respectable" specie-paying banks as federal depositories.

On February 15 Calhoun spoke in favor of the subtreasury bill. He was not a graceful speaker, but his active, bold, and original mind, his brevity, and his exact expressions always assured him a rapt audience. He stood erect, the height of his tall, lean figure augmented by his pompadoured bushy hair. With his eyes fixed on a preselected spot in the carpet in front of him and with his right hand moving methodically up and down "not unlike the motion of a pump-handle," he lectured his colleagues much as a schoolmaster might address a class.[31] For the government to use state banks, he said, would give them a federal character, and this would violate the Constitution. Furthermore, nothing but gold or silver could be used to pay public debts. This speech marked a political about-face for Calhoun. Since

---

[29] James D. Richardson (ed.), *A Compilation of the Messages and Papers of the Presidents, 1789-1897*, 20 vols. (Washington, 1897), IV, 1501-507; Benton, *Thirty Years' View*, I, 705-706.

[30] Hone, *Diary*, 299; Charles Wickliffe to Crittenden, Jan. 13, 1838, in Crittenden Papers.

[31] *Sketches by a Looker On.*

his break with Jackson seven years earlier, he had cooperated with National Republicans (later the Whigs) in opposition to Jackson and Van Buren. Now, to the great bitterness of the Whigs, he joined forces with Democrats.[32]

The following week Crittenden replied to Calhoun. He opposed the subtreasury bill on principle. It would place power "unparalleled in the history of free governments" in the hands of customhouse officials. His real preference was for a national bank, but as between subtreasury and state banks as federal depositories, he favored the latter. He heaped scorn on Calhoun's charge that the government could not employ state banks without giving them a federal character. The government had used state roads continuously to carry mails, he said, and the state had not surrendered jurisdiction over them. He had equal scorn for Calhoun's argument that it was unconstitutional to receive anything but gold and silver in payment of public debts. Good banknotes, he rightly observed, had been used without objection since the beginning of the republic, and had been freely accepted by the government. Obviously Calhoun had witnessed this and even participated in it, yet he "never raised his voice against it— never whispered the indignation of his patriotic and constitution loving heart till now." Besides, since the subtreasury bill called for a gradual approach to a specie standard, the bill itself sanctioned, for a six-year period, practices Calhoun said were unconstitutional. The Rives substitute, Crittenden said, would greatly diminish executive prerogative, and he scored Calhoun's inconsistency in preferring the administration bill to it. Calhoun would indeed, he said, have to compromise with his principles if he could vote for the bill.

"Mr. Calhoun," he added, "may pile his ingenious sophistry mountains high. It may please his new allies, who want some pretext or apology, or defence, for their wretched scheme. But to the public mind, that has grasped the question now at issue, as a practical matter, —as a thing that comes home to the bosoms and business of all—and has *decided* on it *against* the administration, the theory of Mr. Calhoun will appear (as it is) a dream—such *stuff* as dreams are made of. Why should not *paper* be received? Why should good bank notes not be deposited in the Treasury? Where is the limitation of receivability to gold and silver to be found in the Constitution? Where is the ground for limiting the deposites [sic] of taxes, imposts and duties to

[32] *Congressional Globe*, 25 Cong., 2 Sess., 163-65, 183.

gold and silver? It is *money* that is to be received; and bank paper, exchangeable into specie, *is* money."[33]

"I made a speech yesterday," Crittenden wrote to his daughter the next day. "It was no great thing, I think, tho I have received as many congratulations as would turn the head of a man that was much given to vanity." Philip Hone, an ardent admirer of Clay, had heard Clay speak on the same subject for five hours just three days before, but he now recorded that Crittenden's was "the greatest speech I ever heard." "His manners were graceful and animated," he wrote, "his voice clear and distinct, his eye alternatively flaming fire and melting into tenderness." Crittenden had spoken just three hours. The Senate had then adjourned, but "the audience lingered in their seats," Hone confided in his diary, "as if loath to leave the spot of their enchantment."[34] The subtreasury bill finally passed the Senate in late March, twenty-seven to twenty-five, with even Calhoun voting against it in the end; but again it failed to pass the House.[35]

A few months later Crittenden found an opportunity to castigate Van Buren's general fiscal policy. During the preceding months as the economic crisis mounted, the Treasury was emptied, and Congress had approved emergency issue of ten million dollars in Treasury notes. They were a prototype of the greenbacks of the Civil War period. They had no specie to support them and were in the nature of a forced loan. Eight months later, conditions had not improved; the Treasury was again bare, and the administration sought permission to issue another ten million dollars in notes. Crittenden charged both the Jackson and the Van Buren administrations with extravagance. The Adams administration, he said, had been denounced by the Democrats for spending thirteen million dollars a year. Now Van Buren was spending thirty million dollars.

But aside from the extravagance, issuing Treasury notes was unsound financing, he said. The proper way to meet an emergency was by selling bonds with a due date or by taxation. Either method would bring the matter into the open, where it belonged. Then the people would be on notice that the government had borrowed. The issuing of Treasury notes, on the other hand, would deceive them

---

[33] Frankfort *Commonwealth*, March 7, 1838, quoting Baltimore *Patriot*, Feb. 23, 1838; *Niles' Register*, LIV (1838), 43-44; *Congressional Globe*, 25 Cong., 2 Sess., 197.

[34] Crittenden to Mrs. Coleman, Feb. 23, 1838, in Crittenden Papers (Duke); Hone, *Diary*, 305.

[35] *Congressional Globe*, 25 Cong., 2 Sess., 259.

into believing there was no national debt, when actually the notes would constitute a government obligation. If a national debt was to come, let it come openly. He charged that the administration was inconsistent when it denounced banks and banknotes and at the same time issued its own notes. Crittenden's logic was sound and his argument good. He supported an amendment to reduce the issue from ten to two million dollars, but this lost, sixteen to twenty-seven. The bill then passed twenty-seven to thirteen.[36]

During this session of Congress, Crittenden was drawn, as a second, into a duel. After the Burr-Hamilton affair in 1804, dueling in the North had practically ceased. But it had persisted in the South, and by the fourth decade of the century it had become, it seemed, an even more popular method of settling questions of honor between gentlemen than it had been a half century before. Participation in such affairs did not seem to impair the personal or political standing of southerners—quite the reverse. Jackson had killed his man long before he was ever considered as a presidential possibility, and he stood ready to kill countless others, had any been so bold as to openly question the virtue of his beloved Rachel. Clay had tried to kill both Humphrey Marshall and John Randolph, and might have done so, had he been a better marksman. Two of Crittenden's brothers each had killed his man in duels fought years before.

Crittenden, however, had never fought a duel. He had few enemies, and none, it seemed, whom he had given cause to challenge him or who desired his blood. Nor had Crittenden ever issued a challenge, although a few years later in the heat of debate on the Senate floor he would dare a colleague to challenge him. Moreover, Crittenden had shown himself on several occasions opposed to affairs of honor. He had helped accommodate many quarrels that might have led to duels.[37] It is therefore difficult to understand or to excuse Crittenden for allowing himself to be drawn into the Graves-Cilley affair, a duel fought over a provocation so slight as to appear to be pretext.

[36] *Congressional Globe*, 25 Cong., 1 Sess., 388, Appendix, 584-85; Benton, *Thirty Years' View*, II, 35, 36.

[37] T. T. Crittenden, *Memoirs*, 473-78; Moreland, "Some Arkansas Immortals," in Memphis *Commercial Appeal*, Feb. 28, 1926; Crittenden to Clay, April 27, 1826, and n. d., in Crittenden Papers (Duke); Marshall to Crittenden, Nov. 12, 1838, A. B. Wooley to Crittenden, Nov. 11, 1838, Crittenden to S. S. Nicholas, Dec. 18, 1835, in Crittenden Papers.

On the floor of the House in February, Jonathan Cilley, a popular young Democrat of Maine, had questioned the integrity of James Watson Webb, Whig editor of the New York *Courier and Enquirer*. Upon learning of his remarks, Webb sent a demand for retraction through his friend, Congressman William J. Graves of Kentucky. When Cilley declined to receive the communication, Graves declared himself affronted, charging that Cilley's refusal implied that Graves was representing one who was not a man of honor. He demanded that Cilley acknowledge Webb to be a man of honor, but this Cilley would not do. He avowed his ignorance of the state of Webb's honor and took the seemingly unassailable position that it would be a violation of his privilege as a member of Congress to be held accountable to outsiders for words spoken in debate. But this did not satisfy Graves, who thereupon challenged Cilley.

On the night of February 23, the day after his speech against the subtreasury, Crittenden and Maria were dining with Daniel Webster and his wife at the home of Joseph Gales, one of the proprietors of the *National Intelligencer*. About ten o'clock there was a knock at the door. Graves and two of his Whig colleagues, Richard Menefee from Bath County, Kentucky, and Henry A. Wise of Virginia, were seeking Crittenden. They wanted him to act as one of Graves' seconds in the duel, which had already been arranged. Crittenden protested. He had never participated in a duel, he told them, and disapproved on principle. But Graves was insistent. He was anxious, he later explained, that Crittenden be on the ground, "because in Kentucky & wherever else he was well known, no man was more distinguished for his mildness, and humility." Crittenden's presence would be "the best evidence I could offer at home," he added, "that I did not intend to act rashly or go beyond the requirements of those laws under which I went to the field." Reluctantly Crittenden gave in.[38]

Cilley, as challengee, had choice of weapons; he insisted on rifles. The distance agreed on was a hundred yards; the place, Bladensburg, just outside the District in Maryland, the customary site for such affairs. Far more congressional blood had been spilt on that ground

[38] William J. Graves to Henry Clay, Feb. 16, 1842, in Henry Clay Papers, University of Virginia Library; *House Reports*, 25 Cong., 2 Sess., No. 825, pp. 92-101; Crittenden to Mrs. Coleman, Feb. 23, 1838, in Crittenden Papers (Duke).

than from Henry Winder's militia, who ran from the redcoats there in 1814. Graves and Cilley took their posts and, when the word was given, fired. Both missed. A parley was held. Crittenden, Wise, and Menefee insisted that the fight must go on unless Cilley would state that Graves had not "borne the note of a man who is not a man of honor and not a gentleman" or else that he had declined to receive Webb's note because he "did not hold himself accountable to Colonel Webb for words spoken in debate." Cilley had previously made this latter explanation to Graves, but apparently his blood was now up, for he refused to meet either condition fixed by Graves' seconds. Thereupon, Graves asked if Cilley would not state that "in declining to receive the note of Colonel Webb, he meant no disrespect to Mr. Graves, either *directly or indirectly?*" Cilley agreed to do this, but now Graves' seconds were obdurate. They thought this explanation too "*qualified*" and thus unacceptable.

A second exchange was ordered at a shorter distance, and again both marksmen missed. Now Cilley's seconds insisted that the affair must end. At the risk of his life their man had given Graves the satisfaction of two shots. There was no occasion for bad blood between the antagonists; they were merely fighting over a technical point of honor. The code did not call for another shot. Crittenden was understood by all present to agree with this argument, but he later insisted that he was in accord with Wise and Menefee that the fight must go on unless Cilley would disclaim any personal exception to Webb "as a gentleman and a man of honor" or else place his refusal to receive the note on the ground of privilege. Cilley, however, would only state that he "chose to be drawn into no controversy" with Webb. He would add, for good measure, that he meant no disrespect to Graves. But he stubbornly refused either to affirm or to deny anything in regard to Webb's character. A third volley was ordered at still shorter distance, and this time Cilley fell dead before his seconds reached him.

Cilley was thought to have a promising future and was extremely popular on both sides of the House. The shocking announcement that he had been killed spread mixed feelings of sadness at his death and anger at its manner. Both houses adjourned immediately, but next day a committee was set up in the House to inquire into the affair. The committee made an extensive investigation. It took testimony from all participants in the duel and secured copies of all correspondence between principals and seconds. On May 10 it made two reports, each reflecting partisan sympathies. The majority, Democrats, condemned Graves' conduct as "a breach of the highest constitutional privileges of the House . . . without any circumstance of extenuation." Cilley, they said, had given "no offense towards those who pursued him," and performed the part of "the faithful and upright" congressman. His death could not be "vindicated or excused by any circumstance whatsoever," but reflected the "want of the higher attribute of moral courage" of his adversary. The majority report concluded with resolutions calling for the expulsion of Graves and the censure of the House members who acted as seconds.

Even the minority report agreed that the participants had violated the privilege of the House. They objected only to the severity of the punishment recommended by the majority for Graves. After weeks of debate the House voted to publish both reports and lay them on the table indefinitely. This left the resolutions of expulsion and censure hovering over the House participants. They did not apply to Crittenden, of course, since he was not subject to the House's jurisdiction, but it was a strong though indirect censure of him as well as of the congressmen.[39]

Crittenden was disturbed by the public reaction to the affair. Although the Democratic press treated him gently, it strongly condemned Graves and Wise. Nathaniel Hawthorne charged in the *Democratic Review* that "Mr. Graves and . . . Mr. Wise, have gone further than their own dreadful code will warrant them, and overstepped the imaginary distinction which, . . . separates manslaughter from murder."[40] Never before, he added, had a challenge been given or a duel pressed to a fatal close on such a shadowy pretext. Crittenden was unhappy too, even with some of the Kentucky Whig papers, because of their "faint, puny, stunted sort of defence." In a confidential letter Crittenden admitted that Graves "went a step too far." Yet Graves was "a pure minded, noble hearted fellow," who had "acted from a sense of honor." Graves had felt, Crittenden thought,

[39] *House Reports*, 25 Cong., 2 Sess., No. 825, pp. 9-25, 73, 76, 91, 106, 111, 117; *Congressional Globe*, 25 Cong., 2 Sess., 359; Adams, *Memoirs*, IX, 526-27.
[40] Washington *Democratic Review*, Sept., 1838, quoted in Horatio King, *Turning on the Light* . . . (Philadelphia, 1895), 309.

that "The Honor of his State is all in his own hands," and he should be excused because of this worthy sentiment.[41]

Other problems, closer to Crittenden than the matter of Graves, Cilley, or Wise, were disturbing him at this time. Maria had been ill in Washington through most of the winter. As spring came on, however, she was feeling better and the Crittendens were passing the time "quite agreeably," he wrote, although, he added, "her Presbyterianism rejects many invitations to merry-makings, and keeps us very much at home." Meanwhile, his sons were causing him much concern. Robert had been "behaving idly and badly" at Oxford, and Crittenden in January had ordered him to Frankfort, where Mason Brown would keep an eye on him while he spent the remainder of the year in preparatory school there. George was beginning to show the weakness for liquor that was to worry his father the rest of his life.

Crittenden was even more disturbed at this time over his second son, Thomas, who had spent the fall and winter in New Orleans without making a satisfactory business connection. Thomas was thinking of going to Texas, but Crittenden urged him not to do so. He arranged for his son-in-law, Chapman Coleman, to advance money to Thomas and find a place for him in his business in Louisville until "we shall have time to consider & determine on some other course for him." Thomas, he feared, might have acquired "idle habits" and needed a bracer. He sent off a Polonius-like letter, urging him to "*avoid Taverns*, & the *use* of liquors or wines." Thomas had "fine affections & fine principles," but without "fixed employment" he might go astray. "Employment, constant employment, is the only preservative, the only security," for his success.

Not content with admonishing Thomas himself, he called on Ann Mary to assist him. "See that Thomas avoid idleness," he wrote. "If he is not *well* employed, it cannot be but that he will be *ill-employed*." He knew, he told her, that no son of his would ever do anything dishonorable. "That would be [to] throw away their best *inheritance*—the only one that I shall leave them." But this would not be enough. "I must," he added, "see my sons pressing forward with ambitious energy in their pursuits whatever they may be." If Thomas wished to prepare himself for a profession, he would see that he had a chance. "Whatever credit or means I have shall be used

---

[41] Crittenden to General Leslie Combs, March 20, 1838, in Crittenden Papers (Kentucky).

to give him a start. I can make no use of either that can be more satisfactory to me." It was only, he added, in reference to his children "that I have ever regarded poverty as a burthen or evil."[42]

But Crittenden was blessed with an optimistic disposition. "My poor boys," he wrote at the beginning of one letter to his daughter. "My heart has bled over them." Yet, he assured her, she must not think that "because I cannot always controul [sic] my feelings, I therefore make myself miserable. I am not of a cheerless or desponding temper—and my hopes & feelings are not easily or long depressed." Sometimes Crittenden's interest in the doings of his children proved embarrassing to all concerned. Whenever Cornelia received a letter from Ann Mary, Crittenden asked to see it, although these letters frequently contained "sisterly secrets." On one such occasion when he made his request, the girl blurted out to Maria, who was present, that the letter contained "a secret and I could not show it to her." "Pa was obliged to take the hint for the time," she wrote her sister, "but next week it was as bad."[43]

With the adjournment of the Twenty-fifth Congress in early July, the Crittendens returned to Kentucky to a warm welcome from family and friends and another round of barbecues from Crittenden's constituents.[44] The summer was excessively hot and dry, and Crittenden stayed close to home. All his children except George were in Frankfort. Ann Mary had come up from Louisville, bringing her children along, so that the rambling house at Main and Washington was a bright and merry place. Crittenden declined most invitations, so as to spend as much time as possible with his family. However, he could not escape, if he would, another barbecue given by the citizens of Woodford, and he did attend a convention at Maxwell Springs in Lexington to promote the projected railroad from Cincinnati to Charleston.[45]

The next two winters Maria remained in Frankfort while Crit-

[42] Mason Brown to Crittenden, Jan. 24, 1838, Crittenden to Thomas L. Crittenden, April 28, 1838, in Crittenden Papers; Crittenden to Mrs. Coleman, Jan. 14, Feb. 23, April 19, June 1, 1838, in Crittenden Papers (Duke).

[43] Cornelia Crittenden to Mrs. Chapman Coleman, Jan. 15, 1837, in Crittenden Papers (Duke).

[44] Crittenden to My Children at Louisville, June 1, 1838, in Crittenden Papers (Duke); Frankfort Commonwealth, July 18, Aug. 15, Sept. 12, 1838; Woodford County Citizens to Crittenden, July 31, 1838, in Crittenden Papers.

[45] Frankfort Commonwealth, Aug. 1, 15, Sept. 12, 19, Oct. 10, 1838; Mrs. Coleman to Crittenden, Feb. 8, 1839, in Crittenden Papers (Duke).

tenden returned alone to Washington. He messed with Clay and other convivial spirits at the Rush House in January, 1840, paying fifteen dollars a week for board and room for himself and a servant boy. Unrestrained by Maria's Presbyterianism, he enjoyed an extensive social season. He admitted he "was quite a gallant" at the assembly balls that winter. Yet he was always counting the days until he could again be home. "My heart almost leaps forward to meet and to embrace you," he wrote Maria. She was the "tenderest and best of wives," he wrote on another occasion. He felt "that the world was a waste and bore neither fruit nor flowers" for him without her.[46]

Only routine legislation was taken up in the last session of the Twenty-fifth Congress. Democrats controlled the Senate, but Whigs had a majority in the House and could neutralize any administration program that might pass the other branch. The session was chiefly devoted, therefore, to oratory for home consumption and to jockeying for advantage in the coming presidential election. Depression still plagued the country, and Van Buren, the Little Magician in the White House, would indeed need to call on all his necromantic powers to win reelection. Crittenden was busily at work during the session, therefore, seeking to assure that Clay would be the party's nominee. For with the Whig tide flowing, no opportunity must be given other aspirants to gain the nomination Crittenden believed Clay deserved. The outcome would be determined at the Whig convention to be held in Harrisburg in December, 1839. Crittenden looked toward this event with keen anticipation.

[46] Crittenden to Maria, Jan. 29, Feb. 28, 1839, Jan. 2, 5, 8, 1840, in Crittenden Papers; Crittenden to Mrs. Coleman, Jan. 27, 1840, in Crittenden Papers (Duke); Myrta Lockett Avary (ed.), *Recollections of Alexander H. Stephens* (New York, 1910), 49; Clay to Mrs. Clay, Feb. 12, 1840, in Josephine Simpson Collection, Lexington, Kentucky; Crittenden to Thomas, Dec. 10, 1836, in Crittenden Papers; Fessenden, *William Pitt Fessenden*, 13.

CHAPTER VII

The Strategy of Whiggery

THE WHIG party was formed in 1834 from diverse elements opposed to the administration of Andrew Jackson. New England textile manufacturers, Pennsylvania iron manufacturers, Kentucky hemp growers, and Louisiana sugar planters all wanted protection for their specialty; to secure it, they would accept high tariffs all around. Also in the party, on the other hand, were great cotton and rice planters, who desired free trade. There were nationalists of the old Federalist school, who glorified the Union, side by side with nullifiers, who resented Jackson's force bill. There were Bank of the United States men, who thought Jackson's removal of the deposits had destroyed economic stability, and state bank men, opposed to central banks, who had been ruined by his specie circular. Native laborers, whose champions such as Horace Greeley resented the competition of immigrants, were cheek by jowl with manufacturers who imported workers to beat down wages. There were northern farmers, who wanted federal highways to carry their grain and pork to the home market in the cities, and state rights southern planters, who fought internal improvements. There were former anti-Masons or former

Jacksonians like Hugh Lawson White, John Bell, and John Tyler, who had broken with Jackson and who now had no place else to go. A more diverse group had never been gathered together under a political label. The party was strong on talent but so weak in unity that it could rarely indulge itself in the luxury of a campaign platform. The nucleus of the party was the remnant of the Clay-Adams faction, favoring tariff, national bank, and internal improvements. But unless it could straddle all great issues, the party was likely to fly apart, as indeed it did two decades later over the slavery question.[1]

The name Whig appealed to native Americans because of its association with the Revolution, but the historic resistance of the British Whig party to the royal prerogative gave it added significance. The name came to have meaning as a symbol of legislative resistance to executive encroachment and of ministerial independence (of which much was to be made later). The party stigmatized Jackson as King Andrew the First. All the diverse and conflicting elements found it possible to agree at least on the issue of "executive usurpation," with which they attacked Jackson.

Clay was by all odds the strongest Whig leader, but he had not been the party's candidate in 1836, the first national election in which the party participated. Already a two-time loser in presidential races, he had been further discredited among his manufacturing friends by his willingness—which was almost eagerness, some thought —to compromise their interests in order to restore peace in the nullification crisis of 1833. Indeed, it was widely believed that had it not been for the restraining influence of Delaware Senator John M. Clayton, Clay would have permitted Calhoun to drive an even harder bargain than the Compromise Tariff actually was. Long before the election, Clay announced that he would not be a candidate in 1836 unless satisfied that "it was the wish of a probable majority of the people of the States."[2]

Webster, another strong leader, had supported Jackson in the nullification crisis, thus endearing himself to National Republicans.

[1] Winifred E. Binkley, *American Political Parties: Their Natural History* (New York, 1943), 157-68; Lyon G. Tyler, *Letters and Times of the Tylers*, 2 vols. (Richmond, 1885), I, 476-78, 517; William S. Hoffman, "Willie P. Mangum and the Whig Revival of the Doctrine of Instructions," in *Journal of Southern History*, XXII (1956), 342-43; Hone, *Diary*, 104.

[2] George M. Bibb to A. T. Burnley, April 5, 1833, in Crittenden Papers; J. R. Mulvany to Duff Green, May 10, 1834, in Duff Green Papers; E. Malcolm Carroll, *Origins of the Whig Party* (Durham, N. C., 1925), 117; Clay to ———, July 14, 1835, in T. J. Clay Papers.

But although his support of Jackson and the force bill had strengthened Webster in the North, it had made him anathema in the South. Besides, there was something about Webster which detracted from his popular appeal. Charles Dickens, who would meet him a few years later, thought him "the only thoroughly unreal man I have seen on this side of the ocean."

Thus with both Clay and Webster, its two ablest leaders, unacceptable because of sectional feeling in 1836, the inherent weakness of the Whigs was manifest at its very birth. "I do not so much grieve about the *present*," wrote Thurlow Weed two years earlier, "as at the utter hopelessness of the *future*." In upstate New York, he pointed out, the people were unalterably opposed to the Bank of the United States, whereas Webster and Clay were both ardent bank men. "With Clay, Webster or Calhoun, or indeed any man identified with the war against Jackson and in favor of the Bank or the Bank's Shadow . . . the game is up," he added. The party as presently organized was "doomed to fight merely to be beaten," he thought, for "the people" were against them on the only clear-cut issues.[3] Not daring to hold a national convention under the circumstances, the Whigs solved their dilemma, if solution it could be called, by making the election a free-for-all.

The Democratic convention, bowing to Jackson's dictation, had nominated Martin Van Buren. The Tennessee legislature, however, had previously nominated Hugh Lawson White, a former Jackson Democrat who refused to withdraw as a candidate when Van Buren was selected by the national convention. He was, therefore, forced into the Whig camp, and two years later he formally joined the party. Meanwhile, the Massachusetts legislature had nominated Webster, disregarding his unpopularity in the South; a Pennsylvania state convention had nominated William Henry Harrison; and South Carolina was supporting Willie P. Mangum of neighboring North Carolina. No one expected that any one of these candidates could alone defeat Jackson's choice. Rather, the hope was that their combined vote might keep Van Buren from obtaining an electoral majority so that the election would be thrown into the Whig-controlled House of Representatives.[4]

[3] Weed to Francis Granger, Nov. 23, 1834, in Granger Papers; John Forster, *The Life of Charles Dickens* (New York, 1928), 103.
[4] Tyler, *Letters and Times*, I, 517; Crittenden to Morehead, Owsley, Harvie, Brown, Dec. 23, 1835, in Crittenden Papers (Duke).

Crittenden had joined enthusiastically in this strategy. After Pennsylvania nominated Harrison, he urged Kentucky Whigs to work zealously for him. He wanted them to ratify Pennsylvania's action either by legislative caucus or by convention, "or perhaps by both, for it is this quick succession of movements, that indicates & creates activity and zeal." At the same time, he warned, the other Whig candidates must be delicately handled, for it was important that they be kept in the race. After all, they had a common object, the defeat of Van Buren. This goal had produced "a point of union" for their friends in other sections, who were "acting very harmoniously." Webster, for instance, could not possibly win, he said, but keeping him in the contest so as to draw New England votes from Van Buren was imperative. "Say something complimentary & consolatory to him" in the columns of the *Commonwealth*, he urged the editor of that journal. Not only would it be politic, but Webster "deserves it."[5]

To the politically naive, such talk might have a hollow ring. Judged in the court of practical politics, however, Crittenden's motive was not unworthy. He was dedicated to the overthrow of Jacksonism, and he felt that the narrow selfishness of friends of the several candidates threatened defeat for the party. "One is for Webster, & for Webster only," he wrote, "another for White, & another equally exclusive, for Harrison, &. For my own part, though not insensible to personal distinctions & preferences, I care but little comparatively about the individual that is to be advanced." He grieved that John Quincy Adams would support none of the Whig candidates, all of whom, Adams thought, were "at the most third-rate men, whose pretensions rest . . . upon intrigue and political speculation." Adams disapproved also of the new mode of electioneering that seemed to be sweeping the country with the establishment of Jacksonian Democracy. The "peddling for popularity by travelling round the country, gathering crowds together, hawking for public dinners, and spouting empty speeches" completely disgusted the dour old Puritan, and he would have no part of it.[6]

The Whig strategy almost paid off. Van Buren captured 170 electoral votes, just 46 more than the total of his four competitors.

[5] Crittenden to "Dear Sir," Dec. 23, 1835, in Crittenden Papers (Duke); Crittenden to Orlando Brown, Dec. 27, 1835, in Coleman, *Crittenden*, I, 88-89.
[6] Crittenden to David Daggett, Jan. 31, 1836, in Crittenden Papers (Yale); Adams, *Memoirs*, IX, 25, 276-77, 311.

Richard M. Johnson, Van Buren's vice-presidential candidate, did not fare as well as his chief; but no candidate for that office gained an electoral majority, and Johnson was chosen Vice President by the Senate when it met in December.

Putting the election of 1836 behind them, Whigs early turned their thoughts to 1840. By that time the country had been for more than a decade ruled by Jacksonism, a "violent disease" something like the smallpox, according to Hugh Lawson White; "God in his mercy would permit no man, once cured, to have it the second time." To good Whigs like Benjamin Watkins Leigh, the defeat of Van Buren in 1840 became a holy cause. "If I can aid in any way," wrote another, "to rid the country of the plunderers, the knaves, the rascals, the blackguards & fools . . . with whom the administration is infested you may rely upon it."[7]

But who would be the party standard bearer? Adams had been defeated in 1828, and Clay in 1832; in 1836 the multiple-candidacy of Webster, Harrison, White, and Mangum had lost to Van Buren. Who could best challenge the Little Magician of Kinderhook in 1840? Clay had gracefully submitted to party strategy in 1836, and he thought he deserved the nomination now. He was early in the field. A year after Van Buren's election, Crittenden had addressed a giant rally in Louisville. He urged Clay's candidacy and the crowd responded with an enthusiastic endorsement of Clay for President in 1840.[8]

But issues were many and were becoming increasingly acute, and the very qualities of leadership that had brought Clay such a devoted nationwide following were now beginning to militate against him. Over the years his eloquence, his magnetism, his gift for compromise, and his fiery spirit had led him into many battles over most national issues. Even the art of compromise, in which he excelled, produced scars. For in every battle, especially those in which he was victorious, he made enemies who would not forget, extremists at either end not disposed to forgive Clay for taking the middle path. The manufacturing interest had not forgotten the Compromise Tariff of 1833, and anti-Masons, strong in upstate New York and in Pennsylvania, were still smarting because Clay had rebuffed their proferred

[7] White to Crittenden, Sept. 1, 1838, John Campbell to Crittenden, July 12, 1839, in Crittenden Papers.
[8] Louisville *Journal*, Nov. 24, 1837, quoted in Frankfort *Commonwealth*, Nov. 29, 1837.

support in 1832. Thus Clay's brilliance, which had made him by far the strongest of the Whig leaders, was in 1840 to turn out to be a handicap.

Other candidates were further obstacles in Clay's road to the nomination. Webster was especially ambitious. His popularity was confined to New England, but he was holding on desperately, trying to prevent demonstrations in favor of others. "No girl of 25, who saw her charms fading, was ever more anxious to be courted," wrote one of his friends.[9] Harrison's aspirations, too, could not be ignored. He had won more electoral votes in 1836 than Webster, White, and Mangum combined, and his popularity had impressed that great political realist, Thurlow Weed. He was especially strong in Kentucky. He had carried the state against Van Buren in 1836 and could doubtless do so again.

Clay was first choice of most Kentucky Whigs, including Crittenden. Kentucky had supported Harrison in 1836, when Clay was not in the field, and would do so again if Clay were not a candidate. But many Kentucky Whig editors were still carrying Harrison's banner, and this was hurting Clay elsewhere. Means must be found to eliminate this without hurting Harrison's friends, who must be treated, Crittenden thought, with "kindness, respect & conciliation." Harrison's name could not be jostled off without ceremony, lest his friends be antagonized and refuse later to support Clay. To relieve the embarrassment, Crittenden proposed that the Kentucky legislature pass resolutions calling for a national nominating convention and at the same time endorse Clay. This would be ample evidence to all the world that Clay was Kentucky's choice, and would enable the editors to gracefully replace Harrison's name with Clay's. The advice was followed, and in January, 1838, the Kentucky legislature passed the resolutions Crittenden had suggested.[10]

In the months that followed, Clay's fortunes flowed and ebbed. Always an irrepressible optimist where his own political prospects were concerned, Clay was confident. But Francis Granger, whose up-

[9] Clay to John M. Clayton, June 14, 1838, in Clay Papers; Francis Granger to Thurlow Weed, Dec. 26, 1837, Weed to Granger, Dec. 24, 1837, in Granger Papers; Benjamin Watkins Leigh to Crittenden, June 5, 1838, in Crittenden Papers.

[10] Weed to Granger, Dec. 24, 1837, in Granger Papers; Orlando Brown to Crittenden, Dec. 18, 1837, Crittenden to Brown, Jan. 7, 1838, in Crittenden Papers (Duke); Van Deusen, *Henry Clay*, 322; DeWitt Bloodgood to Brown, Dec. 24, 1837, in Brown Papers, Filson Club; Charles A. Wickliffe to Crittenden, Jan. 13, 1838, in Crittenden Papers.

SARAH CRITTENDEN
CRITTENDEN'S FIRST WIFE

ANN MARY CRITTENDEN
MRS. CHAPMAN COLEMAN

Portrait of Mrs. Crittenden courtesy of the J. B. Speed Art Museum, Louisville; portrait of Mrs. Coleman courtesy of Thomas Joyes, Louisville

state New York section was hostile to Clay, thought his "anxiety [for the nomination] had destroyed his judgment. He is more easily duped by sycophants than even W[ebster]," Granger wrote. When Webster gave up the contest early in 1838, his New England and New York followers swung to Clay, much to Van Buren's delight. Clay, he said, was his favorite opponent.[11]

The Whig nominating convention was to meet in December, 1839, in Harrisburg. New York was of crucial importance, and so Clay toured the state the previous summer, from Buffalo east. Outwardly his journey was a triumph. Everywhere he was met by enthusiastic crowds, public dinners, cordial speeches. But this was only surface enthusiasm. Abolitionist strength in the state, together with anti-bank and anti-Mason elements, made it unlikely that Clay could carry New York, and even his friends there opposed his nomination. Thurlow Weed, Whig New York boss, who at least claimed to prefer Clay, was convinced he could not win and set about preventing his nomination.[12] Crittenden was unaware of this. Months before the convention met, Clay had a plurality of delegates pledged to him, and Crittenden took it for granted that he would be nominated. His chief concern was ensuring an enthusiastic public reception for Clay's nomination.[13]

But Weed had arranged things differently. Winfield Scott was demonstrating strength in upstate New York, and Weed was prepared to take either Scott or Harrison, whoever should prove stronger at the convention. He probably inspired the convention to adopt the unit rule, whereby the entire vote of a state would be cast by the majority, in order to neutralize many Clay votes. Thus Clay, who had large minorities in New York, Pennsylvania, and other eastern states, was unable to realize any advantage from them. Scott and Harrison delegates teamed up against him, and after three days of balloting, Harrison had a majority of 148, Clay had 90, and Scott had 16. Weed later claimed that the vice-presidential nomination was offered to Webster, but that he declined the offer. Thereupon, to appease Clay's followers, John Tyler, who although a state-rights

---

11 Granger to Weed, June 7, 1838, in Granger Papers; Van Buren to Andrew Jackson, Feb. 17, 1839, in Van Buren Papers; Alexander Hamilton to Crittenden, July 12, 1839, in Crittenden Papers.

12 John B. Eldredge to William C. Rives, Sept. 6, 1839, Thomas Allen to Rives, Nov. 9, 1839, J. L. Graham to Rives, Nov. 14, 1839, in Rives Papers, Library of Congress.

13 Crittenden to Leslie Combs, Dec. 1, 1839, in Crittenden Papers (Duke).

Virginia Whig was friendly to Clay, was nominated for Vice President.[14] This carefully balanced ticket reflected one of the major divisions within the party, that of a central bank, which Weed and many other Whig leaders, as well as the *National Intelligencer*, the party organ, had long ago abandoned.

Clay accepted his defeat gracefully, although some of his friends were none too pleased at the way in which it had been brought off. "If there has not been some management and deep intrigue about this nomination—then I am mistaken," wrote one Kentuckian. Tennessee Whigs arranged a great ratifying meeting in Nashville, but a leading Democrat there thought Harrison's nomination a "bitter pill to some of the leaders." A loyal friend in New Orleans blamed Clay's defeat on the *"loco focos* of the Whig party."[15] But this was only the first reaction. Soon Clay's friends were assuring themselves that if the ticket were victorious, Clay would control the administration. Besides, there was always the next election to look forward to. If all went well, Clay would surely be the party choice in 1844, perhaps even without the necessity of a convention nomination. They went to work with a will, and even Weed later attested their "conspicuous activity" in the campaign.[16] Convention delegates who were passing through Washington on their return home were dined by members of Congress. Crittenden presided and Clay spoke at this "festival full of patriotic fervor, of burning eloquence, of conquering enthusiasm." This dinner alone, wrote one Whig, would be worth at least two states in the coming election.[17]

There was probably more tomfoolery and humbug in the election

[14] Tyler, *Letters and Times*, I, 594; Van Deusen, *Henry Clay*, 332-33; Robert Gray Gunderson, *The Log-Cabin Campaign* (Lexington, Ky., 1957), 57-66; Hone, *Diary*, 438-39; *The Life of Thurlow Weed*, 2 vols. (Boston, 1883, 1884), Vol. II, Thurlow Weed Barnes, *Memoir of Thurlow Weed*, 167-69 (hereinafter, Barnes, *Memoir of Weed*).

[15] Barnes, *Memoir of Weed*, 76-77; W. L. Marcy and Edwin Crosswell to Martin Van Buren, Dec. 22, 1839, in Van Buren Papers; Duff Green to R. K. Cralle, Monday, 9 [Dec., 1839], in Duff Green Papers; Tyler, *Letters and Times*, II, 4n; James K. Polk to David Hubbard, Dec. 30, 1839, in George Washington Campbell Collection, Library of Congress; Francis Johnson to Crittenden, Dec. 16, 1839, Harrison C. Westervelt to Crittenden, March 26, 1841, Sol Van Rensselaer to Crittenden, Jan. 20, 1844, Alexander Porter to Crittenden, Dec. 18, 1839, in Crittenden Papers.

[16] Alexander C. Bullitt to Crittenden, Dec. 21, 1839, Orlando Brown to Crittenden, Dec. 21, 1839, in Crittenden Papers; *The Life of Thurlow Weed*, Vol. I, Harriet A. Weed (ed.), *Autobiography of Thurlow Weed*, 482 (hereinafter, Weed, *Autobiography*).

[17] Frankfort *Commonwealth*, Dec. 24, 1839; Orlando Brown to Crittenden, Dec. 21, 1839, in Crittenden Papers.

that year than in all presidential elections up to that time. The Whigs at Harrisburg had been careful not to draft a platform that might divide the party, and Harrison in his letter of acceptance carefully refrained from any mention of controversial issues. Nicholas Biddle had advised sometime before that if Harrison should be nominated, it would be "on account of the past, not the future," and he urged that Harrison say nothing about promises, creeds, or principles. "Let no Committee, no Convention—no town meeting," he wrote, "ever extract from him a single word, about what he thinks now, or what he will do hereafter. Let the use of pen and ink be wholly forbidden as if he were a mad poet in Bedlam."[18]

Whig strategy aimed at making Harrison all things to all men. While he maintained silence at North Bend, Whig orators traveled through the highways and byways extolling his virtues. Not only was he a war hero in the mold of Old Hickory, he was a poor man who tilled the soil for his bread. If the speaker addressed a southern audience, Harrison was represented as proslavery and an enemy to abolitionists, whereas New England audiences were told he was heart and soul in the abolitionist fold. Were the audience antibank, so was Harrison; if probank, not more so than the candidate. He could be for high tariff, for low tariff, for state rights, or a nationalist all on the same day, but in different voices.

It was an unusual position the Democrats found themselves in. Heretofore, Whigs had been regarded generally as spokesmen of business and the wealthy against the worker and the poor. Now Whigs were assuming republican garb and pushing Democrats from their arrogated position as champion of the common man. "They are Republican *Democratic* Whigs," complained one Democrat, ". . . and advocates of the poor labourers." An exasperated Democratic reporter wrote that if Harrison were given "a barrel of hard cider" and a pension, he would "sit the remainder of his days in his log cabin . . . and study moral philosophy."[19] Whigs seized upon this. Throughout the West, where many residents had lived at least for a time in log cabins, Whig newspapers echoed and reechoed the sentiment, although not the sarcasm. Soon mobile log cabins were built and

---

[18] Biddle to Herman Cope, Aug. 11, 1835, quoted in Gunderson, *Log-Cabin Campaign*, 73.

[19] Baltimore *Republican*, Dec. 11, 1839, quoted in Gunderson, *Log-Cabin Campaign*, 73; Richard E. Parker to Martin Van Buren, April 6, 1840, William Gear to Van Buren, Nov. 9, 1840, in Van Buren Papers.

drawn by teams cross country to Whig rallies. Cider (or stronger liquid in cider mugs) became the national Whig beverage. Huge parade balls were inflated and rolled hundreds of miles, while paraders chanted:

> Farewell, dear Van
> You're not our man
> To guide the ship
> We'll try Old Tip.[20]

Crittenden contributed his share to these outlandish doings, which set a pattern for subsequent presidential elections. He campaigned in Maryland, Delaware, Pennsylvania, New York, Ohio, Tennessee, and Kentucky. On May 4 he spoke at a giant rally in Monument Square in Baltimore, along with Clay, Webster, William C. Preston, Millard Fillmore, and Tom Corwin. He spoke in Dover in mid-June with John M. Clayton.[21] One of his major efforts was at Livingston, New York, on July 4. A procession of Whigs came from neighboring towns in wagons, and if contemporary accounts are reliable, the nearby communities must have been entirely deserted for the day. For some towns sent as many as a hundred wagonloads "in a solid procession with banners erect & flags flying." Ghent sent a mobile log cabin "filled with 20 . . . log cabin boys . . . drawn by 6 milk white steeds." On top of the cabin was an eagle perched atop the staff of the Stars and Stripes. From Kinderhook, Van Buren's home, came a "Tippecanoe boat . . . manned by 30 good men and true," accompanied by a band and choir, "who made melody in their hearts singing of Harrison and reform." The vast assemblage, estimated at ten thousand persons, gathered in the park in front of the Livingston courthouse.

From a stage erected in the center of the park Crittenden spoke. A disgruntled Whig, who had grown indifferent by reason of "wrongs inflicted on us by our friends," said the effect was "like the application of a Galvanic Battery." At times, he said, Crittenden "poured forth like the mighty cataract of Niagara bearing down everything that seemed to impede his progress. Then again like the smooth and majestic Hudson he seemed to glide . . . along convincing and converting all the *fence men*." His wit and humor would "even call

[20] Gunderson, *Log-Cabin Campaign*, 4, 75-76.
[21] Josiah Morrow (ed.), *Life and Speeches of Thomas Corwin* (Cincinnati, 1896), 33; John M. Clayton to Crittenden, June 13, 1840, James W. Thomson to Crittenden, June 14, 1840, in Crittenden Papers.

forth a smile from the most rigid Hick." Never, he said, were people "better pleased with the Efforts of any man."[22]

From New York, Crittenden returned to Kentucky and plunged at once into the campaign there. Kentucky was safely in the fold, but Whigs wished to pile up an impressive majority. Crittenden spoke at Russellville on July 18, at Hopkinsville two days later, and at Elkton on July 22.[23] He returned home at the end of the month, but left in early August with Clay for Nashville, where a giant rally had been scheduled for mid-August. The Nashville meeting lasted two days. Clay spoke on August 17 and Crittenden the following day. According to Nashville papers, each occasion was such as had never been seen before in the South. Thirty thousand persons, according to David Campbell, "dined at one sitting down, or rather standing . . . except 1000 ladies who were seated."

Avoiding all specific issues, Crittenden took as his theme "executive usurpation," as developed by Jackson and Van Buren. The only issue, he said, was "Liberty against oppression, the people against the office holders." Van Buren, he said, was politically amoral and had stood on every side of every question. He was a "free-trader in politics," a "cologne, whiskered Democrat." He contrasted Van Buren to Harrison, "the plain, clear headed substantial old resident of the West." Harrison had held many offices in which, if he had been less honest than he was, he could have "enriched himself, lived in a costly mansion, and drunk wines, as well as Mr. Van Buren, from the south side of Madeira." Instead, he had been content to perform his duties honestly and faithfully and then retire to his farm and live in his "plain, substantial, and unfashionable house." Crittenden closed with an impassioned and inspirational plea for Tennessee to march side by side with her sister, Kentucky, in "the great struggle for Liberty." He pictured the rising of the people as "an avalanche of popular feeling, rushing down to the east & to the West, from the summit level of the Alleghanies, & carrying all before it." He carried out the figure, wrote one who was present, "until that immense multitude made the welkin resound with their applauding shouts."[24]

[22] Charles Epelstyn to N. P. Tallmadge, July 6, 1840, Tallmadge to Crittenden, July 22, 1840, in Crittenden Papers.

[23] Crittenden to Maria, July 22, 1840, in Crittenden Papers; Frankfort *Commonwealth*, July 30, 1840.

[24] Martin John Spalding to Mrs. Coleman, Dec. 26, 1870, in Crittenden Papers (Duke); Nashville *Whig*, quoted in Frankfort *Commonwealth*, Sept. 1, 1840; David Campbell to William C. Rives, Sept. 9, 1840, in Rives Papers.

The speech reads like sheer demagoguery. Yet it seemed to please his hearers, better conditioned perhaps to that sort of thing than the more sophisticated audiences of modern times. One correspondent said Crittenden that day "far surpassed all the orators I had ever before listened to." The Nashville *Whig* called it "a masterly display of oratory." No pen, it said, could write out the speech, no tongue describe it. Crittenden's friends, the reporter said, freely admitted that they never had heard him on any occasion make a better speech. According to another Whig editor, a thousand sources agreed that no speech had ever been received in Nashville "with greater enthusiasm."[25] Such partisan reports can be discounted. But even the Democrats who were present proclaimed it "the greatest speech they ever listened to." And a distinguished clergyman who professed to be nonpartisan was equally impressed. Thirty years later he remembered it vividly as "one of the most brilliant & impassioned bursts of oratory it has ever been my privilege to listen to." He recalled Crittenden's "silvery voice" and the "acclamations of those thirty thousand people."[26]

Six weeks later Crittenden was the speaker at a great gathering at Cumberland Gap. This was not so large a meeting as the one in Nashville but was featured by "one thousand ladies on horseback from Kentucky all dressed alike."[27] He spoke at Madison, Indiana, in early October, and he and Clay both addressed a large assembly at Shelbyville a week later. The next week Crittenden spoke to a home crowd at Frankfort, and to another gathering in Louisville at the end of the month. Everywhere he met enthusiastic audiences. "Since the world began," he wrote Webster, "there was never before in the West such a glorious excitement & uproar among the people. It is a sort of Popular Insurrection, in which patriotism, intelligence & good order have governed & prevailed in a most exemplary manner."[28]

Such doings were not peculiar to Kentucky and Tennessee. A meeting in Boston drew an estimated crowd of fifty thousand, and one in Dayton, a hundred thousand. In Philadelphia, business was neglected, new enterprises were put off, and people retired from

[25] Baltimore *Patriot*, quoted in Frankfort *Commonwealth*, April 8, 1845; Nashville *Whig*, quoted *ibid.*, Sept. 1, 1840; *ibid.*, Aug. 19, Sept. 1, 1840.

[26] Martin John Spalding to Mrs. Coleman, Dec. 26, 1870, in Crittenden Papers (Duke).

[27] David Campbell to William C. Rives, Sept. 9, 1840, in Rives Papers; Frankfort *Commonwealth*, Sept. 22, 1840.

[28] Frankfort *Commonwealth*, Oct. 20, 27, 1840; Crittenden to Webster, Oct. 27, 1840, in Webster Papers, Library of Congress.

work "to waste time in idleness" and "to listen to the stump speeches of demagogues." Millions were wagered on the outcome. Who could calculate, asked a disgruntled Democrat after the election, "the moral degradation which this contest has produced?" Tom Corwin estimated that he addressed at least seven hundred thousand "men, women, and children, dogs, negroes, and Democrats inclusive," in a hundred speeches. At the New York Whig state convention at Utica, the sober Weed was so rejoiced at harmonious proceedings there that he forgot himself and broke into the chorus of a rollicking campaign song. It was the only time in manhood he was ever known to sing.[29]

Van Buren, the Democratic nominee, was given unintentional aid by the Liberty party candidate, James G. Birney, whose sole program was opposition to slavery. Inasmuch as northern Whigs were more hostile to slavery as a rule than were northern Democrats, Birney would draw more votes from Harrison than from Van Buren. Unless "Abolitionists shall take off some four or five thousand Whig voters," wrote a friend to Van Buren, it would be impossible for Democrats to carry New York. The abolition movement, he added, was "a God-send which God knows . . . we do not deserve."[30]

Birney got 7,000 votes, most of them in New York, but even these were not enough to throw that state to Van Buren. Harrison received an electoral majority of 174, although his popular majority was only 150,000 out of a total of 2,400,000. But it was a great victory for the Whigs, won by running a military chieftain in a campaign without a platform. It was a strategy they would forget to their sorrow four years later, but it would bring victory again in 1848. Meanwhile, there was celebrating to do and planning to undertake.

Harrison's first business was the selection of a cabinet. Clay was so influential in the party and in Congress that no Whig administration could possibly succeed without his support, but Harrison sought to avoid the humiliation of openly asking Clay's advice. Urging Clay to communicate with him through a "mutual friend," he went to Frankfort in late November to visit Crittenden. But Clay would not delegate even to Crittenden authority to speak for him. He hurried down to Frankfort and carried Harrison back to Ashland with him. It may have been well that Clay did insist on a personal meeting, for

---

[29] Hone, *Diary*, 493, 495; Philadelphia *Ledger*, quoted in Lexington *Kentucky Gazette*, Nov. 19, 1840; Tom Corwin to Crittenden, Nov. 20, 1840, in Coleman, *Crittenden*, I, 130-31; Barnes, *Memoir of Weed*, 80.

[30] Jabez D. Hammond to Van Buren, Sept. 21, 1840, in Van Buren Papers.

Robert Wickliffe was in Frankfort still stirring revolt against Clay's leadership. The Old Duke of Town Fork, impatient of Clay's complete dominance of the party, was bent upon displacing him in Kentucky. He had rushed to Frankfort ahead of Clay, eagerly seeking places for his own kin—a cabinet post for his brother Charles and a secretaryship for his son.[31]

The cabinet that eventually emerged was a mixture of Clay's friends and Webster's. Although he declined a cabinet place himself, Clay secured the Attorney Generalship for Crittenden, the War Department for John Bell of Tennessee, the Navy for George Badger of North Carolina, and a place for his Ohio friend, Thomas Ewing. Clay wanted Ewing in the Post Office and John M. Clayton of Delaware in the Treasury, but Webster was opposed to Clayton's appointment. A compromise was effected whereby Ewing was given the Treasury and Francis Granger of New York the Post Office. Webster, with Clay's consent, was made Secretary of State.[32]

When he was offered the Attorney Generalship, Crittenden hesitated. He had just been reelected to a new Senate term of six years and was not certain he should resign his seat for a cabinet post. He sought advice from his friend Letcher, newly elected governor of Kentucky. Letcher, turning the question on all sides, gave ambiguous counsel. He advised Crittenden not to resign until he was satisfied with the general composition of the cabinet. Besides—prophetic thought—what of Harrison's health? If Harrison died shortly, where would Crittenden be? On the other hand, "a good sound and safe administration" was indispensable, and Crittenden's counsel would be needed. "General H. has more confidence in you than anybody," he wrote, "and . . . you will make a safe adviser." Following this advice, Crittenden conferred with Harrison in Washington. Then, his doubts resolved, he sent in his resignation. James T. Morehead, his former law pupil at Russellville, was elected in his place.[33]

[31] W. H. Harrison to Clay, Nov. 15, 1840, Clay to Francis Brooke, Dec. 8, 1840, in Clay Papers; Colton, *Clay*, IV, 446; Martin Beaty to Crittenden, Dec. 1, 1840, in Crittenden Papers; George Rawlings Poage, *Henry Clay and the Whig Party* (Chapel Hill, 1936), 16-21.

[32] Letcher to Crittenden, Nov. 30, Dec. 14, 1840, Jan. 6, Feb. 2, 9, 1841, in Crittenden Papers; Poage, *Henry Clay*, 16-21; Tyler, *Letters and Times*, II, 15.

[33] Letcher to Crittenden, Dec. 26, 1840, in Crittenden Papers (Kentucky); Letcher to Crittenden, Dec. 14, 1840, Jan. 1, 6, 1841, in Crittenden Papers; Crittenden to Letcher, Jan. 11, Feb. 9, 1841, in Coleman, *Crittenden*, I, 132, 134, 138; Collins, *History of Kentucky*, I, 45, 46; *Kentucky Senate Journal*, 1840, p. 85.

There was a mixed reaction to the announcement of the cabinet makeup. Webster's was the biggest name in it, yet a Whig congressman thought his appointment especially unfortunate. Webster was unrivaled in debate, he admitted, yet he had no talent "to lead men." Besides, his private life was subject to censure. "He dont pay his debts and therefore cant be called *a gentleman*," he wrote. Webster was "cold, selfish and out of the Senate by no means a great man," he added. Ewing, he thought, was "overrated," and so was Bell. "They are both vulgar ill bred men and unsuited to their stations." Granger was "conceited." Only Crittenden "and perhaps Badger" met with his approval.[34]

Crittenden's appointment seemed to be generally approved. One disappointed cabinet aspirant thought he was "a noble fellow and will carry much weight of talent and character" in the administration.[35] A sophisticated old capital correspondent agreed. He had been much impressed with Crittenden's Senate behavior, and thought his good intellect, his sound judgment, his eloquence, his knowledge of the law, and his "complete grasp of every case which he examined" would make him a valuable member of the administration.[36] When Crittenden's retirement was announced in the Senate, William C. Preston paid him such a warm and glowing tribute that the galleries broke into unrestrained applause, and Crittenden was so moved that he wept. "I would have given the world to have been Preston," wrote Philip Hone that night, "but I would have given two such worlds to have been Crittenden."[37]

The distribution of patronage is one of the most disagreeable, as well as most difficult, tasks for a new administration. Compared to the number of applicants, the jobs are so few that hundreds are disappointed for every one who is made happy. Also, applicants were from places so widely dispersed geographically that administrators in Washington could not possibly make their own evaluations and consequently had to accept advice from local politicians. Scarcely

[34] J[ohn] C[ampbell] to [David Campbell], Aug. 4, 1841, in David Campbell Papers, Duke University Library.
[35] John Owen to Willie P. Mangum, Jan. 11, 1841, in Henry Thomas Shanks (ed.), *The Papers of Willie Person Mangum* (Raleigh, 1953), III, 91-92 (hereinafter, *Mangum Papers*).
[36] Ben: Perley Poore, *Reminiscences of Sixty Years in the National Metropolis*, 2 vols. (Philadelphia, 1886), I, 250.
[37] Hone, *Diary*, II, 62-63; *Congressional Globe*, 26 Cong., 2 Sess., 199, 222.

were the election returns known in November when applications and endorsements began deluging Harrison and other party leaders. The Whigs as a party had never before tasted victory in a presidential election, and most of their following had been banished from federal patronage for a dozen years. Consequently, they were unusually avid for spoils. Francis Granger found on his arrival in New York City a few weeks after the election that applications were pouring in from all quarters of the state. Busy cliques, he wrote Harrison, were willing to "take upon themselves to designate those . . . they consider as proper persons to fill every honorable or lucrative post in the State."[38]

Shortly after his inaugural, Harrison issued a directive forbidding assessments on salaries of workers or the accepting of contributions from employees for party purposes.[39] But the order was impossible to enforce. What had started as a torrent a few months before was now a flood, and there were dozens of applicants for every office. "The Whigs are almost to a man dissatisfied," wrote one jubilant Democrat. Even the officeholders were unhappy, he added, because they were jealous of those who received better places. John Bell admitted that the Whigs had descended to "a thirst for power and plunder."[40]

Crittenden received his portion of these applications. Most were of little consequence and might be denied with impunity. But how could he refuse to do his utmost for old friends like Balie Peyton, Thomas Swann, Thomas Metcalfe, William J. Graves, Boyd McNairy, Robert J. Ward, John White, Pierce Butler, Joseph Eve, Robert Letcher, or Ogden Edwards?[41] "I begin already to perceive," he wrote Letcher in late January, "that even he who has power to dispose of all the offices, is only made to feel more sensibly the poverty of his means to satisfy the just claims of his friends." The tide was uncontrollable, and Crittenden joined with the rest of the cabinet in revolting against Harrison's directive.[42]

Instead of improving after the inaugural, matters got worse.

[38] Granger to Harrison, Nov. 24, 1840, in Granger Papers.
[39] Webster to Ewing, March 20, 1841, in Crittenden Papers (Duke).
[40] Henry D. Gilpin to Van Buren, June 18, 1841, in Van Buren Papers; Bell to Letcher, Jan. 13, 1841, in Coleman, Crittenden, I, 136.
[41] See Crittenden's correspondence, December, 1840, through May, 1841, in Crittenden Papers.
[42] Crittenden to Letcher, Jan. 25, 1841, in Coleman, Crittenden, I, 139-40; Poore, Reminiscences, I, 257-58.

Now disappointed officeseekers descended on Washington in person. Crittenden was so besieged by applicants, he wrote, that he had not time to say his prayers. "We are laboring along, & endeavoring to keep peace among office-seekers as well as we can," he added. But nothing short of a miracle could "so multiply our . . . patronage as to enable us to feed the hungry crowd that are pressed upon us." It was commonly said that aspirants for office actually slept at night in the White House corridors in order to have first place in line on the morrow. In his efforts to escape them at night, Harrison slipped from the White House by a rear door and took refuge in the home of an old friend.[43]

A few days after taking office, Harrison called a cabinet meeting, but when the cabinet members arrived, the mansion was full of jobseekers and there was no vacant room. The marshal attempted to induce the applicants to leave, but to no avail. He then proposed to rally a force and drive them out, but asked the President first to make them a speech and implore their patience. Harrison did so, explaining that he had public business to attend to and that he could not at that time grant their requests. But they refused to leave unless he would at least receive their letters and pledge himself to attend to them promptly. Harrison agreed, and soon his pockets, then his hat, then his arms, and finally those of the marshal were loaded to capacity, and together they marched upstairs. Even then it was with difficulty that the house could be cleared.[44]

Upstairs the cabinet presented Harrison with more patronage problems. The relationship between Harrison and administration leaders was a curious one. He treated them with great respect, more than he received from them. In all patronage matters he eventually gave way to them, save only in one instance. Crittenden was most anxious to get the governorship of Iowa Territory for his Frankfort neighbor and devoted friend, Orlando Brown. But Harrison had set his heart on this one place for John Chambers of Maysville, Kentucky, the rejected suitor of his daughter, and he held his ground.[45] The

[43] Crittenden to Letcher, March 14, 1841, in Crittenden Papers (Duke); William H. Seward, *An Autobiography from 1801 to 1834, with a Memoir of His Life and Selections of His Letters*, Frederick W. Seward (ed.), 3 vols. (New York, 1891), I, 526; Butler, *Retrospect*, 109-10.

[44] F. P. Blair to Andrew Jackson, April 4, 1841, in Bassett, *Correspondence*, VI, 98. The scene was described to Blair by the marshal, General Hunter.

[45] "Recollections of an Old Stager," XLVII (1873), 753, 754; Crittenden to Letcher, March 14, 1841, in Crittenden Papers (Duke).

case of William C. Rives, whom Jefferson had once described as "the only thoroughly educated young gentleman . . . in Virginia," was more typical. Harrison had attempted to place him in the cabinet but had been prevented, he told Henry A. Wise, by "imperious circumstances."[46]

An "imperious circumstance" in the person of Henry Clay was indeed active. Francis P. Blair, in the *Globe*, called Clay the "Mayor of the Palace," and said Harrison had surrendered both legislative and executive powers to him. Clay was in Washington dispensing patronage, recommending legislative action, and directing its course. He "ostentatiously exhibits himself as master of the new Administration," wrote Blair, and "makes no further reference to General Harrison than an empty compliment once in a while."[47] This was partisan criticism, but not greatly exaggerated. More than once Harrison had to remind Clay that he, Harrison, was President. Clay seemed completely unaware of how dictatorial he was being. On one occasion he wrote out a proclamation for Harrison without consulting him, and he was stunned when the President returned it to him. Rives saw Clay in historical perspective. He thought Clay was aping Jackson, without Jackson's popularity to sustain him. "He has no idea," said Rives, "of the dignity and wisdom of what Burke calls 'a masterly inactivity.' " In fact, said Rives, Clay had "meddled with everything."[48]

Crittenden was another story, and his friends might have fared better with a more ruthless champion. Crittenden had "too much kind feelings to carry points in the Cabinet," as John Bell said. Bell himself, who believed in being a "troublesome fellow," refused to accommodate Crittenden by giving a minor office in the War Department to one of Crittenden's friends. John White agreed that Crittenden had *"too little ambition"* where patronage was concerned, and yielded too willingly to others.[49]

Between the upper millstone of the imperious Clay and a largely

46 "Recollections of an Old Stager," XLV (1872), 573; Rives to Mrs. Rives, Feb. 2, 1841, in Rives Papers.

47 Washington *Globe*, quoted in Lexington *Kentucky Gazette*, Jan. 30, 1841.

48 Harrison to Clay, March 13, 1841, Clay to Harrison, March 15, 1841, in Clay Papers; Jos. M. Sheppard to William C. Rives, Feb. 18, 1841, Rives to Mrs. Rives, Feb. 2, 1841, in Rives Papers; Tyler, *Letters and Times*, II, 10n.

49 John Bell to Letcher, May 2, 1841, John White to Crittenden, April 15, 1841, in Crittenden Papers.

dictatorial cabinet and the lower millstone of importunate jobseekers, Harrison's health was soon shattered. The frank old man, who had learned his manners largely on the frontier, was a touching figure. During his brief weeks in office he continued to be simply himself. With a shawl about his shoulders and a basket on his arm, he frequently did the marketing for the White House. He strolled among the fish counters and vegetable stalls like any middle-class housewife looking for bargains of the day and haggling over price. Once at a formal dinner, described as "a regular hard cider affair— plenty to drink & much noise," he slapped dignified old John Quincy Adams on the back, contributed more than his share of the noise, and drank a toast to Van Buren.[50] Harrison would live exactly one month as President. He was stricken with what his doctors described as "bilious pleurisy" on Saturday, March 27, and died on Palm Sunday, April 4.[51]

The special duties of the Attorney General in that day of uncomplicated government were to represent the United States in actions concerning it before the Supreme Court and to give advisory opinions to the President and department heads regarding the law and their obligations and responsibilities under it. In the few months Crittenden served of his first term as Attorney General, he gave thirteen opinions, only one of which seems noteworthy. It had to do with claims of Florida residents for damages suffered by them when Jackson invaded that Spanish province in 1818. By the spring of 1841 these cases had been in litigation for years. At that time a Florida court ordered the United States government to pay to one claimant damages and interest from the time the claim was first made. Secretary of the Treasury Ewing asked Crittenden's opinion as to whether or not he should pay the interest.

There were two questions involved. First, how much discretion had the Secretary of the Treasury to set aside awards of the courts. Crittenden cited a law of Congress passed in 1834 giving the secretary authority to pay such awards as he deemed "to be just." This, he said, made the secretary "just as much an arbitrator as the judge . . . and his concurrence as essential to the making and validity of any award by them." This brought him to the second question:

[50] "Recollections of an Old Stager," XLVII (1873), 753-54; James K. Paulding to Van Buren, March 22, 1841, in Van Buren Papers.
[51] Adams, *Diary*, X, 456.

was the award of interest rightfully made, and therefore a just debt? Crittenden concluded that it was not. It was not a question of equity or justice, he said, but of whether or not the Florida judges had authority to award interest. They were confined in their jurisdiction only to the question of losses, he said, and this excluded interest. Crittenden's opinion on this subject became a precedent for other Attorneys General in subsequent claims of this nature.[52]

An undertaking altogether distinct from Crittenden's official duty as Attorney General was assigned him by Harrison just a week after he took office. It was a sequel to the *Caroline* affair. Three years earlier, Canadian revolutionists, operating from the American side of the Niagara River, had been annoying Her Majesty's government. One night in December, 1837, a British force crossed the river and seized an American-owned vessel, the *Caroline*, that was being used by the revolutionists for transport purposes. In the attack an American named Durfee was killed. Early in 1841, Alexander McLeod, a British citizen, during a drinking bout in a tavern in western New York, was said to have boasted that he was one of the party that had attacked the *Caroline* and that he had participated in the killing of Durfee. He was arrested by local authorities and indicted for murder.

Just before the Harrison administration was installed, the British government avowed that the attack on the *Caroline* was an official act and demanded McLeod's release. Under the law of nations, avowal of the act by his government excused McLeod from personal responsibility. Had he been charged with an offense against the United States government, he would have been immediately released, and the affair would then have become a matter to be settled between the two governments. But the complex nature of the federal system tied the hands of the United States government. McLeod was being held under the jurisdiction of the sovereign state of New York for a crime committed against her people, and the federal government had no power to interfere. But the British government rejected such a theory, regarding it as an effort by the federal government to avoid its own responsibility. Execution of McLeod, wrote British Minister Henry S. Fox, would mean war. Here matters stood when Harrison took office.

The President instructed Crittenden to go to New York, consult

[52] *Official Opinions of the Attorneys General* . . . 40 vols. (Washington, 1852), III, 635.

with Governor William H. Seward, and ask him to issue a nolle prosequi dismissing the suit. If Seward refused, Crittenden should proceed to Lockport, where McLeod would be tried, and furnish McLeod's counsel with documentary evidence that the British government had avowed destruction of the *Caroline* as a public act. If the prisoner was not ably represented, Crittenden was to procure competent counsel, but he was not to act as counsel himself. He must signify to counsel that it was the federal government's wish, in case of McLeod's conviction, that proper steps be taken at once for appeal to the Supreme Court of the United States.[53] When Crittenden arrived in Albany in mid-March, Seward was conferring with General Winfield Scott concerning New York defenses in the event of hostilities.[54]

At dinner Crittenden discussed the case with Seward and Scott. Crittenden stressed the seriousness of the international situation. Seward said he had no authority to issue a nolle prosequi, nor did New York law permit him to issue a pardon prior to trial and conviction. Besides, there was a civil suit pending against McLeod in addition to the criminal charges, and no governmental authority could interfere with that. Seward was convinced that McLeod's alleged boast of taking part in the *Caroline* expedition was unfounded, that there was ample proof of an alibi, and that McLeod would be acquitted. If he should be convicted, Seward would pardon him. But McLeod must stand trial. Any interference by the federal government would violate the Constitution and would be most damaging to the Whig party in the state. It would be looked upon by the people as "an ignoble submission to an arrogant demand," and New York and perhaps other nearby states "would wheel at once out of the ranks of the supporters of the present administration." Seward was "anxious to act in harmony & concert" with the federal government, but justice must take its course.[55]

[53] Seward, *Autobiography*, I, 527; attested copy of letter of Henry S. Fox to Daniel Webster, March 12, 1841, in Crittenden Papers; Webster to Crittenden, March 15, 1841, Letterbook, 879-88, in Crittenden Papers (Duke).

[54] Crittenden to Letcher, March 1, 1841, in Crittenden Papers (Duke); Seward, *Autobiography*, I, 527; Seward to Francis Granger, March 16, 1841, in Granger Papers; Memorandum (in Crittenden's hand), Letterbook, 1015-18, 1029, in Crittenden Papers (Duke).

[55] Seward, *Autobiography*, I, 527; Memorandum, Crittenden Letterbook, 1015-18, 1023-25, in Crittenden Papers (Duke); J. C. Spencer to Crittenden [March, 1841], Seward to Webster, April 28, 1841, in Webster Papers; Seward to Ewing, May 17, 1841, in Ewing Papers, Library of Congress; Tyler, *Letters and Times*, II, 207-11.

Next day came word that the trial of McLeod had been postponed until October. At that time McLeod's alibi was sufficient to acquit him and the war scare receded.[56] Crittenden, meanwhile, returned to Washington, there to become embroiled in a political struggle which threatened the early destruction of the newly triumphant Whig party.

[56] Tyler, *Letters and Times*, II, 214; Memorandum, Crittenden Letterbook, 1029, in Crittenden Papers (Duke); Seward, *Autobiography*, I, 568.

CHAPTER VIII

The Whig Dilemma

THE DEATH of Harrison and the accession of Tyler to the Presidency exposed the Whig party to the consequences of its own duplicity and demagoguery in the campaign of 1840. The circumspection of party leaders in avoiding a commitment on the issue of a national bank was now undone. Their military hero, acceptable for his lack of a public stand on the question, was dead, and his successor was clearly opposed to the bank.

Before his death Harrison had, at Clay's behest, called a special session of Congress to convene the last of May. Clay and the National Republican element in the Whig party had a four-point program: repeal of the subtreasury bill, which Van Buren had succeeded in getting enacted the year before; establishment of a national bank to replace the subtreasury; distribution among the states of the proceeds of public land sales; and upward revision of the tariff.

Crittenden had given a preview of much of this program just before he retired from the Senate. In January while debating a preemption bill proposed by Benton, he adroitly brought in the completely irrelevant issue of the old Bank of the United States and undertook to defend it as the only measure that could afford relief and provide a sound currency. Any other means, such as state banks or an independent treasury, would be "inefficient, illusory, and inadequate to meet public wants." As Crittenden made point after point, it was noted that Clay sat before him assenting with a nod of the head to Crittenden's arguments. A few days later, Crittenden moved to recommit the preemption bill with instructions to amend it so as to incorporate distribution in it. He argued that distribution was a debt owed the states by the federal government. His amendment lost, but his appointment to the cabinet and his confidential relationship with Clay gave his proposals the stamp of executive policy.[1]

With Tyler now occupying Harrison's chair, Clay immediately recognized a threat not only to his program but to his hopes for the succession in 1844. However, he professed to be sanguine, writing that he had "strong hopes" of Tyler's cooperation. He added that these hopes were "not . . . unmixed with fears."[2] His personal relations with Tyler had been ambiguous. Originally a Jackson Democrat, Tyler had left the party in 1833 because he thought the force bill had "swept away all the barriers of the Constitution, and given us . . . a consolidated . . . despotism."[3] Thereafter, Clay's friends in the Virginia legislature helped elect William C. Rives over Tyler to the United States Senate in 1838. On the other hand, it was through Clay's influence that Tyler had been placed on the ticket with Harrison in 1840. Thus Tyler had reason both to resent Clay and to feel obligated to him.[4]

Tyler's position was not an enviable one. Newly elevated to an office to which he had not been elected, he found himself caught between discordant elements within his own party. Harrison was the first President to die in office, and there followed considerable argument, even among Whigs, as to whether Tyler actually succeeded to the office of President or was merely an acting President until an election could be held to choose another. Tyler, however, stoutly insisted that he inherited the office itself, and his position has been universally accepted since. Burdened with a cabinet not of his own

[1] *Congressional Globe*, 26 Cong., 2 Sess., 90, 91, 114-16, 138, 230, Appendix, 23-27, 47-48, 56-58, 60; Washington *Globe*, Jan. 7, 11, 1841.
[2] Clay to the Rev. H. B. Bascom, May 10, 1841, in Clay Papers (Virginia).
[3] Tyler to Dr. Henry Curtis, Dec. 16, 1827, Tyler to L. W. Tazewell, Feb. 1, 1833, in Tyler, *Letters and Times*, I, 448, II, 379.
[4] William B. Hodgson to William C. Rives, April 4, 1841, in Rives Papers; John Bell to Letcher, May 2, 1841, in Crittenden Papers; Tyler, *Letters and Times*, I, 520-21, 585-92.

choosing, composed of men whose political philosophy was foreign to his, Tyler decided to retain them, probably because of his own weak and uncertain position. But following the example set by Jackson, he continually consulted on official business with his own friends. Judge Beverly Tucker, Lyttleton W. Tazewell, Thomas R. Dew, Henry Wise, and Abel P. Upshur became just as much a kitchen cabinet for him as Blair, Kendall, Eaton, William B. Lewis, and Van Buren had been for Jackson.[5]

It was quite clear to Clay and his friends that Tyler thought the old Bank of the United States "the original sin against the Constitution" and that his state-rights conscience would never permit him to approve a similar measure.[6] However, they also knew that it would be equally contrary to his principles for the President to attempt to instruct Congress on its duties. Clay wrote him almost at once asking his opinion about a bank. He replied that he thought the time not ripe for such an institution and that he had no intention of submitting such a measure to Congress. However, if Clay could frame a bank bill that would be clearly constitutional, and if Congress should pass it, Tyler promised to "resolve my doubts, by the character of the measure proposed." He would "devolve the whole subject in Congress with a reservation of my constitutional power to veto should the same be necessary in my view of the subject," he wrote to an intimate friend.[7]

Early in the session Clay called on Ewing for the draft of a bank plan, and after consultation in the cabinet, Ewing drew one up. Under the circumstances it was assumed to have, and did have, Tyler's approval. It called for Congress to establish a bank in the District of Columbia and provided that branches would be established only with consent of the individual states. Details of the bill were worked out by Ewing, but all members of the cabinet participated in its formulation and approved of the result. It was a compromise between their ultra-Whig views and the state-rights views of the President. Businessmen of the East were content with it, and the party organ, the *National Intelligencer*, endorsed it.[8]

[5] Tyler to Beverly Tucker, July 28 [25?], 1841, Tyler to Sam Rush and others, Feb. 19, 1842, in Tyler Papers, Library of Congress.

[6] Tyler, *Letters and Times*, I, 499.

[7] Tyler to Clay, April 30, 1841, in Clay Papers (Virginia); Tyler to Beverly Tucker, April 25, 1841, in Tyler Papers; Tyler, *Letters and Times*, III, 92-93.

[8] Poage, *Henry Clay*, 45-46; "Diary of Thomas Ewing," in *American Historical Review*, XVIII (1912-1913), 101-102; Tyler, *Letters and Times*, II, 68-69.

Clay's part in what followed seems, in retrospect, inexcusable and suggests that he had determined to ride roughshod over the President's constitutional scruples and to force a break with him. He knew that Tyler would never approve a bill with unrestricted banking privileges. He knew, too, that although there was a nominal majority of seven Whigs in the Senate, at least five of them could not be persuaded to vote for such a bank. However, if he could force the original national bank upon Tyler, Clay felt sure of a veto, and on this he could build the issue of executive usurpation, the only one on which Whigs could unite. This appeared to be a viable course, even though everyone knew Tyler to be friendly, simple, and confiding— hardly a tyrant of Jackson's stature.[9]

Apparently with this course in mind Clay now called a caucus of Whig senators and forced them to agree on a substitute to the Ewing bill giving Congress unlimited branching privileges. Knowing that this would be anathema to Tyler, he nevertheless presented this bill in the Senate June 21. At first some, including many Democrats, thought Clay's bill would pass, and some even thought it would get Tyler's approval.[10] But as it was debated week after week in the Senate, the situation changed. Clay's imperious and dictatorial attitude was offending even loyal friends, so that instead of winning votes, he was losing them. As this became apparent, Tyler's kitchen cabinet encouraged him to stand firm.

By late July, Democrats, ascertaining that the bill's passage was doubtful and its disapproval by Tyler certain, seized upon this opportunity to split the Whigs. Instead of supporting amendments to make the bill more palatable to tender state-rights consciences, they opposed them. They wished to hurry the bill along to the President for his expected veto.[11] As an olive branch to Clay, Tyler had Rives move to substitute Ewing's bill for Clay's, but the motion was overwhelmingly rejected, Democrats voting with Clay Whigs.[12]

To Clay's aid now came John Minor Botts, a Virginia Whig blindly devoted to him. He called on Tyler and proposed still another

[9] Poage, *Henry Clay*, 33, 39-41, 45-47; Eaton, *Henry Clay*, 147; Tyler, *Letters and Times*, II, 41, 43, 47.

[10] Clay to Ewing, June 14, 1841, Clay to Ewing, n. d., Ewing Papers; Clay to Ewing, June 16, 1841, in Clay Papers; *Congressional Globe*, 27 Cong., 1 Sess., 79-80.

[11] Letters to Van Buren from Silas Wright, June 21, Robert McClellan, July 22, C. J. Ingersoll, July 23, 1841, in Van Buren Papers.

[12] *Congressional Globe*, 27 Cong., 1 Sess., Appendix, 354-55, 361-62.

compromise, the Ewing bill with a slight amendment. Branching would be permitted only with state assent, but unless the state legislature at its first session following passage of the bill should positively refuse, its assent should be presumed. Tyler later claimed that he rejected Botts's proposal "emphatically . . . and unequivocally," but Botts represented to the Whig caucus that it had Tyler's approval. Clay thereupon offered it. It was adopted, and the amended bill passed, 26 to 23 in the Senate, and 128 to 97 in the House.[13]

Crittenden, understanding the vital necessity of compromise far better than even Clay, urged Tyler to sign the bill. He saw no difference between the Ewing bill and this, he said. Ewing's bill required that assent be "affirmatively expressed" by the legislature, and the Botts amendment provided that "if such dissent be not expressed" then its assent "may be inferred." Both bills agreed that the consent of the state was necessary, and the only difference was in the *"mode"* of determining its consent. The whole system of our laws was full of analogous instances, he said, and since Tyler had approved Ewing's bill, he saw no reason why he could not approve this. A veto would create a breach between Tyler and the party, would spread discord in Congress, would prevent any other useful legislation, and would bring on the "doom of the *Whig party*." On the other hand, if Tyler would only approve the bill, the success of his administration would be secured. Proponents of the bill had made great sacrifices to meet Tyler's scruples. "I advise, I conjure you," Crittenden wrote, to meet them halfway, and "sign the bill."[14]

The bill went to Tyler on August 7, and four days later it was discussed in cabinet. All gave practically the same advice as Crittenden. All recommended approval, and Ewing read what Webster called a "long & able paper." The bill, he said, did not conflict with the one he had submitted, with Tyler's approval, to Congress. The right to branch was "neither *surrendered* nor *asserted*" in either bill, he wrote.[15]

But Tyler was listening to voices other than those of his cabinet. Like Jackson in 1832, Tyler, without revealing his changed attitude,

---

13 Tyler, *Letters and Times*, II, 55-66 *passim*, 66-70.

14 Crittenden to Tyler, n. d., Crittenden Letterbook, 779-97, in Crittenden Papers (Duke).

15 Webster to Isaac Bates and Rufus Choate [August, 1841], in Webster Papers; Thomas Ewing to President Tyler, undated and unsigned opinion, in Ewing Papers.

now turned against any bank bill at all, even the Ewing bill. On Monday, August 16, he sent the bill back to the Senate with his veto. It was unconstitutional, he said, because under the elastic clause of the Constitution only those unspecified powers that were "necessary and proper" could be exercised by Congress, and this bank was neither necessary nor proper. The Botts amendment had not improved it. Its language was that of "the master to the vassal"; it was "irrational" and unjust. That night the Democratic members of Congress with their wives called on the President en masse and lauded him as the savior of his country. The cellars were opened, champagne was brought out, and there was drinking and hilarity until a late hour.[16]

The Whigs had already decided that in case of a veto they would take up the Ewing bill and pass it. If Tyler took ground in his message against the Ewing bill, the cabinet would resign and the President would be read out of the party. When the veto message came, however, there was no direct reference in it to the Ewing bill. Tyler even disclosed to his cabinet that he would approve a bill that would establish a fiscal institution (he did not like the word "bank") in the District of Columbia with the privilege of issuing its own notes, receiving money on deposit, and dealing in bills of exchange, so long as they were foreign or interstate bills. Such an agency might even establish branches in the states, but must not deal in local discounts. Before the veto message was read in the Senate, Crittenden had written to Clay, telling him that the President would sign such a bill and urging him to accept it.[17]

The day after the veto Congressman Alexander H. H. Stuart called on Tyler with the outline of a compromise bill. The veto had stirred such excitement that Tyler was surprised and alarmed, and he seized the opportunity to get out of his difficulty. He and Stuart agreed in principle on a bill, and he even penciled notes on Stuart's draft. According to Stuart, Tyler had said to him on parting that if Stuart's proposed bill were presented to him, he would "sign it in twenty-four hours." The following day Stuart returned with John M. Berrien. Tyler was not as enthusiastic as on the day before, but still

[16] Richardson, *Messages and Papers of the Presidents*, V, 1916-21; Sargent, *Public Men and Events*, II, 125-26.
[17] J. B. Christian to Beverly Tucker, Aug. 10, 1841, in Tyler Papers; Crittenden to Orlando Brown, Sept. 14, 1841, in Brown Papers, Kentucky Historical Society, Folder 211; Crittenden to Clay, Aug. 16, 1841, in Crittenden Papers.

expressed himself as unopposed to a bank such as Stuart had outlined to him. He urged them to confer with Ewing.

Next day the cabinet discussed the subject thoroughly. Details were agreed on with Tyler, who then urged his cabinet to see that a bill was drawn and presented to John Sergeant, chairman of the House Committee on the Currency. He even asked Webster and Ewing to seek out Sergeant and Berrien but cautioned them not to commit him, for he did not want to be made to appear inconsistent. Webster called on Berrien and Sergeant at once. They met with Ewing later, and by late afternoon a bill that all thought would meet Tyler's approval was drawn up. A copy of the bill was sent to Webster to deliver to Tyler before its introduction. Tyler later claimed that it was not presented to him, although Webster recalled that he read it to Tyler and made several changes in accordance with Tyler's wishes.[18]

Clay and Botts now acted to prevent any *rapprochement* between Tyler and the Whigs. In the Senate on August 19 Clay denounced the President in bitter language. He charged that "a new sort of kitchen cabinet" had been formed whose object was the dissolution of the regular cabinet and even of the Whig party. The same day a letter from Botts published in Tyler's organ, the *Madisonian*, accused Tyler of doubledealing and stated that he would be "headed" by a new bill, stronger than the first.[19] "The President is agitated," Webster wrote. "Mr. Clay's speech & Mr. Botts most extraordinary letter, have much affected him." All the while, Webster added, "violent assaults are made upon him, from certain quarters, to break with the Whigs, change his Cabinet, &, &. . . . We are on the very point of deciding, whether the Whig party & the President shall remain together."[20]

Tyler now contended that he did not understand certain implications of the bill. Despite his claims that he would not dictate to

[18] "Diary of Thomas Ewing," 99-102; Ewing to Tyler, in Frankfort *Commonwealth*, Sept. 21, 1841; Tyler, *Letters and Times*, II, 77-79, 82; Benton, *Thirty Years' View*, II, 353-56; Webster to Bates and Choate, Aug. 25, 1841, Webster to Bates and Choate, n. d., in Webster Papers; Poage, *Henry Clay*, 80-83; Robert J. Morgan, *A Whig Embattled* (Lincoln, Neb., 1954), 25-36.

[19] Morgan, *A Whig Embattled*, 65; *Congressional Globe*, 27 Cong., 1 Sess., 364; "Diary of Thomas Ewing," 102-10; W. B. Campbell to David Campbell, June 17, 1841, in Campbell Papers (Duke).

[20] Webster to Bates and Choate [Aug., 1841], Webster to ———— [Aug. 22, 1841?], in Webster Papers.

Congress, he began frantically buttonholing all who chanced his way, telling them he could not approve of Sergeant's bill unamended. He sent his friend Wise to circulate among congressmen with a similar message. Tyler himself estimated that "Some fifty members of the House were fully apprised of my objections."[21]

Just two days before the rash action of Clay and Botts, Tyler had requested Ewing and Webster to prepare arguments for him justifying the bill's constitutionality. Now he let it be known that under no circumstances would he approve this bill. At Tyler's request Ewing and Webster attempted to persuade Congress to put aside the bill until the regular session, but their efforts were unavailing. Clay insisted that the bill be acted on before the revenue bill was taken up. This stand of Clay's irritated many of his friends, including even Ewing, who regarded it as entirely too dictatorial, but the bill was rushed through nevertheless.[22]

Meanwhile, the cabinet was doing what it could to prevent an open rupture. During the early progress of the second bill Webster gave "a *man* party" in order to keep the Whigs "in good temper," and on the night of August 28 Crittenden gave a supper, inviting representatives of all elements within the party. Maria helped receive, but no other women were present. Tyler had been invited, and when he did not arrive, a deputation was sent to bring him. The White House was closed for the night, and Tyler had retired, but they roused him and brought him to Crittenden's house, where he entered into the spirit of what John Quincy Adams called the "frolicsome agony." Clay met him at the door with the greeting, "Well, Mr. President, show your hand! What are you for, Kentucky whiskey, or champagne?" "Champagne," replied the President, with forced good humor.[23] But these efforts were to no avail. Tyler sent in his veto on September 9, stressing again the unconstitutional features of the agency, which the second bill did not correct.

That night Crittenden, Ewing, Bell, and Badger met at Badger's

[21] Tyler, *Letters and Times*, II, 88, 100, 112; Wise, *Seven Decades*, 188-90.

[22] Webster to Bates and Choate, Aug. 25, 1841, in Webster Papers; "Diary of Thomas Ewing," 105-106; Ewing to Crittenden, Dec. 6, 1842, Crittenden Letterbook, 853-58, in Crittenden Papers (Duke).

[23] Adams, *Memoirs*, X, 544-45; Webster to Mrs. Caroline Webster, Aug. 16, 1841, in C. H. Van Tyne (ed.), *Letters of Daniel Webster* (New York, 1902), 236; Poage, *Henry Clay*, 88; J. F. Simmons to "Dear Wife," Aug. 29, 1841, in Miscellaneous Papers C/S, Filson Club.

home to decide their course. The next morning they told Tyler of their determination to resign. Granger went along with the four, but Webster, bitter over Clay's conduct, decided to remain. Tyler claimed that the other five waited until Saturday afternoon, September 11, to submit their resignations, knowing that Congress would adjourn on Monday and that it would be difficult for him to select their successors in time for the Senate to affirm. The charge merely exposes Tyler's own duplicity, for he had been negotiating for some weeks in anticipation of just this eventuality. He was quite prepared for the resignations, and on the following Monday he presented a new cabinet list to the Senate.[24] Included in the list was one of Clay's Kentucky rivals, Charles A. Wickliffe, brother of the Old Duke.

The Democrats were, of course, delighted at the turn events had taken, and there were mixed reactions to the cabinet disruption, even among Whigs. The *Madisonian*, of course, argued that there was no cause for the break and cited the different reasons given by the several secretaries for their action. It thought that some of their letters of resignation were intemperate and ungentlemanly, although it conceded that Crittenden's was "in good taste and characteristic of a high-toned and honorable gentleman." Some Whigs also questioned the propriety of the mass resignations. Whig members of Congress met in caucus and issued an address to the people to explain their failure to pass measures the congressmen now claimed they had been pledged to. They blamed, of course, Tyler's vetoes. Moreover, they said, these vetoes had not been motivated by "constitutional scruples." Rather, Tyler was attempting to effect "new political combinations." They said that his change of opinion and the "singular want of consistency in his views" had baffled his friends and played into the hands of the Democrats. They closed the address by denying further responsibility for his acts and declared

24 Richardson, *Messages and Papers of the Presidents*, V, 1921-25; Wise, *Seven Decades*, 191; Tyler to Alex Gardner, May 6, 1845, in Tyler Papers; Webster to Hiram Ketchum, Sept. 10, 1841, in Webster, *Correspondence*, II, 110; Ewing to Clay, Nov. 1, 1843, in Clay Papers; Washington *National Intelligencer*, quoted in Frankfort *Commonwealth*, Oct. 5, 1841; Benton, *Thirty Years' View*, II, 350; Tyler, *Letters and Times*, II, 94-97, 121; S. S. Nicholas to Crittenden, Jan. 22, 1842, Reverdy Johnson to Crittenden, Sept. 4, 1841, in Crittenden Papers; Letcher to Crittenden, Sept. 8, 1841, Crittenden to Chapman Coleman, Aug. 25, Sept. 10, 1841, in Crittenden Papers (Duke); Levi S. Fillam to James F. Simmons, Sept. 4, 1841, in Simmons Autograph Collection, Library of Congress; Duff Green to John McLean, Aug. 26, 1841, John Tyler to McLean, Sept. 11, 1841, in McLean Papers, Library of Congress; Hone, *Diary*, 563; Morgan, *A Whig Embattled*, 67-69.

political war upon him. Twenty thousand copies of the address were distributed.[25]

The Whig multitude accepted this "white paper" at face value, and Clay's position as leader in the party, which a week before had seemed tenuous, was restored. The day following the issuance of the manifesto a great demonstration in Baltimore proclaimed Clay the candidate of the party for 1844. Webster, on the other hand, lost stature among Whigs. An editorial in the *Madisonian*, obviously written by him, defended the President and criticized his departed colleagues. A month later in a speech in Boston, Webster tried to justify his action in remaining with Tyler. The Whigs thereupon turned on him. Even Crittenden, who remained personally friendly to Webster, thought he showed "a disposition to yield as circumstances pressed upon him, & to cling to office with a spirit altogether ignoble in a man of his intellect and talent." It would be some time before Webster would make his peace with the party.[26]

From his strategic position in the cabinet, Crittenden must have watched with growing displeasure the development of Clay's attack on Tyler. Tyler had not been quite as intractable and stubborn as Clay represented him. He had, despite conscientious scruples, approved a bill passed that summer distributing proceeds from public land sales in accordance with Crittenden's January proposal. But knowing that Clay hoped to become President himself in 1844, Crittenden could understand his dismay as he watched the President advance himself in the public eye. It was generally known that Tyler lacked vision and leadership, but the Presidency kept him in the spotlight, and he was becoming more and more threatening as Clay's potential rival for 1844. Yet, since Crittenden had first taken a stand in the Old Court fight, he had been an advocate of the national bank, and he could not look gladly upon Clay's cavalier use

[25] Washington *Daily Madisonian*, Sept. 14, 25, 1841; Stephen A. Douglas to Colonel William S. Prentice, Aug. 30, 1841, in Stephen A. Douglas Collection, Illinois State Historical Society, Springfield; Blair to Van Buren, Sept. 27, 1841, in Van Buren Papers; Thomas Newton to Crittenden, Feb. 8, 1842, in Crittenden Papers; Washington *National Intelligencer*, Sept. 13, 1841; Willie P. Mangum to Mrs. Mangum, Sept. 5, 1841, in *Mangum Papers*, III, 230.

[26] Reverdy Johnson to Crittenden, Sept. 15, 1841, George Badger to Crittenden, March 2, 1842, in Crittenden Papers; Francis Granger to J. Meredith, Sept. 20, 1841, L. Saltonstall to Francis Granger, Oct. 22, 1842, in Granger Papers; Van Tyne, *Letters of Daniel Webster*, 237-38; Webster to Letcher, Oct. 23, 1843, in Coleman, *Crittenden*, I, 204-205; P. S. Loughborough to C. A. Wickliffe, Dec. 10, 1842, in Webster Papers; Crittenden to Letcher, Sept. 18, 1841, in Crittenden Papers (Duke); Frankfort *Commonwealth*, Nov. 8, 1842.

of this important issue as an expendable weapon to be employed in demolishing a political rival.

Although the "white paper" publicly restored the Old Chief's ascendancy in the Whig party, Crittenden as one of its strongest leaders knew that scars had been left by the conflict. For knowledgeable Whigs, who sincerely and eagerly desired a stable national bank even at the cost of compromise, knew well that Clay had prevented its establishment. Crittenden was one of those who knew that the national bank would not make a good issue in the coming campaign, for it lacked popular appeal. Crittenden, too, despite his aversion to unrestrained use of the veto and despite Tyler's machinations to advance his own interests, must have had some sympathy for the man; certainly he knew Tyler well enough to recognize that he was not of a stature to justify Clay's ruthless and impetuous attack. This may have been the beginning of Crittenden's decision years later to seek a candidate for the Presidency other than Clay.

With the disruption of the cabinet, Crittenden turned his thoughts homeward. "Before the . . . tenth of next month," he wrote Letcher, "I shall take a drink with you in your own house. Keep your bottles set out and full, and if your liquor be good and your entertainment the same, I will then give you all the particulars about the great affairs at Washington."[27] Although it had cost him great inconvenience, Crittenden was content at the course he had followed. He would have to move his family back to Frankfort and would have no income until he could reestablish his legal business. Besides, his youngest daughter, Sallie Lee, had married Dr. Edward Howe Watson of Frankfort the spring before, and they were living in the family home at Main and Washington. Crittenden was embarrassed about upsetting the plans of the young couple. He insisted that they continue to remain in the house and that "there be as little disturbance of the rest of your household as can be consistent with our admission."[28] The Crittendens arrived home in early October. Many attempts were made to provide public entertainment honoring Crittenden and Clay, but they declined all invitations. Kentucky was already stirred up enough over the "treachery" of Tyler. Clay was now the undisputed candidate for the presidential nomination in 1844, and premature exhibitions could serve no useful purpose.

Soon Crittenden's pecuniary affairs took a turn for the better,

[27] Crittenden to Letcher, Sept. 11, 1841, in Coleman, *Crittenden*, I, 162-67.
[28] Crittenden to Dr. E. Watson, Sept. 13, 1841, in Crittenden Papers (Duke).

and he was once more able to aid relatives and friends in need. Ann
Mary's husband, Chapman Coleman, a successful Louisville merchant
when they married, had been embarrassed by the long depression
following the panic of 1837. Crittenden had lent him money, but
times were hard and he knew his son-in-law was still in difficulty.
Perhaps, he delicately wrote Ann Mary, "even so small a sum" as a
thousand dollars might be of aid to them. Crittenden happened to
have that amount with no particular need for it and enclosed a check
for her husband, setting no time limit on repayment. Six months
later he sent a more modest gift. He understood, he wrote his
daughter, that "you Louisville people are all very hard run for money,
an article which we simple Frankfort folk have little use for."
Accordingly, he enclosed "a present of fifty dollars to make you
rich."[29]

Crittenden's open purse during these years was not restricted to
members of his own family. He and Clay had gone surety for more
than five thousand dollars for an old friend, Balie Peyton, former
Democratic congressman from Tennessee who had gone into business in New Orleans. Hard times had laid Peyton's affairs low, and
he was unable to pay their draft when it came due. Crittenden took
up the draft and wrote Peyton a letter, the kindness of which overwhelmed the poor fellow. He could much better, he wrote, have borne
a rebuke. He did not know when he could repay the debt, but repay
it he would. Crittenden also lent money to his old friend Joseph
Eve, transplanted Kentuckian in Texas. When others on whom Eve
had stronger claims had failed him, Crittenden had stood by him.
"So long as my heart has a single pulsation," Eve wrote, "it will beat
warm with gratitude."

Another beneficiary of Crittenden's generosity was poor, brilliant,
eccentric Tom Marshall, congressman from Clay's Ashland District.
He had been thrown into a debtor's prison in Baltimore in the summer of 1841, and friends, without his knowledge or consent, had paid
his debt of eight hundred dollars and secured his freedom. Marshall,
too embarrassed by his "excesses" to face Crittenden, wrote him for
credit so as to repay his friends.[30]

[29] Crittenden to Chapman Coleman, March 28, 1840, May 16, Aug. 25, 1841,
Crittenden to Mrs. Chapman Coleman, March 19, Sept. 13, 1842, in Crittenden
Papers (Duke).
[30] Clay to James B. Clay, Dec. 24, 1841, Feb. 13, 1842, in T. J. Clay Papers;
Adolphe Mazereau to Crittenden, Jan. 4, 1842, Joseph Eve to Crittenden, Sept. 16,
Dec. 22, 1842, Marshall to Crittenden, July 12, 1841, in Crittenden Papers.

It was during this time, too, that Crittenden was disturbed by the first of many crises brought on by the intemperance of his oldest son. After being graduated from West Point in 1832, George had served a few years in the army. Resigning, he had drifted aimlessly for a time before migrating to Texas with his father's friend, Albert T. Burnley. Prior to annexation, hostilities between Texas and Mexico were frequent, and in an engagement late in 1842 George was taken prisoner.

Crittenden was in Washington when the word reached him, and he called on friend and foe for aid. George might be summarily executed or sent off as a prisoner of state to labor in government mines for the rest of his life. It was not too difficult to seek assistance from his former friends, Webster and Blair, but it must have galled Crittenden to have to plead with Tyler for help. Not one, however, failed him. Webster sent instructions posthaste to the American minister in Mexico City, Waddy Thompson, asking him to "exert every kind of effort which may be in your power" to effect George's release. Webster also called on the British minister in Washington for help, and wrote an urgent letter to the British minister in Mexico City. Meanwhile, Blair had enlisted the aid of Andrew Jackson, who had once befriended the Mexican President, Santa Anna, and it was largely through Jackson's influence that George was released.[31] Crittenden was embarrassed shortly after this to learn that George had borrowed money from Burnley and had not repaid it. Crittenden assumed the debt, and paid it off.[32]

Crittenden had reason to be better pleased with the behavior of his second son, Thomas. After failing to make a New Orleans mercantile connection, he had studied law in Louisville. Thomas returned to Frankfort, married his stepsister Kitty Todd, and started a law practice. In the spring of 1843 he was appointed common-

[31] Crittenden to A. T. Burnley, Jan. 7, 1839, George B. Crittenden to Crittenden, April 31 [?], 1839, Webster to Thompson, Feb. 7, 1843, Thompson to Crittenden, March 17, 1843, Webster to Letcher, Feb. 21, 1843, Crittenden to Thompson, Feb. 6, 1843, Crittenden to Letcher, Feb. 24, 1843, A. L. Santa Anna to Thompson, Feb. 6, March 15, 1843, Sir Richard Pakenham to H. S. Fox, March 18, 1843, in Crittenden Papers (Duke); Webster to Thompson, Feb. 7, 1843 (copy), Webster to Crittenden, Feb. 28, 1843 (copy), Thompson to Santa Anna, March 9, 1843 (copy), Thompson to Webster, March 18, 1843 (copy), in Crittenden Papers; Blair to Jackson, Feb. 12, 1843, Jackson to Blair, Feb. 17, 1843, Jackson to Santa Anna, Feb. 27, 1843, Jackson to James W. Breedlove, Feb. 27, 1843, Jackson to Thompson, July 12, 1843, in Bassett, *Correspondence of Jackson,* VI, 205, 211-13, 224; Tyler, *Letters and Times,* II, 257, 265; Crittenden to Maria, Feb. 5, 1843, in Coleman, *Crittenden,* I, 199.

[32] Crittenden to Burnley, Oct. 31, 1843, in Crittenden Papers (Duke).

wealth's attorney and was awaiting his first prosecution. That opportunity presented itself in the autumn, when Dudley Woolfolk was indicted for murder in the Woodford circuit court. According to reports, Thomas conducted himself very well in the prosecution, but the defendant was acquitted. The defendant's counsel was Thomas' father. Meanwhile, Crittenden's second daughter, Cornelia, had grown into a charming and accomplished woman and had married the Reverend John C. Young, president of Centre, the flourishing young Presbyterian college in Danville. Robert, who had failed at Miami, had transferred there, had gone to work in earnest under his brother-in-law, and had been graduated the year before.[33]

Crittenden returned east the winter after his resignation from Tyler's cabinet to represent the state of Kentucky in a suit against the Schuylkill Bank of Philadelphia, whose cashier had fraudulently issued over a million dollars' worth of counterfeit notes on the Bank of Kentucky. Crittenden had attended to his business by early January and was preparing to return home when he learned that Clay was to resign his Senate seat. It had been assumed generally that Clay would not serve out his term, for the aftermath of the split with Tyler could not benefit any Whig in Congress; but his departure before the end of the session was unexpected.

The Kentucky legislature was in session at the time, and Clay had decided to act before it adjourned so that it could choose his successor. Crittenden wrote his good friend Letcher at once. Letcher spoke to other friends of Crittenden, and it was arranged to fill the vacancy "the very moment [Clay's] resignation should be filed." Crittenden was the logical successor, but Robert Wickliffe, whose brother Charles was now in Tyler's cabinet, attempted to forestall his election. Wickliffe and his friends approached Charles S. Morehead and Joseph R. Underwood and urged each in turn to become a candidate. Both were good Whigs, and both were from the western part of the state, an area which was beginning to feel neglected in political preference. Neither, however, could be induced to oppose Crittenden, nor could any Democrat. When Clay's resignation was received, former Vice President Richard M. Johnson, now a representative in the legislature, asked that the roll be called so that "it

[33] Frankfort *Commonwealth*, May 2, June 20, Sept. 19, 1843; Orlando Brown to Crittenden, Dec. 21, 1839, in Crittenden Papers; Mrs. Coleman to Crittenden, Feb. 11, 1840, Robert Crittenden to Crittenden, May 21, 1841, in Crittenden Papers (Duke).

might go forth to the world that *Mr. Crittenden* was the unanimous choice of his native state." When the roll was called, Crittenden received all of the 120 votes.[34]

Clay hung on for six weeks after his resignation was sent in, as if, Silas Wright thought, he regretted his decision. Meanwhile, Crittenden was impatiently waiting "for the shoes which were to be cast off for his wear." Finally, on March 31, Clay raised his tall, slender figure in the Senate to bid a farewell, he said, to public life. Clay was certainly one of the ablest orators of his day, but his speeches were made to be heard, not read. It was the passion and conviction with which he spoke, rather than what he said, that impressed his hearers. Everyone, including ladies in the galleries, well knew that Clay, far from retiring from public life, was preparing for the coming presidential campaign; that he was, as Letcher put it, "getting off awhile merely to get on better." Yet Clay's voice choked with emotion, and he wept unashamedly as he bade friend and foe a long farewell.

Wright, as he listened, was unmoved, however. He thought he sensed a fear in Clay's mind "that the Gods had determined to gratify him in that wish, even if he should change his mind." But less sophisticated Alexander H. H. Stuart thought it "the most august scene I ever witnessed in my life." Scarcely an eye, he said, was dry in all the assemblage. Even Benton's eyes were moist, and Calhoun, who had not exchanged civilities with Clay since the subtreasury issue five years before, was seen to give way to his feelings "and shed tears like a woman." He and Clay embraced as they passed. "Not a word was spoken by either," wrote an experienced reporter, "for their emotion was too strong for expression." It was an incredible performance, to be understood only in the context of the nineteenth-century love of rhetoric in an America culturally and emotionally undernourished.[35]

[34] Crittenden to Letcher, Jan. 9, 1842, in Crittenden Papers (Duke); Letcher to Crittenden, Feb. 4, 24, 1842, C. S. Morehead to Crittenden, Feb. 9, 23, 1842, in Crittenden Papers; Clay to Lucretia Clay, Feb. 13, 1842, in T. J. Clay Papers; Crittenden to Letcher [Feb., 1842], in Coleman, *Crittenden*, I, 198; Frankfort *Commonwealth*, Feb. 25, March 1, 1842; *Kentucky House Journal, 1841*, p. 586.

[35] Silas Wright to Van Buren, April 2, 1842, in Van Buren Papers; *Sketches by a Looker On*; Letcher to Crittenden, June 21, 1842, in Coleman, *Crittenden*, I, 182-83; Stuart to "Dear Sir," Sunday Evening [April, 1842], in Stuart Papers, University of Virginia Library; Cincinnati *Republican*, quoted in Frankfort *Commonwealth*, April 12, 1842; "Recollections of an Old Stager," XLVII (1873), 758; Poage, *Henry Clay*, 114.

Spring came early to Washington that year. The winter had been a mild one, and by mid-March the grass had a bright freshness and the trees were in full bloom. Tyler was by now quite obviously seeking to head a new party. He had surrounded himself by a cabinet of his own choosing. Webster still hung on in the State Department, although clearly now in a subservient role. Walter Forward was in the Treasury; John C. Spencer, in the War Department; Abel P. Upshur, Navy; Hugh Legarè, Attorney General; and Charles A. Wickliffe, Postmaster General. All except Webster were ardent state-righters.

Tyler had of course proscribed all Whigs of the Clay stripe and was wooing the Locofocos by appointing many of their party to office. But he was having little success. All factions seemed to scorn him. Calhoun, who was shifting back and forth in the Senate, sometimes supporting Tyler, sometimes the Democrats, occasionally the Whigs, thought the conduct of the administration "more like madness than . . . anything I ever saw in public life." Benton remarked on "the absolute imbecility of Tyler [and the] influence of toadeaters & parisites over him." Buchanan thought the administration "a poor concern," living from day to day "upon expedients." Crittenden wrote that "Tyler is as flat here as any poor D—l ever was. The puerility of the man is almost incredible." In Congress he was literally without support, except when he clearly joined Democrats to embarrass Whigs. One Washingtonian, reporting a White House New Year's levee to which practically everyone had been invited, observed that this was the only way Tyler could ever get up a party.[36]

The country had not yet recovered from the depression growing out of the panic of 1837, and the Treasury was in extreme circumstances. As tariff rates declined under the Compromise Tariff of 1833, so did revenue. There was a $3,000,000 deficit in the Treasury the first quarter, and boundary difficulties that created tensions with Great Britain called for increased military expenditures. Whig dreams of distribution of proceeds of land sales had been achieved

[36] Clay to Lucretia Clay, Feb. 13, March 13, 1842, in T. J. Clay Papers; Calhoun to David Hubbard, March 12, 1842, in George W. Campbell Papers; Benton to Van Buren, April 14, 1842, in Van Buren Papers; Buchanan to Letcher, April 17, 1842, in Coleman, *Crittenden*, I, 176; Crittenden to Letcher, Jan. 9, March 6, 1842, in Crittenden Papers (Duke); W. B. Campbell to David Campbell, Dec. 25, 1841, in Campbell Papers (Duke); William C. Preston to Waddy Thompson, Jan. 11, 1842, in Waddy Thompson Papers, Library of Congress; Frankfort *Commonwealth*, Jan. 4, 21, 1842.

in the special session the summer before, thereby depriving the government of that formerly fruitful source of revenue and leaving a higher tariff as the only prospect of relief for the Treasury. It would require months, however, to hammer out a new tariff bill. Meanwhile, Treasury notes were passing at a discount, and the pay of civil servants and of the military was threatened with suspension.

The year before, Congress had authorized the Secretary of the Treasury to sell $12,000,000 worth of bonds, if necessary, and to issue an additional $5,000,000 in Treasury notes payable in one year. The Treasury notes had been issued, but only $5,500,000 of the bonds had been sold. To tide over the emergency, the House early in 1842 passed an administration bill asking for authority to issue the remainder of the $12,000,000, with an additional $5,000,000 to retire the Treasury notes that would soon be due. The bill was reported favorably by the Senate Finance Committee in early April. Then an amendment was offered to it, repealing the land-distribution bill passed only six months before.

Crittenden spoke against the amendment. He reminded his Whig colleagues that distribution was a measure that their party had pursued through prosperity and adversity. He was as sensitive as anyone to government needs for support, but he would "not take one solitary step" to accommodate himself to the administration view on distribution. Whigs no longer had responsibility for Tyler's measures. He chided Democrats for having "whispered away the President from his party" only now to taunt the Whigs for having elevated him to power. Even so, Whigs would support the President "in all that was right." They would not sacrifice the country's interests for mere "gratification of party resentment." But the "imaginary dangers" had only been gotten up to "frighten Congress into a repeal of this law." He would support the loan bill without the land amendment. With it, he would vote against the bill. When the vote was taken, the amendment was defeated. The bill then passed.[37]

Distribution was saved for the time, but now the tariff issue endangered it. The Compromise Tariff of 1833 would expire on July 1, and a revised bill could not be passed by that date. Many thought that in the absence of a new bill, all collections of duties must cease

[37] *Congressional Globe*, 27 Cong., 2 Sess., 385, 398-99, 418, 421; Tyler, *Letters and Times*, II, 158-59.

on July 1. To avoid national bankruptcy, therefore, it was proposed that a provisional tariff, or "Little Tariff," be passed, extending the Compromise Tariff of 1833 for one month while a revised bill was being worked out. One feature of the tariff of 1833 was a provision that by July 1, 1842, average rates must not exceed 20 percent *ad valorem,* a rate commonly accepted as nonprotective. But the average was still above that figure. Furthermore, there had been so much opposition to the distribution bill the year before that the Whigs had only secured its passage by accepting a provision that distribution after July, 1842, be suspended whenever duties on imports were raised above 20 percent. Even with this safeguard, Tyler had accepted distribution somewhat gingerly. Now he insisted that distribution cease on July 1 if rates of the old tariff bill were continued beyond that date.

Crittenden had not had an opportunity before this to vote on a tariff bill. As on most issues, he was a moderate on the tariff, believing protection should be only temporary and that after a few years industry should be able to stand upon its own feet. He had advised Clay in 1832 to accept lower rates than Clay was then willing to accept. Now, however, Crittenden was being pressed from home for upward revision. Hemp manufacturing had been a thriving Kentucky industry a few years before; but with the depression and with the introduction of Indian and Russian hemp products, bagging and rope prices were the lowest they had ever been, and Kentucky growers and manufacturers were facing ruin. They claimed that they needed a tariff of at least five cents a square yard of bagging, which Crittenden thought excessive. "When the Tariff gets to the Senate . . .," Clay had written him, "You and your colleague are expected to take care of this single Kentucky manufacture."

The "Little Tariff" passed the House in mid-June and a week later passed the Senate. At the end of the month Tyler vetoed it because it continued distribution while rates were beyond the stipulated 20 percent. He stated that he would continue to collect duties under the old rates even though the bill had expired.[38] Meantime, the House had hammered out a new bill providing for even higher duties than the old tariff and specifically providing for distribution

[38] Clay to Crittenden, June 3, 1842, in Crittenden Papers; *Congressional Globe,* 27 Cong., 2 Sess., 675-79, 694; Richardson, *Messages and Papers of the Presidents,* V, 2033-66; Tyler, *Letters and Times,* II, 167-70; Sargent, *Public Men and Events,* II, 158.

despite these rates. Crittenden privately disapproved of these higher rates, especially the five cents on bagging, which would infuriate southern cotton planters, the chief purchasers of the product. Nevertheless, he helped beat back all amendments, thinking Tyler would not have the temerity to veto a bill that would provide the revenue he needed to carry on the government. When Tyler did veto the bill, Whig fury could not be contained. John Quincy Adams wanted to adjourn without passing any new revenue bill, and Botts urged impeachment of Tyler.[39]

But Tyler had the Whigs at a great disadvantage, and he knew it. Sectional interests were threatening to split the party. Northern Whigs must obtain higher tariff rates or face ruin at home. Distribution was to them a secondary issue. Southern Whigs, however, were opposed to tariff protection and could accept a bill raising duties only if it were accompanied by distribution. "The surrender of the Land Law or any faltering on the subject," one wrote, "puts an end to all hopes . . . of passing any Tariff Law at all."[40]

Clay's fortunes were involved in the issue; for if his northern friends should surrender distribution to win Tyler's approval of a protective tariff, or if his southern friends should go over to the Democrats and defeat a tariff, he would lose ground in both sections. Despite this, Clay refused to compromise. He insisted that distribution not be given up and urged his friends to stand fast. As the bitter impasse continued through the hot summer months, many thought the days of the republic were numbered. Despite Tyler's declared intention, they argued that if no tariff bill were passed, no revenue could be collected, and the government must go down.[41]

On August 27 the Senate took up the third tariff bill that the House had sent up that session. Its rates also exceeded the 20 per-cent limit, but it made no mention of distribution; for according to terms of the agreement reached the year before, such a bill would bring an end to distribution. Southern Whigs united with southern

[39] Crittenden to Clay, July 2, Aug. 3, 12, to James Harlan, Aug. 16, 1842, in Coleman, *Crittenden*, I, 185-87, 191-94; Alexander Porter to Crittenden, July 6, Letcher to Crittenden, June 21, 1842, in Crittenden Papers.

[40] Willie P. Mangum to Clay, June 15, 1842, in Clay Papers; John White to Letcher, July 11, 1842, in Crittenden Papers; Crittenden to Clay, July 2, 15, Aug. 12, Crittenden to James Harlan, Aug. 16, 1842, in Coleman, *Crittenden*, I, 185-90, 192-93.

[41] Crittenden to Clay, July 2, 15, Clay to Crittenden, July 16, 21, 1842, in Coleman, *Crittenden*, I, 185-90; John White to Clay, Aug. 18, 1842, in Crittenden Papers; Alexander H. H. Stuart to John Newton, Aug. 3 [1842], in Stuart Papers (Virginia).

Democrats in opposing the bill, but Crittenden and his colleague Morehead joined with twenty-two northern Whigs and Democrats in support of it. Protesting against the tyranny of Tyler, Crittenden yielded, he said, to the urgent wants of the nation. He would surrender distribution as he would surrender his purse to the highwayman. And he would pursue that subject later, just as he would pursue the recovery of stolen property. The bill passed by a one-vote margin, twenty-three to twenty-two. Crittenden and Morehead were lauded by the northern press for their patriotism and magnanimity in placing country above party.[42]

With approval of the tariff a separate distribution bill was passed, but Tyler pocket-vetoed it, as everyone had known he would. Congress then adjourned, and Tyler doubtless breathed a sigh of relief. For the first eighteen months of his administration had indeed been conducted "amid earthquake and tornado."[43]

Crittenden's vote on the tariff marks his first division with Clay. Clay had instructed him under no circumstances to surrender to Tyler on the distribution bill.[44] But Crittenden, probably from patriotic motives as well as to save Clay's popularity in the North, had disobeyed. Had he voted against the bill, it would have been defeated, and with it would have gone any chance for Clay to carry a substantial portion of the northern states in the presidential election two years hence. But if Clay resented Crittenden's independence on this occasion, there is no indication of it. For half a dozen years yet, they would remain the most intimate of friends.

Crittenden was completing Clay's unfinished term, which would expire in the spring of 1843. For a time he was uncertain of reelection. Whigs had a substantial majority in both houses, but Robert Wickliffe was still endeavoring by hook or crook to create defections, and Democrats could not again be expected to support Crittenden. A count revealed Crittenden would be defeated if only fifteen Whigs could be prevailed upon to vote with the Democrats. Both senators, Crittenden and Morehead, it was whispered about,

[42] *Congressional Globe*, 27 Cong., 2 Sess., 922, 949-57, 960; Sargent, *Public Men and Events*, II, 186-87; Tyler, *Letters and Times*, II, 167-70, 174, 181-82; Crittenden to Clay, Aug. 2, 1842, in Coleman, *Crittenden*, I, 191; New York *American*, Philadelphia *United States Gazette*, and Washington *National Intelligencer*, all quoted in Frankfort *Commonwealth*, Sept. 13, 1842.
[43] Tyler, *Letters and Times*, II, 181-82; Tyler to L. W. Tazewell, Oct. 24, 1842, *ibid.*, 244.
[44] Clay to Crittenden, July 16, 21, 1842, in Coleman, *Crittenden*, I, 185-90.

were residents of the favored Bluegrass region and the great southern and western portions of the state were entitled to more consideration. Wickliffe's efforts were of no avail. When the election was held in early January, Crittenden received eighty-eight votes to forty-three cast for his Democratic rival, Richard M. Johnson, the former Vice President.[45]

Clay's presidential nomination now seemed almost certain. A mild movement for Winfield Scott was started in Pennsylvania in the spring of 1842, but Crittenden, through mutual friends, was able to prevail upon Scott to withdraw. No sooner was Scott brought into line than Webster created a problem. His reduced stature in the party had still not recovered, and his nomination was out of the question. But he was jealous of Clay's eminence, and he toyed with the idea of defeating him with either Calhoun or John McLean. When these schemes proved hopeless, Webster's friends urged his nomination for Vice President on the ticket with Clay. It was argued that he would greatly strengthen Clay's chances of carrying New England and New York. These obvious advantages had to be balanced against Webster's unpopularity in the South and West, and the scales tipped against him. Clay declined the proposal on the high ground that nominations were the business of the convention, and he refused to make a deal.[46]

By the end of 1843, the mild threats posed by Scott and Webster had been disposed of, and Clay had a clear track for the nomination. His prospects for victory the following November seemed unusually bright. Even the Whig reversals in the New York elections that fall were not too discouraging, for they practically insured the nomination

[45] Letcher to Crittenden, Aug. 8, 1842, Crittenden to Letcher, Dec. 9, 1842, in Coleman, *Crittenden*, I, 170-71, 192; Joseph Eve to Crittenden, Sept. 16, 1842, Eve to Letcher, Dec. 22, 1842, Crittenden to Maria, Dec. 26, 1842, Charles S. Morehead to Crittenden, Jan. 2, 1843, Henry Pirtle to Crittenden, Jan. 2, 1843, in Crittenden Papers; John M. McCalla to Van Buren, Jan. 11, 1843, in Van Buren Papers; Frankfort *Commonwealth*, Nov. 22, 1842, June 27, July 11, 18, 1843; Russellville *Herald and Advertiser* and Frankfort *Kentucky Yeoman*, both quoted *ibid.*, Dec. 20, 1842; Collins, *History of Kentucky*, I, 48.

[46] Crittenden to Letcher, June 23, 1842, Crittenden to Clay, July 3, 1842, Scott to Crittenden, April 5, Oct. 14, 1843, in Coleman, *Crittenden*, I, 184-86, 201-204; Frederick A. Schley to Letcher, July 15, 1842, Scott to Crittenden, July 8, 1843, Peter B. Porter to Clay, Sept. 25, 1843, in Crittenden Papers; Clay to Thomas Ewing, Oct. 29, 1843, in Clay Papers; Clay to John L. Lawrence, Oct. 5, 1843, in Clay Papers (Virginia); Hamilton Fish to John M. Berrien, Oct. 13, 1843, quoted in Savannah *Morning News*, July 22, 1934, in John M. Berrien Papers, Library of Congress; C. G. Greene to Duff Green, July 1, 1843, in Duff Green Papers; H. D. Gilpin to Van Buren, Nov. 5, 1843, in Van Buren Papers.

of Van Buren by the Democrats, and Van Buren would be easy pickings, Clay thought. By early spring, 1844, even such a realist as Thurlow Weed considered Clay's election a certainty.[47] Crittenden was equally confident. Months earlier he had taken to the hustings for his friend.

[47] Clay to John Pendleton Kennedy, Dec. 3, 1843, in John Pendleton Kennedy Papers, Peabody Institute; Weed to Granger, March 11, 15, 1844, in Granger Papers.

CHAPTER IX

Texas and Clay's Epistolary Style

THOSE WHO are disposed to speculate on the narrow turns of fate which decide the course of history might well ponder over the election of 1844, for there have been few, if any, elections more fateful to America. Had a few votes in New York, for example, been changed, Henry Clay would have been elected President of the United States. Under Clay, the Texas issue would certainly have been handled in a manner less inflammatory than under either Tyler or Polk. The Mexican War need not then have occurred, and there would have been no such antislavery agitation as was expressed in the Wilmot Proviso or in the slavocrats' demands for congressional protection of slavery in the territories. There might then have been no new principle of "popular sovercignty" warranting the repeal of the Missouri Compromise a decade later; and there would have been no occasion for the rise of the Republican party to reinstate it. Thus, the election of Lincoln would not have taken place, and possibly the nation need not have been divided by a war whose tragic effects are still evident.

As the campaign got under way, it was generally conceded that

Clay would be a candidate and almost certainly the winner. His star had never shone brighter. That so slim a margin was to separate him from his lifelong dream was to prove not only fateful to Clay's career and to the course of American history, but fateful also to the future of his stanch supporter John J. Crittenden. Well might both Clay and Crittenden reflect on what went wrong here and what could have been changed that might have spelled the difference. The result for Clay was largely vain regret; for Crittenden it was the decision that the tide of fortune had passed for Clay and that it was time for Whig hopes to turn elsewhere.

With Clay acknowledged as the most powerful political figure in the nation, with the effects of the panic of 1837 still present to place the Democrats in an odious light with the people, with most of the great business interests working for him, with his own prestige at its height, and with no formidable leadership among the opponents, we might ask why it was that Clay failed at the moment that triumph seemed surely within his grasp.

The advantage of hindsight permits the student to see, as Crittenden apparently did at last, that Clay's failure lay not altogether with destiny but within Clay himself. For at this supreme moment, Clay's weaknesses were again to lead him to commit errors that were to prove fatal to his cause. His fiery eloquence and love of conflict were to drive him to flay dying horses; his tendency to strike at men instead of at issues was to bring him into a political cul-de-sac; above all, his utter inability to assay the quality and nature of political opinion was to delude him on the great issue of the campaign. It was a trait of Clay's character that he never was to see, as Crittenden now saw, the danger of self-dramatization and the fatal weakness of failing to comprehend political realities. In the events that preceded the election of 1844 we see Clay moving toward disaster with almost the inevitable quality of a character in a Greek drama pursued by the Fates.

Clay had expected that one of the fruits of the battle with Tyler, executive usurpation, would be a campaign issue. Ironically, however, this issue was to disappear along with Tyler, for Clay's too-vehement assault had not left Tyler even the stature of a strawman. Until the spring of 1844, all issues seemed tame and uninspiring. With the bank question pushed into the background, Democrats tried again the old cry of "bargain" against Clay, and on the last day of April, Kentucky Democrat Linn Boyd once more leveled this charge in a full-dress speech in the House of Representatives. But that old refrain was threadbare by this time, and even John Quincy Adams sat and listened "with great complacency" to the recapitulation of his and Clay's old sin.

The tariff question was equally desultory, despite efforts of northern Whigs to create a scare over it. The protective rates established in 1842 were better than even the best friends of protection had anticipated. Prosperity had returned to the country about the time the new tariff was enacted in 1842, and the Whigs gave credit to the tariff. Revenue was now abundant, and northern industrialists like Abbott Lawrence, textile tycoon of Lowell, as well as politicians like Thurlow Weed, feared only that Democrats might force downward revision. By the end of March, though the session had several months to go, Crittenden could reassure them. "Rely on it," he wrote, "the tariff is safe." Any defects in it, he added, would be corrected "hereafter."[1]

When the question of the annexation of Texas arose, however, the whole nature of the campaign was changed, and the basis for the careful strategy Clay and the Whigs had been so long preparing was utterly demolished. Of all national issues it was the one that should have been understood best by a Kentuckian. The deep-seated western urge for expansion was particularly strong among Kentuckians, as was also their natural sympathy with a people struggling for independence. In the case of Texas this was especially true, for many of their own neighbors and friends had settled there. Kentucky papers, including the Clay press, were full of news of Texans and of former Kentuckians like General Leslie Combs and Albert Sidney Johnston. "There can be no doubt," according to Poage, "that the Kentucky Whigs ardently sympathized with the Texans, whom they thought to be only temporarily separated from the United States."[2]

In the eight years since American settlers in Texas had defeated Santa Anna at San Jacinto, the United States had recognized Texas'

---

[1] Augustus Weaver to Crittenden, Feb. 20, 1844, Charles D. Drake to Crittenden, March 28, 1844, Drake to George McDuffie, March 28, 1844, in Crittenden Papers; Amos Kendall to Van Buren, April 30, 1844, in Van Buren Papers; Crittenden to Weed, March 31, 1844, in Thurlow Weed Papers, University of Rochester Library; Lawrence to Granger, March 2, 1844, in Granger Papers; Weed to Crittenden, March 17, 1844, in Crittenden Papers.

[2] Poage, Henry Clay, 125.

independence but had not accepted proffers of union by the Texas government because powerful forces in the northern states were opposed to acquiring additional slave territory. In the summer of 1843, however, a combination of factors revived the question of annexation. Slavery expansionists were looking with longing eyes toward the rich prairie lands of Texas. They justified annexation on the ground that Texas was included in the Louisiana Purchase and that it had been illegally bartered away in the Florida treaty in 1819, a position that Clay himself had held at the time of the negotiations. Their cause was aided by fears that the British intended to establish a protectorate over the republic. In his message to Congress in December, 1843, Tyler, without directly asking for annexation, pointed to the obvious advantages to be reaped from it. Meanwhile, Mexico, who had never recognized Texan independence, let it be known that annexation would lead to war.

Tyler's message broke ground for an annexation treaty that Abel P. Upshur, Webster's successor in the State Department, had worked out with the Texan minister in Washington. Upshur had been assured that the necessary two-thirds vote in the Senate could be secured for ratification. But on the last day of February, before he could submit the treaty, Upshur was accidentally killed in an explosion on the new battleship *Princeton*. Tyler then turned to Calhoun, who already had twice refused the State Department but who now, through the intercession of Henry A. Wise and George McDuffie, was induced to accept the post. On April 22 Calhoun sent the treaty to the Senate.[3]

Accompanying the treaty were documents concerning negotiations, among them a copy of a remarkable letter Calhoun had written to the British minister at Washington. The letter contained a long and irrelevant justification of the institution of slavery and defended United States annexation of Texas as a measure to support that institution. It is difficult even now to understand how Calhoun ever brought himself to write such a letter, or having done so, to include it among the documents sent to the Senate with the treaty. The letter made it impossible for any northern Senator to support the treaty, and thus its defeat was certain. Benton, Alexander H. Stephens, Blair, and other annexationists thought that Calhoun sent

---

[3] Charles M. Wiltse, *John C. Calhoun, Sectionalist, 1840-1850* (Indianapolis and New York, 1951), 159-63, 167; Tyler, *Letters and Times*, II, 278, 294-95.

the letter in order to ensure that Texas be kept out of the Union so that her exclusion could become an issue for southern secession.[4]

Whatever Calhoun's motive, the treaty had rough sledding. Crittenden argued that Texas was not, in fact, an independent nation but was completely dependent upon United States support. "Whatever we may think of *annexation* when properly presented under other circumstances," he wrote, ". . . when this Treaty and documents etc are read & understood there will be felt a general sense of condemnation & shame at the proceedings of our executive government." The treaty was debated for six weeks. When it finally came to a vote on June 8, it was overwhelmingly rejected, sixteen to thirty-five.[5] Now the issue which fate, aided by Calhoun and Tyler, had injected into the campaign would demonstrate its power and would obliterate all others.

For a while, Tyler's vigorous moves toward annexation had propped his faded hopes for the Democratic nomination, for his stand had made him the favorite of southern Democrats. Once more he strove to rally support, but the Tyler banner, which had been reduced to tatters by Clay, could not be restored. For Van Buren and Clay the rise of the issue was also to have an ominous effect. Van Buren had early been a moderate on the slavery question, but when Calhoun linked annexation of Texas with expansion of slavery, he found it impossible to support the treaty. He announced his opposition to annexation in a letter published in the Washington *Globe* on April 27.

Meanwhile, Clay had been considering what course to follow. The genius for compromise that had marked his political career had developed from his hard-won realization that such issues as Manifest Destiny and slavery should not be allowed to burst into open flame. It is hard to understand why he now failed to see the dangers that lay in wait for him in the annexation issue. As early as November 29 Crittenden had warned Clay of Tyler's forthcoming pronouncement and apparently had cautioned Clay against any kind of commitment. As a Kentuckian and a westerner, Clay had no personal feelings

[4] Wiltse, *Calhoun, Sectionalist*, 167-71; Blair to Jackson, May 2, July 7, 1844, Jan. 3, 1845, William B. Lewis to Jackson, Dec. 21, 1844, in Bassett, *Jackson Correspondence*, VI, 281, 299-300, 346; Benton, *Thirty Years' View*, II, 589-90, 619; Stephens to James Thomas, May 17, 1844, in Stephens Papers, Library of Congress.

[5] Justin H. Smith, *The Annexation of Texas* (New York, 1911), 225, 227; Wiltse, *Calhoun, Sectionalist*, 182; Crittenden to Chapman Coleman, May 16, 1844, in Crittenden Papers (Duke).

against annexation, but his Kentucky-bred knowledge of the explosive quality of the issue had given him pause. In answer to a query from Crittenden in December, 1843, Clay enumerated his reasons for opposing annexation: it would not create equality between slave and free states, for the latter would continue to expand even at the expense of Canada; the country already had more territory than it could well govern or occupy; besides, it would provoke war with Mexico. He wrote Crittenden of his resentment against Tyler for raising this issue to arouse "discord and distraction," and he agreed that Tyler's recommendation should be passed over "in absolute silence" if possible. He thought that a united vote of southern Whigs for annexation would destroy the party. The best use to make of the Texas question, he concluded, was as a club against abolitionist agitation; northern Whigs must be made to see that if abolitionists forced secession, then Texas would be joined to the slave states. He completely discounted any British interest in annexing the huge territory.[6]

This vow of silence must have been eminently satisfactory to Crittenden and the Whigs, for Clay's lack of restraint was well known, and equally well understood was the fact that nothing could be gained by a public stand on this issue. In discussing the problem with Crittenden more than a year before, Letcher had remarked that Clay might write "too many letters" and thereby hurt his cause. "He must be *caged*—that's the point—*cage him*."[7]

Two months later Clay's friends were jarred out of complacency by Clay's reaction to reports that a treaty had been negotiated for annexation, and that a careful count revealed a constitutional majority of senators would confirm it. The old chief, scenting battle, showed his inconsistency. "If this be true," he wrote Crittenden, "I shall regret extremely that *I* have had no hand in it."[8]

It was at this point that Clay, impatient of inactivity, determined upon a journey through the South. Learning that he was to visit North Carolina, a Whig Tarheel cried out in anguish. Clay's junketing and letterwriting had already cost the party too much, he said. If he would only stay home and keep quiet, they would have less trouble electing him. He was entirely too fond of his "Epistolary

[6] Clay to Crittenden, Dec. 5, 1843, in Crittenden Papers; Poage, *Henry Clay*, 133, 134.
[7] Letcher to Crittenden, June 24, 1842, in Crittenden Papers.
[8] Clay to Crittenden, Feb. 15, 1844, in Crittenden Papers.

Style," and his letters would soon form a collection as vast as those of Walpole. "If St. Paul had been a candidate for the Presidency," the southerner added, "I should have advised him to cut the Corinthians and not let the Hebrews even see his autograph."[9]

Against these delphic warnings, Clay's actions now appear to have had a tragic quality. As he progressed from New Orleans across the gulf states and north through the Carolinas, he convinced himself that the South regarded Texas with the same un-impassioned view that he did. He could find no excitement on the question anywhere, he wrote. But Thurlow Weed, in his study at Albany, had prescient vision of trouble. "Mr. Clay would be far safer at home," he wrote, "But as that cannot be, we must take what comes."[10]

Clay reached Raleigh on the evening of April 12, in time for a gala reception, with bands playing and thousands cheering. The following day he attended a great barbecue, where the crowd almost overwhelmed him in their eagerness to see and hear the Old Coon. Four days later, sitting under a great white oak, with these plaudits stirring his spirit, he wrote a portentous letter. In it he came out flatly against annexation "at the present time" as dangerous and inexpedient. We would be involved in a war with Mexico; we would have to assume Texas' debt of some thirteen million dollars; we would be divided as a country. He showed the letter to Badger and other Whig leaders, who approved it. He then sent it to Crittenden in Washington, with instructions to have it published in the *National Intelligencer*.[11]

Crittenden was aghast. He had been forewarned that Clay was planning some announcement on the issue and had written, earnestly urging caution. But Clay had crossed the Rubicon. He had told many friends of the letter, promising its appearance by the end of the month. "I wish it to appear accordingly," he wrote somewhat haughtily in reply to Crittenden. He did not, he added, have the slightest apprehension about its reception. The Washington atmosphere was overly timid. Crittenden should get out in the country and talk with the people. "I am perfectly sure," Clay went on, "that the degree of favor which prevails at the South towards annexation

---

9 Edward W. Johnston to Willie P. Mangum, Sept. 14, 1843, in *Mangum Papers*, III, 468.

10 Clay to Crittenden, March 24, 1844, in Crittenden Papers; Weed to Granger, April 8, 1844, in Granger Papers.

11 Van Deusen, *Henry Clay*, 363-65; Clay to Crittenden, April 17, 1844, in Coleman, *Crittenden*, I, 219; Poage, *Henry Clay*, 137.

is far less than is believed at Washington." Besides, Van Buren, who was certain to be the Democratic candidate, was also opposed, and therefore Texas would not be an issue in the campaign.[12] (This letter was written a week before Van Buren's letter appeared and indicates that agreement between him and Clay on the question may have been reached when Van Buren had visited Clay at Ashland two years before.)

There was nothing for Crittenden to do but comply, and the letter appeared in the *Intelligencer* on April 27, the same day Van Buren's appeared in the *Globe*. The coincidence in time suggested that Clay's and Van Buren's friends had agreed on the date of publication; but whatever understanding may have existed between Clay and Van Buren, Crittenden and Silas Wright, who acted as their agents, were not privy to it.[13]

At first it appeared that Clay might have accurately evaluated the political effect of the letter, for when the Whig convention met in Baltimore the following week, Texas was hardly mentioned. Clay was nominated by acclamation, and Theodore Frelinghuysen of New Jersey was named his running mate. Rather significantly the convention did not endorse a national bank.[14]

By the time the Democratic convention was held a month later, however, Van Buren's letter had raised a storm of protest from all parts of the South and even from some northern Democrats. The Democrats, thoroughly alarmed, rose to the occasion with bold and resolute action. They unanimously adopted a platform calling for "reannexation" of Texas and "reoccupation" of Oregon. When Van Buren's try for the nomination ended in a stalemate, a compromise was necessary. George Bancroft led the move to James K. Polk, an enthusiastic annexationist, and the landslide followed. Silas Wright, Van Buren's closest friend (and like him an opponent of annexation), declined the vice-presidential nomination, which then went to George M. Dallas of Pennsylvania.

Polk's nomination was a surprise even to himself. A former Speaker of the House of Representatives, he had served one term as governor of Tennessee but had been defeated for reelection to that office in 1841 and again in 1843. As late as the opening of the

---

[12] Clay to Crittenden, April 21, 1844, in Crittenden Papers.

[13] Tyler, *Letters and Times*, II, 308; Wright to Van Buren, April 29, 1844, in Van Buren Papers.

[14] Frankfort *Commonwealth*, May 21, 1844; Tyler, *Letters and Times*, II, 106.

convention his friends were still eagerly seeking the vice-presidential nomination for him on the ticket with Van Buren.[15]

With Van Buren forced to walk the plank in favor of an annexationist, Clay found himself outflanked. Whig strategy had been based on the assumption that Van Buren would be the Locofoco candidate. "Against him all the documents are prepared and ready," wrote Clay six months before, "and we have nothing to do but to publish another Edition of them, without revisal or correction, organize, and go ahead." Thurlow Weed agreed. "Things certainly look blue for Van . . .," he had written in March, "and unless the party rallies after he is nominated I don't see how he is to get through." Crittenden was of like mind. "The feeling that pervades the whole people is that Van Buren *can not* be *elected*," he wrote, "—that his day is passed—and that Clay's has come."[16]

When they first learned of Polk's nomination, Whigs sneered in contempt. Crittenden referred to him as the John Doe of his party, and said he had no more title to the Presidency than "the said John Doe has to the land he is so everlastingly suing for."[17] Tom Marshall thought the Whigs ought to withdraw Clay in disgust. It was "running a blood horse against a jackass," he said.[18] Even the Democrats were astonished. In Columbia, South Carolina, William C. Preston reported that people cheered Polk's name, then asked who he was. Tyler, thinking Polk's defeat a certainty, now decided to reenter the contest as an independent. His friends called a convention in Baltimore and nominated him. He campaigned through most of the summer but then withdrew in favor of Polk.[19]

Unhappily for the Whigs, the two parties were now squarely divided on the issue of annexation. Having taken his stand, Clay was now in a dilemma. A move in either direction would harm him. When the Democrats took such a positive stand, prominent southern and western Whigs came out openly for annexation; and Clay now

[15] John P. Stewart to Duncan McLaurin, June 8, 1848, in Duncan McLaurin Papers, Duke University Library; Powell Moore, "James K. Polk: Tennessee Politician," in *Journal of Southern History*, XVII (1951), 493-516; Eugene Irving McCormac, *James K. Polk: A Political Biography* (Berkeley, 1922), 232-47.

[16] Clay to J. P. Kennedy, Dec. 3, 1843, in Kennedy Papers, Peabody Institute; Weed to Granger, March 11, 1844, Crittenden to Granger, Feb. 10, 1844, in Granger Papers; Clayton to Crittenden, Dec. 9, 1843, in Crittenden Papers.

[17] Crittenden to T. Childs, Aug. 10, 1844, in Crittenden Papers (Pennsylvania).

[18] Frankfort *Commonwealth*, Aug. 6, 1844.

[19] Preston to Crittenden [June 5, 1844], in Crittenden Papers; Tyler to Mary T. Jones, June [21?], 1844, Tyler to Mrs. Waller, Sept. 5, 1844, in Tyler Papers.

felt forced to try to neutralize the issue. In a letter to the editor of the Tuscaloosa, Alabama, *Monitor*, he confessed to no personal objection to annexation. But it should not be pushed at the time, he said, because it was coupled with slavery and thus was opposed by a large part of the Union. The South replied with a storm of abuse, and Clay issued a second "Alabama letter," in which he indicated his willingness to see annexation if it could be effected in such a manner as not to provoke war with Mexico or too much domestic dissension. Although both of these letters were intelligent and farsighted essays, such a stand, however modified and qualified, could not now fail to arouse opposition from one or the other extremes.[20]

Crittenden had begun organizing Clay's campaign in the autumn of 1842. He first formed a central committee at Washington; from this committee lines of communication led to state committees, and from them to county committees all over the Union. Money was raised from merchants interested in a sound and stable currency, from manufacturers eager to hold on to the benefits coming to them from the tariff of 1842, and from personal friends of Clay devoted to his promotion.[21] Through the fall and winter of 1843-1844 Crittenden carried on an extensive correspondence with Whig leaders, aimed at bringing back into the fold defectors like Rives and Webster. By the end of January he was confident that both could be counted on. He even hoped to capitalize on Calhoun's ancient hostility to Van Buren and to win support for Clay from Calhoun's following. He urged Whig editors to woo the Carolinian. Vindictiveness should be put aside. "The latchstring is always out," he wrote. He even attempted at one time to win Tyler's support, observing that even "a little helps in these hard times."[22]

With the Baltimore convention over, Crittenden hurried home. His presence was demanded at Whig gatherings in Kentucky. A state Whig convention assembled at Lexington on July 3 to ratify the work of the Baltimore convention, and Crittenden must be there. The following week he spoke in Louisville and then went on a tour of the Green River country. Although he had removed from that region more than two decades before, the people there still claimed

[20] Poage, *Henry Clay*, 143, 145.

[21] Clay to Letcher, Aug. 15 [1842], in Crittenden Papers (Duke); Alexander Porter to Crittenden, Dec. 2, 1843, in Crittenden Papers.

[22] Letcher to Crittenden, Jan. 6, Feb. 4, 1844, Abbott Lawrence to Crittenden, April 11, 1844, in Crittenden Papers; Crittenden to Letcher, Dec. 10, 1843, Jan. 28, 1844, in Coleman, *Crittenden*, I, 210, 215.

him as their own. His journey through the region was like a triumphal procession, as he went from burgoo to barbecue, "instructing" the people in the principles of Whiggery. He was back in Bardstown at a great barbecue at the end of July. The month of August he spent in northern Kentucky and in Ohio. In September he went to west Tennessee, where he spoke at Nashville, Jackson, and Memphis.[23] Somehow or other, a Whig congressman there wrote him, Crittenden had his "fingers up to the knuckles in the eyes of the people of Tennessee." He added that meetings there "would have been almost an abortion, if you had refused your presence."[24]

In Polk's own community in west Tennessee, Crittenden heaped scorn upon the Democratic candidate. Polk was, he said, Van Buren "in *miniature*—a small duodecimo edition, full of errors." He would make a suitable successor to Van Buren and Tyler, because he had "the vices of the first and the base littleness of the second." He was trained in Van Buren's school, but the pupil's capacity was "quite inferior to that of his master," and was about the equivalent of Tyler's. What, he asked, could be expected of such a candidate?[25]

By late summer Whig prospects did not seem as certain as they had in June. The first indication that all was not well came in the Kentucky gubernatorial election in early August. Harrison had carried the state four years before by 25,000 votes, and Letcher had won the governor's office the same year by more than 15,000. With Clay the candidate for the Presidency, Whigs expected an even more impressive margin for William Owsley, the Whig candidate for governor, who was opposing Democrat William O. Butler. But when returns were in, it was found that Owsley's margin was a bare 4,600.[26]

Throughout the nation Whigs were stunned, and Crittenden was kept busy explaining that the gubernatorial vote would not influence the presidential race in Kentucky. Clay would still carry the state by 20,000 votes. Owsley's margin, he said, was reduced by "local, trifling & temporary circumstances" that would not be a factor in November. He exhorted Whig leaders to "Keep our friends in your

[23] Crittenden to Clayton, June 17, 1844, in Clayton Papers, Library of Congress, Frankfort *Commonwealth*, June 25, July 16, 30, Sept. 17, 1844; Frankfort *Kentucky Yeoman*, quoted *ibid.*, July 30, 1844; Crittenden's Lexington speech, in Crittenden Papers (in Volume IX).

[24] Ephraim H. Foster to Crittenden, July 13, 1844, in Crittenden Papers.

[25] Notes for speech, in Crittenden Papers (Duke).

[26] Kerr, *History of Kentucky*, II, 717-18; Frankfort *Commonwealth*, Aug. 27, 1844.

state up to the work constantly, in season & out of season." To each man he wrote that his state was crucial and must be carried.[27]

But there was trouble in New York, without which victory was unlikely. Antislavery elements in the western part of the state, unwilling to accept a slaveholder as their candidate, were again supporting the Liberty party, with former Kentuckian James G. Birney as their candidate. Even so, Whigs might have carried New York had it not been for Clay's Alabama letters, which alienated anti-slavery voters. "Ugly letter, that to Alabama," wrote Weed. "Can't stand many such."[28]

To make matters worse, New York Democrats, in an effort to unite Barnburners and Hunkers, had drafted Silas Wright as their gubernatorial candidate. Wright was one of the ablest and most popular men in the state and would add thousands to Polk's vote. "The contest is to be the fiercest ever known, even in our fierce state," Granger wrote. Crittenden wrote daily inspirational messages to Whig leaders there: to Charles A. Davis, to Thomas Childs, to Weed, and to Granger. "Upon your state the Whigs have all along relied with confidence," he wrote one. On the vote of New York "in all probability may depend the Presidential election," he wrote another. "Be in the field constantly, & have no rest but in victory," he wrote a third.[29]

The election was close, so close that if Clay could have obtained a third of the 15,800 votes that went for Birney in New York, he would have carried that state and with it the electoral college. Even so, he received 6,500 more votes in New York than Harrison had received four years before when Harrison carried the state by 13,000. But Polk got 5,000 votes more than Clay and thus carried the state by a small plurality. Clay carried Kentucky by less than half the 20,000 votes Crittenden had predicted. It was the last time Clay would test his strength in a popular election.[30]

[27] Crittenden to Thomas Childs, Aug. 10, 1844, in Crittenden Papers (Pennsylvania); Crittenden to Granger, Sept. 21, 1844, in Granger Papers; Crittenden to Waddy Thompson, Oct. 18, 1844, Charles A. Davis to Crittenden, Aug. 31, Sept. 21, 25, 30, Oct. 1, 1844, Granger to Crittenden, Sept. 29, 1844, in Crittenden Papers.
[28] Weed to Granger, Sept. 3, 1844, in Granger Papers.
[29] Granger to Crittenden, Sept. 29, 1844, Charles A. Davis to Crittenden, Oct. 1, 3, 1844, in Crittenden Papers; Crittenden to Thomas Childs, Aug. 10, Oct. 25, 1844, in Crittenden Papers (Pennsylvania); Crittenden to Granger, Sept. 21, 1844, in Granger Papers.
[30] Ambrose Spencer to Clay, Nov. 21, 1844, in Clay Papers; Frankfort *Commonwealth*, Nov. 26, 1844.

Book Two

PARTY LEADER

CHAPTER X

Mr. Polk's War

Now BEGAN the chain of events leading inexorably to secession and civil war. The election proved the popularity of annexation, and Tyler did not wait for Polk to carry out the mandate of the people. When Congress met in December, he recommended that the Lone Star republic be annexed by joint resolution. Such a resolution passed the House in late January and came before the Senate in early February. There Benton offered a substitute, authorizing a commission to negotiate a treaty of annexation and suggesting pacification of Mexico. A treaty would require ratification by a two-thirds majority in the Senate, whereas the joint resolution would require only a simple majority in each house. Then Robert J. Walker of Mississippi offered an amendment joining Benton's resolution to the House resolution and giving the President discretion to achieve annexation by either method. Crittenden objected, and on the evening of February 26 he spoke against annexation in general and Walker's amendment in particular.[1]

One by one he took up the arguments of the annexationists and examined them. Completely ignoring the Louisiana Purchase, he questioned the power of Congress to admit new states erected out of "foreign" territory. True, he said, Article IV of the Constitution provided for the admission of new states, but the founding fathers had had in mind only the admission of states "arising out of the bosom of the old thirteen States, and territory in the neighborhood . . . belonging to the States, but out of the limits of the State confines." He quoted from the *Federalist*, from Justice Story, and from Jefferson to support this view. Furthermore, he said, the Constitution provided only one method of acquiring foreign territory: by treaty, negotiated by the executive and approved by the Senate. Had there been any other method, the framers of the Constitution, who had carefully weighed the grants of power to the national government, would have explicitly stated it.

Crittenden feared also that annexation would disturb our foreign relations. He urged patience. "The hand that grasps ambitiously, dishonestly, or unlawfully at the plunder of others, particularly when they are in a defenseless condition," he said, "is sure to be festered with the leprosy of dishonor or disgrace." Finally, he condemned the ambiguity that had resulted when Walker joined Benton's substitute to the House resolution. He thought that specifying the mode of annexation was imperative. If the Senate meant to annex Texas by joint resolution, let it say so and not leave the decision to the President.[2]

It was on the whole an able speech, delivered with little preparation, and without even a note to use in marshaling his arguments. The *National Intelligencer* called it a "brilliant speech." A correspondent of the Baltimore *Patriot* called Crittenden "the *first* orator of the Senate," surpassing even Rufus Choate, who had, he thought, "held the palm until that day." This was partisan praise. But an annexationist who heard him was equally impressed. He called it a "splendid speech . . . full of arguments & eloquence & by far the best speech I have heard since I came to Washington." "With all my prejudices in favor of the subject he was speaking *against*," he concluded, "I am satisfied that he is by far the best debater in Congress." However persuasive Crittenden may have been, he was

[1] Richardson, *Messages and Papers of the Presidents*, V, 2193-98; Tyler, *Letters and Times*, II, 360-62; Benton, *Thirty Years' View*, II, 633; *Congressional Globe*, 28 Cong., 2 Sess., 240, 271, 278-80, 287, 308, 315-16, 328-30.

[2] *Congressional Globe*, 28 Cong., 2 Sess., 358-62.

unable to stay the tide. Walker's amendment was adopted twenty-seven to twenty-five, and the amended resolution then passed. The House accepted the Walker amendment, and the President signed the joint resolution on March 1.[3]

Considerable blame for what followed must be attributed to divisions within the Democratic party. Polk was a man of courage and of better-than-average ability, although he lacked true attributes of greatness. Overshadowed by perhaps a dozen men in his own party, he was forced to surrender much to win support in the election from the diverse elements of his party, whose factions were primarily concerned throughout his administration with promoting their leaders, Calhoun, Cass, or Van Buren. Polk was greatly indebted to Silas Wright, Van Buren, and their Barnburners for carrying New York and the election. He attempted to repay them by offering the Treasury Department to Wright; when Wright declined, Polk asked Van Buren to recommend a New Yorker for the War Department. But Van Buren delayed in answering, whereupon Polk named William L. Marcy, whose leadership of the rival Hunker faction in New York made his name anathema to Van Buren and Wright. This action only compounded problems of the party, already split irreconcilably between the Van Buren-Blair-Benton-Wright wing and the Calhoun nullifiers. Needing the support of both factions, Polk decided not to retain Calhoun as Secretary of State. On the other hand, Polk distrusted Blair, who had never been his friend, and against Jackson's advice he abandoned Blair's *Globe* as the official organ of the party. Thus it was that Blair was forced to sell the *Globe* to Thomas Ritchie of the Richmond *Examiner*, who renamed the old paper the *Daily Union*.[4]

Complicating Polk's difficulties with his party was the Oregon question. Since 1818, that vast country, extending from California to Alaska and from the crest of the Rockies to the Pacific, had been jointly occupied by the United States and Great Britain. The recent

[3] Washington *National Intelligencer*, Feb. 28, 1845; Baltimore *Patriot*, quoted in Frankfort *Commonwealth*, April 8, 1845; H. M. Judge to "Dear Wife," March 1, 1845 (copy), in Crittenden Papers; *Congressional Globe*, 28 Cong., 2 Sess., 362, 372, 385; Benton, *Thirty Years' View*, II, 636-37; Tyler, *Letters and Times*, II, 360-62.

[4] McCormac, *Polk*, 254-62 *passim*, 291-98, 323, 328, 331, 333; "Recollections of an Old Stager," XLVII (1873), 253; John M. Clayton to Martin McMichael, March 6, 1845, in Clayton Papers; Duff Green to Polk, Jan. 2, 1845, in Duff Green Papers; Benton, *Thirty Years' View*, II, 650, 651-53; C. F. M. Noland to Crittenden, Nov. 13, 1847, in Crittenden Papers.

influx of American immigrants there, however, had created a population eager for incorporation into the Union. Inspired perhaps by
southern clamor for Texas, northern Democrats began asserting
American claims to all of Oregon months before the Baltimore
convention. Southern delegates to the convention accepted these
claims, and the platform adopted there coupled the "reannexation"
of Texas to the "reoccupation" of all Oregon up to 54° 40', the
southern boundary of Alaska.

Despite this action, Oregon had not been a major issue in the
campaign that year. Its incorporation in the platform may have been
mere sugar coating to make the acquisition of Texas more palatable
to northern tastes. There was no prospect that Britain would
relinquish all of Oregon without a struggle, and after Texas was
annexed in the spring of 1845, southern Democrats were not at all
eager for war with England just to gain a "frozen waste" in the
North. But Polk in his inaugural address had echoed the Baltimore
Platform's statement, that America's right to all of Oregon was
"clear and unquestionable." Meanwhile, Tyler had been negotiating
with Britain and had offered to divide the territory at 49°, with free
navigation of the Columbia River for British vessels. Polk, inheriting
the unfinished negotiations, felt obligated to renew the offer of 49°,
but without the right to use the Columbia. When the British
peremptorily declined, Polk withdrew the offer and reasserted United
States claims to 54° 40'.[5]

Almost at once the British did an about-face and asked for a
resubmission of 49° as a basis for further negotiation, but Polk,
now obligated to the 54° 40' faction in his own party, refused.
Democrats in the Senate were about equally divided between southerners, who advocated compromise at 49°, and midwesterners, who
insisted on 54° 40'. Whigs were generally in favor of compromise,
and together with southern Democrats formed a majority. Polk had
overestimated the zeal of the nation for expansion, and now he faced
a quandary. He must choose between 49° and 54° 40', the very thing
he could not afford to do. To insist upon the latter might lead to
hostilities, with a large congressional majority opposed to war. To

[5] Edwin A. Miles, " 'Fifty-four Forty or Fight'—An American Political Legend,"
in *Mississippi Valley Historical Review*, XLIV (1957-1958), 292, 301-302; Daniel
Webster to Mr. Javen, Feb. 2, 1846, in Webster, *Correspondence*, II, 216; Frederick
Merk, "Presidential Fevers," in *Mississippi Valley Historical Review*, XLVII (1960-
1961), 6-8; McCormac, *Polk*, 554-72.

accept 49° would be an ignominious retreat from the strong position he had already become committed to and would lead to loss of further support for the administration. In this dilemma Polk much preferred that Congress settle the issue and save him embarrassment by directing him to follow one policy or the other.[6]

The Oregon joint-occupation treaty included the provision that it could be terminated by either party on a year's notice, and it was now agreed by all factions that time had come for termination. Polk had urged it in his annual message. But an issue developed over the tone of the resolution calling for termination. Polk's message to Congress had bristled with bellicose claims to all of Oregon as well as with requests for the strengthening of the army and navy looking toward British refusal to give way.[7]

To Polk's support came the chairman of the Senate Committee on Foreign Relations, Democrat William Allen of Ohio. In the brilliant company of the Senate of the 1840s, his was but a dim light. Limited both in education and in ability, he attempted to compensate by an overabundance of brusque and aggressive self-assurance. The vituperative Charles Sumner called him "a tall, tobacco chewing spitting loud voiced ferocious blackguard" who was using his position as chairman to advance his presidential ambitions. Allen introduced for his committee a belligerent resolution which would have given offense to Great Britain. Besides, it would have rescued Polk from his dilemma, for it "authorized and required" the President to give notice of intent to annul the treaty at the end of one year. Crittenden then offered a substitute to the committee resolution. Couched in conciliatory language, it left to the President the final decision as to the giving of notice.[8]

On February 10 Allen opened the debate with a speech extolling American virtue and denouncing British cupidity. England, he predicted, would not dare fight a war over Oregon because she was shrewd enough to know she could not win on that ground against us. He dismissed British pretensions to the disputed territory as "absolute frivolity," and revived old War Hawk cries of 1812,

[6] Merk, "Presidential Fevers," 10-19; Crittenden to Letcher, March 9, 1846, W. C. Rives to Crittenden, March 9, 1846, in Coleman, *Crittenden*, I, 235, 237; Lexington *Observer and Reporter*, April 28, 1846.

[7] *Congressional Globe*, 29 Cong., 1 Sess., 45, 55-56.

[8] Merk, "Presidential Fevers," 12-13; Sumner to [Richard Rathbone], May 14, 1846, quoted *ibid.*, 12-13; *Congressional Globe*, 29 Cong., 1 Sess., 76, 162, 182-83, 198.

accusing Britain of inciting Indians in the Northwest to barbarous attacks on women and children. He even lashed the British for impressing American seamen four decades before.

A fortnight later Crittenden replied, urging arbitration. We were wrong, he said, to insist that our title was unquestionable. "Upon what right," he asked, "do we claim this mighty prerogative above all other nations?" It would be an "elevation of the age" and a "majestic spectacle" if we should submit the dispute to arbitration. Such a course would gain us more in international esteem and honor than the value of all Oregon. Giving only one year's notice of termination would be acting in "intemperate haste"; two years' notice should be given, to allow for further negotiation. Some senators, he said, were urging war to display our courage, but he decried such bellicose talk. "We have no necessity to go to war to make a character," he said. We already had a reputation for courage and need not boast of our might. We had more; we had honor, which was "a grand characteristic of a great nation."[9]

Debate went on for another six weeks. Calhoun, who had now returned to the Senate, came to Crittenden's support. The chief protagonist of the slavery interests had been extremely belligerent with Britain the year before over Texas and had pushed through annexation with complete disregard of all questions of international ethics. Perfectly willing to fight Mexico, Britain, or anyone else for Texas, he was unwilling to fight for a northern wilderness that could never enhance the slave power. On March 16, in an able speech, he advocated an equitable settlement and urged that notice be given in conciliatory language. He was followed by Webster, who spoke in a similar vein, even more effectively. In the House, Jefferson Davis observed that if our title to all of Oregon was as unquestionable as Polk said it was, Polk had erred egregiously in offering to compromise at 49° in the first place. A vote on the resolutions was set for April 16, and Crittenden was chosen by the conservatives to conclude debate for their side.[10]

By this time it was clearly understood that peace or war hung in the balance, and excitement grew as the drama was played out. An

[9] Merk, "Presidential Fevers," 17-19; *Congressional Globe*, 29 Cong., 1 Sess., 350-51, 357, 360-64, 430-31, Appendix, 834-42.

[10] *Congressional Globe*, 29 Cong., 1 Sess., 502-506, 680; Merk, "Presidential Fevers," 23-25; Wiltse, *Calhoun, Sectionalist*, 260-61; McCormac, *Polk*, 59.

immense crowd gathered in the Senate galleries to hear the final debate, and business in the House was suspended as its members crowded into the Senate chamber. Crittenden began with a review of the history of the discovery and exploration of Oregon. Britain's claims, he said, antedated our own and were of a similar nature—discovery and settlement. Accordingly, if we relied on our title, we could not, in reason, refuse to recognize hers. He conceded that notice must be given, but called for language more conciliatory than that suggested by the President's message, which would give offense and would not promote a peaceable settlement.

If war should come, he said, woe unto the President if he had not done all in his power to settle the issue peaceably. A war between the two nations on this question would be a "needless war." Not merely party politicians would be the judges of him who was responsible, nor could "Baltimore resolutions" be pleaded in justification. "The people of the whole civilized world" would be his judges, and consequences of such a war would be incalculable. On the other hand, if we would only be patient, it was inevitable that in time the territory would be ours. Why, he asked, "pluck that fruit green today which tomorrow will fall full ripe into your hand?" He did not, he quickly added, say this in a spirit of aggrandizement. We must be just to all nations and violate no rights. We must submit to no injustices ourselves, but at the same time we must respect the rights of others, the weak as well as the strong.

We must not, therefore, give notice in the spirit of "rash and reckless men." Rather, we should do so as wise men, with moderation, with firmness, and "in such a temper that we may be prepared to meet the issue before both God and man." He would not refuse to accept all of Oregon if we could get it peaceably and honorably. But this could not be. Repeatedly in the past we had offered to settle at 49°. How, in reason, could we now insist on more? Conciliatory notice would enable the two nations to "take each other's hand and to prosecute an effectual negotiation for peace."[11]

When Crittenden finished, Allen took the floor. By now he despaired of passage of the committee resolution. Instead, he wanted to take up a somewhat milder resolution, offered by the House, that "directed" Polk to act, thus saving him the embarrassment of making

[11] *Congressional Globe*, 29 Cong., 1 Sess., Appendix, 842-47.

the decision. Allen explained that since the House had approved its resolution by an overwhelming majority, he thought it best, in deference to that body, to vote on its resolution first. This was agreed to, but Allen's guns were spiked when Reverdy Johnson offered Crittenden's amendment to the House resolution. Not only was Crittenden's amendment more conciliatory than the House resolution, but it placed full responsibility on the President to determine whether or not to give notice. Then Allen countered with a bellicose amendment calling on Congress to provide for the defense of United States citizens in Oregon and repeating our "just title" to all of the territory.

Allen's amendment was defeated twenty-two to thirty-two, and Crittenden's amendment then carried, thirty to twenty-four. Allen was furious. His judgment, never good under the best of circumstances, now deserted him completely. He took the floor and proceeded to lecture the Senate on its shortcomings, much as a frustrated schoolmaster might admonish a class of truant boys. The President, he said, had asked for advice, and senators had told him to use his discretion. The House had shown a patriotic spirit with "a unanimity unparalleled upon any question." The consideration that was due "that great organ of the popular will" should have induced concurrence on the part of the Senate. Not so, however. Now there would be a divided Congress, he predicted, because the House would never accept the despicable Crittenden resolution. The Senate had shown "a frightful unwillingness to meet responsibility." Opposition to 54° 40′ was unpatriotic, pro-British, and even treasonable.[12]

His listeners were stunned. Not only were his words in questionable taste and his manner unbearable, but it was a violation of the rules of the Senate to refer in debate to actions of the House. For what seemed like minutes, not a voice was raised. All were speechless. Finally Crittenden, as chief of the opposition, rose to answer. Allen's bullying had stirred him to a cold fury. Pulling himself to his full height, he proceeded, in a half hour's speech, to administer to Allen "a tongue-lashing such as is seldom heard in the decorous precincts of the Senate."

He rebuked Allen for departing from the spirit of the Constitution

[12] *Congressional Globe*, 29 Cong., 1 Sess., 678-83.

and the rules of the Senate, saying that he had "violated the order of the Senate and treated it with disrespect." Allen's plea for unanimity with the House seemed peculiarly inappropriate, for Allen himself was in a small minority of the Senate and was urging the majority to abandon precipitately their own opinion "and go over to the very small minority to which he belongs." As Crittenden warmed to his subject, his manner became more fervent. His black eyes, ordinarily calm and lacking in radiance, "sparkled like diamonds" and seemed, according to one observer, to penetrate the very vitals of his adversary. Who, he asked, had commissioned Allen to lecture the Senate in such a manner? How dared he denounce as "a miserable paltry thing" a resolution adopted by the body of which he was a member? How could he commit the indignity of condemning the Senate for amending a resolution of the House? Surely he would not ask the House to pass a measure just because the Senate had. How could he demand that the Senate pass a House resolution without amendment? "I cannot and will not sit here and allow such language and see such airs of superiority and supercilious arrogance without a reply," he said.[13]

"I feel proud that I am a Kentuckian," wrote an observer in Washington that night. Crittenden had completely deflated "the bully from Ohio" in a manner that should last Allen for a lifetime, wrote another. The New York *Herald* reporter was also overjoyed. The Kentuckian had riddled "the greater Ajax" with his barbed arrows, while other Democrats sat by speechless, refusing to come to the aid of their comrade. From Boston came word that both Whigs and Democrats were delighted at the castigation of Allen.[14]

The exchange between Allen and Crittenden marked the end of debate. By a vote of forty to fourteen the Senate approved the House resolution, with the Crittenden amendment. Then, in an unprecedented rebuke to Allen, his colleagues deliberately dropped his name from the conference committee to work out differences between the Senate and House versions. The conference committee quickly accepted Crittenden's amendment as a basis for settlement,

[13] *Congressional* Globe, 29 Cong., 1 Sess., 681-83, 692; Merk, "Presidential Fevers," 26.
[14] Washington *National Intelligencer*, April 17, 1846; Baltimore *Patriot*, quoted in Lexington *Observer and Reporter*, April 28, 1846; New York *Herald*, April 17, 1846; Abbott Lawrence to Crittenden, April 23, 1846, in Crittenden Papers.

and both houses approved the committee report, 142 to 46 in the House and 42 to 10 in the Senate. Later, when Polk referred to the Senate a British proposal to divide Oregon at the forty-ninth parallel, that body further humiliated Allen in bypassing his Committee on Foreign Relations, and by taking direct action to accept the British offer.[15]

Crittenden's conduct in the debate had been marked by mature statesmanship. His victory over the northern Democratic expansionists, however, had been aided by changed circumstances. When the British corn laws were repealed, farmers of the Midwest were more disposed to accept compromise on the territorial question. The prospect of increased sales of wheat, rye, and maize was more alluring to many of them than distant wilderness acres. On the other hand, the British became more willing to accept the forty-ninth parallel as the boundary when they perceived that Democratic majorities in Congress would almost certainly press for reduced tariff rates. The prospect of increased sales of British goods, particularly railroad irons, led British Whigs to bring pressure on the Tory ministry of Sir Robert Peel. Nevertheless, it was Crittenden himself, as leader of the opposition to Polk, who forced the Democratic administration to recede from its belligerent position. A Whig editor called his victory the "triumph of wise counsels over turbulent measures." And a southern Democratic editor praised Crittenden's closing speech on April 16, saying it was comparable to the speeches of Charles James Fox and Edmund Burke. "We wish," added the editor, "he was a democrat."[16]

While the Senate was debating the Oregon resolution, the Walker tariff bill was being forged in the House. It provided drastic reductions in rates established in 1842, from over 100 percent *ad valorem* to 30 percent or less on such items as shirtings, cordage, and iron products. Although it was well known that the issue would be close in the Senate, Crittenden showed little interest in it. The mantle of Clay supposedly rested on his shoulders now, but he seemed willing for the bill to pass, provided it could be carried without Whig

---

[15] *Congressional Globe*, 29 Cong., 1 Sess., 683, 692, 703, 717, 721; Merk, "Presidential Fevers," 27; *Senate Documents*, 29 Cong., 1 Sess., No. 489; Benton, *Thirty Years' View*, II, 674-76.

[16] Frankfort *Commonwealth*, May 5, 1846; Marion (Ala.) *News*, quoted *ibid.*, May 19, 1846.

help. Crittenden's lackadaisical attitude toward the Walker bill was consistent with his long-held middle-of-the-road tariff views. Besides, he had been assured by Abbott Lawrence, industrial tycoon and ardent protectionist, that "we can *live*" under the bill. Lawrence even urged placing tea and coffee on the free list, lest Whigs be denounced for "taxing the poor for the benefit of the rich."[17]

Meanwhile, United States relations with Mexico were going from bad to worse. Texas, as a department of Mexico, had extended only to the Nueces River, but after her declaration of independence had claimed territory to the Rio Grande. When Texas was annexed, the Whigs had raised the issue of the boundary in order to spell out United States commitments for defense. The joint resolution of annexation specified no definite boundary, but Polk early made it clear that he would accept Texas' claim. In the fall of 1845, after Texas had ratified the joint annexation bill, Polk sent John Slidell to Mexico City to negotiate agreement on the Rio Grande as boundary and to purchase additional territory, including New Mexico and California. Before Slidell reached Mexico, however, his mission had failed. The Herrera government had been overthrown in a bloodless revolution by General Mariano Paredes, and the new government was committed to assert Mexican sovereignty over all of Texas. Polk had resolved that if Mexico refused to receive Slidell and to agree to territorial cessions as compensation for American claims against her, war would be justified.[18]

Accordingly, when Slidell was brusquely refused recognition by the Paredes government, Polk prepared for war. General Zachary Taylor, already in Texas with an army of several thousand, was dispatched to the Rio Grande, and a United States fleet was stationed off the Mexican coast. Polk had decided to ask Congress for a declaration of war even before dispatches reached him from Taylor on May 9 stating that Mexican troops had crossed to the north bank of the Rio Grande, attacked a small detachment of his force, and killed or captured three score. This message relieved Polk, for he sorely needed a war with Mexico to unite his badly divided party behind his program of expansion to the Pacific. Now he did not need to ask for a declaration of war; war already existed. On Monday,

---

[17] Lawrence to Crittenden, July 24, 1846, in Crittenden Papers.
[18] McCormac, *Polk*, 373, 396, 403, 406, 407.

May 11, he sent a message to Congress stating that Mexico had "invaded our territory and shed American blood upon the American soil." He asked Congress merely to "recognize the existence of the war" and to place at his disposal "the means of prosecuting the war with vigor." There was, indeed, much justification for subsequent Whig charges that Polk purposely provoked the war by ordering Taylor to the Rio Grande.[19]

In response to Polk's request, the House quickly (and almost unanimously) passed a bill providing for prosecution of the war, but the Senate acted with greater deliberation. There, amendment after amendment sought to strike from the preamble language that justified the course of the administration. Crittenden expressed dismay at the President's message, observing that the territory occupied by Taylor's army was claimed also by Mexico. We had been, he said, the first nation of the world to nourish the republics of Latin America. Now we were the first to go to war with one of them, and that one our nearest neighbor, who had been weakened through anarchy and revolution. He feared that the course we had pursued was not "that generous and forbearing policy that ought to be exercised by a powerful and great republic." He saw no reason why our troops should have gone to the Rio Grande. Occupying disputed territory was a warlike act, a "national insult" to Mexico. Why had the government placed its army in such a position? Hostilities must have been foreseen, and they had come.

Nevertheless, "American blood had been spilt," whether on our soil or on Mexico's, and all must now stand by the country while hostilities existed. He was willing to do all that "exigency of the case demands for the defense of the country." He urged, however, that the government send a special mission made up of Clay, Van Buren, Calhoun, and Benton to make peace. Between every blow we struck, he said, we should remember it fell on the head of a neighbor.[20]

Such arguments were to no avail. The Democratic majority in the Senate was united on the war issue, and it voted down all Whig amendments to the preamble, twenty-six to twenty. The bill then

[19] Richardson, *Messages and Papers of the Presidents*, VI, 2287-93; McCormac, *Polk*, 414.
[20] Wiltse, *Calhoun, Sectionalist*, 282; *Congressional Globe*, 29 Cong., 1 Sess., 783, 787-88, 802, 804.

passed forty to two, Clayton of Delaware and John Davis of Massachusetts being the only dissenters. Calhoun, Berrien, and George Evans of Maine were present but did not vote. Crittenden, when his name was called, voted "aye, except for the preamble."

The Congress of this period was wracked by partisanship to an extraordinary degree, and Polk was unable to secure its unqualified support of his war aims. Hardly had hostilities begun, when it became known that the sly, secretive Polk[21] had aided Santa Anna, the exiled Mexican leader, to return to Mexico in order to secure Mexican acceptance of Polk's demands. When Santa Anna's subsequent behavior demonstrated how completely Polk had been duped, Polk's ego, but not his self-confidence, was wounded. Besides, Polk distrusted all Van Buren Democrats, and he thought that all Whigs except Mangum and Crittenden were depraved both morally and politically. He recorded in his diary that Mangum "though a Whig, is a gentleman."[22]

Polk was particularly unhappy with his top military command. Scott and Taylor he thought incompetent, unreliable, "disloyal to the administration and interested solely in their own political advancement."[23] Although Taylor had never been active in politics, he was thought to be a Whig. After Palo Alto, Monterrey, and Buena Vista he became a national hero, and when Polk sought to hold him to a defensive line in northern Mexico, he suspected Polk of ulterior motives. Nor could Polk turn to Scott with greater assurance. Scott was a capable general but a pronounced Whig. He had been a candidate for the Whig nomination in 1844, and he would never cease to yearn for the Presidency.

Scott was naturally eager for the field and began preparations to depart for Mexico. But Polk and Secretary of War Marcy irked Scott by prodding him to get on with the war, without taking time for precautions that Scott thought necessary. Finally, Scott, in a private letter that became public, complained of the "simultaneous fire" against his front and rear, and for this he was ordered to stay at home while Polk looked for a Democratic general. For a time he thought he had found one. Thomas Hart Benton had been a militia lieutenant colonel in the War of 1812 and was ambitious

21 McCormac, *Polk*, 250.
22 Quoted in McCormac, *Polk*, 548. See also Merk, "Presidential Fevers," 12.
23 McCormac, *Polk*, 463.

for further military glory. He quickly made his peace with Polk when war came and suggested that Polk make him lieutenant general, thus elevating him above both Scott and Taylor. Polk was willing to oblige, but there was no legal provision for such a rank, and when Polk asked Congress to create it, Congress refused. Forced to use Whig generals to fight the war, Polk never gave them his full confidence, and his distrust of them was reciprocated. Taylor composed long letters to his friends charging the President with treachery toward him, and Scott years later recorded that he considered Polk "an enemy more to be dreaded than Santa Anna and all his hosts."[24]

Many of the charges against Polk must be attributed to the lively and paranoiac imaginings of his political enemies, for the Mexican War was the most partisan of struggles. One Democrat wrote that the war would manufacture "Presidents, Governors, Judges, and members of Congress for forty years to come." Polk, he added, never dreamed that his order to Taylor to march to the Rio Grande would have such political consequences as it promised.[25]

Although Crittenden believed the war unnecessary, he supported measures to prosecute it to a successful conclusion. When Tom Corwin offered a resolution branding the war as "unjust and dishonorable" and saying that it had been started not by Congress but by the President, Crittenden voted against it. But Crittenden did not support Polk's war aims. From the beginning Polk had dreamed of vast territorial acquisitions. For this purpose he had commissioned Nicholas P. Trist to proceed with Scott's army into Mexico and to treat for such a settlement. But Trist started out by quarreling with Scott, and his mission seemed destined to failure. Disgruntled at Trist's lack of progress, Polk recalled him, only to have his orders coolly disregarded while Trist proceeded to negotiate the Treaty of Guadalupe Hidalgo. By its terms Mexico accepted the Rio Grande as the Texas boundary and ceded New Mexico and California, with all the territory between, to the United States. In return the United States agreed to pay $15,000,000 to Mexico and assumed responsibility for claims of United States citizens against Mexico. Polk decided to

[24] Milo M. Quaife (ed.), *The Diary of James K. Polk during his Presidency, 1845-1849*, 4 vols (Chicago, 1910), II, 217-28, 268-306, 347; Anthony Butler to Crittenden, June 15, 1846, in Crittenden Papers; Richardson, *Messages and Papers of the Presidents*, VI, 2358; Buchanan to Blair, Nov. 27, 1849, in Van Buren Papers; McCormac, *Polk*, 463-64, 494.

[25] R. K. Crallé to Duff Green, June 15, 1847, in Duff Green Papers.

accept the treaty effected by his discredited envoy and on February 22, 1848, submitted it to the Senate.[26]

Crittenden was pleased at the prospect of peace, but he objected to the onerous territorial cession the treaty exacted. He moved to resubmit it with instructions to modify the boundaries. Because of our power and of Mexico's weakness, he said, we should not exact terms that went "beyond the strict measures of our rightful claims." War "should not be waged for the acquisition of territory," he said. If Mexico were willing to settle any "just claims" against her by a cession of land, well and good, but we should be willing to accept territory "of more limited extent." The Wilmot Proviso, which would prohibit slavery in any territory acquired, had already passed the House a number of times, and there was talk of secession if it should pass the Senate. This vast acquisition, Crittenden said, would stimulate the controversy. It was to avert this crisis, as well as to set a "commendable example of justice and moderation . . . before the world," that Crittenden urged adoption of his resolutions. But once more the Democratic majority closed ranks, and with help from a few southern Whigs, they beat back the resolution to resubmit by a vote of eighteen to thirty. The treaty as drawn was then approved by the Senate thirty-eight to fourteen.[27]

Crittenden's reputation and stature were such that he could have a free hand in supporting war measures while at the same time opposing the war itself and the administration's territorial ambitions. But a young congressman from Sangamon County, Illinois, was not permitted to enjoy this same freedom. Abraham Lincoln thought he was governing his own conduct in the House at this time by the example set for him by Crittenden. Actually, however, Lincoln had been less temperate than Crittenden in his criticism of "Mr. Polk's War." In December, 1847, he had introduced a resolution asking for a designation of the "spot" on our soil where American blood had been shed. In speaking on the resolution, he denounced Polk as "a miserably perplexed man." His law partner in Springfield, Billy Herndon, urged him to desist, and a Whig politician there suggested that he be less caustic in his criticism of Polk and model his behavior

[26] *Congressional Globe,* 29 Cong., 2 Sess., 29-30, 131, 171-72; *Niles' Register,* LXXI (1846-1847), 244, 292, 331-33, 339; Morrow, *Life and Speeches of Thomas Corwin,* 48, 51; Richardson, *Messages and Papers of the Presidents,* VI, 2423-24.

[27] Washington *National Intelligencer,* June 10, 1848 (these remarks were made on March 7); *Senate Executive Document No. 52,* 30 Cong., 1 Sess., VII, 36.

after Crittenden. This was too much for the young railsplitter. He had, he replied, been doing precisely that. Crittenden's conduct in the Senate, he added, had indeed been his model. "Wherein," he asked, "is my position different from his?" Crittenden had never approved, he said, of Polk's conduct in bringing on the war, or of his mode of prosecuting it. True, Crittenden voted supply, but so did he. What, then, was the difference between their courses, he asked in frustration, "except that he is a great man and I am a small one?"[28]

It was in the midst of the Mexican War that Crittenden, for the second time in a decade, became involved in an affair of honor. The Graves-Cilley duel had ended in tragedy. This one also brought Crittenden grief, although in a less dramatic way. Alexander Barrow, senator from Louisiana, was one of Crittenden's most intimate friends. In late December, 1847, he and Crittenden were called into consultation by Garret Davis, who said that he had been treated with rank discourtesy in debate in the House with Thomas Bayly of Virginia. After listening to his account, Barrow and Crittenden agreed that Davis must challenge Bayly, and they consented to act as his seconds. A dueling ground in Baltimore was agreed on, and Davis, Barrow, and Crittenden repaired there to keep the engagement. The weather turned bitterly cold en route, and when they reached the ground, their adversaries were nowhere to be found. Actually, Bayly had been arrested on the warrant of a friend and was detained in Washington under a peace bond. After waiting some time in the bitter weather, Barrow suddenly collapsed. His friends carried him to a house nearby, where he sank rapidly and in a few hours was dead.

Announcement of Barrow's death was made to a shocked Senate on December 29. He was widely loved, and Democrat and Whig joined to pay him tribute in eloquent eulogies, as was customary on such occasions. During the early ceremonies Crittenden sat, his head bowed over his desk. When all who were scheduled had spoken, he arose and asked permission to be heard. When his request was granted, he tried to speak, but he was overcome with emotion; for the first and only time in his life he found himself speechless. He could only mutter, "I beg pardon, Mr. President," and sit down. "No words could have equaled the eloquence of this silence," wrote

---

[28] David Donald, *Lincoln's Herndon* (New York, 1948), 26-27; Lincoln to "Friend Linder," March 22, 1848, in Abraham Lincoln Collection, Illinois State Historical Society.

Nathan Sargent. Crittenden's friend Mangum agreed. He would not, he wrote, exchange "such a heart as yours . . . for all your high and brilliant eloquence." Mangum even thought Barrow, could he have witnessed the scene, would "for such a tribute have been almost willing to meet his fate."[29]

Because of family responsibilities it had not been possible for Maria to accompany Crittenden to Washington that winter, and he took bachelor quarters with two young Whig congressmen from Georgia, Alexander H. Stephens and Robert Toombs. In the long winter months of 1846-1847 he missed Maria, but he did not live a hermit's life. William H. Seward, visiting in Washington, reported seeing him at three social functions in the same week: at Major William W. Seaton's "gentleman's sociable," at a Whig dinner given for Seward three nights later, and the following night at Mrs. Tayloe's party for the "gentlemen of Washington." He also attended the grand social affair of that season, a ball given by Buchanan, now Secretary of State, at Carusi's near the end of January. Buchanan sent out thirteen hundred invitations and had to refuse applications for three hundred more because Carusi's assembly room could not accommodate them. Dolly Madison, now eighty years of age, and Alexander Hamilton's widow, ten years her senior, were there. In their starched ruffs and caps they were still the most magnetic females present. They held court, each in her separate station, while the multitude passed from one to the other to pay homage to the distinguished and charming old ladies.[30]

During this long winter Crittenden devoted much thought to the coming presidential election. The course he would follow in that struggle would cause a crisis in his career and would bring about a radical turn in his relations with his old friend and chief, Henry Clay.

29 Henry W. Hilliard, *Politics and Pen Pictures at Home and Abroad* (New York, 1892), 179-80; *Congressional Globe*, 29 Cong., 2 Sess., 97-99; Sargent, *Public Men and Events*, II, 309; Mangum to Crittenden, Dec. 31, 1846, in Coleman, *Crittenden*, I, 265.

30 Seward, *Autobiography*, I, 774-75, 781-82; Crittenden to Maria, Dec. 29, 1845, in Coleman, *Crittenden*, I, 233.

CHAPTER XI

The Kingmaker

THE CAMPAIGN for the presidential election of 1848 began almost simultaneously with the Mexican War. Even before that, party leaders were seeking out available candidates, and the eager ones were planning strategy. Northern Whigs, once hopeful of making an issue of the Walker tariff, were somewhat disarmed by prevailing industrial prosperity. With the coming of the war boom it was difficult to convince businessmen that they were suffering from the tariff. It was equally difficult to persuade midwestern farmers that the tariff was harmful with wheat as high as two dollars a bushel.[1]

Still, 1848 seemed portentious for the Whigs, for the country was tired of war and of the war party. If only the Whigs could come up with a popular candidate who could unite the party, victory might be expected. But where could such a candidate be found? Clay had indicated after his defeat in 1844 that he would not again be a candidate. Besides, even though Clay should change his mind, he would be in his seventy-second year, older even than Harrison had been at the time of his nomination. Yet, as convention time drew near, Clay's friends began to give unmistakable signs that the Old Coon would not let the nomination slip away to a rival by default.

Had Clay withdrawn early, the prize might well have gone to Crittenden. Clay indicated that he would support him. After the tragic debacle of 1844 some of Crittenden's friends regretted that he had not been Polk's adversary. They were convinced that he could have defeated the Democratic John Doe, and they now resolved that he must have the track in 1848. The South and the West, they thought, would go solidly for him. "It will not do to say," wrote one of them, that "you don't care about the office and would not have it. If you are called upon by the Whig party generally . . . you will be *obliged* to run." Ardent Clay men in New York were also insistent that if Clay was not the candidate, Crittenden must be. His nomination would be called for, wrote a last-ditch Clay man there, by "every Whig who knows you." The Nashville *Republican Banner* declared for Crittenden early in 1846, and a year later a Whig meeting in Missouri nominated him for the Presidency. His prospects seemed indeed promising, for not only was he universally popular with Whigs but he would have support even among Democrats, something Clay had always lacked.[2]

As spring gave way to summer in 1847, it seemed certain that Clay was unavailable, and the clamor for Crittenden grew. From Lexington, George B. Kinkead sought Crittenden's permission to have the Kentucky legislature nominate him. Thomas B. Stevenson, Whig editor of the *Atlas* in Cincinnati, who was devoted to Clay, urged Crittenden's candidacy. So also did Joseph L. White from New York, who pledged his own ardent advocacy "of your claims, next to those of Mr. Clay." The Democratic senator from Rhode Island promised his Whig colleague a considerable diversion from the Democratic party to Crittenden if he should be a candidate. Robert Toombs later wrote that in the winter of 1847-1848 Crittenden had had the Presidency "in his grasp" only to thrust it aside in the interest of party success.[3]

[1] J. N. Reynolds to Crittenden, Aug. 4, 1846, in Crittenden Papers; Daniel Ullman to Clay, July 12, 1847, in Clay Papers.

[2] A. T. Burnley to Crittenden, Dec. 3, 1844, Joseph L. White to Crittenden, Sept. 29, 1845, Anthony Butler to Crittenden, June 15, 1846, in Crittenden Papers; Nashville *Republican Banner*, Feb. 20, 1846, quoted in Frankfort *Commonwealth*, March 10, 1846; *Niles' Register*, LXXI (1846-1847), 354.

[3] Kinkead to Crittenden, Jan. 2, 1847, in Crittenden Papers (Duke); Stevenson to Crittenden, May 1, 1847, White to Crittenden, Oct. 30, 1847, in Crittenden Papers; Toombs to Mrs. Chapman Coleman, June 22, 1849, in U. B. Phillips (ed.), *Correspondence of Toombs, Stephens, and Cobb*, in American Historical Association *Report*, 1911, II, 165; James F. Simmons to Crittenden, Nov. 30, 1859, in Coleman, *Crittenden*, II, 178-80.

To all pleas Crittenden refused to listen. "For Heaven's sake," he replied when the subject was first broached, "don't talk to me about the Presidency." As the urgings grew in volume, his feeling was "something more like alarm than gratification" at being spoken of as a candidate. "In all sincerity," he wrote in January, 1847, "I . . . feel no longing, no impatience" for the office. He would not permit the Kentucky legislature to nominate him, nor would he allow his name to be used elsewhere. There were already too many candidates actively in the field, he thought.

Crittenden's reasons for refusing seriously to consider his own candidacy can only be surmised. Perhaps he genuinely shunned the office. Certainly he seemed to lack the burning ambition that marked the careers of Clay, Calhoun, Webster, Scott, McLean, and other perennial candidates. To him men were subordinate to principles, which should not be sacrificed to ambition. Believing that there was no widespread clamor for him, he refused to complicate the party's problem by injecting his own name into the contest. "My opinion, my advice, my wish is that all action be postponed," he wrote. Furthermore, he knew Clay too well to fully credit his assertion, made after defeat in 1844, that he would not again be a candidate. If Old Hal should subsequently change his mind and once more enter the contest, Crittenden would be compelled to step aside and give his chief the track, as he had done in the senatorial election in 1832. "If my feelings were ever so different from what they are," he wrote, "I should think it very bad *policy*, considered in that point of view only, that I or my friends should appear even to *push Mr. Clay* aside."[4]

As doubt of Clay's availability continued, a new star appeared in the national political galaxy. Zachary Taylor had never even so much as voted in all his life, but almost at the beginning of the war his great popularity was discovered and his possible candidacy discussed. By the summer of 1846 he had admirers in factions of both parties. At first he appeared uninterested, but after his victory at Monterrey in late September of that year the siren song seemed more pleasant to his ears. His popularity grew apace. There was something heroic in the image of the doughty old frontier warrior that Winfield Scott's greater military ability and political literacy could hardly

[4] Crittenden to Burnley, Dec. 28, 1844, Crittenden to Kinkead, Jan. 10, 1847, in Crittenden Papers (Duke); Holman Hamilton, *Zachary Taylor, Soldier in the White House* (Indianapolis and New York, 1951), 61.

match. Scott was regarded as a capable and scientific military leader; Taylor's victories had seemed miracles. His image dazzled the public eye like a meteor. Much might be expected of such a man.

Virginia-born like both Scott and Clay, Taylor, now in his sixties, was worn and weatherbeaten by long years on the frontier, fighting in the numerous Indian wars. He had grown to manhood in Kentucky and had many important connections there, among them Crittenden, whose first wife was Taylor's cousin. With Clay seemingly out of the contest, many Kentuckians rallied to Taylor's standard. This by no means detracted from his prestige, for Kentucky was regarded as the heart of Whigdom. In the spring of 1847, when news came of Taylor's astonishing victory over an army many times the size of his own at Buena Vista, his name was on every lip. Philip Hone, devoted Clay follower, wrote of Taylor in disgust: "All parts and parties, professions, sexes, and conditions, call him away from the field of battle to take upon himself the chief magistracy." All other candidates were shoved aside to make way for the hero. Even the Quakers, the lovers of peace, were seduced by the old warrior's fame. Gentlefolk shouted Taylor's name, Hone wrote, and "fair ladies purse up their ruby lips and make his support a passport to their favor." Even the countryfolk were calling for Rough and Ready at the tops of their voices.[5] By May, papers from all sections were urging Taylor for the Presidency. By June, he was threatening Scott's stronghold in Pennsylvania. Abraham Lincoln, one of Taylor's most ardent sponsors, was beguiled into thinking that even Calhoun would support him.[6]

Crittenden and Taylor were lifelong friends, so intimate that when the war came, Tom Crittenden rushed to join Taylor, and the old general made a place for his young kinsman on his staff and moved him into his own household.[7] In early summer of 1846 Taylor, discouraged and resentful of the administration's treatment, planned

[5] Hone, Diary, 795. See also, Hamilton, Zachary Taylor, 38-40; J. F. Levin to McLean, April 17, 1847, James E. Harvey to McLean, June 13, 1847, in McLean Papers.

[6] Frankfort Commonwealth, May 11, 1847, quoting more than a dozen pro-Taylor editors; Stevenson to Letcher [June 20, 1847], in Crittenden Papers; Lincoln to Richard Yates, Dec. 10, 1847, to Taylor Committee of Philadelphia, Feb. 9, 1848, to Thomas S. Flournoy, Feb. 17, 1848, to Asher F. Linder, Feb. 20, 1848, to Archibald Williams, April 30, 1848, in Roy P. Basler (ed.), The Collected Works of Abraham Lincoln, 8 vols. and index (New Brunswick, N. J., 1953-1955), I, 419, 449, 452-53, 467-68 (hereinafter, Lincoln, Works).

[7] Taylor to Crittenden, Jan. 26, 1847, in Coleman, Crittenden, I, 270-76; Crittenden to Taylor, July 5, 1846, in Crittenden Papers (Kentucky).

to leave the army and return home. Crittenden learned of this and in a remarkable letter pleaded with him not to do so. By his victories he had raised the expectations of the country to a high pitch. "You must finish the war," he wrote, and go on "from victory to victory untill [*sic*] peace shall crown all your dangers, & place your fame beyond all the accidents of war." Crittenden then proceeded to matters of military strategy. The large number of volunteers en route to reinforce Taylor, he said, might endanger his chances of victory. For "an unwieldly mass, tho' it might even add to your *strength*, would encumber & impede your *movements*." For the war must be waged with "*activity & audacity*." "It seems to me," he wrote, "that your brave little Army of regulars, reinforced by some selected volunteers, . . . may afford to be *audacious* with such an enemy, & that hardly any thing would be *impossible*." "If I were to hear, therefore, that you had left your masses behind to follow on at their leisure, and that with the whole of your regulars, added to as many chosen Volunteers, you had dashed for Monterey [*sic*], with your provisions in your pocket, I would swear through *thick* and *thin*, that . . . you would beat all before you & get to Monterey without ever being hungry." This would "finish the war, run us all mad with the sudden triumph, & place you where I desire to see you." The letter was written in Scott's office in the War Department and, according to Scott, inspired Taylor, against his own better judgment, to march on Monterrey and capture it.[8]

Soon letters were passing between the senator and the general, and they dealt with more than military affairs. Taylor was convinced that Scott, Marcy, and Polk were trying to discredit him by ordering him to a defensive position while taking the better part of his troops from him to join Scott's expedition against Vera Cruz and Mexico City. Crittenden agreed that Taylor had been mistreated but attempted to mollify him. He was certain Scott had no desire to injure him. Perhaps his treatment was the result of "inadvertence only." In any event, Crittenden wrote, the country would take care of Taylor's honor. And, he added pointedly, he was not referring "merely to your military position." For the people were planning on converting him "into a political leader, when the war is done."

Taylor caught the implication of this and hastily disclaimed

---

[8] Crittenden to Taylor, July 5, 1846, in Crittenden Papers (Kentucky); Arthur D. H. Smith, *Old Fuss and Feathers* (New York, 1937), 257-58.

any political ambition. But he had little chance, if he really had desire, to eschew the plans that the persuasive politician soon set his heart on. For by the spring of 1847 Crittenden, concluding either that Clay was out of the picture or that he should be, saw in Taylor, the guileless military hero, the only chance of saving the weak and badly divided Whig party—and with it, the country—from destruction. In late March he wrote Taylor, frankly outlining his hopes for him and giving him "judicious advice" as to his proper political behavior. Quickly Taylor replied in an equivocal but somewhat eager letter. He had no training or desire for the Presidency. He would much prefer to see the office in other hands, "some able & tried Whig," perhaps Clay. But, he added in the next line, he assumed that Clay "cannot now be considered available." Accordingly, "if my friends deem it for the good of the country that I be a candidate . . . be it so." He would not decline but would do his best to serve honestly and faithfully.[9]

On the surface it may appear strange that a Whig like Crittenden could support for President a military man with no experience in civil affairs, for Whigs had charged that the civil had been subordinated to the military by the Democrats under Jackson. Besides, Crittenden had long abandoned the military zeal he had shown in the War of 1812. "War is a positive evil, even when stripped of all its horrors," he had told the Senate in 1846.[10] Yet Crittenden was a realist, and the problem which confronted him and other Whig leaders was to find a chieftain to lead the party to victory, saving the country from continued "misrule" under the "corrupt" Democratic party. Crittenden and other Whigs who were to join him in promoting Taylor— Weed, Seward, Truman Smith, Alexander H. Stephens, Robert Toombs, Abraham Lincoln—knew what Clay and his idolators were never to learn—that the country was surfeited with old, battle-worn issues of tariff, bank, and distribution. The country was now to be faced with new and greater issues centering around Manifest Destiny and slavery expansion. And these issues must be resolved if the nation was to be saved. To secure national peace and unity, therefore, a new leader with great popular appeal must be found. Lack of ex-

9 Taylor to Crittenden, Oct. 9, 1846, March 25, 1847 [misdated 1846], May 15, 1847, in Crittenden Papers; Crittenden to Taylor, March 23, 1847, in Crittenden Papers (Duke).
10 *Congressional Globe*, 29 Cong., 1 Sess., Appendix, 842.

perience in statecraft need not be fatal, for there would be skilled hands to help guide the ship of state on a new course.

It was not, therefore, because of Taylor's military record but in spite of it that Crittenden decided to support him. The threat to the country in 1848 was not military dictatorship that might enslave the people; on the contrary, the absence of strength in the central government threatened the breakup of the Union. Crittenden sensed this threat even before Clay and most other politicians, and by 1847 he was prepared to abandon Clay and take up the banner of Taylor, in an effort to preserve the Union.

Nor did it disturb Crittenden to find that Taylor had difficulty distinguishing between Democratic and Whig principles. Crittenden himself had little of the ultra party man in his own makeup. "I am no partizan in politics, nor at all ambitious of the character," he had written in 1825 during the height of the court struggle in Kentucky.[11] Since then, in the Senate he had never been a stout supporter of the old issues that had divided Whig and Democrat. From the days of his struggle over relief laws and the court contest he could understand and sympathize with the instinctive hostility of the farmer toward banks and toward the courts that sustained the banks' property rights. As we have seen, he had even protested against what he thought were exorbitant rates for the protection of Kentucky hemp bagging in 1842. The same year he had surrendered distribution in the interest of national solvency. Four years later he had let the protective tariff go almost by default when he might have defeated the Walker bill had he tried.

There were other willing candidates for the Whig presidential nomination, but their hopes soon faded. One of them was John McLean of Ohio, once Jackson's Postmaster General, now turned Whig and serving as Associate Justice of the Supreme Court. McLean was a stout antislavery man and had strong support in New England and in other abolitionist sections. He was, as usual, eager for the nomination. The acid pen of John Quincy Adams had recorded in his diary a decade and a half earlier that McLean "thinks of nothing but the Presidency by day and dreams of nothing else by night."[12] McLean's friends early in 1847 began courting Crittenden's support, for he could "make you more Whig friends, than any other

---

[11] Lexington *Kentucky Reporter*, May 2, 1825.
[12] Adams, *Memoirs*, VIII, 537.

man in Washington now," one of them wrote to McLean. Tom Corwin was being pushed by his friends for the nomination, but McLean was assured that Crittenden and Mangum could silence Corwin, if they were so disposed. Although Crittenden expressed kindness toward McLean, he would promise no support, and six months before the convention, McLean's prospects were gone.[13]

Another irrepressible Whig hopeful was General Winfield Scott. Tall (he was six feet, four inches) and striking, Scott had distinguished himself as a young general in the War of 1812. Commander in chief of the army now, he had long resided in Washington and was highly regarded by many Whig leaders. Scott not only was a brilliant military leader but was remarkably well informed on political matters. He had been considered a possible candidate in 1840 and 1844. Although a native Virginian, he had strong antislavery views and had strength in Pennsylvania and Ohio. By the beginning of 1846 he was in full chase for the nomination. His chief sponsor was Senator John M. Clayton of Delaware, but Thurlow Weed was also taking his candidacy seriously. Much of Scott's strength, however, proved artificial. Friends of other candidates were feigning to support him in order to beat down worthier opponents. When Scott landed at New York in the spring of 1848, fresh from his Mexican conquests, his hopes were high. He was given a brilliant reception, but he soon learned that his cause was flagging and that the star of his fellow war hero, Taylor, was eclipsing his. In an effort to stop Taylor, Scott proposed that he and Clay join forces, with himself as candidate for Vice President, but his offer was never relayed to Clay.[14]

In the end the contest was between Taylor and Clay, but until a few months before the nominating convention, both men backed and filled. Clay's friends, starting a drive in late 1847 to gain the prize for their idol, urged Taylor not to permit his name to be used in rivalry with Clay. Crittenden, on the other hand, was committed to Taylor by that time, and he encouraged Taylor with complimentary messages from Whig leaders. These messages flattered Taylor, yet he doubted his ability to fill the office adequately. If only he

[13] Epes Sargent to Clay, Feb. 27, 1847, in Clay Papers; J. B. Mower to McLean, Feb. 13, Oct. 11, 18, 1847, in McLean Papers.
[14] Seward, *Autobiography*, I, 772; Barnes, *Memoir of Weed*, 167; J. B. Mower to McLean, May 12, 1847, in McLean Papers; Thomas B. Stevenson to Clay, May 22, 27, Aug. 10, 1848, J. L. White to Clay, May 28, 1848, Winfield Scott to Clay, July 15, 1848, in T. J. Clay Papers.

were positive that Clay could be elected, he wrote Crittenden in September, 1847, he would certainly stand aside. On November 1 he wrote that he was convinced Clay could not be elected, yet three days later he wrote Clay of his willingness, even eagerness, to support him "if you . . . were the choice of the party." At the same time he authorized Crittenden to withdraw his name any time he saw fit.[15]

Taylor returned from Mexico in early December, and Crittenden was assured that Old Rough and Ready was in the race to the finish, come what might. Three weeks later Taylor wrote that although he would not voluntarily withdraw himself, he would nevertheless entrust those who had brought him forward to "drop me at the proper time." A month later he repeated this promise, although with even greater ambiguity.[16]

Meanwhile, Clay's plans were going through similar evolutions. Even before the election of 1844 he regarded himself as above contesting for the Whig nomination. "If there is to be any scramble for the office," he wrote in 1842, ". . . I prefer to be left alone in the enjoyment of that repose of which I am in so much need." Shortly after his defeat by Polk he announced that he would not again be a candidate unless he were clearly the choice of a majority of the people. This eventuality was not likely to occur, and many of Clay's friends took his statement at face value. Clay had been at least a potential candidate for the Presidency for a quarter of a century, and he never had been the clear choice of a majority of the people. He had been badly defeated in two contests and had lost to a comparative nonentity in a third. Not even his most ardent followers thought he had a chance to win at his advanced age, but many preferred defeat under his banner to victory under that of another. Crittenden, although personally devoted to Clay, had assumed that his sun had set. After the 1844 election Clay had assured him that he was determined to retire from politics. Whether Crittenden believed Clay really meant this or not, by 1847 he accepted it as a final decision.[17]

In less than a year after his humiliating defeat by Polk, however, some of Clay's devoted friends began scheming to win the nomina-

[15] Taylor to Crittenden, May 15, Sept. 15, Nov. 15, 1847, Jan. 3, 1848, in Crittenden Papers; Taylor to Clay, Nov. 4, 1847, in Clay Papers; Poage, *Henry Clay*, 175-76.
[16] Burnley to Crittenden, Dec. 12, 1847, Taylor to Crittenden, Feb. 13, 1848, in Crittenden Papers.
[17] Clay to J. Watson Webb, Feb. 12, 1842, in Clay Papers (Virginia); Poage, *Henry Clay*, 152, 164; Clay to Crittenden, Nov. 28, 1844, in Coleman, *Crittenden*, I, 224-25; Seward, *Autobiography*, I, 772.

tion for him in 1848. Their hope was that Clay might, after first protesting against his candidacy, be persuaded to *"consent to be run against his consent."*[18] Convinced that Clay could not get an electoral majority, these friends even revived the old 1836 scheme whereby a multiplicity of candidates might throw the election into the House, where Clay could win. By autumn, 1847, their campaign was rolling. If, wrote a friend of McLean's from New York, "The Hones, . . . and Whites, of New York *City*, can effect it, Mr. Clay will be beaten a fourth time for the Presidency. . . . We have but *one* man in the Whig ranks till Mr. Clay dies."[19] This kind of loyalty was flattering to Clay because he had become irritated by what he regarded as the unseemly haste of his Kentucky friends to throw him over for a new and untried candidate. For Taylor meetings were springing up all over Kentucky, two of them in Lexington in the late summer of 1847.[20]

There were abundant reasons why Whigs should look elsewhere than Ashland for their candidate. Age and frustration had taken their toll of Clay's old personal charm, and to many Whigs he now seemed crotchety and overbearing. These were eager to discard him, but others left him with great reluctance. One, pledging support for Taylor, did so with a heavy heart. "I hate to give up Old Hal," he wrote; "I do so love that man, that to see him president I would make any sacrifice." Another wrote that he would support Clay if there were any possibility of his success. He saw none, however, and the predicament of the country called for a Whig victory.[21]

In Kentucky a majority of Whig leaders were opposed to Clay's candidacy. They believed he could not be elected, and some even doubted he could carry the state. Men who had fought for him through the years, who would do so again if it were possible for him to win, were privately praying that he would not run. Thomas Metcalfe was one of these. No living man, he wrote, would have been happier than he to see Clay in the Presidency. Crittenden, too, had

18 White to Crittenden, Sept. 29, 1845, in Crittenden Papers.
19 J. B. Mower to McLean, Sept. 27, 1847, Thomas Dowling to McLean, Oct. 30, 1847, in McLean Papers.
20 Lexington *Observer and Reporter*, Aug. 18, Sept. 15, Nov. 20, 1847.
21 J. B. Mower to McLean, Nov. 14, 1846, David M. Ogden to McLean, Jan. 25, 1848, in McLean Papers; William B. Campbell to Governor David Campbell, Jan. 23, 1848, in Campbell Papers, Duke University Library; Walter Cunningham to Crittenden, Jan. 19, 1848, Waddy Thompson to Crittenden, Feb. 9, 1848, C. F. M. Noland to Crittenden, Nov. 13, 1847, Robert Ritchie to Crittenden, Jan. 26, 1848, in Crittenden Papers.

long been emotionally involved in Clay's career, and regretted that his lifelong ambition to see Clay in the White House would never be realized. Clay, he wrote in the spring of 1847, "ought to be President. . . . I have cherished that wish until it has become part and parcel of me." Another Kentuckian, Thomas B. Stevenson, at the time editor of a Whig paper in Cincinnati, was of like mind. A year before the convention, however, Stevenson wanted someone to persuade Clay to declare for Taylor. Stevenson himself could not do it. He would almost, he said, "as lief propose a divorce to my wife" as to make such a suggestion to Clay. But he loved Clay too much and he had the Whig cause too much at heart to risk seeing both defeated again. Stevenson finally screwed his courage to the point of suggesting to Clay that he regard himself as "a *historic* character."[22]

But Clay was being pressed by other stanch friends to make the race. At the time, the contest between Taylor and Scott was at its height, and they hoped the two generals might destroy one another. They urged Clay to remain quiet until the last moment, as if he would not run. *"Then go it with a vengeance."* The convention would, they hoped, settle on him as a compromise candidate. Acting on their advice, Clay remained noncommital even when Clayton bluntly asked him for a yea-or-nay statement.[23]

Whig victories in Pennsylvania and New York that fall were considered good omens for Clay, and it was agreed that he should make a major policy speech on the Mexican War, after which a great rally honoring him would be held in New York.[24] Clay spoke in Lexington in mid-November. He denounced the war as unjust and unnecessary. He avoided any specific mention of the Wilmot Proviso by advocating no territorial acquisition. The speech threw the Taylor forces into confusion, for it sounded ominously as if Clay was casting his hat into the ring. This fear was increased by a "confidential circular" published by George Robertson and other Bluegrass friends of Clay's.

[22] Kendall, *Autobiography*, 534; Crittenden to Waddy Thompson, May 6, 1847, typescript copy in Waddy Thompson Papers, University of South Carolina Library; George W. Williams to Crittenden, Jan. 7, 1847, Metcalfe to Crittenden, Feb. 8, 1848, Stevenson to Letcher, April 23, June 20, 1847, Stevenson to Crittenden, May 1, 1847, Sept. 7, 1847 [misdated 1848], in Crittenden Papers.

[23] Clay to John L. Littell, Nov. 17, 1846, Epes Sargent to Clay, Feb. 27, 1847, Daniel Ullman to Clay, July 12, 1847, in Clay Papers; Clay to Clayton, April 16, 1847, in Clayton Papers.

[24] Mower to McLean, Oct. 18, Nov. 8, 1847, in McLean Papers; Horace Greeley to Clay, Nov. 30, 1847, in Clay Papers.

The circular denounced Taylor meetings in Kentucky as disloyal to Clay. The effect was to drive a deeper wedge between the friends of Clay and those of Taylor, and to push Taylor to declare his determination to seek the Presidency.[25]

But Clay's Lexington speech did not receive the popular acclaim he hoped for. His opposition to territorial acquisition caused a falling-off of his strength in the South. On the other hand, antislavery men in the North would not support him because he was a slaveholder. He went east in January, fully intending to announce his withdrawal, but Greeley, Daniel Ullman, and others again argued against it. It would lead to prostration of the party in the North, they said, and they persuaded Clay to delay. By late February, therefore, though still disclaiming any desire to run, he was less certain he would withdraw. "My friends appear to increase in confidence," he wrote his son, "that I will obtain the nomination if I desire it." He would postpone final action until he returned home.[26]

Meanwhile, the political situation in his own state was injurious to Clay. Whigs had completely dominated the state for a dozen years, but the party was now torn by factions. Men who thought they had not been adequately recognized were ambitious for preferment, and disaffection had long been smoldering. The party had been divided in 1840 when the Wickliffes were thwarted in their early efforts to obtain a cabinet post for the Old Duke's brother Charles, and when he got the Post Office Department after the cabinet breakup, the split was intensified. The Wickliffes were soon joined by Clay's old enemy John Pope, and by Ben Hardin, Charles Wickliffe's fellow townsman.

Taylor's candidacy gave these old enemies a new opportunity to strike at Clay, and some joined the movement who were more inter-

[25] Manuscript Diary of William M. Pratt, I, 263, University of Kentucky Library; George W. Williams to Crittenden, Nov. 25, 1847, Burnley to Crittenden, Dec. 12, 1847, Letcher to Crittenden, Dec. 23, 1847, Taylor to Crittenden, Jan. 3, 1848, in Crittenden Papers; Poage, *Henry Clay*, 165-66, 168; Will D. Gilliam, "Robert P. Letcher's Appointment as Minister to Mexico," in *Kentucky Register*, XLVII (1949), 118.

[26] Richard M. Johnston and William H. Brown, *Life of Alexander H. Stephens* (Philadelphia, 1883), 225; Seward, *Autobiography*, II, 60-61; letters of Clay to Stevenson, Dec. 2, 1847, Feb. 19, 1848, to James B. Clay, Jan. 16, Feb. 1, 1848, to H. T. Duncan, Feb. 15, 1848, to Leslie Combs, Feb. 18, 1848, in Colton, *Henry Clay*, III, 461, IV, 553-55; Daniel Ullman to Clay, Feb. 18, 1848, McLean to Clay, March 1, 1848, Stevenson to Clay, April 8, 1848, in Clay Papers; Clay to James B. Clay, Feb. 21, 1848, in T. J. Clay Papers; Letcher to Crittenden, Feb. 21, 1848, in Crittenden Papers.

ested in destroying Clay than in advancing Taylor. Crittenden knew this. He knew, too, by this time that an open struggle between Taylor and Clay must be avoided at all cost. When the legislature met in the winter of 1847-1848, it was overwhelmingly opposed to Clay's candidacy and wanted to pass resolutions endorsing Taylor. Such action would split the party irrevocably and would injure Taylor's chances, should he be the nominee, of getting the support of diehard Clay Whigs in the election. If Taylor was to win the party's nomination, it must be without open offense to the Old Coon.

Whig problems in Kentucky were compounded by the coming gubernatorial election. Archibald Dixon of Henderson was eager for the nomination, as also was William J. Graves of Louisville, out of office since his tragic encounter with Cilley. Graves had the support of Governor Owsley, and Letcher was backing Dixon. Neither Dixon nor Graves would make a particularly strong candidate; even with a united party behind him, either might lose to an able Democrat. If a bitter contest for the nomination should develop between them, defeat was almost certain. Such a calamity would influence the presidential election, for if Kentucky elected a Democratic governor in August, a damper would be thrown on Whig hopes for November, both in Kentucky and elsewhere.

"We have our troubles here, and they are not a few," Letcher wrote Crittenden in January. The Whig party was "in the greatest peril." There was "a restless state of feeling . . . which almost amounts to a *delerium*." Dixon proposed that in order to prevent disaster, both he and Graves withdraw in favor of a third man who could unite the party, but Graves refused. "I am no alarmist," wrote Letcher, "but I must tell you . . . we are in great danger of being badly beaten in August." Only "the right man" as a candidate for President could save the state. Metcalfe echoed this sentiment.[27]

When the Whig state convention met in Frankfort, the situation had reached a crisis. A break between the friends of Graves and those of Dixon seemed inevitable. Furthermore, Taylor's supporters were determined to commit the convention openly to Taylor. From Washington, Crittenden wrote Letcher and Metcalfe to prevent this,

[27] Carl R. Fields, "Making Kentucky's Third Constitution, 1830-1850" (doctoral dissertation, University of Kentucky, 1951), 41-44, 55-58; Poage, *Henry Clay,* 171-73; Thomas [Jacob] to Mrs. James B. Clay, Jan. 27, 1847, in T. J. Clay Papers; John L. Helm to Crittenden, Jan. 11, 1848, Letcher to Crittenden, [Jan.] 20, 1848, Metcalfe to Crittenden, Feb. 8, 1848, in Crittenden Papers.

but they despaired of doing so. Letcher was exasperated with Clay. "Great g—d," he exploded, on the eve of the convention, if only Clay could have foreseen "the predicament in which he had placed his friends and his party . . . [he] could not have hesitated a moment about declining."[28]

Next day, when the convention met, lines were drawn. Taylor enthusiasts still insisted on forcing a public endorsement of Old Rough and Ready. Finally, as a last resort, Orlando Brown read letters from Crittenden and Morehead pleading with the delegates not to injure Clay's pride by nominating Taylor. Clay would, they wrote, announce his retirement when he returned home. These letters turned the tide. Without them, a militant Taylor delegate wrote, "We would have carried the nomination of Taylor . . . by an overwhelming majority."[29] But the fact that the convention adjourned without nominating either Clay or Taylor was itself a rebuff to Clay. Worse, as far as Clay's hopes were concerned, eleven of the twelve delegates it chose for the national nominating convention were avowed Taylor men. On top of that, as soon as the convention adjourned in the evening of February 22, a second convention, of Taylor men, met and unanimously endorsed Taylor. The proximity in time and place of the two meetings created the impression abroad that Kentucky Whigs had officially nominated Taylor.[30]

The Frankfort convention also resolved the difficulty over the gubernatorial candidate in a manner most unhappy for Crittenden. Dixon and Graves were withdrawn, and without Crittenden's knowledge or consent, he was drafted. His name was proposed unexpectedly by a delegate from Logan County and was carried in "a perfect storm and hurricane" before Crittenden's friends could marshal their forces to block it. Richard Hawes thought that the move was slyly engineered by a combination of the friends of Graves and Clay, who "aimed to punish Mr. Crittenden for being the friend of General

---

[28] Metcalfe to Crittenden, Feb. 17, 20, 1848, Letcher to Crittenden, Feb. 21, 1848, in Crittenden Papers.

[29] Richard Hawes to Maria Crittenden, Feb. 23, 1848, in Crittenden Papers.

[30] Letcher to Crittenden, Feb. 16, 1848, John W. Russell to Crittenden, March 1, 1848, Philip Swigert to Crittenden, Feb. 24, 1848, in Crittenden Papers; Toombs to James Thomas, April 16, May 1, 1848, in Phillips, *Correspondence of Toombs, Stephens and Cobb*, 103-106; Frankfort *Commonwealth*, March 7, 1848; Cincinnati *Atlas*, quoted *ibid.*, Feb. 29, March 4, 1848; Cassius M. Clay to Clay, April 13, 1848, in New York *Courier and Enquirer*, quoted *ibid.*, April 25, 1848; Lexington *Observer and Reporter*, April 27, 1848; Hamilton, *Zachary Taylor*, 67-68; Poage, *Henry Clay*, 171-73.

Taylor." All Crittenden's friends thought it an unnecessary sacrifice to take Crittenden out of the Senate, which he loved, and place him in the relatively insignificant position of governor. As John Russell wrote, it was "too much like loading a cannon to shoot a pig." "His place cannot be filled here," wrote Charles S. Morehead from Washington; "I have felt prouder of him since I have been here than ever before in my life—He is looked to, by a numerous and most influential band of Whigs as our future President. . . . It was cruel to take him from a theatre where he is winning an immortality of fame." But Crittenden had no choice. It was inevitable that he must answer the call of his Kentucky friends now in such dire distress, and at the end of a week he wired his acceptance.[31]

Meanwhile, Clay left Washington for a visit to Philadelphia on February 23, the day after the Whig convention in Frankfort. John Quincy Adams, stricken at his desk in the House, lay on his deathbed, and the Taylor press made much of Clay's seeming callousness in thus turning his back on his dying friend. But the enthusiasm of Clay's reception in Philadelphia drove all thought of this criticism from his mind. He was greeted at the station by thousands, then by more thousands at the mayor's house, where he was a guest. From Philadelphia he went to New York, there to be feasted and toasted and "kissed by great numbers of ladies of all ages and conditions." Much of this adulation may have been promoted by friends of Scott, Webster, and McLean, using Clay to head off Taylor. But it seemed convincing to Clay. He returned home, and from Ashland on April 10, he took the then-unprecedented step of announcing his own candidacy.[32]

[31] John W. Russell to Crittenden, March 1, 1848, Metcalfe to Crittenden, Feb. 20, 1848, Philip Swigert to Crittenden, Feb. 24, 1848, James Harlan to Crittenden, March 4, 1848, Richard Hawes to Maria Crittenden, Feb. 23, 1848, Harry I. Todd to Crittenden, with postscript from Orlando Brown, Feb. 23, 1848, Leslie Combs to Crittenden, Feb. 27, 1848, in Crittenden Papers; Hamilton, *Zachary Taylor*, 68; Morehead to Orlando Brown, Feb. 26, 1848, in Brown Papers, Filson Club; William B. Preston and others to Crittenden, Feb. 28, 1848, Crittenden to George B. Crittenden, April 14, 1848, in Coleman, *Crittenden*, I, 293-303; Frankfort *Commonwealth*, Feb. 29, 1848; F. P. Blair to Van Buren, March 3, 1848, in Van Buren Papers.

[32] Thomas Dowling to McLean, Feb. 26, March 17, 24, 1848, James E. Harvey to McLean, April 12, 1848, in McLean Papers; Washington *National Intelligencer*, Feb. 26, March 15, April 17, 1848; M. P. Gentry to W. B. Campbell, April 18, 1848, in Campbell Papers (Duke); Stevenson to Clay, Oct. 2, 1848, in T. J. Clay Papers; Lexington *Observer and Reporter*, April 12, 1848; Frankfort *Commonwealth*, April 18, 1848; Richard Hawes to Orlando Brown, March 29, 1848, in Brown Papers, Kentucky Historical Society, Folder 416.

Clay's announcement received a mixed reaction. His strongest supporters, of course, approved. But others thought its tone imperious and haughty. James Harvey, an old friend, thought it betrayed on Clay's part "a morbid passion for the Presidency." Clay had misconstrued, he thought, marks of kindness designed to "give him the opportunity of voluntarily retiring in a blaze of glory." Clay's "false Counsellors," wrote another, should be condemned for misleading him. It was "supreme infatuation," wrote another, for Clay to think of success. His nomination could only result in a fourth defeat "in the evening of his days." Robert Toombs thought Clay's ambition was "as fierce as at any time of his life" and that he was determined "to rule or ruin the party." Years later Gideon Welles was to recall that Lincoln thought Clay a "hard and selfish" leader, whose private personal ambition led to the ruin of his party.[33]

Meanwhile, in early spring of 1848, Taylor's candidacy was experiencing trouble, and had it not been for persistent efforts of three groups, all closely tied to Crittenden, his hopes undoubtedly would have been dashed. In Washington, Crittenden's messmates, Alexander H. Stephens and Robert Toombs, had formed, with Abraham Lincoln, Thomas Flournoy, and William B. Preston, a group called the Young Indians, who succeeded in keeping Taylor's name actively before the public. A second group was in New Orleans: Albert T. Burnley; Alexander C. Bullitt, editor of the *Picayune*; James Love; and Logan Hunton—native Kentuckians all and close friends of Crittenden. A third group in Frankfort, headed by Letcher and Orlando Brown, had deftly swung Whig sentiment in Kentucky to Taylor.[34]

Taylor's naivete, meanwhile, was about to undo the best efforts of his friends. He believed that he could reach the White House without the backing of either of the major political parties, by a "spontaneous movement of the people." In September he had written that he would not accept nomination by a party, for he wanted to be "the president of the nation & not of a party." A few months

[33] John T. Morse (ed.), *The Diary of Gideon Welles*, 3 vols. (Boston, 1911), I, 506-507. See also, Thomas S. James to John R. Desha, May 13, 1848, in Joseph Desha Papers; letters to McLean from Harvey, April 27, 1848, from Caleb B. Smith, April 22, 1848, from John H. Sanders, April 24, 1848, from John Teasdale, April 15, 1848, and from John D. Defrees, April 16, 1848, in McLean Papers; Toombs to James Thomas, April 16, May 1, 1848, in Phillips, *Correspondence of Toombs, Stephens, and Cobb*, 103-106.
[34] Hamilton, *Zachary Taylor*, 63-65; Poage, *Henry Clay*, 157-58.

later he was willing to accept nomination by a national convention "from either the Whigs or Democrats." He hoped, however, that it would be unnecessary to hold such a convention, for the people were "tired of that kind of machinery."[35]

The year before, Taylor had written a guileless letter to the Cincinnati *Signal*, renouncing any territorial acquisition from Mexico. This was interpreted in the South as tantamount to endorsing the Wilmot Proviso, a question then rocking the country to its foundations, and it created grave doubt in southern minds of Taylor's availability. He followed this up with a letter to a Louisiana Whig in which he admitted his ignorance of such matters as bank, tariff, and internal improvements, all sacred subjects in the liturgy of old Whigs of the Henry Clay stamp. When Crittenden tactfully admonished him, he promised to be more cautious. Nevertheless, he insisted that he would not be "a party candidate, or a party president . . . in the general acceptation of the term." He would, however, accept a Whig nomination on his own terms.[36]

Taylor soon demonstrated his independence of party by accepting a nomination from a mass meeting of Whigs and Democrats in Alabama. Indeed, so ambivalent did he seem in party principles that Democrats, as late as March, 1848, were seriously thinking of drafting him as their candidate. "If we could beat Clay with a military chieftain whom the Clayites have been so busy to build up," Blair wrote to Van Buren, "it would [be] 'a consummation most devoutly to be wished.'"[37]

Crittenden was hardpressed to repair damage brought on by Taylor's ill-advised letters. Again and again he wrote the general, counseling him to be cautious, to refrain from all statements on public policy. At the same time he wrote long letters to the press, interpreting and defending Taylor's position, and even putting words into Taylor's mouth. Most revealing was a long letter he wrote Orlando Brown, former editor of the Frankfort *Commonwealth* who still had access to its columns. He had learned, he wrote, from "a

[35] Taylor to Crittenden, Aug. 16, 1847, in Taylor Papers; Taylor to Crittenden, Sept. 15, 1847, in Crittenden Papers; Taylor to Orlando Brown, Dec. 18, 1847, typescript copy in Brown Papers, Kentucky Historical Society.

[36] Taylor to Crittenden, Sept. 15, Nov. 15, 1847, in Crittenden Papers.

[37] Blair to Van Buren, Feb. 29, 1848, in Van Buren Papers. See also, Balie Peyton to Crittenden, Jan. 25, 1848, Stevenson to Crittenden, Sept. 1, 1847, W. S. Archer to Crittenden, Sept. 22, 1847, in Crittenden Papers; John L. Sheafe to Webster, Jan. 20, 1848, in Webster Papers.

confidential friend" of Taylor's that Taylor would soon write Brown a letter for publication, advocating that Mexican territory be annexed as indemnity. Crittenden did not believe that Taylor would advocate such a policy, for it would put him "into direct conflict with the . . . feelings and prejudices of the New England States—a position very much to be avoided at this crisis." Crittenden was sure that this was not Taylor's "true meaning," and that he would not so express himself in the contemplated letter to Brown. If he did, however, it would probably be the result of "carelessness or inadvertance." Taylor's proper policy should be to speak in "general terms, relating to principles rather than measures, & avoiding all *details.*"

Crittenden went on to instruct Brown in what Taylor's true views were, or ought to be: peace was desirable, since the honor of the country had been vindicated; the humiliation Mexico had already suffered should inspire us to magnanimity toward her, and we should exact nothing but a satisfactory adjustment of the Texas boundary, together with a scrupulously honest indemnity for spoilations of the property of our citizens. If it were more suitable and convenient to Mexico to settle our claims by "limited cessions of territory," well and good. But under no consideration should we accept more than would give us the harbor of San Francisco. Other acquisitions would "embroil us with disturbing questions at home." Without going into further details, Crittenden suggested that Orlando could "with your good pen . . . frame something that would exactly do." If Taylor's expected letter should contain different suggestions, Orlando should return it to him "for revision, before its publication." It was important that "all should go smoothly on this subject," he concluded, "so that we may avoid all disadvantages if it should so turn out that he, and not Mr. Clay should be finally our selected candidate."[38]

But Taylor seemed determined that things should not go smoothly. He wrote a letter to a Kentucky Democrat expressing his willingness to accept either a Whig or a Democratic nomination, or both. He followed this up with a letter to the Richmond *Republican,* saying he would accept a nomination by the Whigs if he were left "free of all pledges" and could remain independent of all parties. Otherwise he would refuse. At the same time he stated that he would not withdraw from the race, even if the Whig national convention should choose another candidate. In the previous November

[38] Crittenden to Brown, March 25, 1848, in Crittenden Papers (Duke).

he had written Clay that he would step aside if Clay were the nominee. He now denied ever having made such a statement. Whigs began to regard his candidacy as ridiculous. "The man is certainly demented," wrote Caleb B. Smith.[39]

Whig leaders began seeking a more orthodox candidate, and Crittenden's name was again prominently mentioned, despite his nomination for governor. Most Whigs seemed to favor him or Clayton, and Thurlow Weed developed plans to throw the nomination to either of the two. Weed personally favored Clayton but was assured that Crittenden would be the more popular choice with congressmen. By late March some of Clay's stoutest supporters were conceding that both Clay and Taylor must be withdrawn in favor of Crittenden. Truman Smith was working for Crittenden in Connecticut, and Daniel Goodenow in Maine. The Alabama delegation en route to the national convention innocently sought Clay's advice about switching to Crittenden. Moderate Whigs in the North were willing to accept Crittenden because they regarded him, like Clay, as a southern man with northern views on slavery. For this very reason, however, some southern Whigs opposed him. John Bell, a Tennessee moderate, preferred "a Northern man with Southern feelings to a Southern man with Northern feelings."[40] But Crittenden steadfastly refused to consider his own candidacy.

Had Crittenden merely sat quietly, there is little doubt that Taylor's candidacy would have failed. His fortunes were at a low ebb in April, 1848, when Crittenden and his friends went into action. The impression Taylor gave of his party irregularity would, if permitted to stand, have precluded his nomination. Crittenden and his friends, therefore, prepared to clarify Taylor's party position. Truman Smith wrote the general asking for a statement of true Whig principle but cautioning him to withhold a reply until a proper one could be prepared for him. With help from Stephens and Toombs, Crittenden drafted a reply for Taylor's signature, and dispatched it to Baton

[39] Smith to McLean, April 10, 1848, in McLean Papers; Washington *National Intelligencer*, May 3, 1848; James Harvey to Clay, May 3, 1848, in T. J. Clay Papers; Taylor to Crittenden, March 25, 1848, in Crittenden Papers.

[40] Hamilton, *Zachary Taylor*, 74-75; Thomas Dowling to McLean, March 24, 1848, in McLean Papers; Stevenson to Clay, May 18, 1848, Charles C. Langdon to Clay, May 29, 1848, in T. J. Clay Papers; Daniel Goodenow to Crittenden, April 18, 1848, in Crittenden Papers; John Bell to William B. Campbell, May 23, 1848, in Campbell Papers (Duke).

Rouge by Major William Bliss, Taylor's aide and son-in-law. Their secret was not well kept, for Taylor's rivals soon learned of the ruse. "As soon as Major Bliss reaches Baton Rouge," wrote James Harvey, "we shall probably have another and a final (it is to be hoped) *exposè* from General Taylor. . . . Major B . . . has gone crammed with delightful & refreshing instructions."[41]

On April 23 there appeared in the New Orleans *Picayune* a letter from Taylor addressed to his brother-in-law, Captain John S. Allison, of Louisville. In the letter Taylor professed to be "a Whig but not ultra Whig." If elected, he would try to be President of all the people and be "independent of party domination." The veto power should not be used except in cases of "clear violation of the Constitution, or manifest haste and want of due consideration by Congress." As for internal improvements, a bank, and the tariff, the will of the people as expressed by Congress should prevail. His views on the Mexican War settlement were precisely what Crittenden had written Orlando Brown a month before that they would be.[42]

Until recently, it was believed that this was the same letter that Crittenden had drafted in Washington. It is so similar to Crittenden's that Stephens went to his grave still maintaining that the Allison letter had been prepared in Washington. "The substance of the letter," he wrote Crittenden's daughter many years later, "if not its identical words & form, I am quite sure was written . . . by your father."[43] But Holman Hamilton has shown that Crittenden's New Orleans lieutenants, Peyton, Love, and Hunton, had anticipated him. As alarmed as Crittenden at Taylor's equivocal position, they had gone up to Baton Rouge the day before Bliss reached there. Knowing Crittenden's views, they had worked out with Taylor a draft coinciding so closely with them that perhaps even Crittenden himself was fooled. Completing their work the next day, they hurried to catch the boat to New Orleans. At the landing they met Bliss arriving, and at Taylor's suggestion they showed Bliss the letter. He

[41] Harvey to McLean, April 27, 1848, in McLean Papers; Washington *National Intelligencer*, Oct. 27, 1848; Poage, *Henry Clay*, 157.

[42] Text of the letter can be found in Hamilton, *Zachary Taylor*, 79-81.

[43] A. C. Cole, *The Whig Party in the South* (Washington, 1913), 130n; Poage, *Henry Clay*, 175-76; Stephens to Mrs. Chapman Coleman, June 15, Oct. 13, 1870, Jan. 20, 1871, in Crittenden Papers (Duke). Stephens called this the "second Allison letter," but he was obviously referring to the one of April 22, and not another written by Taylor to Allison on September 4, 1848.

approved it, and no changes were made. They returned to New Orleans, and the next day the letter appeared.[44]

The Allison letter was well received, and at once Taylor's prospects brightened. It was quickly followed up in Kentucky with grassroots Taylor conventions, carefully planned by a central committee of which Orlando Brown and Letcher were the guiding spirits. Then in late April the central committee issued a statement "to the Friends of General Taylor in Kentucky." It expressed astonishment at Clay's announcement of his candidacy and related the circumstances that restrained the Frankfort convention from openly endorsing Taylor in February. The committee pledged its support to the nominee of the Philadelphia convention, whoever he might be.[45]

It had originally been the hope of Taylor Whigs that the general's popularity would make the holding of a national nomination convention unnecessary. Taylor himself was especially opposed to a convention. By February, however, it was manifest that a convention must decide between the rivals, and it was set for Philadelphia in early June.[46] Whigs in Congress, almost to a man, were opposed to Clay, and as southern delegates passed through the national capital en route to Philadelphia, they were persuaded of Clay's unavailability. After watching this brainwashing, a supporter of Clay's despaired of his nomination. "The triggers were all set," he wrote, "and it was impossible to counteract the movements made by members of Congress."[47] If only the delegates could reach the convention by a different route, Horace Greeley thought Clay might win. As it was, he wrote, "we are doomed to be beaten . . . through the machinery at Washington."[48]

[44] [Name obliterated] to Clay, April 26, 1848, in Clay Papers; Logan Hunton to Mrs. Chapman Coleman, Dec. 18, 1871, in Crittenden Papers (Duke); Hamilton, *Zachary Taylor*, 77-79.

[45] Thomas Dowling to McLean, May 4, 1848, in McLean Papers; Charles S. Morehead to [Clay?], May 3, 1848, in Clay Papers; letter of Central Taylor Committee, Folder 31, Brown Papers, Filson Club; Frankfort *Commonwealth*, April 25, 1848.

[46] Taylor to Crittenden, Feb. 13, March 25, 1848, Albert T. Burnley to Crittenden, April 4, 1848, in Crittenden Papers; Malcolm C. McMillan (ed.), "Joseph Glover Baldwin Reports on the Whig National Convention of 1848," in *Journal of Southern History*, XXV (1959), 366-82; Washington *National Intelligencer*, Jan. 27, March 20, 1848; Frankfort *Commonwealth*, Feb. 8, 1848.

[47] James Harlan to Clay, June 2, 15, 1848, in T. J. Clay Papers.

[48] Toombs to James Thomas, April 16, 1848, in Phillips, *Correspondence of Toombs, Stephens, and Cobb*, 103-104; Greeley to Clay, May 29, 1848, in T. J. Clay Papers; Hamilton, *Zachary Taylor*, 87.

By June 6, Philadelphia was overflowing with delegates, official and unofficial. Hotels could not accommodate the multitude, and when boardinghouses also were filled, citizens hospitably opened their doors to the visitors. All seemed mad with excitement. "Such gesticulating, and jabbering you never saw or heard," wrote an Alabama delegate; "Babel could not have beat it far in noise and confusion and many-tongued contention." A Whig reporter described the scene on Chestnut Street that night as "animating beyond anything we have ever had here . . . since the glorious days of 1776." The street was "walled with men," ten thousand having come from New York City alone. Clay, Taylor, and Scott partisans held public meetings on the eve of the convention. Taylor's was held in Independence Square and the crowd was estimated at 20,000.[49]

The convention was called to order in the salon of the Chinese Museum at 11:00 A.M. John M. Morehead, former governor of North Carolina and a friend of Clay's, was chosen president, without opposition from Taylor delegates. Each state was allowed as many votes as it had in the electoral college, but all states were not fully represented, Texas not at all. Confusion resulting from Taylor's early opposition to a national convention had prevented, in some places, the holding of state and district conventions to select delegates. In resolving this problem, the convention acted inconsistently. It refused to let Alabama and South Carolina delegations vote their absentees but permitted the lone Arkansas delegate, a Taylor man, to cast all three of that state's votes and the pro-Taylor delegation from Louisiana to cast Texas' four unrepresented votes. Prior to the beginning of balloting, it was moved that no candidate be considered unless he would pledge "to maintain and carry out the principles of the Whig party." This was aimed, of course, at Taylor, but Morehead ruled the motion out of order, and his decision was sustained. A Louisiana delegate was permitted to read a letter from Taylor, pledging to abide by the decision of the convention and to withdraw from the canvass if he were not chosen.

One hundred and forty votes were required for nomination. On the first ballot Taylor led with 111, followed by Clay with 97, Scott with 43, and Webster with 22. On the second ballot Taylor gained 7, and Scott 7, while Clay lost 11. Clay's fate was sealed when the

[49] Washington *National Intelligencer*, June 8, 9, 1848; McMillan, "Baldwin Reports," 371.

Kentucky delegation failed to vote for him. One of Clay's chief northern supporters had written a week before the convention that everything depended on the Bluegrass state. "If Kentucky hesitates or doubts," he warned, "the north may be discouraged and may yield." And an Alabama delegate later excused his switch from Clay to Taylor on the ground that "The State of Kentucky was . . . against him."[50]

After the second ballot the convention recessed, and party leaders worked through the night to effect combinations that would gain the prize for their favorite. Weed, Fillmore, and Truman Smith battled in Taylor's cause; Greeley, Horace Greeley in Clay's. But if Clay was already defeated, it was also certain that Taylor had won. Three-fourths of his support came from Democratic states, or from Democratic districts in whig states. More than three-fourths of his delegates were from slave states, and support that had been counted on from Ohio and New York did not materialize. So bleak did Taylor's prospects seem that night that Truman Smith proposed to other leaders that the convention adjourn without making a formal nomination. But the proposal was rejected, and balloting was resumed on Friday morning. On the third ballot Smith was able to switch three of Connecticut's votes from Clay to Taylor, and Reverdy Johnson carried three of Clay's Maryland votes into the Taylor camp. This started the stampede, and on the fourth ballot Taylor was nominated, receiving 171 votes to Clay's 32. Only James Harlan, of the Kentucky delegation, supported Clay on the final ballot. Millard Fillmore of New York was nominated for Vice President. Weed wanted Webster for Vice President and claimed that he could have obtained the nomination for him but that Webster declined. If so, it was the second occasion when Webster's own decision kept him out of the White House.[51]

There was much bitterness among Clay's friends over Taylor's nomination. In turning down Clay, wrote Leslie Combs, the convention had refused to accept a "true *Ultra Whig* and a constitutional conservative Slaveholder," and ended by taking "an *Ultra* Slaveholder

---

[50] Joseph L. White to Clay, May 28, 1848, in T. J. Clay Papers; McMillan, "Baldwin Reports," 382.

[51] Full accounts of the convention, both formal and behind the scenes, are in Washington *National Intelligencer*, June 8, 12, 16, 1848; for particular interpretations and insights, see also Poage, *Henry Clay*, 179-80; Hamilton, *Zachary Taylor*, 88-91; Weed, *Autobiography*, 575; Barnes, *Memoir of Weed*, 167-69; Reverdy Johnson to David Campbell, June 5, 1848, in Campbell Papers (Duke).

& no particular Whig." A motion in the convention to make Taylor's nomination unanimous was objected to by delegates from Ohio and Massachusetts. Greeley dubbed the convention the Philadelphia "slaughter-house," and some Clay delegates left vowing that they would exert all their efforts to defeat the nominee. To allay this unhappiness, an immense ratification meeting was held in Independence Square on Friday night, and the walls of old Independence Hall echoed the shouts of ten thousand people. Leslie Combs, Clay's bosom friend, was roused from a sickbed and persuaded to speak. He said a few words, but his heart was not in it. "I never took so hard a pill," he wrote.[52]

Whatever restraints Crittenden may have felt before the nomination were removed by the action of the convention. It was now his duty as a loyal Whig to support the nominee of the party. A ratification meeting was held at once in Washington, and Crittenden spoke. In the course of his remarks he referred to the Spartan life Old Zack had led, saying that he neither drank nor played cards. In an effort to pour gall into Clay's fresh wounds, Democrats interpreted this as a reflection on Clay's well-known fondness for the cup and the gaming table. Crittenden had to deny publicly that his remarks had any reference to Clay.

Before Crittenden left Washington, his friends in Congress tendered him a farewell dinner. All members of the Senate and many from the House joined in sponsoring the event. It was held at the National Hotel on Tuesday, June 13, and was said to be an occasion without parallel. Mangum presided, assisted by Toombs and J. S. Pendleton. Toast after toast was offered, and Democrat rivaled Whig in praise of the affable and suave Kentuckian.[53] With these tributes ringing in his ears, Crittenden took his leave of Washington and hurried home to begin his own belated canvass for governor.

[52] Washington *National Intelligencer*, June 12, 1848; McMillan, "Baldwin Reports," 378; Combs to Clay, June 10, 1848, in T. J. Clay Papers.
[53] Washington *National Intelligencer*, June 15, 1848, copied in Frankfort *Commonwealth*, June 27, 1848.

CHAPTER XII

Kentucky Interlude

BEFORE Crittenden's gubernatorial nomination in the Frankfort convention in February, when it appeared that the feud between Dixon and Graves might split the Whigs, prominent Democrats had contended for the nomination of their party. The leading candidate was Chief Justice Elijah Hise of the court of appeals, but after Crittenden was nominated by the Whigs, Hise withdrew from the contest. The Democratic convention thereupon nominated Linn Boyd, congressman from the First District, but Boyd also declined. Whig editors could not contain their glee at this Democratic reluctance to face their candidate. Who, they asked, would be the next victim? Why not let the election go to Crittenden by default? Anyone would be a fool, they said, to contest the state with him. Finally the Democratic executive committee drafted Lazarus Powell, legislator from Henderson and law partner of Archibald Dixon.[1]

Crittenden arrived at Greenupsburg (Greenup) from Pittsburgh on Monday night, June 19. The following two weeks he campaigned through eastern Kentucky, arriving in the Bluegrass section in early July. In a speech at Versailles he shared the platform with his opponent. Powell, charging that Taylor had no political principles and had no platform, gave Crittenden an opening he seemed to be waiting for, to expose what he regarded as the absurdities of party platforms. Reminding his friend that Polk had to recede from the Baltimore Platform in regard to Oregon, he said that platforms were made by delegates "chosen by nobody knows whom, representing nobody knows whom, and responsible to nobody." The platform committee, he said, generally met "at a tavern over a basket of champagne" and fixed "the principles for the government . . . of the United States." This, he went on, "is popular government with a vengeance." Actually, he said, he considered a "principle" something more profound and more unalterable than could be fixed by "occasional opinions of party meetings." A principle, he concluded, was "an invariable standard in morals and politics . . . by which [actions] are to be tested." Taylor, he said, had principles of this kind.[2]

In the next month Crittenden spoke in southern and western Kentucky, sometimes three times in one day. He was assailed by the Democratic press for having sponsored in the Senate, years before, a bill to prevent federal officials from interfering in elections. This was now denounced as a gag law and interference with freedom of speech. He was also attacked for his support of a bankrupt law passed a decade before and with having opposed the calling of a state constitutional convention. He was blamed, too, for forcing on his party a presidential candidate who was no Whig and whose only qualification for the office consisted "in sleeping forty years in the woods, and cultivating moss on the calves of his legs."[3]

The real issue in the campaign, however, was the relationship between Crittenden and Clay, and whether or not Crittenden's behavior to his old friend had been honorable. Although more responsible than anyone else for launching and guiding Taylor's candidacy, Crittenden had stayed away from Philadelphia during the Whig convention. His position by that time had become most difficult. Already deeply committed to Taylor when he learned of

[1] Lexington *Observer and Reporter*, March 22, 29, 1848; *ibid.*, April 5, quoting Bowling Green *Argus*; Frankfort *Commonwealth*, April 11, 1848.

[2] Maysville *Herald*, quoted in Frankfort *Commonwealth*, July 4, 1848; Frankfort *Yeoman*, July 10, 27, 1848, quoted *ibid.*, Aug. 8, 1848.

[3] Frankfort *Commonwealth*, June 27, Aug. 1, 1848; *ibid.*, July 4, quoting Louisville *Journal*; Stevenson to Clay, May 22, 1848, in T. J. Clay Papers.

Clay's resurging ambition, he attempted to withdraw from active participation in the contest for the nomination. Six months earlier he had been accused by a friend of Clay's of sponsoring Taylor meetings. The letter he wrote in reply is lost, and what he said can only be surmised from a later letter and from collateral correspondence. But it completely satisfied at the time both Clay and his friend.[4] Nevertheless Crittenden continued through that winter and the spring of 1848 to direct the Taylor movement. In early January, 1848, he wrote Burnley, perhaps Taylor's most intimate friend: "My sentiments in relation to Mr. Clay, Genl Taylor & the Presidency have not been concealed—*I prefer Mr. Clay to all men, for the Presidency*—But my conviction—my involuntary conviction—is that he cannot be elected. And that being my belief, I thank God, that he has given us in the person of our noble old friend, Genl Taylor, a man who can be elected, if Mr. Clay cannot."

Crittenden was aware, he added, that the expression of this belief had angered some of Clay's friends. But Clay was "of too noble a nature" to admit of any such feeling or to doubt the sincerity of his friendship because of "my regard for truth & candour." He would consider himself "a false and treacherous friend" if he should advise Clay that he could be elected. Such a course might suit a flatterer, he added, not a friend. He had not believed until recently, he said, that Clay wished the nomination. Clay had told him that he would not be a candidate unless clearly "it was the *general* wish of the people, & that his election was certain." It was manifest, he added, "that that state of things had not occurred." Hence, he concluded that Clay would not even accept a nomination if it were proferred him. He was still confident Clay would "do right" and withdraw when he came to Washington and saw how things really were.[5]

When Clay formally announced his candidacy, Crittenden had written him at once saying that he hoped "it may turn out for the best." However, Clay already knew his opinions and apprehensions on the subject, and, he added, "I must confess that I still retain the same impressions. It has all along seemed to me that there was not that *certainty* of success, which alone could warrant your friends in

[4] J. L. White to Clay, Sept. 4, 1847, in Crittenden Papers (Duke); J. L. White to Crittenden, June 28, Oct. 30, 1847, Clay to Crittenden, Sept. 26, 1847, in Crittenden Papers.
[5] Crittenden to Burnley, Jan. 8, 1848, in Crittenden Papers (Duke).

again presenting your name as a candidate." Clay did not reply, and a coolness developed between the two men that the past years of comradeship could not thaw. In a fury immediately after the convention, Clay had written a bitter denunciation of the Kentucky delegation, charging Crittenden with disloyalty. He gave it to his son James to publish. James delayed until Clay's temper cooled, then persuaded him to suppress it. Had it appeared, it is doubtful that either Crittenden or Taylor could have been elected.[6] No event in Crittenden's life, according to his daughter, "distressed him so much as his alienation from Mr. Clay."[7]

Some of Clay's friends, and more of his and Crittenden's enemies, accused Crittenden of duplicity. Francis P. Blair spoke of vague criticisms he said Crittenden had made of Clay in late April when Blair had been a guest at Crittenden's table. He was convinced that "Our Castor & Pollux of Kentucky were no longer twins—but two."[8] But evidence hardly sustains a charge of doubledealing by Crittenden. He certainly believed in late February, 1848, that Clay intended to announce his withdrawal when he reached home. It was commonly believed in Washington that Clay would do so, and we know from Clay's letters to his son that it was his firm intention until late February to withdraw. Crittenden always maintained that after he learned of Clay's announcement, he took no further action in Taylor's behalf, and his friends vouched for this. George D. Prentice, who had spent the better part of two decades attempting, in the Louisville *Journal*, to advance Clay's cause, later wrote: "When it became manifest that a very large number of Mr. Clay's friends were disposed to nominate him, and that he was not altogether indisposed to be a candidate, neither Mr. Crittenden nor ourselves took the slightest part in any attempt to influence the action of the Whig National Convention as between Mr. Clay and Gen. Taylor."[9]

Clay's warmest friends in Kentucky—Combs, Harlan, Stevenson

[6] Washington *National Intelligencer*, May 17, June 13, 1848; Frankfort *Commonwealth*, May 9, 1848; "Recollections of an Old Stager," XLV (1872), 447, 448; Stevenson to Clay, May 22, June 12, 1848, James Harlan to Clay, June 15, 1848, Clay to Worsley, Throckmorton, Rudd, and Thruston, June 27, 1848, Clay to Nicholas Dean, Aug. 24, 1848, Crittenden to Clay, May 4, 1848, in T. J. Clay Papers; Poage, *Henry Clay*, 157-58, 168, 181; John P. Stewart to Duncan McLaurin, Sept. 14, 1848, in McLaurin Papers (Duke); Hamilton, *Zachary Taylor*, 88-89, 94; Clay to Crittenden, April 10, 1848, in Crittenden Papers.

[7] Coleman, *Crittenden*, I, 281.

[8] Blair to Van Buren, March 3, May 2, 1848, in Van Buren Papers.

[9] Louisville *Journal*, Aug. 24, 1850.

—never wavered in their belief that Crittenden had behaved honorably toward Clay. Stevenson, a month after the convention, wrote Clay's son that Crittenden preferred his father to all men and would "fight under his flag, live or die, while ever it was in the field." Crittenden, he said, had told him before the convention that he believed only Taylor could win for the Whigs in November. Nevertheless, Stevenson was convinced that "neither in public nor in private" did Crittenden use any means to accomplish Taylor's nomination "incompatible with friendship towards [Clay], or with what he owed to himself as a gentleman." One of Clay's kinsmen, Cassius M. Clay, agreed with this. He did not believe Crittenden capable of ingratitude, or of engaging in "a dishonorable intrigue against friend or foe."[10]

In a speech in Lexington a month before the election, Crittenden explained his course in relation to the nomination. With disarming bluntness he confessed that he preferred Clay to Taylor or to anyone else. He stated again that he had supported Taylor initially under the impression that Clay would not be a candidate. After Clay announced, Crittenden said he "assumed a position of perfect neutrality; never attempted to influence a single human being; [and] united in no political organization with a view to the Presidency." He could not, however, retreat from statements already made in support of Taylor, but he had not repeated them thereafter.[11]

The climax of the Clay-Crittenden issue was reached in late July. In a speech in Lexington, Dr. A. K. Marshall, brother of Tom, read what purported to be a letter from Crittenden urging one J. L. Anderson, a Cincinnati lawyer, to procure Taylor delegates from Ohio to the Philadelphia convention. The letter quoted Crittenden as saying that Clay had been "like a millstone" to the Whigs for a quarter of a century; that any other Whig but Clay could have won in 1844; that "everybody had beat him, and anybody could."[12]

The letter created a sensation. Crittenden was in western Ken-

[10] Crittenden to Burnley, Jan. 8, July 30, 1848, in Crittenden Papers (Duke); Crittenden to Winfield Scott, Dec. 9, 1851, in Crittenden Papers; letter of Thomas F. Marshall to Louisville *Journal,* quoted in Frankfort *Commonwealth,* Dec. 2, 1851; Stevenson to James B. Clay, July 19, 1848, in T. J. Clay Papers; Cassius M. Clay, *The Life of Cassius Marcellus Clay: Memoirs, Writings, and Speeches* (Cincinnati, 1886), 213-17 (hereinafter, Cassius Clay, *Memoirs*).

[11] Lexington *Observer and Reporter,* June 28, July 26, 1848.

[12] James Erwin to Burnley, July 18, 1848, in Crittenden Papers; Lexington *Observer and Reporter,* July 26, 1848.

tucky and could not be reached for comment. Clay's son sent off to Cincinnati to find Anderson and the original letter, but Anderson could not be found. There were only two lawyers in Cincinnati named Anderson, neither with the initials J. L., and neither had received such a letter from Crittenden. Furthermore, both were stanch Clay men, and Crittenden would not have dared make such statements to them. Inquiries of all other Andersons in Cincinnati failed to turn up one who had corresponded with Crittenden. Then the letter was examined more closely. It was ungrammatical, and there were anachronisms in it. Finally, its origin was revealed.

Marshall, a Democrat, eager to capitalize for his party on the strained relations of the Whig leaders, had written to Linn Boyd in Washington. Everyone knew, he said, that Crittenden had played Clay false. The problem was to get indisputable and convincing proof. Could not such proof be procured in Washington? "Can no Antony be found," he asked, "to do funeral honors to this modern *Caesar*?" If they could but fix on Crittenden the responsibility for Clay's defeat at Philadelphia, "we will beat him for Governor as sure as God lives."

Boyd responded obligingly. Of course such proof was available. Crittenden's part in Clay's defeat was so notorious in Washington that Boyd was astonished to learn it was doubted anywhere. He had in his possession the very letter Marshall desired. He had obtained it from a man named Snellson. Boyd made excerpts and forwarded them to Marshall with a promise that if Crittenden denied their authenticity, the original would be produced. Marshall was overjoyed. The election, he exulted, was "perfectly in our hands not only in Kentucky but in the United States" as well. But D. C. Wickliffe, editor of the *Observer and Reporter*, refused to believe that Crittenden had ever said the things related or that any Ohio Whig had charged him with writing such a letter. Thereupon, Marshall appealed to Boyd for the original letter of Anderson. But Boyd put him off. In a somewhat incoherent answer he told him that he did not now have the letter.

Marshall smelled a rat. "If it should turn out," he wrote, "that no such letter was ever written or that there is no such man as J. L. Anderson then I shall be in rather an awkward fix." If only he could have had Crittenden's letter or even Anderson's, then "we should have beaten Crittenden 15,000 votes, set Old Hal out against

Gen. Taylor and made the matter easy for us." He now began to fear disgrace and regretted that he had ever become involved in the affair. If Boyd would not certify the excerpts he had made, it was "worse than useless." The only chance to beat Crittenden, he said, was "to get up a war between him & Clay . . . but that 'cock wont fight,' and we will be beaten badly."[13]

The denouement was terrible for Marshall, Boyd, and Boyd's confederate, John M. McCalla, a Kentuckian employed as a government clerk in Washington. Boyd had used McCalla as his amanuensis, and McCalla had gilded the lily by writing to Marshall that John M. Botts had authorized him to state that Crittenden *"alone"* was responsible for Clay's defeat and that Crittenden had "tomahawked and scalped" Clay. When this was published, Botts denied categorically that he had so accused Crittenden. McCalla had to make a complete retraction, exonerating Botts, and Marshall admitted in a speech in Richmond that the Snellson letter was a fabrication. Crittenden, meanwhile, had been reached and had denied having written any such letter. Boyd, hiding behind McCalla's explanations, said nothing.[14]

At the start of the gubernatorial campaign in June, Whigs had been confident of winning an overwhelming victory. The editor of the *Commonwealth* said that a majority for Crittenden of only ten thousand votes would be unsatisfactory. But as the summer wore on with Clay refusing to endorse his old friend, and with great efforts being made to drive the wedge between them deeper, the *Commonwealth* revised its estimate. It now began to fear that Crittenden might be defeated. His defeat would be a party tragedy of the first magnitude in Kentucky, and its reverberation would have disastrous effects on Taylor's chances everywhere. The editor of the *Observer and Reporter* made a special plea to friends of Clay shortly before the August election to come to Crittenden's aid. "If Mr. Crittenden should be defeated, or elected by a very lean majority," wrote editor

[13] Marshall to Boyd, June 24, 1848, Boyd to Marshall, July 6, 1848, Marshall to McCalla, July 18, 1848, in John M. McCalla Papers, Duke University Library; James Erwin to Burnley, July 18, 1848, in Crittenden Papers.

[14] Lexington *Observer and Reporter*, July 26, Aug. 9, 1848; Frankfort *Commonwealth*, Aug. 1, 8, 1848; Washington *Union*, quoted *ibid.*, Aug. 8, 1848; Crittenden statement in Crittenden Papers; Crittenden to Orlando Brown, July 27, 1848, Crittenden to Burnley, July 30, 1848, in Crittenden Papers (Duke); Stevenson to James B. Clay, July 19, 1848, Will R. Hervey to [James B. Clay], July 22, 1848, in T. J. Clay Papers; Boyd and B. L. Clarke to McCalla, July 24, 1848, statement in hand of McCalla, Aug. 1, 1848, unsigned statement of Botts, in McCalla Papers (Duke).

D. C. Wickliffe, "it will act upon our friends everywhere with tremendous power."[15]

Crittenden polled 65,860 votes to Powell's 57,397, a majority for Crittenden of 8,463. Neither side was pleased with the result. Democrats had hoped to hold Crittenden's margin to less than 4,000, perhaps to 2,500. Crittenden called it "a signal victory under all the circumstances of the case," but his friends were not happy.[16]

Wednesday, September 6, 1848, was inauguration day in Frankfort. The sun rose that morning in a cloudless sky, and soon the early morning mist had disappeared. There was a pleasant breeze stirring in the heavy oaks and lindens in Capitol Square as an immense throng gathered there, spilling over onto the slightly terraced lawns on Madison Street. At 11:00 o'clock a procession headed by Willis G. Hughes, chairman of the arrangements committee, moved out from the capitol grounds to the accompaniment of martial music. Proceeding down Washington Street, it stopped at the corner of Main. Crittenden appeared at his doorway and was escorted to the chairman's carriage. The procession then moved up Main Street to Wilkinson, and from there back to Capitol Square. The oath was administered to Crittenden under Inauguration Oak by Chief Justice R. C. McKee, and Crittenden was then conducted to the executive office, where the state seal and the executive archives were handed over to him by retiring Governor Owsley.[17]

With his own affairs settled for the time, Crittenden turned his attention to Taylor's campaign against Democrat Lewis Cass. From the time he had spoken at the ratification meeting in Washington, Crittenden had never ceased to link his own campaign with Taylor's. Indeed, his speeches during the summer had seemed more in Taylor's interest than in his own. Now, however, he returned to the national scene and assumed direction of Taylor's candidacy. It was well that he did, for preconvention wounds were being irritated in places other than Kentucky. Whig papers, whistling by the graveyard, were denying that Clay was unhappy over the results of the Philadelphia convention. He lived, said one editor, only for the victory of the

---

[15] Frankfort *Commonwealth*, June 27, Aug. 15, 1848; Maysville *Herald*, quoted *ibid.*, Aug. 8, 1848; Lexington *Observer and Reporter*, Aug. 9, 1848.

[16] Frankfort *Commonwealth*, Sept. 5, 1848; John Pendleton to Crittenden, Sept. 14, 1848, in Crittenden Papers; John P. Stewart to Duncan McLaurin, Sept. 14, 1848, in McLaurin Papers (Duke); Crittenden to Alexander H. Stephens, Sept. 4, 1848, in Stephens Papers.

[17] Frankfort *Commonwealth*, Sept. 12, 1848.

party. Yet, all the while, Clay remained brooding, refusing to endorse Taylor, and the *National Intelligencer* filled its summer issues with articles attempting to prove to the doubtful that Taylor was a true Whig.[18]

New York, as usual, was a vital state, and a Whig victory there, regarded as certain in the spring because of Democratic divisions between Hunkers and Barnburners, was now in danger. Dissident Whigs, unwilling to accept Taylor, prepared a grand meeting of protest against him in early fall at Vauxhall Gardens. There several hundred Whigs nominated Clay as the True Whig candidate and urged the formation of Clay clubs all over the country. Taylor men in the East were desperate, for New York must be carried if Cass were to be defeated. Appeals were made to Clay to repudiate this defection, and in a letter to the managing committee two weeks later, Clay declined the nomination. In doing so, however, he affirmed his belief that Taylor was no Whig and that the party had been "humiliated" and "degraded" by the Philadelphia convention. Fortunately for Taylor, not all of this was published, but even so, the effect of the temporary schism was not entirely healed. Clay's conduct was bitterly resented. Truman Smith wrote Crittenden that "Mr. Clay's equivocal course in regard to Genl Taylor's nomination is the subject of general remark wherever I go." Robert Toombs thought Clay the most despised man in the nation by all true Whigs.[19]

Crittenden directed the last two months of the campaign with a skill and deftness that might have done credit to such a wizard as Thurlow Weed. There were appeals to him from all sections to come and campaign personally. To have yielded would have dissipated his energies and diluted his influence. Instead, he sent Clayton and Charles S. Todd to Pennsylvania; Clay's friend, Leslie Combs, he sent to New York and New England; and Letcher and Metcalfe were dispatched to Ohio. He kept up a daily correspondence with Whig leaders everywhere: with Truman Smith, who was mailing

[18] Clayton to Crittenden, Aug. 11, 1848, in Crittenden Papers; Frankfort *Commonwealth*, summer of 1848, especially June 13; Washington *National Intelligencer*, summer of 1848.

[19] Nicholas Dean to Clay, Oct. 5, 1848, Morton McMichael to Clay, Sept. 9, 1848, Clay to James Lynch and others, Sept. 20, 1848, in T. J. Clay Papers; O[gden] Hoffman to Crittenden, Sept. 20, 1848, Truman Smith to Crittenden, Sept. 16, 1848, Toombs to Crittenden, Sept. 27, 1848, in Crittenden Papers; ————— to Clayton, n. d., in Clayton Papers. Accounts of Vauxhall meeting are in Washington *National Intelligencer*, Sept. 11, 18, 1848; Frankfort *Commonwealth*, Sept. 19, 1848.

"documents right & left," with Reverdy Johnson in Maryland, with Abbott Lawrence in Massachusetts, with Stephens and Toombs in Georgia. The volume of his correspondence during September and October of that year is appalling.

To all he gave sound advice. By a judicious concentration of effort, success might be assured. "If our exertions are made equally everywhere," he wrote Clayton, they must in many states be wasted and unsuccessful. Pennsylvania, for instance, by late summer, looked doubtful. He asked Clayton to go there and consult with party leaders. If, after "cool & candid calculation," it was decided they could not carry the state, then they should direct all their efforts to other points, such as New Jersey and Ohio. With these states Taylor could be elected without Pennsylvania. On the other hand, if their efforts were divided, all three might be lost and Taylor defeated. When Stephens reported that prospects of carrying Georgia were dim, Crittenden urged him to consult with Toombs and devise new strategy. Georgia, he said, must be carried. Clayton reported, after his conference with Pennsylvanians, that prospects looked good in that state, and Crittenden urged him to attend to all contingencies and to write him often of developments. "You are the Napoleon I rely on," he told him. Ohio, he wrote Ewing, rested on his efforts.[20]

The election was a crisis in Crittenden's career. He well knew that his political head was on the block. For Taylor was everywhere identified as his candidate. In bringing him out, he had offended his old friend Clay. True, Clay's star was setting; but if victory was not won, Crittenden's would never rise again. Over and over he

[20] Files of Crittenden Papers for September, October, and November, 1848, have hundreds of letters from political leaders from all sections reporting on conditions in their sections. See especially letters from Reverdy Johnson, Oct. 5; Joseph Vance, Sept. 21, Oct. 24, Nov. 13; John W. Allen, Sept. 9, Oct. 21; William Woodbridge, Sept. 12; J. Durbin Ward, Sept. 2; James B. Mowrer, Sept. 11, Oct. 22; Moses Grinnell, Sept. 21; Ogden Hoffman, Sept. 20; Thomas Metcalfe, Sept. 2; Truman Smith, Sept. 16, 23, Oct. 3, 17; Leslie Combs, Sept. 17; Alexander Stephens, Sept. 26; Robert Toombs, Sept. 27; Charles S. Todd, Sept. 27; Charles H. Delavan, Oct. 23; R. W. Thompson, Oct. 21; Albert T. Burnley, Oct. 18; George Badger, Oct. 12; Balie Peyton, Oct. 21; Ephraim H. Foster, Oct. 10; Thomas Ewing, Sept. 24, Oct. 6; S. Starkweather, Oct. 21; Clayton, Aug. 11, Oct. 12. See also letters of Crittenden to Clayton, Aug. 30, Oct. 6, 17; Leslie Combs to Clayton, Nov. 12, in Clayton Papers; Crittenden to Burnley, Oct. 19, 27, in Crittenden Papers (Duke); Crittenden to Stephens, Sept. 4, Oct. 6, 1848, Smith to Crittenden, Oct. 2, 1848, in Stephens Papers; Crittenden to Waddy Thompson, Oct. 2, 1848, in possession of Holman Hamilton, Lexington, Kentucky; Abbott Lawrence to Crittenden, Sept. 18, 1848, in Coleman, *Crittenden*, I, 323. For a more detailed account of the campaign state by state, see Hamilton, *Zachary Taylor*, chaps. ix, x, xi.

reminded his associates of the personal consequences for them in case of defeat. Taylor's election, he wrote one lieutenant, was "the great event—of our times. If we fail in that, our Government is but a wreck, and we are given over to proscription." The crisis demanded all their energies and wisdom. He closed a long letter to Thomas Ewing with an even stronger exhortation. "There is, Ewing," he wrote, "one other consideration that must give to you & me a sort of final & concentrated interest in this contest. It is the *last* in which we can hope to share in the triumph. If defeated now, it is final as to us." He urged Ewing to put forth all his effort "in this last struggle, then,—and let nothing be left undone that can contribute to an honorable success."[21]

Taylor gained a plurality in the North and a majority in the South. Van Buren, candidate of the Free Soil party, got not a single electoral vote, but his 290,000 popular votes aided Taylor's cause in the North, particularly in New York. Taylor carried both the Empire State and Pennsylvania, and with them an electoral majority of thirty-six over Cass. His popular vote in Kentucky was 1,200 more than Crittenden's August vote, and almost 6,000 more than Clay's four years before. Clay was ill, and was saved the mortification of casting his ballot, but it was reported that his sons voted for Taylor.

Almost by a thread had Crittenden's political life been spared. So close was the election in most northern states that a switch of a few hundred votes would have given a different result. Each man who played a part could be considered indispensable, but no one had played a larger part than Crittenden, and no one had more at stake than he. Not until the final returns were in could he feel secure. Had Taylor lost, political oblivion would have been Crittenden's reward. "You and I have escaped a great gulf," wrote Clayton. "It was yawning for us. If Taylor had failed you & I were doomed men." With victory achieved, however, and largely through Crittenden's leadership, there might be no limit to his aspirations. The future now looked bright, indeed.[22]

It was not generally believed that Crittenden would long serve as governor, for the routine would be dull indeed to one who had spent so many exciting years in the stimulating company of the United

[21] Crittenden to Clayton, Aug. 30, 1848, in Clayton Papers; Crittenden to Ewing, Sept. 1, 1848, in Ewing Papers.
[22] Clayton to Crittenden, Nov. 11, 1848, in Crittenden Papers (Kentucky).

States Senate. Functions of state government in that pastoral society were quite limited. The governor was little more than the executor of the will of the legislature, and the office offered few opportunities for leadership. State revenues were small, around $450,000 anually, and the governor enjoyed little discretion as to how they should be spent. Patronage was inconsequential. Crittenden had accepted the gubernatorial nomination only to heal a party schism, and at a great personal sacrifice.

After Taylor's election it was taken for granted that Crittenden would become "premier" in the new administration. The President-elect's abysmal ignorance of civil affairs and his limited qualifications were the butt of many a barbed joke of the opposition. He was honest and absolutely incorruptible, but he had been selected only because of his availability. If his administration was to succeed, he must have wise and trustworthy counselors around him to guide him in the school of practical politics. For headmaster in that school no man seemed better equipped than Crittenden. He enjoyed as near the universal confidence of the country as anyone. Enemies he had, but they were relatively few and of recent origin, and the Anderson-Snellson fiasco had gone far to discredit them. He had spent a dozen years in Washington, most of that time in the Senate. There he had distinguished himself as a man of moderation and of great integrity, particularly in the Oregon and the Texas debates. In the Mexican War he had been leader of the "loyal opposition." Although he disavowed the need for the war itself and for territorial acquisition in settlement of it, he had supported all measures for its prosecution. Furthermore, he enjoyed great personal popularity among his colleagues, Democratic as well as Whig. Even Polk trusted and admired him. Only William Allen had reason to dislike him.

Soon, however, rumor spread that Crittenden might refuse to go into the cabinet, and he was bombarded with pleas that he accept a place. He was "implicated" in Taylor's election. People had voted for Taylor under the assumption that if he were elected, Crittenden would be his right arm. Had they suspected otherwise, they would not have voted for him. Furthermore, the party and the country were divided sectionally, and only Crittenden could reunite them. With a Louisiana slaveowner in the White House, only Crittenden's presence in the cabinet would reassure the North. From Abbott Lawrence and Robert Winthrop in Boston, from John Pendleton,

William C. Rives, and William S. Archer in Virginia, from Alexander C. Bullitt in New Orleans, from Francis Granger in New York, from George Badger in North Carolina, from Ephraim Foster in Tennessee, from Tom Corwin in Ohio came these and other pleas. J. Watson Webb warned that Crittenden would be held responsible for the failures of the administration, and that public opinion demanded his presence. One New Englander, hearing that Crittenden could not afford financially to go into the cabinet, offered to raise whatever sum was necessary to provide for him, and to contribute one thousand dollars himself. James Mowrer quoted Cassius' speech to Brutus about "a tide in the affairs of men," but John McClung was more blunt. If Crittenden declined the office, he wrote, it would be a "fatal step." Taylor, through ignorance, would fall into "wrong hands," which would ruin his administration and all who had contributed to his election. There was "no man . . . who will *suffer* half so much from any false step taken by Taylor," he wrote, "as yourself. If Taylor *eats sour grapes*, your teeth will be on edge, although you should be removed a thousand miles from him."[23]

Pressure from members of Congress was especially intense. "We cannot," wrote Clayton, "get along without you. . . . If you were here I should have full faith that we could navigate the ship through all the breakers." William B. Preston wrote that Crittenden's presence in the cabinet *"cannot be dispensed with."* Truman Smith argued that Crittenden was the only veteran politician who should go into the cabinet, but that he must. "This I say," he added, "on grave consideration & I wish to God I had your ear for an hour to assign reasons. If you are willing to take the first . . . place in the Cabinet the country will say Amen but all the rest should be *fresh men.*" Robert Toombs wrote that Washington sentiment was "universal" that he should be in the cabinet. "You must not think of declining," he wrote. ". . . It is of the first importance to the success

[23] Letters to Crittenden from L. H. Arnold, Dec. 5, 1848, from Walter Cunningham, Dec. 24, 1848, from Joseph Blunt, Dec. 8, 1848, from Abbott Lawrence, Nov. [?], 1848, from James B. Mowrer, Oct. 15, Nov. 12, Dec. 3, 1848, from J. Prescott Hall, Dec. 24, 1848, from John Pendleton, Dec. 22, 1848, from E. H. Allen, Nov. 25, 1848, from Francis Granger, Dec. 4, 1848, from William C. Rives, Nov. 25, 1848, from Robert C. Winthrop, Dec. 8, 1848, from Ephraim Foster, Dec. 27, 1848, from Alexander C. Bullitt, Dec. 3, 1848, from Webb, Dec. 21, 1848, from McClung, Jan. 6, 1849, from W. S. Archer, Jan. 7, 1849, from George E. Badger, Jan. 13, 1849, from Garrett Duncan, Jan. 22, 1849, in Crittenden Papers; Corwin to Crittenden, Nov. 29, 1848, in Crittenden Papers (Duke).

of Gen. T's administration and to the country that you should come." "Honest John" Davis of Massachusetts wrote that Crittenden was "by the vote of the people elected Secretary of State."[24]

Even Democrats joined in the clamor. James Buchanan, about to retire as Polk's Secretary of State, pled earnestly both as Crittenden's friend and as a friend of his country that Crittenden not refuse the post. Edward Hannegan, Democratic senator from Indiana, assured Crittenden that his presence in the cabinet would give the country "a feeling of confidence and security which the name of no other man could do." Dire warnings were given that it was now or never for Crittenden.[25]

In late January, Clay was chosen as Crittenden's successor in the Senate, and many now feared that the Old Prince, desperate with disappointment and envy, would seek to embarrass Taylor's administration. "All that hate and *Revenge* can actuate a malignant heart to do will be done by him," wrote Alexander H. Stephens. Crittenden must, therefore, come and protect Taylor. "I do not solicit, or suggest or ask," he added. "I speak in language positive and absolute. For upon your decision in this matter depends more than you are aware of. *You must not Refuse.*" For a time this argument seemed to sway Crittenden. As pressure mounted, it was reported in Frankfort that he would now accept a cabinet post. Even Letcher thought he would.[26]

But Crittenden was not to be persuaded. The gulf that now separated him and Clay recalled to his mind events of a quarter century before, when Clay had made the fatal error of going into Adams' cabinet. The two situations were not precisely the same, but there was similarity enough. Clay had deserted a western man almost as popular as himself in Kentucky and had helped elect a Yankee who, if not despised, was at least distrusted. And Crittenden had abandoned, for a military hero, the man who for almost a half century had been the popular idol of Kentucky as well as the recognized national

[24] Letters to Crittenden from Clayton, Dec. 13, 1848, from Preston, Dec. 6, 1848, from Smith, Dec. 12, 1848, from Davis, Jan. 19, 1849, in Crittenden Papers; Toombs to Crittenden, Jan. 3, 1849, in Phillips, *Correspondence of Toombs, Stephens, and Cobb*, 140.

[25] Letters to Crittenden from Buchanan, Dec. 15, 1848, from Hannegan, Jan. 23, 1849, in Crittenden Papers.

[26] Stephens to Crittenden, Feb. 6, 1849, in Crittenden Papers; Blair to Van Buren, Jan. 27, 1849, in Van Buren Papers; Thomas B. Stevenson to Caleb B. Smith, Feb. 9, 13, 1849, in Caleb B. Smith Papers, Library of Congress.

leader of the Whig party. True, Crittenden's man was much more popular in Kentucky than John Quincy Adams had been. Crittenden well knew, however, that Clay had compounded the injury he had done himself in 1825 by accepting the first place in Adams' cabinet. Had he not made that blunder, he might have been forgiven. Clay, himself, later recognized this as the great error of his career; and Crittenden, who had urged Clay to accept the cabinet post, must long ago have come to regret his bad advice. Now he feared that if he accepted high office from Taylor, he would subject himself to the same charge of bargain that had pursued Clay since that incident of long ago. Indeed, Clay's friends, who were bitter, were eager for Crittenden to repeat Clay's error. They wished, one who communed with them reported, to "charge on [Crittenden] 'bargain sale & corruption' with more fatal effect than the past generations of Locofocoism have done on Mr. Clay."[27]

The memory of Clay's error certainly influenced Crittenden's resolve, but there may have been other motives, too. His one venture into the executive branch of the national government had not been a happy one. He apparently had little taste or talent for administration, particularly for the skillful use of patronage. As head of Taylor's cabinet, he would have vast patronage at his disposal, and perhaps he was appalled at this prospect. Besides, since the days of Jefferson and Madison, the Secretary of State had come to be regarded as the heir apparent to the administration in power, and it is probable that Crittenden had already determined that he did not want to be President. It was the Senate that he had come to love, and it was there that he now longed to return. The surest path to that goal was to serve his term as governor, or at least a major part of it. Then, when a vacancy occurred, his election to the Senate would be assured.

Taylor offered Crittenden the State Department shortly after the election. When the governor declined, Taylor seemed to think he could persuade him to change his mind. He reserved definite commitments of all cabinet places until he could visit Frankfort en route to Washington.[28]

A bitter cold spell descended on Kentucky in late January, and

---

[27] B. B. Meeker to Charles S. Todd, Nov. 20, 1848, in Todd Papers, Filson Club.
[28] A[lexander] C. Bullitt to Crittenden, Dec. 3, Clayton to Crittenden, Dec. 13, 1848, in Crittenden Papers.

ice had formed in the upper reaches of the Kentucky River. Then in mid-February, warm, sunny weather suddenly set the ice floes loose, and they were running thick and heavy when Taylor's boat, the *Sea Gull*, pushed its way upstream from the Ohio. For several days Frankfort had been agog over the arrival of Old Rough and Ready. Visitors from far and near were thronging to the little hill-enclosed village, eager to catch a glimpse of the old hero, now President-elect. About ten o'clock on the morning of February 15, a cannon boomed from the lock a mile below town, announcing the arrival of the *Sea Gull* there. There was a response from guns within the town, and crowds rushed to the riverbanks and gathered on the new bridge crossing the river. As the boat touched the wharf, a shout went up, momentarily drowning out the band that had struck up a martial air.

As Taylor stepped ashore and ascended the stairs to his carriage, he was greeted by members of the legislature and by veterans who had served under him in Mexico. At the statehouse Crittenden welcomed him in a short speech and presented him formally to members of the legislature. At the newly completed First Presbyterian Church on Main Street, across from Crittenden's home, a grand reception was held, and there on a platform erected for the occasion Taylor sat in an armchair between Crittenden and Maria to receive the multitude. That over, Taylor and his host returned in an open carriage to the Mansion House, where serious business awaited them.[29] Their talks ranged deep into the night, and neither man seemed pleased with the result of the conference. Crittenden had no intention of changing his decision and going into the cabinet himself, but he hoped to obtain the Postmaster Generalship for his friend Letcher.

Since 1840 a warm friendship had developed between Crittenden and Letcher. Elected governor in 1840, Letcher remained in Frankfort after his term expired, taking a house on Wapping Street that backed up to Crittenden's on Main. Letcher was noted for his cheerful disposition and for his sense of humor which was intolerant of all melancholy considerations. A decade earlier, even dour old John Quincy Adams had spoken approvingly of his "good temper, playful wit, and shrewd sagacity." Adams deplored Letcher's departure from

[29] Frankfort *Commonwealth*, Feb. 20, 1849; Crittenden to Clayton, Feb. 17, Leslie Combs to Clayton, Feb. 18, 1849, in Clayton Papers; Mrs. Jennie C. Morton, "Governor John J. Crittenden," in *Kentucky Register*, III (1905), 9.

Congress as "a loss to the House, for he laughs at everything; often in the heat of angry and fierce debate he throws in a joke, which turns it all to good humor." Heavy-bodied, with short arms and legs which reminded Cassius Clay of "flappers of a shell fish," Letcher's appearance was almost sufficient to inspire mirth even without his well-developed sense of humor. His round bullethead rested almost directly upon his shoulders, and his mouth seemed capable of unlimited expansion when he talked. His wit together with his physique gave him a Falstaffian character in sharp contrast to Crittenden's, although they were brothers under the skin.

Wise in politics and possessed of balance, Letcher would have been an invaluable aid to Taylor. But Taylor had the strange belief that positions in the cabinet were offered not to men but to states. If Kentucky declined a place, she was not entitled to another offer until aspirations of all other states had been met. He stubbornly refused to consider Crittenden's recommendation of Letcher. On the other hand, he was disappointed and somewhat chagrined that he could not persuade Crittenden to enter his cabinet.

When Taylor left Frankfort at noon next day, the *Commonwealth* made only the terse announcement that Crittenden had declined an appointment because he did not think he should resign so soon after being elected governor. But Thomas Stevenson, who journeyed from Frankfort to Cincinnati with Taylor, learned the true reason. "Taylor reports," he wrote, "that Crittenden's reason to him for not going in, was the apprehension of a cry of bargain & management, and a desire, instead of incurring this, to heal the divisions between Clay & Taylor men." Francis P. Blair, who had borne with Crittenden the agony of an earlier charge of "bargain and management," reached the same conclusion independently.[30]

Crittenden's decision seems in retrospect unfortunate, despite the lesson of the Clay-Adams affair a quarter century before. His sound judgment, his great knowledge and experience in government, and his ready comprehension of complex problems would have been invaluable to Taylor. Furthermore, he would have brought to the administration a prestige that it badly needed. Old Zack's complete

[30] Frankfort *Commonwealth*, Feb. 20, 1849; Stevenson to Caleb B. Smith, Feb. 16, 1849, in Caleb B. Smith Papers; Poage, *Henry Clay*, 183; Blair to Van Buren, Feb. 17, 1849, in Van Buren Papers; Adams, *Memoirs*, VIII, 336, entry of March 5, 1831; Cassius Clay, *Memoirs*, 215.

confidence in him might have prevented the rupture that soon came between Taylor and Clay, for Crittenden was even more of a peacemaker than the Great Pacificator. Crittenden was soon to see the superior wisdom of Clay's plan to settle the sectional crisis, and he probably could have made it palatable to the stolid old warrior. In a way, therefore, blame for the shortcomings of Taylor's brief term rested on Crittenden's head for refusing to go into the cabinet.[31]

During his term as governor, Crittenden was beset by both personal and public problems. Most distressing to him was the behavior of his oldest son, for whose misconduct he now had to appeal to Taylor for clemency. George had drifted aimlessly for a few years after his release by Santa Anna; then in the spring of 1846 he had been recommissioned in the army as captain of dragoons. He had already been disciplined for intemperance, and he promised his father that he would abstain from all intoxicating liquors. But in Mexico in the winter of 1847 he had again been arrested for drunkenness on duty, and fearing to face a court-martial, he had peremptorily resigned his commission. The resignation reached Secretary of War Marcy in March, 1847, but a few days later George himself appeared in Washington and asked to recall it. Marcy permitted him to do so and restored him to command. George returned to Mexico and for a time behaved well. On the expedition against Mexico City he was cited for gallant conduct and promoted to major.

Before the year was out, however, he again was charged with drunkenness, and again he resigned in order to avoid a court-martial. Crittenden's friends prevailed upon Polk to refuse to accept the resignation, and George was restored for the second time to rank. Within three months he was again drunk on duty, and this time his commanding officer did not permit him to resign. A court-martial ordered his dismissal from the service, and Polk approved the sentence of the court and nominated George's successor. Crittenden's former Senate colleagues, including Democrats Benton, Hannegan, Jefferson Davis, and David R. Atchison, urged Polk to reverse his action. George's intoxication was conceded, but it was argued that the court that tried him was incompetent. Polk refused. He took the position that having once approved the court's finding, he could not now

---

[31] See especially Allan Nevins, *Ordeal of the Union*, 2 vols. (New York and London, 1947), I, 231-32; Hamilton, *Zachary Taylor*, 137; Brainerd Dyer, *Zachary Taylor* (Baton Rouge, 1946), 311-13.

reverse it. George was thus out of the army, and Polk could not, he said, jump a civilian to the rank of major over all subordinate officers. Crittenden, frantic at the disgrace to his son and its reflection on the good name of his family, was inconsolable. But the new President came to his relief, and before his term was two weeks old, he reversed the ruling of his predecessor. George was restored to rank, but within a year there would be fresh reports of his intemperance.[32]

In the summer of 1849 even greater tragedy struck. While Robert Crittenden was in Europe on a business trip, his wife, Adeline, died as the result of a miscarriage. Within the same year Ann Mary's husband, Chapman Coleman, died unexpectedly. Crittenden was deeply grieved, for Coleman was not only the husband of his favorite child, he was Crittenden's own friend and confidant. Her husband left her amply provided for, but Ann Mary from that time would lean even more heavily on her father, not only for advice on business affairs, but also in the rearing of her children. His advice on the former she followed, rarely the latter.[33]

As governor, Crittenden had few challenging public problems to deal with. It has been noted that this was an age when the state served as welfare agent for its citizens only in emergencies. Even relief measures had suffered some discredit in the struggles of the 1820s. The state's obligation to the citizen ordinarily consisted of routine measures designed to preserve domestic peace and tranquillity. Given such a philosophy, a governor could do but little to influence the course of his state, and the two years Crittenden spent

[32] Frankfort *Commonwealth*, May 26, 1846; Crittenden to Letcher, May 31, 1847, Marcy to Crittenden, March 27, 1847, Crittenden to A. T. Burnley, Jan. 8, 1848, Crittenden to Chapman Coleman, Aug. 28, 1848, Crittenden to William O. Butler, Nov. 5, 1848, in Crittenden Papers (Duke); Clayton to Crittenden, Jan. 6, 1848, Jan. 23, March 16, 1849, Burnley to Crittenden, April 4, 1848, Garett Duncan to Crittenden, Jan. 3, 15, 22, 25, 1849, Joseph Underwood to Crittenden, Jan. 9, 1849, Thomas Metcalfe to Crittenden, Jan. 14, Feb. 8, 1849, Edward Hannegan to Crittenden, Jan. 23, 1849, Thomas Hart Benton to Crittenden, Feb. 8, 1849, John P. Gaines to Crittenden, Sept. 29, 1850, in Crittenden Papers; Crittenden to Clayton, Jan. 30, Feb. 2, 17, 1849, in Clayton Papers; General W. J. Worth to Crittenden, Dec. 28, 1846, Jefferson Davis to Crittenden, Jan. 30, 1849, in Coleman, *Crittenden*, I, 263, 339-40; Polk, *Diary*, III, 489, IV, 268-69.

[33] Letcher to Orlando Brown, July 23, 25, 1849, in Letcher Papers, Kentucky Historical Society; Crittenden to Brown, July 26, 1849, copy of will of Chapman Coleman, executed July 14, 1850, Crittenden to Burnley, July 19, 1850, Crittenden to Mrs. Coleman, Dec. 9, Oct. 24, 1850, Feb. 23, March 8, Nov. 2, 1851, Mrs. Coleman to Crittenden, Sept. 17, 1850, in Crittenden Papers (Duke); Crittenden to Mrs. Coleman, July 23, 1850, in Crittenden Papers; *Kentucky Register*, XLI (1943), 74.

MARIA CRITTENDEN
CRITTENDEN'S SECOND WIFE

JOHN J. CRITTENDEN
IN HIS EARLY FORTIES

From a banknote of the Farmers Bank of Kentucky, Frankfort, courtesy of the Henry Clay Frick Art Reference Library, University of Pittsburgh

in the office were dull indeed for him. State taxes were nominal, perhaps averaging only a dollar or two per year for each citizen, and were hardly an issue to provoke excitement or controversy. Considerable money had been invested in internal improvements, roads, and canals; but much of this had come from national and state surpluses, from toll collections, and from profits from other state enterprises, such as banks.[34]

One area in which Governor Crittenden gave constructive leadership was in public education. He had long been interested in education. He had served as a trustee of Transylvania in its golden age and had been a warm supporter of President Horace Holley in his difficulties. As speaker of the house in 1830 he had helped push through a bill authorizing local taxes for school purposes. Three years later he was chosen one of ten directors of a state education society formed to stimulate public interest in education.[35] The year before Crittenden became governor, Robert J. Breckinridge had been named superintendent of Kentucky schools, and he had started at once to establish a school system. Crittenden strongly supported his efforts, urging the legislature in his first message to levy a 2 percent property tax for a public school fund. The state, to be true to herself, he said, should afford the people the opportunity to acquire an education that would develop their native abilities. The legislature enacted the measure and also provided that the proceeds from tolls on the Kentucky, Green, and Barren rivers be set aside for education. The foundation was now laid for a soundly financed educational system.[36]

In his second and last annual message to the legislature Crittenden made an eloquent plea for the schools. Nothing would more solidly entrench the doctrines of republicanism, he said, than bringing together in the common schools "the high and the low, the rich and the poor, and uniting them [into] harmonious parts of the Commonwealth." "Educated poverty," he concluded, "will repay a thousand fold and in a thousand ways, its portion of the debt." Although all

34 State financial reports for Crittenden's term as governor are in *Kentucky Senate Journal,* 1849, pp. 9-10; *Kentucky House Journal,* 1848, pp. 7-19.

35 Edsel T. Godbey, "The Governors of Kentucky and Education," in *Bulletin of the Bureau of School Service,* XXXII, No. 4 (June, 1960), 94, 99; Frankfort *Commonwealth,* Oct. 1, 1833, Jan. 14, 28, Feb. 4, 1834.

36 *Kentucky Senate Journal,* 1848, pp. 367-72, 467; *Kentucky House Journal,* 1848, pp. 30-42 (especially 32-33), 399-402, 420.

children who were educated would become more useful citizens, "some poor boy may be sent forth from the humblest of your Common Schools—the People's Schools—singly and alone to redeem the whole debt by his public virtues and his public services."[37]

During Crittenden's term as governor, Kentucky adopted a new constitution, resolving an old issue in state politics. Crittenden, of course, was not a delegate and apparently had little influence on the convention. Whigs generally had opposed a new constitution because legislative districts would be reapportioned therein, endangering Whig dominance of the legislature. Democrats, of course, took the opposite stand, to achieve this very end. Crittenden had been in Washington during the years when the movement for a constitutional convention was gaining popular support, but during the campaign of 1848 he belatedly came out in favor of it. The convention met in Frankfort in October, 1849, but did not complete its work until the next year. Although delegates had not been chosen on party tickets, a majority of them were Democrats, and in spite of Whig efforts, a new constitution was adopted and was overwhelmingly approved by the voters. It supported the institution of slavery but incorporated many democratic reforms. Judges and other officials who had been appointed were now to be elected; legislative districts were reapportioned on a more equitable basis; elections, which formerly had been held over a three-day period, were now to be completed in one day.[38]

Meanwhile, in Washington the slavery issue was becoming more acute as a consequence of the territorial acquisitions of the Mexican War. When Congress convened in December, 1848, Calhoun at once called a caucus of southern congressmen of both parties. He proposed a militant and provocative address to the southern people urging them to withstand what he called "Northern agression," even if it meant dissolution of the Union. This gave Crittenden an opportunity to strike a blow in Kentucky against Calhoun's movement, using his annual message to the Kentucky legislature. He

[37] *Kentucky Senate Journal, 1849*, pp. 10-12.
[38] Crittenden to Mason Brown, Jan. 7, 1838, in Crittenden Papers (Duke); Mason Brown to Crittenden, Feb. 19, 1838, in Crittenden Papers; Wallace B. Turner, "Kentucky in a Decade of Change, 1850-1860" (doctoral dissertation, University of Kentucky, 1954), 2-3; Fields, "Making Kentucky's Third Constitution, 1830-1850," 10, 22-25; Crittenden to Dr. M. Q. Ashby, June 6, 1848, in Frankfort *Commonwealth*, June 28, 1848; *ibid.*, May 28, 1850.

decided to anticipate the argument of the secessionists and speak out boldly for the Union.[39]

Kentucky's attachment for the Union had undergone great change in the half century since James Wilkinson's flirtation with the Spanish governor at New Orleans. In 1828 Crittenden had been one of a legislative committee that replied to South Carolina's Exposition and Protest against the Tariff. Four years later he was speaker of the house when the legislature by a unanimous vote declared South Carolina's nullification ordinance "contrary to the constitution and . . . destructive to the peace and harmony of the Union." The years had brought, if anything, closer ties between Kentucky and the Union. Thomas B. Stevenson, who was in Frankfort during the winter of 1848-1849, thought no one, Whig or Democrat, sympathized with secession. The Union, he added, "is valued above all estimation of slavery."[40]

In his message to the legislature in 1848 Crittenden dwelt on Kentucky's stake in the Union. Her "dearest interests," he said, lay in its preservation. Its dissolution would remedy no ills but would be the *"consummation of the greatest evil that can befall us."* Kentucky, he concluded, would defend the Union to the utmost.[41] In the year that followed, the crisis, instead of abating, deepened. By December, 1849, there were plans for a convention of slave states to decide upon a common policy looking to secession. The border states would be crucial. "Everything is to depend from this day on the course of Kentucky, Tennessee, and Missouri," wrote a Boston editor. Crittenden saw the danger. He was forewarned by friends in Washington, and he determined to speak even more bluntly against the secessionists than he had the year before.

His message to the legislature in December, 1849, was a well-reasoned discourse on constitutional theory. The Constitution, he said, was not the creature of the states, as Calhoun argued, but was made by the people. It was the highest law of the land, and

[39] Toombs to Crittenden, Dec. 3, 1848, Crittenden to Clayton, Jan. 7, 1849, Badger to Crittenden, Jan. 13, 1849, Metcalfe to Crittenden, Jan. 14, 15, 23, 1849, in Crittenden Papers; Stephens to Crittenden, Jan. 17, 1849, in Stephens Papers; Cobb to Buchanan, June 17, 1849, Toombs to Crittenden, Jan. 22, 1849, in Phillips, *Correspondence of Toombs, Stephens, and Cobb*, 164, 141; Blair to Van Buren, Dec. 30, 1848, in Van Buren Papers.

[40] Frankfort *Argus*, Sept. 3, 1828, Dec. 5, 1832; Thomas B. Stevenson to Caleb B. Smith, Feb. 1, 1849, in Caleb B. Smith Papers.

[41] *Kentucky Senate Journal*, 1848, pp. 17-18.

"Inviolable respect and obedience" were due it. It both confirmed all the rights of the states and united "us . . . as one people." All states had pledged to abide by and support the Constitution and the Union it created.

Turning from theory to policy, he reiterated that Kentucky's material well-being was linked to the Union. The state's commercial ties with the Mississippi Valley, he said, were closer than with the gulf states. The great valley would never consent to destruction of the Union, which would close the Mississippi River to its exports. Self-interest, therefore, as well as nobler motives, made the Union a "necessity" to the Mississippi Valley and also to Kentucky. Kentucky sympathized with the southern states, but she would never harbor a thought against the Union and would abide by it to the last. "Dear as Kentucky is to us," he concluded, "she is not our whole country. The Union, the whole Union, is our country; and proud as we justly are of the name of *Kentuckian*, we have a loftier and more far-famed title—that of American Citizen."

It was a noble document, and the legislature gave it solid support. A senate resolution calling on all good citizens to cherish the Union and to denounce all efforts to break "the sacred ties which now . . . link together the various parts" passed by an overwhelming majority. How much the hands of Clay, Webster, Douglas, and other Unionists were strengthened in Washington by stout Unionist voices in Kentucky can only be conjectured. It is a fact, however, that Kentucky gave no encouragement to the Nashville convention in the spring and summer of 1850. And Crittenden played the leading part in aligning his state so solidly with the Union.[42]

[42] H. D. Foster, "Webster's Seventh of March Speech," in *American Historical Review*, XXVII (1921-1922), 253-54; *Kentucky Senate Journal*, 1849, pp. 14-15, 265.

CHAPTER XIII

The Soldier in the White House

RESPONSIBILITY for the relatively limited and undistinguished group of men whom Taylor chose for his cabinet must fall largely on Crittenden. Taylor of course made the final choice, but he discussed all possibilities with Crittenden during his twenty-four-hour visit in Frankfort. Contemporary observers, including Weed, Seward, Stephens, and Toombs, concurred in the belief that Crittenden actually selected the cabinet for Taylor. In this they were mistaken, but Crittenden's own letters are convincing that he suggested some and approved all of Taylor's selections. The day after Taylor left Frankfort, Crittenden assured Clayton that he could speculate "with some degree of confidence" as to the cabinet's makeup. According to Weed, Taylor later complained of the advice he received from one on whom he had relied so heavily. Crittenden was "too good and too forgiving a man & can't say *no* sometimes," said Taylor.[1]

The cabinet included such political nonentities as William M. Meredith of Philadelphia for Treasury, Jacob Collamer of Vermont for Post Office, and William Ballard Preston of Virginia for Navy. George W. Crawford of Georgia, whom Taylor chose for the War

Department, was of more stature, but he would become a source of great embarrassment to the administration, as would also Thomas Ewing, in the newly created Interior Department. Even Clayton, who had showed brilliance as a senator, was but a weak reed for the President in the State Department. And Reverdy Johnson, as Attorney General, hardly measured up to the level expected of so able a lawyer.[2]

The new administration had its first major problem with patronage. Eighty thousand offices scattered over the country were subject to presidential appointment. Postmasters, judges, attorneys, marshals, clerks, revenue collectors, census takers, were distributed in every neighborhood in the land, and troubles that might in isolated cases seem inconsiderable became formidable in the aggregate.

Whigs had never presided over the executive offices except in the brief months between the inauguration of Harrison and the break with Tyler, and the party faithful had developed a ravenous appetite during their long exclusion from federal patronage. One Whig, for example, who had spent more than a quarter century in the Post Office Department before he had been "Polked out," wanted reinstatement. A Kentuckian newly arrived in California wanted to be surveyor general there and asked an intermediary to "see the duck-leged [sic] old fellow" and tell him that "a friend of his half way to China is willing to allot, by metes and bounds, homes to his distant subjects." Another was getting old and "would like to die in a Whig stall well stocked with good fodder"; he asked, "Will there be room for me?" One of Caleb Smith's constituents hoped Smith would be Postmaster General so that he could give some of his friends "a lick at the spoon." Seward, who had a large voice in patronage affairs, divided all people into two classes: those going to California in search of gold, and those going to Washington in search of jobs. Crittenden, whose influence with the administration would not be as great as his friends had expected it to be, found himself converted into "a sort of Home Department, for negotiations & communica-

---

[1] Weed, *Autobiography*, 589-90. See also, Webster to "Dear Sir," Feb. 24, 1849, in Webster Papers; Seward to Weed, Feb. 27, 1849, in Seward, *Autobiography*, II, 100-101; Blair to Van Buren, March 4, 1849, in Van Buren Papers; Burnley to Crittenden, Jan. 12, 1849, Crittenden to Clayton, Dec. 19, 1848, Feb. 17, 1849, in Crittenden Papers; "Recollections of an Old Stager," XLVII (1873), 586.

[2] Toombs to Crittenden, Jan. 9, 1849, Burnley to Crittenden, Jan. 12, 1849, in Crittenden Papers; David Campbell to William Campbell, April 4, 1849, in Campbell Papers (Duke).

tions" relating to government jobs. He would become disillusioned at what he called the "widespread cupidity for office."[3]

One patronage difficulty resulted from a factional struggle among New York Whigs. Seward and Fillmore were rivals for control, and Fillmore's selection for Vice President was embarrassing to both Seward and his *alter ego*, Weed. To forestall the prospect of losing control of New York patronage, Seward had rushed down to Baltimore and Washington after the election. There he had ingratiated himself first with Taylor's brother and in-laws, and later with the general himself. He also assiduously cultivated members of the cabinet, who were already jealous of the consideration Taylor was giving Fillmore. In Taylor's ignorance of political protocol he regarded his Vice President as his chief of staff, consulting him on everything. But few politicians had the skill of Seward at charming patrons, or at undermining rivals, and by the time Taylor was inaugurated, Seward was able to write that "Clayton is becoming confidential with me, and General Taylor improves in favor." He had also established close personal relations with Ewing, Meredith, and Preston.

Through the combined efforts of Seward and the cabinet, Fillmore's influence with Taylor was dissipated, and soon Seward became dispenser of federal patronage not only in New York but in other portions of the North as well. This greatly embittered two important groups—friends of Clay, to whom the nomination of Fillmore had been a concession, and southern Whigs, who were convinced that Seward was using his power to give the Whig party in the North an antislavery bias. Seward was much more radical on the slavery question in 1849 than he would be a dozen years later.[4]

---

3 Numerous letters to Crittenden in winter and spring of 1849, especially those of J. S. Stanner, Jan. 11, of C. F. Clarkson, Jan. 13, and of Charles D. Drake, April 2, in Crittenden Papers; Charles Semple to Orlando Brown, Dec. 28, 1848, in Brown Papers, Filson Club; James Buchanan to George Bancroft, Dec. 18, 1848, in Buchanan, *Works*, XI, 481; William Matton to Caleb Smith, Dec. 14, 1848, Milton Stapp to Smith, Dec. 15, 1848, in Caleb B. Smith Papers; Seward to Mrs. Seward, Feb. 25, 1849, in Seward, *Autobiography*, II, 100; Crittenden to Clayton, March 13, 1849, in Clayton Papers.

4 Harry J. Carman and Reinhard H. Luthin, "The Seward-Fillmore Feud and the Crisis of 1850," in *New York History*, XXIV (1943), 163-69; Weed, *Autobiography*, 586; Seward to Mrs. Seward, Nov. 16, 17, 18, 1848, March 2, 1849, Seward to Weed, Nov. 29, 1848, March 4, 1849, in Seward, *Autobiography*, II, 87-89, 101, 103; Stephens, *Recollections*, 25; "Recollections of an Old Stager," XLVII (1873), 587-90; Poage, *Henry Clay*, 184-85; Hamilton, *Zachary Taylor*, 168-70, 185-86; Toombs to Crittenden, April 25, 1850, in Coleman, *Crittenden*, I, 364-65.

A second problem over patronage must be charged against the chaotic dispensing system that the administration instituted. Advised by Crittenden to follow a broad and liberal course toward all Whig groups and even to favor some deserving Democrats, Taylor seems to have tried to do so. But the old general's staff was unable to execute such a policy. Clay's son James, who had bitterly denounced Crittenden and his friends for betraying his father, was given the important post of chargé at Lisbon. When complaints were made, the administration lost whatever credit it had won with Clay by spreading the word that Clay had solicited the favor.[5] Rewards were given in a haphazard manner to friend and foe alike. Although Taylor's Indiana Whig friend and supporter Caleb Smith was refused any office, Edward Hannegan, lameduck Democratic senator from the same state, was given the choice assignment of minister to Prussia. Lincoln, who as one of the important Young Indians had been among Taylor's first supporters, was slighted in Illinois in favor of Clay's friend Justin Butterfield. On the other hand, Leslie Combs, a Clay man who had done yeoman service for Taylor after the Philadelphia convention, was never shown any consideration even though he applied directly for it.

In justice to Taylor it must be said that he never understood his problem. His native kindness and courtesy were often misinterpreted as promises that Taylor had never intended. Once in exasperation he exclaimed that if he did not "kick a man down stairs he goes away & declares [I] *promised him an office!*" It was also said that appointments were voted on in cabinet, Taylor having one vote the same as his advisers. When one disappointed applicant inquired why he had been passed over, the President was said to have replied that he "stood by him to the last, but was outvoted."[6]

More responsible than all others for the patronage fiasco that developed was Crittenden's friend Clayton. Clayton's difficulty lay in his eagerness to befriend everyone. Beset by countless officeseekers,

[5] Crittenden to Clayton, Dec. 19, 1848, Feb. 17, June 7, 29, 1849, Clayton to Crittenden, May 31, 1849, Combs to Crittenden, May 25, 1849, in Crittenden Papers; Letcher to Orlando Brown, n. d., June 19, 1849, in Letcher Papers, Kentucky Historical Society, Folder 564.

[6] Hamilton, *Zachary Taylor,* 204-15; Poage, *Henry Clay,* 191-92; E. W. McGaughey to Caleb Smith, April 16, 1849, B. F. Wallace to Smith, May 9, 1849, in Caleb B. Smith Papers; Lincoln, *Works,* II, 50, 55n, 93; "Recollections of an Old Stager," XLV (1872), 600; Clayton to Crittenden, July 11, 1849, in Crittenden Papers (Kentucky); Combs to Clayton, April 29, 1849, in Clayton Papers.

he promised more than he could deliver. Soon he was being charged with doubledealing by such Whig stalwarts as George D. Prentice, John Pendleton, Senator James A. Pearce of Maryland, and Robert Toombs.[7] Some of the charges against Clayton could be dismissed as wails of disappointed officeseekers, but much criticism of him went deeper. Burnley wrote Crittenden a few months after the new administration was installed that although he had no personal complaints against Clayton, he was "the most thin skined [*sic*] & the greatest coward—he is selfish, insincere, & will not stick to the truth." Francis P. Blair echoed this sentiment. According to him Clayton lacked "every thing . . . —courage—confidence—popularity."[8]

Crittenden refused to believe such charges against his friend. Even when his own recommendations were ignored, he continued to trust Clayton and to offer disinterested advice to the administration. He was disturbed, however, because Kentucky and other western states were slighted. Many federal jobs were in the East, where large customhouses and navy yards were located. But post offices were everywhere, yet Crittenden's recommendations for Kentucky appointments were ignored. So, too, were his letters to the Interior Department, where his old friend Ewing was treating him with studied coolness.

Crittenden, however, was able to secure the valuable Liverpool consulate for his son Thomas, even though Taylor had planned it for another. This office, with its private business opportunities, was said to be worth at least twenty thousand dollars a year. When this largess was dispensed, however, the awkard hand of Clayton revealed itself, nearly producing a rupture between the two friends. As soon as he learned of his own appointment as Secretary of State, Clayton, knowing he was obliged to Crittenden for it, insisted that Crittenden accept some foreign mission. He might have any he wished; no assignments would be made, he said, until he heard from Crittenden. "Speak freely to me," he wrote, "for I am *devoted* to you. Tell me how I can serve you."

[7] Alexander H. Stephens to Linton Stephens, April 17, 1850, in Johnston and Brown, *Life of Stephens*, 253; John Pendleton to Crittenden, Oct. 12, 1849, Clayton to Crittenden, April 8, May 31, 1849, Crittenden to Clayton, July 23, 1849, in Crittenden Papers; Bernard C. Steiner (ed.), "Some Letters from the Correspondence of James Alfred Pearce," in *Maryland Historical Magazine*, XVI (1921), 181-82; George D. Prentice to Clayton, June 20, 1849, in Clayton Papers.

[8] Burnley to Crittenden, July 22, 1849, Blair to Crittenden, Dec. 20, 1849, in Crittenden Papers.

Crittenden replied that it would be impossible for him to leave Frankfort for at least another year. Then, if it were convenient for the administration, he might accept an assignment in England or France. He realized, he added, that those places might not be available at that time. If so, *"be not embarrassed* in any way on my account," he said. He could wait, or even be content with no assignment for himself.

Soon Clayton, having made too many promises, began a strategic retreat. He wrote Crittenden that he might have any mission he chose, but that if he accepted one, Thomas could not have the consulate. The tone of the letter suggested to Crittenden that either alternative would cancel any claims he had on the administration, and this implication was too much for Crittenden's pride. "You know me well enough," he replied, "to know that I have no 'claims.'" His only interest was the success of the administration. That achieved, he would be amply compensated without any office for himself. He thanked Clayton for the favor shown his son. As for himself, however, he was altogether a *"disinterested friend,* and . . . a *postive non-seeker* of office." He did not desire and would never accept office except when it could be given without embarrassment.[9]

Crittenden had family wounds also to heal over the Liverpool consulate. Ann Mary had wanted the assignment for her husband and understood that Taylor had promised it to him. This was true, but Coleman's affairs would not permit him to accept, although apparently he had not made this clear to his wife. When Ann Mary learned that her brother had received a mission that she had expected for her husband, she wrote her father a petulant letter charging him with discrimination against her in favor of Thomas. Crittenden tried to reassure her. Thomas, he said, would never have accepted, and would resign even now, if he thought Coleman was interested in the appointment. He consoled his daughter with assurances of his affection. "You are," he wrote, "as *near & dear* to me as your brother. . . . Let your good sense . . . banish all these self tormenting & exaggerated feelings. You are capable of better & higher views. . . . Be yourself again."[10]

As spring became summer, patronage was still a problem, and difficulties faced the Whig party in Kentucky. Congressional elec-

---

[9] Clayton to Crittenden, March 16, April 8, 18, 1849, in Crittenden Papers; Crittenden to Clayton, April 6, 16, 17, 23, 1849, in Clayton Papers.
[10] Crittenden to Mrs. Coleman, May 9, 1849, in Crittenden Papers (Duke).

tions were near, and reports of defections were reaching Crittenden in Frankfort. Something must be done to provide better coordination, for it could not even be ascertained who was actually responsible for Kentucky patronage. Some said it was Ewing; others, that Taylor had reserved the state to himself. All Crittenden was sure of was that his voice was not being heard at the national capital. He decided that he must have a trusted agent in Washington who could speak for him to Taylor.

In June, Crittenden succeeded in getting an appointment as Commissioner for Indian Affairs for his dedicated friend Orlando Brown, and he urged Clayton to hold up all Kentucky appointments until Brown could reach Washington. It was of the highest consequence in the coming election, he wrote, that no more mistakes be made. Brown knew all applicants, and his advice could be relied on. It was especially important, he added, that "ultra Clay men" not be excluded from jobs.[11]

When Orlando arrived in Washington, he was received cordially by Taylor and effusively by Clayton. "He called me Brown in less than two minutes," Orlando reported to Crittenden; and Clayton wrote that "Brown is even at first sight, a trump—the king if not the ace." But Orlando soon learned that the "magnificent distances" of Washington were not limited to its spaciousness. There were distances between members of the cabinet and between it and the citizens. He found that the administration was full of "infernal ceremonious checks & balances" in dealings with the public; no one wanted to talk to anybody about appointments, and letters of recommendation were completely ignored "no matter by whom endorsed." The result was much dissatisfaction and "a growing cry for change daily getting louder." The President, he wrote, was looked upon as a figurehead, even the minutest details being settled in cabinet. Something had to be done, but Orlando did not know who was "to bell the cat," for Taylor was perfectly happy with the harmony that seemed to prevail within the cabinet. "If only you were here," Orlando sighed, things might be set aright and the "stately satraps" forced to "drop some of their ridiculous formalities."[12]

Even though he was generally recognized in Washington as the "personal representative of the great Kentucky Kingmaker," Orlando

11 Crittenden to Clayton, June 1, 1849, in Clayton Papers.
12 Brown to Crittenden, June 23, 27, July 10, 1849, in Crittenden Papers; Clayton to Crittenden, July 11, 1849, in Crittenden Papers (Kentucky).

found it difficult to carry out the mission on which Crittenden had sent him. The cabinet had no time to listen to his advice, and Taylor, although fond of Orlando, seemed completely oblivious to the real reason for his presence in Washington. Although he unburdened himself to Crittenden's envoy, Taylor listened very little. Many things could easily be set right, Orlando thought, if only Old Zack would assume the office for which the people chose him. But when Orlando told Taylor of a complete rupture between the cabinet and the editor of Taylor's personal newspaper, the President was unconcerned and seemed to think "all was exactly as it should be in that quarter." Orlando, too, now believed that much of the unhappy situation was due to Clayton, who he thought was totally untrustworthy.[13]

This information, corroborating other reports, was disconcerting to Crittenden. He was convalescing from a serious illness of several weeks, but he went out in a torrential rain at night to confer with Letcher. He walked the floor, and according to Letcher, "he roared at a most tremendous rate." He was indignant with the cabinet, charging that they were not dealing fairly with Taylor. Next day, however, he wrote Orlando in quite a different tone. He rebuked his friend for having caught the contagious "fever" prevalent in Washington, where no one trusted anyone. He must cure himself of this, or his mission would be fruitless. He must not express unfavorable opinions of the cabinet, as this would only antagonize Taylor. Crittenden urged Orlando to cultivate cordial relations with the "satraps," but above all, to win the confidence and friendship of Taylor, "the rock on which you build." As for the cabinet, it was "a good Cabinet," and Clayton was a "noble fellow" who despite his "faults and imperfections" would listen to Orlando with sympathy and understanding. The remedy for errors, he advised, was not to break up the cabinet but to profit from the errors and "do *right* for the future." Orlando must find some way to heal the breach between the cabinet and the press.[14]

Crittenden wrote Clayton of the harm that was being done through the image that had gotten abroad of the administration. The

[13] Brown to Crittenden, June 23, 27, July 10, 1849, in Crittenden Papers; Poage, *Henry Clay*, 186-87.
[14] Letcher to Brown, July 9, 1849, in Brown Papers, Kentucky Historical Society; Crittenden to Brown, July 3, 26, 31, 1849, in Crittenden Papers (Duke); Nathan Sargent to Crittenden, July 15, 1849, in Crittenden Papers.

people, he said, looked to the President as the center of the government. He was more popular than any of his cabinet members, and consequently what was done by him would be more favorably judged and more cheerfully acquiesced in than if done by them. Furthermore, when the cabinet did act, it was not with the "Bold, decided, energetic" course that would capture the imagination of the country. Popular governments depended on the "impulse & sensibilities of the people," and bold action would win their sympathy.[15]

It was soon apparent that Orlando would be unable to smooth out the difficulties, and Crittenden in desperation turned to Letcher. For months he had been dickering with Clayton over a diplomatic mission for Letcher; but although Clayton made brave promises, he would not confirm the appointment. Finally Letcher, in blunter language than Crittenden would have used, forced the issue. He curtly gave the Secretary of State instructions to order him to Washington at once. "There is more in this," he said, "than you may perceive at this first glance. Crittenden . . . wants me there for *your benefit*—I suppose to instruct you."[16] Clayton obeyed. According to Brown, when Letcher arrived in Washington, he went "from house to house, doctoring the sick, feeling pulses and prescribing regimen." Some, he added, "take his prescriptions greedily . . . others make wry faces . . . , but they have let the Doctor hold them by the nose to pour the medicine down their throats. . . . His talks with divers Cabinet officers have had a marked effect."[17] But if this was true, the effect was only temporary. Very shortly Letcher left for Mexico, and affairs moved from bad to worse in Washington.

Crittenden had been particularly disturbed by the obvious breach between the administration and its organ, the newly established *Republic*. Because the *National Intelligencer* was too partial to Clay and Webster to suit some of Taylor's ardent friends, Burnley had put up the money to start the *Republic*, and Alexander Bullitt, editor of the New Orleans *Picayune*, and John O. Sargent, Washington correspondent of the New York *Courier*, were brought in as editors.

Burnley, Bullitt, and Sargent were intensely devoted to Old Zack. But they, like Crittenden, were moderates on the slavery question,

[15] Crittenden to Clayton, July 8, 20, 1849, in Clayton Papers. See also Crittenden to Clayton, Feb. 2, 19, April 6, 11, June 9, 24, 28, 1849, *ibid.*
[16] Letcher to Clayton, July 21, 1849, in Clayton Papers.
[17] Brown to Crittenden, Sept. 14, 1849, in Crittenden Papers; Crittenden to Brown, Aug. 24, 1849, in Crittenden Papers (Duke).

and they were disturbed by Seward's growing influence over the administration. Soon Crittenden was receiving messages from Burnley that confirmed all he had heard from Orlando and others. "This cabinet is incompetent," Burnley wrote in late July. "They *must go out*," he added, "or Genl Taylor's adm. *must go down*, & with it the hopes of the Whig party, for years, if not forever." Crittenden, he said, must put aside his tender scruples and take a place in the cabinet. He could not avoid responsibility for the administration in any event, Burnley said, for it was his administration. If he took an active part, he would be Taylor's successor. If despite his presence the administration failed, then Crittenden would fall in a good cause. But Crittenden was as deaf to these pleas as he had been to the earlier ones.[18]

Meanwhile, Clayton was showing signs of panic. Within a fortnight after he took office, he began sending Crittenden urgent messages, asking him to come to Washington or to some nearby rendezvous. "Tell him," he said to an intermediary, "not to write letters, but to come on himself, and survey the ground, and give us the benefit of his counsel." To Crittenden he wrote direct. "Oh! for one hours talk with you." By July, completely frustrated by administrative problems and severely critical of his colleagues, Clayton was urging Crittenden to replace him. "If you will come here and take my office," he wrote, "I will give it up with a promise to stand by you faithfully all my life."[19]

Crittenden, of course, could not oblige him. To do so, as he pointed out, would "be the theme of a thousand lies." There was no cause for discouragement. Clayton must dismiss any idea of retirement because the country looked to him for leadership. If only he would straighten out the patronage difficulties, all would be well. Clayton did take heart for a time, but soon diplomatic problems came hot after domestic ones. He had been forced to dismiss the French minister for conduct unbecoming a diplomat, and relations with France were strained. The next crisis was the Hungarian revolution kindled by Louis Kossuth. It quickly won American sympathy and promises of support from Clayton, but was

[18] Burnley to Crittenden, July 22, 1849, in Crittenden Papers; Poage, *Henry Clay,* 186-87; Hamilton, *Zachary Taylor,* 170.
[19] Charles D. Drake to Crittenden, April 2, 1849, Clayton to Crittenden, March 16, 1849, in Crittenden Papers; Clayton to Crittenden, July 11, 1849, in Crittenden Papers (Kentucky). See also, Clayton to Crittenden, April 2, 8, May 7, 31, 1849, B. Rowan Hardin to Crittenden, May 8, 1849, in Crittenden Papers.

ruthlessly put down in the summer of 1849. Then Bonaparte marched into Rome to suppress a revolution there. Beset with difficulties growing out of these events, Clayton begged for sympathy. Could not Crittenden, he asked, say a word of encouragement, instead of constantly lecturing him on patronage?[20]

Crittenden was only too happy to do so. It gave him an opportunity he had long sought to urge an image of America as the champion of freedom. He approved of Clayton's dismissal of the French minister. France's attack on Rome he thought "a flagrant outrage" and a violation of the principles of their own Revolution. France should have stood up for the principle of nonintervention in revolutions of other countries, he said, and should have said to Austria, "sword in hand," that she must not interfere with the Roman Republic. France's "pusillanimous conduct" in suffering the fall of Hungary also provoked his disgust. Napoleon was a "despot" who was "deluding the people." He would soon be sweeping over the continent, as his uncle had done, Crittenden predicted, "trampling out every spark of revolution & liberty." If Crittenden were President, he would speak out for the "right of all nations to choose their own government . . . & to denounce the interference of despots with the struggles of the people for free government." "So help me Heaven," he added, "I would make the voice of this people a source of consolation & encouragement to all Nations struggling for liberty." A spirit of "national liberty" was moving in Europe. To remain silent in the great contest would not be "*neutrality*, it would be the *abandonment* & *betrayal* of our principles & of every just & generous & noble sympathy." France in Rome and Russia in Hungary had flagrantly violated the law of nations, and "our protest ought to be entered against these things." He followed up this letter with a message to Orlando, obviously intended for Taylor's ears. "In all commotions & struggles of the *people*, in every foreign land," he wrote, "go for the *people*, & speak it plainly & strongly."[21]

Clayton seemed overjoyed with this. "You never wrote a more sensible letter . . . than that in which you gave me your lessons in diplomacy," he wrote. He promised to follow the advice to the

[20] Crittenden to Clayton, April 6, 11, June 8, 1849, in Clayton Papers; Clayton to Crittenden, April 18, 1849, in Crittenden Papers.

[21] Crittenden to Clayton, June 28, July 21, Sept. 29, 1849, in Clayton Papers; Crittenden to Brown, July 31, 1849, in Thomas L. Crittenden Papers, Kentucky Historical Society, Folder 211.

letter. "You will see by & by that I have sent an agent to recognize the independence of Hungary on the first favorable indication." Sympathy with advancing republican principles would characterize the administration "if the President will allow me," he added. He asked Crittenden to write Taylor on this subject and persuade him "to give me a loose rein." But again Crittenden was doomed to disappointment. Taylor's annual message, prepared a few months later with Clayton's help, made no majestic statement on liberty to reverberate throughout the world. Instead, it was a pedestrian document that professed sympathy for the Hungarians but took pride in the fact that the United States had not become involved. Of the French attack on Rome it said nothing.[22]

The problems of the Taylor administration in foreign affairs grew out of indecision. In domestic affairs, Taylor acted with such force and stubbornness as to endanger the Union itself. As previously indicated, sectional animosities over slavery were already grave when the vast Mexican cession brought threats of disunion. Other issues were dividing the country, such as slave rescues and slavery in the District of Columbia, but the burning issue now became the Wilmot Proviso, which would prohibit slavery in the new territory.

Taylor, as noted, had been willing at the beginning of his campaign to abandon any claim for territory, but Crittenden had persuaded him to endorse a limited acquisition. As the campaign proceeded, however, southerners began to doubt that Taylor would veto the Wilmot Proviso should it pass Congress. To spare him such a decision, his friends resolved to settle the question before he took office. For if he vetoed the Proviso, the Whig party would be destroyed in the North; if he approved it, it would be shattered in the South.[23]

There were many schemes whereby the question might be settled without embarrassment to Taylor. Clayton proposed that California and New Mexico be encouraged to form state constitutions at once and seek admission as states with or without slavery as they chose. Preston had a somewhat similar plan, except that he would incorporate most of New Mexico into California, admit her as a state, then

---

[22] Clayton to Crittenden, July 11, 1849, in Crittenden Papers (Kentucky); Richardson, *Messages and Papers of the Presidents*, VI, 2547-62.

[23] Burnley to Crittenden, Jan. 12, 1849, in Crittenden Papers; C. S. Morehead to Clayton, April 10, 1849, in Clayton Papers; Blair to Van Buren, Jan. 27, 1849, in Van Buren Papers.

ORLANDO BROWN

ROBERT LETCHER

Portrait of Brown courtesy of the Orlando Brown House, Frankfort; portrait of Letcher courtesy of the Kentucky Historical Society, Frankfort

give the small remnant of New Mexico to Texas. Both plans had the advantage of removing the thorny question from the realm of congressional action; states would be created without going through the intermediate territorial stage, wherein Congress would have to legislate on slavery. There was much support from moderate southerners for either scheme. Toombs endorsed the Preston plan enthusiastically. The region could not ever be a slave territory, he said. It was imperative, however, to save southern honor by preventing Congress from forbidding slavery in a territory belonging to all the nation, and he predicted that all southern Whigs and many southern Democrats would vote for a bill based on Preston's plan. Despite Toombs's optimism, Preston's bill died in the House.[24]

Crittenden endorsed Clayton's plan. Not only the safety of the new administration but the safety of the country, he thought, depended upon the prompt admission of California and New Mexico as states. Agreeing with Toombs that the South could never hope to establish slavery in either place, he was anxious only that southerners be "beaten in the least offensive & injurious form" possible. After all, he said, "no sensible man would carry his slaves there if he could." He thought matters would be helped considerably if federal officials in California and New Mexico would *without any formal Instructions* see the importance of promptly organizing state governments, and "act upon it." Clayton assured him that he was *"wide awake"* as to the plan and that "Everything is done as you would wish it. . . . The States will be admitted—free and Whig."[25]

Acting upon Clayton's advice, Taylor dispatched T. Butler King of Georgia to California to help organize a state government without waiting for congressional permission. King carried out his mission, and when Congress met in December, 1849, California had drafted a constitution and sought admission as a free state.[26] In the House,

24 Toombs to Crittenden, Jan. 23, 1849, in Phillips, *Correspondence of Toombs, Stephens, and Cobb,* 141; Hamilton, *Zachary Taylor,* 142-43; Poage, *Henry Clay,* 192-93.

25 Crittenden to Clayton, Dec. 7, 1849 [1848], Dec. 19, 1848, in Clayton Papers; Clayton to Crittenden, April 18, 1849, in Crittenden Papers; Hamilton, *Zachary Taylor,* 142-43; Poage, *Henry Clay,* 193-94.

26 Charles S. Morehead to Crittenden, Dec. 25, 1849, Orlando Brown to Crittenden, Jan. 11, April 19, 1850, in Crittenden Papers; John C. Spencer to Clayton, Aug. 25, 1849, in Clayton Papers, Stephens to Crittenden, Dec. 17, 1849, in Stephens Papers, Duke University Library; Toombs to Crittenden, April 25, 1850, in Coleman, *Crittenden,* I, 364-65; Poage, *Henry Clay,* 195; Hamilton, *Zachary Taylor,* 178-79, 257-58.

Toombs, who had previously endorsed the California bill, now backed off, fearing that after its passage the proviso would be applied to the rest of the Mexican cession. When he and Stephens were unable to obtain assurance from Taylor that he would veto the proposed bill, the two able Georgians joined the opposition alongside moderate southern and northwestern Democrats of the Stephen A. Douglas school.[27]

Opposition to the California bill developed also in the Senate under the leadership of Clay. This seemed to bear out fears of Taylor's friends that if Clay were returned to the Senate, he would use his position to gain vengeance on the President. Crittenden would have preferred that Clay remain contentedly at home, but thought it would be a mistake to oppose his election when he indicated a desire for the office. He was convinced that Clay would cooperate with the administration, and it had been with Crittenden's consent that the Whigs in the legislature chose Clay.[28]

Clay soon saw that sectional bitterness was so great that the California question could not be solved unless all other outstanding questions were also dealt with.[29] In January he proposed his celebrated measures—admission of California under her free constitution; territorial governments in the rest of the Mexican cession, with no congressional restriction as to slavery; reasonable limits to Texas land claims against New Mexico, with $10,000,000 to be paid by the United States in compensation to her; a strong fugitive-slave law; and prohibition of the slave trade in the District of Columbia. Later he agreed to combine these proposals in one bill, the "Omnibus." But Taylor refused to accept the Omnibus Bill, insisting that California be admitted but that no concession be made to the South. Webster gave warm support to Clay, so that defense of the administration from Democratic attack in the Senate was left to younger Whigs like Seward and Truman Smith. Seward's radical stand on the slavery question made his support worse than useless, and Truman

[27] Barnes, *Memoir of Weed*, 177; Poage, *Henry Clay*, 195-96; Hamilton, *Zachary Taylor*, 229-30.

[28] Toombs to Crittenden, Dec. 3, 1848, Reverdy Johnson to Crittenden, Dec. 12, 1848, Burnley to Crittenden, Jan. 12, 1849, in Crittenden Papers; Stephens to Crittenden, Dec. 5, 17, 1848, in Crittenden Papers (Duke); Crittenden to Clayton, Jan. 7, 30, 1849, Leslie Combs to Clayton, Jan. 22, Feb. 4, 1849, in Clayton Papers; Balie Peyton to William B. Campbell, Jan. 20, 1849, in Campbell Papers (Duke); Hamilton, *Zachary Taylor*, 141-42.

[29] Poage, *Henry Clay*, 199-204, 223.

Smith was no match for his veteran adversaries. "Where Elephants can be used in battle," Crittenden wrote of Smith, "he would do well, but modern warfare requires combatants more active and alert."[30]

At this point Taylor's administration was delivered a staggering blow from within. Secretary of War Crawford, attorney for the Galphin family in a pre-Revolutionary claim against the government, secured approval of the claim by the Secretary of the Treasury and by the Attorney General, and pocketed a fee of over $100,000 for himself. The claim seems to have been a valid one, and Crawford had been Galphin's counsel for sixteen years before he entered the cabinet; but opponents of the administration gleefully represented the settlement as a Whig raid on the treasury.[31] Sharply attacked in Congress and finding no one to defend him there, Taylor looked to the Whig press for succor. But even here he was disappointed. The *Republic*, long at odds with the cabinet, went over to Clay. The unhappy Taylor now wanted a change of editors, but Bullitt could not be persuaded to dispose of his interest in the paper.

At this juncture a plea once more went to Crittenden to come to Washington and save the administration and the country. If no change was made in the cabinet, Humphrey Marshall wrote in March, "we shall break down, *beyond a doubt*, before the close of the session." When the cabinet dissolved, as it inevitably must, wrote Morehead, "You will have to come in. . . . There will be no escaping it." Clayton once more made a plaintive appeal. "Come here," he wrote, "and be Secretary of State. . . . Let me go home and plough the ground." Stephens despaired of Crittenden's coming to Washington but urged him at least to write directly to Taylor and save him before he was completely ruined. Even Democrat Francis P. Blair urged him to come on. "For the sake of the country I wish you were here," he wrote. "If I were to consider mere party objects, I would have you stay away."[32]

But as before, Crittenden turned a deaf ear. His refusal is difficult to explain. It is hardly possible that he thought damage

[30] Crittenden to Clayton, Feb. 18, 1850, in Clayton Papers.
[31] Orlando Brown to Crittenden, Feb. 1, April 19, 1850, in Crittenden Papers.
[32] Marshall to Crittenden, March 10, 1850, Morehead to Crittenden, Dec. 25, 1849, Blair to Crittenden, Dec. 20, 1849, in Crittenden Papers; Clayton to Crittenden, Feb. 5, 1850, in Crittenden Papers (Kentucky); Stephens to Crittenden, May 7, 1850, in Stephens Papers (Duke). See also Orlando Brown to Crittenden, April 19, May 18, 1850, in Crittenden Papers.

to the administration was already beyond repair, judging from his letters to Burnley, Brown, Clayton, and others. "The Governor is deeply distressed at the state of affairs at Washington," wrote a friend of Crittenden's from Frankfort at this time. "Yet he never doubts the ultimate triumph of old Zach (D—n it, how I like to hear him swear, when he talks of the *Whigs* (?) who falter, now in the hour of the Administration's trial). . . . If old Zach had but *one* such man in Congress, I would give half I am worth." Undoubtedly, however, Crittenden still feared the vindictive wrath of bitter Clay adherents, who believed he had betrayed their idol. In any event, he remained in Frankfort while Burnley rushed to Washington to reorganize the *Republic*.[33]

Meanwhile, relations between Congress and President, as well as between sectional factions in Congress, were at the breaking point. Congressional action on other business was suspended as Calhoun or Mason, Clay or Webster, Seward or Douglas, and countless others, debated with a montonous fervor through the lengthening spring afternoons every measure conceivably related to slavery. Tom Corwin, exasperated with it all, surmised that if the man in the moon should suddenly drop to earth and observe the workings of Congress, he would probably write in his diary: "Found a Republic of Anglo-Saxons on the Banks of the Potomac, seventeen millions of white people, and three millions of black slaves—with a constitution providing a Govt. whose only business is, to see to the sale, transfer and manumission of said black slaves—Did not learn that any provisions were made for the Govt. of the Whites."[34]

When Clayton's compromise scheme failed, Crittenden endorsed Taylor's. By April, 1850, however, he was convinced that Taylor's laissez faire policy on all issues save California was no longer practicable and that a comprehensive settlement of the slavery question was imperative. The administration must form a plan, he wrote Clayton, and then use all its influence to support it. He suggested as a basis for a settlement "concessions to the South of all that she can *reasonably & constitutionally* ask." Since the South was the

---

[33] John W. Finnell to Orlando Brown, April 28, 1850, in Brown Papers, Filson Club; Crittenden to Burnley, April 29, May 25, 1850, Crittenden to Brown, April 30, 1850, in Crittenden Papers (Duke); Burnley to Crittenden, May 8, 15, 1850, in Crittenden Papers.

[34] Corwin to Pearce, March 28, 1850, in Steiner, "Correspondence of Pearce," XVIII (1923), 347.

"*weaker* & the *aggrieved* party," he urged, "let all the *doubtful* points be granted" to her. If all that she asked were given, he added, "it would amount *eventually* & *practically* to nothing," for all sides agreed that slavery had already reached its geographic limits and never could be successful in any part of the newly acquired territory. If concessions to the South were made, therefore, the northerners would lose nothing in the long run.

This was the very reasoning Clay had advanced for his Omnibus Bill, and Crittenden now endorsed it. Clay's plan, he argued, was not essentially different from Taylor's, and he hoped that Taylor would not be responsible for preventing a compromise. But Taylor thought there was a difference. Besides, in debate in late May, Clay had been severely critical of the President's refusal to consider a comprehensive settlement. After that, Taylor would concede nothing. By July there seemed no prospect of settlement.[35]

At the height of the crisis, almost providentially, Taylor was stricken with a mortal illness after a July 4 celebration and died five days later. Crittenden's ordeal as a kingmaker thus came to a close. It had not been a happy experience for him, nor did it reflect well on his judgment of men. In the first place he had misjudged Taylor. Knowing better than anyone else Taylor's complete ignorance of affairs of state, he had expected to be his guide. When the sequel to the nominating contest made this politically unwise, the President-elect proved to be stubborn, refusing to accept Letcher, Crittenden's personal representative, in his stead. When Taylor would not have Letcher in the cabinet, Crittenden had turned to Clayton, his own choice as well as Taylor's for premier. Here again he sadly misjudged his man. Clayton, who had long been a strong and capable member of the Senate, did not measure up to the new post. Perhaps recent family tragedies had undermined his courage, for he was a weak and unstable leader for an inexperienced President. He constantly solicited Crittenden's advice, but he rarely followed it.

Crittenden failed also to display the toughness that is a necessary ingredient of a good executive. Taylor put his finger on his friend's weakness when he told Weed that Crittenden "can't say *no* some-

[35] Crittenden to Clayton, Feb. 18, April 6, 1850, in Clayton Papers; Crittenden to Orlando Brown, April 30, June 7, 1850, in Crittenden Papers (Duke); Poage, *Henry Clay*, 217; Brown to Crittenden, May 9, 18, 23, 1850, Burnley to Crittenden, May 15, 1850, in Crittenden Papers; Clay to Mrs. Clay, July 6, 1850, in T. J. Clay Papers.

times." Letcher, too, knew that Crittenden could not resist an appeal to his emotions. He vainly tried to persuade his friend not to endorse a woman who wanted to be postmistress of Louisville. Crittenden knew, Letcher said, that "the appointment of the Lady, is entirely objectionable in every respect," but to Letcher's arguments Crittenden only replied: "What could I do or say, [with] such an appeal. . . ?" Crittenden's trouble, Letcher concluded, was that he was moved by "that noble generous feeling, which is altogether too strong for his judgement."[36]

When Taylor's funeral train brought the old warrior to his final resting place at Louisville, Crittenden was there to receive him and to pay tribute to his friend and kinsman in a warm, moving address. But Crittenden must have been aware that his great efforts in Taylor's behalf had led the country to the brink of disaster. For had Taylor lived out his term, the country might well have been torn by disunion and civil war a decade before Lincoln's election.

[36] Letcher to Orlando Brown, June 30, 1849, in Brown Papers, Kentucky Historical Society, Folder 564.

CHAPTER XIV

The Doom of the Whigs

THE DEATH of Taylor and the succession of Fillmore made a cabinet reorganization inevitable, for Seward's influence had built an impossible barrier between Taylor's advisers and the new President. Fillmore wanted Crittenden, and finding that Clay had no objections, he offered him the attorney generalship. The offer was not unwelcome. Secluded in Frankfort during the stirring crisis, Crittenden had felt "as restless as a chained lion or a caged eagle." Not only was he eager to return to Washington, but he had found that expenses of the governor's office were greater than his salary. Some of his friends had tried to place a fund at his disposal, but he would not permit it. When the cabinet offer came, he consulted Burnley, Letcher, Brown, and other friends. All now agreed that there could be no charge of bargain with Fillmore, and so Crittenden accepted the offer.[1]

Washington had grown considerably in the years since Crittenden had started his long period of service there. The population now numbered about forty thousand, mostly government employees or people who served them. The rural beauty that once distinguished the city had vanished and had not yet been succeeded by tasteful elegance. The White House and the Capitol, together with the colonnaded Treasury, stood in contrast to the dull brick edifices that housed the State, War, and Navy departments. Broad, unpaved streets, dusty in summer and muddy in winter, were lighted by only an occasional lamp. Houses were scattered here and there, too far apart even to be numbered. Many of the inhabitants owned slaves, and the slave pen and the auction block were familiar sights.[2]

Tom Corwin, the new Secretary of the Treasury, had taken a house in President's Square opposite the War Department, and when Crittenden arrived in August, Corwin insisted that he and Maria stay there with him until they could find suitable accommodations. By the end of the year, however, the Crittendens had moved to a house on the north side of H Street between Ninth and Tenth, roughly midway between the White House and Capitol Hill.[3]

Besides Crittenden and Corwin, the new cabinet was made up of Webster, in the State Department; William A. Graham, Navy; Alexander H. H. Stuart of Virginia, Interior; C. M. Conrad of Louisiana, War; and Nathan K. Hall, Fillmore's Buffalo law partner, Post Office. Webster, Corwin, and Crittenden were men of national eminence, and the others were not without some stature. Even Blair, a fervent Democrat, conceded that it was "certainly an improvement for the Whigs, though not for us." For, he added acidly, "a more wretched set than the last Cabinet could not be found."[4]

The sectional crisis stood in abeyance during the first weeks after Taylor's death. Then, on July 31, Clay's Omnibus failed in the Senate. Clay went off to a much-needed rest at Newport, while Douglas regrouped the compromise forces and began to push separate bills, embodying the Clay proposals, through Congress. Until this time, Crittenden's absence from Washington had limited his part

[1] "Recollections of an Old Stager," XLVII (1873), 588; John L. Helm to Orlando Brown, Feb. 25, 1850 [misdated 1851], Thomas B. Stevenson to Brown, Sept. 2, 1850, in Brown Papers, Kentucky Historical Society, Folder 427; Crittenden to Burnley, March 23, 1850, Crittenden to Brown, April 3, 1850, in Crittenden Papers (Duke); Humphrey Marshall to Crittenden, March 10, 1850, Richard Hawes to Crittenden, July 26, 1850, in Crittenden Papers; Clay to T. J. Clay, Aug. 6, 1850, in Colton, *Clay*, IV, 611; Crittenden to Fillmore, July 31, 1850, in Crittenden Papers (Kentucky).

[2] Frederick W. Seward, *Reminiscences of a War-Time Statesman and Diplomat, 1830-1915* (New York and London, 1916), 68-69.

[3] *Congressional Directory*, 31 Cong., 1 Sess. (Washington, 1850); *ibid.*, 2 Sess. (Washington, 1851).

[4] Blair to Van Buren, July 20, 1850, in Van Buren Papers.

in the Great Compromise. Now he did good service. Congressmen whose votes were needed hesitated for a time to act on individual bills, fearing to vote a *quid* before receiving their *quo*. Crittenden's presence in the cabinet acted as a guarantee to many, both North and South, that their own measures would be passed and would not be vetoed by Fillmore. In the weeks that followed he, Webster, and Graham worked incessantly to gain hesitant votes for the constantly shifting majorities.[5]

Fillmore promptly signed the Compromise bills as they were presented to him. The Fugitive Slave Act gave him concern. Not only was it repugnant to his own antislavery inclinations, but it would bring down on his administration the wrath of the extreme antislavery men. He asked Crittenden's advice on one clause of the bill that might be considered unconstitutional. Did it suspend the writ of *habeas corpus?* Crittenden held that it did not. The clause, he said, discharged a duty placed on Congress by the Constitution, the obligation to return runaway slaves. Fillmore then signed the bill.[6]

During two and a half years as Attorney General under Fillmore, Crittenden wrote a total of one hundred and thirty-two opinions. Most were of a routine nature, responses to legal questions submitted by the President or by department heads. The opinions were purely advisory, as Crittenden was careful to point out, and were not to be interpreted as definitive. One, however, had to do with the old question in the Florida treaty providing damages for injuries suffered by Spanish claimants when Jackson invaded the province in 1817-1818. Laws of Congress empowered courts at St. Augustine and Pensacola to pass on these claims but reserved to the Secretary of the Treasury the right to reject judgments that he considered not *"just and equitable."* When Corwin refused to pay some judgments and refused to allow interest payments on any, Spanish litigants protested that the treaty would be violated if the law permitted an executive officer to reverse a court decision.

Crittenden's opinion denied this. The treaty, he said, required only that *"some legal proceedings"* be followed in adjudicating the claims and left it entirely to the discretion of the government to determine the particular form of these proceedings. Both secretary and

---

[5] Poage, *Henry Clay,* 196, 261, 263; Hamilton, *Zachary Taylor,* 402-404.

[6] Robert J. Rayback, *Millard Fillmore, Biography of a President,* Vol. XL of *Publications of the Buffalo Historical Society* (New York, 1959), 252; *Official Opinions of the Attorneys General,* V, 254-59.

judges derived their authority from the law passed by Congress, and it was a "play on words," he said, to represent the supervision of the secretary as that of an executive officer overruling a judicial officer. On the contrary, the secretary's ruling was just as much a judicial decision as were those of the judges. As to the question of interest, Crittenden had already advised in 1841 that this could not be allowed. This decision had been followed by subsequent Attorneys General, and he now relied on the rule of *stare decisis*.

Crittenden gave short shrift to the contention of litigants that an act of Congress altering a treaty was null and void. An act of Congress stood on equal footing with a treaty as "the supreme law of the land," and the latest in time must prevail. A treaty might, he said, become so injurious to the interest of one of the parties that it would become the duty of that government to renounce it. True, this power might be abused, but so might all other powers, including that of treatymaking. Despite Crittenden's opinion, a Florida judge awarded interest in a suit. The government appealed to the Supreme Court, and Crittenden appeared as government counsel. This case was decided in December, 1851, and Crittenden's position on all points was upheld.[7]

Fillmore was an amiable, dignified man, not without convictions, but with few strong prejudices. He was large of body, and he had an impressive, intelligent face and a deep, sonorous voice. After his succession, the excitement engendered by the slavery controversy subsided, and soon good relations between northern and southern members of Congress were restored. Crittenden played an important part in this reconciliation. A southerner and the owner of a few household servants, he, like Clay, was opposed at heart to the peculiar institution and looked forward to its ultimate extinction. The tide of history, he thought, was inevitably flowing against slavery, but he believed agitation of the subject unprofitable in the inflamed mood of the times. He was regarded by northerners and southerners alike as a man of sense and moderation. Through his influence Toombs and Stephens returned to the support of the administration and pledged to accept the Compromise of 1850 as final. When Fillmore prepared a statement in his annual message suggesting a slight modification of the Compromise, Stephens appealed to Crittenden, who

[7] *Official Opinions of the Attorneys General*, V, 333, 337-38, 346-47, 353-54, 390-91; David R. Deener, *The United States Attorneys General and International Law* (The Hague, 1957), 96, 289-90, 299-300, 304, 338-39.

was able to prevail upon the President to modify the statement to the Georgian's satisfaction.[8]

Crittenden was awarded the degree of doctor of laws at Harvard graduation exercises in 1851 but was unable to accept in person because a grand tour for Fillmore and his cabinet had been arranged in June to commemorate completion of the Erie Railroad to Buffalo. Crittenden made several speeches during the tour, using this opportunity to plead for adherence to all features of the Compromise as the only salvation for the Union. There was already talk in northern states of nullifying the fugitive-slave law, and Crittenden warned that if the South and the North each accepted only the parts of the Compromise that pleased them, the hard-earned peace won in Congress the preceding year would be lost. He urged all those of tender conscience on the slavery question to "keep their consciences to themselves."[9]

Crittenden returned to Kentucky in mid-July. He had expected to be back in Washington by early September, but in late August, Maria became seriously ill. The nature of her ailment is not revealed. On September 6 Crittenden thought she was out of danger, and he planned to start for Washington "as soon as her recovery will permit." Suddenly she took a turn for the worse, and at 10:30 on the morning of September 8 she died.[10]

Three days later Maria was buried from the Presbyterian Church where she had worshiped devoutly all her life.[11] Maria was by all accounts a charming and excellent woman. Fillmore called her "a most remarkable woman," and thought her "almost indispensable to her husband's happiness." Letcher in Mexico was so overcome with grief that it was more than a month after the news reached him before he was able to write his dearest friend a letter of consolation. Her stepson and son-in-law, Thomas, wrote from Liverpool that

8 H. W. Hilliard, *Politics and Pen Pictures*, 212; Gouverneur Kemble to Van Buren, Feb. 16, 1851, in Van Buren Papers; "Recollections of an Old Stager," XLVII (1873), 588; Stephens to Crittenden, Oct. 24, 1850, in Stephens Papers (Duke); Avary (ed.), *Stephens Recollections*, 27-28; Richardson, *Messages and Papers of the Presidents*, VI, 2628-29.

9 Winthrop to Crittenden, June 25, 1851, in Crittenden Papers; Jared Sparks to Crittenden, Sept. 11, 1851, in Crittenden Papers (Duke); Frankfort *Commonwealth*, June 3, 1851.

10 Frankfort *Commonwealth*, July 15, 28, Sept. 9, 1851; Crittenden to Joseph R. Underwood, Sept. 6, 1851, in Crittenden Papers; Clift, "Kentucky Marriages and Obituaries," XLI (1943), 156.

11 Receipts for funeral expenses dated Sept. 8-11, 1851, Crittenden Papers; Frankfort *Commonwealth*, Sept. 17, 1851.

Frankfort and home "has lost one of its chief charms. . . . We have all lost the best of Mothers," and his father had lost "the most faithful & devoted of wives."[12]

For a time Crittenden was inconsolable. As much as family responsibilities permitted, Maria had been his constant companion. At a time when few wives of congressmen accompanied their husbands to Washington, she generally went there with him. Whenever circumstances made a temporary separation imperative, he wrote her tender and affectionate letters almost daily. Just two years before, Clayton had suffered a similar bereavement, and Crittenden had written him a consoling letter. Death, he said, was directed by a benevolent and wise Providence that man could not understand. Mortals could not see the future and thus could not know what misfortunes death prevented. Now he had to call on all his philosophical resources to save himself from despair.[13]

Crittenden returned to Washington in late September and threw himself into the work that had accumulated during his absence. But his heart was not in it. "I try to forget," he wrote Orlando, "but cannot, & when I think of what I have lost, I almost reproach myself for the patience & resignation with which I have been able to bear such a fate." Webster's health was failing, and Clayton, in an effort to console Crittenden, reported rumors that Crittenden would succeed him. But Crittenden was uninterested. "I don't want the office of Secty. of State," he replied; "I am often very despondent." At the end of October, Crittenden closed the home on H Street that he and Maria had occupied and went to live with Burnley in a pleasant neighborhood near Lafayette Square.[14]

But the world would not stand still for Crittenden's grief, and soon he was involved in international diplomacy. Cuba had long been a restless and unhappy province of once-mighty Spain. From time to time Cuban exiles, with private American backing, led filibustering expeditions from United States ports in attempts to over-

---

[12] Fillmore to Webster, Sept. 10, 1851, in George T. Curtis, *Life of Daniel Webster*, 2 vols. (New York, 1870), II, 532; Letcher to Crittenden, Nov. 20, 1851, in Crittenden Papers; Thomas L. Crittenden to Harry Todd, Oct. 29, 1851, in Thomas L. Crittenden Papers, Kentucky Historical Society, Folder 215.

[13] Crittenden to Clayton, Feb. 17, 1849, in Clayton Papers.

[14] Crittenden to Brown, Sept. 28, 1851, Crittenden to Mrs. Coleman, Nov. 2, 1851, in Crittenden Papers (Duke); Crittenden to Clayton, Oct. 4, 1851, in Clayton Papers; Martha A. Burnley, "Albert Triplett Burnley," in *Texas State Historical Association Quarterly*, XIV (1910), 150-54; *Congressional Directory*, 32 Cong., 1 Sess.; *Washington and Georgetown Directory, Stranger's Guide* (Washington, 1853).

throw Spanish rule in the island. These expeditions were in violation of United States law, and both Taylor and Fillmore had forcibly prevented several from sailing.[15] Despite this, in August, 1851, Narcisco Lopez, an exiled Cuban official, escaped with an expedition from New Orleans. The adventure was poorly planned and ill-fated. The invaders were met on the beaches and wiped out. Lopez himself escaped but left many dead, including fifty-one Americans. Some of these, according to reports, were summarily and brutally executed after capture. Among them was Crittenden's nephew William.

When word of the massacre of the prisoners reached New Orleans, a mob attacked Spanish nationals there, and considerable property belonging to them was destroyed. For this the United States apologized and promised indemnity. Webster was ill at his New England home at Marshfield, and Crittenden, just returned from Kentucky following Maria's death, was acting Secretary of State. Hardly had Crittenden assumed these new responsibilities when first the British minister and then the French called to notify him that their governments' naval forces in West Indian waters had been ordered to assist Spain in preventing further filibusters. Crittenden, after consulting with Fillmore, replied to the French minister, M. de Sartiges.

The President, he said, felt that the timing of the action by the two powers indicated concert in a matter in which neither was directly concerned. The orders, he pointed out, could not be executed without stopping and searching American merchantmen, and such action would imperil peace between the two powers and the United States. Calling attention to the great pains taken by the United States government to prevent filibustering expeditions, as well as to the good faith it had always shown in meeting international obligations, he charged that the attitude of the two powers was unfriendly. The United States, he said, was determined to execute its neutrality laws, but without aid from foreign powers. The escape of Lopez' one small vessel, despite precautions, could not impute bad faith on the part of the United States. Only such minute and insignificant forces could escape, and these, as had been demonstrated,

[15] Ewing to Clayton, Aug. 7, 1849, Crittenden to Clayton, June 22, 1850, in Clayton Papers; Amos Kendall to Crittenden, May 30, 1851 (copy), in Crittenden Papers; Richardson, *Messages and Papers of the Presidents*, VI, 2647-48; Hamilton, *Zachary Taylor*, 199-202, 368-71.

could be dealt with by Spain without aid of her European neighbors. Their concerted movement at this time suggested, Crittenden added, that Britain and France themselves had imperialistic ambitions in Cuba. If so, their hopes would never be realized; for Cuba lay athwart the main road of United States commerce, and its possession by any "powerful European nation" would never be acquiesced in by the United States. He restated the philosophy underlying the Monroe Doctrine and expressed the hope that France would do nothing to interrupt her good relationship with the United States.

It was an able, well-reasoned paper, firm but courteous, and Sartiges was impressed. His reply a few days later was entirely different in tone from his original warning. The position taken by the United States was "so upright," he said, that his government now felt confident that American naval forces would act to prevent an invasion of Cuba. France had never intended her instructions to include the stopping and searching of merchant vessels, on which question she stood in precisely the same position as the United States. She had only regarded her orders as affecting "pirates." She meant no reproach on American conduct, and she agreed that Cuba should never become the property of one of the great maritime powers. Thus the affair closed with all parties in agreement.[16]

Crittenden's handling of the controversy drew praise. Democratic Senator Lewis Cass heartily approved Crittenden's answer to Sartiges, saying that it had laid down "the true doctrine—the doctrine for which we have always contended." But one eager reporter, unwilling to let well enough alone, misrepresented Crittenden as having humiliated Sartiges. This Crittenden denied. Nothing of a "sarcastic or discourteous" nature had transpired, he said, with either the British or the French minister. "I should be ashamed," he added, "to be thought guilty of any rudeness towards either of those gentlemen."[17]

In addition to his duties as Attorney General, Crittenden continued his private law practice before the Supreme Court. He represented Samuel Colt, inventor of the revolver, in all his litigation there. Burnley had secured lucrative practice for Crittenden involving claims for interest on Texas bonds held by descendants of Alexander

[16] *Senate Executive Documents, 1851-1852,* 32 Cong., 1 Sess., I, 4-5, 45, 51, 63, 76-87.
[17] Crittenden to James Harvey, Nov. 3, 1851, in Crittenden Papers (Duke); Clayton to Crittenden, Oct. 27, 1851, Harvey to Crittenden, Oct. 28, Nov. 5, 1851, in Crittenden Papers; Harvey to Crittenden, Nov. 1, 1851, in Coleman, *Crittenden,* II, 17-19; *Congressional Globe,* 32 Cong., 1 Sess., 82.

Hamilton. Letcher in Mexico had secured a retainer of $2,000 for him, with a promise of more, to represent Mexican claimants of rich mining interests in California. Letcher had also found a Mexican claimant to 1,700,000 California acres who wanted Crittenden to represent him when his case came before the Supreme Court. He was promised a $30,000 fee in this case. Land titles in California were the source of as much litigation as they had been in Kentucky a generation before. Spanish, Mexican, and California governments had made extensive grants, often of the same land, to owners who had failed to perfect their titles. A nephew of Crittenden's, Alexander P. Crittenden, was a leading lawyer in California, and he sent Crittenden much business from there.[18]

Meanwhile, Crittenden was concerned about political developments in Kentucky. When he resigned as governor, he had been succeeded by John L. Helm of Hardin County, son-in-law of Crittenden's old friend Ben Hardin. Almost at once division and discord, healed temporarily in 1848, began to reappear in the Whig party. Helm broke with Superintendent Breckinridge over school-fund policies, and some Whigs in the legislature sided with Helm, others with Breckinridge. This split was soon followed by rivalry among ambitious Whigs for the congressional seat from the Ashland District, "the very cradle of Whiggery," as well as for the Whig gubernatorial nomination. Most serious of all was the defection of an antislavery element from the party under the leadership of Cassius M. Clay, brilliant but erratic kinsman of the Sage of Ashland.

For twenty years the Whig party had enjoyed almost undisputed control of the state government; perhaps for that very reason it was difficult for Whigs to heed the warning signals and rouse themselves from their lethargy. Consequently, in August, Lazarus Powell, Democrat, defeated Archibald Dixon by 850 votes. Not since 1832 had the Whigs failed to win the governor's office. Powell was aided by the candidacy of Cassius Clay, who drew 3,621 votes, most of them, presumably, from Dixon. Although Whigs won all other statewide offices, their victories were generally by narrow margins, except that

[18] Contract between Crittenden and Colt, dated Oct. 1, 1850, in Crittenden Papers (Kentucky); H. R. W. Hill to Crittenden, Nov. 2, 1851, Letcher to Crittenden, Nov. 20, 1851, June 4, 1852, Alexander P. Crittenden to Crittenden, May 29, 1854, in Crittenden Papers; Henry G. Connor, *John Archbold Campbell, Associate Justice of the United States Supreme Court, 1853-1861* (Boston, 1920), 83; Crittenden to Fillmore, Jan. 17, 1851, in *Official Opinions of the Attorneys General*, V, 287; Springfield (Mass.) *Post*, quoted in Frankfort *Commonwealth*, May 28, 1852.

of John B. Thompson, who was elected lieutenant governor by more than 6,000 votes. The most significant indication of Whig decline was the contest in the Ashland District, where the veteran Leslie Combs was defeated for Congress by a rising star in the Democratic galaxy, John C. Breckinridge. Breckinridge's majority was 500 votes, whereas the district had usually gone Whig by 1,500 votes. Whigs were able to carry only five of the other nine congressional districts and maintained control in the legislature by a narrow margin: twenty to eighteen in the senate, and fifty-four to forty-five in the house. The election was ominous for the Whig party.[19]

The legislature then chosen was to elect a successor to Joseph R. Underwood, whose term in the United States Senate would expire in March, 1853. In this contest, too, there were many ambitious Whigs in the field. Underwood hoped to be reelected, but Charles S. Morehead, who had won distinction in the House, was eager for promotion to the Senate. So was George Robertson, Clay's stanch friend from Fayette and one of the controversial Old Court judges of a quarter century before. Crittenden's term as Attorney General expired simultaneously with Underwood's as senator, and he, too, wished to return to the Senate. He had always prized a Senate seat more highly than any other office, and before he left Kentucky in September to go back to Washington, he let it be known that he would be a candidate. When Morehead and Underwood learned that Crittenden desired the office, both gracefully stepped aside, and it was thought that he would have little opposition from Robertson. Then the recently defeated Dixon entered the contest.

In the early breach between friends of Clay and Crittenden, Dixon had aligned himself with Crittenden, and it was with Crittenden's backing that he had won the Whig gubernatorial nomination. By entering the senatorial contest in the fall of 1851, however, he showed that he had switched to Clay. The Clay faction still yearned for revenge for the part they believed Crittenden had played in the "Philadelphia slaughterhouse." Clay himself had been civil but cool toward Crittenden since that time. Crittenden had called on Clay when Clay passed through Frankfort en route to New Orleans in

[19] Robert J. Breckinridge to Crittenden, Nov. 23, 1850, John Speed Smith to Crittenden, Jan. 28, 1851 [misdated 1850], in Crittenden Papers; Letcher to Webster, July 5, 1851, in Webster Papers; Frankfort *Commonwealth*, Sept. 16, 1851; Turner, "Kentucky in a Decade of Change, 1850-1860," 16-17; E. Merton Coulter, "The Downfall of the Whig Party in Kentucky," in *Kentucky Register*, XXIII (1925), 163-64; Collins, *History of Kentucky*, II, 534.

December, 1849; and after Crittenden joined Fillmore's cabinet they had met from time to time at Washington social functions.

But hardly was Crittenden settled in office when Clay began charging privately that Crittenden was blocking his patronage recommendations. Even when his charges were refuted, Clay continued to stand aloof. Crittenden was eager to heal the breach with his old friend, the result, he was certain, of a misunderstanding. In a speech in Syracuse, New York, in the summer of 1851 Crittenden had gone out of his way to pay a magnanimous tribute to Clay, and his remarks were copied widely in the Kentucky press. Yet Clay kept at a distance the friend who had fought at his side for the better part of four decades. "The names of Clay and Crittenden have become the *Guelf* and *Gibeline* [sic] of parties," wrote a Kentucky editor in the fall of 1851. "You cannot conceive," wrote another, "of the vastness and immensity of the gulf that yawns between the friends of these two men."[20]

When Dixon refused to withdraw from the contest in favor of Crittenden, Democrats began to have hopes of electing one of their own party. For the slender Whig majority in the legislature might easily be overcome if only a few Whigs could be detached by a bitter intraparty contest. Nor did such defections seem unlikely. Diehard Clay Whigs like George Robertson and Thomas Stevenson, now turned against Crittenden, seemed determined that Crittenden must be defeated at all costs, even though his defeat would weaken the party nationally. For this reason, if for no other, Democratic legislators would vote solidly against Crittenden. His defeat, wrote Orlando Brown, would be "the greatest party triumph they could achieve—great at home and still greater as striking a blow at the Whigs throughout the nation." Crittenden's friends also feared that enough Democrats might, during the balloting, wheel into the support of Dixon and thus elect him.[21]

Foreseeing these dangers, some Whigs proposed postponing the

---

[20] Louisville *Courier*, Nov. 27, 1851; Louisville *Democrat*, Nov. 22, 1851. See also, letters to Crittenden from Julia M. Dickinson Tayloe, March 19, 1851, from John W. Finnell, May 6, 1851, from Orlando Brown, Sept. 18, 1851, from J. B. Temple, Sept. 22, 1851, from Morehead, Oct. 19, 1851, in Crittenden Papers; Crittenden to Brown, Sept. 28, 1851, in Crittenden Papers (Duke); Clay to A. H. H. Stuart, Nov. 7, 1850, in Stuart Papers (Virginia); Crittenden to Leslie Combs, Nov. 1, 1851, in Coleman, *Crittenden*, II, 19-20; Frankfort *Commonwealth*, June 3, 1851; Brown to Thomas L. Crittenden, Dec. 27, 1851, in Brown Papers, Filson Club.

[21] Brown to T. L. Crittenden, Dec. 27, 1851, fragment in Brown's hand but unsigned, in Brown Papers, Filson Club.

election for two years, until the next legislature met in November, 1853. The vacancy would not occur until March of that year, and there would be little business for the Senate to transact between that date and the following December. But there were perils in such a delay, as Tom Marshall, the leader of Crittenden's forces in the house, frankly conceded; a Democratic legislature might be chosen in August, 1853, and then a Democrat would surely be elected to the Senate vacancy. Nothing could more clearly reveal the crumbling of the Whig party than Marshall's open admission.[22]

November 17 had been set as the date for the senatorial election. Before that day arrived, Clay was in Frankfort working openly for the election of his friend Robertson as speaker and covertly, some thought, for Crittenden's defeat. "The contest thickens," wrote a neutral editor. "The man who is seated highest in the affections of the people," he added, "would carry the Legislature by a handsome majority" if unburdened by the calumnies being heaped upon him. Because Crittenden had pardoned Calvin Fairbanks, who had been convicted of assisting some Fayette County slaves to escape a decade before, he was charged with being an abolitionist sympathizer. It was also argued that Crittenden had, for his own interests, quit the Senate in 1848 for the gubernatorial office, that he had resigned that office before expiration of his term to take a "prominent and profitable post" in the cabinet; and that now, "in the grasping spirit of a monopolist" of all honors and offices, he was seeking a Senate seat two years before it would be vacant.[23]

Clay's friends and Dixon's succeeded in electing Robertson speaker, but they adamantly refused to go into a Whig caucus that would bind them to support its choice. This seemed to confirm the general belief that Crittenden was favored by a majority of Whigs. Two ballots were taken in the house on November 17, but Crittenden's friends did not permit his name to be proposed, fearing that Democrats would then rally to Dixon and elect him merely to humiliate Crittenden and the Whig party. They held Crittenden's name back, distributing their votes among other candidates so that none received enough to be elected. Only if they could force the

[22] J. Speed Smith to Crittenden, Dec. 8, 1851, Orlando Brown to Crittenden, Dec. 3, 1851, in Crittenden Papers; Frankfort *Commonwealth*, Dec. 18, 1851; Louisville *Democrat*, Nov. 14, 18, 19, 20, 21, 22, 1851; Louisville *Courier*, Nov. 20, 1851.

[23] Louisville *Courier*, Nov. 20, 25, Dec. 2, 11, 1851; Louisville *Democrat*, Nov. 14, 18, 19, 20, 25, 1851; Frankfort *Commonwealth*, Dec. 2, 9, 1851.

Dixon party into a caucus and there nominate Crittenden could they afford to permit Crittenden's open candidacy.

Despite this cautious strategy Crittenden's name was unexpectedly placed before the house on the third day, possibly by a Dixon adherent or by a Democrat. This brought Tom Marshall hastily to the floor to withdraw the nomination. In a lengthy speech he poured gall in the party's gaping wounds. He accused Dixon's friends of conspiring with Democrats. He pleaded with them, because of the party's national interests, not to make a sacrifice of Crittenden. With consummate sarcasm he pointed out that when a sacrifice had been demanded of Abraham, Isaac was spared at the cost of a sheep. The implication was clear: Dixon was expendable, whereas Crittenden was not.

Clay's friends were infuriated when Marshall reminded them that Crittenden had magnanimously stepped aside in 1832, when he was assured of election to the Senate, so that Clay might have the seat. Thus, said Marshall, Crittenden had saved Clay at a time of crisis from political oblivion. It ill befitted Clay's friends now, he added, to repay Crittenden in the coin they had prepared for him. In his pugnacious, cockpit style, he thus reversed the figures in the picture Clay's friends had painted: Clay became not Crittenden's benefactor but his debtor. The weather turned bitter cold in Frankfort that night, but it was hardly more bitter than the hatred now engendered between the Whig factions. Marshall's lashing tongue had cut deep.

Crittenden's political demise was now openly predicted by Democrats. Up until November 20 all efforts to produce a caucus had failed. Furthermore, it was now ascertained that sixty of the sixty-three Democrats in the two houses would vote to the last against Crittenden if his name should be presented. "Their very bowels are yearning for his nomination" so that they might have at him, wrote one Democrat. Meanwhile, Clay's and Dixon's friends, rallying alternately upon Dixon, Robertson, or Lieutenant Governor Thompson, were holding their ground. A careful check revealed that in a joint vote of the two houses Crittenden could count only forty-three Whig votes to thirty-one for Dixon. The sixty Democratic votes that would surely go for Dixon in a showdown would inundate Crittenden, should his name be openly presented. On the night of the twenty-fourth, Dixon's friends were prevailed upon to go into caucus, but this resulted only in confusion, as both sides claimed victory.

With ruin facing the party, some Whigs attempted to find a solution by a different scheme. Clay's health was precarious, and if he should die after the legislature adjourned, Governor Powell would appoint a Democrat to succeed him. Accordingly he was urged to resign so as to make two vacancies. Then both Crittenden and Dixon could be elected and the deadly feud ended. The election was postponed until December 11, when Clay could be heard from. But no answer came from Clay by that date and the Whigs were still unprepared to vote.

Crittenden in Washington was pained at the controversy over an election that he had thought a mere formality. Early in December he authorized his friends to withdraw his name. He owed the party too much, he wrote privately, to become an obstacle to its success now. Besides, he wanted "no office that is not freely & willingly bestowed," and "no contest in which I am to conquer or be conquered by friends." He had served Kentucky long and, he hoped, faithfully and not discreditably. But, he added, "When my services should cease to be acceptable to her, to hold office under her would no longer be an object of ambition for me.[24]

On the night of December 11 the Whigs went once more into caucus. By now it was conclusive that neither Crittenden nor Dixon could be elected, and both were withdrawn. The caucus then balloted on a dozen other candidates before finally settling on Thompson, a man of little talent. Next day, as Thompson's election was assured, Dixon was said to resemble "a motherless calf," and Crittenden's friends were now referring to the caucus as "the slaughterhouse convention."[25]

Thompson was a friend of Crittenden's, and his election was admittedly a triumph for Crittenden over Clay's partisans. Yet a Democratic observer thought that the satisfaction of diehard Clay men over having prevented Crittenden's election almost compensated them for their own defeat. In many ways, too, it was a costly victory for Crittenden. Thompson was so clearly below the stature of the

[24] Crittenden to Brown, Dec. 8, 1851, in Coleman, *Crittenden*, II, 24-25; Crittenden to [Burnley], Dec. 5, 1851, unsigned copy in Crittenden's hand, in Crittenden Papers (Duke).

[25] *Kentucky Senate Journal, 1851*, pp. 62-72, 77, 80, 109-11, 192, 202; Louisville *Courier*, Nov. 20, 22, 25, 27, Dec. 11, 12, 15, 1851; Louisville *Democrat*, Nov. 18, 19, 20, 21, 22, 24, 25, 26, 27, Dec. 12, 13, 15, 1851; Frankfort *Commonwealth*, Dec. 2, 1851; Orlando Brown to Crittenden, Dec. 3, 1851, in Crittenden Papers; Brown to Thomas L. Crittenden, Dec. 27, 1851, in Brown Papers, Filson Club; Little, *Ben Hardin*, 588-89.

men whom Kentucky had been sending to the Senate that few Whigs could rejoice over his election. One reporter, noting that twenty-five legislative days had been devoted entirely to the contest, estimated that Thompson's election had cost the state $12,500 in legislative expenses. He wondered if Thompson's service in the Senate would be worth that much to the commonwealth.

The futility of the contest was demonstrated a week later when Clay's resignation was received. Crittenden now declined to be a candidate for the remainder of Clay's term, and Dixon, on December 31, was chosen by a party vote of seventy-one to fifty-eight over Democrat James Guthrie. Ironically, Dixon, who owed his seat to Clay's friends, would play a significant role two years later in the repeal of the Missouri Compromise, reopening the slavery controversy that Clay had done so much to allay the year before.[26]

The senatorial contest showed conclusively that the rupture produced by the struggle over the 1848 presidential nomination had not been healed in Kentucky, and since Kentucky had always been regarded as the bedrock of the Whig party nationally, the future seemed bleak. New issues would soon crowd old Whig programs of bank, tariff, and internal improvements off the national stage. By 1852 the party was floundering aimlessly, striving only to preserve the status quo. It was a paradox that despite so much individual brilliance in its second-generation leaders—Toombs, Stephens, Clayton, Ewing, Seward, Weed, Winthrop, Corwin, Lincoln, Crittenden, Bates, Curtis, to name only the most prominent—the party itself had so little vigor. The plethora of talent was unable to counter the centrifugal force generated in the party by divisive sectional issues. By the winter of 1851-1852 both Clay and Webster were tottering to their graves, and the party they had done so much to create would not long survive them.

Fillmore's administration was generally successful, although not studded with brilliant achievements. Having just passed through the greatest crisis since its founding, the nation was in need more of calm readjustment than of great enterprise or activity. Fillmore's advisers, according to even the most partisan of Democrats, were "men of sense," and they governed the country satisfactorily if not brilliantly. Under the circumstances it seems strange that Fillmore was not chosen to lead the party in 1852. As usual, there were many

[26] *Kentucky Senate Journal, 1851*, p. 414; Little, *Ben Hardin*, 590; Poage, *Henry Clay*, 271-72.

aspirants for the nomination. Webster, although he would not be alive on election day, was early in the field. Winfield Scott was again eager. Clayton, Seward, and Weed were promoting him, and for a time it was thought that Crittenden was, too. They were old friends, and Crittenden had sometimes lived at Scott's when Maria did not accompany him to Washington.[27]

But southern Whigs were suspicious of Scott's free-soil associations. They insisted that the platform and the candidate stipulate the finality of the Compromise of 1850. Since Fillmore was identified with the Compromise, Crittenden regarded his reelection as vital to prevent the reopening of the slavery controversy. Most Kentucky Whigs agreed, and in the winter of 1852 local Whig meetings in all parts of the state endorsed both Fillmore and the Compromise. Clay, too, on the eve of his departure for his last journey to Washington, announced for Fillmore.

Meanwhile, a move had been generated by some of Crittenden's friends to have the Kentucky Whig convention, which would meet in Frankfort in late February, nominate him for the Presidency. But Crittenden refused, perhaps wisely, to entertain any serious belief in his own availability. Learning that county meetings had endorsed him, he wrote Orlando Brown that "If any purpose of that sort should be manifested in the Convention, I beg you and all my friends to suppress it." He urged instead that Fillmore be endorsed. When the convention met and Crittenden's letter was read, his name was withdrawn from consideration. But before Fillmore was nominated, the meeting passed by acclamation a resolution honoring Crittenden.[28]

But Fillmore was regarded by many northern antislavery men as a "doughface"; they refused to accept the Compromise as a final settlement of the slavery issue, and they would not have him as their

[27] "Recollections of an Old Stager," XLVII (1873), 588; Blair to Van Buren, Dec. 26, 1850, June 17, 1851, Feb. 22, 1852, Gouverneur Kemble to Van Buren, Feb. 16, 1851, in Van Buren Papers; E. G. Squires to Clayton, Sept. 2, 1850, Elisha Whittlesey to Clayton, Nov. 23, 1850, John W. Houston to Clayton, Feb. 27, 1851, in Clayton Papers.

[28] Scott to Clayton, Aug. 4, 1851, in Clayton Papers; Richard Hawes to Crittenden, Feb. 26, 1852, R. C. Wintersmith to Crittenden, Feb. 27, 1852, in Crittenden Papers; Crittenden to Brown, Feb. 6, 1852, in Crittenden Papers (Duke); Brown to Thomas L. Crittenden, Dec. 27, 1851, Brown to W. B. Haldeman, March 20, 1852, in Brown Papers, Filson Club; Frankfort *Commonwealth*, Feb. 3, 13, 17, 24, March 2, 24, 1852; Louisville *Courier*, Dec. 15, 1851, Feb. 18, 21, 23, 1852; Cole, *Whig Party in the South*, 253.

candidate. Disruption of the party thus seemed inevitable. For Seward and other northern extremists were bitterly opposed to the fugitive-slave law and were avowing that where human freedom was concerned, there was a higher law than the Constitution. On the eve of the national convention Crittenden was frequently mentioned as a middle-of-the-road candidate. George D. Prentice openly advocated his nomination as a moderate between the extremes, and Joseph R. Underwood, a few days before the convention met, thought Crittenden's nomination almost inevitable. Clay's approval was sought and obtained.[29]

But compromise was effected in a more extraordinary manner. When the convention met, southerners sought a resolution endorsing the Compromise, and northern moderates supported them. As a result of their combined efforts, the convention passed the resolution. Nominating Fillmore would logically have been the next step. But to this Weed and Seward would not agree. Scott was their man, and a deadlock between him and Fillmore ensued for fifty-two ballots before Scott was nominated on the fifty-third. It was then asked if Crittenden would accept nomination for second place, and a letter from him was produced, declining. Thereupon, William A. Graham was nominated.[30]

Democrats were equally hard pressed to find a candidate. George M. Dallas of Pennsylvania, Polk's Vice President, was not acceptable because his vote had broken the tie that was preventing passage of the Walker Tariff in 1846, and thus even his own state would not support him. Lewis Cass, defeated by Taylor in 1848, was eager for another try, and Daniel Dickinson of New York and Stephen Douglas were also ambitious. Buchanan, in retirement at Wheatland, felt that the time was not propitious for him. After a long contest, Democrats chose Franklin Pierce of New Hampshire, undistinguished in politics but like Scott a Mexican War hero.

Pierce won the election in a landslide, getting 254 electoral votes to Scott's 42. It was the last time the Whigs would contest for the Presidency. The party had been hopelessly broken by the nomination of Scott, as most southern Whigs deserted to the Democrats. Curiously, almost like the last glow of a dying ember, the party showed

[29] Cole, *Whig Party in the South*, 246-47, 253; Poage, *Henry Clay*, 276; Underwood to Thomas H. Clay, Aug. 3, 1852, in T. J. Clay Papers.
[30] Louisville *Journal*, quoted in Frankfort *Commonwealth*, May 28, 1852; *ibid.*, June 30, 1852.

vitality in Kentucky that year. It elected a majority of the legislature in August, and in November, Scott carried the state by 3,000 votes. Subsequent events, however, would dissipate any expectations of a Whig resurgence.[31]

Personal affairs occupied much of Crittenden's time during the closing months of the Fillmore administration. Ann Mary was finding it difficult in her widowhood to manage her business affairs and to rear her children in a way she thought worthy of them. One of her sons John Crittenden Coleman, although only fourteen years old, was a student at Centre College. He had become a discipline problem and had been suspended by his uncle, President Young. Ann Mary asked for advice, and Crittenden gave it. She must treat her son with "*severity* mixed with . . . kindness." He must be made to feel that he had brought disgrace on his family but that he could redeem himself by good conduct in the future. "It is just the want of this exercise of parental authority," he said, "that fills the country with so many dissolute & miserable sons."[32]

Thomas and Robert Crittenden were settled in business in Frankfort and were prospering, but Crittenden was once more hearing bad reports of George. He was so afraid that George would again be dismissed from the army in disgrace that he urged him to resign. Yet when George promised to reform, Crittenden was eager to believe him. "It does not take much to rekindle my hopes of what I so much desire," he wrote. Eugene, his youngest son, was also drifting idly, accumulating debts which his father had to redeem.[33]

In the closing months of his term as Attorney General, Crittenden began paying court to a wealthy widow. As a child, Elizabeth Moss had moved with her family from Mason County, Kentucky, to Missouri. There she had been twice married, first to Dr. Daniel P. Wilcox, by whom she had two daughters, and after his death to

[31] Dallas to Duff Green, Nov. 20, 1850, W. L. Marcy to Green, April 16, 1852, in Duff Green Papers; Howell Cobb to Orion Stroud, Aug. 4, 1852, in Phillips, *Correspondence of Toombs, Stephens, and Cobb*, 312-13; Binkley, *American Political Parties*, 179-80; Poage, *Henry Clay*, 276; Coulter, "Downfall of the Whig Party in Kentucky," 165; Frankfort *Commonwealth*, Dec. 3, 1852.

[32] Mrs. Coleman to Crittenden, July 31, 1852, in Crittenden Papers; Crittenden to Mrs. Coleman, Feb. 14, 1852, in Crittenden Papers (Duke).

[33] Maria Crittenden to Harry Todd, Jan. 28, 1851, in Harry I. Todd Papers, Filson Club; letters to Crittenden from R. C. Wintersmith, Feb. 27, 1852, from J. Thomas McDuffie, March 31, 1852, and Crittenden to Mrs. Coleman, Oct. 28, 1852, in Crittenden Papers; Crittenden to Mrs. Coleman, Jan. 9, May 17, Aug. 8, 1852, in Crittenden Papers (Duke); Mrs. Phillip S. Fall to Carrie Fall, Dec. 29, 1853, Albert B. Fall Papers, Kentucky Historical Society, Folder 275.

General William H. Ashley, explorer, wealthy fur trader, and congressman from Missouri. From Ashley she inherited a large estate—six thousand acres of Missouri lands, some of it valuable mining property, real estate in the business district of St. Louis, and property in Washington assessed at more than $120,000. Elizabeth Ashley reveled in Washington social life, and the middle-aged widow and the aging widower—Crittenden was now sixty-five—became attracted to one another. By all accounts she was a woman of style and of considerable charm. One who had traveled extensively compared her to cultured European women he had met. She was described as "refined, intelligent and accomplished," with a "noble, natural elegance." She was handsome, too. A much younger rival for social precedence spoke admiringly of Elizabeth's "superbly moulded" neck and shoulders that, "even in middle age, excited the envy of her less fortunate sisters." According to this account, Elizabeth was "a sweet type of the elderly fashionable woman, her face reflecting the utmost kindness, her corsage and silvery hair gleaming with brilliants."[34]

Crittenden and Elizabeth Ashley were married quietly on Sunday evening, February 27, 1853, at St. Paul's Cathedral. Before that date, however, Crittenden, who despite his lucrative Supreme Court practice had accumulated little property, insisted upon the execution of a contract guaranteeing Elizabeth complete control over her estate. A longtime friend of bride and groom, acquainted with the past happiness of each, declared the match ideal. "When till now," he asked, "did any man have three *such* wives? or any woman, three such husbands?"[35] There can be little doubt that Crittenden's affection for Elizabeth was as ardent as had been his love for Maria and Sarah Lee. In the ten years of their life together, she accompanied Crittenden on his travels whenever possible. When circumstances sometimes briefly separated them, his warm letters to her were as impatient for their reunion as those of any youthful swain in the throes of his first great passion.[36]

34 Washington *National Intelligencer*, Sept. 20, 1851; T. C. Flournoy to Elizabeth Ashley Crittenden, June 18, 1853, in Crittenden Papers (Duke); Virginia Clay-Clopton, *A Belle of the Fifties* (New York, 1905), 83-84.

35 T. C. Flournoy to Elizabeth Crittenden, June 18, 1853, in Crittenden Papers (Duke); Frankfort *Commonwealth*, Sept. 8, 1854.

36 Biographical sketch of Elizabeth Ashley Crittenden, Crittenden to Elizabeth Ashley Crittenden, Dec. 6, 1853, in Crittenden Papers (Duke); Peter G. Camden to Alexander [Andrew] McKinley, Jan. 24, 1846, Freeman Wing to Mrs. Elizabeth Ashley, Aug. 4, 1849, Crittenden to Elizabeth Ashley Crittenden, Nov. 29, Dec. 2, 1853 (copies), E. C. Cabell to Crittenden, March 19, 1860, in Crittenden Papers.

When Crittenden's term expired with Fillmore's administration in March, he took his bride home to Frankfort. They went by sea, stopping for visits at Mobile and New Orleans. Arriving in Kentucky in late spring, they spent a quiet summer with Crittenden's old friends there, the Letchers, Browns, Swigerts, Todds, and others. In October a public dinner was given in Crittenden's honor in St. Louis, and the couple visited there for several weeks. They were back in Frankfort by mid-November, however, where Crittenden had important business with the legislature.[37]

Clay had died in Washington a year and a half before—not, however, before a reconciliation with his old friend was effected. Crittenden had made repeated overtures to Clay during the four years of their estrangement, but all were rebuffed until three weeks before Clay died. He sent for Crittenden, and they held a prolonged conversation, after which Clay instructed his son Thomas, his constant companion in his last illness, to "treat him [Crittenden] kindly." It was at that time, too, that Clay had approved Crittenden's proposed nomination by the Whig convention at Baltimore in 1852. According to Orlando Brown, Clay told another friend at this time that he had been "greatly troubled" that Crittenden "should have suffered in the public estimation for his conduct in relation to the election of General Taylor and I regret that I was in error about it even for a moment myself." Clay added, said Brown, that he was "now satisfied that his whole conduct in that matter was what Mr. Crittenden's friends would have expected of him." Last vestiges of the feud were dispelled when Crittenden delivered an eulogy of Clay before a large Louisville audience in September.[38]

All this smoothed the way for Crittenden's return to the Senate. It will be recalled that Clay had resigned in the winter of 1851-1852 in time for the legislature to elect Dixon to the remainder of his term, which would expire in March, 1855. The legislature of 1853-1854

[37] Collins, *History of Kentucky*, I, 240; Frankfort *Commonwealth*, April 25, Nov. 18, 1853.

[38] Thomas H. Clay to ————, June 7, 1852, in Colton, *Clay*, IV, 634; Crittenden to Orlando Brown, May 5, 1852, in Brown Papers, Filson Club; Brown to Thomas H. Clay, July 19, 1852, in Thomas Hart Clay and Ellis P. Oberholtzer, *Henry Clay* (Philadelphia, 1910), 336n; Joseph R. Underwood to Crittenden, June 19, 1852, Ben Adams to Burnley, July 9, 1852, Adams to Crittenden, July 31, 1852, in Crittenden Papers; Underwood to Thomas J. Clay, Aug. 3, 1852, in T. J. Clay Papers; Frankfort *Commonwealth*, June 3, 1851; New York *Express*, quoted *ibid.*, July 19, 1852; Louisville *Courier*, quoted *ibid.*, Oct. 1, 1852.

was to choose a successor for the full term, and Dixon, now content, declined to enter the contest again. Crittenden, therefore, had no Whig opposition, and since Whigs still controlled the legislature, despite Tom Marshall's forebodings of two years earlier, his election was assured. He was chosen over Governor Powell on January 10 by a joint vote of the two houses, seventy-eight to fifty-nine. His election was celebrated by a great dinner at the Mansion House in Frankfort by Whigs and Democrats alike. Powell himself presided over a gathering of nearly two hundred and fifty, and Crittenden was toasted for "His purity, his wisdom, his patriotism." A strange turn, indeed, in the wheel of fortune since the bitter struggle of two years before.[39]

It was well for Crittenden that the election came when it did, for if it had been delayed three months, he probably could not have been chosen. In the intervening period he was to engage as counsel in a trial that brought his popularity to its lowest ebb. On a November morning the year before, Matt Ward, son of a wealthy Louisville businessman, had armed himself with a pistol and gone to the Male High School to demand satisfaction of the principal, William H. A. Butler, who had disciplined Matt's younger brother the day before. In the encounter that followed, Matt shot and killed Butler, and was indicted for murder. As public sentiment became aroused against him for what seemed an unprovoked attack, venue was changed to Hardin County and the trial was set for mid-April, 1854.

Crittenden was a lifelong friend of Matt's father, Robert J. Ward. Learning Ward wished him to represent his son but was hesitating to ask it because it was an unpopular cause, Crittenden volunteered his services. The trial lasted more than a week. The prosecution asked for the death penalty and rested heavily on the testimony of the students who had witnessed the assault. In a skillful defense Crittenden sowed doubt as to the value of their statements. When he found discrepancies, he emphasized them; where the testimony of several witnesses agreed on minute details, he suggested that the boys had been coached. He also presented an impressive array of character witnesses, including Louisville Mayor James Speed, William Preston, George D. Prentice, and Larz Anderson. All testified to Matt's mild temper and good character.

In his plea to the jury Crittenden reviewed the evidence, empha-

---

[39] *Kentucky House Journal,* 1853, p. 76; *Kentucky Senate Journal,* 1853, p. 67; Frankfort *Commonwealth,* Jan. 19, Feb. 18, March 22, 1854.

sizing those features that tended to support his plea of self-defense. Then he appealed eloquently to the merciful instincts of the jury. If they were in doubt, he said, they must find for the defendant. If they did not and later learned that they had erred, peace of mind would be impossible. "If you err," he said, ". . . keep on the side of humanity, and save him from so dishonorable a fate" as death by hanging. He closed with a sentimental but moving allegory of Creation, saying that Mercy had promised to follow Man's wayward steps and preserve in him the spark of Divinity. When he had concluded, the prosecutor paid tribute to his oratorical powers and added that he had just made "perhaps *the* greatest" speech of his life, for no man "could make two such speeches in the course of an ordinary lifetime." The result was acquittal. As the verdict was rendered, the crowd burst into cheers, and Matt Ward was borne triumphantly from the room.[40]

There had been no more sensational trial in Kentucky in a generation, and at the news of Matt Ward's acquittal, a shocked public raised a protest of indignation. Crittenden was roundly denounced by the press both within and without the state. He was charged with defending a man known to be guilty and attempting to impose false testimony upon the jury and was attacked for his "false reasoning, erroneous deductions, and absurd conclusion." Even the *Commonwealth*, a prime supporter of Crittenden for several decades, spoke out against the verdict. The only question, according to the *Commonwealth*, was whether the crime was murder or manslaughter. The Boston *Mail* compared the Wards to Russian despots, saying that the "hireling lawyers" were their "aristocratic servants bent on warping the so-called law." The Pittsburgh *Gazette* thought that Crittenden would never outlive the memory of the trial, and that he had lost forever his influence with his constituents. No southern Whig, it said, had "stood a fairer chance for the Presidency than he did. He was spoken of at the North with great favor for that office."

[40] A. D. Richardson, *A Full and Authentic Report of the Testimony on the Trial of Matt F. Ward* (New York, 1854), especially 8-33, 37-38, 43-45, 49-51, 53-54, 125-54, 175-76; George Cole, *Trial of Matt F. Ward* (Louisville, 1854), 6, 13-19, 37-38, 51-54, 135-51; Louisville *Democrat*, April 19, 20, 22, 26, 1854; Detroit *Free Press*, quoted *ibid.*, April 29, 1854; Louisville *Journal*, May 25, July 22, 1854; Crittenden to Elizabeth Crittenden, April 17, 19, 26, 1854, Crittenden to Logan Hunton, May 14, 1854, Crittenden to Larz Anderson, May 30, 1854, in Crittenden Papers (Duke); Matt F. Ward to Crittenden, March 17, 1854, Crittenden to Garret Davis and others, Dec. 30, 1854, in Crittenden Papers; Coleman, *Crittenden*, II, 72-87.

Now, "he could not carry one Northern State." The Detroit *Free Press* and the Cincinnati *Times* expressed shock at the verdict, convinced that Ward money had influenced the jury's verdict. Much was made of the fact that Crittenden's services had not been sought, but that he had volunteered, and that he had accepted no fee. Only Prentice, in the Louisville *Journal*, defended him and the Wards.

Protest meetings were held all over the state, in Hardin, Henderson, Henry, and Harrison counties. At Elizabethtown, and in neighboring Meade and McLean counties, the verdict was denounced as corrupt, and Crittenden's resignation from his recently won Senate seat was demanded. At Madison, Indiana, a mass meeting requested their county board to recall an invitation that had been extended Crittenden to address the county agricultural fair. He had, the resolution pontificated, "prostituted his great talents in an unworthy cause."

Most threatening of all was a meeting held at the courthouse in Louisville on Saturday night, April 29. Resolutions were passed denouncing the verdict as contrary to justice, requesting the Wards to leave the city, and demanding that Crittenden resign from the Senate. The meeting itself was orderly, but after it adjourned, a mob gathered and burned effigies of the twelve jurors, Prentice, Crittenden, and defense witnesses. The mob then proceeded to the Ward home, where effigies of the Ward brothers were hung and the house was set on fire.[41]

Crittenden was astonished at the reaction. Often before he had represented unpopular clients, but there had never been such an outburst as this. He defended himself forthrightly but ineffectively against all charges. It was not only his "professional *right*" to appear in the case, but under the circumstances, his "*duty*." If he had refused because of the great prejudice against Ward or from "any merely selfish calculations," then, he said, "I should have felt myself degraded—unworthy the name of *Friend*—unworthy of my profession—unworthy of the respect of honorable men—unworthy of *old Kentucky*." He did not think Matt guilty, he said, but guilty or innocent, he was entitled to counsel. His critics, he said, seemed to

41 Louisville *Democrat*, April 28, 29, May 1, 2, 3, 4, 5, 6, 9, 11, 1854; Detroit *Free Press*, quoted *ibid.*, April 29, 1854; Boston *Mail* and Pittsburgh *Gazette*, quoted *ibid.*, May 6, 1854; Frankfort *Commonwealth*, May 3, 5, 12, July 21, 1854; Louisville *Courier*, April 30, June 19, 1854; Louisville *Journal*, issues of April, 1854.

confuse the duties of counsel with those of judge. It was the duty of counsel to marshall all arguments and evidence in behalf of his client and submit them to the court for decision. As to not accepting a fee, he said his feelings "reviled from *bargaining* with a friend . . . in distress about a fee," especially when he knew that "it would be a bargain on my side only." For Ward would have assented to any sum he named. He could not be a "speculator" in his friend's distresses.[42]

Crittenden admitted that in criminal law his sympathies were always with the accused. In a long career at the bar, he said, he had never appeared as prosecutor. He feared to do so, he said, "lest in the spirit of controversy & pride for professional victory," he might be instrumental in unjustly convicting "some unfortunate fellow creature." The accused, he added, are always wretched, whether innocent or guilty. They drew his sympathy, "not because I favor or approve the guilty, but because I hope they may be innocent, or not so guilty as charged to be." In the course of his practice he had defended many persons charged with crime, often without fee. In retrospect he was not disturbed by the probability that he might have enabled a guilty client to escape the law. If so, "only one more poor offending child of humanity, . . . escaping the punishment & vengeance of man," would be "left to the mercy & justice of his God."[43]

But the abuse heaped on Crittenden continued through the summer and on into the autumn. Some of Crittenden's friends circulated a letter vindicating his conduct, signed by thirty-four leading members of the Kentucky bar. But Louisville lawyers refused to sign. They entertained the kindliest feelings toward Crittenden, they said, but they did not wish "to mix themselves up with that Ward business."[44]

[42] Crittenden to James Harlan and others, Dec. 30, 1854, Letterbook, 675-703, in Crittenden Papers (Duke).

[43] Crittenden to Logan Hunton, May 14, 1854, to [Larz] Anderson, May 30, 1854, in Crittenden Papers (Duke); Matt F. Ward to Crittenden, March 17, 1854, Crittenden to Larz Anderson, May 29, 1854, Crittenden to Garret Davis and others, Dec. 30, 1854, in Crittenden Papers; Coleman, *Crittenden*, II, 91-100.

[44] James Harlan and others to Crittenden, Sept. 12, 1854, in Crittenden Papers (Duke); Garret Davis and others to Crittenden, Sept. 12, 1854, in Coleman, *Crittenden*, II, 89; Letcher to Crittenden, Jan. 16, 1855, in Crittenden Papers.

CHAPTER XV

The Know-Nothings

THE MIDDLE of the nineteenth century was peculiarly a time of party flux in the United States, for conflicting sectional interests were bringing both parties dangerously close to dissolution. Both had divided, North and South, over the annexation of Texas, the Mexican War, and the question of slavery in the territories. Antislavery sentiment was present in northern wings of both parties, but among Whigs this feeling ran much deeper than it did with Democrats. For this reason, southern Whigs found it harder to unite with their northern brethren in election years than did southern Democrats. Thus, party collapse was more imminent for the Whigs than for the rival party.

Unionist Whigs in the South, like Toombs and Stephens, felt especially mistreated. They had combined with unionist Democrats in 1850 to prevent secessionists from undoing the Compromise just passed by Congress, and they felt ill repaid for their efforts two years later when antislavery Whigs forced the nomination of Scott. Such action convinced Toombs, Stephens, and other southern Whigs that if the Union were to be preserved, the Whig party must go. The two Georgians went into the Democratic party the following year.

In the lower South, by this time, slavery had become so deeply engrained into the social fiber that people had come to regard the institution as their way of life and of more consequence than the Union itself. Even in the border states this sentiment existed, but to a lesser degree. In Kentucky, one of the principal reasons for the decline of the Whigs was the heavy shadow which the northern, anti-slavery wing of the party cast over the state.[1]

Slavery was an issue so wrapped in emotion that no truly national party dared to take a strong stand for or against it. To do so would result only in certain loss in one of the sections. In their efforts to preserve the Union, therefore, Whigs had attempted to distract themselves and the nation from this burning issue by advocating national rather than sectional programs. But they soon found that protection, internal improvements, distribution of proceeds from land sales, and a national bank could become sectional issues, too, less bitter only than slavery. By 1850 many Whigs were convinced that these issues had no further appeal to voters. Richard Hawes, requesting Orlando Brown to address the convention of Kentucky Whigs in 1853, pleaded with him to "say as little about the old issues as possible."[2]

Party flux was taking place in the North as well as in the South, and among Democrats as well as Whigs. In New York, free-soil Democrats, under the name of "Softs," controlled federal patronage under Pierce and demonstrated their disdain for the nationalistic views of the old Hunkers. On the other hand, free-soil Whigs controlled the state government and were treating the nationalist "Silver Grays" with equal disdain. To Crittenden, Fillmore, and others, it seemed a propitious time to unite conservative factions of both parties into a new Union party, casting off both abolitionists and secessionists. It was clear that a union of their radical adversaries— free-soilers and secessionists—was impossible.[3]

Had such realignment taken place, the conservative party might for a time have enjoyed the success that its proponents envisioned;

[1] New York *Express*, Nov. 9, 1852, quoted in Frankfort *Commonwealth*, Nov. 19, 1852; *ibid.*, Aug. 3, 1853; Toombs to Crittenden, Oct. 9, Dec. 5, 1852, in Crittenden Papers; Coulter, "Downfall of the Whig Party in Kentucky," 163-64; William M. Pratt, Manuscript Diary (Kentucky).

[2] Hawes to Brown, Feb. 19, 1853, in Brown Papers, Kentucky Historical Society.

[3] Burnley to Crittenden, July 22, 1849, in Crittenden Papers; Fillmore to Kennedy, Oct. 14, 1853, Kennedy to Fillmore, Nov. 26, 1853, in Kennedy Papers, Peabody Institute.

and the nation might then have had time to try to avert the ordeal of fire and blood then preparing. But in periods of political disorganization, politicians seem to feel so insecure that they grasp at every issue, however transitory, that might bring even temporary personal advantage. Controversial legislation of any kind is particularly promising, and this was provided in the winter of 1853-1854 by Stephen Douglas' Kansas-Nebraska bill. This bill, in establishing territorial governments for the region, expressly repealed the Missouri Compromise, which for a third of a century had prohibited slavery in the Louisiana Purchase north of 36° 30′ north latitude. The new bill provided that the decision for or against slavery there would be left to future settlers—"popular sovereignty," it was called.

Few acts of Congress have started such a tragic chain of events as did this one. Some northern Democrats and almost all northern Whigs denounced it as a betrayal of a sacred agreement. The Democratic party, though shaken to its foundations, managed to hold itself together for another half-dozen years, partly because its control of national patronage was a unifying influence. Whigs, however, lacking any such common bond and more deeply divided on the merits of the issue than the Democrats, could not survive. Disintegration of the Whig party brought the nation to a crisis, and moderate Whigs, particularly those in border states, would be faced with a personal dilemma. Southern Whigs might unite with southern Democrats on a program of slavery expansion, as espoused by the national Democratic administration; and northern Whigs could go into the newly formed Republican party, dedicated to repeal of the Kansas-Nebraska Act and to the prevention of the spread of the peculiar institution. But border Whigs, like Crittenden, located in states where slavery was an accepted tradition even though it was not nearly so vital to the social and economic order as it was farther south, could unite with neither. They needed a new party.[4]

While the Whig party was deteriorating, a movement had been growing that would offer at least a temporary refuge for many of its members. This movement went under various names at different times and places, but it is generally referred to as nativism. There were some manifestations of nativism as early as Revolutionary days, a

[4] Roy F. Nichols, "The Kansas-Nebraska Act: A Century of Historiography," in *Mississippi Valley Historical Review*, XLIII (1956-1957), 197-99; Binkley, *American Political Parties*, 169-71.

result of Protestant antecedents of most colonials. The movement was fed from time to time by the increased flow of immigrants, particularly of Germans and Irish in the late 1840s.

All groups of immigrants had an impulse to carry with them and to reestablish in their new communities the customs and cultures they were leaving in the old. There were social and religious implications, therefore, as well as political, in the antiforeign, or nativist, movement. In early days, when immigration was a mere trickle, a lone immigrant settled in a community where he was surrounded by native Americans, and under their influence he soon became Americanized. The great numbers that came in the 1840s, however, settled in communities with slightly older immigrants with the same origins as themselves. Here they lived closely together, preserving old customs, languages, prejudices. Few of them were intellectuals. Almost none from continental Europe could speak English, and many could not even write their own native language. Their clergymen, who sometimes accompanied them, often discouraged the study of English in order to maintain influence over them. These conditions shut them off from all Americanizing influences, and at the end of the five-year period that the naturalization law required before citizenship could be granted, they were still as German or Irish as when they first landed.[5]

Some customs of the immigrants were particularly offensive to natives when they could be identified as ethnic activities. Thus, Germans seemed inclined to beer drinking and to too much merry-making on Sunday. The Irish drank too much whisky and seemed addicted to brawling. Many of the more literate and articulate of the immigrants were freethinkers and were likely to be atheists; and they as well as devout Roman Catholic immigrants demanded reforms in Sunday blue laws. A midwestern Congregationalist minister wrote of immigrants in his section, "The tide is swelling that rolls in upon us, drifting to our shores an incalculable amount of infidelity, superstition, and error, which threatens to lay waste and destroy our institutions." Even tolerant and liberal Unitarians, like

---

[5] Oscar Handlin, "Immigration and American Life; a Reappraisal," in Henry Steele Commager (ed.), *Immigration and American History: Essays in Honor of Theodore C. Blegen* (Minneapolis, 1961), 12-15; John T. Flanagan, "The Immigrant in Western Fiction," *ibid.*, 90; Ingrid Semmingsen, "Emigration and the Image of America in Europe," *ibid.*, 27; Franklin D. Scott, "The Immigration Theme in the Framework of National Groups," *ibid.*, 123.

Amos Lawrence and William Ellery Channing, regarded immigrants as one of the evils of this world that must be endured.[6]

It was inevitable that the immigrants should be drawn, more often than not as pawns, into the factional struggles inherent in American politics and extraordinarily bitter at midcentury. Both parties at first courted the new arrivals and voted them illegally whenever they could to advance the interests of the local machine. This bloc voting was more spectacular than the indigenous irregularities that had become commonplace in American elections. Since both parties seemed equally guilty of encouraging it, the first reaction of the natives was to form an independent party to put it down.

As competition developed between the two parties for the votes of the immigrants, Whigs found themselves at a disadvantage, for their party was generally considered the spokesman of property and business. Besides, Whig businessmen were forced into a nativist attitude by their native workers, who feared that efforts to improve their status would be undermined by the "half-famished, ignorant" foreigners, who would "toil for any wage and would never devote an hour to personal improvement." Democratic bosses, on the other hand, were uninhibited in welcoming the newcomers.[7] Many states permitted immigrants to vote prior to naturalization and sometimes after a residence of only a few months. Whig protest against this practice reached a high pitch after Clay's defeat in 1844. The election of Polk over their idol seemed to them a betrayal of true American democratic principles.

Whigs were unable to agree on all factors that contributed to their humiliating defeat, but there was one theory which most Whigs came to accept: the foreign vote had been the deciding factor. From large cities everywhere, particularly from New York, Baltimore, Philadelphia, Cincinnati, and St. Louis, came reports that corrupt federal courts were permitting the unlawful naturalization of newly arrived immigrants. The Cincinnati *Enquirer* reported a month before the election that at least twelve hundred immigrants had been illegally naturalized there and that all would vote for Polk. A week after the election the New York *Express* attributed the Democratic victory in

[6] Philip D. Jordan, "The Stranger Looks at the Yankee," in Commager, *Immigration*, 64-66; W. Darrell Overdyke, *The Know-Nothing Party in the South* (Baton Rouge, 1950), 17, 19.

[7] Jordan, "The Stranger Looks at the Yankee," in Commager, *Immigration*, 66; Overdyke, *The Know-Nothing Party in the South*, 8-9, 11-16.

the pivotal Empire State to the Democratic party's *"manufacturing [of] voters."* It estimated that in the two weeks before the election, not fewer than twenty-five hundred persons had been naturalizd in New York City alone. Thus, it concluded, "The votes of men just *admitted* to the sacred right of citizenship have settled the political character both of this city and the Empire State!"[8]

These partisan statements by Whig journals are to be regarded with skepticism; but that Whigs believed them is hardly to be doubted. "The foreign vote . . . destroyed your election," wrote one Albany Whig to Clay. "We have been robbed of our lawful President by the seven thousand fraudulent votes cast for Mr. Polk in this city," wrote a New Yorker. Horace Greeley charged that many immigrants were allowed to vote without even submitting to the formality of illegal naturalization. "The glaring frauds by which the election was consummated afford a sad predicament of what must be expected hereafter," wrote John Quincy Adams. Webster, in a speech at Faneuil Hall, boldly attributed the loss of both New York and Pennsylvania to the foreign vote and recommended a "thorough reformation of the naturalization laws" before the next election. From New Orleans, Albert Burnley wrote Crittenden that steamboats had been chartered to carry foreigners up and down the rivers and bayous voting again and again at the various polling places for Polk. Plaquemines Parish, which never before had polled more than 340 votes, gave Polk a majority of 970. From Baltimore came word that almost a thousand foreigners had been naturalized prior to the election and that nearly all had voted for Polk. "Thus men who could not speak our language," wrote an outraged Baltimore Whig, "were made citizens and became politicians too." Burnley echoed the sentiment. Democrats, he wrote Crittenden, "will beat us forever—unless, indeed, we can check them by restraining, if not destroying the influence of foreigners."[9]

[8] Quoted in Wallace Turner, "Henry Clay and the Campaign of 1844" (Master's thesis, University of Kentucky, 1933), 60-61.

[9] Ambrose Spencer to Clay, Nov. 21, 1844, Epes Sargent to Clay, Nov. 26, 1844, John H. Westwood to Clay, Nov. 28, 1844, A. B. Roman to Clay, Dec. 2, 1844, in Clay Papers; W. Bouligny to Clay, Dec. 4, 1844, in T. J. Clay Papers; John Quincy Adams to Clay, Jan. 4, 1845, in Colton, *Clay*, IV, 520; Greeley, *Recollections*, 165; Binkley, *American Political Parties*, 162-63, 187; Harry J. Carman and Reinhard H. Luthin, "Some Aspects of the Know-Nothing Movement Reconsidered," in *South Atlantic Quarterly*, XXXIX (1940), 216; Buchanan, *Works*, VI, 73; Sargent, *Public Men and Events*, II, 249; Burnley to Crittenden, Dec. 3, 1844, in Crittenden Papers; Cole, *Whig Party in the South*, 309.

Since most of the Irish and many of the German immigrants were Catholic, nativism contained heavy overtones of anti-Catholicism. It was not only the foreign voter, therefore, who in Whig eyes had done this mischief—it was the foreign Catholic voter. In Baltimore, Catholic votes overcame a fusion of Whigs and Native Americans. In New York, Archbishop John Hughes' influence was thought to be decisive for Polk. Millard Fillmore wrote that a combination of "abolitionists and foreign Catholics have defeated us in this state." It was German and Irish Catholic laborers, according to Thomas Ewing, who were the backbone of the organization against Clay in Ohio. Even from Maine a distraught Whig wrote that "We are to be prostrated in the dust by an army of Irish paupers, set on and marshaled by their infernal priest!!! God Almighty Save us!!!"[10]

Thus, the belief that immigrants, and particularly the Catholic immigrants, had contributed substantially to their defeat in 1844 produced a trauma in Whig mentality from which the party did not recover. From all sections came Whig pleas for reform in naturalization and election laws, a move not altogether unwarranted. Within a few weeks after the election, Whig gatherings in places as remote from one another as New Haven, Connecticut, and Alton, Illinois, passed resolutions deploring foreign influences in elections and calling for reforms which would prevent "The illegal foreign votes that are thrown against us in the larger cities."[11]

Increasingly, and to an alarming degree after this election, Whigs came to regard themselves as the true guardians of the American heritage, and their opponents as champions of an alien host, dedicated only to political plunder. Some regarded the defeat as a greater national humiliation than the burning of Washington by the British in the War of 1812. Philip Hone believed fervently that the "respectable" people, "who have wives whom they cherish and children whom they strive to educate, men who go to church on Sundays, respect the laws and love their Country," had voted in overwhelming numbers for Clay, whereas men who had no stake in the country's future had robbed them of their birthright. "The 'Sceptre has de-

---

10 C. A. Davis to Crittenden, Oct. 4, 1844, in Crittenden Papers; John S. Wendell to Clay, March 11, 1848, Thomas Ewing to Clay, Nov. 1, 1843, Millard Fillmore to Clay, Nov. 11, 1844, J. D. Mighels to Clay, Nov. 11, 1844, in Clay Papers; Overdyke, *The Know-Nothing Party in the South*, 20.
11 Resolutions of New Haven [Conn.] Whigs, Nov. 14, 1844, Resolutions of citizens of Alton, Ill., Nov. 19, 1844, in Clay Papers.

parted from Israel,' " he wailed. "Ireland has reconquered the Country which England lost." Corrupt and dishonest demagogues, another wrote, had by the aid of "a foreign legion" overpowered true patriotic citizens. The country for which their forefathers fought and bled was now governed "by Foreign Barbarians," wrote another, *for the President is their President.*" Clay was the choice of "the American People."[12]

Pierce's landslide victory in 1852 alarmed Protestants of all sects to a fear of foreign Catholic ascendancy in the government. Two weeks before that election, Tom Corwin in Ohio had been confident, as were all Whigs there, he said, that Scott would get the immigrant vote. Yet after the election he wrote, "we know they *all* voted the other ticket." It was believed by many, he added, that the about-face had resulted from orders received from Archbishop John Hughes in New York, and as a consequence, there was "a most ferocious and fearful opposition to those of the Romish faith who are foreigners."[13]

By 1853 a new Native American party had been formed. At first it was a secret organization, and members pleaded ignorance whenever questioned about it. This led to their popular designation as Know-Nothings. The party's first successes were in New York and Massachusetts. New York moderate Whigs, led by Fillmore, had been eclipsed after 1853 by Seward's radicals, and the Fillmore group, but not Fillmore himself, then combined with the American party. In Massachusetts, free-soil Whigs and Democrats, convinced that only a new party could prevent the spread of slavery, left the older parties and joined the Know-Nothings.

In the South the swing of Whigs to the new party was stimulated by other motives. There were few Catholics in the South and, consequently, little hostility to foreigners on account of their religion. But the census of 1850 revealed that almost all foreigners, regardless of where they landed, settled in the North and were largely responsible for the additional eighteen representatives that northern states would have in the new Congress. Furthermore, because of the

[12] George T. Davis to Crittenden, Nov. 25, 1844, in Crittenden Papers; Thomas Nevitt to Clay, Nov. 23, 1844, Philip Hone to Clay, Nov. 28, 1844, Dr. Bronson to Clay [n. d.], Mrs. Levert to Clay, Dec. 6, 1844, in Clay Papers; Sergeant Perry (ed.), *The Life and Letters of Francis Lieber* (Boston, 1882), 245; Clay to Crittenden, Nov. 28, 1844, in Coleman, *Crittenden*, I, 223-24.

[13] Corwin to James A. Pearce, Oct. 20, 1854, in Steiner, "Correspondence of Pearce," 40-41.

strong antislavery views of the immigrants, their votes would naturally go to the most radical antislavery candidates. "The mistake with us," growled a slaveholder, "has been that it was not made a felony to bring in an Irishman when it was made piracy to bring in an African." Thus the Know-Nothings were linked to the slavery issue in both North and South, but on opposite sides.[14]

In the border states, however, Know-Nothings were influenced more by fear of sectional conflict over slavery than by eagerness for its protection or by an aversion to Catholics. They regarded the foreigner as a disturber of the peace won in 1850, and they knew that in any war between the sections their region would be the battleground. The Know-Nothing party offered them an alternative, a delay of violent civil war. They sought to preserve the Union by pushing aside the slavery issue. There were therefore two elements in the Native American party of the mid-1850s. One was a healthy, respectable element, made up of such people as the amiable Clayton and Orestes A. Brownson, himself a convert to Catholicism. Distressed at the corruption of the ballot box and at the sectional conflict threatening the Union, these men went into the party as the only vehicle they saw that might possibly preserve the national integrity and the Union. On the other hand, there was a rough, rowdy element, bigoted and narrowly nationalistic, who left a stigma of disrepute on all in communion with them.[15]

Despite their sectional division, Know-Nothings soon had phenomenal success in local elections. By the spring of 1854 they were firmly entrenched in most eastern cities, including the national capital, and they captured state governments in all sections. In Philadelphia and New York the party soon absorbed almost all Whigs and many Democrats. In the New York gubernatorial election in 1854, Know-Nothings, despite many handicaps, polled 25 percent of the

[14] Carman and Luthin, "Some Aspects of the Know-Nothing Movement Reconsidered," 217-21; Louisville *Journal*, Nov. 21, 1854; George M. Stephenson, "Nativism in the 40's and 50's with Special Reference to the Mississippi Valley," in *Mississippi Valley Historical Review*, IX (1922-1923), 194-95; Cole, *Whig Party in the South*, 309-13; A. C. Cole, *The Irrepressible Conflict* (New York, 1934), 144-46; Binkley, *American Political Parties*, 189-94.

[15] Carman and Luthin, "Some Aspects of the Know-Nothing Movement Reconsidered," 221-24; Ray Allen Billington, *The Protestant Crusade, 1800-1860: A Study in the Origins of American Nativism* (New York, 1938), 394; Wallace B. Turner, "The Know-Nothing Movement in Kentucky," in *Filson Club Quarterly*, XXVIII (1954), 270.

vote. In Massachusetts they elected the governor by an overwhelming majority, almost the entire legislature, a solid congressional delegation, and a new United States senator, Henry Wilson. By the following winter Clayton and other leaders thought they were destined to capture control of the national government.[16]

Know-Nothing growth was rapid in Kentucky, and with the decline of the Whigs there, its force fell with a staggering impact on the now resurgent Democracy. In Lexington and in Louisville, Know-Nothings, made up largely of old Whigs, carried city elections overwhelmingly in 1854. By January, 1855, it was reliably estimated that there were 50,000 Know-Nothing voters in the state. Leadership of the Native American party in Kentucky early devolved on three prominent old Whigs: Robert J. Breckinridge, Garret Davis, and George D. Prentice. Prentice, who earlier had denounced nativist principles as "preposterous," by the spring of 1855 was defending the party against charges that it was linked with abolitionists. He now called the American party "the true, the formidable, and the *only* . . . antagonist of abolitionism." Northern states, he said, were attempting to break down constitutional protection for the rights of the states. The American party had assumed the task of safeguarding these rights.[17]

In June the first national convention of the party was held in Philadelphia behind closed doors, and at once the slavery issue raised its controversial form. Delegates agreed on planks proscribing aliens from public office, on a twenty-one-year period before citizenship could be bestowed on aliens, and on a policy of resistance to Catholicism's "corrupting and aggressive" practices. But on slavery they could not agree. New England delegations wanted a strong anti-Nebraska resolution. Such a resolution, of course, could not be accepted by either southerners or border-state men. Eventually a platform was adopted deploring agitation of the slavery issue, calling for preservation of the Union, and endorsing, by implication, the Kansas-Nebraska Act. Thereupon, delegates of twelve northern states withdrew.

Through it all sat Burnley, listening, he wrote Crittenden, to "a

[16] George W. Mitchell to Alexander H. H. Stuart, June 20, 1854, in A. H. H. Stuart Papers; Edward Jay Morris to Clayton, Feb. 21, 1855, in Clayton Papers; Binkley, *American Political Parties*, 189-94.

[17] Louisville *Journal*, Dec. 30, 1854, March 20, 24, April 16, May 3, 7, 1855.

great deal of immaterial talk, by immaterial men, about immaterial things. . . . I suppose such a pitiful convention never assembled," he added. "It is full of fools & demagogues—most of them forgetting all the nationality which ought to belong to them in their representative character, & trying to make a little miserable personal popularity at home to enable them to be elected constables, members of the Legislature, & some of them even aspire to Congressmen." Burnley had hoped the party might be the agency for saving the Union, and he and Prentice had proposed to solve the slavery question by reestablishing the old Missouri line and having it extended through the Mexican cession. When this was rejected in favor of the proslavery proposal, he despaired of the future of the party.[18]

Nor were Crittenden's other Kentucky friends better impressed with the party's beginning. Letcher wrote of a Know-Nothing meeting in Louisville in January, a "boisterous affair"; the party would not, he wrote Crittenden, "amount to anything." A month later, reports of a state convention held in Louisville had done little to change Letcher's opinion. "I am in ill humor about that movement," he wrote Crittenden. The following November, Letcher went as an observer to a Louisville meeting. Tom Crittenden was there and made a speech, but Letcher thought the "whole order of the affair was bad, very bad."[19]

If Crittenden had had any hopes for the future of the American party as then constituted, reports he received from Burnley and Letcher must have disillusioned him. His faith in the Whig party was unshaken. A party reorganized and revitalized along conservative lines was the only salvation for the country, he thought. Yet it would be foolish intentionally to drive Americans away. After all, they were Whigs, under strange colors and with some extreme doctrines on aliens and Catholics, but nevertheless Whigs. A way must be found to win them back to the true faith. In 1856 a President would be chosen, and on the outcome of that election would hinge the safety

[18] J. R. Robertson, "Sectionalism in Kentucky from 1855 to 1865," in *Mississippi Valley Historical Review*, IV (1917-1918), 50-51; Turner, "Kentucky in a Decade of Change," 41; Coulter, "Downfall of the Whig Party in Kentucky," 166-68; Louisville *Journal*, quoted in Lexington *Observer and Reporter*, Aug. 18, 1847; Frankfort *Commonwealth*, Jan. 10, 17, 1855; Burnley to Crittenden, June 12, 1855, in Crittenden Papers.
[19] Letcher to Crittenden, Jan. 16, 25, 29, Feb. 25, Nov. 30, 1855, in Crittenden Papers.

of the Union. Both Democratic and Republican parties were too radical on the slavery question to govern a united country. If the country was to be saved, therefore, help of Know-Nothings was imperative. A complete break with them was out of the question. On the other hand, the party had no chance of winning unless it could unite with old Whigs and other conservatives.

By midsummer, 1855, Crittenden was lending support to the Know-Nothing candidate for governor, Charles S. Morehead. In a speech in Frankfort on July 24 Crittenden endorsed his old friend but went out of his way to repudiate the anti-Catholic tenets of the Know-Nothings. He declared himself "utterly hostile to imposing any penalties, proscription, or disability upon any man on account of his religion." He had fullest confidence, he added, in native Catholics as much as in any men of any faith. He was certain they acknowledged no allegiance to the Pope superior to that owed their country. However, he confessed, naturalization laws should be reformed to prepare immigrants more thoroughly for their duties as citizens before the franchise was given them.[20]

In the August election in Kentucky the Know-Nothings swept the state. Morehead was elected governor over his Democratic rival, Beverly L. Clarke, by 4,400 votes. The party also chose six of ten congressmen and won lopsided majorities in the legislature. It is noteworthy that forty counties that had voted Whig in 1852 were carried now by Know-Nothings. It was in this election, too, that riots in Louisville resulted in a score of fatalities, practically all of them among foreigners. Final responsibility for these riots has never been clearly established. Know-Nothings blamed Democrats and Democrats blamed Know-Nothings, but popular revulsion soon set in against the latter.[21]

The remarkable success of the Know-Nothings in Massachusetts, New York, Pennsylvania, Ohio, and Kentucky in 1854 and 1855 encouraged their hope that they would capture the Presidency in 1856. By playing down the slavery issue and by emphasizing preservation of the Union and elimination of corruption, they would be-

[20] Frankfort *Commonwealth*, July 27, Aug. 6, 1855; Overdyke, *The Know-Nothing Party in the South*, 78, 86.
[21] Turner, "Kentucky in a Decade of Change," 51; Kerr, *Kentucky*, II, 847-50. For accounts of Louisville riots see Louisville *Journal*, Louisville *Democrat*, and Louisville *Courier*, Aug. 7-20, 1855.

come the truly national party. Their prospects were not without promise. Republicans seemed so likely to break up the Union by their antislavery program that it was believed all northern moderates would unite to prevent their success. At the same time, the Pierce administration had been captured so completely by extreme proslavery southerners that the Democratic party was weakened in the North. Besides, Democratic prestige was at a low ebb because of a firm belief that the party was rotten through and through with corruption in high places. It was not at all strange, therefore, that "the betting odds in 1855 were in favor of the Know-Nothings as the coming major party of the opposition."[22]

The problem of the Know-Nothings, as with most new political parties, was to find the right man to lead them. There was much talk of Fillmore, who was on a European tour at the time and not even a member of the party, and of Daniel Dickinson, a New York Democrat. Many, however, thought it would be a mistake to take any northern man. It would be difficult to find one with enough appeal to southerners to draw them from the "doughface" candidate the Democrats were sure to choose. If only Know-Nothings could find a southern man, one "truly national without being too ultra on *Negroes*," wrote a New Yorker to Crittenden, he could carry enough northern states to put him over.[23]

Crittenden, John Bell, or Clayton might fit this description, but quiet, diminutive Garret Davis, who had done much to establish the new party in Kentucky, was ambitious, even though he had been inactive in national politics for many years. Crittenden's name was proposed, although, like Fillmore, he still claimed allegiance to the moribund Whig party. Clayton was for him, according to Prentice, and so were many influential former Whigs, both in the border and in the South. "Many—*very many*—desire you to allow yourself to be made President," wrote Tom Corwin in 1854.[24] Crittenden and his Kentucky friends, however, were more concerned with the election of a conservative Unionist to the Presidency than with the promotion of Crittenden's personal fortunes. Their problem

---

[22] Binkley, *American Political Parties*, 195, 207; George Pepper Norris to Clayton, Dec. 17, 1855, in Clayton Papers.

[23] J. N. Reynolds to Crittenden, Oct. 5, 1855, Letcher to Crittenden, Nov. 30, 1855, in Crittenden Papers.

[24] Corwin to Crittenden, March 10, 1854, in Coleman, *Crittenden*, II, 104-105.

was to win Know-Nothing support for a conservative old Whig, perhaps for Crittenden, without at the same time tainting him with the
religious bigotry and antiforeign extremism of the party.

By December, Burnley, working with Letcher, Prentice, and
George Robertson (now reconciled to Crittenden), had formed a
plan. Details purposely were left obscure by the principals in their
correspondence, but veiled hints there, as well as their recorded behavior, give a reasonably accurate picture. The American party
was scheduled to hold its nominating convention in Philadelphia in
February, 1856. A month before that date a convention would be
held at Frankfort for the purpose of selecting delegates and, perhaps,
recommending a candidate to the Philadelphia convention. If the
state convention could be dissuaded from naming a favorite son,
and if the Philadelphia convention could be postponed until July,
a Whig national convention in June could nominate Fillmore, Crittenden, or some other conservative old Whig. Then the postponed
American convention might be persuaded to accept the nominee
of the Whigs. At the same time, conservative Democrats, alarmed
at radical drifts in their own party as well as in the Republican, might
be won to suport a reinvigorated Whig party. Robertson went off
to Washington in mid-December, and Crittenden was cryptically
instructed by Letcher only to *See him*, and attend to him." Crittenden did so, and two weeks later Robertson was back in Kentucky
reporting himself "very much delighted with everybody & everything
in Washington."[25]

Bitter cold descended on Kentucky in late January. Temperatures
dropped to zero and below and remained there for several weeks.
River transportation was at a standstill because of ice, and travel
over the frozen, rutted roads was extremely uncomfortable and even
dangerous. It was feared that only a handful of local "councils" of
the American party would be able to send delegates to the Frankfort
convention. Shortly before it was scheduled to meet, Garret Davis
sought out Burnley and Letcher in a bid for the support of Crittenden's friends for his own presidential aspirations. But Davis had

25 W. G. Brownlow to John Bell, Jan. 15, 1856, Balie Peyton to Bell, Feb. 3,
May 5, 1856, in John Bell Papers, Library of Congress; John A. Rogers to Clayton, Jan.
19, 1855, in Clayton Papers; Frankfort *Commonwealth*, May 25, 1853; Martha A.
Burnley, "Albert Triplett Burnley," 153; letters to Crittenden from J. C. A. Kennedy,
May 8, 1855, from Letcher, Dec. 13, 1855, from Burnley, Jan. 7, 1856, from A. F.
Hopkins, Feb. 22, 1856, in Crittenden Papers.

been too militantly antiforeign and anti-Catholic to fit into their plans, and they managed to prevent his nomination by the convention without incurring his wrath. A week after the convention, Davis conceded that the conduct of Crittenden's friends had been wise and that Crittenden himself was a "model of magnanimity & generosity & moderation," completely untouched by selfishness or ambition. Davis himself was won over to Burnley's plan of postponing the national nominating convention until July.[26]

But Burnley's plan would not continue to move so smoothly. The national council of the American party convened in Philadelphia on the eve of the convention, and trouble started when rival Pennsylvania delegations sought recognition. When the free-soil group was admitted by a vote of almost two to one, the embittered southern delegates determined to insist that the council reendorse the Kansas-Nebraska Act. Under the undemocratic regulations of the party, the national council, and not the convention, was authorized to fix the party's tenets, although state councils customarily disregarded such statements of doctrine as they chose.

The council, beset with confusion and insurrection on both fronts, attempted compromise. Some southern councils objected to proscription of Catholics, and so the council modified its rigid anti-Catholic position by declaring merely that no one should be eligible for office who recognized fealty to any foreign potentate or who did not consider the Constitution the supreme law of the land. Most councils could accept this. But the slavery issue was more difficult of a solution. The former specific endorsement of the Kansas-Nebraska Act was eliminated in a new statement that verbosely but obscurely approved of popular sovereignty. This pleased neither side. Southerners charged that the party had become abolitionized, and many of them now withdrew. Meanwhile, northern delegates declared that the party was ruined in their states by the popular-sovereignty plank.

When the convention opened two days later with three hundred delegates present, the battle over the slavery plank was resumed. Resolutions declaring that the national council had no authority to prescribe a platform and that no candidate favoring introduction

26 Burnley to Crittenden, Jan. 28, 1856, Davis to Burnley, Jan. 27, 1856 [misdated 1855] (copy), Feb. 8, 1856 (copy), Robertson to Crittenden, March 8, 1856, in Crittenden Papers.

of slavery north of 36° 30′ would be nominated were both tabled by overwhelming majorities. Thereupon, fifty northern delegates walked out and went over to the Republican party.[27]

In the confusion and disorder that followed, a proposal was made to adjourn until July 4 and was debated all day on February 23. Southern delegates feared that delay would cause the northern wing of the party to go over to the Republicans, and northerners feared the southern wing might join the Democrats. In the end the resolution was voted down by a decisive majority, and the convention then proceeded to nominate a candidate. On the second ballot Fillmore, still unaffiliated actively with the party and still absent in Europe, was nominated. Andrew Jackson Donelson of Tennessee was nominated for Vice President. Seventy "North Americans," unhappy with these choices, now withdrew and ultimately joined the Republicans.[28]

The American party had thus broken apart over the slavery issue, just as had the Whigs. Had Burnley succeeded in postponing the Know-Nothing convention until after the old Whigs had nominated Fillmore, and had Know-Nothings then endorsed him, Fillmore's position would have been strong. For he would then have stood before the country as the candidate of an old, respected, and respectable party. Know-Nothing endorsement would have rallied countless legions to his standard without injury to his prestige. As it was, however, he was the candidate of a new and questionable party, endorsed by the remnants of the Whigs. This would identify Whigs with Know-Nothingism rather than the other way around, and Fillmore could hardly hope to win. Even in the South his support would be meager. For ultraslavery interests by now had forced acceptance there of more extreme views than Fillmore could avow, and many southerners were no longer willing to accept the Compromise of 1850 as final. They now insisted that popular sovereignty must prevail in all territories, not just in the Mexican cession. The only hope for Fillmore was that he might win enough electoral votes in the border states to throw the election into the House.[29]

[27] Washington *National Intelligencer*, Feb. 21, 22, 25, 26, 1856; Binkley, *American Political Parties*, 195; Carman and Luthin, "Some Aspects of the Know-Nothing Movement Reconsidered," 224-28; Nevins, *Ordeal of the Union*, II, 466-67.

[28] George P. Norris to Clayton, Feb. 23, 1856, in Clayton Papers; Carman and Luthin, "Some Aspects of the Know-Nothing Movement Reconsidered," 226.

[29] Lewis Condict to Crittenden, Oct. 13, 1856, in Crittenden Papers.

Despite the miscarriage of Burnley's plans, Crittenden had little choice but to support Fillmore, even though he would have preferred him under a different banner; for as one observer noted, the border people were "truly between hawk and buzzard." A week after the nomination, Crittenden arrived late at a ratification meeting at Capp's Saloon in Washington. Called on for a speech, he responded. "We strive," he said, "for our native-born sovereignty, our native born supremacy in that land which a beneficent God has given us." These principles were insisted upon by nativists "not because they loved the foreigner less, but because they loved their country more." He would be glad to give the foreigner "a share of all [we] had, but for the good of the foreigner as well as the good of ourselves this Government must be kept in our own hands, or it would fall to dilapidation and ruin." This, however, must not be the "great and paramount object of their party." That should be "the maintenance of the Constitution and the Union, and to this [aim] all others were subordinate." There was no hope of restoring harmony, he said, save through the election of Fillmore.

Shortly thereafter in debate in Congress, Crittenden elaborated on this doctrine. He denounced the practice of "reaching out a hand to foreigners to get in their votes." The Constitution contemplated the exercise of governmental functions only by citizens, and he was unwilling to extend suffrage to any others. It would be a "species of sacrilege" to do so. The right to vote, he added, was "the sceptre, the crown," of the citizen. "Let him be my fellow citizen, whether by birth or by adoption, according to the laws of my country. To him belongs this right."[30]

It was late summer before Congress adjourned and Crittenden could return to Kentucky. When he did, he threw himself into the campaign for Fillmore. He toured the western part of the state in October, speaking at Glasgow, Bowling Green, Hopkinsville, Russellville, and Elkton. He was received everywhere with great affection. At Bowling Green he shared the platform with Andrew Ewing, Tennessee Democrat. The Louisville *Journal*, an out-and-out American sheet by now, claimed that Crittenden triumphed completely over his adversary, demonstrating conclusively that the Democratic

---

[30] Washington *National Intelligencer*, March 1, July 19, 1856; William D. Lewis to Clayton, July 28, 1856, in Clayton Papers; Cole, *Whig Party in the South*, 324-25; *Congressional Globe*, 34 Cong., 1 Sess., 1522.

party was responsible for the agitation of the slavery question that was threatening destruction of the Union.[31]

Democratic editors, however, who formerly had conceded Crittenden's powers as a speaker, disagreed. They thought they now noted an inability on Crittenden's part to transmit to this new party the enthusiasm and fire that had inspired him when preaching the Whig cause. His Know-Nothing efforts, they claimed, were "failures." Almost sadly they reflected on his "former gallant bearing," his former "accustomed eloquence," the absence now of "burning sentences" in his speeches. "His heart is not in the cause," wrote one, "and his keen sense of honor teaches him that his hypocrisy ought to degrade him in the eyes of all true men." Another, likening him to "the galvanized corpse of his former self," said his speeches had about them "the damp and mill dew of a new made grave."[32]

By this time, however, Kentucky was already lost to Fillmore. Old Whigs in the state, fearful that a division in anti-Republican votes might result in Frémont's victory, crossed over into the Democratic party and voted in great numbers for Buchanan. The process was repeated in other border and southern states. In North Carolina, Badger wrote Crittenden, Whigs had "behaved like apes —have turned democrats and ruined the State—Heaven help us!" For a time in Kentucky it had been expected that Buchanan's part in the embarrassment of Clay three decades before would cause Clay's old friends now to declare a holy war on the Democratic candidate. Many, like John Minor Botts of Virginia, would take even Frémont—or the devil himself—in preference to Buchanan. In the end, however, Buchanan carried the state by more than six thousand votes. It was the first time Kentucky had cast her electoral vote for a Democrat since 1828, when Jacksonians had broken Clay's domination of the state.[33]

If there had been any chance of victory for the Whig-American

[31] Frankfort *Commonwealth*, Aug. 29, Sept. 5, 12, 22, 1856; Louisville *Journal*, Oct. 15, 1856.

[32] Louisville *Times* and St. Louis *Democrat*, quoted in Frankfort *Commonwealth*, Nov. 2, 5, 1855.

[33] Carman and Luthin, "Some Aspects of the Know-Nothing Movement Reconsidered," 228-29; H. T. Duncan to Crittenden, June 24, 1856, Letcher to Crittenden, July 1, 1856, Badger to Crittenden, Aug. 9, 1856, in Crittenden Papers; John Tyler to Robert Tyler, Sept. 27, 1856, in Tyler, *Letters and Times*, II, 532; Coulter, "Downfall of the Whig Party in Kentucky," 170-71; Turner, "Kentucky in a Decade of Change," 58-61.

candidate in northern states, it was lost by mismanagement. Old Whigs in Massachusetts, embarrassed by their denunciation of the coalition of free-soil Democrats and Whigs that had elected Charles Sumner to the Senate a few years before, were reluctant to combine with Americans now. In Connecticut, fusion was effected with Democrats, but this infuriated Pennsylvania Republicans, who had agreed to support Fillmore in exchange for American support of the state Republican ticket. "It was a horrible blunder," wrote a Pennsylvania American, for Republicans were *"mad* as devils about the Connecticut fusion." Republicans now withdrew from the agreement, throwing the state to Buchanan. Frémont, meanwhile, carried Connecticut, along with the rest of New England.[34] Americans had high hopes in New York and optimistically spoke of the state as certain. But Letcher, on a speaking tour for Fillmore there in October, assured Crittenden this was not so. He had canvassed the entire state, had talked to the people, and was convinced the rural vote would carry the state for Frémont. It did.[35]

In the final result, Fillmore received 875,000 votes to 1,838,000 for Buchanan and 1,340,000 for Frémont. But the only electoral votes Fillmore received were Maryland's 8, whereas Buchanan received 174 and Frémont, 114. Buchanan was thus elected President, the last Democrat to reside in the White House for almost three decades.

The American party's decline after the 1856 election was even more rapid than its rise. The reaction of naturalized voters to it was so bitter that henceforth a candidate for office with a strong Know-Nothing record had little chance of election wherever the foreign vote was significant. Within a short time the very name of the party was used as an epithet by rival Republican and Democratic politicians to belabor one another. Fortunately for Crittenden, perhaps, his Senate term still had four years to run. Even though he had come to the party late, and with obvious reluctance, and had emphasized the Union-preserving principles in its platform rather than its proscription of Catholics and foreigners, he could hardly have won reelection to the Senate after 1856. For the following

[34] George T. Curtis to Crittenden, July 3, 1856, Jacob Dewees to Crittenden, Feb. 10, 1860, in Crittenden Papers; Curtis to Crittenden, July 10, 1856, in Coleman, *Crittenden*, II, 130-31; Vespasian Ellis to Alexander H. H. Stuart, Oct. 10, 1856, in Stuart Papers (Virginia).

[35] Letcher to Crittenden, Oct. 20, 1856, in Crittenden Papers.

year the legislature was captured by the Democrats. Meanwhile, Crittenden had become absorbed in the titanic struggle to save the Union. The struggle was being waged on all fronts, from Kansas to Georgia to New England. Its focal point, however, was of course Washington.[36]

[36] Stephenson, "Nativism in the Mississippi Valley," 197-99; Coulter, "Downfall of the Whig Party in Kentucky," 171-73.

Book Three

THE PATRIOT

CHAPTER XVI

Dark Shadows

As THE Thirty-fourth Congress assembled for its first session in December, 1855, Kansas was the center of attention almost to the exclusion of other business. Douglas in 1854 had had no conception of the fury that his Kansas-Nebraska bill would unleash. It had been all but universally conceded, save by a few southern extremists, that slavery had reached its natural limits and would never extend into the bleak western plains with their long frigid winters and dry summers. Douglas had sought to resolve both a complex constitutional question regarding slavery as well as conflicting sectional interests in a Pacific railroad by organizing territorial governments on the principle established in the compromise of 1850. It had seemed to him that repealing the prohibition against the introduction of slavery into the territories merely removed from federal statutes a gratuitous and humiliating insult to a large and respected portion of the nation's citizens. After all, had not Webster said in his Seventh of March speech that it was needless to reenact a law of God and Nature? If the Back Bay Boston sage could entertain such conciliatory sentiments, surely they must be excused in a self-made lawyer with presidential aspirations from the Illinois prairies.[1]

No sooner was the Kansas bill introduced, than a storm of protest arose in all sections of the North among men as far apart politically as Thomas Hart Benton and Moses H. Grinnell. An alarmed Benton wrote Crittenden. "Is the country to be convulsed worse than war . . . ?" he asked. "Is all Clay's labor to be buried with him?" To Grinnell it was the most villainous proposal ever presented to Congress and would be fatal to any northern man who supported it. The day after the bill in final form was reported to the Senate, Salmon P. Chase and Joshua Giddings issued an appeal to the people of the country, pontifically denouncing it as a betrayal of a sacred pledge and a plot to exclude free laborers from the territory and convert it into "a dreary region of despotism, inhabited by masters and slaves." It charged that the bill was designed to spread slavery eventually even into the free states.[2]

It was useless for Douglas to attempt to reason with his critics. Emotions were now stirred, North and South, and the controversy fed on itself. Each side insisted that victory for its opponents in the western territories meant an end to its own way of life. Southerners, who would never have taken slaves to the plains territories even if they could, now demanded a "right" to take them there. Northerners, who in their rational moments knew the region would never support slavery, fought with equal bitterness for a law to prohibit the "peculiar institution" there.[3]

Verbal controversy in the East over Kansas was punctuated by sporadic violence in the territory itself. Even before the bill was passed, Eli Thayer had persuaded the Massachusetts legislature to charter the Massachusetts Emigrant Aid Company to subsidize the establishment of free-soil colonies in Kansas. By the end of 1854 several thousand free-soil settlers had reached there, many of them men without families, armed with Sharps rifles. At the same time, emigrants from the South were moving into the region, the most notable a colony of about three hundred led by an Alabama planter named Jefferson Buford.

[1] Charles W. Ramsdell, "The Natural Limits of Slavery Expansion," in *Mississippi Valley Historical Review*, XVI (1929-1930), 163; George Fort Milton, *The Eve of Conflict: Stephen A. Douglas and the Needless War* (Boston, 1934), 187-91.

[2] Benton to Crittenden, Jan. 30, 1854, in Crittenden Papers (Duke); Grinnell to Crittenden, Feb. 22, 1854, in Coleman, *Crittenden*, II, 10; *Congressional Globe*, 33 Cong., 1 Sess., 275-80.

[3] Ramsdell, "The Natural Limits of Slavery Expansion," 163.

Much Kansas violence grew out of ordinary frontier brawls over disputed land claims, liquor, or women, and was unassociated with slavery. But there were unmistakable signs that some of the disorders of the territory did indeed grow out of the slavery issue. The first territorial delegate to Congress was chosen in November, 1854, at a time when there were probably not more than two thousand adult males in all Kansas. Yet almost three thousand votes were cast, seventeen hundred of them by Missourians who crossed over the border on election day. If the election judges questioned the qualifications of the Missourians, the judges were set aside, and the Border Ruffians themselves became judges and voters, too.[4]

This election was only the first in a series of lawless acts by the Border Ruffians. In March, 1855, five thousand Missourians poured across the border and helped elect a proslavery legislature, which proceeded to enact a slave code for the territory. The free-soil settlers retaliated by calling a convention to meet at Topeka in the fall of 1855 and draw up a state constitution. A few months later the constitution was ratified and state officers were chosen in an election boycotted by the slavery faction. The Topeka group then sought admission as a free state.[5]

This was the situation with which the Thirty-fourth Congress must deal when Crittenden returned to the Senate in December, 1855. This was the first Congress elected since formation of the Republican party in the summer of 1854. Because of party flux of the period, it is impossible to fix precisely the political affiliation of each member. No party, however, had a majority in the House. There were somewhat more than a hundred Republicans, approximately eighty Democrats, and about forty-five Americans or Know-Nothings. A bitter and prolonged struggle at once developed in the House over the speakership, paralyzing all legislation for two months. Finally, in February, rules had to be changed so as to permit election by a plurality. Only then was Nathaniel Banks of Massachusetts, former Democrat and present Know-Nothing, chosen speaker over William Aiken of South Carolina.

In the Senate, where there was a Democratic majority, there

4 *House Report*, No. 200 ("Howard Report"), 34 Cong., 1 Sess., 3-92.
5 "Howard Report," 9, 30-33, 357-58, 933-47, 1042-65; J. C. Malin, *John Brown and the Legend of '56* (Philadelphia, 1942), 514-18; G. J. Park to Crittenden, Dec. 20, 1855, in Crittenden Papers; Milton, *The Eve of Conflict*, 187-91.

were many new faces. Most notable of the newcomers were Lyman Trumbull of Illinois, Democrat turned Republican, and Henry Wilson, Massachusetts Know-Nothing who would soon join the Republicans. Seward, a recent convert to the Republican party, was the principal spokesman of the antislavery forces. Stephen Douglas, short of stature but strongly knit and with a massive head, was leader of the northern Democrats. In his forty-second year, skilled in parliamentary strategy, he was a brilliant and pugnacious debater. He had his eye on the Presidency, in 1856 if possible, by 1860 for certain.

The immediate problem confronting Congress was adjustment of the confused, anarchic conditions in Kansas, with its rival governments—the proslavery legislature, corruptly elected but nevertheless legitimate, and the Topeka state government, more honestly chosen but patently revolutionary. By March there were two Kansas proposals before Congress. One, advanced by Douglas, called for organization of a state government when population reached the federal ratio of representation, 93,420; the other, sponsored by Seward, called for immediate admission under the Topeka constitution.

Crittenden, who had been out of office when the Kansas-Nebraska Act was passed, had made no secret of his opposition to it. Archibald Dixon, Clay's successor in the Senate and the man who forced into the bill an explicit repeal of the Missouri Compromise, had urged Crittenden not to commit himself while the bill was pending in Congress. Whigs were talking of Crittenden for the Presidency, he wrote, and opposing the bill would drive southern support from him.[6] Disregarding this advice, Crittenden expressed his opposition quite frankly. The Missouri Compromise, he wrote Dixon, had long been regarded as a sacred compact between the sections. The South should not press for its repeal unless the North would concur in substituting popular sovereignty for the exclusion of slavery north of 36° 30′ fixed in the Compromise. Should the South force the issue, serious disturbances were sure to result. As for his own presidential prospects, "I do not cherish or entertain the least expectation, wish or aspiration to become a candidate for the Presidency," he wrote.[7]

In the weeks following his return to the Senate, Crittenden was

[6] Dixon to Crittenden, Feb. 7, 1854, in Coleman, *Crittenden*, II, 101.
[7] Crittenden to Dixon, March 7, 1854, in Crittenden Letterbook, 48 (Duke).

dismayed at the sharp divisions developing there; there were scathing denunciations of parties and sections, bitter personal insults,
rigid, unyielding, uncompromising partisanship. Statecraft seemed
to have disappeared and to have been replaced by political warfare
to the hilt. Northern moderates urged him to use his great influence
as a southerner who was opposed to slavery expansion to calm the
troubled waters, but he took little part in early debates. He seemed
content with making conciliatory efforts whenever an opportunity
presented itself. Once, when Douglas became offensive in debate
with Sumner, Crittenden called the Little Giant to order. His words
are not recorded in the *Globe*, but they must have carried a sting.
An unfriendly constituent of Douglas' was so gratified at the "decided and dignified manner" of Crittenden's rebuke that it caused
him to "wish to live a little longer in our country."[8]

Although Crittenden had little in common with Sumner, he
rushed to his aid again that spring. A learned but coldly pedantic
man, Sumner was utterly intolerant of views incompatible with his
own. His airs of superiority were irritating to friend and foe alike,
and the lashings of his vitriolic tongue drove its victims to violent
fury. Absolutely convinced of the moral evil of slavery, he entertained no proposals of a temporizing or compromising nature where
it was concerned. Already he had made so many personal attacks
on southerners that he was at this time the most-hated man in the
chamber. On May 19 and 20 he delivered a long and well-rehearsed
philippic which he later entitled "The Crime Against Kansas." Elab-
orately adorned with classical quotations, the speech contained nothing that had not already been said in regard to Kansas conditions; it
was purely a rhetorical exercise, perhaps designed to inspire the
reaction it got. In it Sumner personified slavery as a moral perver-
sion, and called its introduction into Kansas the "rape of a virgin
territory." Federal officials, including even the President, he said,
were its tools.[9]

Sumner heaped personal abuse upon Douglas and Andrew P.

8 Edward L. Pierce, *Memoirs and Letters of Charles Sumner*, 4 vols. (Boston,
1877-1893), III, 435; Russell Hinckley to Crittenden, March 19, 1856, in Crittenden
Papers (Duke); Corwin to James A. Pearce, May 16, 1856, in Steiner, "Some Letters from the Correspondence of James Alfred Pearce," 167; Amos A. Lawrence to
Crittenden, May 24, 1856, Robert Winthrop to Crittenden, June 13, 1856, in Crittenden Papers; *Congressional Globe*, 34 Cong., 1 Sess., 639, 1387-95.

9 David Donald, *Charles Sumner and the Coming of the Civil War* (New York,
1960), 293-96.

Butler, a courteous and cultured Senator from South Carolina, who was absent at the time from the chamber. Butler he likened to Don Quixote, and Douglas was his Sancho Panza, both of them panting after and in the service of the harlot Slavery. In the grossest of bad taste he referred to a physical infirmity of the elderly Butler, a paralysis of muscles of the face whereby he was unable to control in his speech the spewing of tiny droplets of saliva. South Carolina and Virginia, too, he said, had become cancerous growths on the body politic. Were both now blotted out, civilization would lose little. Such language had never before been heard within the Senate chamber, certainly not since the time of John Randolph. Cass called it the "most un-American and unpatriotic" speech ever uttered there, and hoped never to hear its like again "here or elsewhere."[10]

Had matters ended there, the speech would have had little effect, save, perhaps, to discredit Sumner. Two days later, however, after the Senate adjourned, Sumner remained in his chair near the center aisle on the back row busily engaged in writing. Crittenden also remained in his seat in the row in front of Sumner and some distance to his right. He was deeply absorbed in conversation with Senator Pearce and did not notice when two men entered the chamber. One was the tall, robust Preston Brooks, representative from the Edgefield District of South Carolina, kinsman and neighbor of Butler's; the other was Brooks' colleague, Lawrence Keitt.

Suddenly Crittenden heard a disturbance, and turned to look. He saw Brooks raining blows with his cane on the head of Sumner. Jumping to his feet, Crittenden lunged at Brooks, calling on him to desist. Meanwhile Sumner, wrenching his writing table from its fastenings, had struggled to his feet. Another blow descended on Sumner's head, and he fell unconscious just as Crittenden sprang between him and his assailant. Anticipating Crittenden's intervention, Keitt stepped to Brooks' side, his cane uplifted, threatening the Kentuckian. But before he could assault Crittenden, Toombs, who appeared, prevented him. Crittenden reached out and took from Brooks' hand the remnant of the now-broken cane, then helped lift the unconscious Sumner and carry him into the Vice President's room.[11]

---

[10] *Congressional Globe*, 34 Cong., 1 Sess., Appendix, 529-44.
[11] *Congressional Globe*, 34 Cong., 1 Sess., 1279; *Senate Report*, No. 191, *House Report*, No. 182, 34 Cong., 1 Sess.; Pierce, *Memoirs and Letters of Charles Sumner*, III, 470-74.

The extent of Sumner's injuries have long been disputed. He was absent from the Senate for the next two and a half years, part of the time traveling in Europe, seeking to regain his health. Some charged, however, that for partisan effect he simulated greater injury than he actually suffered. Massachusetts, nevertheless, sympathized with him, and the state legislature refused to choose a successor to him during his long absence.

Meanwhile, a House resolution to expel Brooks failed to receive the necessary two-thirds vote, although a resolution of censure passed. Brooks thereupon resigned, returned to South Carolina for a triumphal reception, stood for reelection, and was unanimously chosen to the seat he had vacated. The effect of all this was to widen the breach between the sections. To southerners, northern justification of Sumner's studied calumnies and vulgarities branded all northerners with his guilt. Almost simultaneously came news of John Brown's brutal murders of five proslavery settlers in Kansas, and southerners soon came to think of all northerners as being at least partially to blame for Brown's atrocities. To northerners, southern approval of Brooks' brutal attack stamped all southerners as men of violence hardly different from the Missouri Border Ruffians, whose sacking of Lawrence, Kansas, was revealed in the eastern press at almost the same time. Robert Winthrop, dignified, austere, but moderate New Englander, was probably right in thinking Brooks' attack rivaled the Kansas-Nebraska Act in building northern hostility to slavery. Brooks and Douglas, he wrote Crittenden, "deserve statues from the Free Soil party. The cane of the former & the Kansas Bill of the latter . . . have secured a success to the Agitators which they never could have accomplished without them."[12]

The shock of these events had hardly abated when debate was resumed on the question of statehood for Kansas. Douglas' bill, which provided for admission only when the population of the territory should reach the federal ratio, had been withdrawn in favor of a substitute prepared by Toombs. Toombs' bill provided for an immediate census of all bona fide white settlers; a five-man commission, appointed by the President, which would supervise the election of delegates to a constitutional convention; and the admission of Kansas, regardless of population, as soon as this convention completed its work. There was much to recommend the Toombs

[12] Winthrop to Crittenden, June 3, July 18, 1856, in Crittenden Papers.

bill. Speedy admission of Kansas under a constitution whose delegates were fairly chosen would remove the burning issue of slavery expansion from congressional strife and partisan agitation. The drawback was that by this time northerners were unwilling to trust the weak and vacillating Pierce to implement objectively such a bill as Toombs proposed. For Republicans believed, as the fair-minded and reasonable John P. Hale of Maine charged, that the President was *"particeps criminis"* to conditions in Kansas.[13]

Debate on the Toombs bill began July 1, and the following day rough, arrogant Ben Wade of Ohio spent several hours denouncing the repeal of the Missouri Compromise, quite properly blaming it for the current troubles. Like Hale, he did not trust the President to appoint honest and fair election officials, although he had other objections to the bill, too. It was an attempt, he said, to "steal" Kansas for slavery and, if successful, would bring an end to the republic. He was followed by Asa Beggs of North Carolina, who justified slavery in general and its progress in Kansas in particular.

Night was coming on, and members had drifted out, so that there was no quorum. Efforts to adjourn were refused, and the sergeant was sent for absent members. When a quorum had been brought in, Henry Wilson moved to insert a provision nullifying all acts passed by the proslavery territorial legislature. Crittenden spoke against this. Were they, he asked, to correct lawless conditions by passing laws to create a lawless state? How could extending impunity to future violence remedy present violence? Seward, Toombs, and Clayton joined in the debate, Seward supporting the amendment, the others opposed.

At 10:30 Trumbull moved adjournment, but the motion was voted down. Then Trumbull spoke for an hour, and John Bell for two. At 12:30 Crittenden interrupted Bell to move adjournment, but the motion was again overwhelmingly voted down. At 2:00 A.M. Seward took the floor and spoke until nearly four, advocating the Topeka constitution as adequate and proper for Kansas. Seward yielded from time to time to Wilson and other Republicans, who stated they would never, under any circumstances, vote for Kansas to come into the Union as a slave state. This brought the ominous rejoinder from southerners that if ever a party came to power pledged to prohibition of slavery from the territories, the South would leave

[13] *Congressional Globe*, 34 Cong., 1 Sess., 1519.

the Union. The stage was being prepared for the events that would follow the Republican victory a few years hence.

In the course of his remarks Seward stated that the time for compromise had passed, and Crittenden took the floor at dawn and chided him for his harsh and unyielding attitude. He would compromise, he said, "to the last moment of time" in order to preserve the Union and its integrity. He rebuked Seward, also, for attempting to substitute the Topeka bill instead of improving the Toombs bill with amendments. He denounced the Topeka constitution as unjust, the work of only a fraction of the voters in the territory. They constituted a population much smaller than that in the smallest New York county, yet Seward would make a state of them.

Turning to the entire body of the Senate, Crittenden pleaded for an end to recrimination and invective. Instead of acrimony he urged moderation and conciliation to stay the current of ill feeling spreading over the land. On all sides people were asking: "Will the North stand this and will the South stand that? . . . There was once a people of the United States," he went on, "there was once a common country that filled and swelled the hearts of patriots. . . . Now I am told Senators will do for a part of my country nothing at all." He disapproved himself of many features of the Toombs bill. The small population of Kansas indicated that the territory was unprepared for statehood, and the haste in rushing admission of the territory was deplorable. Nevertheless, he would vote for the bill in order to restore sanity to the country. Talk of disunion was evil and foolish. He trusted in the good sense of the people to preserve the Union.[14]

When Crittenden sat down, Trumbull, William Bigler, and Richard Broadhead, the latter two from Pennsylvania, offered a series of amendments, all of a rearguard nature. All were overwhelmingly voted down. Finally the vote was taken, and the bill passed, thirty-three to twelve. The tired Senators adjourned and went home to their beds. They had been in session twenty hours. But the long night and the forty days previously spent in debate had all been in vain. Members of the House, a majority of whom had free-soil sentiments, refused even to consider the Toombs bill. They passed, instead, a bill providing for the admission of Kansas under the

[14] *Congressional Globe*, 34 Cong., 1 Sess., 663, 693, 1439, 1467, 1506, 1519, 1539, 1786, Appendix, 740-805 *passim* (Crittenden's remarks, 761-63, 794).

Topeka constitution. Efforts at adjustment were unsuccessful, and Congress adjourned on August 11 with the question of Kansas no closer to a solution than it had been more than eight months before.[15]

When Congress adjourned, the controversy subsided. Even in Kansas, turmoil ended temporarily, largely through the efforts of a vigorous and fair-minded new governor, John W. Geary. Geary gained the confidence of both factions in the territory, disbanded both the free-staters and the Border Ruffians, and brought peace for a time to the distracted land. The storm revived, however, in the autumn of 1857, when the proslavery legislature called a constitutional convention entirely on its own initiative, without benefit of an enabling act of Congress. Free-staters, having already established their own constitution in an even less legitimate manner at Topeka two years before, refrained from voting for delegates, and the convention that met at Lecompton in September was made up entirely of proslavery men. Led by a federal territorial official named John Calhoun, the convention proceeded to draw up and adopt a constitution declaring slave property inviolable and forbidding the legislature to prohibit the importation of slaves or to emancipate them without compensation or without consent of their owners. It further declared that once in force, the constitution could not be amended before 1865.

Pierce and Governor Geary, and later Buchanan and his new governor, Robert J. Walker, had all pledged that any constitution for Kansas should be submitted to the voters of the territory in a free plebiscite. Such democratic procedure had not always been followed in creating the score of states that had been admitted since formation of the Union, but Kansas had been settled under unusual conditions. A state government there, in order to succeed, had to have the backing of a solid majority of the people.

By the fall of 1857, however, free-state immigrants pouring into the territory greatly outnumbered proslavery newcomers. Unmistakable proof of this was revealed when the free-staters overwhelmingly won control of the new territorial legislature in October. It was certain, therefore, that a constitution containing a slave code would never win majority approval in a free election. Knowing this, the convention called an election for December 21 that allowed very little discretion to voters, although it had the facade of a plebi-

---

[15] *Congressional Globe*, 34 Cong., 1 Sess., 1786, 2019, Appendix, 805.

scite. Voters were allowed merely to register their approval of the constitution; they could not reject it in its entirety. They could vote against the introduction of additional slaves, but they could not vote to free the handful already there. Furthermore, before voting, they had to swear to uphold and abide by the constitution or a ballot would be denied them. There were many other features of the constitution that were objectionable to the free-staters. Under the restrictions imposed, they stayed away from the polls, and the constitution was ratified on December 21 by six thousand proslavery votes.

Meanwhile, the newly elected legislature with its free-state majority had passed a bill calling for postponement of the plebiscite from December 21 to January 4, at which time a governor and other state officers would also be chosen. On January 4 the proslavery party, which had defied this law in holding the plebiscite in December, stayed away from the polls. The free-staters thereupon rejected the constitution by ten thousand votes. Despite this, the Lecompton convention had forwarded its constitution to the President with a petition that the territory be admitted under it. The legislature, on the other hand, now petitioned Congress not to admit the terriory under the Lecompton constitution, charging that it was obnoxious to nine-tenths of the people, that most of the votes cast for it on December 21 were fraudulent and fictitious, and that the election itself had been held under conditions that violated all prior pledges.[16]

In his first message to Congress on December 8, Buchanan had discussed the Kansas situation in such ambiguous language that no one quite understood his views. On February 2, however, he submitted to Congress the Lecompton constitution with the express request that Kansas be admitted under its terms. In doing so, he made the astonishing statement that "It is impossible that any people could have proceeded with more regularity in the formation of a constitution than the people of Kansas have done." He particularly urged prompt admission in order to restore peace and quiet to the country.[17]

The Senate of the Thirty-fifth Congress was a distinguished com-

16 *Congressional Globe*, 35 Cong., 1 Sess., 16-17, 1155-66 *passim*; Adam Beatty to Crittenden, April 3, 1858, in Crittenden Papers.
17 Richardson, *Messages and Papers of the Presidents*, VII, 2980-85, 3002-12; *Congressional Globe*, 35 Cong., 1 Sess., 14-22, 42-52, 113-42, 158-65.

pany. Although there were no senators who could match the spectacular brilliance of Clay or Webster or who enjoyed the intellectual reputation of Calhoun, yet the caliber of the membership was high. Actually, four political parties were represented instead of three, for the Democrats were divided by the slavery question into two wings, each pushing its own program. Douglas, perhaps the most dynamic and skillful parliamentarian in the chamber, was leader of the northern Democracy. His program called for popular sovereignty in the territories, letting the people there decide whether to prohibit slavery or not. There was a lack of intimacy, however, between Douglas and the President that soon would widen into a chasm, and Douglas was not, therefore, spokesman for the administration. That position more nearly devolved upon William Bigler, Buchanan's fellow Pennsylvanian. Reared in the rough political school of the Keystone State, Bigler was a cautious, uninspired, and uninspiring counselor for the President. Of far more consequence among northern Democrats was the learned and cultured George Pugh of Ohio.

There was considerable talent among southern Democrats. Jefferson Davis of Mississippi, by no means the ablest of the group, was in effect their spokesman. He seemed to inspire more confidence than the far more brilliant Toombs, or the vacillating Robert M. T. Hunter of Virginia, or Hunter's colleague, the ardent state-righter James M. Mason. John Slidell of Louisiana was closer to Buchanan than any other senator, but he did not exert much influence in the chamber because of his seeming lack of political principle. More brilliant perhaps than all other southerners was Judah P. Benjamin, Slidell's Louisiana colleague.

Among Republicans, Seward was regarded the leader. He was ably advised by his lifelong friend and fellow New Yorker, the shrewd political manipulator and boss, Thurlow Weed. Salmon P. Chase of Ohio, former Democrat, was an envious rival of Seward for leadership in the party. A brilliant lawyer who was almost fanatical on slavery, he was less resilient than the more affable Seward. Ben Wade, Chase's Ohio colleague, and Zach Chandler of Michigan, were more rough spoken than Chase, but equally as inflexible on slavery.

The Nestor of the Senate was Crittenden. Eminently a man of peace, unable to follow his Whig friends into either Democratic or Republican party, he remained a less than enthusiastic member of that vanishing tribe, the Americans. Few would describe him as brilliant, yet he was loved and universally respected for his affability, his good sense, his patriotism, and his moderation. Careless in dress and in grooming, he, like most American males in that rural age, was rarely seen without a tobacco quid in his jaw. His spare, erect, vigorous frame belied his seventy years. His dark hair had long ago turned to an iron gray and would soon be white. Beneath heavy gray brows and long lashes, his dark eyes still sparkled, often with ebullience, less frequently with deep emotion. Calm and thoughtful in bearing, his aquiline nose, large mouth, square chin, and massive forehead lent his countenance a character that was described by a Charleston *Courier* reporter as "inelegant but keen . . . giving an idea of decision, promptness, and mental power."[18] Forty years had passed since he had first entered the Senate. His first term had begun the day of Monroe's inaugural, before Webster, Calhoun, Benton, or Wright had entered the chamber, and long before any other of the present members. A Baltimore editor called him the "connecting link between the glorious past and the doubtful present."[19]

He spoke on almost any occasion with fluency and with what one observer called a "calm, gentlemanly ease, which is evidently the result of habitual intercourse with the most cultivated society." When Clayton died the year before, he had been chosen to deliver a eulogy. Although his friendship for Clayton had been long and deep, his speech was brief and restrained, a "calm, manly, discriminating eulogy, fit to be spoken by a great man over the corpse of a great man." When he spoke, he always rose above sectional interests and personalities, and because of this, he was eagerly listened to and was more than ordinarily effective. His only passion, now that its existence was threatened, was the Union.[20]

The day before Buchanan's Lecompton message was received, Crittenden had spoken in the Senate, calling once more for an end to sectional conflict. A bill to admit Minnesota was pending, and southerners urged delay until a Kansas bill could be agreed on, so that both could be admitted together. Crittenden opposed delay as unjust to the people of Minnesota, who had met all conditions for admission. They should not now be held back, he said, just because

18 Quoted in Frankfort *Commonwealth*, Jan. 12, 1857.
19 Quoted in Frankfort *Commonwealth*, April 9, 1858.
20 Cincinnati *Daily Commercial*, June 21, 1858, quoted in Coleman, *Crittenden*, II, 153-54; *ibid.*, 362-65.

Kansas had problems that could not be easily solved. He denounced such a manifestation of sectional feeling along with threats, now daily occurrences, of a breakup of the Union. It was a dangerous and ominous sign, he said, that such language could be so familiarly used. For himself, he believed the Union was to exist forever, "not because I wish it, . . . but it is to live for ages [because] it is enshrined in the hearts of the people." The people would sustain it, even if the statesmen of the country were recreant. "It is not in our power," he said, "thank God it is not in the power of the Senate, or the Congress . . . to overthrow this Government; and I rejoice in it." The galleries responded with deafening applause.[21]

On February 18 Senator James S. Green of Missouri presented a bill from the Committee on Territories calling for admission of Kansas under the Lecompton constitution. Douglas, chairman of the committee, thereupon presented a minority report charging that the Lecompton constitution was secured by fraud. He urged defeat of the committee's bill. Douglas, four years too late, saw the ugly fruit of his Kansas-Nebraska Act. Yet, measuring full up to his reputation for courageous independence, he now broke completely with the administration and took the lead in opposition to the bill.

Debate raged daily for more than a month, with hardly a member unrecorded in at least one major address, several making many. On March 4 Green offered a substitute providing for joint admission of Minnesota and Kansas, the latter under Lecompton. The same day James H. Hammond, South Carolina cotton grandee and for a quarter of a century one of the most ardent of secessionists, made his famous King Cotton speech, in answer to Seward's statement of the day before that the war between slavery and freedom had already been won by freedom. Seward was speaking figuratively, but Hammond, purposely taking Seward's figure literally, defied the North to make war on slavery. Slavery meant cotton, and without cotton to feed New England and European textile mills, economic blight and political revolution would follow in those regions. No, he said, the North dared not make war on slavery. Their own people would rise up against them. During the course of the debate, northern extremists stated they would never "under any circumstances" vote to admit a slave state. Southerners rejoined that unless the Lecomp-

[21] *Congressional Globe*, 35 Cong., 1 Sess., 501-502.

ton bill was adopted, their states would leave the Union. It was against this background that Crittenden, on March 16, announced that he would speak the following day.[22]

Crittenden was well informed on conditions in Kansas. Kentuckians who had settled there originally as proslavery advocates had written him of the outrageous conduct of the Border Ruffians. They told him that free-staters now outnumbered proslavery men in the territory five to one. The proslavery legislature, wrote one, had by its "infamous laws" made many converts to Republicanism. The South, said another, was represented in the territory by "unprincipled men" who would not stop short of any excess.[23]

Word had been passed that Crittenden would speak, and the galleries filled early. It was one of the largest and most distinguished audiences of the year. Lord Napier, Baron Edward de Stoeckl, the Russian minister, and other members of the diplomatic corps were there, and Elizabeth had been honored with a seat among the senators. Members of the House, abandoning their own business, crowded into the chamber, filling every nook and corner.

Calmly, unburdened with notes, Crittenden arose and addressed the chair, occupied by his Kentucky neighbor, Vice President John C. Breckinridge. He reviewed the now heavily documented charges of fraud in Kansas elections. From the beginning, he said, the territory had been carried by armed invaders from Missouri. The ten thousand votes cast against the Lecompton constitution on January 4 proved that it did not have the support of the people. To impose such a constitution on them against their will would be to deprive them of the right of self-government, the principle that was the very foundation of our nation. He reminded the Senate that less than six months before, a legislature had been popularly elected and was now urging Congress not to admit Kansas under Lecompton, charging that the constitution had been obtained by fraud and had the backing of only a small minority. On the other hand, many of the voters in the December election, he said, voted under assumed names: Thomas Hart Benton, James Buchanan,

22 *Congressional Globe*, 35 Cong., 1 Sess., 524, 544-53, 570-78, 608-21, 755, 802, 828, 901, 920, 939, 959-64, 981-87, 1123.

23 G. J. Park to Crittenden, Dec. 20, 1855, May 20, 1856, Adam Beatty to Crittenden, April 3, 1858, Letcher to Crittenden, Dec. 26, 1857, Leslie Combs to Crittenden, March 16, 1858, in Crittenden Papers; W. H. Settle to Orlando Brown, April 6, 1857, in Brown Papers, Filson Club.

William Seward. In one precinct where only thirty or forty qualified voters lived, twelve hundred votes were counted. Rejection of the bill, he said, would be upholding the true principle of popular sovereignty.

Repeal of the Missouri Compromise he regarded as a mischievous error, for it had become "hallowed" by thirty years' acquiescence and had produced nothing but good. True, the Supreme Court had declared it unconstitutional three years after its repeal, but he had never doubted its constitutionality. Under it, the country had been able to preserve substantial harmony on the slavery question. Then the Kansas-Nebraska Act had been passed, to achieve still greater peace by localizing the question. Unfortunately, it had had the opposite effect.

Lecompton, he said, was regarded as a sectional question, and he, a Kentuckian, was called by some a traitor to the South because he opposed the bill. But "I do not want to know any such thing as a section in my conduct here," he said. He would be governed by the Constitution and by a just spirit, regardless of whether North or South was favored. The Constitution was intended to wipe out all sections, and it would do so if only politicians would let it. "It is we," he said, "that make sectional lines to divide and distract the country."

He scorned as revolutionary Buchanan's assertion that Kansas could, after admission, amend her constitution prior to 1865, despite the prohibition in the Lecompton constitution. This, said Crittenden, was dangerous doctrine. It would completely refute the American political principle that a constitutional convention can restrict the will of a future majority. He appealed to southerners to be reasonable. He reminded them that in 1854, during debates on the Kansas-Nebraska bill, many now in the chamber had conceded that there was no chance that Kansas could ever support slavery. Thus, even if the Lecompton bill now passed, the victory would be a barren one for the South, for slavery would languish in Kansas. At the same time, to force passage of the bill would aggravate the slavery issue and bring additional strife and bitterness.

Turning to Hammond's King Cotton speech, Crittenden conceded that both sections had boundless resources. But these should supplement each other, not tend to create independent sections.

"What a magnificent country is made," he exclaimed, "when we put it all together." It was such a country "as the Almighty never gave to any other people, and never [before] placed on the surface of the earth." North and South made a natural union, each supplementing the other. "The very diversity of our resources is the natural cause of union between us." It would not do for us all to make cotton, nor would it be wise for all of us to work in manufactures. Nature herself had sanctioned the Union. Only lawmakers were attempting to destroy it.

Unjust and fraudulent as Crittenden knew the Lecompton bill to be, he would vote for it if he thought it would bring peace. But he did not believe it would, and he served notice that he would later offer an amendment that he hoped would perfect it. He closed with an eloquent plea for a return to the spirit of tolerance and moderation that had been demonstrated by the founding fathers of the republic. The bonds of union—language, blood, country, memories of the past, and hopes of the future—were much stronger than the forces attempting to divide the sections.

As Crittenden sat down, there was a spontaneous and deafening burst of applause that could not be quieted until Breckinridge threatened to clear the galleries. As soon as order was restored, Trumbull jumped to his feet. He called Crittenden's exposition "eloquent and conclusive," and urged an immediate vote on the bill. No one, he said, could have listened to that masterful account without the conviction that Lecompton was "an iniquitous and infamous thing." But a vote was not taken then, and Trumbull's extreme confidence proved to be unwarranted. The following day Toombs answered Crittenden. The South, he said, had been degraded from her position of equality. Perhaps Kentucky herself might some day be called on to evaluate the importance of the Union, he said.[24]

Crittenden replied to Toombs. As a true friend of the South, he said, it was his duty to give her "the best counsel and advice I can." He wished that the South had been more magnanimous when the Lecompton bill was first introduced and that she had spurned the opportunity to press her claims on a reluctant Kansas. Even if she carried her point, he repeated, it would be but a hollow victory. How much better if the South had said, "We go upon great principles,

24 *Congressional Globe*, 35 Cong., 1 Sess., 1153-59.

and we go for the truth." That would have been the noblest position for her to take. No, he had not deserted the South, as Toombs and others charged. "She has no truer or more faithful son than I." He spoke, he said, not as a party man nor as a sectional one. "I thought I had grown old enough to rid myself of the misconceptions and the prejudices that belong to the partisan." He was not only a true son of the South, he said, he was also a true citizen of the United States. He acted as he did "simply because I believe it to be my duty to the South and my duty to the whole country and to my own integrity and my own convictions."[25]

Green next appealed to Crittenden as a member of the American party to help put down the Republicans, "the common enemy of us both," by supporting the Lecompton bill. But Crittenden repeated that he was not a party man on this issue and was uninterested in advancing or putting down either of the parties. He was there as "the independent Senator" of his native state. He wished only to wipe out sectional lines and do what was best for all parts of the country. As for the American party, he embraced the principle of reforming the ballot box "by preventing foreigners who have just arrived on our shores, from . . . putting their votes in with mine . . . [and] with our naturalized fellow citizens, who have as deep an interest in this Government as I have." He would change the naturalization laws "not at all in hostility or unkind feeling toward foreigners," but because he wished to preserve the sanctity of the ballot box. On the same principle he would protect it "against anybody who undertakes to stuff it, or to put frauds into it," as had been done in Kansas. For the ballot was "the crown and the sceptre of that sovereignty which the people possess."[26]

A week later Crittenden offered his substitute bill. It provided for resubmission of the entire Lecompton constitution to a vote of the people. To ensure fairness for both factions, a four-man commission, composed of the proslavery governor, his secretary, and the presiding officers of the two houses of the free-state legislature, would conduct the election. If a majority of voters approved the constitution, the territory would be admitted forthwith. If a majority rejected it, another convention would be called at once and a new

---

[25] *Congressional Globe*, 35 Cong., 1 Sess., Appendix, 124-31.
[26] *Congressional Globe*, 35 Cong., 1 Sess., Appendix, 212-14.

constitution would be drawn and submitted to the voters. Critten-den's bill also greatly reduced the generous land grants that the Le-compton bill had provided. Even so, two sections were set aside in every township for support of public schools and a total of seventy-two sections for a state university. In addition, 5 percent of the pro-ceeds of the sale of public lands in Kansas were to go to the state for the building of roads and other public improvements. Crittenden's substitute had the solid backing of Republicans, but it was known that it could not pass. It was brought quickly to a vote and rejected, twenty-four to thirty-four. Thereupon the Lecompton bill was passed immediately, thirty-three to twenty-five.[27]

In the House, however, the anti-Lecompton forces were more successful. When the Senate bill came before them on April 1, Re-publicans joined with Douglas Democrats in passing the Crittenden substitute by a vote of 120 to 112, and returned it to the Senate. The *National Intelligencer* hailed the House bill as the true imple-mentation of the principle of popular sovereignty and a triumph over fraud and usurpation of constitutional liberty. Even the New York *Herald*, previously a supporter of Buchanan, urged "conservative" Democratic senators to vote for Crittenden's substitute, or at least let it pass by default when it came once more before the Senate.[28]

But the Buchanan forces held, and the House bill was rejected on April 2. The Senate then asked for a conference. Anti-Lecompton senators were opposed to a conference, but were voted down thirty to twenty-four. In the House, too, a strong effort was made to block the conference, but a tie vote there was broken by the affirmative vote of the Speaker, and committees from the two houses held meet-ings for a week. Out of these meetings came a compromise bill, largely the work of Congressman William H. English of Indiana. It, too, provided for resubmission of the Lecompton constitution to a plebiscite but with the proviso that if it were rejected, the territory would not again have an opportunity for statehood until its popula-tion reached the federal ratio. It contained the same land grants as Crittenden's substitute, but the provision for delay in statehood in case the Lecompton constitution was rejected offered a strong in-ducement for approval.

27 *Congressional Globe*, 35 Cong., 1 Sess., 1264-65.
28 New York *Herald*, April 6, 1858, quoted in Louisville *Journal*, April 10, 1858.

When the Senate conference committee made its report, the bill itself was in possession of the House. The report merely called for the striking of certain parts of the Lecompton bill and the addition of the new material. There was an attempt to force a vote at once, but Crittenden objected. He wanted to compare the English bill with the Lecompton bill and with his amendment. It was unparliamentary, he said, to proceed while the original bill was in the other house. He asked postponement until the next day; the bill's advocates would not agree. Seward and Douglas, who were following Crittenden's lead, protested against this inconsiderate treatment of the venerable Kentucky senator, but to no avail. Four motions to adjourn were made but were beaten back. Finally, on the plea of Simon Cameron of Pennsylvania that Crittenden be given time to discuss the issues, postponement to the following day was agreed to.

When he arose to speak next day, Crittenden again faced a full chamber and crowded galleries. In a frontal attack upon the bill, he objected to the implied threats of the English bill, both as to land grants and as to undue prolongation of territorial status. The election would not be a free one, for there was "a great bonus offered" to the people to accept the Lecompton constitution. The bill was inconsistent with Buchanan's original plea for a quick admission of the territory in order to calm the country. Kansans, he was sure, would reject the offer, and their territorial status and consequent sectional friction would then be continued indefinitely. A further objection to the bill was that it added a fifth member, the district attorney (a presidential appointee), to the election commission. Thus, the proslavery faction would have a three to two majority, and the impartiality provided in his substitute would be abandoned.

Crittenden asked only that justice be done, for only justice could give security to all sections. "Evil generates nothing but evil; injustice generates nothing but injustice." Was the country, with its glorious prospects, to be constantly distracted by "these little things that disturb our peace?" He called on senators from the West to join in an effort to reduce frictions and thus preserve the Union. They of all people had the greatest interest in its preservation, for if separation took place, the West would be cut off from markets of the world through tolls and taxes charged at New York and New Orleans. In their very geographical position, therefore, there was "a natural, a destined patriotism" so far as the Union was concerned. They were bound by "an everlasting and perpetual bond" to stand by the Union. Commerce and trade demanded it, if loftier motives did not. The people of the West must be "the appointed guardians of this particular interest," just as North and South had their particular interests. If they would but raise their eyes from the ground and look to the future, they would see enough there "to swell the heart of the nation, to give it a dignity and consequence . . . to raise it above all the little mists and fretful policies of the day."

Debate continued throughout that day and the next. Hale pointed out that the principal argument used against Crittenden's substitute had been that the plebiscite it called for would create unnecessary expense, delay, and agitation. Now the English bill accepted all these. He suggested that it was a face-saving device for the administration, which truly it was. Wade protested against striking out "the just arrangement . . . made by that just man . . . the Senator from Kentucky," for the impartial election commission. Wilson, too, paid tribute to Crittenden. "If the proposition made by the Senator from Kentucky had been adopted, this whole question would have been settled today."

The bill was made the special order for April 30. On that day the Senate approved the English bill, thirty-one to twenty-two. On the same day the House accepted the bill, 112 to 103. In the House all Republicans voted consistently with Crittenden and against both the Lecompton and the English bills to the end. In the Senate the story was the same. All eighteen Republicans sustained Crittenden's efforts. His bill was defeated by a combination of administration Democrats and "South Americans."[29] Despite his opposition to the English bill, Crittenden considered it better than the unjust Lecompton bill and its passage a personal victory. The English bill itself he regarded as "a *little, shabby Lecompton like trick*," but he did not think of it as final. It could be amended in the next Congress. The Lecompton bill, if passed, could not.

Crittenden's prediction as to the fate of the English bill proved true. When the plebiscite was held on August 2, the Lecompton constitution was rejected by a vote of 11,800 to 1,900. The people

[29] *Congressional Globe*, 35 Cong., 1 Sess., 1433, 1437, 1442, 1444, 1551, 1557-59, 1762, 1792, 1795, 1798, 1800-1802, 1804, 1814-24, 1876, 1899, 1905, 1907, 1929; Louisville *Journal*, April 13, 1858; Washington *National Intelligencer*, April 2, 3, 6, 9, 14, 15, May 1, 1858; Preston King to Crittenden, April 15, 1858, in Crittenden Papers; Charles Robinson to Thomas Ewing, March 29, 1858, in Ewing Papers.

of Kansas preferred to remain under their own territorial government rather than accept statehood under a constitution imposed on them by slaveholders from without.

Reactions to Crittenden's part in the defeat of Lecompton were, of course, varied. He was reviled as an abolitionist both in the South and by Buchanan supporters in the North as well. Even his former bosom friend Toombs denounced him as a traitor and reported that all parties in Georgia so regarded him. Burnley, on a visit to New Orleans, found that no paper there dared print Crittenden's March 17 speech, although Whigs, Americans, and even some Democrats privately approved his stand. Even in Kentucky, opinion was divided. John C. Breckinridge charged him with deserting slavery and southern rights and with going over to the Republican party. So did James B. Clay, although another son of Henry Clay, Thomas, stated that had their father been living, he would have acted with Crittenden. Another Clay, Cassius Marcellus, now a Republican, denied that Crittenden had gone over to the Republicans. On the contrary, he said, Crittenden had forced them to "*come down*" and join him. Actually, he added, Crittenden's position was the same as that enunciated in the Democratic platform, but the Democrats deserted their own platform on Lecompton. He defended Crittenden's stand as "right and noble," saying he had prevented civil war.[30]

The Louisville *Courier*, an extreme southern-rights sheet, said Crittenden had "missed the popular mind" in Kentucky and was "dead for good and forever" there. The *Kentucky Statesman* called him a "superannuated traitor," and an indignation meeting in Trimble County branded him as "John Judas Crittenden." But Crittenden knew he was not dead in Kentucky. Already he had heard from his friends there, from Letcher, Orlando Brown, and A. G. Hodges. "You stand upon the proud eminence of a true patriot, and need not be fearful of consequences," wrote Letcher. Hodges added, "I would rather occupy your position . . . before the American people, than to be President for twenty years." The approval of his friends pleased Crittenden. He wrote he had dealt the administration some hard blows in "some very important and great debates, in

[30] Lexington *Kentucky Statesman*, quoted in Louisville *Journal*, July 31, 1858; Crittenden to Thomas H. Clay, July 1, 1858, in Crittenden Papers (Duke); Richmond (Ky.) *Democrat*, quoted in Frankfort *Commonwealth*, July 23, 1858; Crittenden to S. S. Nicholas, April 28, 1858 (copy), in Crittenden Papers.

which I may say that I have been greatly *distinguished.*" He had received, he said, both applause and abuse, but he had done his duty, and was satisfied.[31]

Scores of letters from all sections, some even from the South, came to him asking for copies of his March 17 speech. All these letters were laudatory, many urging him for the Presidency. He was elected to dozens of college literary societies, and he received invitations to speak in Boston, New York, Philadelphia, and many lesser places. His Senate speeches drew enthusiastic praise from Douglas, John Tyler, Chase, and many other public men. Douglas ordered twenty-five thousand copies printed of the March 17 speech, calling it "a great and patriotic speech" which would "live, and be read, and admired, when we have all passed away." He generously credited Crittenden, along with some "glorious Americans and old line Whigs from the South," with defeating Lecompton. Chase wrote Crittenden that he was impressed "by the great force of your argument, and the liberal and patriotic character of your sentiments."[32]

When Congress adjourned in June, the journey home was a triumphal procession for the venerable Kentucky senator. Crowds welcomed him wherever his train stopped. A committee of Cincinnati gentlemen met him at Columbus and escorted him to the Queen City. When his train arrived at the depot of the Little Miami Railroad, a crowd of thousands was waiting with a band, and he was conveyed in an open carriage up Broadway to the Spencer House, where his old friend Tom Corwin, now governor of Ohio, welcomed him. The welcome was not a partisan affair, Corwin said, but one where all parties combined to honor "a statesman who has proved true to the Constitution and the Union." Truly, Crittenden replied, he was now a man without a party, although he still held to his old Whig principles. But, he added, "I speak to no party. I have none

---

[31] Crittenden to Mrs. Coleman, April 27, 1858, in Crittenden Papers (Duke). See also, Crittenden to Orlando Brown, May 14, 1858, *ibid.*; Toombs to Stephens, March 28, 1858, in Phillips, *Correspondence of Toombs, Stephens, and Cobb*, 433; Burnley to Crittenden, April 3, 1858, Letcher to Crittenden, March 29, April 1, 1858, Hodges to Crittenden, March 23, 1858, in Crittenden Papers; Louisville *Courier*, quoted in Frankfort *Commonwealth*, March 19, 1858; Lexington *Kentucky Statesman*, quoted *ibid.*, April 19, 1858; Maysville *Eagle*, quoted *ibid.*, April 23, 1858.

[32] Letters to Crittenden during spring and summer, 1858, especially those from Tyler, April 29 (copy), from Chase, April 9 (copy), and from Douglas, March 14 [misdated 1848], in Crittenden Papers; Albert J. Beveridge, *Abraham Lincoln*, 2 vols. (Boston, 1928), II, 593.

to influence." He had arrived at an age when he resolved to be "more of a patriot and less of a politician." As far as it was possible to do so, he thought, he had divested himself of partisanship.

A delegation from Louisville arrived at the Spencer House with an invitation to visit the Falls City, where a public reception was planned. But Crittenden was tired and said he would proceed to his home as quickly as possible. The delegation thereupon presented him with resolutions designating him a "grand monument to our country's greatness . . . [whose] voice has risen far above the smoke and clash of party strife, in favor of the people's rights."

After this ceremony and a reception, Crittenden was scheduled for a similar meeting that night at Covington, across the river, and at 7:30 a procession conducted him to the wharf, where a Kentucky committee awaited him aboard the ferryboat. Cannon boomed as the boat approached the Kentucky shore, where a torchlight procession, led by a band, made its way through downtown Covington, which was lavishly decorated for the occasion. Banners inscribed to "J. J. Crittenden, the Incorruptible Statesman" were stretched across Scott Street. As the procession turned into Madison Square, bonfires were lighted, and cheers from ten thousand echoed and reechoed. When quiet was restored, Judge W. B. Kinkead delivered a welcoming address and Crittenden responded.

The Kentucky Central Railroad had put a special train at the service of a committee to escort him from Covington to Lexington. Along the road the next day, the train stopped at Falmouth, Cynthiana, and Paris, at all of which Crittenden was given a tumultuous welcome. Monday evening, June 21, the train arrived in Lexington. On its approach, cannon were fired, and as it entered the station, Menter's Band struck up the national anthem. Crittenden was preceded by the gathered multitude to the capacious Odd Fellows Hall, which was crowded with fifteen hundred men and women. Here George Robertson presented the old statesman, and Crittenden responded in a speech of almost an hour's length. When he had finished, according to a reporter, "The very walls were made to echo with prolonged . . . cheering."

An immense celebration had been planned for Crittenden in Frankfort for the next afternoon, but he foiled the plans of his friends there by slipping in on a morning train. When news of his arrival spread, however, a committee marched to the house at the corner of Washington and Main and, accompanied by a band brought from Cincinnati for the occasion, took him to the state-house, where a crowd had gathered. There his friend Governor Morehead welcomed him, and again Crittenden responded.

A month later a grand festival was held in Woodford County, within sight of Crittenden's birthplace. The crowd was said to exceed five thousand persons. Crittenden was assured that his course on Kansas was approved by all who knew him, and that the meeting was called to express the people's gratitude for "the honor he had reflected upon Kentucky by his noble stand in favor of right, truth, and justice, against fraud, violence and oppression."[33]

33 Cincinnati *Daily Commercial*, June 21, 1858, quoted in Coleman, *Crittenden*, II, 154-57; Louisville *Journal*, June 21, 1858; Frankfort *Commonwealth*, June 16, 18, 25, July 26, 1858; Lexington *Observer and Reporter*, quoted *ibid.*, June 25, 1858.

CHAPTER XVII

The Election of 1860

THE DEMOCRATIC party, already badly divided when Buchanan took office, was further demoralized by Buchanan's weak and ill-advised policies during the first year of his administration. By his espousal of the Lecompton bill he drove many northern Democrats out of the party. Then, by his unrelenting attacks on Douglas for his part in defeating the bill, he had hopelessly divided remnants of the party.

Reverberations of the Lecompton struggle echoed through the country in the summer and autumn of 1858. A seemingly inconsequential election was underway in Illinois, and the Republican nominee for Douglas' Senate seat, the chief prize in the contest, insisted on talking about Kansas and Lecompton. To Republicans outside the state it seemed strange that their party in Illinois should attack Douglas' position on Lecompton, which coincided with their own, and as a result of which he had lost all federal patronage in the state. Greeley, Banks, Wilson, and other Republican leaders in the East thought that Illinois Republicans should take Douglas up and send him back to the Senate, where his great abilities could be used to prevent the spread of slavery.

Such talk was disconcerting to Abraham Lincoln, for he had determined to challenge his old rival, Douglas. There was actually little practical difference between the positions of Lincoln and Douglas on Kansas or on slavery. Douglas personally disapproved of slavery, just as did Lincoln. Neither believed Congress could or should interfere with it in the states; both thought Congress could constitutionally prevent its introduction into the territories. Lincoln would have Congress implement this authority by direct legislation. Douglas, confident that slavery could never exist in the remaining territories, hoped to calm national agitation by establishing the principle of popular sovereignty. The one real difference between them on slavery was philosophical. Lincoln thought slavery was a moral evil. Douglas thought it amoral; to him it was only a political issue, to be decided by legislation and by judicial decision.

Lincoln, a latecomer to the Republican party, claimed to be the disciple of Clay; and one of his chief problems in the contest with Douglas was winning the support of old Clay Whigs. James B. Clay, now gone over to the Democrats, had announced in Lexington his support of Douglas. It was rumored that Crittenden, too, desired Douglas' reelection and that he would write to Illinois friends in Douglas' behalf. To forestall this, Lincoln wrote Crittenden in early July telling him that his Illinois friends would be "mortified exceedingly" if he should do so. But already Crittenden's advice had been sought and he had endorsed Douglas. By Douglas' sacrifice of his personal interests on Lecompton, Crittenden said, he merited the support of the people of Illinois. During the Lecompton struggle, Crittenden had spoken freely in Washington of the high regard he entertained for Douglas and of his belief that Douglas deserved reelection. He was now receiving letters asking confirmation of these statements, and although he did not want to interfere or to give offense to Lincoln, he must answer these letters "in a proper manner."

At Crittenden's request, Douglas' friends did not at first publish any of his letters. But Lincoln's friends, either by design or through ignorance, made claims that all Clay's old supporters, including Crittenden, were eager for Lincoln's election; and Lincoln failed to deny this. The matter came to a head in late October when Lincoln's organ, the *Illinois State Journal*, claimed Crittenden had written to a gentleman in Springfield saying he "wanted Douglas crushed." Now the Douglas press published a letter from Crittenden confirming his support of Douglas and stating that he had written no such letter as Lincoln's friends were claiming.[1]

Douglas won a narrow victory, but Lincoln had not lost. The reputation he gained in the contest would set the stage for a greater victory for him two years hence. At the time, however, he was depressed at his defeat, and he did not forget that Crittenden played a major part in it, although he exonerated Crittenden of any malicious intent. A year later he reminded a Cincinnati audience that "a Senator from Kentucky, whom I have always loved with an affection as tender and endearing as I have ever loved any man . . . was writing letters into Illinois to secure the re-election of Douglas." One of Lincoln's most distinguished biographers thought the defeat itself was not as bitter to the future president as the refusal of Crittenden and other old friends to support him. For Mary Lincoln it must have been especially painful, for Crittenden had been one of her father's dearest friends and his groomsman at his second marriage.[2]

When Congress reconvened in December, 1858, the Kansas question had subsided and there seemed some prospect that the country might experience a period of comparative calm. The new wings of the Capitol had been completed, and before the Senate moved to its new chamber, Crittenden, as the veteran of the Senate, was called upon for a valedictory address. In responding, he referred to the great men and great events he had known there. In leaving the chamber, senators would not be leaving behind the many sentiments of patriotism that had been expressed there but would carry them with them. The future course of the Senate, he said, must not dishonor the memories of the past. On the contrary, all must discharge their proper duties to preserve the Union, the source of all their country's greatness "in times to come, as it has been in the time that is past."[3]

[1] Lincoln to Crittenden, July 7, 1858, in Lincoln, *Works*, II, 483-84; Crittenden to Lincoln, July 29, 1858, in Robert Todd Lincoln Papers, Library of Congress; Springfield *Illinois State Register*, Springfield *Illinois State Journal*, quoted in William H. Townsend, *Lincoln and the Blue Grass* (Lexington, Ky., 1955), 234-36.

[2] Letters to Crittenden from T. Lyle Dickey, July 19 (copy), from Herndon, Nov. 1, from Owen G. Cates, Nov. 4, 1858, in Crittenden Papers; Cates to Crittenden, Oct. 22 (copy), Crittenden to Dickey, Aug. 1, 1858 (copy signed by Crittenden), in Crittenden Papers (Duke); Crittenden to Lincoln, Oct. 27, 1858, in Robert Todd Lincoln Papers; Lincoln to Crittenden, Nov. 4, 1858, in Coleman, *Crittenden*, II, 164; Carl Sandburg, *Abraham Lincoln: The Prairie Years*, 2 vols. (New York, 1926), II, 167.

[3] Washington *National Intelligencer*, Jan. 5, 1859; *Congressional Globe*, 35 Cong., 2 Sess., 202.

But Buchanan once more acted to dash Crittenden's hopes of sectional peace. Apparently in an effort to unite the factions of his badly divided party, Buchanan now undertook an aggressive foreign policy. In his annual message he urged Congress to authorize military occupation of portions of Mexico and other Latin American countries that had allegedly mistreated American nationals. Really a man who abhorred war, Buchanan was being pushed by partisan leaders to desperate measures. "We may have to intervene in Mexico," wrote Caleb Cushing to Franklin Pierce. "I live in hope that something will turn up to animate and justify the [Democratic] party."[4]

More specific were Buchanan's complaints against Spain. Insults to the American flag and to American nationals in Cuba, he said, called for a settlement of grievances. Cuba was "a constant source of injury and annoyance to the American people," and until it was ours, our relations with Spain would be troubled. He asked that a sum of money be placed at his disposal to expedite negotiations for its purchase. Shortly thereafter, Slidell, for the Committee on Foreign Relations, reported a bill appropriating thirty million dollars for this purpose. He argued speciously that transfer of the island would benefit Spain, Cuba, the United States, and world trade. It was a foolish move, for it was well known that Spain would not sell Cuba for thirty million dollars, or for any amount. Furthermore, Buchanan's proposal to buy it merely heaped one insult on another. Four years before at Ostend, Buchanan had been one of the authors of the jingoistic document which advised the taking of Cuba from Spain by force should she refuse to part with it peaceably. Nevertheless, southern expansionists, led by Slidell, Benjamin, and Toombs, now took up the bill and pressed it eagerly.[5]

Again the old sectional cleavage appeared, even though Douglas and a few northern Democrats now supported the Cuba bill. But Republican senators who had fought to keep Kansas from becoming a slave state would not be parties to making Cuba one. Seward, Wade, Collamer, Dixon, and others led the onslaught, and enough northern Democrats joined in to defeat the bill.

[4] Cushing to Pierce, April 9, 1858, quoted in Allan Nevins, *Emergence of Lincoln,* 2 vols. (New York and London, 1950), I, 446; Richardson, *Messages and Papers of the Presidents,* VII, 3042-51.

[5] Richardson, *Messages and Papers of the Presidents,* VII, 3039-42; *Senate Committee Reports,* No. 351, 35 Cong., 2 Sess.

Of all miscues for which Buchanan has been blamed, perhaps none was of more fateful consequence than his Cuban proposal. For it struck fear in Republicans, although probably to an unwarranted degree, that the slave states were determined to expand the peculiar institution by acquiring territory in the Caribbean and elsewhere in Latin America. A despondent and defeated Lincoln, sitting in his dingy office in Springfield, followed the debates closely in the columns of the New York *Tribune* and the *Intelligencer*. He would remember the Cuba affair two years later when he was asked to support a compromise proposal in order to stay southern secession.

Crittenden's part in the Cuba debate was not decisive; nevertheless, his remarks are revealing. Although he was a member of the Foreign Relations Committee, he expressd his disapproval when the committee reported the bill. He thought the proposal at the time utterly impractical, and he objected to the chauvinistic tone of the preamble. On February 15 he spoke at length against passage of the bill. Although he was not opposed in the abstract to acquiring Cuba, he thought the time most unpropitious for negotiations. The Cuban people themselves, he said, resented the President's proposal. They did not want "to be meted out and bought and sold in the market." Besides, England and France were vitally concerned in Cuba. They had recently proposed a treaty with the United States wherein all three nations would renounce any pretensions of their own and guarantee the island forever to Spain. Certainly they would not sit by now and see it pass to us. Even if Cuba could be acquired peaceably, however, Crittenden thought she should be given her independence. There was a time, he said, when our policy had been to promote goodwill with Latin American nations. Buchanan now seemed bent upon searching out causes for quarrels with them. "It seems that a Yankee can no sooner go traveling abroad," he said, "than somebody imposes on him, cheats him, or strikes him, and he comes to the government and makes a claim."[6]

By the summer of 1859 a schism had developed in the Democratic party over the issue of slavery in the territories. Southern Democrats generally had accepted the principle of popular sovereignty in 1850, and thereafter many northern Democrats had been won to its support. Gradually, however, southern Democrats had shifted to

[6] *Congressional Globe*, 35 Cong., 2 Sess., 908, Appendix, 155-60, 168-69.

the view that the power to restrict slavery could not be exercised by the territorial legislature but only by a convention called to draw up a state constitution. Not until then, they argued, did sovereignty pass from the national government to the people of the new state, and until then territories belonged not to the national government but to all the states, slave as well as free. Congress, therefore, instead of acting itself, or permitting its creature the territorial government to act for it, to exclude slavery, was obliged to take positive action to uphold property in slaves during the territorial period. This position had become strongly buttressed in 1857 when the Supreme Court rendered the Dred Scott decision. Paradoxically, it was argued that federal support of slavery in the territories was a manifestation of "state rights."

The summer of 1859 was torrid in Kentucky, temperatures in the upper nineties prevailing throughout July and August. But Crittenden could not sit quietly at home. A governor would be chosen in August, and Crittenden believed that the fate of the state and even of the nation was at stake. Kentucky Democrats had been won to the southern view that the national government must protect slavery in the territories, and they had nominated for governor Beriah Magoffin, who subscribed wholeheartedly to that principle. The Republican party, practically nonexistent south of the Ohio River, nominated no candidate to oppose Magoffin, but remnants of Whigs and Americans formed a loose association called the opposition and chose Joshua Fry Bell of Boyle County. Crittenden supported Bell.

Bell proved a phlegmatic candidate. Reluctantly accepting the nomination at first, he withdrew, then reentered the contest. Instead of taking issue with Magoffin on the territorial status of slavery, he disappointed his followers by trying to outdo Magoffin in urging federal support of the institution. Under the circumstances, therefore, it is not surprising that the election produced little excitement and that Magoffin won by a healthy margin of nine thousand votes. Democrats elected all other state officials and six of ten congressmen and won overwhelming control of the legislature.[7]

[7] Joseph R. Underwood to Crittenden, July 14, Charles Ripley to Crittenden, July 21, 1859, in Crittenden Papers; Burnley to Crittenden, May 11, 1859, in Crittenden Papers (Duke); Washington *National Intelligencer*, Aug. 13, 1859; Louisville *Courier*, Feb. 23, July 19, 20, 1859; Louisville *Journal*, May 4, 1859; Turner, "Kentucky in a Decade of Change," 69-70.

A storm in mid-November turned Indian summer in Kentucky abruptly into winter, with heavy snow and bitter cold. When the storm abated, Crittenden and Elizabeth left for Washington, where they took rooms once more at the National Hotel. There was little prospect of any important legislation that year. Washington then as now was a political community whose main concentration was on the preserving or destroying of political power. Politicians were thinking principally of the coming presidential election, and besides, parties were too evenly balanced in Congress to pass any measure of consequence, save for a homestead bill that Buchanan would veto. Three days before Congress met, John Brown had been executed in Virginia for his mad, abortive attack on Harper's Ferry two months before. To southerners, Brown's plot seemed the logical fruit of seeds long ago sown by abolitionists. Actually the Republican party would officially repudiate Brown six months later at the Chicago convention, but to a host of northerners, including intellectuals like Emerson, Thoreau, and Whittier, he seemed a man of God, martyred on the altar of human freedom. It was against this background that the Thirty-sixth Congress convened.

To compound its difficulties, a contest over the speakership developed again between the proslavery and antislavery factions. Two years earlier, Hinton Rowan Helper had published *The Impending Crisis of the South*, attempting to demonstrate that slavery was responsible for the relative poverty of the section. He urged abolition of slavery as the only salvation for the southern economy. This was farther even than Republicans, as a party, had gone, although many individual Republicans had endorsed the book. One of these was John Sherman of Ohio, Republican choice for Speaker. Republicans had a plurality but no majority in the House, and now a resolution aimed at Sherman stated that no one who had endorsed Helper's book was fit to be Speaker.

Debate on the resolution raged for two months. Tempers became frayed, talk of secession grew more familiar, and representatives, fearing for their lives, came armed into the chamber. When Owen P. Lovejoy, Illinois abolitionist, was interrupted by Roger Pryor of Virginia in the midst of an antislavery speech, men sprang from their places, drawing guns and knives as if by signal, all resolved to sell their blood as dearly as possible. By some miracle, peace was restored without violence, but the incident was not forgotten. Throughout the session, men continued to go armed to both House and Senate. "Some with 2 revolvers & a bowie knife as I happen to know," wrote South Carolina's James Hammond.[8]

In early February, in an effort to discredit Douglas' principle of popular sovereignty, Jefferson Davis introduced in the Senate a series of resolutions expounding the constitutional theories of state-rights southerners. These resolutions held that sovereign states created the Constitution; that territories were the common possession of all states; that neither Congress nor territorial legislatures had power to prohibit slavery; that, on the contrary, the federal government had the duty of protecting slavery in the territories; that not until the drafting of a state constitution could slavery be excluded from a territory; that the fugitive-slave law was constitutional, and that attempts of state legislatures or of individuals to nullify it or in any other way to interfere with slavery in the states or territories where it was established was revolutionary and would lead slave states to "seek proper redress."[9]

Davis' resolutions were foolish and ill considered, as even Toombs privately admitted, for the issue had already been faced and settled in existing territories. Slave codes had been adopted almost a decade earlier by territorial legislatures in New Mexico and Utah, yet there was only a handful of slaves in either territory, perhaps two dozen in each. There was now no chance whatever that slavery would be established in Kansas, Nebraska, or Washington, the only other territories, nor was there much prospect under the circumstances that more territories would be acquired. The issue was therefore an artificial one, and the only effect of the Davis resolutions was to agitate the matter further and to drive a wedge deeper between northern and southern wings of the Democratic party.

Debate on the resolutions dragged on for months, until speakers and arguments were exhausted. Davis based his theories not on natural rights, as had the Revolutionary fathers, but on constitutional rights. He denied that the United States was a government of "one people." On the contrary, it was "a compact between the sovereign

---

[8] Louisville *Courier*, Nov. 14, 1859; Hiram Ketchum to Crittenden, Jan. 17, 1860, in Crittenden Papers; Martin J. Crawford to Alexander H. Stephens, April 8, Hammond to Stephens, April 19, 1859, in Stephens Papers.

[9] *Congressional Globe*, 36 Cong., 1 Sess., 658.

members who formed it." The colonies in 1776 had not declared their independence as a people but separately as independent sovereignties, just as they had ratified the Constitution separately and over a period of several years. He quoted from Mason, Madison, Hamilton, and other framers of the Constitution to show that they considered it a compact of states. He conceded that the United States had sovereignty over the territories, but the federal government was not the United States. It was merely its agent. The government had only such power as the Constitution gave it, and it had not been given power to legislate slavery out of a territory.[10]

Davis' arguments seemed to Crittenden to be abstractions. He had long regarded slavery as "a great evil," but he thought, with a majority of Kentuckians, that sudden and forced emancipation would only compound the evil. During his mature life he had owned nine slaves. Some he had inherited from his father's estate, the remainder from that of his wife Sarah. But as early as 1833 he had voted in the Kentucky legislature to restrict the importation of slaves into the state. Five years later he was one of fifty members of Congress who signed an address to the people of the United States reciting the accomplishments of the American Colonization Society and soliciting funds for it.[11] About the same time in the Senate he had denounced certain resolutions offered by Calhoun warning northern state legislatures not to attempt to interfere with slavery; Crittenden declared that these resolutions were "indecorous" and calculated only to irritate. He was not in sympathy with abolitionist efforts to disturb domestic peace, but Calhoun's resolutions would bring the South to trial over theories "on which no two men could agree."[12]

Now, a decade and a half later, Crittenden saw Davis' resolutions in a similar light. They were firebrands that would provoke retaliation and agitate the country but would accomplish no useful purpose. He took little part in the early debates, but when the resolutions came to a vote in late May, he spoke not against their

[10] *Congressional Globe*, 36 Cong., 1 Sess., 2320-22.

[11] Crittenden to James G. Birney, March 10, 1834, in Crittenden Papers (Pennsylvania); Crittenden to Chapman Coleman, Dec. 1, 1833, in Crittenden Papers (Duke); Woodford County Deed Book C, 365; Woodford County Deed Book D, 153; Birney to Crittenden, Feb. 11, 1834, in Crittenden Papers (Kentucky); Birney to Crittenden, May 14, 1841, in Crittenden Papers; *Kentucky House Journal, 1832*, p. 500; Washington *National Intelligencer*, quoted in Frankfort *Commonwealth*, June 20, 1838.

[12] *Congressional Globe*, 25 Cong., 2 Sess., Appendix, 53-56.

passage but against the useless strife that they promoted. Whether the Constitution was "made by people through the states or by the states for the people" was immaterial, he said, for it "was not the less sacred" for being the creature of either. In either case it had "supreme authority of the people" for its sanction. "My opinion is," he said, "that it was made by the people of the United States, [for] the States themselves derived their authority from the people."

Crittenden had always believed, he continued, that Congress had power to prohibit slavery in the territories. He still believed it should have that power, but inasmuch as the Supreme Court had ruled otherwise in the Dred Scott case, he would bow to that decision. It would naturally follow from that decision, he conceded, that Congress had the duty to protect slave property in the territories. However, actual interference by Congress should only be undertaken in cases of extreme exigency. It was better, he argued, "that a particular wrong shall be endured than a great public inconvenience incurred." All agreed, he went on, that there was no present occasion for interference, nor was there apt to be in the future, for the existing territories were not likely to have controversies over slavery. Why, then, agitate the country about an evil so remote? The Davis resolutions were "making a present evil out of an apprehension of a future one . . . never likely to occur." To make a case for the resolutions, one must suppose a territory, slaves to fill it, hostility to the slaves, and an attack upon the constitutional rights of the owners.

Turning to the Republicans, he charged them equally with the Democrats for disturbing the peace of the country over a chimera. Had their party never been formed, slavery would have stood precisely where it now stood, restricted for all practical purposes to the southern states. Since Republicans disclaimed any intent to interfere with it there, their professed purpose was already accomplished. Slavery expansion was ended. Why disturb the peace longer by their denunciations of slavery, if they themselves recognized the right of slavery to exist in the states and proposed to do nothing about it there? Their denunciations were only inciting unrest and violence. Yet, he added, the Republicans were not alone at fault. "There have been indiscretions on both sides," and these should teach lessons of moderation. He pleaded with both parties to work for reconciliation so that the Union would be preserved. It must not and could not be overthrown. The following day the resolutions passed by overwhelming majorities, Crittenden himself voting for them.[13]

To Crittenden, the remarkable growth of the Republican party seemed ominous for the future of the Union. Southern Democrats, now in almost undisputed control of their section, had made it clear that election of a Republican President would drive their states to secession, and by the winter of 1859-1860 Republican success seemed not unlikely. The party had captured undisputed control in New England, had substantial majorities in Ohio, Michigan, Wisconsin, Minnesota, Iowa, and had large pluralities in most other northern states. Even in Illinois only gerrymandered legislative districts had enabled the spokesman of northern Democracy, Douglas, narrowly to defeat the comparatively unknown Lincoln in 1858. To win in 1860, the Democrats must carry several large northern states in addition to the entire South and border. Only Douglas of the prominent candidates had any substantial strength in the north. Yet control of the party in the South was passing from moderates like Stephens, Toombs, Hunter, Cobb, and others, to radicals of the stamp of Robert Barnwell Rhett and William L. Yancy. These latter men, with Buchanan's support, were determined to prevent Douglas' nomination at Charleston in April. Buchanan's behavior seems inexplicable. He should have known it was impossible for northern Democrats to accept extreme state-rights demands, for to do so would bring about defeat in their own states.[14]

The split between Buchanan and Douglas Democrats encouraged conservatives with visions of a new party opposed to both northern and southern extremists. For more than a year, many public-spirited men from all parts of the Union had been telling Crittenden that time was ripe for such a movement, and that he must take the lead in it: from Washington Hunt and Francis Granger in New York; from Winthrop, Everett, and A. A. Lawrence in Boston; from Balie Peyton and John Bell in Tennessee; from Rives and Preston in Virginia; from John Pendleton Kennedy in Maryland; from William A. Graham in North Carolina; from George D. Prentice, S. S.

[13] *Congressional Globe*, 36 Cong., 1 Sess., 2320-22, 2342-43, 2350-52; Toombs to Stephens, Feb. 10, 1860, in Phillips, *Correspondence of Toombs, Stephens, and Cobb*, 461; Washington *National Intelligencer*, May 31, 1860.

[14] Roy F. Nichols, *Disruption of American Democracy* (New York, 1948), 219, 223, 242, 264-66; Georgia Lee Tatum, *Disloyalty in the Confederacy* (Chapel Hill, 1934), 4-13; Louisville *Journal*, April 18, 1859.

Nicholas, Madison C. Johnson in Kentucky. All were certain that a new party, with a new name, without fanaticism or proscription, could unite patriotic and conservative men of all parties to check sectionalism and disloyalty to the Union.[15]

Crittenden had reached a similar decision more than a year before. Listening to the Kansas debates in the first session of the Thirty-fifth Congress, he became convinced of the utter incapacity of either the Republican or the Democratic party to heal the gaping sectional wounds brought on by the slavery issue. Neither could bring peace to the distracted country, for the program of neither would be accepted by the other. Threats of revolution and secession had become so commonplace and so open that he no longer doubted that the national Union was in peril. If the Union was to be saved, therefore, it must be through the medium of a new party which would inspire none of the sectional bitterness identified with the older parties. The time had come, as Letcher wrote, for patriots to forget old political affiliations and rally to the Union. Clay had anticipated just such a movement a decade before. Speaking to the Kentucky legislature after the crisis of 1850 had subsided, he suggested that salvation of the Union might call for the formation of a new party, and he pledged his support if such a move became necessary.[16]

In the autumn of 1858 Crittenden began a frontal assault on the two great parties. Their leaders he regarded as selfish, grasping, intolerant; and their programs were inevitably leading, he believed, to the breakup of the republic he had served so long and whose preservation was now the all-consuming purpose of his life. It was for this very reason he had gone three years before, somewhat late and with some reluctance, into the American party. Despite its alien and religious antipathies, he had then regarded it as the only possible medium for securing national unity. It had failed, but out of its ashes he hoped now to mold a new organization dedicated to the preservation of the Union.

At New York City in November, 1858, Crittenden attacked both

[15] Letters to Crittenden from Hunt, March 18, 1858, from Johnson, March 22, 1858, from Justin Jones, April 6, 1858, from Nicholas, April 12, 1858, and from Rives, Jan. 9, 1860, in Crittenden Papers; Nathan Sargent to A. H. H. Stuart, Oct. 31, 1858, in Stuart Papers; Balie Peyton to John Bell, Dec. 17, 1859, in Bell Papers; Louisville *Journal*, March 9, 1859.

[16] Nichols, *Disruption of American Democracy*, 249; Letcher to Crittenden, June 16, 1858, in Crittenden Papers; Poage, *Henry Clay*, 266.

Republicans and Democrats for their constant slavery agitation. The country was founded, he said, on the belief that the people were competent to govern themselves, but party management and maneuvering left little opportunity for them to do so. Two or three bosses managed party machinery, he said, and the machine controlled elections. The people were fed up with the slavery issue. They could settle it if no barrier were placed in their way; or, if they could not, then there was no hope for the country anyway. If they should fail, then "our scheme of government, the mighty promises of self-government that we have held out to the world, and liberty, all fall to the ground."[17]

He followed this up three months later in a Senate speech. Again the subject of debate was slavery, and statements by speakers of their commitments to party platforms on the subject aroused Crittenden's ire. He was sick to death, he said, of parties and their platforms, too. The country had come to be regarded as the servant of party, rather than the other way around, and the consequence was that parties were threatening the interests of the people. Politicians seemed to lose sight of the fact that it was the Constitution which was supreme, not party platforms. How were platforms made? Why "a parcel of gentlemen get themselves elected to a convention; they go there, and a few leading men hover about the outskirts and dictate all that is done, and then set up a platform, and that platform is infallible for four years." He wanted "to hear no more of platforms instead of the Constitution, or of conventions that are the masters of the people."[18]

Crittenden had already called a meeting of fifty members of the "Opposition" in Congress. To them he summarized his views on the ills of the country, of which slavery was foremost. Never before had he felt such anxiety for the nation's future. Breakup of the Union was being threatened, but it was a calamity too horrible to contemplate. It would shock the civilized world, and he refused to believe that "God in his providence" would permit it. Aggressive talk in and out of Congress had led to aggressive acts. Witness John Brown's raid. Brown's behavior proved that threats were not all idle but would influence "certain deluded people" in the North as well as impatient southerners.

[17] Quoted in Frankfort *Commonwealth*, Dec. 8, 1858.
[18] *Congressional Globe*, 35 Cong., 2 Sess., 1274.

Agitators, he continued, would be found in all societies, but if leaders would only retain their reason, delusions fed by fanatics would pass away. Traitors there were both North and South, but he did not believe their numbers great. A recent Union meeting in New York that adopted conciliatory resolutions endorsed by former Presidents Van Buren, Fillmore, and Pierce was evidence of returning fraternal feeling there. He urged southerners to receive these manifestations of goodwill in the spirit in which they were made. Talk of disunion was absurd, for evils unredressed in the Union certainly would not be solved out of it.

Before the meeting adjourned, a committee was appointed to confer with the central committees of the all-but-moribund Whig and American parties with the purpose of forming a political organization whose platform would be merely "the Union and the Constitution." Next evening in Philadelphia the national committee of the American party met to consider the proposal. It appointed Crittenden chairman of a committee of ten to act for it.[19] By mid-January the organizational structure of the new party had been agreed on. It stood, according to Crittenden, in "that *middle-ground* & *temperate* region, where all who are opposed to both Democrats & Republicans might freely & properly meet. . . . From that position they might defend the country against the madness of those parties, their sectionalism, secession, & disunion tendencies." At the suggestion of William C. Rives it took the name Constitutional Union party.[20] At the direction of the party's central committee Crittenden appointed a special committee to prepare an address to the public on the purpose of the party. It was important that this be published early in order to give Union men a rallying point, for in the South particularly these lacked a common ground and were fast drifting into the Democratic party simply because they had nowhere else to go.

It was planned that state conventions meet shortly after publication of the address and endorse the Constitutional Union party and its aims. But difficulties arose from the beginning. For one reason

[19] Washington *National Intelligencer*, Dec. 22, 24, 26, 1859; New York *Herald*, Dec. 22, 1859, quoted *ibid.*, Dec. 23, 1859; Washington *Globe* and Boston *Journal*, quoted *ibid.*, Dec. 22, 1859; J. E. Plautz to Crittenden, Feb. 16, 1860, in Crittenden Papers.
[20] Crittenden to S. S. Nicholas, Jan. 29, 1860 (copy misdated 1840), W. C. Rives to Crittenden, Jan. 9, 1860, in Crittenden Papers.

or another many of those whom Crittenden appointed to the special committee were unable to serve. Crittenden assigned the actual drafting of the address to John Pendleton Kennedy, wealthy and distinguished former Whig congressman and man of letters in Baltimore. Crittenden urged haste, but Kennedy was delayed by illness. Crittenden then appealed to Erastus Brooks of the New York *Express*. Brooks responded, but his product did not satisfy Crittenden. It lacked "stateliness & dignity," and was "too party-like." Kennedy, now recovered, was again called on, but Crittenden was not entirely happy with Kennedy's draft and revised it himself. Finally, on February 22, the address was issued. It denounced both major parties, detailed reasons why neither was capable of governing, and called on the people to rally to the new organization. It urged state conventions to recommend two men for the consideration of a national nominating convention.[21]

Its reception was encouraging. From North Carolina, Kentucky, Virginia, Massachusetts, and Pennsylvania came enthusiastic accounts of ratification meetings, some held, incongruously, before the address was received. In Boston, old Websterites like George S. Hilliard, George T. Curtis, and Leverett Saltonstall joined with A. A. Lawrence in promoting a mammoth meeting at Faneuil Hall, where more than eight hundred delegates from over two hundred Massachusetts towns recommended Crittenden and Everett for the presidential nomination. A meeting in Frankfort, Kentucky, on February 22 resolved that the people of the state were "for the Union and the Constitution intact," and that they would redress any wrongs they might suffer "inside of the Union and not out of it." They, too, recommended Crittenden for the Presidency. In Philadelphia a "monster meeting" in early February "fairly set the city in." The politicians, wrote one of its organizers, "are astounded and the masses delighted." In Tennessee the convention was one of the largest as well as one of the most enthusiastic that had ever met there, and if Balie Peyton's account may be credited, it was marked by "the most perfect unanimity." Even from Mississippi came re-

[21] Crittenden to Kennedy, Jan. 24, Feb. 8, 9, 1860, in Kennedy Papers, Peabody Institute; Kennedy to William A. Graham, Feb. 7, Kennedy to Crittenden, Feb. 15, 1860, in Crittenden Papers (Duke); Alexander H. H. Stuart to Crittenden, Jan. 22, Kennedy to Crittenden, Jan. 31, March 5, 1860, in Crittenden Papers; Crittenden to Francis Granger, Jan. 24, 1860, in Granger Papers; Crittenden to Jacob Brown, Jan. 24, 1860, in Crittenden Papers (Chicago).

ports that "The movement is running through the country like fire upon the prairies."[22]

Intermixed with such enthusiastic accounts were a few discouraging notes. From New Jersey came word that prospects for the party there were poor. Outside of Philadelphia, news from Pennsylvania was discouraging. Former Know-Nothings there thought the movement "humbug" and refused to support it. They still remembered the fusion fiasco with Democrats in 1856, so that some regarded the new party as a secret ally of the Democrats, and newspapers refused it publicity. In late April came bad news from Philadelphia, too. Practical politicians among old Whigs there had not joined the movement, and consequently leadership had devolved upon amateurs who were then easily outwitted by professionals in the older parties. Much the same was true in Georgia, where Toombs and Stephens remained aloof. Stephens thought the party aims were impractical and too vague. So, too, did Abraham Lincoln in Illinois. By mid-April in Louisiana, national committeeman Charles M. Conrad had become completely disillusioned. Convinced of the utter impracticability of the party's carrying any northern state, he urged abandonment of the whole project, for dividing the Democratic vote would only lead to Republican victory.[23]

From the beginning of the movement it had been generally assumed that Crittenden, despite his age, would be the new party's candidate. His Lecompton position in 1858, although it cost him much of his following in the South, had given him great stature in the North. Even so, he still retained strength among old Whigs

[22] Letters to Crittenden from Edmund C. Pechin, Feb. 7, from William P. Burwell, Feb. 18, from Balie Peyton, Feb. 25, from William A. Graham, Feb. 27, from A. A. Lawrence, March 19 (copy), 30, and from John P. Kennedy, March 5, 1860, in Crittenden Papers; Collins, *History of Kentucky*, I, 83; Frankfort *Commonwealth*, Feb. 23, 1860; Louisville *Journal*, April 9, 1860; Vicksburg *Whig*, Raymond (Miss.) *Gazette*, and Philadelphia *Journal*, quoted *ibid.*, Feb. 9, 1860. Washington *National Intelligencer*, December, 1859, and January, February, March, 1860, has numerous accounts of local and state organizational meetings.

[23] Letters to Crittenden from Joseph F. Randolph, Jan. 30, from Jacob Dewees, Feb. 10, from J. E. Plautz, Feb. 16, from C. M. Conrad, April 19, and from Edmund C. Pechin, April 30, 1860, in Crittenden Papers; Conrad to Crittenden, May 4, 1860, in Crittenden Papers (Duke); Stephens to Crittenden, Jan. 21, 1860, in Henry Cleveland (ed.), *Alexander H. Stephens, in Public and Private, with Letters and Speeches, before, during and since the War* (Philadelphia, 1866), 659; Lincoln to Stephens, Jan. 19, 1860, in *Some Lincoln Correspondence with Southern Leaders before the Outbreak of the Civil War, from the Collection of Judd Stewart* (New York, 1909), 4.

in the South, and this was the group mainly counted on by the
new party in that section. From the Northwest came reports of his
great popularity in Illinois, Indiana, and Iowa. Lawrence was confident Massachusetts could be carried with him as the candidate.
When Crittenden's name was proposed at the convention in Faneuil
Hall, he wrote, "the severe decorum of the assembly completely
broke down."[24] At the same time, newspapers in all sections were
endorsing him. The New York *Journal of Commerce*, the Philadelphia *Enquirer*, the Philadelphia *News*, the Alexandria (Va.)
Gazette, the Wilmington (Del.) *Commonwealth*, the Lexington
(Mo.) *Express*, the St. Louis *News*, and the Louisville *Journal* all
urged his nomination.[25]

Crittenden, however, had resolved at the start that he would
not be a candidate. When the Lecompton debates in the spring of
1858 stirred many to urge his nomination, he had written his daughter
that "no ambition for the Presidency guides or troubles me." The
following December he gave a flat refusal to a group of New York
old Whigs who urged him to accept leadership of the party then
being projected. He would serve the party, he said, but he would
never be its presidential candidate. "I wish you to understand that
distinctly," he said. "No ambition of that sort has ever yet disturbed one moment of my lifetime, nor will it ever deprive me of
one moment's sleep. That you may rely on." A year later his resolution was unchanged.[26]

Such renunciation seemed to many to lack finality, although
Crittenden's own organ repeated it. "We assume the responsibility," said the *Commonwealth*, "of stating that he is not a candidate for the Presidency." Even after this, moves to draft him
persisted, and Nathan Sargent, at the urging of some of Crittenden's

[24] Lawrence to Crittenden, March 30, 1860, in Crittenden Papers.
[25] Letters to Crittenden from Oscar Tyler, March 24, 1858, from Sam Carpenter,
March 29, 1858, from Leslie Combs, April 11, 1858, from Robert Letcher, May 31,
1858, from Joseph P. Letcher, July 7, 1858, from C. W. Weaver, July 19, 1858, and
from J. M. Barr, April 24, 1860, in Crittenden Papers; New York *Journal of Com-
merce*, quoted in Washington *National Intelligencer*, July 20, 1858; *ibid.*, March 6,
April 3, 1860; St. Louis *News*, quoted in Frankfort *Commonwealth*, April 26, 1858;
Lexington (Mo.) *Express*, quoted in Howard K. Beale (ed.), *The Diary of Edward
Bates, 1859-1866*, in American Historical Association, *Annual Report, 1930*, IV
(Washington, 1933), 45. The St. Louis *News* advocated either Edward Bates or
Crittenden.
[26] Crittenden to Mrs. Coleman, April 27, 1858, July 2, 1859, in Crittenden Papers
(Duke); Washington *National Intelligencer*, Dec. 4, 1858; Frankfort *Commonwealth*,
Dec. 20, 1858.

friends, published a letter advocating his candidacy. Crittenden was vexed. In some annoyance he answered that he would not accept nomination except as "the spontaneous choice of the people . . . without any caucusing, or caballing." Finally, on the eve of the Baltimore convention, he made an unqualified renunciation. At a public dinner gotten up to honor him at Alexandria, Virginia, he was toasted as the next President. In responding, Crittenden disclaimed any wish for the office. He had "served out his time and it was time to retire," he said. He would not accept the office if he could have it, and he knew he could not have it.[27]

It was Crittenden's modesty that inspired the last statement, for he privately admitted that he could have the nomination if he would accept. But he would soon be seventy-four years old, and no longer did he aspire to place or power. His one ambition now was to preserve the Union, and to do that, he would rise above the pettiness and rivalries of partisan politics. Besides, he was disillusioned with party, as well he might be. "I am tired of public life," he wrote an old friend, "disgusted with the low party politics of the day, and the miserable scramble for place & plunder." He did not know who would be nominated, nor did he care so long as the candidate was respectable, and so long as he himself could "escape & get off smoothly." Of his old friends only Letcher seemed to understand this. "You are right to have nothing to do with the nomination for the Presidency," Letcher wrote. "Let Everett or Hunt or somebody else take the place." But Orlando Brown, equally devoted to Crittenden, did not agree. For many years, Brown's chief aim in life had been the advancement of his great friend. When Crittenden had refused to permit his candidacy in 1852, Brown had written in a spirit of dejection, "It was his [Crittenden's] weakness always to press forward others to the exclusion of himself and . . . if he had been of a more ambitious temperament he would probably have been President of the United States before this." Now Brown realized that the last fleeting chance of seeing Crittenden reach that goal was gone, and he was despondent.[28]

With Crittenden unavailable, the field was wide open. Winfield

27 Nathan Sargent to Crittenden, Aug. 12, 1858, in Crittenden Papers; Frankfort *Commonwealth*, June 23, July 14, Dec. 20, 1858, May 2, 1860.
28 Crittenden to Logan Hunton, April 15, 1860, in Crittenden Papers (Duke); Letcher to Crittenden, April 2, 1860, in Crittenden Papers; Brown to W. B. Haldeman, March 20, 1852, in Brown Papers, Filson Club.

Scott let it be known that "if nominated, & if elected—two tall gates to be leaped by an old horse," he would accept. Crittenden apparently tried to interest Lincoln in the nomination, but without success. Lincoln thought the platform of the party meaningless, a compromise of principles. For a time Edward Bates was considered a prospect. He was the choice of many in Missouri, and he had strength in Kentucky and Tennessee, too. Bates seemed eager for the nomination, but he was fishing also for the Republican nomination. According to one critic, he wanted to "run with the hare and hold with the hounds." To smoke him out, Republicans in Missouri asked for a clear-cut statement of his principles on slavery. When he subscribed to the Republican creed, he was eliminated from further consideration by Constitutional Unionists.[29]

It was a distinguished group of delegates who gathered in Baltimore the second week in May, bent on saving their country. From New York came Governor Washington Hunt and Erastus Brooks. From Pennsylvania came Joseph R. Ingersoll. Balie Peyton, Andrew Jackson Donelson, and G. A. Henry, grandson of Patrick Henry, came from Tennessee; John Todd Stuart, former Lincoln law partner, from Illinois; Alexander H. H. Stuart, from Virginia; Governor William L. Sharkey, from Mississippi; Leverett Saltonstall, from Massachusetts; Leslie Combs, from Kentucky; Governor John M. Morehead, from North Carolina. Conspicuously absent were Lawrence, Rives, and Hiram Ketchum, all of whom found it impossible at the last moment to attend. Ten of the thirty-three states were entirely unrepresented, but at that time most were relatively small and unimportant: California, Florida, Michigan, Iowa, Louisiana, New Hampshire, Rhode Island, Oregon, Wisconsin, and South Carolina.[30]

The convention assembled in the old Presbyterian Church at the corner of Fayette and North streets. The theme was patriotism, and it was graphically displayed. Spectator galleries on three sides were decorated with red, white, and blue bunting. Behind the president's

[29] Scott to Crittenden, Jan. 27, 1860, in Crittenden Papers (Duke); Lincoln to Crittenden, Dec. 22, 1859, in Some Lincoln Correspondence with Southern Leaders, 4; Louisville Journal, March 22, 1860; Louisville Courier, March 23, 1860.

[30] Letters to Crittenden from Lawrence, May 5, from Rives, May 5, and from Ketchum, May 7, 1860, in Crittenden Papers; Murat Halstead, A History of the National Political Conventions of the Current Presidential Campaign (Columbus, Ohio, 1860), 104-105 (hereinafter, Halstead, Conventions of 1860); Washington National Intelligencer, May 10, 1860.

chair two large American flags, surmounted by an eagle, framed a huge portrait of George Washington. Crittenden, as chairman of the executive committee, opened the convention; and his appearance was greeted by deafening applause from galleries and floor. Three times three cheers were given for the venerable statesman, handkerchiefs were waved, and hats tossed into the air by the otherwise sedate gathering. At Crittenden's suggestion Washington Hunt was chosen temporary chairman, and that evening he was elected permanent chairman. Leslie Combs was named chairman of the platform committee.

It had been generally agreed that the platform should be brief and should dodge all sectional issues that might, in Edward Everett's words, "lose in one quarter what it gains in the other." Combs' report followed this plan. It called for "The Constitution as it is, and the Union under it now and forever." It pledged protection from domestic and foreign enemies and a restoration of the rights of the states. It was adopted by acclamation, somewhat to the annoyance of Murat Halstead, just returned from the boisterous Charleston convention. He thought there was "too much unity here . . . to be interesting." Everybody, he added, was "eminently respectable, intensely virtuous, devotedly patriotic, and fully resolved to save the country."[31]

Balloting began on the second day. One hundred and twenty-eight votes were necessary to nominate. On the first ballot John Bell led with 68½, Sam Houston was next with 57, and Crittenden, despite his renunciation, was third with 28. The remainder of the votes were divided among Edward Everett, William A. Graham, John McLean, William C. Rives, John Minor Botts, and William L. Sharkey, Mississippi Unionist. Crittenden's votes came from Kentucky, Missouri, and Vermont. The chairman of the Kentucky delegation explained that although Crittenden had repeatedly refused to permit his candidacy, Kentucky delegates nevertheless were instructed to vote for him. The Missouri delegation announced that "whether he is a candidate or not," Missouri would cast her votes for him. Ohio also was instructed to vote for him but, deferring to his wishes, did not. Bell was nominated on the second ballot, after New York, Pennsylvania, Ohio, Massachusetts, and Virginia

31 Halsted, *Conventions of 1860*, pp. 104-107.

swung to his support. When Hunt declined to be a candidate for the vice-presidential nomination, Edward Everett was nominated by acclamation.[32]

It was the misfortune of the party that it chose two candidates who lacked great popular appeal. Both were intelligent and well educated, and Everett could even lay claim to distinction as a scholar and an orator. Bell did not have a mind of the first order, although he was a student of philosophy, law, literature, and the history of government. But he lacked mental agility, which seemed to correlate with his physical obesity and his stiff, formal bearing. He created an image of solemnity and glumness that repelled rather than attracted. His biographer says of him that "he could smile but he had no hearty laugh. To him life, public and private, was a serious business." But Bell's was an honest and blameless life, and even John Quincy Adams, who had little praise for most of his colleagues, many years before had conceded that Bell was "on the whole, a good Speaker [of the House]," even though, he added, he was "occasionally subservient from timidity." Adams had not so neutral an opinion of his neighbor, Everett, whom he described as a reed "shaken with the wind."[33]

Originally Crittenden and other party leaders had hoped to effect a merger with moderate Republicans. There was not great dissimilarity in philosophy of Republicans and old Whigs on economic programs, and Whigs were the backbone of the new party. Three months before the Chicago convention, Crittenden's old friend Blair, now influential in Republican councils, promised to support him for the Republican nomination if only Crittenden would accept the principle of slavery exclusion from the territories. A year earlier reports were widespread that an entente had been reached between Crittenden and Seward, and that Crittenden would be the presidential candidate of all factions opposed to the Buchanan administration. Both the Republican New York *Times* and the Democratic New York *Herald* professed to believe this rumor. Even Greeley was

---

[32] Halsted, *Conventions of 1860*, pp. 104-107, 110, 114-20; Washington *National Intelligencer*, May 10, 11, 12, 1860; Dwight L. Dumond, *The Secession Movement, 1860-1861* (New York, 1931), 92-94; Everett to Crittenden, May 7, 1860, in Crittenden Papers (Duke); Crittenden to Washington Hunt, April 24, 1860, in Coleman, *Crittenden*, II, 195-96.

[33] Joseph H. Parks, *John Bell of Tennessee* (Baton Rouge, 1950), 7; J. W. Caldwell, "John Bell of Tennessee," in *American Historical Review*, IV (1898-1899), 659; Adams, *Memoirs*, IX, 39, 214.

willing to accept Crittenden as a fusion candidate, and George D. Prentice spoke optimistically of the probability of the Republican convention at Chicago accepting the candidate of the new party, who at the time he believed would be Crittenden. In Missouri, fusion of all opposition parties was effected in December, 1859, and continued through the following spring.[34]

Such a merger on a national scale seems, in retrospect, not unreasonable, and might well have been effected except for the territorial question. Seward, the chief Republican spokesman, who was still regarded as a radical, was not nearly so certain in 1860 that the country faced an "irrepressible conflict" as he had been the year before, when he made the ominous prophecy at Rochester. Without making a complete about-face, his radicalism had by now become considerably tempered. Although he yearned for the Republican nomination (and the Presidency) for himself, he well might have been won to a plan of fusion behind some border-state old Whig, had Republican prospects seemed less promising. But Republican confidence had been bolstered by northern elections in 1858 and 1859. By 1860 party leaders believed they could win the election without aid from the border, and so the move failed.[35]

By the winter of 1859-1860 came rumors of another possible union, between Constitutional Unionists and Douglas Democrats. By midsummer of 1860 there was little doubt among the well-informed that the election of Lincoln would be the signal for the withdrawal of at least the gulf states. Soon, too, it became certain that if Lincoln could carry the doubtful states of New York and Pennsylvania, he would win. The strategy of Bell and Douglas leaders was therefore aimed at carrying these states.

Bell and Douglas both knew that neither, working singly, could hope to win a majority in the electoral college; their one hope was

[34] Letters to Crittenden from Thomas H. Clay, June 24, 1858, from John O. Sargent, Dec. 9, 1859, from C. H. Bressler, Feb. 2, 1860, from James Collins, Feb. 2, 1860, and from S. S. Nicholas, April 3, 1860, in Crittenden Papers; Nathan Sargent to Alexander H. H. Stuart, Feb. 18, 1859, in A. H. H. Stuart Papers; Francis P. Blair to Crittenden, Feb. 16, 1860, in Crittenden Papers (Duke); Beale, *Diary of Edward Bates*, 70, 72, 74, 106; Greeley to George E. Baker, April 28, 1859, in Barnes, *Memoir of Weed*, 255; Ollinger Crenshaw, *The Slave States in the Presidential Election of 1860* (Baltimore, 1945), 12, 31; Louisville *Courier*, Feb. 19, April 16, 30, June 11, 1859; New York *Courier and Enquirer*, quoted *ibid.*, July 20, 1859; Louisville *Journal*, Feb. 10, 1860; New York *Herald*, quoted *ibid.*, June 7, 1859; New York *Times*, quoted in Frankfort *Commonwealth*, Feb. 21, 1859; Glyndon G. Van Deusen, *Horace Greeley, Nineteenth Century Crusader* (Philadelphia, 1953), 223-24.

[35] Crenshaw, *The Slave States in the Election of 1860*, p. 304.

to prevent Lincoln from receiving a majority. Their friends therefore planned a fusion between their electoral tickets in doubtful states, so that state electoral ballots would be cast for whichever candidate seemed to have the better chance of getting a majority of the electoral vote of the nation. In case a majority in the electoral college was unattainable for either Bell or Douglas, they still might, by uniting on Bell, prevent Lincoln's carrying closely divided states by pluralities. If successful, this strategy would throw the election into the House, where Bell would probably be chosen, simply because he was the least objectionable to the partisan followers of the other candidates. Should the House be unable to reach a decision, the Presidency would devolve upon the man whom the Senate would choose as Vice President. It was almost certain that this choice would fall on Oregon Senator Joseph Lane, Breckinridge's secessionist running mate.

By August the scheme was fully developed. The two parties in New York had agreed on one electoral ticket of ten Bell supporters and twenty-five Douglas men, who if elected would vote as a unit. Douglas leaders assured Bell that "if we succeed, & if it shall appear that the whole [Electoral] College of N. Y. is necessary & sufficient to elect you their men will vote for you rather than send the election to the H. of Reps." At the same time Bell men in New Jersey had "a perfect understanding with the democrats." A similar arrangement was made in Rhode Island.

The plan had remarkable possibilities of success. In late July, Weed, and probably Seward, were seriously considering joining in the movement. Had they done so, the main stream of American history would have been altered. "We have the power," Weed wrote a national committeeman of the Constitutional Unionists, "to take this state from the Repns. & send the election to the House of Reps. provided the national men can be united on one Electoral ticket. Shall we do it?"[36]

[36] Washington Hunt to Bell, June 7, Aug. 19, 1860, in John Bell Papers; Weed to Granger, July 23, 1860, in Granger Papers. See also, Charles S. Morehead to Crittenden, Oct. 4, 1860, in Crittenden Papers; Mary Scrugham, *The Peaceable Americans of 1860-1861, A Study in Public Opinion* (New York, 1921), 49; Dumond, *Secession Movement*, 99-105, 109-11; Cincinnati *Enquirer*, quoted in Louisville *Courier*, Dec. 31, 1859; August Belmont to Blanton Duncan, Aug. 9, 1860, in John Bell Papers; John Tyler to Robert Tyler, Aug. 27, 1860, in Tyler, *Letters and Times*, II, 560-61; Horace Greeley, *The American Conflict*, 2 vols. (Hartford, Conn., 1864), I, 324; James G. Blaine, *Twenty Years of Congress: From Lincoln to Garfield*, 2 vols. (Norwich, Conn., 1884-1886), I, 171.

Similar fusion movements were effected in Virginia, Kentucky, Tennessee, and Georgia. In late August, Alexander H. H. Stuart reported an *"entente cordiale"* between Douglas men and Bell men in the Old Dominion. In Kentucky a Breckinridge paper reported "Billing and cooing . . . upon every stump" between followers of Bell and Douglas. In Alabama, although no formal fusion took place, there was open sympathy between Bell men and Douglas men. A Bell supporter in October reported "our Douglas cousins" gaining. "Every vote they get," he added, "is half a vote for us." In mid-September, Douglas, according to his running mate, had hopes of victory for himself, and supreme confidence that he would at least prevent Lincoln's election. A month later Alexander H. Stephens, who had refused to go into the Bell movement, was almost ready to concede that Bell would carry Georgia, and that the election would go to the House of Representatives.[37] As the campaign tempo increased, even Breckinridge, despite the deep enmity between his followers and those of Douglas, was brought into the fusion movement. In New York seven of Douglas' electors were replaced on the fusion ticket by Breckinridge electors, and a similar policy was followed in New Jersey and Pennsylvania.

Throughout the campaign Douglas and Bell stood firmly for adjustment of sectional difficulties. Election of either of the other candidates, they claimed, would break up the Union. On the other hand, Breckinridge followers denounced Douglas and Bell for truckling to the abolitionist tendencies of the Republican party. At the same time Breckinridge himself disavowed secession. Laurels for doubletalk in the campaign, however, must be awarded the Republicans. Lincoln, like Harrison two decades earlier, was represented as all things to all men. Where it was profitable to do so, the slavery issue was played down and more popular programs advanced—in the Northwest, a homestead law and internal improvements; in the East, particularly in Pennsylvania, tariff protection. Where protection was unpopular, however, the vague Republican plank on the subject could be quoted to prove that the party stood for free trade. Where vestiges of old Whig strength remained, Lincoln was portrayed as the disciple of Clay; in Democratic strongholds he was pictured as

[37] Stuart to Blanton Duncan, Aug. 23, 1860, Jere Clemens to John Bell, Oct. 1, 14, 1860, in John Bell Papers; "From the Autobiography of Herschel V. Johnson, 1856-1867," in *American Historical Review*, XXX (1924-1925), 321; Stephens to J. Henley Smith, Sept. 12, Oct. 13, 1860, in Phillips, *Correspondence of Toombs, Stephens, and Cobb*, 496, 502.

unequivocally opposed to the compromising proclivities of the great Kentuckian.

But New York's thirty-five electoral votes could be decisive, and it became vital for Republicans to frustrate the fusion movement there. Greeley and other Republican editors flooded the state with denunciation of it. The *Tribune* branded the movement as a "humbug," a "nasty swindle," a "cheat," a "corrupt bargain and sale." It reminded the Germans and Irish of the Know-Nothing antecedents of the fusionists, ignoring the fact that Lincoln had been chosen over Seward at Chicago largely because Seward was more outspoken than Lincoln in his opposition to Know-Nothings. Greeley warned the voters that the fusion movement was designed to sell them out like slaves. He and other Republican editors warned, too, that fusion success would result in the election of Joe Lane, another "Northern man with Southern principles," to the Presidency; that it was the question of an honest Republican or a corrupt Democrat, and that no other candidate but Lincoln had a chance for a majority in the electoral college.[38]

Despite his years, Crittenden's aid was sought by party leaders in all sections, and he took an extraordinarily active part in the campaign. After Congress adjourned, he had gone to Boston at Lawrence's urging, to stimulate efforts there before he returned home. In September, Washington Hunt pleaded with him to come to New York. Even one speech by Crittenden, according to Hunt, might turn the scale there and result in victory. Charles S. Morehead, just returned from campaigning in Pennsylvania, wrote him, "Not less than one thousand persons" begged him to persuade Crittenden to come to that state.[39]

But Crittenden concentrated his efforts mostly in Kentucky and in other border states. In all his speeches he emphasized how inconsequential were the party platforms. The slavery issue was a mere shibboleth, for there was not and there would not be a practical occasion calling for congressional intervention in the territories. There was no territory, nor was there apt to be, where slavery would be attracted. At its last session all in Congress had agreed, he said,

[38] Scrugham, *Peaceable Americans*, 50-51.

[39] Letters to Crittenden from J. P. Comegyns, April 27, from James De Peyster Ogden, May 25, from Morehead, Oct. 4, 1860, in Crittenden Papers; from Lawrence, May 25, from Mrs. Coleman, June 3, 1860, in Crittenden Papers (Duke); from Lawrence, May 26, and from Hunt, Sept. 3, 1860, in Coleman, *Crittenden*, II, 207, 217-18.

that there was no occasion for Congress to interfere at the present time. Why, therefore, should an issue be raised over some problem that would arise only in the distant future if at all? Sufficient to the day was the evil thereof. Popular sovereignty was "a mere abstraction." The question in Kansas and the other territories had already been settled, since none of them had a climate conducive to slavery. To speak of slavery in the great Rocky Mountain area was to dismiss it. There was not "one single spot of any considerable extent in any Territory . . . where any man would desire to carry his slaves, and yet the whole contest is as to what is to be done when the people carry their slaves where they don't want to carry them."

In Louisville, in August, he made a stirring plea for Bell as the only candidate capable of calming sectional antagonisms and bringing peace to the country. Bell had no platform "to ensnare men." He had no feuds to settle, no enemies to punish. If elected, he would bring all together, not in a party triumph, but in a triumph for the country. What, he asked, was the alternative? Lincoln, although an upright man, if elected would be governed by the antislavery party that brought him to power. Crittenden acknowledged that the "wise leaders" of that party were not abolitionists, but there were enough abolitionists in it to alarm the South. Even though Lincoln would not do any positive act against slavery, his mere election would be a "great calamity to the country"; for it would quicken the antislavery impulse and thus increase agitation and cause apprehension in the South.

As for Douglas, Crittenden trusted him as a "loyal, courageous Union man," who had sacrificed his future to principle in the Lecompton struggle. His election could not, however, calm the country either. His party not only was feuding with the Republican party but it had complex internal divisions. The Buchanan-Breckinridge faction would prevent it from pursuing a stable, conservative course, despite what Douglas might do.

Turning to Breckinridge, Crittenden charged that if he was not a secessionist himself, he was the candidate of every disunionist in the South. His nomination had been inspired only by the desire of the conspirators to draw Kentucky into a southern confederacy. They knew that Breckinridge had no chance of carrying the election, or even a single northern state. "They would rather have Kentucky for their ally," he said, "than Mr. Breckinridge for their President."

Despite this conspiracy, Crittenden went on, Kentucky would never secede. She was the very "heart of the Union," and prudence, patriotism, and reason all combined to dictate that she support Bell. He painted a glowing picture of the future of the country if the Union should be preserved intact: a nation of 100,000,000 by the turn of the century, where every man would be "free to think, free to speak, free to work." His generation should leave to their children such a country as their fathers had left them. The time had come for patriots to abandon parties and cling to their country instead. The great virtue of Bell's party, he said, was the absence of a platform. Platforms meant nothing to Presidents, for once elected, they disregarded the parts that did not appeal to them.[40]

In late September, Crittenden went to Nashville. He was already exhausted from his labors and urged his friends there to spare him the ordeal of public receptions other than his address. But it was impossible. The "*vox populi*," one of them wrote, demanded otherwise. A delegation from Nashville, headed by John Bell, met him in Bowling Green and accompanied him from there. In Nashville he was drawn through cheering crowds in an open carriage, feeling as honored, he wrote, as if he had been "twenty Presidents." The Nashville *Banner* reported that it had never seen such enthusiasm and excitement in the community "from the hour that the great Crittenden arrived."[41]

His speech, delivered to an estimated fifteen thousand at Watkins Park, was in sharp contrast to the one he had made there just twenty years before. Then he had not scrupled to stoop to demagoguery in depicting Van Buren as degenerate and Harrison as the poor but honest frontier soldier and farmer. But now he must rise above such shallow flights, for his life had almost run its course, and perhaps his country's life was also drawing to a close. In Tennessee the issue was between Breckinridge and Bell, and Crittenden denounced the Breckinridge party as "men of selfish ambition," conspiring for personal reasons to break up the Union. They were men for whom the republic was not large enough, who preferred the country's destruction to "the non-attainment of their own selfish ends." They called themselves Democrats, but their relation with democracy was "shal-

[40] Louisville *Journal*, Aug. 4, 1860; New York *Times*, Sept. 18, 1860, quoted in Crenshaw, *Slave States in the Election of 1860*, p. 38; Railey, *History of Woodford County*, 240-41; Lexington (Ky.) *Leader*, Aug. 20, 1960.
[41] Nashville *Banner*, quoted in Frankfort *Commonwealth*, Oct. 3, 1860.

low—hollow—superficial." They well knew they could not win, and they were trying only to divide the anti-Republican vote so that Lincoln would be elected. They would then use his election as an excuse to break up the Union. In moving terms he pictured the results of disunion. "The respect of the world would be lost, our flag disgraced, and the glorious title of American citizen would be no protection abroad." Our ships then would "skulk in out of the way bays and rivers . . . and fear to meet a flag upon the open sea." He urged all his hearers to come to the aid of their common country in maintaining the Constitution and the Union that made them all free. "Come," he implored, "let us go locked in hands as one family."[42]

In October he campaigned in Missouri. He dined with Edward Bates in St. Louis and urged him to persuade Lincoln, who was maintaining an ominous silence, despite southern charges of radicalism, "to make a soothing address." Bates was surprised that Crittenden believed "there really will be an attempt to break up the Union" in the event of Lincoln's election.[43]

The people went to the polls on Tuesday, November 6. Through their ballots Lincoln received 180 electoral votes, 28 more than were necessary for his election. His victory was fairly and constitutionally won and was achieved over powerful combinations of his opponents. It is one of the ironies of the American political system, however, that despite this decisive Republican victory in the electoral college, Lincoln had 1,000,000 fewer popular votes than the sum of those for Douglas, Breckinridge and Bell. Nor was his victory the result simply of a division of the opposition votes among three different candidates. Under the American electoral system, majorities in the large, populous states were sufficient to have carried him into the Presidency even if all opposition votes had been concentrated on one man. This is not to say that the split in the Democratic party was without influence in Lincoln's election; it is impossible to estimate what a united Democratic party might have achieved. The mere fact of the party's division and consequent poor prospects of victory probably drove many doubtful supporters over to the enemy. Horatio Seymour concluded that "thousands and thousands" who voted for Lincoln

[42] Letters to Crittenden from Nashville citizens, Aug. 29, from Edwin Ewing, Sept. 5, and from W. A. Cunningham, Sept. 14, 1860, in Crittenden Papers; Nashville *Banner*, quoted in Frankfort *Commonwealth*, Oct. 3, 1860.

[43] Beale, *Diary of Edward Bates*, 154-55.

in New York had no confidence in Republican doctrine, but feared that a vote against him would result in throwing the election to Joseph Lane.[44]

Another ironic result of the election was the ridiculously small vote Douglas received in the electoral college, Missouri's nine votes and three of New Jersey's seven. Lincoln got fifteen times as many electoral votes as Douglas, although his popular plurality over Douglas was in the ratio of only four to three. Thus, practically all Douglas' 1,377,000 popular votes were entirely unrepresented in the electoral college.

The election turned on the contest in New York. Lincoln could have lost any other doubtful state and still have won. He could not have won without the Empire State. After waging a bitter and determined struggle, Republicans won there by a relatively narrow margin of 50,000 in a total vote of more than 750,000. Had Weed followed his midsummer impulse and thrown in his lot with the fusionists, it seems certain that Lincoln would have been defeated.

Lincoln also carried Pennsylvania, where the issue was the tariff, slavery hardly drawing mention throughout the canvass. David Wilmot, the embodiment of free-soil sentiment, had been defeated there three years before. Lincoln's cause was helped materially by the election of Andrew G. Curtin as governor, on an out-and-out high tariff platform, a month before the presidential election. Such an acute Republican observer as James G. Blaine later concluded that if Curtin had lost in October, the resulting demoralization would have been disastrous to Lincoln not only in Pennsylvania, but in Indiana, Oregon, California, and New Jersey. Loss of these states would have precluded his election.[45]

Despite their defeat, Constitutional Unionists did not play an insignificant part in the election. The contest south of the Mason-Dixon line was largely between Bell and Breckinridge, with Douglas playing a very minor role, and Lincoln none whatever. Bell's electoral vote was thirty-nine to Breckinridge's seventy-two; yet Bell polled

[44] Seymour to Crittenden, Jan. 18, 1861, in Coleman, *Crittenden*, II, 255. There is a thoughtful and penetrating analysis of the election returns by James G. Randall in *Lincoln the President*, 2 vols. (Boston, 1916), I, chap. xxi; Nevins, *Emergence of Lincoln*, II, chap. x; Emerson D. Fite, *The Presidential Campaign of 1860* (New York, 1911), 276-300.

[45] Horace Greeley, *Recollections of a Busy Life* (New York, 1868), 392; Washington Hunt to John Bell, Nov. 21, 1860, in John Bell Papers; Blaine, *Twenty Years of Congress*, I, 206-207.

almost 600,000 popular votes to Breckinridge's 850,000. Bell's vote and Douglas' vote together exceeded Breckinridge's in the slave states by almost 100,000. Shifts of about 300 votes in Missouri and about 700 in Maryland would have carried both those states for Bell, and would have given him a total electoral vote of fifty-six.[46]

What it all added up to, however, was that Lincoln was a minority President with less than 40 percent of the popular vote. Not a single vote did he get in ten of the eleven states that would soon make up the southern Confederacy, and only a very insignificant vote was cast for him in all the border slave states except Missouri. His support was almost altogether from the free states and was more sectional, even, than Breckinridge's.

It is another strange anomaly of the American political system that a man with the political acumen of Abraham Lincoln should have been almost completely ignored on the national scene until after he was fifty years of age. Equally ironic was it that he should then have been catapulted, almost without preparation and in considerable ignorance of the true political situation in the country, into the Presidency, where his decisions would control its destinies. That he was completely misinformed as to the true sentiment in the South and in the border, his own letters as well as unfolding events would soon demonstrate. Lincoln was fundamentally a man of peace and a man of compromise. But his information at this time came only at second hand, and too much of it from stubborn and unyielding men. Secession and Civil War and the loss of a half million lives would follow as a result of his election. Meanwhile, there was to be one last chance for adjustment and reconciliation between the sections.

[46] Binkley, *American Political Parties*, 204; Edward Stanwood, *History of the Presidency*, 2 vols. (rev. ed., Boston, 1921), I, 297; Cole, *Whig Party in the South*, 339.

CHAPTER XVIII

Toward the Abyss

THE LAST session of the Thirty-sixth Congress convened on December 3 in an atmosphere of intense excitement. A majority of Washington residents were ardently prosouthern. Buchanan's organ, the *Constitution*, despite its name was now openly advocating the forceful prevention of Lincoln's inauguration. Government officers and clerks paraded in the streets, disunion cockades in their hats. "Political affairs here look most gloomy," wrote Crittenden, "they are *mixed* up with darkness."[1] Buchanan's behavior was unsatisfactory to his contemporaries, just as it would be to later generations. A large, phlegmatic man, he inspired little confidence or affection, and many regarded him as cold and calculating. One associate claimed he never did "an unkind thing from impulse, or without hoping to gain from it." Even the ardent prosouthern John Tyler, visiting in Washington that winter, thought Buchanan did not present "that calm and intrepid appearance" that he had hoped to see.[2]

Rarely, however, has any public man faced responsibilities as delicate and difficult as were now thrust on Buchanan. His was a more difficult task even than Lincoln's. For Lincoln would have some influence over the course of events and might make or refuse to make an adjustment with the South. Buchanan had no such choice. He was the retiring head of the minority wing of a divided party that had just been repudiated at the polls. Tugged at from all directions by divided counselors in his official family, it is little wonder that he temporized. By January the southern members of his cabinet would withdraw, and he would then be able to create a more forceful image of the government. For the time being, however, he remained passive, not daring to take bold measures to preserve peace in a divided country. His difficulties cannot be equated with those of Jackson during the nullification controversy without grossly exaggerating Jackson's problems and minimizing his.

By the time Congress met, South Carolina had already started the machinery leading to secession, and it was well known that other states were preparing to follow her. Even men who during the recent election had led the fight for Unionism in southern states were now joining the secessionists. A Kentucky Unionist visiting in Memphis in early December found Bell men there now as ardent for secession as those who had supported Breckinridge. And about the same time, one of the stoutest of Alabama Unionists announced his willingness to secede unless southern grievances were redressed.[3]

As southern senators and representatives reached Washington, they began holding secret meetings in an effort to effect a concerted disunion plan. Specially invited to these caucuses were southern Unionists, and heavy pressure was exerted to force them into the secession party. On December 6 Albert Gallatin Brown of Mississippi, Louis T. Wigfall of Texas, and Alfred Iverson of Georgia spoke, as if by prearrangement, in the Senate. All three agreed that attempts at reconciliation were now useless and that secession was inevitable. On the same day the Secretary of the Treasury, Howell Cobb, issued an address to the people of Georgia urging speedy secession as the only alternative to degradation and ruin. On December 13, thirty southern members of Congress wired their constituents: "The argu-

[1] Crittenden to Orlando Brown, Dec. 6, 1860, in Brown Papers, Filson Club. See also Horatio King to James Buchanan, Nov. 7, to Nahum Capen, Dec. 10, 31, and to Isaac Toucey, Dec. 30, 1860, in King, *Turning on the Light*, 25, 32, 37, 39.

[2] "Recollections of an Old Stager," XLVI (1872-1873), 704; Nat Vose to E. B. Washburne, Dec. 15, 1860, in E. B. Washburne Papers, Library of Congress; Tyler, *Letters and Times*, II, 615.

[3] Garret Davis to Crittenden, Dec. 10, 1860, Jere Clemens to Crittenden, Nov. 24, Dec. 25, 1860, in Crittenden Papers.

ment is exhausted. All hope of relief in the Union . . . is extinguished. . . . We are satisfied the honor, safety, and independence of the Southern people are to be found only in a Southern Confederacy."[4]

Just what practical advantage southern extremists hoped to gain from secession is not clear. Fire-eaters declaimed incessantly on "Southern rights," but none of them ever explained how secession could ensure slavery further than federal and local law already did. The slavery controversy had many facets, but the right to expand into the territories was the most critical issue. Yet this right had been guaranteed by the Dred Scott decision, and favorable territorial legislation in New Mexico, Utah, and Kansas implemented it. Nothing could more clearly reveal the shallowness of expansionist talk. For the census of 1860 would soon show only two slaves in Kansas, fifteen in Nebraska, twenty-nine in Utah, and twenty-four in New Mexico, seventy in all, and about half of them the property of government officials on temporary duty.

Another great source of controversy had to do with fugitive slaves. Only 803 slaves escaped from the South in 1860—approximately one-fiftieth of one percent of the slave population—and practically all of this group fled from the border states, the very region where secession had least support. Indeed, it is most unlikely that more than a handful of slaveowners from the Deep South had ever lost a slave into northern territory. Yet secessionists from the Deep South cited violation of the fugitive-slave law most often as the grievance that must be redressed if they were to remain in the Union.[5]

Even had this latter complaint been a just one, it is again impossible that secession could have relieved the problem. As long as slave states remained in the Union, a harsh federal law made it possible for claimants to recover fugitives when they were apprehended, and occasionally even to kidnap northern Negroes who were not slaves. As a North Carolina Unionist pointed out, secession would therefore, in effect, move the Canadian border to the Ohio River.[6]

It seems not unreasonable to conclude that secession was a hasty, ill-considered, impetuous act, and that those responsible for it were

[4] Martin J. Crawford to Alexander H. Stephens, Dec. 8, 1860, J. Henley Smith to Stephens, Dec. 9, 1860, in Stephens Papers; James G. Randall, *The Civil War and Reconstruction* (New York, 1937), 200-201.

[5] United States *Census, 1860, Population* (Washington, 1864), 16, 161, 557, 575; *American Annual Cyclopedia, 1861* (New York, 1864), 696.

[6] J. G. deRoulhac Hamilton, *The Correspondence of Jonathan Worth*, 2 vols. (Raleigh, 1909), I, 124.

lacking in true statesmanship, however pure their motives may have been. Furthermore, it was carried out in rather an unfortunate and slipshod manner. At the time, no state in the Union could modify its constitution in less than a year's time. This provision had been made purposely so that people might take a long, hard look before making even minute changes in their fundamental law. Yet South Carolina and other states, within a matter of a few weeks, in a time when their political psyches were emotionally disturbed, called conventions, and these conventions took action that would have incalculable effects not only upon the living but upon the lives of their descendants for generations to come. Rarely has a people with such a rich political heritage acted in such an irresponsible manner.

But those now charged with conduct of the national destiny were almost as irresponsible. Transition of authority from one administration to another is awkward and difficult under ideal conditions. Its difficulties were increased in this country at that time by the long interval between election and inaugural. In November, 1860, the Republican party found itself chosen to lead the country when it was not yet in control of the Presidency and was a minority in Congress. The party lacked organizational leadership and had no clearly defined program. As previously noted, its platform was a catchall, designed to attract voters of diverse views.

Actually there were three courses open to the Republican party in November, 1860: compromise and preserve the Union, let the seceding states go in peace, or crush them by force. There were two wings of the party, one radical and one conservative. The conservatives at first were divided on whether to compromise or accept secession. The radicals, represented in Congress by men like Sumner, Wade, Chandler, and Chase, were opposed to either of these alternatives. They regarded both as weakness and timidity, and they came to Washington in an unyielding mood. "I think the country is ready for war," wrote a constituent of one of these, as "it is the only thing that will put an end to slavery." Another wrote that "the Republican pulse beats high for War but a back down to Traitors & Slavery will Ruin our Party and prospects."[7]

---

[7] W. S. Baldwin to E. B. Washburne, Jan. 25, 1861, Alvin Armstrong to Washburne, Feb. 12, 1861, in Washburne Papers. See also, Randall, *Lincoln the President*, I, 230; Dumond, *Secession Movement*, 149-50; Nevins, *Emergence of Lincoln*, II, 387; David M. Potter, *Lincoln and His Party in the Secession Crisis* (New Haven, 1942), 20-44; Scrugham, *Peaceable Americans*, 69.

The "go in peace" advocates probably never expected that secession would materialize. If, as David Potter believes, this is true, their position was insincere and was aimed merely at soothing southern anger and preventing northern concession. Unhappily, their stand further obscured an already complex and difficult situation and prevented the real alternatives of compromise or coercion from being promptly dealt with. Horace Greeley originally belonged to this group, but he soon joined the advocates of coercion.

The compromise element in the party was perhaps best represented by Seward, Thurlow Weed, Charles Francis Adams, and John Sherman. In late November a debate began between Weed's Albany *Evening Journal* and Greeley's *Tribune* on the value of preserving the Union. Weed was willing to compromise the Chicago platform, which had taken a firm stand against slavery expansion into the territories. Greeley would sever the Union if necessary to adhere to the platform.

With the party thus divided, all action that might further divide its forces must be avoided. Leaders in Congress were afraid to act without assurance of support from the grassroots, or without approval of the President-elect, but the people could not instruct Congress of their will unless Congress submitted some program to them, and Republican congressmen feared that submission of such a program would indicate approval or uncertainty on their part. Nor could Lincoln be of much help under the circumstances. Basically a conservative and a man willing to compromise most issues, he now utterly misjudged the temper of the South. Furthermore, he had become so committed on the moral evil of slavery that compromise on his part would appear not only weak but wicked. At a time, therefore, when a strong and a resolute course was necessary to save the country from disaster, the party called to assume leadership found itself completely immobilized. As James G. Blaine noted, it was as if the Republicans, having gained the object of their efforts, were aghast at the reaction their success had produced. "I am without schemes, or plans, hopes, desires, or fears for the future," Seward wrote Weed two weeks after the November election.[8]

In their predicament the Republicans procrastinated. Meanwhile,

---

[8] Seward to Weed, Nov. 18, 1860, in Seward, *Autobiography*, II, 478. See also, Potter, *Lincoln and His Party*, 50-51, 56-57; Scrugham, *Peaceable Americans*, 72; Dumond, *Secession Movement*, 149-50; Blaine, *Twenty Years of Congress*, I, 273-74.

Lincoln added to their indecision by his secretive behavior. As John Sherman wrote, "We are powerless here because we don't know *what Lincoln wants*. . . . He communicates nothing even to his friends here & so we drift along." In a caucus held on December 3 the Republicans formally agreed on a policy of "masterly inactivity." They were to "shun all exciting discussions, push forward the public business, and await future developments." They would "sit quietly by while their opponents held the floor."[9]

The truth was that not only Lincoln but most Republican leaders completely misjudged the secession crisis, believing it to be all bluff and bluster. Charles Francis Adams, Jr., closely associated with his father and with Seward during the election campaign and after, later confessed this. "We all dwelt in a fool's Paradise," he wrote. All, he added, were "of average blindness. I know it was so in the case of Seward and my father; as it was absolutely so in that of Sumner. We knew nothing of the South, and had no realizing sense of the intensity of feeling which there prevailed; we fully believed it would all end in gasconade."[10]

It is ironical that Republican leaders should be so exercised over the altogether meaningless issue of slavery in the territories but were utterly unconcerned about the really important issue of slavery in the states. To a distinguished modern scholar their attitude suggests that they regarded the territorial question "not as a thing to settle but as a thing to agitate, so that politicians could merely skirt a subject they were really not essentially grappling with." For by 1860, as has been noted, there were only threescore and ten slaves among a population of several hundred thousand whites in all the region between Missouri and California, and Canada and Mexico. In a well-reasoned article published at this time, Charles Francis Adams, Jr., demonstrated convincingly that the laws of economics would shortly bring an end to the cotton monopoly of the South, and thus of slave labor, according to his view the most extravagant form of labor. Thus, he concluded, "the peaceful laws of trade may do the work which agitation has attempted in vain."[11]

[9] Kenneth M. Stampp, *And the War Came* (Baton Rouge, 1950), 65, 110-11.
[10] Potter, *Lincoln and His Party*, 80.
[11] J. G. Randall, "The Civil War Restudied," in *Journal of Southern History*, VI (1940), 447; [Charles Francis Adams, Jr.], "The Reign of King Cotton," in *Atlantic Monthly*, VII (1861), 451-65.

Many Republicans opposed the spread of slavery for humane reasons. Others, equally opposed to the institution, were impelled by less worthy motives. "Let them keep their niggers if they will," wrote one Illinois Republican, "but they must not bring them in contact with us." Admitting that many in his state had a "hatred of niggers," he said that all Illinoisans were "terably" opposed to the extension of slavery. Others seemed reluctant to compromise on the territorial question for fear that "the party will go to smash."[12] This mood was probably not that of the majority, for compromise was in the American political tradition. Every great issue from the creation of the Constitution, itself a compromise, had been settled by compromise: the nature of the Union, as disputed in the Kentucky and Virginia resolutions and in the Hartford convention; the tariff; disposal of public lands; internal improvements—all of these issues had followed a regular pattern of proposal, resistance, and compromise. Compromise had settled the Missouri question in 1819-1820, the nullification controversy in 1833, and the great issues following the Mexican War a decade before the secession crisis.

Furthermore, as conciliators were quick to note, the election of 1860 had demonstrated great popular support for compromise. By unanimous vote in ten states, by overwhelming majority in five more, and by powerful minorities in the remainder, Lincoln had been rejected by the people. Besides, in the view of those who sought conciliation, even the pro-Lincoln vote did not mean support of war. It was one thing that a plurality of the people in some states and a majority in some others had chosen the Chicago platform over either popular sovereignty or congressional protection as a settlement of the slavery question. But their votes had been cast when the country was at peace and when rumblings of possible secession, if heard at all, seemed remote, indeed, to northern people. Whether or not that northern plurality would choose that same platform if it meant breaking up the Union and precipitating war was an entirely different question. Save for a relatively small number of all-out secessionists, it could be assumed that the 60 percent of the people who voted against Lincoln were for compromise. Likewise it is certain that many of the 40 percent who voted for him also favored it. It is, therefore, a safe assumption that "an overwhelming majority of both

12 V. Armour to E. B. Washburne, Dec. 21, 1860, Alexander Stewart to Washburne, Feb. 9, 1861, in Washburne Papers.

the Northern and the Southern people preferred compromise to either a dissolution of the Union or Civil War."[13]

The country was thus prepared for reconciliation, and with the convening of Congress, all eyes turned to Crittenden to work out the details of compromise. Long before Congress met, rumors had him filling many roles. A few days after the election, Republican papers were predicting that Lincoln would offer him the State Department. It was also rumored that he had rushed to South Carolina to plead for delay there. Another report, with considerably more substance, had southern leaders preparing for him a statement of their minimum demands so that he might discuss these demands with northern leaders.[14]

Crittenden was working quietly all the while, attempting to keep himself unidentified with any sectional or partisan faction. "The best services of your best day will be needed as a pacificator," an old friend wrote him at this time. "Preserve yourself for that." Dozens of compromise proposals were submitted to him, and his advice was sought by correspondents as far apart geographically and politically as Robert Winthrop, Martin Van Buren, Governor Thomas H. Hicks of Maryland, and a member of the Mississippi secessionist convention. Some suggested dividing the Union into two equal parts, some suggested improvements in the fugitive-slave law, one proposed emancipation of all slaves in thirty years, another the holding of a plebiscite on an undisclosed compromise. All said that they relied on him to save the country.[15]

During the first two weeks of the session Crittenden spoke only twice, both times briefly. When Buchanan's message was read, Thomas Clingman, North Carolina fire-eater, made an inflammatory speech justifying secession on the grounds of Lincoln's election. Crittenden took the floor to refute him, calling on all senators to re-

---

[13] Frank Klingberg, "James Buchanan and the Crisis of the Union," in *Journal of Southern History*, IX (1943), 470-71; Dumond, *Secession Movement*, 165; Scrugham, *Peaceable Americans*, 69.

[14] St. Louis *Missouri Republican*, Nov. 11, 1860, quoted in William E. Baringer, *A House Dividing: Lincoln as President Elect* (Springfield, Ill., 1945), 53-54; New York *Herald*, Nov. 2, Dec. 3, 4, New York *Times*, Dec. 6, New York *Tribune*, Dec. 8, 10, 1860, quoted in Potter, *Lincoln and His Party*, 101-104, 148.

[15] S. S. Nicholas to Crittenden, Dec. 21 [1860], in Crittenden Papers (Duke). See also letters in Crittenden Papers, Volume 23, especially from Martin Van Buren, F. M. Aldridge, Thomas H. Hicks, John A. Campbell, Daniel Lord, Jeremiah Clemens, Robert Winthrop, Archibald Dixon, Garret Davis, Charles A. Davis, James D. Ogden.

strain their passions during the period ahead, which everyone recognized would be a trying one. At the same time he disagreed with Buchanan's statement that the federal government had no power to coerce a seceding state. "To say that no State has a right to secede, and that it is a wrong to the Union, and yet that the Union has no right to interpose any obstacles to its secession," he said, "seems to me to be altogether contradictory." Privately he wrote that Buchanan's message constituted "a base surrender of the Union."[16]

Two days later Lazarus Powell, Crittenden's newly chosen colleague from Kentucky, moved the appointment of a special committee of thirteen to consider that part of the President's message relating to the sectional issues. The motion instructed the committee to report whether additional legislation or constitutional amendments were needed to ensure protection of property and rights of citizens and equality among the states.

The resolution met with Republican opposition, for the party shrank from admitting publicly that it had no program to meet the crisis. Two weeks were spent debating Powell's resolution, with delay as the objective. As the debate generated heat, Crittenden made a second brief speech, urging that the resolution be speedily adopted. He again spoke of the need for calmness and restraint, pointing out that it was important to avoid debates on substantive matters at this time. Despite Crittenden's plea for moderation, Wigfall of Texas made an incendiary speech on December 13, praising South Carolina for making preparations to secede. A few days later Ben Wade of Ohio responded, in a harsh and vindictive speech. He sneered at the petty insignificance of South Carolina, denied the right of secession, and predicted that Lincoln would use force against seceding states and that secessionists would eventually meet the fate of traitors. He renounced all talk of compromise as humiliating to Republicans.[17]

Meanwhile, Crittenden had been carefully formulating what he hoped might be a final settlement of the slavery issue. All compromises on the question since 1787 had been mere legislative acts, subject to alteration by later congressional action. Thus the Missouri Compromise had been repealed by the Kansas-Nebraska Act, which sabotaged the peace so dearly won in 1850. Compromise agreements

[16] *Congressional Globe*, 36 Cong., 2 Sess., 5; Crittenden to Orlando Brown, Dec. 6, 1860, in Brown Papers, Filson Club.
[17] *Congressional Globe*, 36 Cong., 2 Sess., 19, 24, 32, 47-59, 71-76, 85-87, 99-104.

reached this time must be more permanent; they must be embodied in amendments to the Constitution itself. In preparing his plan, Crittenden consulted with friends from all sections. It was certain now that South Carolina would secede, but he hoped, as he had written Orlando Brown, that conciliatory measures might dissuade other states "from following her bad example."[18]

On Wednesday, December 18, Crittenden arose in the Senate to present his proposals for compromise. They consisted of a series of unamendable amendments to the Constitution:

1. Restore the Missouri Compromise line (36° 30′) and extend it to California. Slavery, during the territorial stage, would be recognized south and prohibited north of the line. When states were created from the territories, they could come in as free or slave as they chose.
2. Prohibit Congress from abolishing slavery on government property in slave states.
3. Prohibit Congress from abolishing slavery in the District of Columbia so long as it existed in Maryland or Virginia. Even then it could not be done without consent of inhabitants or without compensation.
4. Prohibit Congress from interfering with the interstate transportation of slaves.
5. Compensate claimants of fugitive slaves rescued by mobs.
6. Prohibit future constitutional amendments that would (a) reduce the additional representation allowed states for three-fifths of their slaves, (b) alter the fugitive-slave requirement of the Constitution, or (c) give Congress power to interfere with slavery in the states.

The plan also called for a series of congressional resolutions:

1. The present fugitive-slave law was constitutional, should not be repealed, and ought to be enforced.
2. State laws conflicting with the act were null and void and ought to be repealed by the states.
3. Congress should amend the fugitive-slave law so as to delete certain clauses obnoxious to northern citizens.

[18] Crittenden to Orlando Brown, Dec. 6, 1860, in Brown Papers, Filson Club. See also Garret Davis to Crittenden, Dec. 10, 1860, in Crittenden Papers; Madison C. Johnson to Mrs. Coleman, July 17, 1867, in Crittenden Papers (Duke); Crittenden to Larz Anderson, March 29, 1861, in Frankfort *Commonwealth*, April 5, 1861.

4. Congress should strengthen and enforce laws prohibiting the foreign slave trade.

Crittenden explained that in preparing his proposals, he had looked impartially from section to section in order to seek out the causes of discontent as well as the means to remedy them. He did not regard his proposals as definitive, but he hoped that with amendments they might be made acceptable to the country. The question, he said, was not partisan; it was a question of the very life of the republic, "the life of this great people." He realized that northern men would find it difficult to sanction the legality of slavery south of the 36° 30′ line. Yet this was a mere trifle if it would prevent the breakup of the Union. The overthrow of the Union would be "the greatest shock that civilization and free government have received," more momentous in its consequences and "more fatal to mankind" even than the French Revolution.

What if the southern states should reject this line, he asked Republicans, and should peaceably separate and then ask for a fair division of the territories? Could the northern states offer less than he proposed, and could not southerners then take their slaves into their portion of the divided territories? Should the North refuse a fair division, there would be a struggle for possession, and war would result. Much better, he said, to settle the question amicably on the Missouri line. For thirty years, he reminded them, the country had lived peacefully under the Missouri Compromise. Its repeal had inspired the formation of the Republican party, whose chief aim at its founding was the restoration of the line. Separation and a divided country within six months would follow unless this proposal or an amended form of it, was accepted. Compromise would be the "cheapest price at which such a blessing as this Union was ever purchased."

Crittenden reviewed the progress of the free-soil movement in the territories. At the end of the Revolution, he said, the southern states had owned 600,000 square miles of western lands, and northern states only 164,000. Then Virginia ceded the Northwest Territory to the federal government, which soon excluded slavery there, and the free region then had 425,000 square miles, whereas the South had only 385,000 square miles. Subsequent acquisitions had increased the disparity, so that the North had now 2,200,000 square miles, whereas the South had less than 1,000,000 square miles of territory. Division along the Missouri line, he said, would still leave the North with three times as much territory as would go to the South.

Crittenden avoided any discussion of the right or wrong of the controversy, except to observe that "Right and wrong, in this world, and in all such controversies, are mingled together." He urged the sacrifice of party views in the interest of preserving the Union. Party in such a crisis "ceases to deserve consideration," because the preservation of the Union "demands our highest and our greatest exertions." He would gladly give up any opinions he held if by so doing he could save the Union. He asked Republicans to do no more. Come, he pleaded to his northern colleagues, accept this proposal, and "we shall go on again in our great career of national prosperity and national glory."[19]

Throughout his speech there was not a sound in the chamber other than his calm, resonant voice. All seemed fearful of missing even one syllable that fell from the lips of the aged statesman now beginning the climactic effort of his career. All knew that he would retire from public life at the end of the session and that this was likely the last issue on which he would be heard. Five times the Kentucky legislature had chosen him to full Senate terms, and he had also served for the remnant of a term when Clay had resigned during Tyler's administration. Only William R. King of Alabama had been as many times elected to the Senate. Crittenden's career had been characterized by moderation and fair dealing, and he was on good terms with all groups, from southern extremists to radical Republicans. A young Democratic congressman who crowded into the chamber thought Crittenden spoke on this occasion "as if the muse of history were listening to him."[20] James G. Blaine, who was also present, said no member of the opposition would be listened to with as much respect and sympathy by Republicans. He praised the venerable Kentuckian's purity of motive, his disinterestedness, and his patriotism. "Everybody," he said, "accords to him that." Blaine himself could support at least some of the proposals.[21]

19 *Congressional Globe*, 36 Cong., 2 Sess., 112-14; Greeley, *American Conflict*, I, 376; S. S. Cox, *Three Decades of Federal Legislation* (Providence, R. I., 1888), 67.
20 Cox, *Three Decades*, 67.
21 Blaine, *Twenty Years of Congress*, I, 330-31; *Congressional Globe*, 36 Cong., 2 Sess., 115-16.

Crittenden's speech came at a time when Republican ranks were breaking on the issue of conciliation. New York Republicans, Buchanan was reliably informed, were preparing to "cut loose entirely from Greeley and the abolitionists." James Dixon of Connecticut as well as Rhode Islanders Henry B. Anthony and James F. Simmons had already made conciliatory speeches. In the House, John Sherman had made the ingenious proposal that all the western territory be admitted forthwith as a single state and on a basis of popular sovereignty, with provision for later subdivision into numerous states. The House had created a committee of one member from each state to consider proposals for adjustment, the Committee of Thirty-three. That committee was controlled by Republicans, but Lincoln's close personal friend, William B. Kellogg of Illinois, spoke there, promising concessions. Charles Francis Adams, also a member of the committee, was convinced that Crittenden and other moderate old Whigs in the border states would be repudiated by their constituents unless the North manifested a spirit of concession and compromise. And if the moderates were repudiated, secession in the Upper South and in the border states would follow. In the committee and later in the House, Adams urged modification of the personal-liberty laws, constitutional prohibition of congressional interference with slavery in the states, and admission of New Mexico as a slave state. On December 13 the committee endorsed in principle certain of these mollifying constitutional remedies. Indeed, when, following Crittenden's speech on the eighteenth the Senate approved Powell's resolution calling for a special committee, radical Republicans seemed in retreat on all fronts and conciliation seemed triumphant.

Two days later, at almost the same hour South Carolina was passing her ordinance of secession, Vice President Breckinridge appointed the Committee of Thirteen. There were four southern Democrats, three northern Democrats, five Republicans, and Crittenden, who now had no party. Toombs and Davis represented the Deep South; R. M. T. Hunter of Virginia, Powell, and Crittenden, the Upper South. Northern Democrats were represented by Douglas, Bigler, and Henry M. Rice of Minnesota; Republicans had Seward, Wade, Collamer of Vermont, James R. Doolittle of Wisconsin, and James W. Grimes of Iowa. It was a strong committee. Crittenden, Douglas and Seward had the greatest stature, but the others were not undistinguished. No legislative body, in the opinion of Buchanan, here or elsewhere, had ever created a committee of such fateful significance, for upon its success or failure rested the preservation of the Union.

Much was expected of the moderate, scholarly Hunter in efforts to stay the impending revolution. Some help was hoped for from the talented Toombs, too, who was far more amenable to reason than his rough exterior and boisterous behavior indicated. He was a large man—six feet tall, broad-shouldered and firmly proportioned—and his expressive face, dark eyes, and commanding bearing reminded at least one of his contemporaries of Mirabeau. Toombs' great ability had never been truly appreciated in the House, just as it was somewhat discounted now in the Senate. He was haughty, imperious, overbearing, and impatient of contradiction. He was a man to reckon with in any intellectual contest, and he certainly was not lacking in courage.[22]

The committee held its first meeting on Saturday, December 22. The tide of sentiment favoring conciliation was now swelling in influential Republican ranks outside of Congress. As has been seen, Thurlow Weed had already urged acceptance of the line of 36° 30', the most important part of Crittenden's proposal. Now, with Seward's approval, Weed renewed this proposal in his Albany *Evening Journal*, and it was endorsed by two other powerful and influential Republican papers, the New York *Times* and the New York *Courier and Enquirer*. On the Tuesday night preceding the committee's first meeting, a group of thirty influential New Yorkers of all parties, including such men as August Belmont, William B. Astor, William H. Aspinwall, Moses H. Grinnell, and Hamilton Fish, met in New York and unanimously urged conciliation by the North. More important than all, Seward, the Republican spokesman, was known to favor Crittenden's proposal. He had told James Barbour, Virginia Unionist, that nothing short of Crittenden's plan would calm the South and that he would support it. On December 20 a New York Democrat reported to Buchanan that Seward had told him the Republicans were willing for the sake of peace "to have the territorial question settled by the Missouri Compromise

[22] Donald, *Sumner*, 373-74; Potter, *Lincoln and His Party*, 129-30; Cox, *Three Decades*, 70; Hilliard, *Politics and Pen Pictures*, 131; "Recollections of an Old Stager," XLVIII (1873-1874), 254; Buchanan, *Works*, XII, 117; Klein, *Buchanan*, 384.

Bill running it to the Pacific."[23] Furthermore, Lincoln had offered Seward the State Department, and Seward was in New York awaiting the return of Weed, who had gone to Springfield to win Lincoln's support for Crittenden's plan.[24]

But the long shadow of the President-elect would cast a gloom over the meeting of the committee. What was not commonly known even by Republicans of moderate views, such as John Sherman and Charles Francis Adams, and what certainly Seward and Weed did not know, was that Lincoln had already taken an inflexible position against the heart of the Crittenden plan, restoration of the Missouri line. Moreover, he had already informed trusted lieutenants in Washington of his sentiments, and they had passed the word to their colleagues after Seward had left for his rendezvous with Weed. "Let there be no compromise on the question of *extending* slavery," Lincoln wrote Trumbull on December 10. "If there be," he continued, "all our labor is lost, and, ere long, must be done again. . . . Have none of it. Stand firm. The tug has to come, & better now, than any time hereafter." The following day he wrote almost the identical message to Kellogg. "Entertain no proposition for a compromise in regard to the extension of *slavery*. The instant you do, they have us under again; all our labor is lost, and sooner or later must be done over." Two days later he wrote Washburne: "Prevent, as far as possible, any of our friends from demoralizing themselves, and our cause, by entertaining propositions for compromise of any sort, on 'slavery extention.' There is no possible compromise upon it. . . . Whether it be the M[iss]o[uri] line, or Eli Thayer's Pop[ular] Sov[ereignty] it is all the same. . . . [H]old firm as with a chain of steel."[25]

When the committee met, therefore, the eight non-Republicans were surprised at the rigidly irreconcilable position taken by their Republican colleagues. Seward, of course, was absent in New York, receiving Weed's report on his mission to Springfield. But Wade, Grimes, Doolittle, and Collamer, offering no proposal of their own,

[23] James Ford Rhodes, *History of the United States from the Compromise of 1850*, 7 vols., III (New York, 1895), 27, 32, 43-44 and n; Burton J. Hendrick, *Lincoln's War Cabinet* (Boston, 1946), 132-33; Potter, *Lincoln and His Party*, 78-87 *passim*, 183-84; Klein, *Buchanan*, 384.
[24] Rhodes, *History of the United States*, III, 45-46; Potter, *Lincoln and His Party*, 162-66; Klein, *Buchanan*, 384.
[25] Lincoln to Trumbull, Dec. 10, to Kellogg, Dec. 11, to Washburne, Dec. 13, 1860, in Lincoln, *Works*, IV, 149-51.

voted uniformly against all propositions made by the others. Crittenden's was only one of seven plans presented to the committee, but all were voted down, most of them getting little support. None but Crittenden's later received serious consideration in deliberations of the Senate.

As a practical matter, the committee had agreed at the outset that unless a majority of Republicans as well as a majority of Democrats on the committee agreed to any proposal, it should be considered rejected. In other words, three Republicans or four Democrats could negate any proposal even though all other members of the committee approved. The numerous parts of Crittenden's proposal were voted on separately. No part got fewer than six votes; most got eight. Toombs and Davis had stated that they would accept Crittenden's plan if the Republicans would, but the four Republicans voted against most parts, including the main one, restoration of the Missouri line. Davis and Toombs thereupon also voted against it. Toombs at the time stated that although he himself was not satisfied with the proposal, he knew his state would be, and he would therefore vote for it provided the Republicans would. Davis professed his entire satisfaction with the proposal.[26]

Crittenden had been confident that his plan would receive sympathetic Republican consideration. When Republican members of the committee refused to support him, therefore, he was in despair. The Republicans "refuse to lower their . . . party standard a single hair's breadth, and present their Chicago platform as their ultimatum," he told a group of friends. They seemed convinced, he wrote, that the South was only bluffing and that their best policy was "to stand firm & *do nothing*."[27]

Seward returned to Washington and to the committee deliberations on Christmas Eve. An ordinary man might have felt some embarrassment at the part he now had to play, but not this wily and devious protege of Thurlow Weed. Weed had found Lincoln entirely unreceptive to the Crittenden territorial proposal, and Seward was faced with the alternative of declining the State Department and embracing the compromise plan, or of rejecting the compromise

[26] *Senate Reports*, 36 Cong., 2 Sess., No. 288 (hereinafter, *Journal of the Committee of Thirteen*), 2-18; *Congressional Globe*, 36 Cong., 2 Sess., 270, 1390, Appendix, 41; Cox, *Three Decades*, 77-78, 114-15.

[27] Crittenden to S. S. Nicholas, Dec. [22], 1860 (copy), in Crittenden Papers; letter of L. A. W., in Louisville *Journal*, Dec. 28, 1860.

and accepting the first position in the cabinet of the new President. He chose the latter.

His attitude was friendly and conciliatory, however. On the preceding Saturday night, en route to Washington, he had stopped off in New York and addressed the gentlemen of the New England Society, dining at the Astor House. He assured them jauntily that there would be no trouble. Secession he dismissed as humbug. Kind treatment and cool tempers North, he said, would bring an end to it. Now, before the committee, he was equally conciliatory, but firm. Republicans could not, he said, accept the principle of slavery expansion implied in Crittenden's first resolution. They would not reject all of his proposals, however. Specifically he proposed resolutions guaranteeing slavery in the states where it existed, seeking repeal of the personal liberty laws, and modification of the Fugitive Slave Act.[28] These proposals were insufficient to satisfy Toombs and Davis and were voted down. The committee continued to meet through the week of December 24, but without success. On the last day of the dying year it reported to the Senate its inability to agree on any plan of adjustment.[29]

The failure of the Crittenden proposals in the Committee of Thirteen must be charged to its Republican members. Had Seward asked, when he returned to Washington on December 24, for a reconsideration of the vote on Crittenden's proposals, it is highly probable that Collamer and Doolittle would have joined him in voting for them. If so, the proposals would have passed the committee with at least eleven votes. Reported to the Senate by such a majority, they would have been brought to a speedy vote and approval there, probably by a constitutional majority. The House then, with all the pressures of the incoming administration, would probably have been compelled to follow suit.

It is conceded by some contemporary historians as well as by most modern scholars that this would have put a stop to secession. "No fact is clearer," wrote James Ford Rhodes, "than that the Republicans in December defeated the Crittenden Compromise; few historic probabilities have better evidence to support them," he added, "than the one which asserts that the adoption of this measure

[28] Rhodes, *History of the United States*, III, 49-50; *Journal of the Committee of Thirteen*, 10, 12; Potter, *Lincoln and His Party*, 167-68, 242-43.
[29] *Congressional Globe*, 36 Cong., 2 Sess., 211; *Journal of the Committee of Thirteen*, 10-14.

would have prevented the secession of the cotton States, other than South Carolina, and the beginning of the Civil War in 1861."[30] Even had Seward not been able to persuade two Republican colleagues on the committee to join him in support of Crittenden's proposals, it would not have been fatal to the plan. For, as we shall see, his influence in subsequent Senate deliberations would have been sufficient to order a national plebiscite on Crittenden's proposals that might well have stayed the bitter strife that followed their rejection.

The refusal of Republicans to accept division of the territories into slave and free-soil sections seems, even in light of the knowledge they possessed, as shortsighted and unstatesmanlike as was the conduct of southern extremists in urging secession because of the refusal. It had long been conceded by all knowing men, North as well as South, that slavery would never prosper there. Popular sovereignty, for all the Republican denunciation of it, actually was working to exclude slavery in the territories as effectively as congressional prohibition could. But Republicans had taken their position on the question long before, some of them decades before, at a time when the eventual triumph of the free-soil element had not yet been demonstrated as it had been everywhere by 1860. The party had been formed to prevent the spread of slavery into the territories at a time when that prospect seemed an imminent probability in Kansas. To concede now that the danger no longer existed for which they had organized would be an admission that popular sovereignty had already achieved the end for which they had waged their battle. In the absence of any program as a substitute, such an admission might result in dissolution of the party.

It needs to be emphasized, also, that the terms the South was willing to accept were actually a restriction of the lawful limits of slavery. For the Supreme Court had ruled in 1857, in the Dred Scott case, that Congress could put no restriction on slavery in any of the territories. Within two months the Republicans would demonstrate the hollowness of their own cries of alarm. Before the inauguration of Lincoln, the Republican-controlled Congress passed bills for territorial governments in Colorado, Nevada, and Dakota, containing no prohibition of slavery. Even such a stouthearted Re-

[30] Rhodes, *History of the United States*, III, 41-42; Richard N. Current, *The Lincoln Nobody Knows* (New York, 1958), 94.

publican as James G. Blaine commented in afteryears on this strange anomaly—Republicans disregarding their very *raison d'être* with never a word of protest. Washburne, Thaddeus Stevens, Owen Lovejoy, Wade, Sumner—all of them were thundering at that very moment that Crittenden's proposal was a betrayal of the principles on which the country was founded, but none raised his voice against the omission of an antislavery provision in these bills. Daniel Sickles in the House called attention to the omission. He asked that the Colorado bill be read again before a vote was taken, not believing he properly understood it. When it was read, he pointed out that the Wilmot principle of the Republicans had been abandoned. No Republican offered an explanation.[31]

Even Seward admitted, after passage of these bills, that the territorial question was settled and that it had "ceased to be a practical question." Douglas, too, though not vindictively, could not refrain from pointing out to his Republican colleagues that they had abandoned in these bills the position of their President-elect, who claimed to have voted for the Wilmot Proviso forty-two times in his one congressional term. "The whole doctrine for which the Republican party contended as to the Territories is abandoned," said Douglas. "Non-interference is substituted in its place." He rightly maintained that this was the very principle enunciated in his Kansas-Nebraska bill, and Blaine conceded that this was so. Douglas called the territorial bills the "apotheosis of Popular Sovereignty."[32]

In the light of all this, the refusal of the five Republican senators on the Committee of Thirteen to concede the heart of Crittenden's propositions calls for closer scrutiny. Three of them were radicals, Wade, Grimes, and Doolittle, the latter a less vindictive one than the other two. But Seward and Collamer were not. As we have seen, Seward's position, and in turn Collamer's also, was determined by Lincoln, and it now becomes necessary to try to analyze Lincoln's reason for assuming such an inflexible position.

The stature that Lincoln would gain in the ensuing four years has created a legend about him that all but obscures the fact that at the time of his election, and for some months thereafter, he was a plain country lawyer with a narrowly limited background. He would

---

[31] *Congressional Globe*, 36 Cong., 2 Sess., 729, 1003, 1005, 1207-208, 1334-35, Appendix, 326-28, 337-38, 346-48; Blaine, *Twenty Years of Congress*, I, 269-70.
[32] *Congressional Globe*, 36 Cong., 2 Sess., 1391, 1460; Blaine, *Twenty Years of Congress*, I, 270; Seward, *Autobiography*, II, 499.

soon prove that he had great undeveloped capacities for leadership and for sensing the feelings of the great masses of the people. In the winter of 1860-1861, however, he was being led by, rather than leading, his party. He was not regarded by most of his contemporaries as more than what he seemed to be. Orville Browning, perhaps his closest friend, never regarded him as a great man, and thought Edward Bates much abler. Jeremiah Black, Buchanan's stout Secretary of State, thought him "very small potatoes and few in a hill."[33] Charles Francis Adams thought that Lincoln, by refusing to agree to Seward's desire for compromise, was "ruining everything" and was making Seward's position unbearable.[34] Seward, however, acceded for the time to his chief's strong sentiments regarding the territories, hoping until the very last moment that in the end he would be able to control the man who had been chosen over him and bring the ship of state safely to shore.[35]

In the ominous public silence that Lincoln maintained from his nomination until his inaugural, he revealed somewhat his failure to understand the temper of the southern people. He apparently thought that the average southerner could distinguish between Lincoln's own philosophy on the slavery question and that of abolitionists like William Lloyd Garrison. When asked to publicize his views, he refused, repeatedly. He also seemed to think that secession was largely talk on the part of a few hotheads, and would be easily put down by an overwhelming Unionist sentiment in the South. The Upper South he believed so steadfast that there was patently no danger of secession there. If there were, the border states would smother the sentiment.[36] Meantime, he would hold his counsel until March 4, and then in a conciliatory message, he would give such assurances that all fear of him and his party would dissipate. Only twice between his election and his inaugural did he permit himself the luxury of a public statement on the troubled condition of the country, both times by proxy. On the first of these occasions he wrote an insertion for a speech Trumbull delivered in Springfield,

[33] Theodore C. Pease and James G. Randall (eds.), *The Diary of Orville Hickman Browning*, 2 vols., (Springfield, Ill., 1925), I, 601; Randall, *Lincoln the President*, I, 160; Black to Charles R. Bucklaw, Jan. 28, 1861 (typescript copy), in Black Papers.
[34] Stampp, *And the War Came*, 196-97.
[35] Randall, *Lincoln the President*, I, 160.
[36] Baringer, *A House Dividing*, 214-15; Potter, *Lincoln and His Party*, 140; Stampp, *And the War Came*, 179-203.

expressing pleasure over the military preparations that were underway in southern states. These would offer, he said, means for Unionists there more easily to suppress secession.[37]

It was on December 20 that Weed had made his vain attempt to persuade Lincoln to recede on the territorial question, and on that very day South Carolina passed her ordinance of secession. When news of it reached Lincoln, he dismissed it as "loud threats and much muttering." A week later Duff Green arrived in Springfield as Buchanan's envoy, on a mission similar to Weed's. Green carried a copy of Crittenden's resolutions, and he and Lincoln discussed them for several hours. According to Green, Lincoln acknowledged that adoption of the Missouri line would calm southerners for a time, but soon they would renew the agitation by attempts to annex Mexico. Lincoln gave Green to understand that although he and his party were committed to resisting the expansion of slavery into the territories, he would both acquiesce in and "give full force and effect" to any decision by the people to adopt Crittenden's proposal as an amendment to the Constitution. He promised to write Green a letter the next day referring Crittenden's proposals "to the action of the people in the several states."[38] Lincoln did write a letter addressed to Green, but he sent it to Trumbull in Washington to deliver to Green, if Trumbull and "our discreet friends" thought it would do no harm.

Apparently Trumbull and the friends did not approve of the letter, for they never delivered it to Green. Green thereupon gave a statement to the New York *Herald*, repeating what he understood Lincoln's position to be. The publication of this created consternation among radical Republicans in Washington, and Kellogg was dispatched to Springfield to confer with the President-elect. Then, on January 28, Kellogg published in the *Herald* a qualified retraction of Green's report. Kellogg was authorized to say that Lincoln would "suffer death" rather than enter into a bargain that would have the appearance of "buying the privilege of taking possession" of the government. This was the second and last of Lincoln's statements prior to his inaugural.[39]

[37] Potter, *Lincoln and His Party*, 140.

[38] Green to Buchanan, Dec. 28, 1860, in Buchanan, *Works*, XII, 119n; Klein, *Buchanan*, 385.

[39] Lincoln, *Works*, IV, 175-76, 183; Rhodes, *History of the United States*, III, 67; New York *Herald*, Jan. 8, 1861, quoted in Baringer, *A House Dividing*, 210-11.

ELIZABETH CRITTENDEN
CRITTENDEN'S THIRD WIFE

JOHN J. CRITTENDEN
IN HIS EARLY SEVENTIES

Portrait of Mrs. Crittenden from "A Belle of the Fifties," by Mrs. Virginia Clay-Clopton; engraving of Crittenden owned by the author

Lincoln had other visitors in Springfield. An unidentified Kentuckian, possibly Robert J. Breckinridge, went there in early December to suggest that Lincoln place three southern Unionists in his cabinet. Lincoln amazed his visitor by replying that he would appoint neither an "enemy" nor anyone who had voted against him. The Kentuckian argued for two hours, with Lincoln silent for the most part. At the end he thanked his visitor "for your counsel," but the latter was unhappy. His report of the interview caused Kentucky Unionist George Robertson to fear that if Lincoln's position should become known, southern fears of a "subterranean design to wage an exterminating crusade" against their section would be confirmed, and they would speedily secede.[40]

Orville Browning, too, visited Lincoln at this time and found him firmer on the territorial question than he expected. According to Browning, Lincoln thought "no concession by the free states short of a surrender of everything worth preserving, and contending for would satisfy the South, and that Crittenden's proposed amendment . . . ought not to be made."[41] Herndon, too, although frequently an unreliable witness, stated that Lincoln that winter said he "apprehended no such grave danger to the Union as the mass of people supposed would result from the Southern threats," and that he "could not in his heart believe that the South designed the overthrow of the government." Another Lincoln intimate, Ward Lamon, said Lincoln hoped for a peaceful reconstruction "even after the formation of the Southern Confederacy." Lincoln himself, in his journey east to his inaugural, demonstrated in speech after speech his belief that the secession movement was artificial and of little consequence.[42]

Testimony of other contemporaries supports the belief that Lincoln was hopelessly confused and misinformed about political conditions in the South at this time. Horace Greeley wrote a few years later: "Mr. Lincoln entered Washington the victim of a grave delusion. . . . [H]e fully believed that there would be no civil war—no serious effort to consummate the Union. . . . [H]e did not cherish a doubt that his Inaugural Address . . . would, when read throughout the South, dissolve the Confederacy as frost is dissipated by a vernal sun." No less convincing are the words of Charles Francis Adams,

---

[40] George Robertson to Crittenden, Dec. 16, 1860, in Coleman, *Crittenden*, II, 222-23.
[41] Pease and Randall, *Browning Diary*, I, 453.
[42] Potter, *Lincoln and His Party*, 247, 316-17.

Jr. "As to the tremendous crisis which then confronted the country and himself individually,—the catastrophe immediately impending—if at that time Mr. Lincoln realized the situation he certainly . . . gave no indication of the fact." Almost all recent scholarship agrees with these conclusions.[43]

Believing that secession was only gasconade, Lincoln saw no purpose in stirring up the radicals in his own party by making unnecessary concessions. Many of these radicals, like Lincoln, thought secession a bluff. But many influential Republicans who thought it might result in war were unconcerned if it should. Herndon, returning from a tour of central Illinois, reported that the sentiment everywhere was for a firm stand on the platform regardless of consequences, and Trumbull's correspondence confirms this. It was "the very life blood—the corner stone of the party," wrote one constituent. If the party should surrender on the territorial question, "We are gone hook & line." Another wrote that surrender of the principle of the Chicago platform "would be the annihilation of the party." To yield one new guaranty to the South, wrote another Republican, would "destroy the Republican party."

Equally unconcerned as to consequences was Senator Zachariah Chandler of Michigan. "Without a little blood-letting," he wrote Governor Austin Blair, "this Union will not . . . be worth a rush." And Governor Oliver Morton of Indiana, in a November speech urging coercion of South Carolina, said, "If it was worth a bloody struggle to establish this Nation, it is worth one to preserve it." These were powerful men in Republican circles, and Lincoln was not entirely impervious to their influence.[44]

Lincoln expressed the fear to Duff Green that restoration of the Missouri line would lead to southern demands for territorial acquisition to the South, in Mexico, in the Caribbean, and in Central

[43] Greeley, *Recollections of a Busy Life*, 404; Charles F. Adams, Jr., "Lincoln's First Inauguration," in *Proceedings of the Massachusetts Historical Society*, XLII (1884), 151-52; Potter, *Lincoln and His Party*, 140-42, 245, 314, 316-17; Current, *Lincoln Nobody Knows*, 77, 84-86, 94; Nichols, *Disruption of American Democracy*, 456; Hendrick, *Lincoln's War Cabinet*, 135, 137; Baringer, *A House Dividing*, 214-15; Randall, *Lincoln the President*, I, 231; Stampp, *And the War Came*, 179-203.

[44] Letters to Trumbull, December, 1860—January, 1861, especially from Wait Talcott, Dec. 16, from John R. Woods, Dec. 20, and from W. H. Herndon, Dec. 21, in Trumbull Papers, Library of Congress; V. Armour to E. B. Washburne, Dec. 21, 1860, in Washburne Papers; *Congressional Globe*, 36 Cong., 2 Sess., 1247; Kenneth Stampp, "Letters from the Washington Peace Conference, of 1861," in *Journal of Southern History*, IX (1943), 395n.; Randall, *Lincoln the President*, I, 231-34.

America. Crittenden's original proposal implied that any future acquisitions either south or north would be subject to terms of the division, and he subsequently accepted an amendment by Powell that made this explicit. Lincoln's fears on this score were not altogether imaginary. For years southern expansionists had dreamed of annexing additional territory in Mexico, as well as the island of Cuba. Filibustering expeditions in the past decade had not been uncommon occurrences, and just the year before, as we have seen, southern members of Congress had backed a bill to put $30,000,000 into Buchanan's hands to negotiate the acquisition of Cuba.

But sober reflection should have given Lincoln some reassurance on this point. Filibustering had been put down by both Whig and Democratic administrations; and if Cuban or Mexican territory could not be acquired under Pierce or Buchanan, there was little likelihood that it could be under a Republican President. Besides, as we shall see, Lincoln and the Republicans would not recede from their position even when Crittenden offered to add to his proposals a provision making future acquisitions of territory impossible without the express approval of northern members of Congress.

Thus it was that Crittenden's proposals were put to death in the Senate Committee of Thirteen in late December. Directly, their failure was due to the opposition of the five Republican members of the committee. Indirectly, the responsibility for their rejection was Lincoln's, who exerted from Springfield the vast influence that was his as President-elect.

South Carolina, as already noted, had seceded two days before the Committee of Thirteen's first meeting, and conventions already had been called in five other gulf states. When the Committee of Thirteen was created and Crittenden's proposals were given an enthusiastic popular reception, the prospect of adjustment brightened and it was expected that further secession would not take place. The volatile Robert Toombs, by now an ardent secessionist himself, was sure that Georgia would not secede if Crittenden's proposals were adopted in the committee. When they failed, however, Toombs wired an address to the people of Georgia. He told of the rejection of Crittenden's proposals and of the refusal of the Republicans to offer any of their own, and he urged immediate secession as the "best guarantee for liberty, security, tranquility, and glory." Similar messages went out to other states from their representatives, and proved effective.[45] "The Republicans are defiant and have resolved to make war on us," wrote a Georgian who up until this time had been a stanch Unionist. They intended, he wrote, to pass a force bill and "subdue us into submission."[46]

As if awaiting these messages, the secessionists went into action. Within three weeks after the committee reported failure, Florida, Mississippi, Alabama, and Georgia had followed South Carolina in passing ordinances of secession. Two more weeks, and Louisiana and Texas would join them, and a convention at Montgomery would give birth to the southern Confederacy. Another two months, and the shot would be fired at Sumter which would precipitate the war.

Meanwhile, Crittenden's efforts at compromise had taken a new and more dramatic turn.

[45] Phillips, *Correspondence of Toombs, Stephens, and Cobb*, 525; Cox, *Three Decades*, 80-81.
[46] J. Henley Smith to Alexander H. Stephens, Dec. 26, 1860, in Stephens Papers.

CHAPTER XIX

Mad Men North and South

NEW YEAR'S, 1861, came to a sorely disturbed and divided nation. "Panic has already risen to a fever heat," wrote young Henry Adams from Washington. It seemed inevitable that before long there would be fighting in the streets. The chorus of disunionists who brazenly predicted that Lincoln would never be inaugurated had grown prodigiously both in number and in volume.[1]

Strangely, Crittenden's spirits now revived, despite darkening clouds of separation. Rejection of his proposals in the committee, he decided, need not be final. He was now convinced that many Republicans in both Senate and House were eager for reconciliation. Heretofore they had found it impossible to resist pressures exerted by the President-elect and by radical leaders because there had been no direct expression from their constituents, urging compromise. If they were assured of grassroots support, however, they could vote their sentiments without fear of reprisal. Thus when a group of conservative Georgians, dismayed over Toombs' fatalistic message, asked Crittenden and Douglas if there was any hope for "the rights of the South in the Union," both answered promptly that there was. "Don't give up the ship," they wired. "Don't despair of the Republic."[2]

Such hopes were not unwarranted. From New York on New Year's Day came reliable reports that Seward would support Crittenden's proposals if they should be brought before the Senate. This had created a "buoyant feeling" in Wall Street, where financiers now feared only that the South might reject northern overtures. The following day a group of New York business and professional men, headed by Peter Cooper, William H. Aspinwall, A. A. Low, Hamilton Fish, and Moses Grinnell, journeyed to Washington to urge Republican leaders to compromise. They gave a dinner at Willard's for the eighty or more Republican congressmen and senators. Arguing that circumstances had changed since adoption of the Chicago platform, the New Yorkers urged their guests to abandon it. Simon Cameron, John Sherman, and several others agreed with them. Meanwhile, Weed in the Albany *Journal*, Henry J. Raymond in the *Times*, and J. Watson Webb in the *Courier and Enquirer* were increasing the tempo of their conciliation crusade.[3]

His proposals having failed of adoption in the Committee of Thirteen, Crittenden now resolved to bring them directly before the Senate. On January 3 he did so, coupling with his original resolutions two proposals offered by Douglas: one prohibited Negro suffrage in the territories; the other made provisions for colonization of free Negroes. Explaining that circumstances made it impossible for constitutional majorities in Congress to adopt the amendments to the Constitution that were "necessary and proper" to save the Union, he now proposed a resolution calling for a national plebiscite on his proposals. The people, he said, ought to be heard from. Their opinion would be the best and surest guide for their representatives to follow. After all, they were the source of the government's power. Although such procedure was unprecedented, he argued, it would not impinge upon the Senate's dignity. He himself had too long shared its honors to propose now to humble it. But preservation of the Union was cause enough to depart from tradi-

[1] Henry Adams, "The Great Secession Winter of 1860-1861," in *Massachusetts Historical Society Papers*, XLIII (1885), 663-64.
[2] Thomas S. Powell to Alexander H. Stephens, Dec. 30, 1860, in Stephens Papers; Phillips, *Correspondence of Toombs, Stephens and Cobb*, 528n.
[3] J. S. Anderson to Alexander H. Stephens, Jan. 2, 1861, in Stephens Papers; Potter, *Lincoln and His Party*, 125-26, 128.

tion. The people would give good advice on how the difficulties should be settled. He looked with full confidence to them, and he would walk proudly upon the road that they pointed out "more surely and more firmly when I am strengthened with their strength, and honored with their advice." As for the sacrifice called for in his compromise plan, it was a trifle, a scruple "of as little value as a barley corn that stands between us and reconciliation." While the Congress sat paralyzed about "that little atom which is to be sacrificed," the nation was being destroyed. "We are spell-bound," he said, "in our party politics, and in opinions which they have generated and fastened . . . upon us against our will."[4]

As Crittenden sat down, Douglas arose in support of the unique proposal. He did not believe Lincoln intended to do anything about slavery in the southern states, he said, but he could well understand that the South feared he would. Republican speakers during the recent election had made much of Lincoln's "House Divided" speech, as well as others which seemed to threaten the very fundamentals of slavery. Besides, Seward's proposal before the Committee of Thirteen of an *unamendable* amendment to the Constitution forbidding Congress from interfering with slavery in the states was a cause for southern uneasiness. Republican unwillingness to give the same assurance for the District of Columbia and the territories created a presumption that they had designs on slavery there. The offering of that one amendment while refusing all others was creating apprehension in the South. He urged Republicans to vote for submission of Crittenden's proposals to the people. To arguments that the people had already voted on the issue in November he replied, as had the recent visitors from New York, that the people had not then been faced with secession and war. Now they were.[5]

Seward, in rebuttal, dismissed the plebiscite proposal as unconstitutional, charging that it was a delegation of Congress' power. But Crittenden's resolution clearly provided that the plebiscite was to be regarded merely as advisory, with Congress to retain freedom of action. To an extreme state-righter, a captive of his own restrictionist philosophy, a plebiscite might appear unconstitutional inasmuch as Congress had not been delegated specific power to call for one. It is surprising, however, that one with the general latitudinarian philos-

[4] *Congressional Globe*, 36 Cong., 2 Sess., 211, 237.
[5] *Congressional Globe*, 36 Cong., 2 Sess., Appendix, 38-42.

ophy that Seward avowed should have raised such a question. In a lengthy speech on January 7 Crittenden answered Seward. He again conceded that his proposal was extraordinary, but insisted that it was necessary and not in violation of the Constitution.

Turning then to a discussion of the merits of his proposals, Crittenden maintained that they would not extend slavery, since slavery already existed in both New Mexico and the Indian Territory, the only territories south of 36° 30'. Recognition of this fact would not compromise Republican principles. Besides, all recognized, he said, that slavery would never survive in that "arid and sterile" region, and it would be a matter of "ten or fifteen years" at the most until it would disappear entirely there. Southerners, he said, knew slavery would not survive in the region, but they were concerned over the principle of the equal rights of the states. The territories had been acquired by conquest in which the South had paid her full share in blood and treasure, and the people of the North had no more right to insist on all the territory than they had to claim that all the money in the Treasury should be used for their benefit. As for slavery in the District of Columbia, that stood "upon a ground that no man can deny," for at the time Maryland and Virginia had ceded that land it was never contemplated that Congress would ever abolish slavery there and it would be bad faith to do so now.

Crittenden conceded that South Carolina had acted rashly, for there was no right of secession. Her conduct had been revolution and "a lawless violation of the Constitution." A constitutional right to destroy the Union would indeed be a strange provision for any government. The Constitution was "a grand and inviolable instrument upon which no man should lay his unhallowed hand." If oppressed beyond endurance, let him take the responsibilities and the consequences of revolution. "Let him defy the war; let him proclaim himself a revolutionist, and not attempt to hide his revolution in the little subtilties [sic] of law."

But Republican denunciation of slavery had given alarm to southerners, and now that they were victors, if they should refuse to give security to the South and, planting themselves sternly on dogmas, say "We will take no step backward," the South could not but fear for their very society. Crittenden was not addressing his Republican colleagues in a vindictive spirit. He appealed to them rather as his countrymen, as statesmen, and as victors in a great political strife. They could now save their country, not by making concessions but by merely granting justice. The trouble was that Republicans, with the aid of the pulpit, had turned a political question into a moral issue. He did not want to speak disrespectfully of the clergy, but he could not help but observe that "the pulpit has become the minister of politicians, and the politicians have ministered to ministers of the Gospel, neither to the benefit nor profit of the Gospel." As a consequence, there had been such a mixing of political and religious questions that people were being taught, "not of political improvidence . . . of slavery," which Crittenden freely acknowledged, but that "it is a great sin." They were wrong to apply such principles to government, for conscience was a good enough guide of conduct for the individual. "You have no right," he said, to "condemn my conscience, and put the penalty upon it of a forfeiture of my political rights, if I continue to act upon it."

It was not enough, he went on, for Republicans to aver that they had no designs upon slavery in the states. He would not attempt to justify slavery, but his fellow Kentuckians believed they had as much right to go into the territories with slaves as "you, who do not choose to hold such property, have to go without them." He implored them to be generous, for it would be "a noble starting point" for the new administration. Would they rather encounter the destruction of the Union and civil war than to "recede one hair's breadth from a particular, prescribed doctrine?" Woe to them if they should. "If the sword is to be the only weapon relied upon, then woe to your Administration! Your victory will be turned to blood and ashes." Surely dogma could not exact such a price.[6]

Response to Crittenden's plea was heartening. Already a committee of congressmen, largely from the border states but including Texas, North Carolina, Arkansas, New York, New Jersey, and Pennsylvania, had endorsed his proposals. Now, on the day following Crittenden's speech, in a special message to Congress, Buchanan endorsed both the Crittenden compromise plan and the submission of it to the people. It was too late, Buchanan wrote privately, for mere resolutions of kindness. There must now be something "tangible" presented, "and this has been done by Mr. Crittenden." News-

6 *Congressional Globe*, 36 Cong., 2 Sess., 264-67.

paper dispatches from Washington reported general confidence there that the plebiscite would be held and that the people would endorse Crittenden's proposals.[7]

But time was running out. Action was needed, and action was difficult to get. Republican senators were in a dilemma. Assured that the people would overwhelmingly approve Crittenden's proposals, they did not dare permit his resolution of January 3 to come to a vote. A vote against the resolution would be denounced as undemocratic, and they would be charged with preventing the people from expressing their sentiments on a vital question. On the other hand, a vote to refer the proposals to the people would suggest tacit approval on their own part, or at least uncertainty. Either course would make them anathema, not only to the radicals in their party but, strange as it may seem, to Lincoln himself. Under the circumstances, Republicans procrastinated, amended, and postponed, hoping to ride out the storm until the inaugural was successfully achieved and the executive department firmly in their grasp.[8]

On January 9 Crittenden moved action on his resolution. Then Daniel Clark of New Hampshire moved a noteworthy substitute. It declared that the Constitution already was ample to preserve the Union and needed to be obeyed rather than amended, that the present danger would be obviated by enforcement of the laws rather than by "new guarantees for particular interests, or compromises for particular difficulties, or concessions to unreasonable demands." Henry Wilson of Massachusetts then moved postponement of debate. Pugh of Ohio, Bigler of Pennsylvania, and Willard Saulsbury of Delaware all objected. Time was of the essence, Bigler said, and every other question sank into insignificance when compared to Crittenden's proposal. Only seven weeks of the session remained; prompt action was called for. Saulsbury stated that if a future Gibbon should write the history of the decline of the republic, he would date its fall "from the rejection of the resolutions offered by the Senator from Kentucky." Despite these warnings, Wilson's motion to postpone carried.[9] That very day, Mississippi passed her ordinance of secession, and the following day, January 10, Jefferson

[7] Frankfort *Commonwealth*, Jan. 9, 1861; Richardson, *Messages and Papers of the Presidents*, VII, 3169; Buchanan, *Works*, XI, 73, XII, 123-24.

[8] Cox, *Three Decades*, 78-79.

[9] *Congressional Globe*, 36 Cong., 2 Sess., 289-90.

Davis made the melancholy announcement in the Senate. Then, once more on Wilson's motion, Crittenden's resolution was again put aside, as it was also on the following day.[10]

During all this time Seward had maintained a silence strange for the acknowledged spokesman of a triumphant party. When he announced, therefore, that he would speak on January 12, the galleries filled early, for it was already known that he would occupy the first place in the new cabinet, and for that reason his words would carry great import. He would be speaking for the new administration. Though he had refused to support Crittenden's proposals in the Committee of Thirteen, it was by now common knowledge that he sympathized with them. "Everybody," according to David Donald, "believed that he was cooperating with Douglas and Crittenden to work out a new compromise scheme."[11] Now, it seemed to Crittenden and other conciliators, any inhibition on Seward in the Committee was removed. Here he was not being called on to give the resolutions his stamp of approval. All that was being asked was his consent to transmit them to the people so that they might express their sentiment concerning them.

There have been few senators more astute or more agile in political tactics than this canny and inscrutable former Whig from upstate New York. Governor of his state in Tyler's time and senator since Taylor's, he had early risen to a position of primacy in the Republican party largely because of his radical antislavery pronouncements. Though he scorned pomposity or oratorical flourishes, he had coined such ringing phrases as "the higher law" and the "irreconcilable conflict." Now more than middle-aged, he loved to sit, a cigar perpetually in his mouth, talking in a light and offhand manner while he coolly sized up his man. Visitors who were unacquainted with him were sometimes beguiled by his casual manner, his slouching figure, his disorderly hair. His beaked nose and his owlish manner of tilting his head to one side distracted attention from the sharp, penetrating eyes, hidden somewhat from view by their heavy, shaggy brows.[12]

It was partly because of his reputation for radical views on slavery that Seward had been passed over for Lincoln in the Wig-

10 *Congressional Globe*, 36 Cong., 2 Sess., 305-306, 308.
11 Donald, *Sumner*, 372.
12 Henry Adams, "The Great Secession Winter," 659.

wam Convention. Actually, he had been striving to change the revolutionary image he had earlier created, and in the winter of 1860-
1861 he was spokesman for the conciliatory wing of his party. When
he rose to speak on January 12, therefore, all ears were turned to hear
what clue he might give of future policy. Crittenden sat directly in
front. The tone of Seward's message was conciliatory. Lincoln's
election, he said, was no cause for alarm at the South, for his party
would not have a majority in either branch of Congress. Consequently, there would be such restraints on the new President that
even if he wished, which he did not, he could do nothing to injure
slavery. He could not "appoint a minister or even a police agent,
negotiate a treaty, or procure the passage of a law," without consent
of the opposition parties. Nay, without their consent he could
"hardly draw a musket from the public arsenals to defend his own
person."

He spoke for two hours, emphasizing the horrors of disunion and
civil war and urging reconciliation. As he did so, the aged Crittenden
was overcome with emotion. He bowed his white head and wept
unashamedly. As a conciliatory gesture, Seward offered again to support an *unamendable* amendment to the Constitution prohibiting
Congress from interfering with slavery in the states. He favored, also,
repeal by the northern states of their personal liberty laws. He made
a somewhat qualified proposal to divide the western territories into
two parts and admit one immediately as a free state and the other
as slave. He urged the calling of a national constitutional convention
to deal finally with all issues, after tempers had cooled. But back off
from the Chicago platform he would not.[13]

Seward's offer to divide the territories into a free and a slave state
was more of a practical concession than even Crittenden's plan called
for. But by this time the issue was clearly an abstraction. Southerners
now insisted on northern recognition of a theoretical right for taking
their slaves where they had already demonstrated they did not wish
to take them. Northerners were unwilling to recognize any such
right in theory, but at the same time indicated a willingness to admit
the disputed territory as a slave state.

After Seward spoke, Crittenden tried to bring his resolution to
a vote, but it was again postponed. Since four more states had now
seceded, Republicans were in a majority, and Douglas charged that

---

[13] *Congressional Globe*, 36 Cong., 2 Sess., 341-46; Seward, *Autobiography*, II, 494.

they were conspiring to prevent a vote on Crittenden's resolution "by points of order and by giving it the go-by and taking up other questions." When James F. Simmons of Rhode Island protested that there were half a dozen different solutions proposed and that it was difficult to give priority to one over another, Douglas replied that he and all other authors of proposals would "agree to follow the lead of the venerable Senator from Kentucky." He pointed out that if only Crittenden's proposition were permitted to come to a vote, others could be offered as amendments, and thus a vote could be had on each in turn and a solution found that would pacify the country.

On January 15 Crittenden's resolution was postponed, sidetracked in order to take up a Pacific railroad bill. Crittenden professed himself a friend of the railroad bill, yet he could not vote for it while this vital matter was pending. For it was utter foolishness, he said, to prepare a railroad for posterity when the Union itself was dying. Railroads would be "utterly useless, utterly vain, if the Union is to be destroyed." Until the safety of the Union was assured, "What do I want with railroads?" he asked. "What do I want with all the great improvements that would become a mighty empire. . . ?"

On January 16 Powell offered an amendment to Crittenden's first article. It provided explicitly for inclusion of all territory acquired in the future. Crittenden accepted this but pointed out that the acquisition of future slave territory was impossible, because sufficient northern votes could always block it. Douglas and Pugh, however, knowing that there was northern apprehension on this point, protested that it would unnecessarily encumber the bill and make passing it more difficult. During debate on this amendment, time again came for consideration of the Pacific railroad bill. Bigler moved to postpone the railroad bill, and his motion carried twenty-seven to twenty-six. All twenty-six of the negative votes were Republican except those of the two Democratic senators from California, Gwin and Latham, who wanted action on the railroad bill. Powell's amendment then passed, twenty-nine to twenty-four.

It now seemed impossible to prevent a direct vote on Crittenden's resolution. Then, unexpectedly, Clark moved to substitute his own resolution of January 9, the one that stated that amending the Constitution was unnecessary. A vote was quickly called, and Clark's resolution passed, twenty-five to twenty-three. Douglas, who had stepped momentarily from the chamber just before the vote was called, returned and asked to be recorded against Clark's resolution but was refused. All twenty-five affirmative votes were Republican. Not one Republican voted in the negative.

Of even greater significance is the fact that six southern senators from Texas, Louisiana, Arkansas, and Georgia, states that had not yet seceded, were in the chamber but refused to vote on the Clark motion. Their motives can only be surmised. Perhaps, like Toombs and Davis in the Committee of Thirteen, they did not want to mislead their constituents with an illusion that compromise was possible when Republicans voted solidly against it. Perhaps their pride would not permit them to exact compromise by their own votes. But had they voted against Clark's substitute, it would have been defeated by four votes. These twenty-nine votes, with the addition of Douglas' vote, would have enabled Crittenden's resolution to pass with a majority of five. Since this resolution was not a vote to amend the Constitution, a simple majority would have been sufficient to pass it on to the House. Its fate there can only be surmised. Senator Latham and Congressman S. S. Cox were confident that it would pass. In any event, the door would have been held open to reconciliation, while tremendous popular pressure was being built up to sustain a compromise.

It is noteworthy, too, that the eight senators from the four states that had already seceded were still in Washington. Their withdrawal from Senate deliberations was a voluntary act on their own part, and their right to participate and vote could not have been questioned by Republicans who denied the right of secession. Their votes, added to those of the six senators who were present but not voting and to Douglas' vote, would have increased the majority for Crittenden's proposal to thirteen, thirty-eight to twenty-five. Such a majority in the Senate might well have been decisive in swinging support for the proposal in the House.

Even though the secessionist senators refused to vote, however, primary responsibility for the defeat of the Crittenden compromise at this stage must fall on the twenty-five Republicans who voted to substitute Clark's resolution for it. Modern scholars are in agreement on this. With victory already won, they could well have afforded to accept the principle of slavery in the territories. According to James G. Randall they "raised huge clouds of controversy out of precisely those phases of slavery that lacked substance—slavery in

Kansas for instance, which never had any true bearing upon Kansas itself. They created opposition out of a highly artificial, almost a fabricated, issue. They produced quarrels out of things that would have settled themselves were it not for political agitation." James G. Blaine later wrote that Republicans in this period were talking about "an imaginary negro in an impossible place." As to future territories, the conclusion of Allan Nevins is persuasive. "Nor was it likely, though it was certainly possible," Nevins says, "that the Southern expansionists who had signally failed to gain any Cuban, Mexican, or Central American soil during the eight years of Pierce and Buchanan would be able to do so in the near future. . . . So far as the actual diffusion of slavery went, the Republicans could have afforded to swallow the Crittenden Compromise—for the possibilities of slavery expansion were near the end."[14]

Meantime, there had been accumulating in the northern states a vast reservoir of sentiment in support of Crittenden's proposals, and it now began to overflow. Already a meeting in Pine Street in New York City had adopted resolutions promising that if the South would refrain from precipitate action, northern conservatives would force Republicans to recede on the territorial question. Now came letters by the hundreds to Crittenden, endorsing his efforts and his program—letters from Charles A. Davis, the iron manufacturer; from John Brodhead, railroad president; from Anthony B. Allen, farm machinery manufacturer; from A. A. Lawrence, Boston textile magnate; from Edward Everett and George T. Curtis; from Edwin Croswell, Albany printer; from August Belmont and Jay Gould, financiers; from Winfield Scott; from Governor Thomas Hicks of Maryland; from David Lord, distinguished lawyer; from James de Peyster Ogden and James W. Beckman, aristocratic New Yorkers; from Horatio Seymour and John A. Dix; and from humbler folk in the farms and factories. All reported a great change of sentiment in their neighborhood since the election.[15]

Press reports confirmed this. A correspondent of Greeley's

14 Nevins, *Emergence of Lincoln*, II, 403-404. See also *Congressional Globe*, 36 Cong., 2 Sess., 305-306, 326, 351-52, 361-63, 379-81, 386-87, 402-410; *ibid.*, 37 Cong., 1 Sess., 19-22; Potter, *Lincoln and His Party*, 184-85, 206; Rhodes, *History of the United States*, III, 153-54; Randall, "The Civil War Restudied," 447; Blaine, *Twenty Years of Congress*, I, 272.

15 See Crittenden Papers, January and February, 1861, especially Vol. XXV; King, *Turning on the Light*, 40; Potter, *Lincoln and His Party*, 121-22; Buchanan, *Works*, XI, 300; Coleman, *Crittenden*, II, 254-55.

Tribune conceded that there was great pressure for compromise, and the Albany *Atlas and Argus* said that extremists, both North and South, would be "crushed out, by the patriotic, Union-loving sentiment of the country." It demanded that the Republicans cease their policy of "masterly inactivity" and begin the "work of conciliation and compromise." Thurlow Weed had also "stepped out like a man" in support of the plan, and his influence was such, wrote J. W. Murray, that "when he speaks, no dog except that cur Greeley dare to bark." Weed thought Crittenden's plan "fair and reasonable, and the one most likely to succeed." For weeks he commuted between Albany and Washington, urging Republican support for it, and he tried to promote a conference of governors to work in its behalf, but in both efforts he failed.[16]

From Indiana came reliable reports that Crittenden's compromise would be endorsed there by a majority of fifty thousand votes. Conventions of the Constitutional Union party and the Democratic Union party in Louisville on January 7-8 endorsed it as "a fair and honorable adjustment." Ten days later the legislatures of Delaware, Virginia, and Kentucky urged Congress to approve it. A week later, in Philadelphia, six thousand workmen stood in Independence Square at night during a snowstorm and voted unanimously to endorse it. At almost the same time in Mayfield, Kentucky, one of the largest meetings ever gotten together there endorsed it with "unparalled [*sic*] unanimity." A record-size meeting in Van Buren, Arkansas, did likewise. The board of aldermen of Boston unanimously adopted resolutions thanking Crittenden for his services and inviting him to visit there as the guest of the city. Four days after Georgia seceded, a Unionist there wrote Crittenden that Georgians "would [still] vote for your proposed amendments if they had a chance to do so by an overwhelming majority."[17]

---

[16] Barnes, *Memoir of Weed*, 312. See also, Robert G. Gunderson (ed.), "Letters from the Washington Peace Conference of 1861," in *Journal of Southern History*, XVII (1951), 382; J. W. B. Murray to Crittenden, Jan. 5, 1861, in Crittenden Papers; Glyndon G. Van Deusen, *Thurlow Weed, Wizard of the Lobby* (Boston, 1947), 266-69; Greeley, *Recollections*, 396.

[17] Letters to Crittenden from John D. Defrees, Jan. 5, from Rufus K. Williams, Jan. 23, and from Edmund Dumas, Jan. 23, 1861, in Crittenden Papers; *House Miscellaneous Documents*, 36 Cong., 2 Sess., No. 21; *House Executive Documents*, 36 Cong., 2 Sess., No. 55; Buchanan, *Works*, XI, 119, 124-25; George T. Curtis to Crittenden, Feb. 12, 1861, in Coleman, *Crittenden*, II, 263-64; Louisville *Courier*, Jan. 10, 1861; Louisville *Journal*, Jan. 10, 1861; Frankfort *Commonwealth*, Jan. 9, 29, 1861.

GEORGE B. CRITTENDEN
MAJOR GENERAL, C.S.A.

THOMAS L. CRITTENDEN
MAJOR GENERAL, U.S.A.

Courtesy of Thomas Joyes, Louisville

Support for Crittenden's proposals did not end with editorials and mass meetings. On January 3, the very day Crittenden offered his plebiscite resolution, there began to descend on Congress such a flood of petitions as had not been seen in that body since the abolitionist petitions of Theodore Dwight Weld, two decades before. From Harrisburg, Carlisle, Philadelphia, Port Clinton, Lehigh County, Easton, Monongahela County, Upper Mount Bethel, Neville, Berlin, Wayne County, Snyder County, Chester, Montour County, Lancaster, Safe Harbor, Bradford County, Elk City, Luzerne County, Alleghany County, Mercer County, and Blair City, all in Pennsylvania, came petitions for Congress to speedily adopt Crittenden's proposals. From Annapolis and Frederick, Maryland, came others, and still more from Wilmington, Delaware; thirty different petitions from Michigan; from Coles County, Illinois, the home of Lincoln's aged stepmother; from Guernsey City and Portsmouth, Ohio; from St. Anthony, St. Cloud, and Stillwater, Minnesota; from Superior, Wisconsin; from Jefferson, Illinois; from Liberty Corner, New Jersey; from Muhlenberg County, Kentucky; from Lincoln, Maine; from a hundred other northern cities and towns. The mere listing of the places of origin of the petitions requires four pages of the *Senate Journal.*

On January 21 Senator Polk of Missouri presented a petition from St. Louis praying for the passage of the Crittenden compromise, or else its "substance." More than ninety-five sheets of foolscap paper were required to record all the names. The following week Seward presented a petition from New York, containing almost forty thousand names. Extended to its full length, he said, it would have reached across the Senate chamber eighteen times. Seward had previously presented one of twenty-five thousand names. Both asked that Crittenden's or some similar plan be adopted.[18]

The Massachusetts legislature as early as 1837 had declared with near unanimity that new slave states should not be admitted, and during the crisis over Texas, the legislature had resolved that Massachusetts would never consent to the "further extension of slavery to any portion of the world."[19] Now from Massachusetts came pe-

[18] *Congressional Globe,* 36 Cong., 2 Sess., 237, 352, 378-79, 401, 442, 483, 500, 516, 537, 586-89, 634, 839-40, 1126, 1243; *Senate Journal,* 36 Cong., 2 Sess., 494-97; Seward, *Autobiography,* II, 498.
[19] Donald, *Sumner,* 132, 136, 370.

titions by the dozen. A delegation of Bostonians, headed by Everett, Winthrop, and Lawrence, brought a huge petition and tried vainly to win Sumner's support for Crittenden's proposals. On Lincoln's birthday, Crittenden presented petitions from 182 cities and towns of the Bay State, signed by more than twenty-two thousand persons. All had been obtained, so petitioners said, in a great hurry and under other handicaps. In nearly every case the petition noted that "if we had only had time to present it to the voters . . . the number of signatures would have been doubled."[20]

Horace Greeley, by now bitterly opposed to any compromise, later conceded that "if a popular vote could have been had . . . on the Crittenden Compromise, it would have prevailed by an overwhelming majority." James Ford Rhodes, writing three decades later, agreed. "No doubt can now exist," he wrote in 1895, "and but little could have existed in January, 1861, that if it had been submitted to the people it would have carried the Northern States by a great majority; that it would have obtained the vote of almost every man in the Border States; and that it would have received the preponderating voice of all the cotton States but South Carolina."[21]

With such evidence of overwhelming support, it is not surprising that Crittenden remained hopeful of working out a satisfactory settlement, even after the substitution of Clark's resolution for his own on January 16. Two days after that event, Crittenden secured a reconsideration of the Clark resolution by a vote of twenty-seven to twenty-four. Then Bigler offered Crittenden's resolution as an amendment to Clark's, and the Crittenden compromise was once more on the Senate calendar. Rumors were renewed that with the aid of influential Republicans the compromise would be effected. On the night of January 18 Crittenden and Douglas met with Seward and Dixon and came to an agreement; the exact nature of it has never been revealed but Crittenden was further encouraged. Charles Francis Adams thought it impossible for Republicans to defeat Crittenden's resolution, and Greeley in late January conceded that only *"a very few more Republicans"* were needed to secure its passage. He, too, believed that Seward favored it. "We will pass in substance Mr. Crittenden's plans," wired John A. Gilmer, North

---

[20] *Congressional Globe*, 36 Cong., 2 Sess., 862.
[21] Greeley, *Recollections*, 397; Greeley, *American Conflict*, I, 380; Rhodes, *History of the United States*, III, 148, 149-50, 150n.

Carolina Unionist congressman, to a constituent on January 22. "Give no ear to alarms."[22]

Had they been privy to Seward's private correspondence, they would have been less certain. "Two-thirds of the Republican Senators are as reckless in action as the South," he wrote on January 13. He could not compromise if he would, he added, for "there is nobody to go with me." He was already thinking of "clearing my conscience of responsibility" for the war he feared might come. In a Republican caucus he attended a few nights later there was "not one word said to disarm prejudice and passion, and encourage loyalty." Distraction, he added, ruled the hour. "Mad men North, and mad men South, are working together to produce a dissolution of the Union by civil war." Weed, on a visit to Washington about the same time, confirmed this. He could not find ten Republicans there "who either comprehended the real question or appreciated its consequences." The trouble was that Lincoln's closest associates at this time were radicals, who were telling him that compromise was not necessary to hold the Union together.[23]

After he secured reconsideration of the Clark substitute on January 18, Crittenden was again faced with the same tactics of delay that Republicans had used to frustrate his efforts since Congress first met. More than half of the session had now elapsed, and yet a direct vote on his proposal could not be secured. Day after day he and his allies, Douglas, Bigler, Pugh, sought to get his resolution to the floor, but as often as they tried, they found themselves put off. First there would be the railroad bill, then the tariff, then private bills, then a territorial bill, then the railroad bill again. On rare occasions when they could get it on the calendar as a special order, filibustering harangues on the propriety of the personal liberty laws and on the iniquity of secession would consume its allotted time and thus prevent a vote.[24]

22 *Congressional Globe*, 36 Cong., 2 Sess., 443, 494-96; Milton, *The Eve of Conflict*, 534; Rhodes, *History of the United States*, III, 174-75; Gilmer to Jesse J. Yeates, Jan. 22, 1861, in *War of the Rebellion: A Compilation of the Official Records of the Union and Confederate Armies*, 128 vols. and index (Washington, 1880-1901), Series I, vol. LI, pt. 2, p. 7 (hereinafter *Official Records*).

23 Seward, *Autobiography*, II, 496-97; Weed to Francis Granger, Jan. 26, 1861, in Granger Papers; Jeremiah Black to Charles R. Bucklaw, Jan. 28, 1861, in Black Papers.

24 *Congressional Globe*, 36 Cong., 2 Sess., 443, 489-96, 506-508, 518-21, 542, 554-60, 589-96, 608-18, 634, 667-70, 680-90, 864-65.

In view of all this, it is remarkable that Crittenden did not give up hope. Yet at the end of January he and Douglas sent optimistic messages to Virginia Unionists, and Crittenden wrote privately that "the passion for disunion has partly subsided." Finding that Republicans were centering their attack on the Powell amendment, which included in the settlement territory to be acquired in the future, Crittenden, on February 12, moved to have this stricken from his resolutions. He had accepted it in the first place, he said, only to indicate the finality of the settlement. He had reasoned that since northern states would never agree to acquire territory south of 36° 30′ and southern states would never agree to acquire any north of the line, there would be an end to territorial expansion. Since the provision was obnoxious to the North, however, he would strike it out. But parliamentary procedure prevented action, and the false issue of Powell's amendment continued to plague Crittenden, despite his disavowal. As we shall soon see, when he later moved to substitute resolutions which did not contain the Powell amendment for his own, his efforts were equally fruitless.[25]

Meanwhile, the Virginia legislature had called a peace conference. In issuing the call, the legislature endorsed Crittenden's proposals as a basis for compromise. All thirty-three states had been invited, but the seven gulf states that had already seceded, together with Michigan, Wisconsin, and Minnesota, refused to send delegates. Distance and time combined to prevent Oregon and California from doing so, so that only twenty-one states were actually represented. In many instances Republican-controlled legislatures were reluctant to send representatives, and only fear of popular reaction persuaded them to do so. The Republican minority in the New York legislature resolved that "There is no difference between the proposed meeting of commissioners at Washington and the Secession Convention to be held . . . at Montgomery, Alabama."[26] Illinois Republican legislators voted to send delegates only "as a matter of political necessity. . . . We did not approve of the policy," one of them wrote Trumbull. He added that he believed Lincoln preferred that they not be

[25] Published letter of Crittenden and Douglas to James Barbour in Frankfort *Commonwealth,* Jan. 31, 1861; Crittenden to S. S. Nicholas, Dec. [?], 1860 (copy), in Crittenden Papers; *Congressional Globe,* 36 Cong., 2 Sess., 862-65; Crittenden to Larz Anderson, March 29, 1861, in Coleman, *Crittenden,* II, 296; Louisville *Journal,* March 19, 1861.

[26] Gunderson, "Letters from the Washington Peace Conference," 383.

sent. "Yet our sister states would act, and it might be unwise in us, not to join them." Only Democratic pressure in the Indiana legislature caused that state to send a delegation. Before appointing five stanch Republicans, however, Governor Oliver P. Morton obtained assurances that they would not favor amending the Constitution; that they would not accept any proposition recognizing slavery in the territories; and that they would not entertain any additional guarantees for slavery. According to one authority, the Republicans agreed to send delegates to the conference only in order to fix the responsibility of secession and war on the South. They had no interest to compromise, and their real aim was "to appease their northern critics more than their southern foes."[27]

As the delegates arrived in Washington in early February, they were astonished at the preparations they saw going forward there. Already, to secure the city from secessionist attack, General Scott had deployed troops and cannon in strategic locations. The wildest of rumors were afloat—there was talk of plots to prevent Lincoln's inauguration and plots to poison horses of the military; the mayor of the city was said to be in league with two thousand armed secessionists. Attorney General Edwin M. Stanton publicly warned that southern troops would occupy the capital before March 4. Some Washingtonians had already removed their wives and children from the city, and one Massachusetts delegate to the convention became so alarmed at what he saw and heard that he immediately secured asylum for his wife and daughter in the Russian embassy. So great was the tension that early one morning when an artillery company sounded the usual reveille, people rushed into the street half-clad but fully armed, thinking war had come. A few days later, when a peaceful salute was fired to honor creation of the new state of Kansas, another panic ensued.[28]

On February 4, the same day that delegates from six seceded states began deliberations at Montgomery leading to creation of the southern confederacy, the peace convention began its sessions be-

[27] Stampp, And the War Came, 172-75. See also Virginia Acts, 1861 (Richmond, 1861), 337-39; E. Peck to Trumbull, Feb. 2, 1861, in Trumbull Papers; Senate Miscellaneous Documents, 36 Cong., 2 Sess., No. 20; Kenneth Stampp (ed.), "Letters from the Washington Peace Conference," in Journal of Southern History, IX (1943), 395-96.
[28] Robert G. Gunderson, "William C. Rives and the Old Gentlemen's Convention," in Journal of Southern History, XVII (1951), 466; Seward, Autobiography, II, 497, 502; Dumond, Secession Movement, 241-44.

hind closed doors in Washington. Among the 133 delegates were a former President, six former cabinet members, eleven former United States senators, fifty former congressmen, twelve state supreme court justices, five former ambassadors. Despite this distinguished membership, Horace Greeley dubbed it the "Old Gentlemen's Convention," because, he said, it was made up of "political fossils." Twelve of the delegates were over seventy years of age, thirty-four were past sixty, seventy-four were past fifty.[29]

The inflexible position agreed on by Republican delegates was reinforced by signs of seeming Unionist strength in states of the Upper South and the border, signs that the Republicans completely misread. When delegates to state conventions had been elected in Virginia and Tennessee, Unionists had won a majority, whereas in Kentucky the legislature had even refused to call a convention. This gave a false reassurance to Republicans, already overly complacent about southern Unionism. There was little chance, therefore, that a decisive majority of delegates could be found for any substantial compromise proposal. Yet, as Julia Tyler wrote, "People are catching at straws . . . and look to the Peace Commissioners as if they possessed some divine power to restore harmony." Even her husband, the president of the convention, was in suspense and doubt.[30]

When the convention assembled, a committee of one delegate from each state was set up to screen proposals. Prime measures considered by the committee were the restoration of the Missouri line and the calling of a national constitutional convention—the latter, apparently, a delaying action promoted by Republicans. Reverdy Johnson, a member of the screening committee, later reported that all proposals to give reasonable guarantees to the South were frustrated by Republican members. He and James Guthrie, Kentucky Unionist and chairman of the committee, vainly implored Republicans to agree to something conciliatory. Secession was no longer a mere threat but an accomplished fact. What the Upper South and border Unionists now needed was some indication of a compromise spirit at the North, in order to reduce sympathy in their own states for the seceders. But their appeals were rebuffed with a stubborn, callous coldness.

[29] Gunderson, "Rives and the Old Gentlemen's Convention," 467; *Senate Miscellaneous Documents*, 36 Cong., 2 Sess., No. 20.
[30] Julia Tyler to "Dear Mama," Feb. 13, 1861, in Tyler Papers; Tyler, *Letters and Times*, II, 613; Dumond, *Secession Movement*, 245.

As the crisis deepened and excitement in Washington grew, however, some northern delegations began to waver. They were, one delegate wrote, "a little weaker in the knees" than when they first arrived in Washington. There were reports that the New York delegation would accept a compromise were it not for the fact that "certain men of that State are more interested in killing Seward [politically] than in saving the Union." Indeed, wrote Reuben Hitchcock, an Ohio delegate, "there is too general a feeling that party is paramount to Union." Hitchcock pointed out that restoration of the Missouri line would actually eliminate the little slavery then existing in Nebraska, Utah, and that part of New Mexico which extended above 36° 30'. But, he added, "political cabals & intrigues" were working to make sure that the patent issue of slavery in the territories not "be taken out of the political arena." That was the only reason, he thought, that Republicans opposed the measure, for Crittenden's proposal "Neither extends slavery, nor makes free territory slave, but it does curtail slavery & make Slave territory free." Besides, he added, the whole business would be controlled by the Lincoln administration for the next four years, and they could settle it for freedom, unless "the aspirants for office are determined to keep the question open, as their stock in trade."[31]

The committee report, made on February 15, agreed substantially with Crittenden's resolutions except that it restricted the territorial settlement to present territory. (Crittenden, as has been seen, had attempted three days earlier in the Senate to restore this modification to his own plan.) After receiving the committee's report, the convention wrangled for two weeks over it. Voting was by states, each state, regardless of size, having one vote, to be cast by the delegation majority. When the vote was taken on February 26, the critical question of dividing the territories at 36° 30' was defeated, eleven to eight. Illinois then moved a reconsideration, and it was carried. The territorial division then passed nine to eight. This reversal was effected only after a most remarkable set of circumstances. Not only did Illinois change her vote, but Missouri,

31 Reuben Hitchcock to Peter Hitchcock, Jr., Feb. 6, 10, 16, [25?], March 4, 1861, in Gunderson, "Letters from the Washington Peace Conference," 386-89; [James Buchanan], Mr. Buchanan's Administration on the Eve of the Rebellion (New York, 1866), 146-47; Lucius E. Chittenden, A Report of the Debates and Proceedings . . . of the Conference Convention held at Washington, D. C., in February, 1861 (New York, 1864), 9-10, 21, 42, 70; Stampp, "Letters from the Washington Peace Conference," 399-400; Buchanan, Works, XII, 128.

Kansas, and Indiana abstained, and New York lost her vote when a tie developed in her delegation, brought about by the absence of one member. Then, in substance, Crittenden's other proposals were also adopted. One significant addition was the provision that no new territory should ever be acquired without the approval of separate majorities of slave-state and free-state senators.[32]

Not one of the resolutions received overwhelming support in the convention. Only five of fourteen northern states voted for the territorial resolution, and even Virginia and North Carolina voted against it when the restriction to present territory was added. Tyler and his fellow Virginian, James Seddon, denounced the report as "a delusion and a sham," as did also the New York *Tribune* and the New York *Times*.[33] Nevertheless, Tyler dutifully reported the resolutions to Congress, with the recommendation that they be adopted and submitted to the states as amendments to the Constitution. In the Senate they were referred to a select committee of five, with Crittenden as chairman, with instructions to report the next day, February 28.

On that day Crittenden reported them favorably and moved that they be substituted for his own on the Senate calendar. But Trumbull and Seward moved a substitute resolution requesting the states to express their views on the wisdom of calling a national constitutional convention. Hale then insisted that under the rules of the Senate a second reading of the resolutions would have to lie over until the next day. Crittenden was exasperated, for time was running out. He marveled, he said, at the way in which obstructionists attempted to evade "by indirection and by little petty special pleading . . . the consideration of a great subject." Only two working days remained before the Thirty-sixth Congress would expire, and with it, probably, the life of the nation. Yet punctilios, "these nice questions of order," could not be set aside. But Hale's point of order was sustained, and action on the resolutions was postponed.[34]

That day the House passed and sent to the Senate a proposed constitutional amendment identical with the one Seward had of-

[32] *Senate Miscellaneous Documents*, 36 Cong., 2 Sess., No. 20; Tyler, *Letters and Times*, II, 608; *Congressional Globe*, 36 Cong., 2 Sess., 1254-55; Chittenden, *Report*, 42, 70; Stampp, *And the War Came*, 129-30.

[33] Dumond, *Secession Movement*, 248-51; Gunderson, "Letters from the Washington Peace Conference," 384-85.

[34] *Congressional Globe*, 36 Cong., 2 Sess., 1255, 1269-74.

fered in the Committee of Thirteen, prohibiting any amendment to the Constitution that would give Congress power to interfere with slavery in the states. Lincoln, who by now was convinced that northern opinion was misrepresented in the South and that some assurance must be given the border states, had consented to such an amendment. The resolution passed the House by a vote of 133 to 65, with some Republican support, but with all 65 opposition votes being Republican.[35]

On Friday, March 1, when the peace conference resolutions were taken up, Douglas moved that this House resolution be considered at the same time. Crittenden supported him, urging that the House resolution now be given precedence over the peace conference resolutions as well as over his own. Douglas' motion was given a first reading, and unanimous consent was asked that it be ordered also to a second reading so that it could be taken up the next day for final action. No objection being heard, the clerk entered the order.[36]

Meanwhile, all through that Friday a three-cornered debate raged over the relative merits of Crittenden's proposals, those of the peace conference, and Seward's substitute recommending a national constitutional convention. Crittenden now supported the peace conference resolutions in preference to his own. They were, he said, substantially the same. The only difference had to do with future territory, and he was opposed to annexing more territory. We had too much already, and it was the source of all our trouble. He now regretted that he had ever accepted the Powell amendment regarding future territory in the first place and explained again that he had done so only as a symbol of permanence to the settlement. He had since changed his mind as to the value of the provision, but even if he had not, he would accept the peace conference resolutions over his own. They were the result of the deliberations of representatives of more than twenty states. It would be presumptuous of him to place his own opinion over theirs. Let us settle our present difficulties, he begged, and if we must have future acquisitions, leave their troubles to the future. Now was the time to omit from the resolutions every word that might give offense and impede their passage.

[35] *House Reports,* 36 Cong., 2 Sess., No. 31; Gunderson, "Letters from the Washington Peace Conference," 391; Randall, *The Civil War and Reconstruction,* 201; *Congressional Globe,* 36 Cong., 2 Sess., 1284-85.

[36] *Congressional Globe,* 36 Cong., 2 Sess., 1255, 1305; James M. Mason to John Tyler, March 2, 1861, in Tyler Papers.

His argument won two converts. The diminutive George E. Pugh, who until that time had been holding out for Crittenden's resolutions, now announced that for expediency's sake he would support the peace conference resolutions. So would Edward D. Baker of Oregon, a great friend of Lincoln's. Previously he had voted against Crittenden on every dilatory motion. Now, impressed by "the noble expression" of the Kentuckian, he would vote to submit either Crittenden's or the peace conference proposals to the people. If they were supported by the border states, he would vote for them at the polls himself. If this meant abandonment of the Chicago platform, so be it. He now stood, he said, "in the presence of greater events than those which attend the making of a President." He was ready to put country over party. The Chicago platform, after all, was not the Constitution.

But Baker, who would give up his life at Ball's Bluff only eight months hence, was the only Republican Crittenden could convert. Others would not budge. Debate proceeded for hours with monotonous repetition. Again and again Republican motions to adjourn were made, withdrawn, made again, and beaten back. Late in the evening Douglas asked unanimous consent to make the House resolution the special order for the next day. This was agreed to, and adjournment was carried.

But when Douglas called the resolution up the following day, Sumner objected that under the rules it could not be considered, for it had not been given a second reading. The *Journal* was appealed to, and it corroborated statements of Democrats that a second reading the day before had been ordered by unanimous consent. But Sumner insisted that he had objected the previous evening and that the second reading had been put off. His motion to correct the *Journal* to conform with his memory now carried, twenty-four to seventeen. This act alone is ample support for Kenneth Stampp's statement that during the last week of the session the Republicans "slaughtered every meaningful compromise that had been presented."[37]

Sumner's unexpected action was indeed a blow to Crittenden's hopes. For this was Saturday, March 2. The Senate would meet for only two hours Monday morning before its term expired at noon, and

[37] *Congressional Globe*, 36 Cong., 2 Sess., 1306-12, 1314, 1316-18, 1338-40; Stampp, *And the War Came*, 139.

the House resolution could not be voted on in that time. On the other hand, there was now no chance of Congress passing either his or the peace conference resolutions, for even if they should pass the Senate, the House would have no time to act on them. Passage of the House resolution, although far less than Crittenden had originally hoped to achieve, was needed now to hold the states of the Upper South and the border in the Union. For with the secession of the seven gulf states, the remaining slave states feared that a constitutional amendment freeing their slaves soon might be forced upon them.

Sumner's stubborn insistence on delay, therefore, forced Crittenden to move for a Sunday meeting, a thing unprecedented. For all practical purposes, he said, it would be the last day of the session, and it might also be the last day of the Union. "If we may help an ox out of the pit on Sunday," he said, "we shall be excused for helping a nation out of its difficulties." But Republicans Harlan, Fessenden, Clark, King, Collamer, and Doolittle all raised objection after objection to prevent the Sunday motion from coming to a vote. A vote was finally ordered at seven o'clock in the evening, when many senators were out of the chamber. Crittenden's motion lost, fifteen to twenty-one.

But the Republican ranks could not hold forever at such high-handed behavior. When Bigler moved to amend the rules so that resolutions proposing constitutional amendments could be excepted from the rule requiring readings on three separate days, the motion passed, twenty to sixteen. This cleared the way for consideration of the House resolution, but Virginia's Mason and Hunter now objected. They insisted on a vote on Crittenden's resolution—nothing less. Crittenden protested. It was now too late, he said, for either his resolutions or those of the peace conference to be effective. On the other hand, the House resolution, if now passed by the Senate, would do some good. Those now clamoring for precedence of his resolutions were trying by subterfuge, he said, to defeat the one resolution that had chance of passage. Long hours were now spent in filibustering argument, but finally it was agreed to take up the House resolution.

Pugh, who until this moment had given Crittenden yeoman support, now inexplicably joined in the dilatory tactics. Pugh had the reputation of being an able lawyer and an excellent logician, but the syntax of the House resolution did not please him and he moved to amend so as to improve its style. Douglas objected that the wording was sufficiently clear, and that even a minor amendment would require returning the resolution to the House for reconsideration there. This was tantamount to killing it, for the House had already adjourned. Crittenden pleaded with Pugh to bear with bad grammar if it expressed a good thought. "I prefer bad English expressing a good thing," he said, "to good English expressing a bad thing."

Pugh's amendment was voted down on a voice vote, but on a call for a division, votes were changed so that it resulted in a tie, nineteen to nineteen. Breckinridge then voted for the amendment, and it passed. Crittenden in his desperation momentarily forgot that he had voted in the negative and moved reconsideration. He was called to order, but Pugh now came to his relief and made the motion himself, and it carried. Gwin, who had previously voted against Pugh's amendment, announced that he would vote for it. His purpose, he said, was to kill the House resolution and then vote for Crittenden's. This would take away one of the precious nineteen votes that had effected the tie. Then Clingman, who had voted for Pugh's amendment, now switched against it, balancing Gwin.

Tedious debate now followed. A motion to adjourn was beaten back at eleven o'clock. Then Clingman switched again and announced that he would vote for Pugh's amendment. This triggered a mad scene. Dozens of senators, their patience exhausted, jumped to their feet, shouting arguments without either seeking or getting recognition from the chair. When order was restored, Baker got the floor and came once more to Crittenden's aid. The House resolution was not "a delusion," not "meaningless," as had been charged, he said. It was merely an assurance to reasonable men on a matter about which they were in doubt. If it were not passed, it could be justly said that Republicans really did, "in our secret hearts, intend to interfere with slavery in the States." He would vote for the resolution "to help quiet things in Virginia," as well as to "sustain good Union men in Kentucky." If his fellow Republicans were determined to kill the House resolution, he called on them to do so by a direct vote on it, not by passing Pugh's ill-conceived grammatical amendment. Let not the epitaph of the Union be "died of bad grammar."

A vote was then taken on Pugh's amendment, and it was defeated, seventeen to twenty. Now Pugh offered Crittenden's resolution as a substitute for the House resolution. More debate followed, running out the clock. When Powell stated that he was unalterably opposed to coercion of the seceded states, Chandler repeated his earlier assertion that the nation would not be worth preserving without "a little blood-letting." He charged Virginia with treason, and Floyd, who had resigned from Buchanan's cabinet under a personal cloud, with robbery. Wigfall responded angrily, ridiculing in biting sarcasm Lincoln's recent flight through Baltimore, "in disguise," and defying the North to attempt coercion of the seceded states.

When Wigfall sat down, Crittenden got the floor. It would be, he said, the last time he would ever speak in that chamber, and he would say a word in parting. Before he could continue, however, Hunter moved for a recess until seven o'clock, Sunday evening, so that the elderly Crittenden might get some rest before giving his farewell message. The motion was agreed to. It was within seven minutes of midnight, and the Senate had been in constant session since noon.

Long before the Senate reassembled on Sunday evening, the galleries were filled with spectators. The women of Washington, alarmed for the nation's safety, were now daily visitors in the galleries of Senate and House, coming before noon and remaining until night. This Sunday evening the galleries had filled early, and strangers had crowded onto the Senate floor to hear the venerable Kentuckian's valedictory. The chamber itself was so crowded that it had to be cleared in order to permit senators to reach their seats. Lincoln, who had come to hear his onetime idol, remained, an interested spectator. As those ejected from the floor crowded into the galleries, great confusion developed, for all space there was already occupied. A man who fainted had to be passed to the exit over the heads of the crowd, for passage could not be forced through it.[38]

As Crittenden arose, all were hushed to hear him. Despite his three months of frustration, his speech was a message of hope. Con-

[38] *Congressional Globe*, 36 Cong., 2 Sess., 1349, 1356-70, 1372-76, 1380; Mrs. Roger (Sara Agnes Rice) Pryor, *Reminiscences in Peace and War* (New York, 1904), 98; Washington *Evening Star*, March 4, 1861, quoted in Baringer, *A House Dividing*, 330.

gress and the government sometimes failed to govern justly, he said, but such failures were transitory. Secession was evil and had wronged the country. A solution had not yet been found for the crisis, but he was confident that it would be. A quarter million people in the North had petitioned for acceptance of his resolutions. Never before had such sentiment for reconciliation been expressed in so short a time. These petitioners were the common people, and his confidence in them was greater than in their representatives. The people had assured him that "right will eventually be done, that they, the true sovereigns of the country," would not allow their children, "scattered about through all this land, to go to war with one another upon such a comparative trifle." For "through this great nation common blood flows. What man is there here that is not of a blood, flowing . . . through every State in the Union? and we talk about not compromising a family quarrel. . . . In the name of God, who is it that will adopt that policy? We are one people in blood; in language one; in thoughts one; we read the same books; we feed on the same meats; we go to the same school; we belong to the same communion. . . . It is our infirmity to have . . . difficulties. Let it be our magnanimity and our wisdom to compromise and settle them."

Sadly Crittenden rebuked his colleagues for three months of procrastination. They were now about to adjourn, having accomplished absolutely nothing. The Senate of the United States, beholding the dismemberment of the nation and the threat of civil war, had been unable to resolve the difficulty. "Sir," he asked, "is this not a remarkable spectacle? How does it happen that not even a bare majority here, when the country trusted to our hands is going to ruin, have been competent to devise any measure of public safety? How does it happen that we have not had unanimity enough to agree on any measure . . . ? We see the danger; we acknowledge our duty; and yet, with all this before us, we are acknowledging before the world that we can do nothing. . . . Some are for coercion; yet no army has been raised, no navy has been equipped. Some are for pacification; yet they have been able to do nothing; the dissent of their colleagues prevents them; and here we are in the midst of a falling country, . . . presenting to the eyes of the world the saddest spectacle it ever has seen. Cato . . . fell struggling. We fall with the ignominy on our heads of doing nothing, like the man who stands by and sees his house in flames, and says to himself, 'perhaps the fire will stop before it consumes all.' "

Only the Republicans could prevent complete disaster. Seven states from the Deep South were already gone. Eight slave states, including his own, still tottered on the brink. Something yet might be done to save them, he pleaded. The only question of slavery in the territories now or hereafter was in New Mexico. "What are the worth and value of that Territory to white or to black? It is the most sterile region of country belonging to the United States, the least happy. It has been open to slavery for ten years, and there is a controversy . . . whether there are twenty-four or twenty-six or twenty-eight slaves within the whole Territory. . . . [I]t can never be made a slave state."

The same question now confronting them had faced the country in 1820 over Missouri. Wise men then had divided the territory, even as he had sought to do in his proposals, on the line of 36° 30'. It had been charged, he said, that his proposition would have established slavery in New Mexico forever, but this was not so. It was very easy to make speeches in that round and unmeasured language, but that was not what he proposed. He only asked that slavery be left in New Mexico as it was. "Until this Territory of more than one hundred thousand square miles . . . shall contain in its borders a hundred thousand . . . inhabitants. . . . For that short period, let things remain as they are just now. . . . When it does come in, . . . then . . . we will give them the right to form themselves into a State and be admitted into the Union; and when so admitted, they shall have the right to dispose of this question of slavery just as they please; only, for the sake of peace, let this question rest in silence for that short time."

Surely they must realize that his proposal called for no sacrifice of Republican scruples. The Chicago platform pledged only that "slavery shall not be extended in any Territory." He did not ask that slavery be extended. For "slavery does exist there now, and probably to almost as great an extent as ever it will be in the future. . . . Do not believe, my fellow-citizens of the North, my brother Senators of the North, that I am urging this on you as a bargain. . . . I would not take the most paltry right from you to give it to the South. I would not detract a particle from your honor, in order to give anything like a triumph to any section of the country. You are as much my country men as anybody. I claim the whole country as my country."

He did not wish, Crittenden said, to appear as the advocate of slavery, nor of a party, nor of the South. He was not attempting to show that the South was right in its demands. It was no longer a question of party or section. It was a question of country and Union. His northern colleagues must realize, however, that the South had cause for discontent and fear of a victorious Republican party that insisted on a policy that gave the North all. "From that discontent and long irritation has now grown this flame which is consuming our country, and has severed from us a valuable and important portion of it. . . . Was there ever a revolution so permitted to go on, —ever the dismemberment of a great country so allowed to take place —ever the overthrow of a mighty nation like this allowed in the face of the whole world, plainly and obviously to the sight of its Legislature, and all allowed to go to wreck and ruin, when it could have been preserved in peace, by a grant no larger than that which I have shown you[?]"

He observed that all senators from the seceded states had agreed to accept his proposition, yet the Republicans had refused it. Was it not worth something, he asked, to prevent the secession of Kentucky, Maryland, North Carolina, Missouri, Tennessee, Arkansas? "Or is an idea, is a dogma, to prevail—a dogma not of the Constitution, . . . a dogma having its origin . . . in one section of the country, and which is attempted to be placed above the Constitution . . . ?" Crittenden spoke of the greatness of the Union in the times past, of the respect and esteem it had all over the world, of the protection it threw around its citizens. Should they not show patience and forbearance before discarding such a priceless jewel? It was truly "a marvel in the history of the world" that secession should have been permitted to take place.

He had previously asked for a vote on his resolutions—not that he expected their passage by a two-thirds majority. But even if they got only a bare majority, they might contribute to the pacification of the country, might create a disposition of forbearance. Now that he could not expect even that, he hoped for a favorable vote on the House resolution to amend the Constitution. He did not think it went far enough as a general remedy, but it might have some good effects. Surely there could be no objection to it. He asked that all amendments to it be withdrawn so that it might pass and lead the way to peace by demonstrating that there was no blind and unreasoning opposition to constitutional amendments.

As for Kentucky, he would not agree to secession. "I was born and bred in the State of Kentucky; and as to my native state, old Kentucky, I shall say to her more freely than to others: I desire to see you stand by the Union . . . ; give to the world a long continued evidence of your constancy, your patriotism, and your fidelity to the Constitution. . . . There is nothing . . . in all the hopes and all the triumphs that secession can promise itself, equal to the proud swelling of the heart at these noble and patriotic sentiments. . . . Let Kentucky . . . be the last to leave that Union which has conferred upon her so much honor, so much glory, so much liberty, and so much happiness; and, abused as it has been, mal-administered as it has been, it is as yet the best Government on earth; the only Government on earth in which a man commands his own actions, can speak his own thoughts in any work which he pleases, where no man is imprisoned unlawfully, from one end of it to the other. . . . It is only here in the arms of this great and mighty Republic that liberty was ever presented to the world in all her height and all her majesty."

The Constitution, Crittenden pointed out, made it possible to change governments frequently, and in this way wrongs could be righted within the Union. Even though some groups must suffer temporary wrong, therefore, they should bear with it. But if efforts at reconciliation should fail and war should come, then "when rebellion and revolution shall have passed over this whole land, I want to see old Kentucky, even in that day of desolation, standing up, if left alone on the wasted field, brave and collected, with the flag of the Union in her hands, standing . . . like the last hero of a battle; and then, when the Union is no more, and she stands there the image of patriotism, of honor, and of heroism and of fidelity to the Union, it will be time enough for her to consider what next shall be done."[39]

Crittenden was interrupted again and again by applause from spectators. Once Senator Jesse D. Bright, in the chair, attempted to have the galleries cleared, but after five minutes the sergeant returned and reported it was impossible to do so. He and his assist-

[39] *Congressional Globe*, 36 Cong., 2 Sess., 1375-80.

ants were "physically tossed about" and themselves removed by the people in the galleries. The interruptions prolonged Crittenden's speech, and it was past nine o'clock when he sat down. The Senate was hushed—moved to silence, according to a member of the House who had crowded into the chamber, "by the glorious beauty of his last earnest . . . appeal for conciliation."[40]

Then Trumbull broke the silence. Why, he wanted to know, did not Crittenden turn his pleas to the seceders? Why were only Republicans at fault? Baker came once more to Crittenden's defense and, in doing so, confessed Republican miscalculation. At the beginning of the session, he said, secession had been regarded as only a bluff. Now it was a reality in seven states and was threatened in eight more. Crittenden, who was "Union to the very core," asked only that the Senate reassure his people. Baker would give reassurance. If war came, the government would have need of those people.

Douglas asked for a vote on several propositions in order: first on the House resolution, next on the peace conference resolutions, next on Crittenden's, and finally on the substitute of Seward and Trumbull. He asked that all amendments be withdrawn: their passage would in effect defeat any proposals, for the House had adjourned and would be unable to consider amendments. Then ensued a long debate in which nearly every senator except Crittenden engaged. Some thought passage of Crittenden's resolutions by the Senate, even though not acted on in the House, would do more to pacify the border states than would the House resolution. Others expressed preference for one of the other measures. Some wanted nothing done. The *unamendable* feature of the several proposals was attacked and defended.

Midnight came and went. It was now Monday, March 4. Within twelve hours the life of the Thirty-sixth Congress would come to an end. Yet the arguments went on. Pugh insisted that the Senate vote Crittenden's compromise. It had been endorsed, he said, by greater numbers than "any proposition that was ever before Congress." For two months they had fought to get a vote on it, but it had been brushed aside for railroads, tariffs, and pensions. He had heard Jefferson Davis say before he left that it would "maintain the Union if . . . [it] could receive the vote it ought to receive from the other side of this chamber." Even now, he added, if it could be voted, it

---

[40] *Congressional Globe*, 36 Cong., 2 Sess., 1375-77, 1380; Cox, *Three Decades*, 72.

would bring back all seceded states but South Carolina within twelve months, and even South Carolina soon thereafter. Douglas conceded all Pugh's arguments and vouched for Davis' statement, too. But, he repeated, it was now too late to get House action on Crittenden's propositions. Pass the House resolution, he urged; then the next Congress could take up once more the Crittenden proposals.

Four o'clock came and then five. Pugh moved to table all proposals and amendments but withdrew the motion when promised that he could get a vote on his motion to substitute Crittenden's proposals for the House resolution. His motion to substitute then lost, fourteen to twenty-five, Crittenden, Douglas, and Bigler voting with the majority against it. Bingham then offered another substitute for the House resolution. Bingham's substitute stated that no amendment to the Constitution was necessary, but it was defeated, thirteen to twenty-five. The Seward-Trumbull substitute was defeated by a like vote, and then the peace conference resolution. Finally, the House resolution could no longer be put aside, and a vote was taken. It passed by the two-thirds margin required for a constitutional amendment, twenty-four to twelve. All twelve negative votes were Republican. Thus was the proposed thirteenth amendment to the Constitution adopted by Congress and prepared for submission to the states for ratification. The war, of course, would intervene to prevent action by the states. At the war's close would come another thirteenth amendment, doing the very thing this resolution said must never be done.

After the passage of the House resolution, Mason moved to take up Crittenden's resolution, and it was finally before the Senate for a vote, at dawn on March 4. Crittenden moved to substitute the peace conference resolutions. This was agreed to, but the peace conference resolutions were then defeated. A vote was then taken on Crittenden's resolutions, and they were defeated nineteen to twenty. Not a single Republican was included in the nineteen affirmative votes, and all twenty opposition votes were Republican. Seward and four other moderate Republicans, Hale, Simmons, Collamer, and Cameron, were present but did not vote. The president's gavel fell. The turbulent life of the Thirty-sixth Congress was at an end. So, too, was Crittenden's long Senate career.[41]

---

[41] *Congressional Globe,* 36 Cong., 2 Sess., 1380-1405.

CHAPTER XX

Stand by the Union

DESPITE the failure of Congress to accept his proposals, Crittenden was lauded for his efforts. John Tyler, who had now forgiven Crittenden for their differences of two decades earlier, called the proposals "open and manly, like the man himself." Buchanan paid "a just tribute" to his vigor and perseverance in attempting to save the country from "the direful calamity of disunion and civil war." Jefferson Davis praised his wisdom, his "patriotic zeal," his "ardor and ability." The Baltimore *American* doubted if there had ever been, "even in the war of the Revolution, a grander and more impressive spectacle of true heroism . . . than that of this aged patriot, struggling upon the verge of that fearful precipice . . . , to save his country from disunion and civil strife." It bestowed the title long borne by John Quincy Adams on the Kentuckian. "Old man eloquent," it said, "a thousand blessings on thy venerable head!" Whatever befell, it added, "the noble efforts of Crittenden will command the respect of mankind and the admiration of posterity." If the Union survived the storm, it predicted, he would be regarded as the second savior of his country. The Kentucky senate thanked Crittenden, as also did the Virginia legislature, by an all but unanimous vote. The Washington city council formally expressed its gratitude for his long years of service to the Union.[1] So did the city councils of Cincinnati, Boston, and Wheeling, and public dinners were proffered him by citizens in Philadelphia and in Louisville.[2]

On March 7 Crittenden was serenaded by a large group of Washington citizens, and he responded in a stout Unionist speech. He said it was not the people who had caused the crisis, but "petty politicians" who misled the people. He pleaded with his audience to remain loyal to the Union. There was no profit for anyone in secession, for "The vision of disunion is anarchy, disorder, and ultimate war." Despotism would follow, he said, and instead of a Congress with free representation, the country would have a dictator who would rule. "Do not be deceived," he cautioned, "let no delusive scheme or glittering hopes that may be held out of advantages to be derived from our separation—breaking up into little States— let no idea of that sort delude you for a single moment." The working people, the mechanics, the bone and sinew of the land, would be withered and wasted. For after separation would come war, and the people would be called upon for taxes and for military service. There were some who thrived on disorder and war, and they would eat out the substance of the common people. Armies would be concentrated in their little villages, and they would be made "the packhorses and burden-bearers in time of war." Liberty, they would find, was a luxury to be enjoyed only in peace.[3]

Most contemporaries agreed that early adoption of Crittenden's proposals would have stayed secession in all states but South Carolina and thus would have averted the bloody war that followed. Nearly all recent scholarship has agreed with that conclusion. From December to March, however, Republicans stood as a solid phalanx of resistance to all conciliatory measures in the Senate Committee of Thirteen, in the House Committee of Thirty-three, in the peace convention called by Virginia, and on the floor of the two houses of Congress. According to Thurlow Weed, Republicans convinced

[1] Tyler, *Letters and Times*, II, 629; Buchanan, *Buchanan's Administration*, 131; Jefferson Davis to Mrs. Coleman, Sept. 17, 1871, in Crittenden Papers (Duke); Baltimore *American*, quoted in Louisville *Journal*, March 5, 20, 1861; *ibid.*, Feb. 11, 13, 1861; Frankfort *Commonwealth*, Jan. 24, 1861.

[2] Crittenden Papers, Letterbook, 1091, 1095, 1097-98, 1205-207, 1213-15 (Duke).

[3] Louisville *Journal*, March 13, 16, 1861.

southerners, particularly in the border states, that the North cared nothing for conciliation.[4]

In defense, Republicans stated that Crittenden's proposals entailed acceptance of the Breckinridge platform, but this was not accurate. The Breckinridge platform had called for federal protection of slavery in all the territories, north of 36° 30′ as well as south. Crittenden's proposal called for slaveholders to surrender the theoretical right, underwritten by the Supreme Court and by Congress as well as by legislatures in territories already organized, to take slaves north of the old Missouri line. As Buchanan pointed out, the Crittenden territorial compromise actually yielded everything to the North "except a mere abstraction." Restoration of the Missouri line had been the principal goal for which the Republican party had been founded, and had been its main stock in trade for the seven years since formation of the party. James Ford Rhodes has concluded that if the North had fully understood that failure of the Committee of Thirteen to agree on this issue meant that the cotton states would secede, "pressure from the North . . . would have been so great as to lead to the adoption of the Crittenden Compromise pure and simple." Rhodes concluded also that Lincoln never comprehended "the peril that menaced the nation should a settlement not be reached."[5]

Nor could Republicans honestly justify their refusal to compromise on the ground that the people had voted in November to sustain the Chicago platform at all hazards. As David Potter has shown, the proponents of slavery exclusion in the territories "lacked a majority, even before the secession crisis." To the 60 percent of the voters who cast ballots against Lincoln should be added, he says, thousands who voted for him for reasons other than slavery. Manufacturers wanting a protective tariff, homesteaders, transcontinental railroad advocates, all voted for him for reasons other than their concern about slavery in the territories. If to all these we add the voters who opposed the Democratic party because of its corruption, and those who voted for Lincoln for personal reasons, the vote on the slavery-exclusion issue is reduced even further.

Moreover, many Republicans who had endorsed the Chicago

---

4 Potter, *Lincoln and His Party*, 302; Barnes, *Memoir of Weed*, 312.

5 Rhodes, *History of the United States*, III, 61, 66; Buchanan, *Buchanan's Administration*, 135-36; Scrugham, *Peaceable Americans*, 61-62, 67; Blaine, *Twenty Years in Congress*, I, 269-70.

platform in November defected on a large scale in December, January, and February. Many good Republicans reported this to Crittenden, and Martin Van Buren predicted that although some Republicans might never openly support Crittenden's compromise proposal, they would nevertheless acquiesce in it when convinced that it would be acceptable to a large minority of their constituents. Buchanan, who gave the proposals what aid he could, was also certain they would have passed and would have prevented secession in all states except South Carolina. Potter's conclusion that "when Lincoln moved to defeat the compromise, he did not move as the champion of democracy, but as a partisan leader" is therefore almost irresistible.[6]

Had not the ground been cut from under them by the rigidity of the incoming administration, there were strong Unionist forces in the South that would have rallied to suppress secession. But Lincoln's refusal to permit passage of the conciliatory but intrinsically valueless territorial compromise drove southern Unionists into the camp of the secessionists. Had Republicans searched for the most effective device for promoting secession, as Stephen Douglas pointed out, they could not have found a better one than the refusal of conciliation while threatening coercion. "While conservative Southern men were exerting every effort to delay immediate action," says Dwight Dumond, "the Republicans . . . were fighting the battle for the unconditional secessionists." It was a fearful responsibility Lincoln and his party had assumed, "a breakdown of constructive statesmanship," James G. Randall called it.[7]

Crittenden tarried in Washington a few weeks after Congress adjourned. The Kentucky senate had requested him to remain and continue his work for conciliation as long as he judged it worthwhile. Hope of effecting a settlement no longer existed, but there was another reason for his remaining. Justice John A. Campbell, an Alabama Unionist, determined to resign from the Supreme Court after his state seceded, and Lincoln had decided to appoint Crittenden to the vacancy. The new cabinet approved, and an order was drawn up for his nomination. It was rumored that there was opposition from radical Republican senators, particularly from Sum-

---

[6] Potter, *Lincoln and His Party*, 189-92, 200; Van Buren to Crittenden, Dec. 24, 1860, in Van Buren Papers; Buchanan, *Buchanan's Administration*, 138, 140; Rhodes, *History of the United States*, III, 158-66.

[7] Dumond, *Secession Movement*, 168; Randall, *Lincoln the President*, II, 3.

ner, but Sumner publicly denied that he opposed the appointment. All obstacles seemed cleared when Campbell suddenly reconsidered, deciding not to resign at once. The court adjourned shortly thereafter and the nomination was never sent in. By the time the court reassembled, conditions had changed and Lincoln made other plans. Thus, for the second time, Crittenden was denied a place on the Supreme Court, even after he had been appointed.[8] But he was probably not greatly disappointed. Three decades earlier he had eagerly sought a Supreme Court appointment. Now old, tired, discouraged, worldly honors had long ceased to have great attraction for him. A year before, he had written Logan Hunton that he was eager to retire from public life. Many of his friends, men who had helped him shape historic events, had now passed from the scene and had been replaced by a younger generation.[9]

There remained, however, one final service Crittenden must perform for his country. Kentuckians were a divided and confused people, disturbed both at the unreasoning precipitancy with which the South had rushed into secession as well as with the folly and shortsightedness with which the North had rejected all compromise efforts. Fast-moving events combined with ancient ties, social mores, and economic interests to bewilder them to the point of political paralysis. But Kentuckians would have to choose, and their decision would be crucial for the nation. Lincoln himself best expressed the importance of Kentucky to the Union cause when he wrote Orville Browning: "I think to lose Kentucky is nearly the same as to lose the whole game. Kentucky gone, we cannot hold Missouri, nor, as I think, Maryland. These all against us, and the job on our hands is too big for us. We would as well consent to separation at once, including the surrender of this capital."[10] It was to save Kentucky for the Union that Crittenden hurried home in mid-March.

The homecoming at Frankfort was a sad one, for the dearest of old friends were no longer there. Burnley lingered on, racked and wasted by a fatal pulmonary ailment, but Letcher and Thomas Carneal, both of whom had shared Crittenden's inmost thoughts for

[8] Frederic Bancroft, *Life of William H. Seward*, 2 vols. (New York and London, 1900), II, 97; Stanton to Lincoln, March 6, 1861, in John G. Nicolay Papers, Library of Congress; New York *Times*, March 8, 9, 15, 20, 1861; Stanton to Buchanan, March 10, 14, 1861, in Buchanan, *Works*, XI, 163, 169.

[9] Crittenden to Logan Hunton, April 15, 1860 [?], in Crittenden Papers (Duke).

[10] John G. Nicolay and John Hay (eds.), *Complete Works of Abraham Lincoln*, 12 vols. (New York, 1895), VI, 359-60.

more than a quarter century, had passed away during Crittenden's great ordeal in Washington. At the time of Letcher's death Burnley had written Crittenden a plaintive message: "I never wanted to see you at home as much in my life; but I am willing never to see you in this world again if you can save the Union."[11]

Since the abortive separation movement in Kentucky during the first decade of statehood, Unionist sentiment had grown there sturdy as an oak. Unionism had been nourished by the part played by pioneer Kentuckians in conquering the forest from the forces of nature and in defending their newly won Eden from Indian reprisals. It had matured during the War of 1812, when Kentuckians had reclaimed at the Thames the great northwestern empire surrendered by William Hull the year before. It had been renewed by the blood of Kentuckians spilled at Monterrey, at Buena Vista, and at Palo Alto. The average Kentuckian was not given to reasoning about the Union; his feeling was like a religious devotion that he accepted without delving into the why or the wherefore. "I am a *National man*," wrote Orlando Brown as the secession crisis deepened, "and hate, from the bottom of my soul, every man who has been in any way instrumental in robbing me of my nationality."[12]

All political parties in Kentucky in the 1860 election, even Breckinridge's, had pledged unqualified devotion to the Union. The people were "for the Union and Constitution intact," stated a resolution of the Constitutional Union party that year. Kentucky, it added, "will redress her wrongs inside of the Union and not out of it." But even here, as in the other border states, slavery produced a dichotomy in this fervent support of the Union. During the 1850s, Kentucky was growing more reactionary as to slavery. In December, 1859, John G. Fee and his abolitionist associates were driven by a mob from Madison County, and the action was enthusiastically approved by mass meetings throughout the state. Thereafter, as if in endorsement, the legislature repealed a law prohibiting the importation of slaves into the state and passed a law making it a crime to write, print, or circulate incendiary documents. Another law prohibited the emancipation of slaves without providing for their re-

[11] Burnley to Crittenden, Feb. 12, 1861, in Crittenden Papers (Duke). See also, Thomas H. Clay to Crittenden, Jan. 4, 1861, in Coleman, *Crittenden*, II, 253; John B. Bibb to Crittenden, Dec. 15, 1860, in Crittenden Papers.

[12] Brown to Crittenden, March 7, 1861, in Crittenden Papers; Collins, *History of Kentucky*, II, 895.

moval from the state, and also forbade free Negroes to enter the state.[13]

But slavery cut both ways on the issue of union or secession. There were some slaves in every county, but the largest numbers were concentrated in the Bluegrass region, in Jefferson County, and in a rich agricultural region of southwestern Kentucky, from Warren County to the Jackson Purchase. The conservative landed aristocracy, who owned most of the slaves, were in most cases Unionist. They could see no advantage in secession, for there would no longer be a fugitive-slave law to catch and return their runaways. The large middle class were not as a rule concerned about slavery, but the poorer farmers and mechanics "hated slaves and . . . their owners."[14]

Even though it may be an oversimplification, it is not far off the mark to say that at the beginning of 1861 there were three main divisions within the state. First of all there was the relatively small group that was Unionist to the core. No matter what the provocation, they could not be won to secession. These people were concentrated largely on the northern border of the state, although there were individuals of this opinion in all sections. They would sacrifice anything, one of their critics wrote, "slaves, territory—almost the right of suffrage," in order to remain in the Union. Next was a small but vociferous group who were for immediate secession, and who did not seek or want northern concessions. Ties with southern states and with what, for lack of a better term, was and is called the southern way of life drew them to the South. Located generally in the southern and western part of the state, they too had a few sympathizers in all sections.

In between these extremes was a larger group, undoubtedly a majority, who loved the Union and peace and who believed that by concession and mediation, grievances might be redressed. They did not believe in coercion of the seceded states, and they took their stand on the Crittenden compromise. Amos Kendall, a skilled judge of public opinion, thought that all the 92,000 Kentuckians who had voted for Douglas and Bell as well as three-fourths of the 52,000 who had voted for Breckinridge were at one and the same time "staunch supporters of the Union, and adversaries to Northern

---

[13] Collins, *History of Kentucky*, I, 82-83.
[14] Arndt M. Stickles, *Simon Bolivar Buckner, Borderland Knight* (Chapel Hill, 1940), 47-49; Wilson P. Shortridge, "Kentucky Neutrality in 1861," in *Mississippi Valley Historical Review*, IX (1922-1923), 287-88.

interference with Southern institutions."[15] Another political observer thought these people wanted "all their rights but believe they can get them in the Union. They want Revolution to be the last resort." There would be time enough for that in the future, if it were found necessary.[16] Ten years of negotiation, wrote another, was "preferable to the shedding of one drop of blood." They were for the Union, he added, "as long as it is honorable to stay in it. We are against coercion. We are for making peace before war is declared."[17]

Economic forces unassociated directly with slavery were also influencing sentiment for or against secession. Secessionists argued that the prosperity of Kentucky depended upon merchandising to the South and that unless Kentucky joined the Confederacy, the southern market would be lost. Unionists replied that if Kentucky seceded, she could not import through the East and that her commerce would thus be limited to one section. Furthermore, they argued, railroads built in the past decade had considerably modified Kentucky's marketing. These railroads now made it possible for vast quantities of Kentucky pork and grain to reach eastern and European markets. But these markets would be lost by secession and the consequent imposition of the northern tariff. Business interests, therefore, particularly the railroads, were inclined to Unionism.[18]

Another economic factor worked for the Union. Expenses of the federal government had generally been borne by import duties and public land sales. Only under unusual circumstances, and then but briefly, had direct taxation of the people been resorted to. But southerners were historically opposed to a tariff, and it was taken for granted that the Confederacy would adopt a free-trade policy. That would necessitate a direct property tax that would be ruinous to property holders. One Hardin County farmer estimated that his own property would have to pay an annual tax of a thousand dollars to the Confederate government if Kentucky should secede.[19]

Geography, too, tended to draw Kentucky away from the Confederacy. If she should secede and war should follow, her elongated

15 Kendall, *Autobiography*, 581.

16 A. M. Brown to Samuel Haycraft, Jan. 19, 1861 (photostat), in Haycraft Papers, University of Kentucky Library.

17 E. F. Nattall to Crittenden, Jan. 11, 1861, in Crittenden Papers.

18 Shortridge, "Kentucky Neutrality," 288-89; Charles A. Davis to Crittenden, Feb. 14, 1861, in Crittenden Papers; Stickles, *Buckner*, 49-50.

19 Samuel Haycraft to Mrs. Samuel Haycraft, Feb. 6, 1861, in Haycraft Papers (Kentucky).

boundary of some seven hundred miles would adjoin the free states of Ohio, Indiana, and Illinois, and their five-and-a-half million people would be pitted against Kentucky's population of fewer than a million. Furthermore, seven railroads in those states had terminal points on the Ohio, so that the Northwest could speedily throw overwhelming numbers of troops across Kentucky's border.

The struggle in Kentucky first centered on the question of calling a convention, the accepted method of effecting secession. In the excited state of the time, such a convention might well have been swept into secession by the overpowering momentum already created by southern nationalism. Unionists, therefore, aimed at preventing the call. They pointed out that if the purpose of such a convention was to keep Kentucky in the Union, a convention was unnecessary, for, one editor said, "we are thank God already there." On the other hand, if its purpose was to take the state out of the Union, it was "pernicious."[20]

But Governor Beriah Magoffin had strong southern sympathies. Furthermore, he assumed that the Union was already irretrievably dissolved, and he was certain that there was little sentiment in Kentucky for coercing the seceded states. Consequently, while Crittenden was struggling to bring his proposals to a vote in the Senate, Magoffin called the legislature into special session on January 17 and urged it to call a convention to consider Kentucky's proper course. At the same time he urged a border-state convention to provide for a peaceable solution of the problems facing the dissolved Union.[21]

At first it was difficult to tell which party, Southern Rights or Unionist, was stronger in the legislature. Douglas men and Bell men, who had now joined forces, were almost equal in number to the Breckinridge men in the senate but were a decided minority in the house. Had all Breckinridge men been secessionists, a convention bill would have been quickly passed. But some of the Breckinridge party refused to join at once the secession movement, and their refusal gave Unionists the opportunity they needed to fight a delaying action, hoping that the next elections would return a solid and

---

[20] Crittenden to Leslie Combs, Jan. 28, 1861, in Frankfort *Commonwealth*, Feb. 2, 1861; *ibid.*, Jan. 26, 1861, quoted in J. R. Robertson, "Sectionalism in Kentucky from 1855 to 1865," 60; Thomas H. Clay to Crittenden, Jan. 9, 1861, in Coleman, *Crittenden*, II, 253.

[21] *Kentucky House Journal, January Session, 1861*, p. 9; Collins, *History of Kentucky*, I, 86; Shortridge, "Kentucky Neutrality," 289-90.

dependable Union majority. The greatest fear of Unionists was that the contagious enthusiasm aroused by the emerging southern Confederacy might impetuously sweep the state out of the Union.[22]

The Union cause won an early victory when both houses voted to raise the Stars and Stripes over the capitol dome. A few days later, however, a house resolution denouncing northern threats of coercion passed unanimously and another resolution, passed by a vote of eighty-seven to six, warned that Kentucky would resist armed invasion of the South. In the senate these resolutions were tabled in favor of one accepting Virginia's invitation to the Washington peace conference. Both houses had already endorsed the Crittenden compromise then pending in Congress; but the house included in its endorsement a clause stating that if the northern states rejected it, Kentucky would "consider herself forever absolved from all allegiance to the Federal Constitution." But in a test vote in the house in mid-February on a convention bill, the Unionists won fifty-four to thirty-six. The legislature then adjourned until March 20.[23]

When it reconvened, both Lincoln and Jefferson Davis had been inaugurated and pressure for decisive action was mounting. Crittenden, now returned from Washington, was invited to address a joint session, and on March 26 he did so. He spoke for nearly two hours, reviewing the history of the slavery controversy and explaining his efforts to effect a compromise. He conceded that Congress had the right and duty to govern the territories but argued that it should not discriminate in exercising this right. Excluding by federal law any class of property, including slaves, from the territories was unjust. "The North was in the wrong and the South was in the right in respect to this question," he said. However, he was convinced, from the thousands of petitions that had come to Congress, that northern people did not hate the South. Human nature was such that man was incapable of "hating" whole classes of people "for the sins of a few." He was sure that a majority of northern people differed with their representatives and that if given a

[22] Shortridge, "Kentucky Neutrality," 290-91; Robert M. McElroy, *Kentucky in the Nation's History* (New York, 1909), 509-11.

[23] *Kentucky House Journal, January Session, 1861,* pp. 43, 65; Collins, *History of Kentucky,* I, 86; Shortridge, "Kentucky Neutrality," 290-91; McElroy, *Kentucky,* 511-14; Leslie Combs to Robert Anderson, Jan. 18, 1861, in Robert Anderson Papers, Library of Congress.

chance, they would save the Union. Party loyalty and party discipline, however, prevented them from voting as they wished. They were elected as partisans, on party platforms, and were "subject to the control of their party."

The Chicago platform, "a thing no bigger than my hand," he said, had been set up "like an idol of old, and worshipped, and a great country . . . sacrificed upon its altars." But he had faith in the people, more than he had in Presidents, senators, or congressmen. "I believe in the intelligence of the people," he said; "I believe in the public virtue of the people. . . . I find that there is a wisdom, a generosity, and a public virtue, that will not allow this country . . . to go down in ruins." Meanwhile, he said, the object of everyone should be to bring back seceders, some of whom were "of our families—some of them our brothers." They might secede from the government, but they could not secede from "those thousand affections that bind them to us." Nature had tied bonds that could not be untied, least of all by party difficulties and political troubles. The seceders had "greatly erred"; they had done "wrong to themselves, wrong to us, and wrong to all mankind," by breaking up the government "whose promises reached humanity in every region of the world."

Secession, he told his audience, was not legal. What the seceders had done was revolution. The Union was not legally broken, therefore, but still existed. However, the national government should not employ force but should follow a policy of "forbearance and peace," in order to win back the affection of the southern people. "Let them go in peace with their experiment," he said. When it proved too costly and too difficult, as it surely would, they would wish to return. "Do not excite them," he urged, "by war or bloodshed," for that would forever exclude reconciliation. As for Kentucky's course, although she should show forbearance toward the erring seceded states, her interest was with the Union, "whose blessings we have so long experienced."[24]

Crittenden's argument was persuasive, and the legislature adjourned on April 4, again without calling a convention. It was doubtless fortunate for the Union cause that it was not in session

[24] *Kentucky House Journal, January Session, 1861,* p. 378; Louisville *Journal,* March 27, 1861; Frankfort *Commonwealth,* March 27, 29, 1861; McElroy, *Kentucky,* 514.

eight days later, when Fort Sumter was attacked. Had it been, the contagion of excitement might have forced through a convention bill that would have led to secession.[25] But the attack on Sumter, and Lincoln's call for troops to put down the rebellion, only increased the confusion of Kentuckians; and southern sympathizers now took advantage of this confusion in an intensified drive for secession. At a meeting in Louisville on April 16 they advocated arming the state to resist any federal troops that might enter Kentucky in an effort to coerce the seceded states. Neutrality meetings and petitions were gotten up in all parts of the state, and such a wise and patriotic man as Madison C. Johnson of Lexington actually wrote out a resolution to present in the legislature, urging Congress to recognize the independence of the southern states.[26]

It was difficult for Kentuckians to distinguish between the attitudes taken by some northern states, on the one hand, and that of the federal government, now under the control of a northern sectional party. Slavery in the territories was the core of the conflict between the sections, and Kentuckians agreed with Crittenden that the South was right on that question. Consequently, coercion looked very much to Kentucky Unionists "like a war upon the part of the Free States against Slavery, in which the General Government was . . . made the instrument of attacking the people of the . . . Slave States on account of their having this property."[27] To have attempted to force Kentucky in the spring or summer of 1861 into a war against the South would have resulted in throwing the state into the Confederacy. Unionist leaders, therefore, advocated neutrality as the only alternative to secession. George D. Prentice and James Speed, members of a joint central committee of the Bell and Douglas parties, issued an address to the public approving Magoffin's refusal of Lincoln's call for troops and urging, curiously, the taking of sides "not with the Government and not with the seceding states, but with the Union against them both." A Union held together "by the sword," they said, was "not worth preserving."[28]

Crittenden agreed with them that neutrality was the proper

[25] Collins, *History*, I, 86-87; McElroy, *Kentucky*, 515-20; Frankfort *Commonwealth*, April 15, May 1, 1861.

[26] Shortridge, "Kentucky Neutrality," 294-95; copy of Johnson resolution, with notations by Crittenden, in Crittenden Papers.

[27] Garret Davis to Robert Anderson, April 20, 1861, in Robert Anderson Papers.

[28] Collins, *History of Kentucky*, I, 85-88.

course for Kentucky. In mid-April he started on a tour of the central part of the state advocating such a program. He told a large crowd at the Odd Fellows Hall in Lexington that Kentucky's honor was in no way obligated to support the Confederacy, for Kentucky had had no part in formulating the Confederate policies that had brought secession and war. On the other hand, he said, it was unthinkable that Kentucky would make active war on the South. Her proper course was neutrality, holding herself ready at all times to act as mediator. Neither side should cross her borders. But if Kentucky should secede, he warned, she would be in a war the conclusion of which no man could foresee. He called upon his audience to think long before casting their lot with the Confederacy.[29]

Loyalty to the Union, he told another group, who called upon him to clarify the position of Union men, needed no defense. Union men stood "where God & their fathers placed them." They stood "by that *Constitution & Union,* under which they have always lived," under which they had grown in freedom, in prosperity, and in happiness. Those "who come to seduce Union men to *desert* their Union" were the ones from whom explanations should be demanded. What wrongs had they suffered within the Union that could be more readily redressed outside of it?[30]

In early May, Magoffin called the legislature into a third session. Lincoln's conciliatory inaugural address together with statements he made to Congressmen Garret Davis and Warner L. Underwood encouraged Kentucky Unionists to hope that he would respect a neutral policy in the state. To Davis he had said that he had no plans to move troops across Kentucky, and he assured Underwood that if the state would "stand still," he would make no move against her. At the legislature's suggestion, Unionists and Southern Rightists each appointed three prominent citizens to meet and formulate a program that the legislature could agree on. Unionists named Crittenden, Archibald Dixon, and S. S. Nicholas; the Southern Rights party named John C. Breckinridge, Magoffin, and Richard Hawes. The latter group proposed calling a convention, but the Unionists flatly refused. Instead, they suggested a declaration of neutrality, and

[29] Louisville *Journal,* April 22, 1861; Frankfort *Commonwealth,* April 15, 1861; Danville (Ky.) *Tribune,* quoted *ibid.,* May 1, 1861.
[30] Crittenden to Gentlemen of Jessamine County, April 8, 1861, Letterbook, 807-808, in Crittenden Papers (Duke).

this was finally agreed to. Both houses thereupon resolved that Kentucky should remain neutral and work for mediation, and Magoffin followed their action with a neutrality proclamation. This was a clear-cut victory for the Union cause, for the legislature now adjourned sine die. Immediate danger of secession was past, and there was now time to work for a more solid adherence to the Union cause.[31]

But neutrality was an anomalous position and was clearly only a temporary expedient. Actually it was just as much a declaration of state sovereignty as was secession, and it was only a slightly different manifestation of the very principle that South Carolina and other southern states had avowed in seceding from the Union. It would soon bring Kentucky, however, to an entirely different course from that of her sisters to the South. As Crittenden explained to General Scott at the time, Kentucky was, under the confused conditions, "rendering better service . . . than she could by becoming an active party in the contest."[32]

Meanwhile, Kentucky Unionists were faced with another problem. During the preceding year, the state militia, under the name of State Guard, had been thoroughly reorganized by Simon Bolivar Buckner. By the spring of 1861 it numbered about five thousand well-trained men from all parts of the state. With the exception of the United States Army, which was little more than twice as large, it was perhaps "the best drilled and best officered" military force in the country.[33] Its very efficiency, however, was disturbing to Unionists. For Buckner and most of his corps of officers were believed to be prosouthern, and Unionists feared the Guard might be used to promote secession. Indeed, it was largely because of this fear that Unionists generally approved of Magoffin's refusal to respond to Lincoln's call for troops after Sumter. All Union men were needed at home, Crittenden wrote, to prevent a State Guard coup from seizing the state in the interest of the Confederacy.[34]

By a patently unconstitutional procedure, the legislature now took control of the State Guard from the governor and from Buckner, placing it under a board of five commissioners. This board, fearing at

[31] Collins, History of Kentucky, I, 88-91; McElroy, Kentucky, 523-26.
[32] Crittenden to Scott, May 17, 1861, in Robert Todd Lincoln Papers.
[33] Stickles, Buckner, 46; E. Merton Coulter, The Civil War and Readjustment in Kentucky (Chapel Hill, 1926), 82-83.
[34] Crittenden to Scott, May 17, 1861, in Robert Todd Lincoln Papers.

first to take such drastic action as the disbanding of the State Guard, raised a new class of militia to counter its influence and to serve only in the home county of the militiamen. These were called Home Guards, to distinguish them from the prosouthern militia. In late April a company was formed in Frankfort, and Crittenden, along with 161 others, joined as a private.[35]

But all arms were in possession of the State Guard, and there were none to be purchased for the Home Guard. Lincoln was appealed to, and he responded. On the night of May 7, Crittenden, James Harlan, Charles A. Wickliffe, Garret Davis, and Thornton F. Marshall met secretly in a room of the Capitol Hotel in Frankfort. Here they were joined by James and Joshua F. Speed from Louisville. With the Speeds was an emissary from Lincoln, naval Lieutenant William Nelson, a native Kentuckian and a man of gigantic physical proportions. Nelson brought a promise from Lincoln to furnish all arms needed, provided precautions were taken to ensure that they not fall into the hands of secessionists. The little group formed themselves into a "Union Defense Committee," and within ten days five thousand muskets were surreptitiously delivered into the hands of Home Guardsmen, and three weeks later came another five thousand. From central points they were conveyed by wagon to outlying regions. These arms gave assurance and confidence to Kentucky Unionists and may have been a decisive factor in saving the state from secession.[36]

By early May, therefore, public sentiment, which only a few weeks before had hung in the balance, had swung decidedly against secession. At its meeting in April the legislature had issued a call for a border-states convention to meet in Frankfort the following month. Crittenden was unenthusiastic about prospects of its accomplishing anything substantial, but reluctantly he consented to be a candidate.[37]

Election of delegates was set for May 4, and two separate tickets,

[35] Collins, History of Kentucky, I, 90-91; Coulter, Civil War and Readjustment, 86-89; McElroy, Kentucky, 523-24; Frankfort Commonwealth, April 29, 1861.

[36] Captain Thomas Speed, The Union Cause in Kentucky (New York and London, 1907), 100-10; Robert L. Kincaid, "Joshua Fry Speed—1814-1882, Abraham Lincoln's Most Intimate Friend," in Filson Quarterly, XVII (1944), 78; William H. Seward to the Union Defense Committee [of Kentucky], May 9, 1861, in Seward Collection, Chicago Historical Society; Letters to General Robert Anderson from John A. Dix, May 20, from Seward, May 31, from Garret Davis, June 5, from Thornton F. Marshall, June 6, from J. M. Delph, June 6, and from James Harlan, July 27, 1861, in Robert Anderson Papers.

[37] Crittenden to S. S. Nicholas, Dec. [?], 1860 (copy), in Crittenden Papers.

Unionist and Southern Rights, were made up. The Unionist slate, headed by Crittenden, recommended the Crittenden compromise as a basis of readjustment but expressed willingness to accept any plan the convention agreed to, provided that it was endorsed by the people of the North and then incorporated into the Constitution. The Southern Rights party also advocated the Crittenden compromise but with different implications. All through the winter and spring this party had been working to win Crittenden to its support. While making vitriolic attacks on other Unionists—Prentice, Garret Davis, Guthrie, the Speeds, Robert J. Breckinridge—they had treated Crittenden gently. For if they could but gain his support, one of their editors admitted, "the last vestige to opposition [to secession] in Kentucky would be swept away." Now they advocated his compromise proposals, not as a basis for negotiation, but as an ultimatum. If the proposals were refused by the North, they said, Kentucky should join the southern Confederacy. Before the election of delegates, however, the Southern Rights party withdrew their ticket. War had already come, they explained, so that talk of readjustment was now futile. The Unionist ticket, therefore, won by default. Yet even without opposition, its twelve candidates received a total of 104,000 votes, two-thirds as many as were cast in the Kentucky presidential election six months before. This was, indeed, encouraging to Unionists.[38]

Other than the moral effect produced by this vote, the convention was devoid of accomplishment. Crittenden was chosen president and called the first session to order on the morning of May 27 in the chamber of the court of appeals. Only nine of Kentucky's twelve delegates were present, only four of Missouri's seven, only one from Tennessee and he somewhat irregularly chosen. Tennessee, as well as Virginia, had already thrown in her lot with the Confederacy, and Maryland was apparently too disturbed by events there to send delegates. Delaware was also unrepresented.

To the people of the nation the convention issued an address that denied the right of secession and recommended the Crittenden compromise as a basis of reconstruction of the Union. It pledged Kentucky's loyalty to the Union but advocated her neutrality in the conflict. To the people of Kentucky it issued a separate address.

[38] Louisville *Courier*, issues through winter and spring, especially March 21, April 4, 27, June 3, 1861; Frankfort *Commonwealth*, April 12, May 1, June 17, 1861; Louisville *Journal*, March 19, 27, 1861; Coulter, *Civil War and Readjustment*, 51-52.

Both sides in the controversy were wrong, it said, and both had acted with "madness and folly." Kentucky had no cause of quarrel with the Constitution and no wish to quarrel with her neighbors. All she asked was permission to remain aloof from "this unnatural strife." The war had come as a result of "the ambitions of men, rather than from the wrongs done the people."[39]

Soon another election would further confirm the still somewhat qualified Unionism of Kentucky. Lincoln had called a special session of Congress to meet July 4, and the Kentucky delegation, which normally would have been elected in August, had to be chosen in a special election set for June 20. Before Crittenden's return from Washington, a move had been started to persuade him to run for Congress from the old Ashland District. Crittenden, long resolved to retire from public life, at first refused to consider the suggestion. By March, however, pressure to win his consent was mounting. No one else would satisfy the Union men, and mass meetings in the district were ignoring his refusal to become a candidate and were declaring for him. Even the Louisville *Democrat*, until then a dedicated and bitter critic of Crittenden, joined in. Crittenden's course in the secession crisis, wrote editor J. H. Harney, deserved the commendation of every patriot. He had neither abandoned the rights of the South nor given any quarter to the extremists who had broken the Union, and the overwhelming opinion of the state supported him. "We want good service and wise service in Congress," said the patriotic Harney, and to secure "such services as those of Crittenden, we shall give up all past party predilections." Crittenden, he added, was "a power in this State . . . on the right side—a power that extends from one end of the Union to the other."[40]

Finally, at the end of May, Crittenden yielded to the pressure and consented to become the candidate of the Unionist party. His opponent was the incumbent, William E. Simms, an ardent Southern Rights advocate, and secessionists now concentrated their efforts on defeating Crittenden. If they could do so, they believed there would still be hope of taking the state into the Confederacy. Union

[39] Frankfort *Commonwealth*, May 29, June 5, 1861; Collins, *History of Kentucky*, I, 91.

[40] Letters to Crittenden from C. J. Blackburn, Feb. 21, from Orlando Brown, March 7, from D. C. Wickliffe, May 7, and from Garret Davis, May 11, 1861, in Crittenden Papers; Louisville *Democrat*, March 4, 1861; Louisville *Journal*, March 5, 1861; *ibid.*, June 13, copying letter of Morehead to W. A. Dudley, June 7, 1861; Frankfort *Commonwealth*, March 11, 1861.

men, however, were aware of the significance of the contest, and they, too, were thoroughly aroused. There was little time to campaign, but Crittenden moved through the district. Crowds gathered about him, as "with all the vigor and spirit of a young man, unbent by age, his . . . form erect, his voice clear and thrilling, his eye blazing with all the fervor the high responsibility of his position inspired," he appealed to their patriotism. He told them that he believed the rebellion should and would be suppressed. The South, he said, by attacking Sumter had become the aggressor.[41]

The election was an overwhelming Union triumph throughout the state. Unionist candidates won nine of the ten congressional districts, losing only in the First District. Their total margin over the Southern Rights party was 50,000 votes. Crittenden's majority was 2,566 more than twice the margin by which the Unionist candidates would carry the district in the legislative election in August. Had Crittenden faltered or had he pursued any other course than the one he did, according to William B. Kinkead, Kentucky would have been lost to the Union.[42]

Crittenden, a veteran of the Senate but a seventy-five-year-old freshman in the House, took the oath as a member of the Thirty-seventh Congress on July 5, and was assigned at once to the important Committee on Foreign Affairs. Four days later he was asked to deliver a eulogy of Douglas, whose sudden death had occurred a month before. He paid tribute to his late companion in the compromise struggle as "an honorable and patriotic man . . . ready to sacrifice his personal interests for the good of his country." Douglas would be sorely missed, he said, in the crisis ahead. When he sat down, S. S. Cox of Ohio arose and, pointing to Crittenden, reminded the House that he had been spared "to guide our storm-tossed and storm-tattered vessel to its haven of rest." In the order of nature he would not be long with them, but while he was, "let us . . . learn from his lips the lessons of moderation and loyalty."[43]

Many Kentuckians were looking to Crittenden to resume his efforts at conciliation, hoping the war might thus be brought to a speedy conclusion. He sought advice from trusted friends, most of

[41] Frankfort *Commonwealth*, May 14, 23, June 3, 7, 14, 19, 28, 1861; Letter of William B. Kinkead in New York *Sun*, Aug. 21, 1887.
[42] Kinkead in New York *Sun*, Aug. 21, 1887; Frankfort *Yeoman*, Aug. 8, 1861; Shortridge, "Kentucky Neutrality," 296-97.
[43] *Congressional Globe*, 37 Cong., 1 Sess., 22, 35-36; Cox, *Three Decades*, 68.

whom urged that he delay such a move, for neither of the adversaries would listen to talk of peace without the clash of arms for which they were preparing. Moreover, his return to Congress was received with mixed sentiments in the North, where many feared that if he renewed his compromise proposals the war effort would be weakened. Some even believed that his election had been shrewdly contrived by Confederate sympathizers with that very purpose in mind. Consequently, many of the conservatives who had rallied to his standard the winter before would now desert him should he renew his compromise plan. Better to let someone else take the lead, his friends now advised. Crittenden could then sustain that effort.[44]

But there was another matter of pressing concern. Kentuckians and other border Unionists, suspicious of northern intentions, were eager to clarify issues. For what purpose was the federal government girding for war: was it to preserve the integrity of the Union, or was it to put an end to slavery? Kentuckians were alarmed, too, at Lincoln's seeming inclination to disregard restrictions imposed on him by the Constitution. Already he had moved by decree to expand the regular army, a power delegated by the Constitution to Congress. Also, unsure of the loyalty of certain government officials, the President had on his own authority directed the Secretary of the Treasury to advance $2,000,000 without security to some New York businessmen to pay for "military and naval measures necessary for the defense and support of the Government." This was a clear violation of the constitutional provision that no money should be drawn from the Treasury except by act of Congress. He had suspended issuance of the writ of habeas corpus in Maryland and defied a ruling of Chief Justice Roger B. Taney that only Congress could exercise such a power. Following that, he instructed General George Cadwallader to refuse service of a writ issued by the Chief Justice that ordered the military to surrender a political prisoner to the marshal. This was, indeed, strange conduct for a government professing to wage a war to uphold the Constitution.[45]

To calm the fears of border Unionists, as well as to gain their

---

[44] Thomas Ewing to Crittenden, June 25, 1861, in Crittenden Papers (Duke); Garret Davis to Larz Anderson, in Frankfort *Commonwealth*, July 12, 1861; Joseph R. Underwood to Crittenden, July 13, 1861, in Crittenden Papers; Cincinnati *Press* and New York *World*, quoted in Louisville *Courier*, June 26, 1861.

[45] Randall, *Civil War and Reconstruction*, 360-62, 394-95. See also, Charles S. Morehead to Crittenden, June 30, 1861, in Crittenden Papers.

cooperation in the war effort, Crittenden decided to offer in the House a resolution clearly defining federal war aims. On July 19 he gave notice of such a resolution, and three days later, as Irvin McDowell's army was reeling back from its demoralizing repulse at Bull Run, he called it up. It declared: "That the present deplorable civil war has been forced upon the country by the disunionists of the southern States, . . . that . . . Congress, banishing all feelings of mere passion or resentment, will recollect only its duty to the whole country; that this war is not waged on their part in any spirit of oppression, or for any purpose of conquest or subjugation, or . . . of overthrowing or interfering with the rights or established institutions of those States, but to defend and maintain the *supremacy* of the Constitution, and to preserve the Union with all the dignity, equality, and rights of the several States unimpaired; and that as soon as these objects are accomplished the war ought to cease."[46]

Henry C. Burnett, the one Southern Rights representative from Kentucky, asked that the resolution be divided, and it was. On the first part, that stating that the war was the work of southern disunionists, only Burnett and one other voted in the negative as it passed, 122 to 2. On the remainder, only Representatives John F. Potter from Wisconsin and Albert G. Riddle of Ohio cast negative votes as it passed, 117 to 2. Two days later the resolution was passed in the Senate, thirty to five, Breckinridge and Powell from Kentucky joining Trumbull, and Walden P. Johnson and Trusten Polk of Missouri in the minority.[47]

The northern press enthusiastically endorsed the resolution. The New York *Times*, until then unsure of Crittenden's intentions, now acquitted him of any leaning to disloyalty. The resolution, it said, went "to the very core of the questions at issue" and would have a good psychological effect in the border states.[48] Quite clearly this resolution meant that the war would not be an antislavery war; it meant, equally clearly, that the Union would later be restored as it was before secession. Although those sentiments would be repudiated in less than two weeks, Crittenden thought that a significant victory had been won in the cause of reconciliation.[49]

[46] *Congressional Globe*, 37 Cong., 1 Sess., 209, 222-23.
[47] *Congressional Globe*, 37 Cong., 1 Sess., 222-23, 243, 265.
[48] New York *Times*, July 28, 1861.
[49] Crittenden to Elizabeth Crittenden, July 19, 1861, in Coleman, *Crittenden*, II, 329.

Crittenden now stoutly supported all measures for the furnishing of men and supplies to prosecute the war, just as he had in the Mexican War a decade and a half before. But when the first of a series of acts confiscating the property of citizens in the seceding states was proposed, he spoke out against it. Slaves were being used in Confederate camps as servants and in the building of fortifications, and frequently these slaves had been impressed from unwilling masters. As early as May, General Benjamin F. Butler, commanding at Fortress Monroe in Virginia, had classed them as contraband and had refused to return to their masters three such slaves who fled into his lines. On August 2 a Senate bill providing for confiscation of all slaves used in promoting insurrection was reported in the House.[50]

Crittenden argued that the confiscation bill was unconstitutional. It was universally admitted, he said, that Congress had no power in time of peace to legislate on slavery in a state, and war did not modify that restriction in any way. William Kellogg of Illinois interrupted to point out that some southern slaveowners had committed treason, and that for that reason their property could be confiscated. The Constitution, Crittenden replied, defined treason and provided punishment for it. Many of the slaveowners who would be affected by the bill could not be adjudged guilty of treason in a fair trial, but even if they could be, their slaves could not be legally confiscated. The Constitution forbade forfeiture of property "of any description" beyond the lifetime of the offender, and the bill under discussion provided for a forfeiture "forever" of the slaves.

Aside from its unconstitutionality, he said, the bill was impolitic. For it would be charged that "we are making an anti-slavery war." Furthermore, the bill contradicted his resolution, passed just the week before, and would undo the good work that resolution had already accomplished. They should not descend to such "small, petty means" of annoyance. "Let us do no act," he begged, "that shall degrade this struggle from its national character." But his plea was overridden. The great haste with which the bill was passed suggests that either the vote on Crittenden's resolution was a meaningless gesture or else the mood of Congress had experienced a speedy and unexplained reversal. The Senate bill, with minor amendments, passed the House

---

[50] *Congressional Globe*, 37 Cong., 1 Sess., 231, 409-15; Randall, *Civil War and Reconstruction*, 478.

on August 3 by a margin of sixty to forty-eight. Two days later the amended bill passed the Senate, twenty-four to eleven.[51]

Meanwhile, conciliatory Unionist tactics in Kentucky were increasing Union sentiment there. Lincoln had shrewdly sent a native Kentuckian, Robert Anderson, of Fort Sumter fame, now promoted to brigadier general, to command the Department of Kentucky. Anderson was a brother of Crittenden's friend Larz Anderson of Cincinnati. Advised of the delicate balance of sentiment in Kentucky, Anderson refused to sanction open recruiting within the state prior to the August elections, and Lincoln supported him in this, even against the wishes of the War Department.[52] By early July, therefore, Kentuckians were more and more pleased with their decision against secession. "We are losing no votes," Orlando Brown wrote, "while the *secession* voters are moving off to Virginia, to Tennessee, or to the Devil." And Joseph Holt, after a visit to Louisville, was equally sure of Union triumph in the state.[53]

Emboldened by these gains, Lincoln now began to recede from the tacit recognition he had given to a neutral Kentucky. Buckner, as agent for Magoffin, had in early June secured from Union General George B. McClellan, commander of the Department of Ohio, an agreement respecting Kentucky's recently proclaimed neutrality quite similar to the assurances Lincoln had earlier given Garret Davis and Warner Underwood. A month later, however, McClellan repudiated the agreement, and Buckner was sent to Washington to obtain renewed promises from Lincoln. Buckner called on Crittenden, and together they met Lincoln on July 10. Lincoln wrote an equivocal statement to the effect that although he had no present plans for sending an armed force into Kentucky, he would make no promise that would bind his future course. He refused even to sign the statement but gave it to Crittenden to identify in any way he saw fit. Crittenden initialed it.[54]

At the time, Lincoln's action was reassuring enough to Ken-

[51] *Congressional Globe*, 37 Cong., 1 Sess., 411-13, 430-31, 434.

[52] Anderson to his wife, June 6, 27, 1861, Anderson to Crittenden, July 8, 1861, Joshua F. Speed to Lincoln, June 3, 1861, W. G. Terrell to Anderson, July 9, 1861, in Robert Anderson Papers.

[53] Brown to Crittenden, July 9, 1861, in Crittenden Papers; Joseph Holt to Larz Anderson, July 24, 1861, in Robert Anderson Papers.

[54] McElroy, *Kentucky*, 531-37; Stickles, *Buckner*, 76; Coulter, *Civil War and Readjustment*, 99.

tuckians. Ill-conceived statements by Howell Cobb and Confederate Secretary of War L. P. Walker further aided the Unionists. Cobb and Walker expressed the hope that Kentucky would not secede but would remain neutral so as to be a buffer battleground. The result was that in the August elections, Unionists won seventy-six of one hundred seats in the house and, including holdovers, had a senate majority of twenty-seven to eleven.[55]

The Unionist victories showed that the people wanted peace and that they were endorsing, as the surest means of achieving it, the neutral position advocated by the Unionist party. Even at the time, however, the elections were misinterpreted as endorsements of Lincoln's war policy. The War Department in Washington now ordered William Nelson, the supplier of Lincoln guns to the Home Guard, to open a recruiting and training camp in Garrard County, in central Kentucky. Secessionists hoped to take advantage of this seeming violation of neutrality and to provoke an incident that would create a clash between the State Guard and Nelson's recruits.

Crittenden returned home from Congress in mid-August just as this new excitement was arousing Unionist fears. Failing to persuade Nelson to delay his activities, he appealed to Lincoln. Kentucky's position, he reminded Lincoln, was "peculiar and exceptional." The Unionist legislature would soon meet and adopt measures which would give "more firmness & stability to the Union Party, and a more definite form & character to its policy." Until then, however, it would be wise "to forbear all Federal action, not indispensable, that could possibly produce division or irritation."[56] But this time Lincoln refused. The result of his refusal would have been uncertain had not the Confederates now rashly decided to disregard Kentucky neutrality. Early in September, first at Columbus on the Mississippi, and then in a line eastward to Cumberland Gap, Confederates entered the state in force. Unionist troops then moved in along the northern border, and the figment of Kentucky neutrality had come to an end.

When the legislature met, it quickly passed resolutions instructing the governor to insist on the unconditional withdrawal of Confed-

[55] McElroy, *Kentucky*, 536-37; Collins, *History of Kentucky*, I, 92.

[56] Crittenden to Lincoln, Aug. 19, 1861, in Letterbook, 821-24, Crittenden Papers (Duke). See also, James Harlan to Robert Anderson, Aug. 19, 1861, Oliver P. Beard to Anderson, Aug. 28, 1861, in Robert Anderson Papers; Garret Davis to Crittenden, Aug. 12, 1861, William Nelson to Crittenden, Aug. 16, 1861, in Crittenden Papers.

erate troops, and it voted down a resolution instructing him to make a similar demand of the Union forces. When Magoffin vetoed the first resolution, it was promptly passed over his veto. One week later the legislature declared officially that the Confederacy had invaded the state, and it now called on General Anderson to take command of all Kentucky volunteers. The State Guard was ordered disbanded, whereupon most of them crossed into Tennessee and joined the Confederate Army.[57]

Which side first violated Kentucky's neutrality is of little importance. Neutrality was an untenable position from the beginning, but Unionist leaders had accepted it as the only alternative to secession. Although a majority of the people of the state would doubtless have preferred to remain neutral throughout the war, Unionist leaders well knew that they could not. Crittenden's part in effecting the transition from neutrality to Union cooperation was of vital importance to the Union cause. A leading authority called him "the outstanding conservative Unionist leader" and said his influence "unquestionably became one of the strongest forces making for the Union."[58] James G. Blaine thought Crittenden "more than . . . any other man" saved Kentucky from rebellion. "But for his strong hold upon the sympathy and pride of Kentucky," Blaine later wrote, "the malign influence of Breckinridge might have forced the State into the Confederacy." Lincoln, he added, thought Crittenden's course entitled him to "the admiration and gratitude" of all loyal Unionists.[59]

[57] Collins, *History of Kentucky*, I, 92-94; Coulter, *Civil War and Readjustment*, 100-19; letters to Robert Anderson from Nat Wolfe, Sept. 16, and from James Speed, Sept. 19, 1861, in Robert Anderson Papers.
[58] Coulter, *Civil War and Readjustment*, 92.
[59] Blaine, *Twenty Years of Congress*, I, 330-31.

CHAPTER XXI

A Nation Divided

THE WAR brought Crittenden great personal sorrow. Like many other Kentuckians—Breckinridges, Clays, Moreheads, Prentices, Bufords—Crittenden's ties with the closest of kin were severed by war. The chief source of his grief was the weak and unstable George. By the beginning of 1861 George had risen to the rank of lieutenant colonel in the United States army. Officers of southern background now began resigning from the army to go into Confederate service. Curious as this procedure might seem today, it was then considered normal and was freely permitted. This was to be in many respects a gentleman's war, and bloodletting must not start until sides had been chosen. Suspecting George's Confederate inclinations, Crittenden implored him not to follow his southern comrades. Kentucky, he wrote, had not seceded, and George's position was different from that of officers from the Deep South. "Be true to the government that has trusted in you, and stand fast to the nation's flag," he pleaded. Besides, the cause of secession was hopeless. The rebellion would surely be crushed, and all who participated in it would only make "a useless sacrifice of themselves."[1]

Without so much as communicating with his father, however, George sent in his resignation and joined the Confederate army. He quickly rose to the rank of major general and was given command of the right wing of the Confederate Army of the West when it moved into Kentucky in September. Six months later he suffered a disastrous repulse of his ill-disciplined troops at Mill Springs, and as a result, he was censured by a military court. Under this cloud George resigned his commission in the fall and served for a time as voluntary aide on the staff of General John S. Williams. In the last year of the war he rose again to the rank of colonel and commanded a brigade in east Tennessee. George's defection to the Confederacy, Crittenden wrote, caused him "shame & sorrow." In the spring of 1862 George D. Prentice, soon to be embarrassed by the defection of his own son, wrote a scathing editorial on George in the *Journal*, which drew from Crittenden a letter of complaint. Conceding that George's conduct was unjustifiable, he could see no profit to the Union cause now by the humiliation of George's loyal kin.[2]

A year before the war, Crittenden had given Ann Mary's son, John Crittenden Coleman, $1,500 to establish himself in business. Shortly after the attack on Fort Sumter, however, the young man joined the Confederacy and was sent to training camp near Pensacola, Florida. There, in February, 1862, he became involved in an affair of honor while under the influence of liquor, and a duel was avoided only through the intercession of a cousin. Then, suddenly, young Coleman died under mysterious circumstances, and his grief-stricken mother wanted Crittenden to obtain permission for her to go to Florida to investigate. With difficulty Crittenden dissuaded her, pointing out that she could do no more for her son, whereas she still had duties to her living children. He urged her to "resist the vain grief" that would only serve to distract her from this duty. His own affection for his grandson, he assured her, was not dimin-

[1] Crittenden to George Crittenden, April 30, July 19, 1861, in Coleman, *Crittenden*, II, 321-22, 328-29.

[2] Acceptance of resignation [dated May 19, 1861] of Lieut. Col. George B. Crittenden, June 11, 1861, Headquarters Department of New Mexico, United States Army, Special Orders No. 69, in Crittenden Papers (Duke); Crittenden to Mrs. Coleman, Feb. 23, 1862, *ibid.*; J. Stoddard Johnston, *Confederate Military History*, Vol. IX, *Kentucky* (Atlanta, 1899), 233-34; *Kentucky Register*, LII (1954), 120-21; Harriet Crittenden to "Dear Mother," April 20, 1862, Bibb-Burnley Papers, Folder 65, Kentucky Historical Society; *Report of the Adjutant-General of the State of Kentucky— Confederate Kentucky Volunteers, War of 1861-1865* (Frankfort, 1918), 344; Crittenden to Prentice, May 14, 1862, in Coleman, *Crittenden*, II, 347.

ished by his joining the Confederacy. "I thought it was an *error* on his part. But that did not affect my attachment to him."[3]

His other sons and grandsons were a source of pride to Crittenden. Thomas had been a high-ranking officer in Buckner's prosouthern State Guard, and for a time had been suspect because of the association. When the Guard was disbanded in September, however, the legislature, assured of his loyalty, instructed the military board to reorganize it with Thomas as commander. When it was mustered into Union service that fall, Thomas was advanced to brigadier general and assigned to Buell's Army of the Ohio. He won distinction at Shiloh two months after George's disgrace at Mill Springs, and was promoted to major general. Crittenden thus had the unique experience of having sons in each army rise to the rank of major general.[4]

Eugene, already in the Union service, rose to the rank of colonel. In the summer of 1863 he took part in the pursuit and capture of John Hunt Morgan in Ohio. John Crittenden Watson, a grandson and a graduate of the Naval Academy in 1860, participated in the capture of New Orleans by Admiral David G. Farragut at almost the same time his uncle Thomas was winning promotion at Shiloh. Young Watson later would be Farragut's flag lieutenant at the Battle of Mobile Bay.[5]

When Crittenden returned to Washington in late November for the second session of the Thirty-seventh Congress, it soon became manifest that radicals in the Republican party, unhappy at the course of the administration in prosecuting the war, had laid plans to seize the initiative from Lincoln. Leader of their forces in the House was the able but unlovable Thaddeus Stevens, lawyer and iron manufacturer of Gettysburg, Pennsylvania. Stevens' vindictive attitude toward the South had been revealed the summer before in an outburst during debate on the Confiscation Act. If the entire South "must be laid waste, and made a desert, in order to save this Union from destruction," he said, "so let it be. I would rather, sir, reduce them to a condition where their whole country

[3] W. Call to Crittenden, March 4, 1861, in Crittenden Papers; unsigned fragment of letter from Call to Patrick Joyes, July 1, 1861, Mrs. Coleman to Crittenden, Oct. 30 [1861], Crittenden to Mrs. Coleman, Nov. 11, 1861, in Crittenden Papers (Duke).

[4] Letters to Crittenden from Winfield Scott, Oct. 7, 1861, from Jeremiah T. Boyle, April 16, 26, 1862, from John N. Finnell, April 26, 1862, from Joshua F. Speed, Feb. 17, April 26, 1862, and from Lyne Starling, April 28, 1862, in Crittenden Papers.

[5] Speed, *Union Cause in Kentucky*, 235; Rhoads, *Colonial Families*, VII, 490-91.

is to be repeopled by a band of freemen than to see them perpetrate the destruction of this people through our agency."[6]

On the first day of the session Roscoe Conkling, New York radical, proposed a resolution to investigate the Union disaster of six weeks before at Ball's Bluff. The resolution was really aimed at McClellan, Scott's successor as commander in chief. McClellan was a Democrat and was far too moderate in his attitude toward the seceded states to suit the radicals. On January 6 Crittenden spoke against the resolution. Congress, he said, should not interfere in the conduct of the war or in the management of the army. The Constitution gave it no authority to do so, nor could war be properly conducted in such a manner. Committees were not competent to judge generals. Passage of Conkling's resolution would set a precedent, for thereafter everyone who lost a loved one in battle would bring charges that the battle had been mishandled.[7]

But the radical tide was too strong, and the resolution passed, seventy-nine to fifty-four. This was only the beginning. Soon, true to Crittenden's prediction, a flood of complaints about incompetence of the high command called again and again for investigations. In mid-February the radicals proposed to set up a permanent Committee on the Conduct of the War, composed of members from both houses. Again Crittenden protested. Investigating battles already fought was bad enough, he said, but such a committee as was now proposed could subpoena President and generals and look into plans of campaign. Even though the committee might tread lightly at first, in time "they will become used to the sceptre," and "What they handle delicately at first they may come to handle without delicacy before they get through with it."[8]

Crittenden's protests were again brushed aside, and the committee was set up to pursue what would soon become an infamous course. It would inquire into not only Ball's Bluff but also Bull Run, Fredericksburg, Chancellorsville, Gettysburg, and the Petersburg crater. It would investigate the administration of the Army of the Potomac under all its numerous commanders until Grant began traveling with that army in the spring of 1864. It would damage, almost beyond repair, the reputations of able, patriotic soldiers. Most notable of these victims were General Charles P. Stone, whom

[6] Quoted in Randall, *Civil War and Reconstruction*, 371.
[7] *Congressional Globe*, 37 Cong., 2 Sess., 192-94.
[8] *Congressional Globe*, 37 Cong., 2 Sess., 852-55.

the committee made the goat of the Ball's Bluff disaster, and General Fitz-John Porter, charged with responsibility for the calamity of Second Bull Run.

Next on the agenda of the radicals was a more severe confiscation measure than the one passed the preceding August. That called only for forfeiture of property, including slaves, actually used in the rebellion. The new bill, proposed by John A. Bingham of Ohio, provided for forfeiture of all the slaves of any person who aided the rebellion in any way, regardless of whether or not the slaves had been used for military purposes. Accompanying the bill was a resolution proclaiming that the President and all officers under him had the right and duty, "whenever [it] will avail to weaken the power of the rebels . . . or to strengthen the military power of the loyal forces," to emancipate slaves in rebel territory. This was aimed at Lincoln, for John C. Frémont had issued such a proclamation in Missouri the preceding summer only to have Lincoln revoke it when mutiny in a company of Kentucky volunteers spread fear that the still unsettled Kentucky situation would deteriorate as a result. It was reported that the Kentucky legislature "would not budge until that proclamation was modified."[9]

During debate on Bingham's bill Representative John Hickman of Pennsylvania attacked Lincoln for the soft policy he was using toward the rebels. No bill would be necessary, he said, if only Lincoln would do his duty. And no matter how strong a bill Congress might pass, Lincoln would not enforce it. Crittenden rose to Lincoln's defense. He had opposed Lincoln's election, he said, but Lincoln had since won him to his side. "There is a niche in the temple of fame," he said, with almost prophetic vision, "a niche near to Washington, which should be occupied by the statue of him who shall save this country. Mr. Lincoln has a mighty destiny," and well might "step into that niche." But if he should turn into a mere party man, a sectarian, the place would be reserved for some "future and better patriot." Lincoln was no "coward," as Hickman charged, simply because he would not do what the Constitution forbade his doing. If he should act in violation of it, he would be a despot.

Both Hickman's proposals and Bingham's bill were unconstitutional, Crittenden said, for courts and Congress both had said re-

[9] *Congressional Globe*, 37 Cong., 2 Sess., 1303, 1788; Randall, *Civil War and Reconstruction*, 478-79; Shortridge, "Kentucky Neutrality," 298.

peatedly that Congress had no authority over slavery in the states. How then could the President, who was without positive legislative power, have any? Some slave states, he said, were not in rebellion. Some of them had laws forbidding the bringing of free Negroes into their limits. "Can you," he asked, "contrary to the laws in those States, turn these emancipated slaves into their midst?"

It had been argued by Stevens and others in justification of confiscation that the South should be made to pay the cost of the war. This was barbarous, Crittenden said; there was no instance in history where such a thing had been done. It was unwise, too, because it would drive the South to desperation and would thus prolong the war. Bring about peace, he urged, and then make rebels pay their proportionate share of the war. By driving them to extremity, the nation would lose more in blood and treasure than it would gain. The proposed bill was also a bill of attainder, he said, and unconstitutional for that reason. If adopted, it would be fatal to the republic. It would deprive citizens of property without due process. It was unnecessary because the Union had the power to suppress the rebellion without such measures. Since slavery was constitutional, its merits need not be argued. If slavery were dangerous to future peace, remedies should come in due time and in proper manner.

One thing at a time, Crittenden urged. First restore the Union and preserve the integrity of the Constitution. Then take care of the slavery issue, constitutionally. He reminded the House that it had already declared that the war was being waged only for the Union. Congress had pledged to cease fighting without assailing the institutions of any state, once the rebellion was put down. He pointed to the difficulties attending the freeing of all slaves. The Union had only six hundred thousand troops at the time, and yet there were complaints about the cost of supplying them. How could they feed and clothe four million slaves? He asked Stevens to answer this, for he was chairman of Ways and Means.[10]

The Bingham bill was tabled, but in its place was passed an even harsher act. Under it all property of officers of the Confederate government was to be immediately confiscated and, after a period of sixty days, that of all other persons who aided the rebellion. This would have been less objectionable had it applied only to those

[10] *Congressional Globe*, 37 Cong., 2 Sess., 1802-805, 1815-20.

actually guilty of giving aid to the rebellion. But the law was made applicable to all persons living in any of the seceded states, even those actually loyal to the United States, as well as to foreigners residing in the Confederacy. Thus, in the words of James G. Randall, "The guilty thing during the war was mere *residence* in an 'insurrectionary state.'"

At the same time efforts were being made to enforce this extraordinary measure, the Supreme Court of the United States ruled that the states which had seceded were nevertheless *de facto* governments, and that persons residing in them had a duty to obey them in "civil and local matters." This was such a fine distinction that had all southerners been possessed of the wisdom of Solomon, they would have found it impossible to follow the diverging rules of law prescribed for them. They must obey their state governments while at the same time they were refusing obedience to the Confederate government of which the state was a cooperating part. The bill passed the House, eighty-two to forty-two, and was approved by the Senate July 12.[11]

It was known during debate that Lincoln was opposed to the bill and that he was preparing a veto message for it. His objections were based on the difficulty of discriminating justly between loyal and disloyal persons in the application of the bill. He agreed with Crittenden's view that the bill was clearly an attainder and therefore unconstitutional, since it provided forfeiture beyond the life of the accused. Learning of his intended veto, Congress thereupon did a remarkable thing. It rushed through a joint resolution explaining that the law was not expected to forfeit property beyond the life of the accused. This extraordinary procedure, whereby Congress passed a resolution explaining the meaning of an act previously passed, was now matched by equally strange behavior on the part of Lincoln. Although the explanatory resolution met only part of his objection, he now approved the bill but attached his intended message of veto to it as explanation of his own understanding of it. Under such strange circumstances did this questionable act become the law of the land.[12]

When Congress adjourned in July, Crittenden and Elizabeth re-

---

[11] *Congressional Globe*, 37 Cong., 2 Sess., 3106-107, 3188, 3267, 3293; Blaine, *Twenty Years of Congress*, I, 375; Randall, *Civil War and Reconstruction*, 371-72.

[12] *Congressional Globe*, 37 Cong., 2 Sess., 3406; Richardson, *Messages and Papers of the Presidents*, VIII, 3286-88; Randall, *Civil War and Reconstruction*, 373.

turned home by way of West Point. Some cadets there from border states were planning to resign from the academy to join the rebellion, and Crittenden wanted to make a personal appeal to each of the Kentucky cadets not to do so. He did not publish his intentions, for he feared that if his visit were known, it would be interpreted as distrust of his young fellow Kentuckians. He knew the families of most of them, and as he spoke to them of the Union, according to Robert Winthrop who was present, his "eye kindled, and his voice trembled with emotion." Winthrop said he had never seen a man more in earnest than Crittenden was that day, and that he "seemed to excite an electric sympathy in all whom he addressed." Winthrop himself had "rarely been more moved."[13]

Crittenden and Elizabeth arrived home in mid-August. Already Generals Braxton Bragg and Kirby Smith had started out from east Tennessee to liberate Kentucky from Union control. By the end of the month Smith would send William Nelson's force reeling back in panic from the Battle of Richmond, and in early September Confederate forces would occupy Lexington and Frankfort and would threaten Cincinnati and Louisville.

The Crittendens fled to Louisville. They were offered refuge by friends in Ohio, but Crittenden declined to leave the state "in her present troubles & perils." Even if he could serve no useful purpose, he would at least share in the dangers. "Here I am, & shall be till the present crisis is over," he wrote. He never doubted that "victory will be on our side." Crittenden sent Elizabeth to visit her daughter in St. Louis, while he put up at the Galt House. As Bragg's army approached Louisville, panic spread from there to the high command at Washington. Bragg had outmaneuvered Union General Don Carlos Buell and had placed his army across Buell's line of march toward Louisville. So desperate was the Unionist plight that rumors that the War Department planned to abandon Louisville and withdraw troops from there to help defend Cincinnati were generally believed. On September 10 Crittenden and Governor James Robinson wired a joint protest against such a plan to General Henry W. Halleck. "If Louisville is taken," they said, "the State is gone."

How influential this message was is not known, but the Washington government now hesitated, neither withdrawing troops or

13 Winthrop to Mrs. Coleman, Dec. 26, 1870, in Coleman, *Crittenden*, II, 350-52. See also, Crittenden to Mrs. Coleman, Aug. 5, 1862, Winthrop to Mrs. Coleman, Jan. 6, 1871, in Crittenden Papers (Duke).

sending reinforcements. Thereupon, a week later, Crittenden and Robinson, now joined by Garret Davis, urged Halleck to speed aid at once. Buell was still prevented from reaching the city, his army was in great peril, and the fate of Kentucky, they said, hung in the balance. They asked that Nelson be placed in command of the defenses of the city. This was done, but only ten days later Nelson was assassinated in the Galt House within Crittenden's presence. Almost simultaneously came word from Washington, ordering Buell, who had gained access to the city through Bragg's blundering, to turn over his command to George H. Thomas. Again Crittenden and his associates protested, this time to Lincoln. Not only did the army have confidence in Buell, they said, so did the people of the city. To remove him at such a time would be a great error. Again their prayer was heard, and Buell was retained in command until Bragg was driven from the state. After Perryville and the retreat of the Confederates, Crittenden and Elizabeth returned to Frankfort.[14]

Meanwhile, Union commanders in Kentucky had again upset the political equilibrium by interfering with local government and with the civil liberties of the people. Because of divided sentiment in the border states, it could not be assumed that all citizens were loyal, and overzealous but inexperienced officers began taking extreme security measures, contrary to law and despite claims of civil authorities that they were dealing with the problem adequately. Since the invasion by the Confederates in September, 1861, the state had acted promptly to meet its obligations. The legislature had voted overwhelmingly to adhere to the Union, turning over to the federal government not only state troops but all volunteers as well. It assumed Kentucky's portion of the direct tax imposed by Congress in August, 1861. It extended extraordinary privileges to citizens absent from the state in the service of the federal government and stripped of citizenship all Kentuckians in the service of the Confederacy. In February, 1862, it gave an almost unanimous vote of thanks to Union officers for driving Confederate forces from the state.

The courts were equally zealous in manifestations of loyalty. In October, 1861, many prominent citizens, including James B. Clay,

---

14 Frankfort *Commonwealth*, Aug. 15, 1862; F. Daniels to Crittenden, Sept. 11, 1862, in Crittenden Papers; Crittenden to S. S. Cox, Oct. 7, 1862, in Crittenden Papers (Yale); Crittenden to Mrs. Coleman, Oct. 27, 1862, in Crittenden Papers (Duke); *Official Records*, 1, XVI, pt. 2, pp. 504, 529, 557-58; Hambleton Tapp, "The Assassination of General William Nelson, September 29, 1862, and Its Ramifications," in *Filson Quarterly*, XIX (1945), 197.

were imprisoned by court order. A month later the federal district court at Frankfort indicted for treason more than thirty of the leading citizens of the state who had gone into the Confederacy. The list included Breckinridges, Browns, Burnleys, Deshas, Dudleys, and Marshalls. At its April term in 1862 the Bourbon circuit court indicted 46 of its citizens for disloyalty, and at the next term, 195. At the same time the Fayette grand jury indicted 260.[15]

Most of those indicted were actually in Confederate service, but this was insufficient to suit military officials, who proceeded to order the arrest of hundreds who were guilty of no misconduct and against whom there was no evidence save the unsworn statement of suspicious or jealous neighbors. All that was necessary to procure an arrest, wrote one who had suffered, was "Simply a Statement to an officer that Such an one was a rebel. . . . No specific charges were necessary, but the broad term of Rebel was all that was required."[16] Some Union commanders deplored such abuses. General Anderson early issued orders forbidding arrests except on conclusive evidence of an overt act of disloyalty, and William T. Sherman, who succeeded him, ordered that any person arrested on charges of disloyalty must be taken before a United States commissioner and dealt with according to law.[17]

From the beginning, however, these orders were disregarded. Charles S. Morehead had long served the state as legislator, as governor, and in Congress. He had valuable property, however, in Tennessee and Alabama, and although there was no evidence that he had ever committed a disloyal act, he was known to have southern sympathies. He was seized in his Louisville home in the dead of night and without charge or indictment hustled off to Fort Lafayette in New York harbor. Kept there for months without trial, he was released only after Crittenden made a personal appeal to Lincoln. Returned to Louisville, Morehead learned a few months later that he was about to be seized again, and he fled into the Confederacy.[18]

Morehead's case is only one of more than thirteen thousand unconstitutional military arrests listed on the records of the federal commissary general of prisoners. Estimates of the total number of

[15] Collins, *History of Kentucky*, I, 95-116, *passim*.
[16] R. W. Blackburn to Crittenden, Nov. 20, 1862, in Crittenden Papers.
[17] Collins, *History of Kentucky*, I, 96-97.
[18] Crittenden to Morehead, Jan. 12, 1862, Morehead to Crittenden, June 18, 1862, in Coleman, *Crittenden*, II, 343-44, 348-49.

such persons seized in this manner run almost to forty thousand, the vast majority in the border states. Christopher Rogers of Paris, Kentucky, like Morehead, was taken from the bosom of his family ten days before Christmas and rushed to Fort Lafayette. John M. Harlan, Crittenden's Frankfort neighbor and future Supreme Court justice, secured affidavits attesting Rogers' loyalty and forwarded them to Crittenden. Rogers was perfectly willing to take a loyalty oath, but he had never been given the opportunity. He would guarantee bond in any amount to appear before any court to answer any charges that might be preferred.[19] Crittenden protested to both Seward and Lincoln in regard to these despotic practices and was able to obtain relief in individual cases like Morehead's and Rogers'.

But the general situation, instead of improving, got worse. General Jeremiah T. Boyle was appointed commander of the Kentucky District in the spring of 1862 and at once issued orders for wholesale arrests on mere suspicion and hearsay. Soon outrage was piled on outrage. Governor Magoffin's brother was sentenced to death for violating parole, although he swore he had never given his parole. The federal commander at Lexington in the spring of 1862 arrested many people without warrant, refused to honor *habeas corpus* writs in their behalf, and rushed his prisoners off to Camp Chase at Columbus, Ohio. About the same time, Judges W. P. Fowler and G. A. Flournoy were seized while holding court in western Kentucky. They had refused to take a loyalty oath that included a stipulation which waived their right to a civil trial and admitted jurisdiction of a military court in event of their subsequent arrests. They had, of course, previously taken oaths to preserve and defend the Constitution. Meanwhile, half a dozen newspapers of the state had been suspended for what commanders called expressions of disloyal sentiments. By the summer of 1862 two religious periodicals had been suspended, and clergymen from all parts of the state were in military prisons.[20]

By this time also, federal military authorities were controlling

[19] Christopher C. Rogers to Crittenden, Jan. 17, 1862, in Crittenden Papers; Randall, *Civil War and Reconstruction*, 387-94.

[20] Letters to Crittenden from James F. Robinson, Feb. 6, from Richard A. Buckner, March 4, from Leslie Combs, May 13, from William A. Dudley, May 14, and from Beriah Magoffin, May 29, 1862, W. P. Fowler to Magoffin, May 23, 1862, in Crittenden Papers; Crittenden to Lincoln, April 4, 1862, in Robert Todd Lincoln Papers; *Kentucky House Journal, 1861-62-63*, 2 Vols., I, 901-15, 918-21; Collins, *History of Kentucky*, I, 95, 105-107; Frankfort *Commonwealth*, Aug. 15, 1862.

elections. On July 21, Boyle, who had political ambitions, issued an order forbidding persons "hostile in opinions" to stand for office under threat of being charged with an overt act of treason. As a result, the elections on August 4 polled a very small vote, and Unionist candidates won everywhere. In Owen County all candidates who were not avowed supporters of the Lincoln administration were imprisoned.[21] After Morgan's raid in July, 1862, military officials took an ever harsher course. Boyle issued a decree that "disloyal" persons in each neighborhood were to be assessed for property damages or losses suffered by guerilla raids. He appointed provost marshals in every county of the state to carry out the order, under the threat of "your money or Camp Chase."[22]

Crittenden was Kentucky's most influential representative in Congress, and complaints of most of these abuses were channeled through him. He conducted a lengthy correspondence with both Secretary of War Stanton and with Seward, protesting against these violations of constitutional rights, but his efforts were generally frustrated by procrastination.[23] Moreover, protests were followed only by more abuses, and as Congress seemed inclined toward more extreme measures, Crittenden once again resolved that a new party must be formed to save the nation from the radicals. He called a meeting of conservative members of Congress in Washington in the summer of 1862. Resolutions were adopted calling for: limiting the war to suppression of the rebellion while preserving the Constitution; fair treatment of the South at the war's close; condemnation of both northern and southern extremists; recognition that Congress was without power to confiscate property; and a reaffirmation of the Crittenden resolution of July, 1861. The House had expressly refused to reaffirm that resolution by a vote of sixty-five to seventy-one at the beginning of the session the previous December, all but one of the adverse votes being cast by Republicans.[24]

21 Collins, *History of Kentucky*, I, 104-105; Charles Morehead to Crittenden, June 18, 1862, in Coleman, *Crittenden*, II, 348-49.
22 Collins, *History of Kentucky*, I, 102-105.
23 George Robertson to Crittenden, Nov. 26, 1862, Fitz-John Porter to Crittenden, Feb. 10, 1863, in Crittenden Papers; Crittenden to Stanton [Dec., 1862], in Crittenden letterbook, 813, Crittenden Papers (Duke); Crittenden to Lincoln, Jan. 19, 1863, in Robert Todd Lincoln Papers; *Kentucky House Journal, 1861-62-63*, I, 902.
24 Letters to Crittenden from John Reynolds, May 8, from John C. Ham, May 12, from Hiram Ketchum, May 13, and from Oliver G. Carter, May 14, 1862, in Crittenden Papers; Frankfort *Commonwealth*, July 11, 1862; *Congressional Globe*, 37 Cong., 2 Sess., 15.

The movement for a conservative party received strong support. Many Unionists agreed with Crittenden that if the 1862 congressional elections were favorable to radicals, all hope of preserving constitutional liberties was gone. The Thirty-seventh Congress had been completely dominated by radicals, but the election of the Thirty-eighth Congress in the autumn of 1862 reflected an astonishing reversal of public sentiment in the North.[25] In Ohio, Indiana, Illinois, Pennsylvania, New York, and New Jersey, Democrats won control, and even in rock-ribbed New England, Republican majorities were greatly reduced. Ironically, had it not been for the border states, the Republicans would have lost control of Congress. But military interference in those states secured election of a number of representatives pledged to radical programs. James G. Blaine later conceded that "But for the aid of the Border slave States the anti-slavery positions of Mr. Lincoln might have been overthrown by a hostile House of Representatives."[26]

Crittenden was thoroughly unhappy at the radical course being followed both by the administration and by Congress when he returned to Washington for the last session of the Thirty-seventh Congress. He and Elizabeth spent a melancholy Christmas. He had not fully recovered from a long illness of the previous spring, and they took a house on F Street in order to avoid the excitement of life in the National Hotel. Crittenden was in his seventy-seventh year, and age was taking its toll of his former optimism. The nation's destiny now hung in the balance, and he feared for the country's future. The war had not been going well, and there was much talk of revolution. Extremists in Congress and in the army were plotting a military dictatorship to supplant what seemed to them a bumbling and blundering administration. It was possible, Crittenden feared, that the Union might be broken up and several confederations formed.

He wrote of his fears to Thomas and cautioned him to prepare for "all possible contingencies that these strange and revolutionary times may produce." Should a coup develop either in Congress or in the army, Thomas must take no part in it. He must remember

[25] Crittenden to S. S. Cox, Oct. 7, 1862, in Crittenden Papers (Yale); letters to Crittenden from W. R. Henley, Oct. 3, and from Thomas Dowling, Dec. 1, 1862, in Crittenden Papers; Frankfort *Commonwealth*, Aug. 1, 1862.

[26] Thomas Dowling to Crittenden, Dec. 1, 1862, in Crittenden Papers; Blaine, *Twenty Years of Congress*, I, 444; Randall, *Civil War and Reconstruction*, 599-603.

that political representatives and civil government "are the primary guardians of public liberty and the constitution. . . . The case must be strong, indeed, to . . . manifest . . . the *necessity* that would justify or excuse the military for interfering with or resisting the authority of the Civil government to which its rule of action is subordination." Even where the government had failed and was broken down, and "was plainly using the Army to betray the Country, the Army should stand still, and leave revolution to the civil population, and then follow them." As for Crittenden's own course, "I am inflexibly for the Union," he wrote. "I can never subscribe to a separation of the United States—It is possible that I may be obliged to submit to it, but I cannot assent to it. It will be in itself, the surrender and distruction [*sic*] of our great country."[27]

Five weeks later Crittenden's uneasiness about his son was put to rest by the renown Thomas gained at Stone's River, when his corps held fast while the rest of the army broke under the savage Confederate attack. The stubborn resistance of Thomas' corps turned defeat into victory and won great credit for him. Crittenden would never learn of his son's less than brilliant performance in the Chickamauga campaign eight months later.

The final session of the Thirty-seventh Congress had to deal with a constitutional difficulty over the western section of Virginia. Ancient rivalries between the people of the mountains and those of tidewater and piedmont reached a climax when the Virginia convention voted secession. Union mass meetings in the western section led to a convention at Wheeling in the summer of 1861, when a new state government was formed claiming to be the government of Virginia. Although this was actually a movement of secession from Virginia, the Wheeling government soon won recognition at Washington as the legitimate government of the state of Virginia.

Under conditions almost of anarchy in the region, this Wheeling government, speaking for all Virginia, decreed that a new state be set up in fifty counties of western Virginia, and a convention was called in November, 1861. This convention adopted a constitution for the new state of West Virginia. The Wheeling government, again speaking for the entire state of Virginia, now gave its consent to the formation of the new state, thus fictitiously observing the constitutional requirement that no state be created out of the

[27] Crittenden to Thomas Crittenden, Nov. 28, 1862, in Crittenden Papers (Duke).

territory of another without its consent. The new state then applied to Congress for admission to the Union.[28]

In early December the House took up a Senate bill to admit West Virginia, and on December 9 Crittenden spoke against it. He sympathized, he said, with the plight of the people of western Virginia and honored their patriotism. But only an elastic imagination could construe the action of the Wheeling government as giving Virginia's consent to creation of the new state. To the charge that Virginia was out of the Union by her own act and that the Wheeling government was therefore legitimate, Crittenden responded that both Congress and the administration were fighting the war on the principle that the Union could not be broken and that a state could not withdraw. He had sworn to uphold the Constitution. When the war was over, he wanted the Union restored, but this bill would prevent it. It would be a new-made Union "cut and slashed by passion, by war."[29]

Even Thaddeus Stevens, high priest of radicals, conceded when voting for the bill that he did so on the theory that war gave Congress "absolute power" to act in an irregular manner. "I will not stultify myself by supposing," he said, "that we have any warrant in the Constitution for this proceeding." The bill passed ninety-six to fifty-five. Lincoln, too, had grave doubts about the bill's constitutionality and propriety, but reluctantly he gave his consent, and the new state was proclaimed on April 20, 1863. Not until 1920 would all its constitutional entanglements with the Richmond government be straightened out.[30]

It was in this session, too, that an issue arose over the right of a military officer to serve in Congress. Francis P. Blair, Jr., although a high-ranking officer, had served in Congress the preceding session but now was absent in the field. William Vandever, however, just elected to Congress from Iowa, recently had been mustered into service as colonel of the Ninth Iowa Infantry. He obtained leave, came to Washington, and claimed his seat. The House Committee on Elections reported that he was not entitled to the seat. The report was first upheld but later reconsidered.

[28] Randall, *Civil War and Reconstruction,* 329-35.
[29] *Congressional Globe,* 37 Cong., 2 Sess., 3396; *ibid.,* 3 Sess., 37, 46-48; Blaine, *Twenty Years of Congress,* I, 462-65.
[30] *Congressional Globe,* 37 Cong., 3 Sess., 59; Randall, *Civil War and Reconstruction,* 335-37.

On January 21 Crittenden spoke against a resolution to seat Vandever. Schuyler Colfax of Indiana argued that "brave defenders" of the country should not be thus discriminated against, but Crittenden replied that it was simply a matter of upholding the Constitution. That instrument provided that "no person holding any office under the United States shall be a member of this body." To the argument that "brave defenders" should not be suspect, Crittenden replied that the Constitution had settled that question, and that "they may be suspected . . . or that they may be guilty." Otherwise a brigade of soldiers might supply several Congresses, and Colfax's patriotism would sustain all of them in their seats. How easy it would then be for the President to order them to the field if they became troublesome. "It does not accord with the independence of a member of this House," he said, "to be subject to the orders of the President." But again Crittenden was overridden, and the House refused, eighty-four to twenty-eight, to unseat Vandever.[31]

Lincoln's attitude toward emancipation had undergone considerable change after Confederate authorities had rejected the somewhat tardy olive branch he offered in his inaugural. For political reasons he had revoked Frémont's proclamation of emancipation in Missouri because of its bad effect on the situation in Kentucky. He followed this up in the spring of 1862 by revoking another emancipation proclamation issued by General David Hunter and applying to portions of South Carolina, Georgia, and Florida. But if the Union forces should triumph in the war, slavery was doomed, and Lincoln by the summer of 1862 had become convinced of it. How much he was influenced in his course by pressure from radicals, how much by humanitarian motives, and how much by military expediency cannot be determined. Doubtless all were factors, even though he justified his conduct eventually on the ground of military necessity. But it seems that he would have preferred a more gradual and a more orderly approach to a solution of the problem than the one he actually settled on in the end.

In March, 1862, against the advice of Crittenden and other border Unionists, Lincoln persuaded Congress to offer compensation to any state that would voluntarily emancipate its slaves. Crittenden protested. Why, he asked, was more exacted of his state than she had done already in proving her loyalty? She had parted with kin-

---

[31] *Congressional Globe*, 37 Cong., 3 Sess., 432, 971.

dred and natural allies and made war on them in support of the Union. She had encouraged enlistment of her sons, and her representatives in Congress had voted men, money, and supplies to prosecute the war. Why must she also surrender her domestic institution?[32]

After Congress passed the bill that Lincoln requested, the loyal slave states did not respond. Meanwhile, Lincoln decided by mid-July to issue a proclamation of emancipation at an appropriate time. This would, of course, apply only to the states in rebellion. At the same time, Lincoln continued to work on a plan of voluntary, gradual, and compensated emancipation for the loyal slave states, and he was seeking Crittenden's cooperation and advice in devising such a plan.[33]

In September, after Lee's repulse at Antietam, Lincoln issued the preliminary proclamation, warning that on January 1 he would free slaves in rebel-held territory of seceded states. In his message to Congress on December 1 he called attention to this proclamation as well as to his plan of compensated emancipation in other states.[34] Because of the recent election reverses the administration had suffered, however, it was believed by many, including so intimate a friend of the President's as Orville Browning, that Lincoln should not and would not issue the final proclamation. Much pressure, both from those advocating and those opposed to the measure, was brought to bear on him.[35]

Crittenden and other border-state congressmen met in early December to devise an attack on the proclamation, and Crittenden was selected as one of a committee of three to call on the President in protest. They told Lincoln that the proclamation would be fatal to the restoration of peace, prejudicial to loyal slaveholders, and subversive of principles of the Constitution. When their protest was disregarded, a critical situation developed in Kentucky and other border states.[36]

Already the Kentucky legislature had defiantly turned down any proposal of compensated emancipation, threatening even armed opposition to any attempt at what it considered a violation of the Con-

[32] Frankfort *Commonwealth*, July 25, 1862. See also Richardson, *Messages and Papers of the Presidents*, VIII, 3269-70; Blaine, *Twenty Years of Congress*, I, 372-73.
[33] F. P. Blair to Crittenden, July 12, 1862, in Crittenden Papers.
[34] Richardson, *Messages and Papers of the Presidents*, VIII, 3334-43.
[35] Randall, *Lincoln the President*, II, 166-67.
[36] Lincoln, *Works*, VI, 8; Louisville *Journal*, Dec. 24, 1862, Feb. 6, 1863.

stitution. The proclamation soon threatened to unite many Kentucky Unionists with their old secession enemies, whose warnings of a year before now seemed prophetic. Treason to the Constitution in abolishing slavery was considered by Kentucky Unionists just as evil as treason through secession, and stanch Union men like George D. Prentice and Robert J. Breckinridge joined in denunciation of the proclamation. They believed Lincoln had gone over completely to the abolitionists. Crittenden, too, protested, although his loyalty to the Union never wavered for a moment. "Fight the proclamation with resolutions," he wrote Governor J. F. Robinson, "and the rebels with bayonets."[37]

In his message to the legislature Robinson denounced the proclamation, and Crittenden's letter to him was later read in the senate. Although the proclamation did not apply to Kentucky, all knew that when slavery was abolished in ten states of the Deep South, it could never survive in Kentucky. Some legislators advocated calling Kentucky troops home from federal service, and some even urged changing sides and joining the rebellion.[38] Finally, in early March a calm and dignified set of resolutions was adopted, recounting the many grievances the state had suffered through confiscation acts and military excesses. The resolutions drew a distinction between the administration and the government. The former could be opposed without hostility to the latter. They branded the proclamation as "unwise, unconstitutional, and void."[39]

Closely linked to emancipation was the question of the enlistment of Negro soldiers. There were three different categories of Union troops: the regular army, which consisted of little more than fifteen thousand officers and men at the start of the war and which was not greatly enlarged during it; the state militia, normally under the command of the governor, but with an anomalous relation to the federal government so that it could be called into national service; and the volunteers, who constituted the vast majority of Union soldiers. Until 1863 the raising of all Union troops was left to governors in the several states.[40]

[37] Coulter, *Civil War and Readjustment*, 158-60; Louisville *Journal*, Dec. 24, 1862, Feb. 6, 1863.
[38] Coulter, *Civil War and Readjustment*, 161-63; John W. Finnell to Crittenden, Jan. 26, 1863, in Crittenden Papers.
[39] Coulter, *Civil War and Readjustment*, 162.
[40] Randall, *Civil War and Reconstruction*, 406-409.

Most states, however, did not have established systems of conscription; and as volunteering lagged in the spring and summer of 1862 a militia act, passed in July, provided the states with a system devised by the War Department. This act was administered in each state by the governor, with much discretion being left him as to policies and procedures. The inefficiency of this system was notorious, and when it failed to meet expectations of the War Department, there began talk of raising troops among Negroes, either slave or free.

General David Hunter experimented with a Negro regiment in South Carolina in the spring of 1862, and news of this agitated Kentucky Union soldiers. The colonel and six other officers of the Second Kentucky Cavalry wrote Crittenden from Tennessee shortly after the Battle of Shiloh that Kentucky soldiers were increasingly dissatisfied. They regarded Negro enlistment as a step toward emancipation and as a repudiation of Crittenden's resolution, adopted almost unanimously by Congress the summer before. If the government would follow the policy promised in that resolution without meddling with such matters as confiscation and emancipation, they said, "our confidence would be restored." On the other hand, if it intended to trample on the Constitution by freeing and arming slaves, these men would promise "nothing in regard to our future actions."[41]

By January 1, 1863, several Negro regiments were already in the field, and Lincoln's emancipation proclamation on that day declared that all emancipated slaves "of suitable condition" would be received into the armed services for garrison duty. Then, on January 12, Thaddeus Stevens introduced in the House a bill authorizing the enlistment of 150,000 Negro troops, with provision for emancipation of slaves and their families after service and with compensation to loyal masters. Stevens explained that some Negro troops already had been raised under the act of July, 1862, but that his bill was designed to regularize their position and give them protection against summary reprisals by Confederates.[42]

On January 29 Crittenden spoke against the bill. It indicated, he thought, degeneracy of the whites in that it was an appeal to the

[41] Buckner Board and others to Crittenden, May 12, 1862, in Crittenden Papers (Duke).

[42] Randall, *Civil War and Reconstruction*, 503-504; Richardson, *Messages and Papers of the Presidents*, VIII, 3359; *Congressional Globe*, 37 Cong., 3 Sess., 282, 598.

black man to protect the "liberties of the white man." At the same time, the bill stigmatized the Negro in that it provided only half pay and excluded him from all positions of command. Nor could it be defended on the grounds of necessity, Crittenden said, for there were a million white volunteers under arms at the time. It could only be, therefore, an abolition scheme to secure freedom of slaves. Abolitionists had proceeded, step by step, toward one end—complete abolition. It was universally believed, North as well as South, that the white man was superior to the Negro, he said. Whether or not this was true, not one of his listeners would admit a Negro to social equality.

The army would consider enlistment of 150,000 slaves "an insult and a degradation," he said, for it would be cowardice to shelter white men behind slaves. Even Sparta and Athens had never resorted to such practices. If the bill should pass, recruiting officers would be "driven pell-mell" out of Kentucky. Instead of helping to restore the Union, the bill would "enlarge and embitter the war," for it would violate the Constitution. For nearly three centuries slaves had been considered property, and since the formation of the Constitution, domestic institutions had been subject to only state regulation. But the President had been pressed into the proclamation, and now this bill would extend emancipation into the loyal states. Crittenden was still for the Union, he said, but he was for prosecuting the war "like a brave heroic nation, by the hands of freemen." He had sworn to uphold the Constitution, but he had not sworn to uphold "the abolition party."[43]

But Crittenden's protests again were disregarded, and the bill passed in early February, eighty-three to fifty-four. It failed in the Senate, however—not because of opposition to its principle but because senators concluded that the Militia Act of July, 1862, gave the authority requested in Stevens' bill.[44] Meanwhile, that militia act had proved so ineffective that in mid-February the Senate passed and sent to the House a national conscription law, the first conscription act ever to come before Congress. The bill was debated extensively in the House on February 23. Its inadequacies, too, would become notorious, but they need not detain us here. On February 25 Crittenden arose to speak against the bill.[45]

[43] *Congressional Globe*, 37 Cong., 3 Sess., 604, Appendix, 72-73.
[44] *Congressional Globe*, 37 Cong., 3 Sess., 690, 924, 1309.
[45] *Congressional Globe*, 37 Cong., 3 Sess., 1029, 1213-34, 1252.

It was his last address before either house of Congress. His tall form was now bowed, and the luster of his eye was gone. He drew a parallel between the approaching end of the Thirty-seventh Congress and the close of his own career, reviewing briefly his efforts to avoid the struggle and, after they failed, his efforts to direct the course of the war so that at its end the republic would be restored as it was before. He reminded his listeners of his war-aims resolution, passed all but unanimously only eighteen months before. Had the government upheld the sentiments then avowed, he said, the war would long have been over. For that resolution had united the country, and men had flocked to the colors by hundreds of thousands. But this very session of Congress had deprived the loyal people of the South of all protection of their property. Now Union men were disillusioned, whereas the South had become united. Confiscation of property, forcible emancipation, conscription—these and other oppressive acts had sown deep seeds of future disaster to the country.

War could not be carried on more successfully by violating the Constitution than by obeying it, he said. For the Constitution was "our bulwark, our best defense." But Congress, influenced by "the petty spirit of party, rather than by patriotism," had assumed powers denied by the Constitution. By so doing, it had lost the hearts of the people, and they would no longer volunteer but must be drafted. Their hearts would not be won by further departures from the Constitution. Only by returning to its principles would the people's confidence be restored. "For the distrust that now exists you must substitute faith." The true purpose of the war was to save the country, not abolish slavery. Abolitionists had clouded the picture, and unless their progress was halted, all would soon be lost. He attacked as sophistry the abolitionist charge that the Union could not be saved without destroying slavery.

The bill passed that day, however, with only minor amendments, 115 to 49. Five days later the Senate accepted the amendments, and Lincoln signed the conscription act. Congress adjourned, and Crittenden, for the last time, left Washington for home.[46]

[46] A. K. McClure, *Recollections of Half a Century* (Salem, Mass., 1902), 375; *Congressional Globe*, 37 Cong., 3 Sess., 1289-91, 1293, 1478.

CHAPTER XXII

In the Midst of Battle

DURING the winter just past, Crittenden's health had not been good, and he again determined to retire from Congress. Symptoms of his declining vitality had been general rather than specific, but according to an intimate acquaintance, he was conscious of his approaching death and made frequent references to it. He was probably suffering from coronary disease, because he complained of shortness of breath and frequent chest pains. Before leaving Washington, he turned over to Seward's care a little slave boy who had made his way into Union lines and had been brought to Washington, where he had become Crittenden's servant.[1]

These last months were busy ones. His concern for his family and friends was as keen as ever. He admonished Ann Mary, who had moved to Baltimore and was fraternizing with Confederate sympathizers there. "I entreat you," he wrote, "to be on your guard— have nothing to say on politics. It hardly seems to me to become one to live in the *Union*—to take its protection, and at [the] same time to give . . . sympathy & voice to the Rebellion against it." He could not understand how she "should have allowed such feelings of favour for this Rebellion to possess your intelligent mind."[2]

He found time, too, to write Lincoln, on behalf of a grand-daughter of his old friend Isaac Shelby, whose life had become enmeshed in the web of war. She had been left in Kentucky with six small children when her husband had followed Bragg into the Confederate service after Perryville. Four of the children had since died, and the distraught mother was seeking permission to visit her husband within Confederate lines. "Her broken heart," he wrote the President, "seems to be held together only by the hope of [once] more seeing her husband." Yet she could not go unless assured she could return to care for her remaining children.[3]

It was probably at this time, too, that he prepared resolutions on the reconstruction of the Union after the war should end. These emphasized that the states of the Confederacy, despite their acts of secession, retained their federal relationship and were entitled to resume their constitutional positions in the Union as soon as possible, with "all the rights and powers they ever possessed under the Union." Measures must be taken to heal divisions in the country, and there should be no punishment of Confederates other than a small group of guilty leaders.[4]

Meanwhile, new troubles faced Kentucky. There was no longer danger of secession, but radicals under the banner of the Republican party had arisen in the state and were eager to gain control. Relatively few in number, they were quite vocal and were most vindictive toward rebels or anyone who advocated leniency toward them. Crittenden's course in Congress had been too moderate for these radicals, who now would replace him with one of their own kind. In this effort they were joined by remnants of the secessionist party, who also opposed him. These blamed him for frustrating their ambitions and denounced him for voting money to carry on the war against the South. They called him and other Unionist leaders "dastardly political knaves," who by their "rascality" had "brought Ky. to the degrading position she now occupies."[5]

    [1] Letter of William B. Kinkead in New York *Sun*, Aug. 21, 1887; Crittenden to Seward, March 17, 1863, in Seward Collection, University of Rochester Library.
    [2] Crittenden to Mrs. Coleman, April, 1863, in Crittenden Papers (Duke).
    [3] Crittenden to Lincoln, April 16, 1863, in Robert Todd Lincoln Papers.
    [4] Coleman, *Crittenden*, II, 369.
    [5] Kurt F. Leidecker, "Amid the Strife, Further Correspondence of George Clinton Stedman," in *Kentucky Register*, LI (1953), 191-217.

Crittenden's friends, learning of his intention to retire, insisted that he not do so. "Y[ou]r presence there is of the highest interest to the State and to the Nation," wrote Joshua F. Bell. Congressman Robert Mallory from Louisville wrote that Crittenden had no right to refuse his service in such critical times. From Scott County came word that Unionists there would accept no other candidate, and a leading Union journal insisted that Crittenden be returned to Congress. "Kentucky expects it, the nation expects it, and the people intend it." Reluctantly, Crittenden again bowed to their demands.[6]

Republicans of the Ashland District had called a convention for mid-May to nominate a congressional candidate. To counter this action, Fayette County conservatives induced Crittenden to address them at the spacious Odd Fellows Hall, on the corner of Short and Walnut streets in Lexington. Crittenden walked to the hall accompanied by William B. Kinkead and D. C. Wickliffe, editor of the *Observer and Reporter*. After climbing the stairs, Crittenden had to sit and rest in the anteroom because of shortness of breath. When he entered the hall, a tumultous welcome greeted him, and age and feebleness seemed to fall from him as he arose to speak. His voice was clear and resonant now, and his eye once more sparkled with the old flame of combat. It would be his last speech, and he may have surmised as much, for he reviewed the history of the sectional quarrel and gave advice for the future as if leaving a final legacy to the people he had served so long. According to Kinkead, he had never been more eloquent.[7]

Crittenden vindicated his course in the late Congress. He had changed no opinions, he said, during the war. He had done what he could to prevent secession and war, but it had come. Secession was not constitutional. On the contrary, it was rebellion, "a rebellion without cause," for the Lincoln administration had committed no act that could justify it. The secessionists had acted merely upon an apprehension of future harm to be done their section by Lincoln; they feared that slavery would be abolished in the states, despite the pledge of the Republican platform. Furthermore, he

[6] Frankfort *Commonwealth*, May 1, 1863. See also, Kinkead in New York *Sun*, Aug. 21, 1887; letters to Crittenden from Bell, April 23, from Mallory, April 28, and from M. C. Graves, May 11, 1863, in Crittenden Papers; Frankfort *Commonwealth*, May 13, 18, 1863.
[7] Kinkead in New York *Sun*, Aug. 21, 1887.

added, had southern states not seceded, votes of their representatives in Congress could have prevented any Republican attempts to interfere with slavery.

Secessionists had therefore provoked an unjust war upon whose outcome hung "the destiny of mankind, the liberty and welfare of the human race." "Of course I was for the war," he exclaimed. "What war could be more just? . . . Where could we ever hope to find a better Government? . . . How could I . . . be otherwise than for the war to defend and preserve this glorious Government of ours against the rebellion?" It had seemed to him that under our form of government, rebellion was impossible, for the people were our government, and "Who was there . . . to rebel against the people?"

But he wanted to pursue the war as "a national objective, with no mean party scheming." To that end he had offered his war-aims resolution. This, too, had proved ineffective. Even so, he was still for the war, notwithstanding confiscation acts, emancipation, the raising of Negro troops, and "the talk about negro equality." He had voted against all these acts, but when they passed, he had continued to support the war.

Some argued that Kentucky should withdraw its support of the war because the federal government had acted unconstitutionally. This, said Crittenden, would be fatal; if they should cease to fight, they would surrender all rights to a voice in a final settlement. If they would but win the war first, the people "in their wisdom" would later right the wrongs suffered during the war. Their duty was "to save our country first, and then turn around and save the Constitution." He conceded that the measures of the radicals were obnoxious, "but the rebellion is more so." The great issue was the preservation of the country, and in that great undertaking, crushing the rebellion had first priority.

Even while supporting the war, however, he had felt free to protest against violations of personal liberty. Lincoln he regarded as "a most well-meaning and excellent man." Nevertheless, errors in public affairs must be pointed out, or there would be no liberty. He had no desire to return to Congress and would not sacrifice "a hair's breadth" of any of his opinions for "a dozen seats in Congress." He had voted for all bills to raise money and troops except the recent conscription act. His reason for opposing that measure was that it was obviously intended not to raise troops but to draft slaves and free them. He had only the kindliest of feelings for Negroes, but he believed whites "a superior race." As such they should protect their own liberties, not rely upon slaves for protection. He would rather see his own sons brought home corpses than saved by the sacrifice of a Negro's life.

As for the treatment of actual rebels, Crittenden thought they deserved the penalties the radical measures imposed. But it was wise to bring the war to a quick end, and those measures had the opposite effect, for they drove the enemy to desperation and thus prolonged the war. He did not "hate the South," as some of his secessionist opponents were charging; he merely hated the principles they were attempting to carry out. When the war was over and the erring brothers returned, however, all should endeavor, "as a matter of policy, and for humanity's sake, to treat it as a family feud." They should "endeavor to forgive and forget, on all sides the wounds and disasters that have fallen upon us." Then the nation could "take a new start." The country had learned what civil war was, and he thought there would be "no more rebellions after this one was disposed of."

Meanwhile, the war must go on. He had no doubt of ultimate victory, for the people had the power and the will to win, "and we shall accomplish it." Providence, he thought, had not yet played out the destiny of this nation and would surely lead it to victory. But the people must be prepared to fight through to the end. There was much talk of foreign intervention on the side of the Confederacy, but that must not deter them. They must prosecute the war "without an armistice, regardless of foreign intervention—fighting all the world, if necessary, even England and France—as long as there is a rebel in arms threatening [the] Government, and threatening Kentucky."[8]

As he swung into his peroration, it was apparent that he had captured the huge audience with the forthright earnestness of his appeal. Noting this, Wickliffe and Kinkead made whispered plans to offer, as soon as Crittenden concluded, a resolution approving his course in Congress and recommending him to the district for re-election. When it was done, the resolution was approved with a mighty shout. Someone in the crowd called out that Woodford County was present and asked that the vote be put to them. It was, and then to Scott and other counties, and the response came again

[8] Frankfort *Commonwealth*, May 18, 1863; Cincinnati *Commercial*, quoted in Louisville *Journal*, May 18, 1863.

and again with a roar of "Ayes." Never did a statesman, Kinkead later wrote, receive "a more splendid testimonial of the confidence and admiration of his countrymen. It was a last and most glorious tribute to the worth and nobleness of one who had so long and so faithfully served them." The demonstration utterly routed the radicals. When the district convention met a few days later, Crittenden was nominated without opposition.[9]

But Crittenden did not live to see election day. The end came quickly for him, and with little suffering. He was exhausted after the Lexington speech and retired to Frankfort for a long rest, hoping to regain his strength. On July 4 he was able to attend the annual Independence Day ceremonies at Cove Spring, where he had so often thrilled the gatherings with flights of patriotic oratory. Now he was too feeble to make such an effort, but he was toasted as "The Last of the great men who gave to the Senate of the United States its lustre." He responded briefly, but in a voice so feeble that many of the throng could not hear. He planned to visit the Indiana alum springs, and he and Elizabeth were on their way there a week later, when he collapsed in Louisville, probably from a coronary thrombosis. He was taken to the home of Dr. Bush, where he remained bedfast for a week.

He was visited there by an old Logan County friend, John B. Bibb, and they talked of old times in Russellville, of the War of 1812, and of the militia company formed in Logan after the war and named for Crittenden. Thomas Bramlette, Unionist candidate for governor passing through Louisville, called to see him, and they talked long of the condition of the country. As Bramlette was taking his leave, Crittenden grasped his hand. He would not live, he said, to see the end of his country's troubles, but he charged Bramlette in a fervent and affecting manner, to "save our beloved State & . . . preserve the Union."[10]

The next day, July 22, Crittenden was sufficiently recovered to travel, and Elizabeth took him back to Frankfort to the home in which he had lived for more than forty years. His youngest sister, Lucy Thornton, was visiting from California, where she now lived. Thomas was called home from his command in Tennessee, and he

---

[9] Kinkead in New York *Sun*, Aug. 21, 1887.
[10] Bramlette to Mrs. Coleman, March 13, 1872, in Crittenden Papers (Duke). See also, John B. Bibb to Mrs. Coleman, Nov. 26, 1867, *ibid.*; Frankfort *Commonwealth*, July 8, 27, 1863.

reached Frankfort on Friday, July 24. Robert was already there.

Lucy sat with Crittenden through much of the day on Saturday. His mind wandered, and he talked a great deal, more to himself than to her, of his youth and of his early friends. "How many families," she heard him murmur, "I have known rise to the heights of prosperity, and then decline and pass away; and I *have helped them!* I have helped them!" He spoke of his brothers, all of them long dead. Then he spoke lucidly and earnestly of the embattled state of the country, and his eyes flashed with a feverish luster. Then, looking about him, he exclaimed with religious fervor: "Let all the ends thou aimest at be thy country's, thy God's and truth's." Lucy became alarmed and asked if he could not put his trust in the Saviour. "Ah Lucy," he replied, "I have thought a great deal more about that than you or anyone knows, and I am satisfied! I am satisfied!"

Late that evening the family gathered in the room when John S. Hays, the Presbyterian minister called. Crittenden looked up and said, "Mr. Hays, I have been wanting to speak with you." The minister drew near the bed, but Crittenden waved him away. "Not tonight, Mr. Hays, not to-night; I am too weak; to-morrow."

Thomas and Robert sat with him that night as Crittenden composed himself for sleep. He dozed fitfully past midnight and through the early morning of Sunday, July 26. About three o'clock he awoke in some discomfort and asked to have his pillow arranged. When Thomas smoothed it, he thanked his son, turned on his side, and gently passed away.[11]

As news of his death went out, the press of the country seemed to vie with one another in paying him eloquent tribute. In 1851 Thomas Marshall had spoken of Crittenden's selflessness, his courage, and fearlessness when fighting for a cause or in the interest of his friends, but of his lack of zeal for a contest in his own behalf. He called him a "mirror in which the young chivalry of Kentucky may . . . fashion itself to all manly virtue and every gentlemanly grace." Now this figure would be repeated, in slight variations, over and over again.

The Providence, Rhode Island, *Post* said that "No man's integrity was more unquestioned, and few, even among the great men with whom the larger part of his service was passed ranked as his equals." The Boston *Daily Advertiser*, long his political enemy, said

---

[11] Coleman, *Crittenden*, II, 367-68.

there were few statesmen whose death could cause such genuine emotion. His position was unparalleled, it continued, in that he had practically no enemies. He was devoid of all charges of personal ambition, it added. "No man suspected him," it said, "of devotion to party interests. . . . His devotion to the interests of the whole country, prevented any charge of sectional selfishness." His life had been spent in "generous public service." The Republican New York *Times* saluted his patriotism and integrity, as did also the *Tribune*. The *National Intelligencer* called his death a "national calamity which has rarely been exceeded" and eulogized the "purity and exaltation of his patriotism, the nobility and elevation of his personal character." He belonged to a race, the *Intelligencer* added, "who always adorn the land which gave them birth." He had fallen when the country "stood most in need of his wise counsel and unselfish devotion."

The *Commonwealth* called him the "last of the great men of the post-Revolutionary time, who kept alive, . . . the great truth that man was capable of self-government." Nor did he leave "his equal behind him in this nation, and scarcely in the world." In all that constituted greatness, added the *Commonwealth*, "he had no superior. Great without ambition for place or prominence; patriotic, without any selfish inducement; brave, virtuous, and self-denying, . . . he was the model of a citizen, a patriot, and a gentleman." His death would cause Kentuckians to feel "as if [they] stood alone to mourn the loss of her well-beloved son."

George D. Prentice in the Louisville *Journal* called him "the good angel of our country." He was a man, said Prentice, "of the loftiest integrity, a patriot of unsurpassed fidelity and of unequalled magnanimity, . . . an orator whose golden eloquence was the thrice-refined spirit of a just and honorable conciliation." More than any other man in the land, he added, Crittenden "embodied the spirit and the principle to which . . . every enlightened American looks for the salvation of the Republic. . . . He was indeed the glass wherein true patriots did dress themselves." But this mirror now lay "broken upon the earth." For "The true and princely Crittenden is dead."[12]

[12] Marshall's letter in Frankfort *Commonwealth*, Dec. 2, 1851; *ibid.*, July 27, 1863; Providence *Post* and Boston *Daily Advertiser*, quoted *ibid.*, Aug. 7, 1863; New York *Times*, July 28, 1863; New York *Tribune*, July 28, 1863; Washington *National Intelligencer*, July 28, 1863; Louisville *Journal*, July 27, 28, 1863.

Crittenden's last will was made shortly before his death. He owed no debts, but his estate was appraised at only $8,000. Considering the lucrative legal practice he had enjoyed through a long career, this was remarkably little property for him to have accumulated. But he had an expensive family, many of them in maturity still dependent upon his generosity. Crittenden himself was prodigal of money and seemed little interested in accumulating it.[13]

The estate also contained a claim of several thousand dollars still due Crittenden as a fee for legal services rendered to John C. Frémont, which Crittenden had pressed with a vigor unusual for him in money matters. Crittenden had won for Frémont a verdict before the Supreme Court in 1855 perfecting title to more than a million dollars' worth of California land. Part of the fee agreed upon had been paid, but Frémont procrastinated about the remainder. After Crittenden's death, he claimed that the fee had been paid and refused, even when Crittenden's sons threatened suit, to arbitrate the claim.[14]

Crittenden, who had drawn wills by the hundreds, perhaps by the thousands, failed to have his own witnessed. His friends Mason Brown and Alexander Renick, however, identified his handwriting, and the will was admitted to probate. To Elizabeth he gave for life the house, furniture, silver, and a bust of himself by Hart; and he gave her outright portraits of herself and of him by Healy. At her death the silver was to be divided between his daughters, the marble bust was to go to Thomas, and the house was to be sold and the proceeds divided equally among his children, except that debts owed him by Thomas, Robert, and Cornelia were to be charged against them in the distribution. His ten slaves were "not to be sold except to some one or other of my children," so that "a proper & kind treatment thereby [be] assured to them." A silver service, given Crittenden by Robert J. Ward when he refused a fee for the defense of Matt, was bequeathed to George. To Robert he gave an early portrait of himself by Healy, and to his stepson Harry S. Todd he gave his watch. Thomas and Robert were appointed executors.[15]

[13] Miscellaneous Crittenden Papers; Coleman, *Crittenden*, II, 367.
[14] Letters to Crittenden from Andrew McKinley, Sept. 18, from Logan Hunton, Nov. 13, 22, and from Frémont, Nov. 14, 1861, Thomas L. Crittenden to Frémont, Dec. 23, 28, 1864 (copies), E. N. Faucher to Thomas L. Crittenden, Dec. 24, 1864, in Crittenden Papers.
[15] Franklin County Will Book, No. 3, p. 100, extract in Kentucky Historical Society; Franklin County Tax List, 1863; Memorandum, Crittenden Papers (Duke).

The funeral was set for Wednesday, July 29, at ten o'clock. Private business houses were closed all that day by common agreement, and public offices by order of the governor. "When a great man dies," the governor's proclamation said, "a nation mourns." General John W. Finnell, Colonel James H. Garrard, and Orlando Brown, all old friends of Crittenden were appointed a committee to make arrangements for the funeral. In Louisville the city council and aldermen met in special session. They resolved that "The Bayard of America is gone! . . . Yet his great acts, his wisdom, and voice, still thunder in our ears for the right." They decreed that the city hall should be draped in mourning for thirty days and agreed to attend the funeral as a group. A special train carried them to Frankfort on Wednesday morning.[16]

Services were held at the Presbyterian church across the street from Crittenden's home. The church was filled to overflowing and thousands of people stood in the street outside. The funeral was the largest and most impressive ever seen in Frankfort. The Reverend Daniel Stevenson, pastor of the Methodist church, gave the invocation. The Reverend John R. Hendrick preached the sermon, and the Reverend Mr. Hays gave the closing benediction.

Then the procession formed. General Boyle was chief marshal, with the Second Regiment of Maryland Volunteers as military escort. Behind the pallbearers came the family in carriages, escorted by the assistant marshal. Next came the governor and his staff, followed by officers of the state government. Then came judges and officers of state courts, Louisville's mayor, aldermen, and council, then Frankfort's mayor and council. General Ambrose Burnside, commander of the Department of Ohio followed with his staff. Finally came citizens by the hundreds, in carriages, on horseback, and on foot. From the church on Main Street the procession moved through the city. As it wound up the hill to the cemetery, cannon placed on surrounding hills thundered forth, and reverberations were heard for miles around. Through it all there was a continuous tolling of bells from churches all over the city. When the journey's end was reached, Crittenden was laid between Maria and his mother, close by the grave of his son John.[17]

---

[16] Coleman, *Crittenden*, II, 372; Frankfort *Commonwealth*, July 29, 1863.
[17] Frankfort *Commonwealth*, July 29, 31, 1863.

CHAPTER XXIII

Epilogue

THE CAREER of John Jordan Crittenden was steeped in irony, although his innate modesty and his discernment of the realities of life were such that he viewed his career always with a kind of mellow, philosophic content. To have been prominent in public affairs for more than half a century, to have moved as an equal among the most powerful leaders during the formative years of the nation, to have had a voice in selecting Presidents and in deciding the issues which shaped the course of national history are attainments not reached by many men. Yet Crittenden must sometimes have pondered over that irony which poets and dramatists from the time of the Greeks have held to be the central theme of life, especially for men of large affairs. In Crittenden's case the very virtues which led to his highest achievements were in part responsible for denying him an even larger role than he attained in public life, perhaps even the Presidency. And nowhere is this irony more apparent than in Crittenden's relations with Henry Clay.

It was Crittenden's fate to be ten years the junior of a leader who came upon the scene in an era when personal magnetism was the essential quality for political success. Moreover, as often is the way with fiery and imperious natures, Clay could never suffer others to share the spotlight with him. No other public man of the period, unless perhaps Jackson, so completely dominated his followers as did Clay. Jackson, however, was elected President shortly after the founding of his party and then passed into the background, leaving the center of the political stage to his lieutenants—Van Buren, Benton, Blair, Polk. It was Crittenden's fortune to be second in line to a man who never reached the White House, yet who never ceased to yearn for it. Eighteen forty-eight should have been Crittenden's year to lead the Whig party in person instead of by proxy as he did, if only Clay had already attained his great objective or else were content to renounce the effort. But Clay was not able, when the times were going past him, to step aside gracefully; and the bitterness engendered by Taylor's election, together with the declining fortunes of the Whigs, decreed that Crittenden would never again have a chance for the Presidency, even had he wished it.

This was the initial irony in Crittenden's life, although he reconciled himself to it with no apparent regret. With Clay and Webster too old and battle-scarred for serious consideration in 1848, there was no other Whig politician of sufficient stature to win save Crittenden himself. But Clay's reluctance early to announce his withdrawal made it impossible for Crittenden to permit his own candidacy. Yet, as the party's leader in Congress to whom all younger Whigs were turning, it was Crittenden's duty to produce a candidate who could win. It was almost a bizarre spectacle, therefore, to see a man as knowledgeable and as devoted to party as Crittenden choosing and grooming for the Presidency one as ignorant of party principles as Taylor. Crittenden was thinking of the appeal of a military reputation, the potency of which he had ample evidence in the success of Jackson and Harrison; and Taylor's military reputation in 1848 was at least as eminent as theirs had been. That Taylor was abysmally ignorant of political affairs was clear to Crittenden, just as he must have realized how gravely the nation at this critical time stood in need of astute leadership by one familiar with the issues. That Crittenden's hopes of being helmsman under Old Zack's nominal leadership were to be dashed was another irony; for who could have foretold that one as devoid of experience in politics as this doughty old warrior would so stubbornly refuse to listen to

Crittenden simply because Crittenden felt it unwise to accept a place in the cabinet?

The supreme irony for Crittenden, however, came at the climax of his career in his relations with Lincoln. History has established Lincoln as the statesman devoted most loftily to the cause of peace and Union. Yet in the months between Lincoln's election and inauguration it was Crittenden who was cast in the role of peacemaker and preserver of the Union, and Lincoln, unwittingly, in the opposite role. No other man except Crittenden had then the stature and the reputation for disinterested patriotism sufficient to rally conservatives from both embittered sections to accept a compromise after Lincoln's election had precipitated the secession crisis. It was a role for which Crittenden was fitted by both temperament and experience. That failure was to be the result of his endeavors here when he came so close to achieving compromise which would have delayed, and thus might have prevented, the dissolution of the Union and civil war was the great tragedy of his life. But the cruelest irony was that Lincoln, who later would show his greatness, had not at this moment the discernment to give Crittenden's proposals his support.

In reality, however, defeat for Crittenden's agonized struggle for compromise should not be set down as a failure alone for him nor be laid solely at Lincoln's door. The narrow margin by which his proposals lost meant that others had also failed the nation. It was the failure of the southern senators who refused to vote for them when Clark's substitute won over them on January 16. It was the failure of the Republicans who refused to support the compromise or to allow the country to vote on the issue of war—of Seward who surrendered to Lincoln and the radicals in his party, of Weed, of Buchanan, of Duff Green, unable to convince Lincoln of his error. It was the failure of New York financiers like August Belmont, fearful of losing the millions owed them by southern planters, though fearful, too, for the fate of the country. It was the failure of William Cullen Bryant, who warned Lincoln in December to beware of compromise plans which "would disband the Republican Party."[1] It was the failure of the quarter of a million northern men whose names are now forgotten, who petitioned Congress in January to accept the Crittenden proposals.

It is not difficult for historians to trace the antecedents of the

---

[1] Lincoln, *Works*, IV, 164n.

Civil War, to attribute to these antecedents the status of cause, and to conclude that this war was therefore irrepressible. There is no way to demonstrate logically that the course of events might have been altered had one man, or a few men, acted differently.

It can be shown, however, that in the winter of 1860-1861 only a slight change on the part of a few men would have given the compromise a different outcome. Secession and war would then have been delayed, at least for a while. Almost all students of the period are today agreed on this. Then might passions have begun to cool and the nation have had time to prepare for the gradual and peaceable end to slavery, which in retrospect seems to have been destined for not many more years. Then might the tragic conflict of our history have been averted and our national destiny changed.

But Crittenden was not altogether unsuccessful in his efforts for the Union. He spent the last two years of his life in the struggle to hold Kentucky in the Union, and if Lincoln's judgment was correct and Kentucky was the key to the saving of the nation, then these last years did contain a glorious, if unheralded, achievement.

It must not be thought that Crittenden's life was without blemishes. His early career was marked sometimes by excessive partisanship, and he was frequently guilty of acting from the prejudices of his age and class. Yet, in the great crises that tore the nation in the last decade of his life, his patriotism rose above either partisan or personal ambition. His thoughtful, sober reasoning and wise counsel would be sorely missed in the postwar Congress. His plea for his fellow countrymen "to forgive and forget . . . disasters that have befallen us" so that the nation could take a new start toward reconciliation and peace would be rejected. But the larger image that John J. Crittenden creates for the student of his career is that of a man of great simplicity, of high integrity, and of truly noble patriotism—a man who earned the name of statesman.

CRITICAL ESSAY ON AUTHORITIES

THE HALF century that encompasses Crittenden's public life includes both the consolidation of the federal union and the oft-recurring crises that threatened that union and which led at last to the Civil War. It is enriched by the presence and influence of such figures as John Marshall, John C. Calhoun, Henry Clay, Andrew Jackson, John Quincy Adams, Martin Van Buren, James K. Polk, Thomas Hart Benton, Daniel Webster, Stephen A. Douglas, Jefferson Davis, Thurlow Weed, William H. Seward, and Abraham Lincoln. The period has been studied intensively. Almost every man of national stature has had at least one scholarly biography; many have had several. The correspondence of many of them, as well as that of lesser figures, has been preserved, and published editions of more than a few of them are available. Furthermore, many of the men at the center of political action, or else on the fringes, kept diaries or wrote memoirs of the events in which they participated. Consequently, the period is one extraordinarily rich in materials which the student must examine with care. In this essay only the sources most significant for an understanding of Crittenden's long and complex career are included.

Manuscripts

There are two principal collections of Crittenden's letters. One, at the Library of Congress, consisting of several thousand items, has been used again and again by historians investigating special periods and events; never before, I think, has the entire collection been used in a study encompassing the whole period. There is hardly a national issue, from the War of 1812 down to the Civil War, which is not discussed by knowledgeable correspondents of Crittenden's in this large collection. At Duke University, however, is a collection which, while barely half as large as that at the Library of Congress, has been carefully winnowed of chaff and contains many letters indispensable to an understanding of both Crittenden and the period in which he lived. In addition to these depositories there is a scattering of Crittenden letters in libraries at the University of Kentucky, in the State Historical Society of Pennsylvania, in the Chicago Historical Society, at Yale University, and in the possession of Thomas Joyes of Louisville, Kentucky, who is a lineal descendant of Crittenden. There is an unpublished family history of real merit by Francis Hudson Oxx, "The Kentucky Crittendens. The History of a Family Including Genealogy of Descendants in Both the Male and Female Lives, Biographical Sketches of Its Members, and Their Descent from Other Colonial Families." A microfilm copy of this was examined in the Kentucky Historical Society, Frankfort.

Next in importance as sources for this study are the numerous collections of letters of friends and associates of Crittenden's. In this category the papers of Henry Clay would take first rank. Largest of the Clay collections are the Henry Clay Papers and the T. J. Clay Papers, both in the Library of Congress. My colleague, Professor James F. Hopkins, is engaged in the publication of a most comprehensive collection of *The Papers of Henry Clay.* He has secured copies or reproductions of not only the Clay letters in the Library of Congress but from less extensive collections in this country and in Europe. These he has generously made available to me, and for this I am greatly indebted to him.

Other manuscript collections of Crittenden's close associates which were indispensable to this study were the two collections of Orlando Brown Papers, one in the Filson Club in Louisville, the other in the Kentucky Historical Society in Frankfort; the papers of John M. Clayton, especially important for the period of the election of 1848 and the administration of Zachary Taylor; and the collections of John Bell, Thomas Corwin, Thomas Ewing, Francis Granger, William C. Rives, Caleb B. Smith, Alexander H. Stephens, and Zachary Taylor, all in the Library of Congress. At Duke University a second collection of Alexander H. Stephens Papers is especially valuable. In the University of Kentucky Library the Samuel Haycraft Papers throw light on the confused situation in Kentucky during the secession crisis, as does the William Moody Pratt Diary for the decade before and the Isaac Shelby Papers for the period of the War of 1812. In the Filson Club the Charles Stuart Todd Papers and the Harry Innes Todd Papers give an insight into Kentucky politics as well as social life in Frankfort. The John Pendleton Kennedy Papers in the Peabody Institute in Baltimore are valuable for the Constitutional Union movement and the election of 1860.

Of hardly less importance for an understanding of Crittenden and his times is the correspondence of his political adversaries, Martin Van Buren, Franklin Preston Blair, Salmon P. Chase, Joseph Desha, Duff Green, John McLean, Lyman Trumbull, John Tyler, E. B. Washburne, all in the Library of Congress. There are many significant items among the unpublished Lincoln letters in the Robert Todd Lincoln collection in the Library of Congress. The John M. McCalla Papers at Duke University Library are valuable for the exposé of the Snellson-Anderson forgery.

Government Publications

Most important of many federal governmental publications used in this study are the *Annals of Congress* and its successor, the *Congressional Globe*. Also important are various congressional committee reports and documents, especially the Report of the Committee of Thirty-three in the *House Miscellaneous Documents*, 36 Cong. 2 Sess., No. 31; *House Report* No. 181, 34 Cong. 1 Sess., for the Sumner-Brooks affair; *Senate Miscellaneous Documents*, 36 Cong. 2 Sess., No. 20, for the report of the Washington Peace Conference in February, 1861; and *Senate Reports*, 36 Cong. 2 Sess., for the proceedings of the Committee of Thirteen to consider compromise proposals in December, 1860. Crittenden's opinions as Attorney General are found in *Official Opinions of the Attorneys General* . . ., 40 vols. (Washington, 1852, 1856), III, V. The Kentucky legislative journals of the period are important for a record of state political activity.

Newspapers

The Washington *National Intelligencer* and the New York *Tribune* were the most influential Whig newspapers nationally, and *Niles Weekly Register* published in Baltimore, had a wide coverage of press reports from all sections of the country. Whig journals in Kentucky of great importance were the Louisville *Journal*, published by George D. Prentice; the Frankfort *Commonwealth*, published by Crittenden's devoted friend, A. G. Hodges, and edited for a time by an even closer friend, Orlando Brown; and the Lexington *Observer* (later the *Observer and Reporter*). The Louisville *Courier* and the Louisville *Democrat* were opposed to the Whig party, as also was the Frankfort *Argus of Western America*, published by Amos Kendall until he moved to Washington in Jackson's administration.

Published Diaries, Correspondence, and Memoirs

For an understanding of this period the student must examine the published writings of men active in public affairs. Charles Francis Adams (ed.), *John Quincy Adams, Comprising Portions of His Diary from 1795 to 1848*, 12 vols. (Philadelphia, 1874-1877), is biased but indispensable. So also is Thomas Hart Benton, *Thirty Years' View; or a History of the Working of the American Government for Thirty Years from 1820 to 1850*, 2 vols. (New York, 1854). Of more limited value is John Bassett Moore (ed.), *The Works of James Buchanan Comprising His Speeches, State Papers, and Private Correspondence*, 12 vols. (Philadelphia, 1911); Frederick W. Seward, *Reminiscences of a War-Time Statesman and Diplomat 1830-1915* (New York, 1916); S. S. Cox, *Three Decades of Federal Legislation* (Providence, R. I., 1888); Horace Greeley, *Recollections of a Busy Life* (New York, 1868); William Stickney (ed.), *Autobiography of Amos Kendall* (1872; reprinted, New York, 1949); E. D. Keyes, *Fifty Years' Observation of Men and Events Civil and Military* (New York, 1884); Josiah Morrow (ed.), *Life and Speeches of Thomas Corwin* (Cincinnati, 1890); Henry W. Hilliard, *Politics and Pen Pictures at Home and Abroad* (New York, 1892); A. K. McClure, *Abraham Lincoln and Men of War Times* (Philadelphia, 1892); and McClure, *Recollections of Half a Century* (Salem, Mass., 1902). Calvin Colton's *Life, Correspondence, and Speeches of Henry Clay*, 6 vols. (New York, 1864), and his *Private Correspondence of Henry Clay* (Cincinnati, 1856) are most valuable but will soon be outdated by Professor Hopkins' volumes. Of less value for this study than was anticipated was Mrs. Chapman Coleman (ed.), *The Life of John J. Crittenden, with Selections from His Correspondence and Speeches*, 2 vols. (Philadelphia, 1871). Mrs. Coleman took too many liberties with her father's correspondence.

For an insight into Whig politics in New York, as well as for commentary on the national scene, the student will need to examine *The Life of Thurlow Weed, Including His Autobiography and a Memoir*, 2 vols., I, Harriet A. Weed (ed.), *Autobiography of Thurlow Weed* (Boston, 1883), II, Thurlow Weed Barnes (ed.), *Memoir of Thurlow Weed* (Boston, 1884), even though the canny politician is at times inscrutable in this seemingly confidential narration. Equally unwilling to reveal his inmost thoughts is Weed's friend William H. Seward, although the student neglects at his peril Seward's *Autobiography from 1801 to 1834, with a Memoir of His Life and Selections of His Letters*, edited by Frederick W. Seward, 3 vols. (New York, 1891). This work, together with Seward's writings in three volumes, gives much detail on behind-the-scenes events in the national capital from 1848 to 1861. Also important for general background on the period are: Allan Nevins (ed.), *The Diary of Philip Hone, 1828-1851* (New York, 1936); John S. Bassett (ed.), *Correspondence of Andrew Jackson*, 6 vols. and index (Washington, 1926-1935); Ben: Perley Poore, *Reminiscences of Sixty Years in the National Metropolis*, 2 vols. (Philadelphia, 1886); "Recollections of an Old Stager," published anonymously in *Harper's Monthly*, XLV-XLVIII (1872-1874); Nathan Sargent, *Public Men and Events from the Commencement of Mr. Monroe's Administration, in 1817, to the Close of Mr. Fillmore's Administration, in 1853*, 2 vols. (Philadelphia, 1875); and Ulrich B. Phillips (ed.), *The Correspondence of Robert Toombs, Alexander H. Stephens, and Howell Cobb* (Annual Report of the American Historical Association, 1911, II; Washington, 1913). Alexander H. Stephens, *Recollections*, Myrta Lockett Avary (ed.) (New York, 1910); Henry Cleveland (ed.), *Alexander H. Stephens, in Public and Private . . .* (Philadelphia, 1910); and Stephens, *Constitutional View of the Late War between the States . . .*, 2 vols. (Philadelphia, 1868-1870), are also valuable.

Important for special periods or events are the following personal accounts: Logan Esarey (ed.), *Messages and Letters of William Henry Harrison*, 2 vols. (Indianapolis, 1922), for the Thames River campaign; Thomas Ewing, "Diary of Thomas Ewing," in *American Historical Review*, XVIII (1912-1913), 97-112, which gives a splendid account of the cabinet crisis in the Tyler administration; and Lyon

G. Tyler (ed.), *Letters and Times of the Tylers,* 3 vols. (Richmond, 1884-1896), which tells the same story but from a different point of view. The Washington Peace Conference of February, 1861, is well covered in Volume III of *Letters and Times of the Tylers,* and also in Kenneth M. Stampp (ed.), "Letters from the Washington Peace Conference of 1861," in *Journal of Southern History,* IX (1943), 394-403; in an article of the same title edited by Robert G. Gunderson, *ibid.,* XVII (1951), 382-92; and in another article edited by Gunderson entitled "William C. Rives and the 'Old Gentlemen's Convention,'" *ibid.,* XXII (1956), 459-76. The secession winter itself is given interesting sidelights in [James Buchanan], *Mr. Buchanan's Administration on the Eve of the Rebellion* (New York, 1866); in Horatio King, *Turning on the Light* . . . (Philadelphia, 1895); and in Roy P. Basler (ed.), *The Collected Works of Abraham Lincoln,* 8 vols. and index (New Brunswick, 1953-1955). The four-volume *Diary of James K. Polk during his Presidency, 1845-1849,* Milo M. Quaife (ed.), (Chicago, 1910), is a valuable account of national affairs and Democratic party difficulties for the four years of Polk's administration from a not-unbiased participant.

Monographs and Special Studies

Valuable for a view of personalities, events, or special topics in the period are numerous articles in periodicals. Deserving special notice in the *American Historical Review* are articles by: T. P. Abernethy, "Andrew Jackson and the Rise of Southern Democracy," XXXIII (1927-1928), 64-77; J. W. Caldwell, "John Bell of Tennessee," IV (1898-1899), 652-64; and St. George L. Sioussat, "Some Phases of Tennessee Politics in the Jackson Period," XIV (1908-1909), 51-69. In the *Mississippi Valley Historical Review* are: R. P. Brooks, "Howell Cobb and the Crisis of 1850," IV (1917-1918), 279-98; Arthur C. Cole, "The South and the Right of Secession in the Early Fifties," I (1914-1915), 376-99; Dorothy Ganfield Fowler, "Precursors of the Hatch Act," XLVII (1960-1961), 247-62; Frederick Merk, "Presidential Fevers," XLVII (1960-1961), 3-33, a scholarly study of the Oregon question in 1846; Edwin A. Miles, "'Fifty-four Forty or Fight'—An American Political Legend," XLIV (1957-1958), 291-309; Roy F. Nichols, "The Kansas-Nebraska Act: A Century of Historiography," XLIII (1956-1957), 187-212; Charles W. Ramsdell, "The

Natural Limits of Slavery Expansion," XVI (1929-1930), 151-71; James G. Randall, "The Blundering Generation," XXVII (1940-1941), 3-28; J. R. Robertson, "Sectionalism in Kentucky from 1855 to 1865," IV (1917-1918), 48-63; Wilson P. Shortridge, "Kentucky Neutrality in 1861," IX (1922-1923), 283-301; St. George L. Sioussat, "Tennessee, the Compromise of 1850, and the Nashville Convention," II (1915-1916), 313-47; and George M. Stephenson, "Nativism in the 40s and 50s with Special Reference to the Mississippi Valley," IX (1922-1923), 183-202. Significant articles in the *Journal of Southern History* are: Frank H. Heck, "John C. Breckinridge in the Crisis of 1860-1861," XXI (1955), 316-46; Frank Klingberg, "James Buchanan and the Crisis of the Union," IX (1943), 455-74; Powell Moore, "James K. Polk: Tennessee Politician," XVII (1951), 493-516; and James G. Randall, "The Civil War Restudied," VI (1940), 440-57. Charles Francis Adams, Jr., made a well-reasoned prediction of the end of slavery in "The Reign of King Cotton," in *Atlantic Monthly*, VII (1861), 451-65.

In the *Filson Club History Quarterly* are many articles which throw light on Crittenden's career in Kentucky: W. C. Barrickman, "Political Nominating Convention," XVIII (1944), 37-51; Milo M. Quaife, "Governor Shelby's Army in the River Thames Campaign," X (1936), 136-65; Allen E. Ragan, "John J. Crittenden, 1787-1863," XVIII (1944), 3-28; Otto A. Rothert, "Browsing in Our Archives: A Glimpse of Alfred Pirtle, 1837-1926," XI (1937), 211-17, which gives a picture of ante bellum Frankfort society; E. G. Swen, "Kentuckians at William and Mary College before 1861 with a Sketch of the College before That Date," XXIII (1949), 173-98, giving an account of college life at Williamsburg during Crittenden's student days; Charles G. Talbert, "A Roof for Kentucky," XXIX (1955), 145-65, which tells of Indian warfare in Kentucky in the time of Crittenden's father; and Wallace B. Turner, "The Know-Nothing Movement in Kentucky," XXVIII (1954), 266-81.

Even more prolific of local history is the *Register of the Kentucky State Historical Society*, with articles by: Orlando Brown, "The Governors of Kentucky [1792-1824] with Biographical Sketch and Notes," G. Glenn Clift (ed.), XLIX (1949), 5-24, 202-24; Clift, "Kentucky Marriages and Obituaries—1787-1860," XXXVI (1939), XXXIX (1941), XLI (1943); E. M. Coulter, "The Downfall of the Whig Party in Kentucky," XXIII (1925), 162-74; Leonard Curry, "Election

Year—Kentucky, 1828," LV (1957), 196-212; George C. Downing, "Governor Robert Letcher," III (Jan., 1905), 13-16; Downing, "The Home of Governor Crittenden, Frankfort, Kentucky," III (Sept., 1905), 23-24; Ella Hutchinson Ellwanger, "George D. Prentice," XIII (1915), 15-33; "Excerpts from the Executive Journal of Governor James Garrard," XXIX (1931), 197-200; Will D. Gilliam, "Robert P. Letcher's Appointment as Minister to Mexico," XLVII (1949), 116-24; Gilliam, "The Schuylkill Bank Fraud," L (1952), 249-55; Holman Hamilton, "Kentucky's Linn Boyd and the Dramatic Days of 1850," LV (1957), 185-95; Willard R. Jillson, "A Glimpse of Frankfort," XL (1942), 155-217; William Leavy, "Memoir of Lexington and Its Vicinity," XLIII (1945), 44-62, 107-37, 250-60, 310-46; Kurt F. Leidecker, "Amid the Strife. Further Correspondence of George Clinton Stedman," LI (1953), 191-217; Mrs. Jennie C. Morton, "Governor John J. Crittenden," III (Sept., 1905), 11-20; James A. Padgett (ed.), "The Letters of James Taylor to the Presidents of the United States," XXXIV (1936), 318-46; A. C. Quisenberry, "Kentucky's Neutrality in 1861," XV (1917), 9-21; Quisenberry, "One Hundred Years Ago—The Battle of the Thames," XI (1913), 9-28; Quisenberry, "Kentucky Troops in the War of 1812," X (1912), 49-66; and Charles G. Talbert, "Kentucky Invades Ohio—1782," LIII (1955), 288-96.

Other articles of special interest are: Martha A. Burnley, "Albert Triplett Burnley," in *Quarterly of the Texas State Historical Association,* XIV (1910-1911), 150-54; Harry J. Carman and Reinhard H. Luthin, "The Seward-Fillmore Feud and the Crisis of 1850," in *New York History,* XXIV (1943), 163-84; Carman and Luthin, "Some Aspects of the Know-Nothing Movement Reconsidered," in *South Atlantic Quarterly,* XXXIX (1940), 213-34; Richard R. Stenberg, "Jackson, Buchanan, and the 'Corrupt Bargain' Calumny," in *Pennsylvania Magazine of History and Biography,* LVIII (1934), 61-85; W. E. Tilberg, "Responsibility for the Failure of the Crittenden Compromise," in *Historical Outlook,* XIV (1923), 85-93.

Biographical and General Works

Biographical dictionaries of Kentuckians of general use in a study of this kind are: *Biographical Encyclopaedia of Kentucky of the Dead and Living Men of the Nineteenth Century* (Cincinnati, 1878); Thomas M. Green, *Historic Families of Kentucky* (Cincinnati, 1889);

Bishop William Meade, *Old Churches, Ministers and Families of Virginia*, 2 vols. (Philadelphia, 1861), II; and Nelson Osgood Rhoades, *Colonial Families of the United States of America . . .*, 10 vols. (Baltimore and Los Angeles, 1907-1920), VII. Lewis and Richard Collins, *History of Kentucky*, 2 vols. (Covington, 1874), is a treasury of information about early Kentucky history, including a prodigious amount of biographical data. The two most scholarly histories of Kentucky are Thomas D. Clark, *A History of Kentucky* (New York, 1937); and E. Merton Coulter and William E. Connelly, *History of Kentucky* (Chicago and New York, 1922). The latter work is the second volume of a five-volume edition with the same title edited by Judge Charles Kerr. Penetrating and thoughtful studies of early Kentucky society are Arthur K. Moore, *The Frontier Mind, a Cultural Analysis of the Kentucky Frontiersman* (Lexington, Ky., 1957); and Bernard Mayo, *Henry Clay, Spokesman of the New West* (Boston, 1937). Lucius P. Little, *Ben Hardin: His Times and Contemporaries* (Louisville, 1887), is of some value, as also is Arndt M. Stickles, *The Critical Court Struggle in Kentucky, 1819-1829* (Bloomington, Ind., 1929).

General works dealing with politics and political parties during Crittenden's career as Clay's lieutenant are: W. E. Smith, *The Francis Preston Blair Family in Politics*, 2 vols. (New York, 1933), II; Wilfred E. Binkley, *American Political Parties: Their Natural History* (New York, 1943); E. Malcolm Carroll, *Origins of the Whig Party* (Durham, 1925); A. C. Cole, *The Whig Party in the South* (Washington, 1913); Arthur M. Schlesinger, Jr., *The Age of Jackson* (Boston, 1945); and Glyndon G. Van Deusen, *The Jacksonian Era, 1828-1848* (New York, 1959). Biographies of special value for this period are: C. M. Wiltse, *John C. Calhoun*, 3 vols. (Indianapolis and New York, 1944-1951), II, III; John A. Garraty, *Silas Wright* (New York, 1949); Charles H. Ambler, *Thomas Ritchie: A Study in Virginia Politics* (Richmond, 1913); John S. Bassett, *Life of Jackson*, 2 vols. (New York, 1911); George T. Curtis, *Life of Daniel Webster*, 2 vols. (New York, 1870); Claude M. Fuess, *Daniel Webster*, 2 vols. (Boston, 1930); George R. Poage, *Henry Clay and the Whig Party* (Chapel Hill, 1936), an excellent political study of the latter decades of Clay's life; and Clement Eaton, *Henry Clay and the Art of American Politics* (Boston, 1957). Glyndon G. Van Deusen's biographies of three great Whigs, *Life of Henry Clay* (Boston, 1937); *Thurlow Weed: Wizard of the Lobby* (Boston, 1947); and *Horace Greeley*,

Nineteenth Century Crusader (Philadelphia, 1953), are indispensable. The first volume of Charles G. Sellers, *James K. Polk: Jacksonian, 1795-1843* (Princeton, 1957), is a scholarly study of Tennessee and national politics in this period but is not concerned with Crittenden. Eugene I. McCormac, *James K. Polk, a Political Biography* (Berkeley, 1922), is still a most excellent biography. Works of special interest for this period but more limited in scope are: Robert Gray Gunderson, *The Log-Cabin Campaign* (Lexington, Ky., 1957); and Robert J. Morgan, *A Whig Embattled: The Presidency of John Tyler* (Lincoln, Neb., 1954). David R. Deener, *The United States Attorneys General and International Law* (The Hague, 1957), has an account of Crittenden's part in the settlement of the Florida claims.

Important for background material on the period of Crittenden's decade as Whig leader from 1845 to 1855 are two biographies of Zachary Taylor, the first by Brainerd Dyer, *Zachary Taylor* (Baton Rouge, 1946); the second by Holman Hamilton, volume II of a more detailed study, *Zachary Taylor, Soldier in the White House* (Indianapolis and New York, 1951). Important also for this period is the second volume of Frederic Bancroft, *Life of William H. Seward* (New York, 1900); Robert J. Rayback, *Millard Fillmore, Biography of a President*, volume XL of the *Publications of the Buffalo Historical Society* (New York, 1959); A. D. H. Smith's life of Winfield Scott entitled *Old Fuss and Feathers* . . . (New York, 1937); and Ulrich B. Phillips, *Life of Robert Toombs* (New York, 1913).

The standard work on the nativist movement and the Know-Nothing party is Ray Allen Billington, *The Protestant Crusade* (New York, 1938). Of considerable importance, too, are more recent studies by William D. Overdyke, *The Know-Nothing Party in the South* (Baton Rouge, 1950); and Henry Steele Commager (ed.), *Immigration and American History: Essays in Honor of Theodore C. Blegen* (Minneapolis, 1961), especially essays in the latter work by John T. Flanagan, Oscar Handlin, Philip D. Jordan, Franklin D. Scott, and Ingrid Semmingsen.

Scholarly literature on the growing sectional crisis over slavery in the territories after 1848 is so abundant that only a fraction of it can be mentioned here. The second volume of Albert J. Beveridge, *Abraham Lincoln, 1809-1858* (Boston, 1928), is still valuable as also are: Avery Craven, *The Coming of the Civil War* (New York, 1942); David Donald, *Charles Sumner and the Coming of the Civil War*

(New York, 1960); James C. Malin, *John Brown and the Legend of Fifty-six* (Philadelphia, 1942); Allan Nevins' two splendid studies, *Ordeal of the Union*, 2 vols. (New York, 1947), and *The Emergence of Lincoln*, 2 vols. (New York, 1950); Roy F. Nichols, *The Disruption of American Democracy* (New York, 1948); and Carl Sandburg, *Abraham Lincoln: The Prairie Years*, 2 vols. (New York, 1926). James Ford Rhodes' classic *History of the United States from the Compromise of 1850 . . .*, 9 vols. (New York, 1893-1922), volumes I and II, are somewhat outdated but still of value.

Equally prolific has been scholarship concerning the secession crisis produced by the election of 1860. Drawn on most heavily in the present work are three studies of depth and insight: David M. Potter, *Lincoln and His Party in the Secession Crisis* (New Haven, 1942); James G. Randall, *Lincoln the President: Springfield to Gettysburg*, 2 vols. (New York, 1946), I; and Kenneth M. Stampp, *And the War Came: The North and the Secession Crisis* (Baton Rouge, 1950). Important also are: G. P. Auchampaugh, *James Buchanan and His Cabinet on the Eve of Secession* (Lancaster, Pa., 1926); William E. Baringer, *A House Dividing: Lincoln as President Elect* (Springfield, Ill., 1945); Ollinger Crenshaw, *Slave States in the Presidential Election of 1860* (Baltimore, 1945); Richard N. Current, *The Lincoln Nobody Knows* (New York, 1958); Dwight Dumond, *The Secession Movement* (New York, 1931); Emerson D. Fite, *The Presidential Campaign of 1860* (New York, 1911); Murat Halstead, *Caucuses of 1860. A History of the National Political Conventions of the Current Presidential Campaign . . .* (Columbus, Ohio, 1860); Philip S. Klein, *President James Buchanan: A Biography* (University Park, Pa., 1962); George Fort Milton, *The Eve of Conflict: Stephen A. Douglas and the Needless War* (Boston, 1934); Joseph H. Parks, *John Bell of Tennessee* (Baton Rouge, 1950); and Mary Scrugham, *The Peaceable Americans of 1860-1861: A Study in Public Opinion* (New York, 1921).

Scholarly works dealing with Kentucky's internal struggle in the secession crisis are: E. Merton Coulter, *The Civil War and Readjustment in Kentucky* (Chapel Hill, 1926); Robert M. McElroy, *Kentucky in the Nation's History* (New York, 1909); and Arndt M. Stickles, *Simon Bolivar Buckner, Borderland Knight* (Chapel Hill, 1940).

INDEX